Post-Systematic Theology I

Markus Mühling

Post-Systematic Theology I

Ways of Thinking – A Theological Philosophy

BRILL | WILHELM FINK

Cover illustration: Photo by Tom Gainer on Unsplash.com.

Bibliographic information published by the Deutsche Nationalbibliothek

The Deutsche Nationalbibliothek lists this publication in the Deutsche Nationalbibliografie; detailed bibliographic data available online: http://dnb.d-nb.de

www.fink.de

Cover design: Anna Braungart, Tübingen
Production: Brill Deutschland GmbH, Paderborn

ISBN 978-3-7705-6585-6 (hardback)
ISBN 978-3-8467-6585-2 (e-book)

Table of Contents

Preface

I am glad to present here the first volume of a three-volume 'Post-Systematic Theology', which is a comprehensive description of the Christian way of perceiving truth and value. This first volume is presented as 'Ways of Thinking': a theological philosophy based on a narrative ontology. However, this ontology is not so much a science of being than it is a science of becoming, a kind of 'gignomenology'. Not only are classical questions of a philosophy of religion and of a prolegomena to dogmatics treated, but also important approaches oriented towards phenomena are discussed, partially by interdisciplinary means, which amounts to a partial convergence of perception and revelation. Part 1 discusses 'preparations', in part 2 the genuine narrative ontology is explicated, part 3 explains 'divine self-presentation', and part 4 presents the 'equipment' necessary for the following material volumes.

I have to say thanks to all who helped to realize the ways of this project: Werner and Betty Jeanrond enabled a period of research in Oxford, where I wrote the major part of this manuscript. Philipp Stoellger provided critical discussions about individual themes. Similarly, I am grateful to Martin Wendte and Tim Ingold. Pre-eminent thanks go to Carsten Card-Hyatt, who transformed the English version into a readable one. Corrections were done by Johanna Knotte, Bich nhi Dang, Charlotte Fischer, David Kannemann, and Brandon Watson. I am extraordinarily grateful to my colleagues and students at the Protestant University of Barmen (Wuppertal) and Bethel. Without the joyful atmosphere provided by them on campus – where research and life are organically connected – this volume could not have been published. As if that was not a great gift in itself, the university administration also provided financial funds that enabled the work on a double original manuscript, both in German and English. Thanks also to the publisher Brill, especially to Jörg Persch and Martin Illert, who supported this project in an extraordinarily manner. I owe special thanks to my wife Anke and my daughter, Pia Laetitia Johanna. They provided the free spaces which are necessary to write such a work. It is dedicated to Pia.

Epiphany 2020 *Markus Mühling*

PART 1

Preparations

CHAPTER 1

'Post-Systematic' Theology

The term 'systematic theology' is a relatively recent one. The first use of 'system' to designate a work explicating the Christian faith was by Bartholomew Keckermann (*Systema SS. Theologiae tribus libris adornatum*, 1602), which was followed by the appearance of 'systematic theologies' by Buddeus and others in the 18th century in response to the growing independence of the theological disciplines. And of course, in the 20th century, 'systematic theology' has become a very common term.[1]

In Keckermann's theology, the use of the term 'system' simply means that the presentation of the material is ordered, along with the assumption that the subject-matter could be understood as an organic whole. Keckermann was influenced by Melanchthon,[2] who referred to the Hellenistic and especially Stoic concept of *techné*: an art of presentation based on knowledge and for the sake of a fruitful life.[3]

Apart from the idea of an ordered presentation for the sake of practical, i.e. beneficial aims, the historic roots of the concept do not specify the content that would come to be implied by the technical use of 'system'. Rather, the background for Keckermann was the distinction between the analytic and synthetic methods developed by Giacomo Zabarella. Keckermann distinguished practical from theoretical sciences, such that the analytical method was proper to the former and the synthetic method to the latter. Since he conceived theology as a practical science that is directed to the end of salvation for humans, the explication of theology made use of the analytical method and therefore theology is a system in the sense of a *techné*.[4] As such, the best way of understanding the term 'system' in its original use as part of the term 'systematic theology' is as a form of presentation oriented towards salvation.

1 Cf. Schwöbel, C., Art. Systematic Theology.
2 Cf. Melanchthon, P., CR 11, 257.
3 Cf. Strub, C., Art. System, 824.
4 Cf. Rohls, J., Protestantische Theologie der Neuzeit, Bd. 1, 80.

 | DOI:10.30965/9783846765852_002

1.1 Technical Concepts of 'System' in Kant and Hegel

In modernity, the concept of a 'system' was more and more technically defined and it became a very specific concept in the philosophy of Kant. He defines a 'system' as follows:

> By an architectonic I understand the art of systems. Since systematic unity is that which first makes ordinary cognition into science, i.e., makes a system out of a mere aggregate of it, architectonic is the doctrine of that which is scientific in our cognition in general, and therefore necessarily belongs to the doctrine of method.
>
> Under the government of reason our cognitions cannot at all constitute a rhapsody but must constitute a system, in which alone they can support and advance its essential ends. I understand by a system, however, the unity of the manifold cognitions under one idea. This is the rational concept of the form of a whole, insofar as through this the domain of the manifold as well as the position of the parts with respect to each other is determined *a priori*. [...|
>
> The whole is therefore articulated (*articulatio*) and not heaped together (*coacervatio*); it can, to be sure, grow internally (*per intus susceptionem*) but not externally (*per appostitionem*), like an animal body, whose growth does not add a limb but rather makes each limb stronger and fitter for its end without any alteration of proportion.
>
> For its execution the idea needs a schema, i.e., an essential manifoldness and order of the parts determined *a priori* from the principle of the end. A schema that is not outlined in accordance with an idea, i.e., from the chief end of reason, but empirically, in accordance with aims occurring contingently (whose number one cannot know in advance), yields technical unity, but that which arises only in consequence of an idea (where reason provides the ends a priori and does not await them empirically) grounds architectonic unity. What we call science, whose schema contains the outline (*monogramma*) and the division of the whole into members in conformity with the idea, i.e., a priori, cannot arise technically [...] but arises architectonally [...]; such a science must be distinguished from all others with certainty and in accordance with principles.[5]

We can summarize this by identifying four essential elements in Kant's use of system:

1. A system refers to the rational *apriori*, not to the distinct reality of the 'thing in itself' (*noumenon*). This presupposes the subject-object distinction, if not their separation. Insofar as reason is truly rational, i.e. reason that is *apriori*, reason always functions systematically.
2. The manifold contents of cognition are not isolated objects, but are connected to one another relationally.

---

5 KANT, I., Critique of Pure Reason, A832–834, B860–862.

3. These relational connections are organized with the help of one idea or principle, making the system a totality. For Kant, a system always refers to a totality that can be described using one idea. Furthermore, a system is always closed, meaning that a system is not able to grow or to alter. All apparent or possible changes do not affect the system itself but only its explication.
4. Kant calls the methodological explication of the relata that are gathered under one idea by the subject of reason 'architectonics', which he distinguishes from 'technics'. The consequence for Kant is that what while we are used to referring to the 'empirical' or 'hard sciences simply as 'science', they ought to be grouped under the heading of 'technics' and not under the heading of science.

Kant's rigorous understanding of the concept of system implies that there is only a single system of reason, since reason is also seen as a single thing. Therefore, written explications of systems – including Kant's *Critique of Pure Reason* itself – have to be distinguished from the one genuine system. For Kant, this distinction is based on the expectation of progress, meaning that all explications will supersede each other in a process that will get closer and closer to the one true system.[6]

In the following era, that of the so-called German Idealism, Kant's concept of a system was presupposed and partly radicalized. Since the principles of a system were seen as autonomous – that is, based in nothing else but the system itself – J.G. Fichte thought that every proper system had to have a cyclical structure.[7]

In the early Hegel, we can find a critique of the idea of systems hand in hand with its most demanding conceptual form:

> Philosophy, as a totality of knowledge produced by reflection becomes a system, that is, an organic whole of concepts, whose highest law is not the intellect but Reason. The intellect has to exhibit correctly the opposites of what it has posited, as well as its bounds, ground and condition. Reason, on the other hand, unites these contradictories, posits both together and suspends them both. One might demand that the system as an organization of propositions should present the Absolute which lies at the basis of reflection in the fashion of reflection, that is, as the highest, or absolutely fundamental proposition. But such a demand at once entails its own nullity. For a proposition, as something posited by reflection, is something limited and conditioned on its own account.[8]

6 Cf. Strub, C., Art. System, 832.
7 Cf. Strub, C., Art. System, 841.
8 Hegel, G.W.F., Difference, 103.

The solution to the problem in Hegel's later philosophy consists in the fact that what a system promises is the sublation into the absolute itself, wherein the whole is identical with its own becoming.[9]

What is significant in Hegel's use of the term system here is a move that can be seen as decisive in the step from Kant to Idealism. In contrast to Kant, who presupposed the subject-object distinction and at once distinguished the system of reason from its explications, Hegel saw correctly that any constitution of a system necessarily had to exclude the other from itself and thereby produce contradictions. As an activity of reason, the *noumenon*, to which it is directed, is excluded; the subject matter of real constructions should be the system of reason, but at the same time the system of reason is excluded, so that the Kantian system of reason becomes an unrecognizable *noumenon* on a second level. The only way to avoid abandoning the idea of the system is thus what Hegel indeed did: the system has to include the antinomy and it has to be seen as embedded in the reality of the sublation of the absolute itself.

1.2 Technical Concept of 'System' in Systems Theory

The second technical concept of a system worth mentioning is the one used in Systems Theory. Here, the idea of a system is not restricted to rationality, as in Kant, but refers to empirical states of affairs and their regulation. Therefore, a system is understood as a set of cybernetic rules. Nevertheless, the system is not identical with the empirical reality, but rather is the model-like explication of the empirical field in question. What is seen as subject and what is seen as object is defined within the system: both are constituted by the system itself. Niklas Luhmann claims that systems can overlap and contain each other and, most importantly, that every system is related to its environment, which itself can consist of systems. What is significant here is Luhmann's insight that all systems possess a kind of 'double' contingency: Both what of the environment a system can accommodate, and therefore can be regulated by the system, as well as what the system cannot accommodate, and so cannot be regulated, is contingent.[10] The ultimate environment of any possible system is the world itself, which is not a system. The world is therefore, following Luhmann, a limit-concept like the Kantian *noumenon*. Once more, what of the world can be grasped by systems and what cannot is due to contingency. A complete systematization of the world is therefore impossible.

9 Cf. Strub, C., Art. System, 842.
10 Cf. Luhmann, N., Funktion der Religion, 81.

Of relevance to this point are the interlocking of systems in the second-order cybernetics of Heinz von Förster.[11] First-order systems are all systems that order and regulate empirical observations. What can be placed in the system is therefore determined by the system-building scientist. More precisely, first-order systems are not really concerned with objects, but with the properties of the first-order systems themselves, and that means with the properties of the method chosen by the scientist for the system. A first-order system thus works with representations and the relations among representations. Far more interesting is the second-order system, in which empirical objects, subjects, and research communities are all equally embedded. This embedding is conceived as real and the constructivist feature of the first-order systems is transferred onto the second level. The cognitive systems of the second level therefore replace the classically-conceived cognitive subject. The inner-systemic distinctions and inner-systemic entities that emerge within the systems network are therefore conceived as autopoietic,[12] i.e. self-organized. As a consequence, an important contrast to Kant's understanding of a system emerges. The systems understood through systems-theory are open, can develop, and change. Yet, it is still impossible for systems to be identical with the world.

The great difficulty here seems to be the transfer of the concept of system from the first level to the second level. It is one thing to say that our own academic use of concepts appears in systems (first-order systems), and a completely different thing to claim that the same is going on in reality. This claim is at best a postulate. And slice the pie anyway you like, there is no empirical basis and no rational basis for demanding such a transfer. The language of second-order systems is nothing but a metaphor that has been universalized.

1.3 Critiques of Systems

All concepts of systems, be it the Kantian, the Idealist, or the systems-theoretic, have been subject to a variety of meaningful criticism. In the first case, we might consider the Romantics, although in this case there was a desire to at least partly save the idea of the system.[13] Schleiermacher declared the historicity of all systems, with the consequence that the development of any system

11 Cf. FOERSTER, H.v., Cybernetics of Cybernetics.

12 The concept of autopoiesis was identified and popularized by MATURANA, H., Neurophysiology of Cognition. Cf. also MATURANA, H./VARELA, F.J., Autopoiesis and Cognition, xvii.

13 Cf. STRUB, C., Art. System, 845.

cannot come to an end. Nevertheless, he tries to save the idea of a system insofar as he distinguishes natural from artificial systems. Natural systems endure, whereas artificial systems, in contrast, may be complete but not lasting; they lie within the realm of temporary validity.[14]

Kierkegaard uses Hegel's concept of a system as a starting point by turning it against Hegel. A system of existence is unthinkable because a system must be conceived of as closed. But then existence itself would have to be conceived of as sublated and negated.[15] In this way, Hegel and Kierkegaard can be seen as dealing with the same problem, but in a very different manner. Whereas Hegel arrives at the concept of a dynamic system through sublation into the absolute, Kierkegaard uses the figure of sublation, and the concept of negation implied by it, in order to abandon the idea of the system entirely. In modern terminology, we can understand Kierkegaard as claiming that a system is necessarily a well-founded set, although this is nothing like reality (see ch. 18).

The following set of critiques are also well known. In his *Will to Power*, Nietzsche reduces all forms of system-building to questions of power;[16] Heidegger conceives the end of thinking in systems as the end of modernity;[17] Derrida – although he acknowledges the impossibility to think without any system – saw that system-immanent, emergent differences are driven by something, which, as *différance*, is beyond any systematization.[18] Further, whereas these thinkers criticized the features of unity and closeness of a system, Bertrand Russel challenged a system's organic traits. Since he denied that there are any internal or essential relations, the world dissociates into unrelated individuals (see ch. 7). The consequence is that any notion of a system becomes superficial. Of course, positions that do not share this radical kind of individualism may draw different conclusions. For example, Nicholas Rescher no longer claims that systematicity is a sufficient condition of truth, unlike Hegel, but nevertheless argues that it is a necessary one.[19] But clearly this, in the end, signals a shift in the whole concept of a system.

14 Cf. Schleiermacher, F.D.E., Dialektik (1811), 49.

15 Cf. Kierkegaard, S., Abschließende unwissenschaftliche Nachschrift (1846), 111.

16 Cf. Strub, C., Art. System, 847f.

17 Cf. Heidegger, M., Vom Ereignis, 81–90.

18 Cf. Derrida, J., Margins of Philosophy, 1–28.

19 Cf. Rescher, N., Cognitive Systematization, 33–38.

1.4 Post-Systematic Theology

Why have we abandoned the system by substituting it for a 'Post-Systematic Theology'? The answer is less spectacular than a respected colleague, Hans-Peter Großhans supposed, who accused me of undermining our own discipline; this is far from my intention. The claim behind the title is, on the contrary, that by the standards of the technical accounts of systems that have been provided by Kant, Hegel, and Systems theory, one cannot really find a work of 'Systematic Theology' that justifies its title, which is really good news.

All of the technical accounts of the system we considered are highly problematic. Kant presupposes the subject-object distinction, if not their separation, which is criticized in this book and has been criticized by contemporary theology as a whole. A system that relies on the concepts of well-founded sets is also in that case not one in which systems are understood to be open and developable. This downfall is one more reason not to use the term, since we will see that theology does not deal with well-founded sets of entities, but is concerned with a mode of perceiving (see ch. 5, 18, 22 and 23). Above all, there is no unified idea that is serviceable for theology. Of course, it has been claimed that the unity of God serves in this role, and that theology's subject-matter is everything, as long as it is considered *coram Deo*. While the thrust of the argument might be true, the current study is not an objection to denying the validity of theological systems. In the first instance, God is not an idea. Christian faith confesses and proclaims God as Father, Son, and Holy Spirit in dynamic love, and as creator, redeemer, and perfector. There are historical examples of attempts to sum this up under a single idea. But, as for example in Anselm's radical attempt in *Proslogion* to use *unum argumentum* for the whole framework of theology, this does not imply its reduction to a single idea, as everything that is said has to be seen as bracketed by prayer – no matter what general value one finds in Anselm's and other similar attempts at theology. Second, divine *unity* is not a principle given to theology but a non-basic and problematic feature of theology, as we will learn in the second volume.

Instead of using the concepts of Kant and Hegel, one could try to use a concept of system similar to that found in Systems theory, but this would be no improvement. In this case, one would not only have to subscribe to an [unsupported] representationalism, as Karen Barad observed,[20] but also have to agree to a highly problematic and incoherent constructivism. Yet, most importantly, one would have to accept a very specific metaphor: The reality in which we

20 Cf. BARAD, K., Meeting the Universe Halfway, 133–135.

have our becoming is to be understood as nothing but a second-order system. But this would amount to an ontologization and a transfer of what academics might do in their day jobs to reality. There is not only no basis for such a move, it also requires one to suppress some essential features of reality. More sophisticated system-theories, such as Luhmann's, might show awareness of this fact by claiming that the function of religion consists in turning non-describable complexity into describable complexity.[21] Arguments like these might serve to support the social necessity of religions, but one would still easily become a victim of legitimate critics of religion (see ch. 21.).

Nevertheless, theology cannot be entirely un-systematic, without any order to its work, either. And a post-systematic theology is also not without order. What then can it mean? In arguing for his concept of post-democracy, Colin Crouch uses the image of a parable in order to explain different phenomena with the prefix 'post': The parable approximates an ideal but comes to an inflection point before the ideal can be reached in order to then veer away from it. This movement after the inflection point, which is denoted by the prefix 'post', does not mean to fall back on something old, but to reach towards something new.[22] Can we also use this image to describe what post-systematic theology might mean? It is tempting to do so, but it is still impossible, since it presupposes a technical concept of system, at least as an ideal or a regulative principle, which is impossible due to the critique of the system explained above.

One might be suspect that post-systematic theology is just another one of the many 'post-modern' theologies. But this is also not the case. An appreciator of such theologies as a whole or even if only some of those philosophies usually called 'post-modern' will see that, although we will occasionally interact with such philosophies, they will nevertheless come in for clear criticism. My own previous work, of which this is a development, has been described as 'post-liberal', out of a need to provide some sort of classification.[23] But this is, in the end, a meaningless category, since all that is said by it is that it is neither pre-modern nor that it shares the premises of what is usually called 'liberal theology'.

In regard to the material features of the technical concepts of systems referred to above, we must stress that not everything attributed to systems has to be criticized. The idea that the presentation, as well as the subject-matter, of theology is relational is a very fruitful one. But we cannot express this relationality with only the help of one single idea, which would be a misleading

21 Cf. LUHMANN, N., Funktion der Religion, 26.

22 Cf. CROUCH, C., Post-Democracy, 20f.

23 Cf. WALTER, G., Rev. Mühling, Liebesgeschichte Gott.

reduction. In the face of the Kantian concept of a system, 'post-systematic' can be easily explained in a modest way: Whereas we abandon totality, we retain and stress relationality. Our concern is therefore a kind of relationality that does not reduce irreducible difference and alterity to unity, but allows them to appear together and remain. One of the main theses of this work is that the best means to do so is to make use of a 'narrative ontology', as we shall see, though narrative ontology is not a single idea.

Although it would had been in principle possible to do without the word 'system' entirely, in the end there was no meaningful alternative. 'Dogmatics' has negative connotations and is not materially appropriate to this work, as 'Dogmatics' is normally understood to be a subset of Systematic Theology, excluding Ethics and Philosophy of Religion. For similar reasons, the term 'Christian doctrine' would be a poor fit, but in fact it is far worse since it would suggest that the subject matter would be a 'doctrine', a *doctrina christiana*. But the concept of a doctrine has so many meanings that it would not be easy to employ just one. One would have to define it in such a way that a sufficiently qualified concept of doctrine would have nothing in common with what 'doctrine' means in everyday language.

It is also worth asking whether such a 'Post-Systematic Theology' is much different in intent than the original use of the term 'Systematic Theology' by Keckermann, Melanchthon, and the traditional use of the term system in classical culture. Insofar as merely some kind of order is implied, there are similarities. But there are important differences. First, we do not share the epistemological presuppositions of the post-reformatorian era, which can be found in Keckermann. Second, although our presentation is directed towards the living of a fruitful life, as the Stoics understood systems, there is also a decisive difference. Our presentation is not based on knowledge, but on perception (cf. ch. 5). And it is a basic thesis of this book that neither knowledge nor experience, but rather perception is the very starting point for theology. Third, the ancient definition of *techné* as the art of presentation for the sake of a fruitful life is not a neutral statement of intent, and it is one against which theology has to protest for the sake of the integrity of Christian faith (cf. ch. 4).

A 'Post-Systematic Theology' does not intend to give a completely new presentation of what theology has to say. The intention is to use a more adequate name for what is usually done under the heading of 'Systematic Theology'. The precise features of this 'Post-Systematic Theology' cannot be explained in advance; they are not the subject of theoretical reflection. Therefore, what 'Post-Systematic Theology' really means can only be observed step by step while it proceeds along the way, precisely what this book intends to offer.

1.5 Stages of the Way

This first volume is dedicated to the reflection on these ways as ways of perceiving and thinking. It replaces what is normally called 'Prolegomena', 'Principles of Doctrine' or 'fundamental theology'. But on the one hand, the reader will find more themes than one usually finds in works on *prolegomena*. And on the other hand, where the themes presented here intersect with those of a *prolegomena*, they are not treated as extensively as would be necessary for such a work. Any explication of the themes of classical *prolegomena* cannot avoid the problem that one would be better off presenting them as *epilegomena*, since a real concise presentation of such themes would presuppose the material content of Christian faith – which will be the subject-matter of the following volumes. It is decisive for any theology to recognize that it is impossible for methodology to direct the material, whereas it is in fact strictly the other way around. Therefore, presenting the content of this book not at the beginning, but at the end would be appropriate. But there would also be a disadvantage: it would become nearly unreadable, since the reader would be confronted with a series of terminological decisions and necessary neologism which would only be explained in the last volume. Therefore, we will not follow this logical order but start instead with the 'ways of perceiving'.

In addition to themes found in classical *prolegomena*, the reader will find here topics usually treated within the realm of the philosophy of religion. But once more, not all the themes of a classical philosophy of religion will be treated here. The reason for this is that if there were a kind of philosophy of religion that would really function without the basis of revelation, it could not say anything very meaningful. Rather, philosophy of religion works best when it understands itself to be proceeding toward revelation.

Just as this volume surpasses what classically would be part of a work on *prolegomena*, it also surpasses what would be presented as philosophy of religion. Many of the themes presented in part two of this book can neither be classified as *prolegomena* nor as philosophy of religion, since they treat a series of genuine philosophical problems. Formally, we set aside the concept of God in these passages, since we will introduce the concept of God in part three. Nevertheless, this does not mean that these passages strive simply to agree with professional philosophers. In reality, the decisions made here are not independent from the material decisions of the following volumes, but are implied by the latter ones. If the reader has the impression that some decisions made in part two of this book do not seem to follow in a strictly logical or necessary way, then she might be reminded that these passages are also passages on theology, not on philosophy. One could begin considering these ways of perceiving from two starting points: directly with reflection on revelation or, quasi-independently from revelation, with reflection on perception. Both of these ways converge in the material parts of this volume. In part 2, we will go a part of the way independently from reflection on revelation in order to merge ways with the subsequent volumes on revelation. Perhaps the reader will then also see that, in this first part, revelation is not ignored. Therefore, part 2 of these ways of perceiving could be called 'theological philosophy' or 'Christian philosophy'. But such a title would also be misleading, since the latter expression is a classical one used in Roman-Catholic, especially neo-thomist traditions,[24] and this tradition does not play a large role in this work.

These ways of perceiving consist of four simple stages.

The first stage (Part 1) serves as preparation for the journey. Apart from this chapter, this will involve short chapters on the history of stories, on the subject-matter of theology, and on the question of Christian practice.

The second stage (Part 2) is the start of the journey, beginning with a discussion of a phenomena-based narrative ontology. The concept of perceiving, or better of perceiving truth and value, the terminology of a narrative ontology, the concepts of relations, of ways and wayformational lines, of events, of time and space, of signs, metaphors, concepts and names, theories and models, of dramatic coherence, of rules and causality, contingency and other modalities, of the subject-object distinction und of truth are all visited *en route* in an ordered manner. Terminologically, this part is foundational for the entire work.

In the third stage (Part 3) we will first set out the minimal conditions for a concept of God. Second, during a discussion of the concepts of revelation, it will become clear how the whole journey is a theological one. We will then get our first glimpse of the terrain of the following volumes, and as such the course of our journey.

The fourth and last stage (Part 4), however, reminds us that it might be meaningful not to move to this new terrain too quickly, but to first ensure that we have gathered the necessary equipment for this journey by discussing themes such as faith and religion, historicity and Holy Scripture, reason and faith, interdisciplinarity, and (post-)systematic criteriology.

---

24 Cf. e.g. BÖHNER, P./GILSON, E., Christliche Philosophie.

CHAPTER 2

The Problem with a History of Stories

This post-systematic proposal for a systematic theology is based on a narrative ontology. What this means will be explicated primarily in Part 2, chapters 5–19, though in truth it will require the whole work. As in the case of all methodologies, so here: Following a method means to become located in a history. And it is a useful academic practice to explicate such histories at the beginning of a work. But in this particular case it also causes a problem: a narrative ontology is not identical with narratology. If it wants to satisfy the claims implied by its name, it has to be comprehensive. But then it is obvious that no particular era of the history of thought or the history of theology can claim to be the original ancestor of such an approach. It would be easy to write a history of stories that only refers to those that have the word 'narrative' in their names, or to refer to those that use such related expressions like 'history' or 'history of salvation'. If such was the case, one could easily go from the 17th century onwards. However, to proceed this way would be a mistake, since not only the history of the term, but also the history of the facts, is at stake.[1]

And this means that the real ancestors of a narrative ontology are nothing less than the oldest scriptural sources available. In the case of theology, we can restrict ourselves in this regard to the biblical witnesses, the Scriptures of the Old Testament or the Hebrew Bible. There are different ways of describing the constitution and growth of the Old Testament. But it is obvious that in all these models, the different Scriptures are not only narrations or narratives. Also, other genre-like collections, such as laws in the Pentateuch, are important. However, these other genres are imbedded in real or fictive narrative relations. It is significant that the transmission of these other genres was only possible within their narrative frameworks, whereas their original *Sitz im Leben* is in many cases unreconstructable. We can assume that there were other collections of laws in the ancient Near East that have not been passed on. To be embedded in a narrative context is not, perhaps, a guarantee that something will be passed on throughout the centuries, but it increases its probability.

1 FREI, H., Theology and Narrative, 119 already refers to this: 'The association of narrative with religion generally and Christianity in particular has always been close, although the self-consciously systematic use of the concept "narrative" in Christian theology is a modern invention. Reference to "the sacred story" or "sacred" or "salvation history" as a category to describe what was taken to be the do- minant content of the Bible did not arise until the seventeenth century.'

 | DOI:10.30965/9783846765852_003

We might also suggest that this could be the case for collections of prophetic words, psalms, and texts of wisdom.

Further, in the material aspect, it is noteworthy that not only do narratives play an important role in the Old Testament, but that there might be something like a narrative understanding of the world's becoming. In the middle of the 20th century, Gerhard von Rad and his school stressed the 'historical' character of Hebrew thought by claiming that this kind of theology could be found in an exemplary way in the so called 'little historical credo' of Deuteronomy 26,5–9.[2] Current Old Testament research does not consider this text to be the beginning of Hebrew theology, as von Rad had claimed, but rather as the summary of a transition point in the growth of the tradition.[3] Nevertheless, there can be no doubt that Hebrew thinking and the character of Hebrew theology consists in the fact that it is not doctrinal, that the Hebrew language uses far less abstract terms in comparison with other languages (such as Greek), and that ontological and substantializing terms appear late, if they appear at all. Therefore, it is still possible to follow von Rad at least partly by claiming the character of Hebrew thinking is broadly 'historic'. It is therefore not surprising that in the 20th century such historical thinking was also prominent in systematic theology, for example in Wolfhart Pannenberg's claim that revelation happens as history. In such cases, one normally uses the terms 'history' or 'history of salvation'. But are these really the correct terms? In Hebrew, there are no abstract terms for 'history' or 'being'. It is also worth mentioning that von Rad's characterization of Hebrew thinking is not as 'historical' in a genuine sense. He identified the uniqueness of the 'little historical credo' in the fact that this text pronounced YHWH's deeds of salvation, except without any report of how these deeds were received or interpreted by humans. Therefore, it is questionable whether summaries like these are really 'historical' at all, but it is undoubtably the case that they are narrations and narratives. Therefore, one can conclude that its unique features are less 'historical' than narratival.

What we have found by a look at the Hebrew and Greek tradition of the Old Testament can be supported by a look at the New Testament. Although the majority of the Scriptures might consist of letters, one might ask whether these letters would had been passed on without the Gospels and Acts. But, even if one supposes they would have been, one cannot deny that letters are also narratively constituted in another sense. Letters capture parts of correspondences which possess a narrative sequence and consist of narrative events.

2 Cf. von Rad, G., Theologie des AT 1, 136.

3 Cf. exemplarily the subsumption of Gertz, J.C., Stellung des kleinen geschichtlichen Credos, 44f.

A side-ways glance at the Hellenistic heritage of Christianity shows that abstract thinking might be here much more prominent than in Hebrew thinking. Nevertheless, this part of the Christian heritage is also unthinkable without stories. Plato might be skeptical of the poetic theology of Homer's stories about the gods.[4] Nevertheless, his own dialogues include collections of stories, traditional ones and invented ones. What then, is Plato, if not a great storyteller? Of course, one cannot say that in regard to Aristotle's known works. But in another sense, he is also an ancestor of narrative thinking, if not of narrative ontology, by reflecting conceptually in his *Poetics* on some of the important insights of narrative thinking. These considerations might be only loosely, or too loosely, connected with his considerations on first philosophy and his ethics. Nevertheless, it also is important to see Aristotle as an important ancestor of narrative thinking.

The whole subsequent tradition of Christian theology, independently of which traditions might here or there play leading roles in particular periods, is in all cases a history of the interpretation of the biblical witnesses, with the consequence that theology's narrative roots cannot denied.

Let us have a look at the philosophy and theology of modernity. Hume and Kant might not offer examples of narrative approaches, but this state of affairs changes in Idealism. Does Hegel really teach the sublation of religion and theology into philosophy and is he really explicating the concept of the Absolute? Or is his dynamization of, for example, logic not more than a hint that his thinking – its claim to be dealing with the conceptual notwithstanding – pulls ineluctably in a narrative direction? Whatever one makes of Hegel, this narrative focus was recently explicitly affirmed in the case of Schelling by the philosopher Axel Hutter:

> [T]he critical transition from a negative to a positive philosophy [...] requires a transition from a timeless ontology of objective being to a radically temporal ontology of narrative meaning. The being of the world thereby becomes the temporally articulated meaning of a narrative or story that cannot be grasped 'in a single word', since it is never the individual but only the whole that leads to genuine meaning, to the solution of the riddle. The positive philosophy of Schelling leads at last to a *narrative ontology*, which places meaning prior to being.[5]

---

4 Cf. PLATON, Politeia, 379a.

5 HUTTER, A., Der kritische Sinn des Gottesbegriffs, 175: „[Der] kritische Übergang von einer negativen zu einer positiven Philosophie [... erfordert] den Übergang von einer zeitlosen Ontologie des objektiven Seins zu einer radikal zeitlichen Ontologie des narrativen Sinns. Das Sein der Welt wird so zum zeitlich artikulierten Sinn einer Erzählung oder Geschichte, der nicht ‚mit Einem Wort' gefaßt werden kann, da nie das Einzelne, sondern nur das Ganze auf den eigentlichen Sinn, auf die Lösung des Rätsels führt. Die positive Philosophie

Therefore, the outcome of Idealistic thinking is a narrative thinking, which is explicitly found, if not in the mouth of Schelling himself, but in the terms of one of Idealism's contemporary interpreters, as a *narrative ontology*. Of course, we have not yet discovered what a narrative ontology might be.[6] Nevertheless, we may find clues by looking at dynamization, temporality, and the insufficiency of pure conceptual work.

By beginning with hallmarks such as these, it would be easy to find more modern ancestors, for example in process philosophy and in the phenomenological tradition.

Narrative thinking becomes explicitly categorised as such during the so-called 'narrative turn'[7] from the second half of the 20th century onwards. But defining the precise meaning of this narrative turn is not so easy. One of its most important sources is Alistair MacIntyre's *After Virtue*[8], published in 1981. But, as influential as *After Virtue* might have been and may still be, MacIntyre's thinking is not the origin of the narrative turn, but more a mill where different heritages, approaches, and disciplinary positions come together and where they might be processed. Therefore, there is no single conception that could serve as a blueprint for what the 'narrative turn' means. With his background in the phenomenological-hermeneutical tradition, Paul Ricœur's theory of narrative was an important influence, especially in theology, and was perhaps facilitated by the fact that he touched on many issues shared with theology as he pursued his questions.[9] We should also mention that long before one could speak of something like a 'narrative turn' we can find programmatically narrative approaches like Wilhelm Schapp's philosophy of stories in the phenomenological tradition, despite the fact that these examples have been later

Schellings führt so am Ende auf eine *narrative Ontologie*, die dem Sinn einen Vorrang vor dem Sein einräumt."

6 With HUTTER, A., Narrative Ontologie Hutter has also written a version of a narrative ontology and it is the only use of this specific term that I know of. Though it is notewrothy that Hutter here understands philosopy as human self-awareness which concentrates on the terms of freedom, God, and immortality and enables a life in allegory. But Hutter's version of a 'narrative ontology' unfolds as a philosophical analysis of Thomas Mann's "Joseph and His Brothers". So his version of narrative ontology is something completely different from what we provide in part 2 of this book, even if there may be some overlap.

7 For this term and its history cf. GOODSON, I.F./SCHERTO, R.G., Narrative Turn.

8 MACINTYRE, A., After Virtue.

9 Cf. RICŒUR, P., Time and Narrative I; RICŒUR, P., Time and Narrative II; RICŒUR, P., Time and Narrative III. Examples of recent theological work that interacts with Ricœur can be found in HILLER, D., Gottes Geschichte; KREITZSCHECK, D., Zeitgewinn; SCHLARB, V., Narrative Freiheit.

ignored.[10] Be that it as it may, at the beginning of the 21st century the academic situation could be characterized comprehensively as one 'after' the narrative turn:

> Talk of narrative is intensely fashionable in a wide variety of disciplines including philosophy, psychology, theology, anthropology, sociology, political theory, literary studies, religious studies, psychotherapy and even medicine. There is widespread agreement, that human beings typically see or live or experience their lives as a narrative or story of some sort, or at least as a collection of stories.[11]

I am not sure whether this description of the omnipresence of narrativity in academics is really accurate. But in any event, this quotation suggests that narrative thinking has become widespread enough to cause a backlash. Galen Strawson, who offered this diagnosis of the state of academics at the beginning of the 21st century, argues that the narrative paradigm is only an insubstantial fashion, and he tries to show how this is exemplified in talk of narrative identity. He is not alone in his critique,[12] and this shows that there are, of course, alternatives to narrative thinking. Whether it is really possible for these critiques – as legitimate as they might be in particular – to escape narrativity completely, or whether they only propose another kind of narrative thinking, is another question (cf. ch. 19).

It is significant that the natural sciences remain unmentioned in Galen Strawson's list. Does this mean that they are something like the last bastion resisting narrativity? That is by no means the case. On the one hand, the historization of the natural sciences, accomplished with the help of the concept of paradigms introduced by Thomas Kuhn,[13] can be conceived as being bound up in different, changing narratives. On the other hand, the work of the natural sciences also has an undeniable narrative dimension, in two ways. Narrations and narratives serve as heuristics for the development of new theories, as, for example, in the case of thought experiments, which are nothing but miniature narratives. Much more important, however, is that the work of the natural sciences, in the case of experiments and their documentation, follows an irreversible narrative sequence. The sequence of theoretical background, description of the apparatuses of the experiment, description of its observations, and their interpretation, cannot be rearranged completely at will. This sequence

---

10 Cf. SCHAPP, W., In Geschichten verstrickt (1953) und SCHAPP, W., Philosophie der Geschichten (1959).

11 STRAWSON, G., Against Narrativity, 428.

12 Cf. exemplarily LIPPITT, J., Getting the Story Straight and WILLIAMS, B., Life as Narrative.

13 Cf. KUHN, T.S., Structure of Scientific Revolutions. Cf. also MÜHLING, M., Art. Paradigm III+IV.

therefore has a transitive order. But transitivity is also an important feature of all narratives. Whereas this narrative order is still visible in original research articles, it vanishes in the presentation in the text book presentations used in academic teaching. Whether this is simply the result of incidental or pragmatic reasons without any important implications or the deformation of what may legitimately be called 'the natural sciences', is a question to which we have to devote ourselves in a later section[14] (cf. ch. 8.5).

Let us now look at the role of narrativity in the theology of the 20th century. Once again, it is decisive that we do not conceive of narratives too narrowly. First of all, we must mention Karl Barth and his *Church Dogmatics*, which has been understood at different points as a paradigm of a narrative theology.[15] On the Roman Catholic side, Hans Urs von Balthasar is of similar interest.[16] He rejects narrativity in the shape of epics, but supports narrativity in the shape of the dramatic (cf. ch. 16). In German Protestant theology during the second half of the 20th century, the theologies of Wolfhart Pannenberg, Dietrich Ritschl, Eberhard Jüngel, and Jürgen Moltmann can be seen as ancestors of narrative thinking. Even though Pannenberg claims that it is the history of salvation and not the narration of salvation that is primary for theological thinking, it is, however, also able to represent the object of history adequately, in contrast to a profane history that cannot satisfy its object. But if one conceives of Pannenberg's theology primarily as narratival instead as historical,[17] a number of sham attacks from philosophy of science against his position become dispensable. In the case of Dietrich Ritschl, narrativity appears explicitly by way of his *Story Konzept*.[18] Nevertheless, he is not promoting something like a narrative ontology since he conceives of stories as only the 'raw material' of theology. As such, he at once acknowledges the important role of narrativity while nevertheless devaluing it by fencing it off in a restricted and narrow area.[19] In *God as the Mystery of the World* (*Gott als Geheimnis der Welt*), Eberhard Jüngel more than once described the divine being as a love story.[20] And yet, he also

14 Cf. INGOLD, T., Impediments of Objectivity.

15 Cf. FREI, H., Eclipse of Biblical Narrative, viii; MAURER, E., Narrative Strukturen, insbes. 13 and for more evidence MEYER ZU HÖRSTE-BÜHRER, R., Gott und Menschen in Beziehungen, 102f. With reservations here can also be named RITSCHL, D., Theologie ist explikativ und argumentativ, 32, although a narrative method is here rejected in the last conclusion of Barth.

16 Cf. BALTHASAR, H.U.v., Theo-Drama I; BALTHASAR, H.U.v., Theo-Drama II; BALTHASAR, H.U.v., Theo-Drama III; BALTHASAR, H.U.v., Theo-Drama IV; BALTHASAR, H.U.v., Theo-Drama V.

17 Cf. PANNENBERG, W., Gott der Geschichte.

18 Cf. RITSCHL, D./JONES, H.O., "Story" als Rohmaterial der Theologie.

19 Cf. RITSCHL, D., Theologie ist explikativ und argumentativ.

20 Cf. JÜNGEL, E., God as the Mystery of the World, xi, 317, 374.

conceives of narrative speech more as a kind of proclamation of faith than one suitable for the work of systematic theology.[21] In the Anglophone tradition, different 'post-liberal' theologies were developed at the same time, empahsizing narrativity in different ways. Significant here is Hans Frei's approach, drawing on biblical theology,[22] George Lindbeck, who conceives of theology as the grammar of faith,[23] and particularly Stanley Hauerwas' ethical theology, whose core is determined by narrativity.[24] Finally, Robert W. Jenson's systematic theology has accorded perhaps highest conceptual value to narrativity of all.[25]

In light of Jenson's theology, mention should also be made of the different theologies associated with the 'Trinitarian Renaissance', in so far as they have not been mentioned already.[26] Most of them would not conceive of themselves as explicitly narrative approaches. Nevertheless, it is striking that even in those cases, such as in the Eastern Orthodox tradition, where the immanent trinity occupies the center of theological work, the result is not simply abstract thinking, but a kind of thinking that is at least akin to narrative approaches.[27]

In contemporary theology, one could cite theologies as different as Klaas Huizuing's aesthetic theology[28] and Celia Deane-Drummond's dialogue between theology and the natural sciences,[29] both of which would be inconceivable without reflections on narrativity. Further, one may even ask whether or not that branch of theology that restricts itself to research on the history of theology can also be seen as following a narrative approach in the widest sense. Such a suggestion becomes plausible if it can be shown that historicity has to be conceived of as a type of narrativity (cf. ch. 24). Also those positions that stress the phenomenality of the life-world,[30] those that give a central role

21 Cf. JÜNGEL, E., God as the Mystery of the World, xii.

22 Cf. FREI, H., Theology and Narrative.

23 Cf. LINDBECK, G.A., Nature of Doctrine.

24 Cf. HAUERWAS, S., Community of Character; HAUERWAS, S., Peaceble Kingdom.

25 Cf. JENSON, R.W., Triune God; JENSON, R.W., ST I.

26 Cf. e.g. RAHNER, K., Der dreifaltige Gott als transzendenter Urgrund; MOLTMANN, J., Trinity and the Kingdom of God; GUNTON, C.E., Promise of Trinitarian Theology; ZIZIOULAS, J.D., Being as Communion; SCHWÖBEL, C., Gott in Beziehung; GRESHAKE, G., Der dreieine Gott; TORRANCE, A., Persons in Communion.

27 Cf. ZIZIOULAS, J.D., Signifikanz des kappadozischen Beitrags, especially 77, where the intra-trinitarian person and its ontological freedom is the focus. So the classic *processiones* are no longer understood as abstract relations, but acquire the characteristic traits of occurrences.

28 Cf. HUIZING, K., Ästhetische Theologie.

29 Cf. DEANE-DRUMMOND, C., Christ and Evolution.

30 Cf. e.g. STOELLGER, P., Passivität aus Passion; DALFERTH, I.U., Radikale Theologie; EVERS, D., Gott und mögliche Welten; HENRIKSEN, J.-O., Life, Love and Hope; MOXTER, M., Kultur als Lebenswelt.

to metaphor,[31] or are built around relationality,[32] all belong to narrative approaches in the widest sense. Process theology[33] and open theism[34] might also be reasonably described as narrative approaches, or at least they share interests with narrative theology.

Furthermore, one should not restrict oneself to the field of systematic theology alone. The exegetical disciplines have also rediscovered the eminent significance of narrativity by, for example, stressing the history of redaction – the phenomena of the rewritten bible – and by taking literary criticism into account, as well as other literary narratologies. In the realm of ethics[35] and practical theology[36], narrative must either be explicitly studied or come into play through the important role given to biography in those disciplines.[37]

We are now at a point where the notion of narrativity is broad enough that one may ask how useful narrativity can be if it is given such a wide compass. Two responses suggest themselves. On the one hand, we have not broadened the concept infinitely, as there remain many approaches that do not belong under the umbrella of narrative, such as the revival of ontologies of subjectivity in theology[38] or positions that reanimate classical metaphysics. Further, a constructive critique of explicitly narrative concepts[39] suggests that the concept is not an empty one. On the other hand, 'narrativity' does not mean the same thing in all cases. Therefore, it is a legitimate question if these are all mere equivocations of different phenomena or if we have indeed discovered an important dimension of theological thinking itself.

Of course, we would argue for the second thesis: Narrativity is an irreducible dimension of every theological work. We cannot prove this thesis with a short argument of only a few sentences. Rather, this entire work will be its

---

31 Cf. SOSKICE, J.M., Metaphor and Religious Language; STOELLGER, P., Metapher und Lebenswelt; MCFAGUE, S., Metaphorical Theology.

32 Cf. z.B. HERMS, E., ST I; HERMS, E., ST II; HERMS, E., ST III.

33 Besides the essential philosophical approaches in WHITEHEAD, A.N., Process and Reality and HARTSHORNE, C., Logic of Perfection those considering process-philosophical approaches can also be mentioned here, e.g. COBB, J./GRIFFIN, D.R., Process Theology; GRIFFIN, D.R., Process Theology; KELLER, J.A., Problems of Evil; KELLER, C., On the Mystery; FORD, L.S., Transforming Process Theism, as well as theologies influenced by Whitehead, e.g. WELKER, M., Universalität Gottes.

34 Cf. PINNOCK, C./RICE, R./SANDERS, J./HASKER, W./BASINGER, D., Openness of God.

35 Cf. e.g. HOFHEINZ, M./MATHWIG, F./ZEINDLER, M. (Hg.), Ethik und Erzählung; FISCHER, J., Theologische Ethik; BROCK, B., Singing the Ethos of God.

36 Cf. e.g. SCHLARB, V., Narrative Freiheit; SWINTON, J., Dementia.

37 Cf. e.g. DRECHSEL, W., Lebensgeschichte.

38 Cf. exemplarily BARTH, U., Religion in der Moderne; DANZ, C., Systematische Theologie et al.

39 Cf. NÜSSEL, F., Narrative Identität?.

proof. The first step in doing so is to explicate the main features of a narrative ontology, which occupies part two of this volume. At first glance, the notion of 'narrative ontology' might appear self-contradictory, but this is not the case. The phrase 'narrative ontology' is motivated by the following state of affairs. It can be argued that a feature of many post-liberal, narrative positions is that they devalue – if not denounce – classical conceptual work. Here, we want to explicitly reject this anti-conceptual drive. If one wants to show that narrativity is a dimension of every possible theological work, one has a twofold task: First, one has to show that stories and concepts are not opposed, but that at the base and at the borders of concepts, stories appear. Second, we have to reject the relativistic implications for reality-claims and truth-claims that entail such a devaluing of concepts. Therefore, in order to express both, we use the expression 'narrative ontology'. It is designed to distinguish our position from anti-conceptual or relativistic uses of narrativity and in order to stress – although there is a high amount of truth in the phenomenological and theological critics of ontological or metaphysical thinking – that such criticisms are not directed towards every kind of ontology. The exception is the most convincing kind of ontological thinking, which is the proposed narrative ontology understood as irreplaceable for all theological reflection.

We cannot give a history of this narrative ontology. It would only be possible if its material content were also explicated. But, in this case, it would also not be a meaningful endeavor because one would nevertheless have had to make use of the most diverse theological and philosophical traditions. Therefore, we resisted the temptation to provide a history of such research and instead offer a rather a short description of the problem of a history of stories. And this problem consists precisely in the fact that no dimension of any theological work can be told through the particular history of its research.

CHAPTER 3

The Subject-Matter of Post-Systematic Theology

We begin with a double-thesis:

1. Post-Systematic Theology is the criteria-based, (self-)involving, second-level narrative explication (as well as im-plication and com-plication) of the perception of the truth and value of the Trinitarian God. This God is understood as the integration of all wayformational perspectives within a particular wayformational perspective.
2. Post-Systematic Theology is the criteria-based, (self-)involving, second-level narrative explication (as well as im-plication and com-plication) of Christian practice with respect to its truth-claims, as well as pursuing the im-plications and com-plications of this explication.

This two-fold definition is not self-evident and will be explained in due course. However, a single chapter will not suffice for such an explanation, since the definition of the subject-matter, in both cases, presupposes so much. Many aspects of the definition will receive detailed discussions in chapters of their own throughout the course of this book. The concepts of perceiving truth and value, of wayformational perspectives, of secondary narrativity, of the relevant criteria, of truth, of practice, and of 'Christian' will only be clarified by the extensive discussions in this volume. We will deal with the concept of perceiving truth and value at the beginning of Part Two in chapter 5, and we will end with the discussion of criteria in chapter 27 as the last chapter of the first volume. Therefore, the reference to the subject-matter in the title is not restricted to the present chapter alone, but in principle applies to the whole work. The present chapter is thus in fact the shortest of all, and we will concentrate our efforts on the presentation of this twofold thesis.

That being said, some general comments may be helpful in order to understand the relationship of our theses to other possible definitions of systematic theology.

3.1 Post-Systematic Theology is an Activity

If it is correct that post-systematic theology explicates a perception, while also tracing this perception's im-plications and com-plications, it is an activity or a *praxis*. This means that some things are excluded: Post-systematic theology is not a system of doctrines, not a collection of propositions, not a *doctrina*, not

 | DOI:10.30965/9783846765852_004

Christian doctrine, not a *summa*, and not a catechism.[1] As an activity or *praxis*, it is an aspect of Christian practice, which is seen as part of its subject-matter according to the second definition. In this sense, post-systematic theology is indispensable, and it is practiced because the Christian faith exists insofar as it consists in its secondary narrative explication, along with perusing its im-plications and com-plications. In distinction from the other kinds of secondary narratives that belong to Christian practice, it is led by criteria. These criteria, as we will see in chapter 27, are not foreign to Christian practice but derived from it. However, the concrete, organizational shape of this criteria-led activity is relatively open. It is, for example, not necessarily an academic discipline. Nevertheless, due to social and ecclesial requirements such *adiaphora*, like being an academic discipline, are significant. The fact that (post-)systematic theology is an academic discipline is therefore, relatively speaking, a given due to the contingencies of our concrete life-world.

As a practice that explicates, im-plicates, and com-plicates, post-systematic theology is a hermeneutical practice in the broadest sense of the term. Its task is principally open. This openness has nothing to do with our isolated faculties, but is an implication of its subject matter. This matter is itself an open state of affairs, as we will see during the course of the book.

As an activity led by specific criteria, post-systematic theology needs the formation of skills and capabilities that may be called 'competencies'. However, the problem with using this term is that it has enjoyed a specific, far too narrow use by the educational sciences at the beginning of the 21st century.[2] It is not this narrow concept we have in mind when talking about 'competencies', but rather those skills that are internalized and habituated, which are quite similar to those skills required by craftspeople.[3] And yet, this metaphor also possesses some negative implications. Obviously, in many cases, craftspeople need to develop specific manual skills that of course do not belong to the practice of post-systematic theology. Far more problematic is that the skills needed by craftspeople are often derived from the performance of a technique.[4] But

1 There is no consensus concerning the term catechism. Usually, an instructive abstract is meant. However, Luther in DINGEL, I./U.A. (Hg.), BSELK, 915 (BSLK 545) and ibid., 916 (BSLK 547f) speaks about "catechism" as a verb (*Catechismum treiben*), not in the sense of an instruction, but as an active practice of permanently following the self-involving ways of the Gospel, which is clearly evocative of the form of the *verbum externum*.

2 Although one can also derive the term of competencies from the new educational science, it appears as though the position was influenced by the media and therefore by economics, which as such refers to the very opposite of *praxis*. For critiques, see, e.g., KRAUTZ, J., Bildung als Anpassung.

3 Cf. SCHWÖBEL, C., Doing Systematic Theology (engl.).

4 Cf. HOYE, W.J., Emergence of Eternal Life, 45.

if there is one thing that post-systematic theology definitively is not, it is that of a technique. Could the competencies required by post-systematic theology then be compared to skills needed in arts? Perhaps, but this metaphor also has its limits. Furthermore, today some conceptions of art are still bound to the understanding of the arts preeminent in the 19th century, including the idea that an artist has to be a genius.[5] Whatever this term might mean, in order to practice post-systematic theology, one does not have to be or to become one.

A possible compromise would be to compare the work of post-systematic theology to neither the arts nor the crafts, but to arts and crafts. But here also there would be so many misleading connotations – one is reminded of exhibitions at arts and crafts markets, whose products often resemble more kitsch than anything else – that we should refrain from this comparison. Rather, post-systematic theology requires reflection, discussion, and the practice of narration. One can surely describe this as "*Nach-denken*"[6], too. But it is not a purely mental activity in the usual sense, but also a bodily practice. This can be seen in the element of involvement in our definitions: It is not simply explicating, but *committed* explicating, im-plicating, and com-plicating. In the first place, this feature precludes post-systematic theology from being a disengaged[7] activity, which could be done quasi-mechanically or that could be separated from the person or her identity. As a (self-)involving activity, the identity, the becoming, and the formation of those who are doing post-systematic theology is included. Although it is an activity that is primarily pursued by professional theologians within academia, as well as in parishes and schools, one cannot separate the office and person. Of course, every theologian would need more than those skills required by post-systematic theology in order to do their specific profession. Therefore, we cannot make an *a priori* claim that the theological profession specifically does not allow for the separation of the office from the person. But insofar as post-systematic skills are required by the theological profession as such, a separation is impossible. In this respect, the theologian will always be a witness to and for her work, inclusive of her own identity-claims. Obviously, this demands a specific kind of responsibility which exceeds those of many other professions.

---

5 Cf. SCHMIDT, J., Geschichte des Genie-Gedankens.

6 In this context, Barth speaks of theology as „Nachdenken des vorgesagten und vorbejahten *Credo*" (BARTH, K., Fides quaerens intellectum, 26) or that theology is a matter of „ein vertieftes *legere*, um ein *intus legere*, um ein Nachdenken" (BARTH, K., Fides quaerens intellectum, 40).

7 The concept of disengaged reason was developed by Charles Taylor: "Disengagement is always corelative of an 'objectification' […]. Objectifying a given domain involves depriving it of its normative force for us." (TAYLOR, C., Sources of the Self, 160).

We called this specific kind of activity an explication, but we also included exploring the 'im-plicating' and 'com-plicating' of this activity. At this stage of our inquiry, these terms cannot be explained, since to do so would presuppose the whole course of the coming inquiry. The patient reader will find the explanation in ch. 27.

3.2 The Subject-Matter of Post-Systematic Theology

There is only one subject-matter of post-systematic theology. Nevertheless, there are two definitions. The reason is the following:

The first definition – the 'explication of the perception of the truth and value of the Trinitarian God, as well as pursuing the implications and complications of this perception. This God is understood as the integration of all wayformational perspectives within a particular wayformational perspective' – resembles classical definitions, which conceived systematic theology as speech about God (and all things related to God).[8] The second definition – 'explication of Christian practice with respect to its truth-claims, as well as pursuing the implications and complications of this explication' – resembles functionalistic definitions, such as can be found in, for example, the realm of the so-called analytical method and its notion of theology as practical science (cf. ch. 1), as well as definitions like Schleiermacher's, who held that theology 'is the collective embodiment of those branches of scientific knowledge and those rules of art, without the possession and application of which a harmonious Guidance of the Christian Church, that is a Christian Church-Government, is not possible.'[9] The intent was indeed to make use of these two kinds of definitions, not because they represent parallel or alternative definitions, but in order to describe the same subject-matter from different perspectives. On the one hand, speech about God and divine self-presentation appears only in, with, and through Christian practice. Therefore, to explicate, im-plicate, and com-plicate Christian practice implies speech about God. On the other hand, Christian practice conceives of the self-presentation of the Triune God as the condition of its possibility. Therefore, without claiming the truth of divine revelation there would be nothing that could be called Christian practice. In other words: 'all things related to God' includes Christian practice. Therefore, Christian practice is included in the task of explicating, im-plicating, and com-plicating divine self-presentation. Consequently, both definitions or both

8 For example, see the classic description found in THOMAS VON AQUIN, s.th.I, 1a 7.

9 SCHLEIERMACHER, F., Brief Outline, §5, 93.

versions of the definition refer to the same subject-matter. What is denied, however, is the possibility of speaking of God abstractly, divorced from Christian practice. Further, the subject matter is not concerned with purely human thoughts, or the pure content of consciousness, or exclusively human practice. In order to preclude such misunderstandings, it seems necessary to place the double perspective given by these two definitions at the very beginning of the project.

If post-systematic theology is itself an activity and *praxis* that finds its subject-matter in a (Christian) *praxis*, then we can say that post-systematic theology is preeminently a practical science. However, the correct understanding of this claim depends on *how* one conceives of (Christian) *praxis*.

CHAPTER 4

Christian Practice

4.1 The Practice-Prejudice in the Technical Narrative of Modernity

As we noted in the previous chapter, post-systematic theology is an eminently practical endeavor. This claim may appear counter-intuitive, as systematic theology is often seen as highly theoretical. Indeed, the material content of systematic theology in general suggests that systematic theology has to do with the construction, analysis, critique, and reconstruction of numerous theories. Is there a contradiction here? No. The contradiction is only apparent and its cause lies in contemporary usage, especially regarding practice and *praxis* on the one hand, and regarding theory on the other hand. Contemporary usage is too narrow and makes the phenomena at stake opaque. William Hoye called this opaqueness the praxis-prejudice.[1] What does this mean?

In everyday language, an activity counts as 'practical' if it serves as a means to an end that is distinct from the activity itself. It is practical to use cars, since this activity is a means to arrive somewhere, such as work. It is practical to have a knowledge of psychology, since it enables a minister to do pastoral counselling. According to this argument, every theory receives its value through its *praxis*: The theory of electrodynamics is practical since it allows for the realization of electro-mobility. The Christian faith – along with other religions – are practical, since they provide an ethical orientation, contribute much to personal and social well-being, or something along these lines. Faith serves a person or societies.[2] Faith serves morality. If this practice-relevance is missing, then an activity is called 'purely theoretical,' 'abstract,' or 'speculative' – expressions normally used with negative connotations.

If one shares this praxis-prejudice, one would expect that the claim that theology is an eminently practical endeavor would mean that it is useful for particular humans or societies. And the definition of theology given above as a practical science can indeed be understood within this line of thinking. When Keckermann calls theology a practical science since its end is beatitude,[3] then

1 Cf. HOYE, W.J., Emergence of Eternal Life, 42–58.

2 To avoid misunderstandigs: indeed theology, just as church in general, can serve the world. But the fact that this is can be done by church or theology does not consequently mean that this function defines or legitimates theology or the church.

3 Cf. ROHLS, J., Protestantische Theologie der Neuzeit, Bd. 1, 80.

 | DOI:10.30965/9783846765852_005

it seems that theology amounts to something like a technique for realizing felicity. When Schleiermacher mentions the skills without which the guidance of the church is impossible, it appears as though theology provides the techniques one has to master in order to do a specific job.

This praxis-prejudice not only determines our use of language, but also determines our ability to perceive phenomena, including that of human life and its environment. Hoye suggests that this praxis-prejudice can be seen in, for example, a Marxist anthropology that is based on a technical paradigm:

> The labour process [...] is human action with a view to the production of use values, appropriation of natural substances to human requirements;[4] At the end of every labour process, we get a result that already existed in the imagination of the laborer at its commencement.[5]

We can call this the 'technical narrative of modernity', that is a narrative structure that appears in different ways and in particular shapes throughout modernity, including where Marxist thinking is rejected. This narrative has the following parts. Human beings and their culture are opposed to nature. The culture that defines humanity is a culture of labor, i.e. activities that alter natural ends (and thereby also human nature itself) in favor of ends determined by humans, which are necessary to put nature to use. The ends of technical work are chosen by humanity *before* they put a particular process in motion. At the same time, humans also make use of themselves as a means in these processes; they cannot stay outside of it. Humans, therefore, have to submit themselves to this process. Later we will see that this technical narrative of modernity may be better conceived of as intentional transport in a network (ch. 8). Here, it will suffice to stress two points: This narrative determines not only the manner in which we relate practice and theory, it also determines our perception of phenomena.

With Hoye, we can illustrate this paradigm with the help of a simple example.[6] The parable of the Good Samaritan (Lk 10:25–37) can be seen as representing a common good in western culture. Explicated in the light of the technical narrative, its meaning would consist of a paradigm of the practice-relevance of Christian neighborly love. Understood in this way, the purpose of the parable appears to be the following: It wants to give an answer to the question who or what a neighbor is (V.29). And the answer is: the neighbor is someone in the need of help, as is in the parable, it is the one who has

---

4 MARX, K., Capital, vol. I, 194.
5 MARX, K., Capital, vol. I, 188.
6 Cf. HOYE, W.J., Emergence of Eternal Life, 50–53

been robbed. This person is the natural material, who must be supported or changed by my activity in order to keep him alive. This aim has been chosen in advance. Christian neighborly love would therefore be a practice, which is to say a technique in the sense of the praxis-prejudice. It is a technique, an activity that serves a pre-determined use. This use is the criterion for neighborly love and for what counts as Christian value.

However, this does not reflect what is said in the parable itself.[7] Exegetical and theological considerations of this parable are also at risk of perceiving the parable in light of the technical narrative of modernity. This risk can be seen in what is often said, that 'neighbor' is defined in a universal and general way as everyone that may need something from me.[8] But the parable itself completely resists this interpretation. It is not the one in need who is called the neighbor, but the Samaritan (v. 36).[9] The question of the parable is: which one *became* a neighbor to him that fell among the robbers? Therefore, the point of the parable is not that the Samaritan has to intentionally perform an act, but deals with the passive process of becoming, which of the three persons involved, the Samaritan alone undergoes. In meeting the robbed man, the Samaritan develops the ability to empathize by being moved in his inner being in a particularly visceral manner. It is this movement that is decisive; the active deed simply follows from this movement. It is a kind of doing by undergoing. The parable does not favor constituting one's identity by active deeds in contrast to finding one's identity by following traditions.[10] It favors the constitution of one's identity by perceiving truth and value. The Samaritan does not act *intentionally*, but *attentionally* (cf. ch. 8). It is the affective attention to his environment that first determines his own becoming and personal formation, and thereafter his choice of ends. As such, it describes the complete opposite of the technical narrative of modernity as exemplified by Marx. On the contrary, intentional action determined by pre-chosen ends appears in the case of the two who passed by. They did not become neighbors because they were not passively affected by their environment, but were simply controlled by their intentional rules and the intentions they had before they made their way. They walked their way only as a necessary means to an end and were not interwoven in their way.

7 An excellent interpretation that also acknowledges the relative right of the traditional allegorical and christological interpretation is given by BOVON, F., Lukas II, 81–99.

8 Cf. for example KÜNG, H., On Being a Christian, 258.

9 Cf. for example SELLIN, G., Lukas der Gleichniserzähler, 23ff. However this meaning is relativized by noticing that the relation of neighbors is reciprocal with the result that the Samaritan and the harmed man would be neighbors for each other. Cf. YOUNG, N.Y., The Commandment to Love your Neighbor.

10 Cf. for a different view WOLTER, M., Lukasevangelium, 398.

Of course, this biblical parable alone does not suffice to correct the technical narrative of modernity. And of course, there are many other criticisms of the technical narrative, for example Heidegger's radical analysis and critique of modernity.[11] Suppose critics such as these are justified. What would this mean for the relation of practice and theory? It sounds like a thought experiment, but it is far more than that. In the pre-modern period, especially in the ancient and medieval use of the concepts, we find another way of relating practice and theory. For Aristotle, *praxis* does not mean an activity intentionally chosen for the sake of a distinct end, but in contrast to *poiesis* is an activity that is an end in itself and resists any mediation.[12] Further, the expression of 'pure theory' in the contemporary sense would have been impossible for the tradition, since *theoria* may be derived from *theos* and *horao*[13], meaning God's own vision. This meaning is also reflected in the Latin translation of *theoria* as *speculatio*: *Speculatio* does not refer to abstract and hypothetical considerations, whose value for reality is in doubt, but simply the vision of God.[14] Further, terms like *contemplatio* and *meditatio* did not, unlike the modern terms of contemplation or meditation, refer to a kind of turn to an inner self by the shutting out the environment. Rather, they referred to a particular way of perceiving that resonates reality in a qualified manner.[15] Whereas in the technical narrative of the praxis-prejudice, practice refers to an activity that leads to a use different from itself and theory is nothing but a means for the practice that is determined by the practice, the relation appears to be exactly the reverse in the traditional use of the concepts. *Praxis* is *not* an activity that leads to an intentionally chosen use, but an end in itself, which finally leads, without technical necessity, to *theoria* as perfection.

4.2 Christian Practice

The purpose of the previous section should not be misunderstood. My intention is not simply to deliver a repristination of traditional use of the language of practice and theory (whose details are much more complex than can be

11 Cf. for example HEIDEGGER, M., Question Concerning Technology, and for a description WENDTE, M., Die Gabe und das Gestell, 26–59.

12 Cf. ARISTOTLE, Nicomachean Ethics, VI,5; 1140b, 6–7 (*poiesis* is translated as 'making', *praxis* as 'action'). For an interpretation that objects to the common exclusivist defintion of the relation of *praxis* and *poiesis* cf. EBERT, T., Praxis und Poiesis.

13 Cf. KÖNIG, G., Art. Theorie.

14 Cf. EBBERSMEYER, S., Art. Spekulation.

15 Cf. KERSTIENS, L., Art. Kontemplation.

discussed here) and abandon the use given to it by the praxis-prejudice completely. Nevertheless, the examples given in the last section may illustrate what Christian practice might mean:

1. Christian practice does not refer to the sum of all the actions that humans called Christians or humans calling themselves Christians do. Therefore, quasi-empirical surveys given to believers are not an appropriate means of explicating what Christian practice ought to be.
2. Christian practice is not something that can be conceived of by the praxis-prejudice. Also, post-systematic theology as an eminently practical endeavor is not called practical because it has a use, be it an individual, a civic, or a moral one, but since it is a *praxis* in the Aristotelian sense: it precludes any functionalization.
3. Christian practice is a *praxis*, in as much as it consists in an attentional activity that harmonically resonates with the life-world through the formation of a perception that is adequate to this life-world. It is *praxis*, because it is above all an undergoing and becoming instead of primarily a doing. It is a doing only insofar as it is a becoming and developing *reaction* to an antecedent *pathos*.
4. Post-systematic theology as an explication (and im-plication and complication) of this *praxis* is itself practical as it supports the *praxis* of the perceiving of Christian practice. As a criteria-based reflection it does not primarily explicate the actions or the being of agents, but their becoming. It is not primarily ethics, if one conceives of ethics as a science of action. It is not a view of reality and also not an ontology, if one conceives of ontology as the science of being. It would be better to call it a 'gignomenology,' a science of becoming. But we will be forced to introduce so many neologisms in this volume that we will refrain from the use of this word and rather speak of a phenomenology or ontology of becoming – or more precisely, of a narrative ontology.
5. Christian practice is called Christian because it conceives itself as enabled and circumscribed by the self-presentation of the Trinitarian God. To make it still more explicit: It is Christian practice since it perceives itself as interwoven with the story of Jesus Christ in a way that acknowledges the story of Jesus Christ as the canon, norm, and rule of its own identity claims. It is Christian because it leads one to perceive one's own life in the light of the Gospel.

With these introductory comments, we complete the preparation for the journey. What awaits us is the first stage of the ways of perceiving: the explication of a phenomenologically-based narrative ontology.

PART 2

Narrative Ontology

CHAPTER 5

Perception and Narration

To begin with, perception is not as trivial as it may appear. It is often the case that the focus quickly shifts from perceiving to the perceived, to the capacity of perception or to its physiological conditions. Far too quickly one might be tempted to speak of perception instead of perceiving. It is impossible for animals, both nonhuman and human, not to perceive – even during sleep. Because it is a continuous phenomenon that accompanies all other phenomena, it is difficult to describe it as opposed to any of the other associated phenomena. There can be no phenomenon that is free from perceiving. The first task is therefore not to analyze or define what it means to perceive, but 'simply' to describe it. In order to describe it thoroughly, however, it will be necessary to set aside what seems to be self-evident and what our experience seems to take for granted – at least in a preliminary way. In order to describe the phenomenon of perception it is necessary to de-self-evidentialize it.

The term 'de-self-evidentialization' may appear very artificial, but perhaps it is the best way to say what is meant. It does not labor under any preconceptions, unlike similar terms such as *epoché* or phenomenological reduction. The disadvantage of these latter terms is that they are enmeshed with research on particular theories in the history of phenomenology or with the thought of certain phenomenologists. Of course, de-self-evidentialization is also not free from such connotations. But in contrast to the other terms mentioned, it is not necessary to know those connotations in order to understand the meaning. It simply means to put aside what one desires to know about the phenomenon in question in order to describe the phenomenon, which in our case is perception. Therefore, it is not necessary to put aside any connotations that may also be present. A complete de-self-evidentialization is as impossible as a complete phenomenological reduction is.[1] Further, even if it would be possible, it would not desirable. What would a complete de-self-evidentialization mean? It would mean the liberation of perception from any presuppositions rooted in specific stories. However, at the end of our description we will see that the point of perceiving is that

1 The term de-self-evidentialization has especially been used to characterize the modern period. Already BLUMENBERG, H., Lebenswelt und Technisierung, 48 recognized that the modern period can be described as an enduring process of de-self-evidentialization. However he also saw that a complete de-self-evidentialization is impossible as it is itself based on new self-evidences. For on the one hand, the term life-world is a limit concept, similar to that of black holes (cf. BLUMENBERG, H., Theorie der Lebenswelt, 54), on the other hand any observation or critique of the de-self-evidentialization of life-world can only take place from within it (cf. BLUMENBERG, H., Theorie der Lebenswelt, 49). Cf. also DALFERTH, I.U., Gott, 218.

 | DOI:10.30965/9783846765852_006

it is intermeshed in stories. To insist on a complete de-self-evidentialization is to produce a (pragmatic) contradiction.

In perception, something appears. And that which appears, has a specific and, at least relative, priority over everything else, as we will see shortly. This priority of the appearing means that the appearing determines me as perceiver in an almost complete way. It seems that I am immersed into that which is perceived. One can show this easily with the help of a thought-experiment (which always involves a little abstraction from the phenomena). Imagine viewing mountains from an elevated point of position. One would see mountains, valleys, the sky with its weather, and immediately in front of oneself: stony ground. What does not at first appear? I, myself, the perceiver. Only after my attention is drawn to myself will I recognize that in my visual field my nose and my cheeks also appear. However, they remain somehow transparent, fuzzy, and vague. Perhaps I will put my finger, which will first appear sharply at arm's length, between my eyes.[2] And now it appears translucent, and spooky, too. Further, should the perceiver want to turn herself into the perceived, the perceiver vanishes on the margin of the other things I that perceive in my visual field. Let us introduce another level of abstraction into our thought experiment. Imagine that the perceiver is not able to move at all, so that it is not possible to turn one's head or to change one's focus to one's hands and knees. Would it be possible for such a perceiver to develop the notion of herself, or a self at all? Perhaps it would, as the nose and cheeks still appear in their spooky manner; they would, so to speak, be invisibly visible. And in contrast to everything else that would appear, this translucent visibility would appear permanently and seemingly without any change or division into different sequences. In this case, the perceiver would perceive herself only as a horizon of the perceived, which can never be reached and which resembles rather the limit of perception. Such a creature would be completely determined by the other that is perceived in almost complete passivity. But remember, this unmoved perceiver is an abstraction from reality and does not really exist. In reality, the perceiver is constantly on the move. Add this permanent motion to the creature that has only the sense of sight. Now, it would be possible to perceive two relatively connected movements, the movement of the other that is perceived and the movement of oneself. But since these movements are connected, how can I know that it is two movements and not only one that belongs to the appearing? If there were only the visual sense, could we know the duality? Not immediately through perception but only by inference could we identify that there are two movements

2 Cf. INGOLD, T., Life of Lines, 99.

instead of one. Imagine now another scenario. Hearing is your only sense, and you hear an orchestra playing. What appears in this scenario? In contrast to the spooky appearance of oneself in the visual field, nothing of oneself appears, at least if the orchestra is loud enough. The perceiver appears now as completely determined by the perceived. Imagine that this perceiver moves in front of the orchestra. Besides the progression of the melodies she can perceive changes of dynamics and of frequency, dependent on whether she moves close to an instrument or away from an instrument. Perhaps such a perceiver could get the idea that it is not the instrument itself that changes the alterations of dynamics and frequency, but that it is some other movement. However, even if this would be possible, how should the perceiver know whether it is her own movement or the movement of the orchestra? Would such a perceiver be capable of developing such a notion herself? Perhaps not. Now imagine a creature with only the haptic sense. Changes of hot and cold and different pressures from being caressed to being injured painfully would be all that appear. But there would be no way of distinguishing whether these impressions are caused by one's own movement or another's. The distinction between self-motion and other-motion would be meaningless for such a perceiver. Let us return from the abstract notion of a single sense to the reality of actual perceivers, including their many, intermeshed senses. In such cases, self-motion is as immediate as the motion of the perceived, even when one does not draw one's attention to one's own motion. What can we infer from these considerations?

First: perception is initially without a differentiation between perceiver and perceived.

Second: when perceiver and perceived are differentiated, it is in such a way that the perceiver is determined by the perceived. Therefore, the perceived has some priority over the perceiver. In this regard, the phenomenological tradition claims that all kinds of perception are intentional.

It is doubtful whether the language of intentionality is truly meaningful. On the one hand, the concept of intentionality is ambivalent in more ways than one, as we will observe later. On the other hand, this term could be misunderstood to imply that the perceiver is antecedent in relation to the perceived. Such an antecedence, however, is the opposite of what we have found. Such a false priority of the perceiver over the perceived can perhaps be found in Husserl's thinking, who was accused of falling back from phenomenology into subjectivity-theory.[3]

3 Husserl always treats constitutive questions within the framework of questions of consciousness, cf. BERMES, C., Merleau-Ponty, Pos. 969 and FÖRSTER-BEUTHAN, Y., Zeiterfahrung und Ontologie, 48.

Third: self-motion is immediately present with the motion of the other that is perceived. It appears in the second-order-movement of the other that one perceives.

Fourth: perception always has to be in motion. A tone without movement and sequence is not a tone at all. Though it is possible to imagine a perceptible world consisting of one single tone without any modulation in frequency or dynamics, nonetheless such a tone must have a duration.

Perception is always dynamic, and it is not imaginable in another way. Initially, perception happens without the differentiation of the perceived from the perceiver. How should one think about this primordial unity and what should it be called?

There are a number of proposed answers to these questions. In his later work, Merleau-Ponty called this primordial unity 'flesh', which denotes the lack of distinction between perceived and perceiving.[4] The idea is that 'flesh', in this sense, has the ability to be incarnated, because it manifests or incarnates itself either in the form of the perceived or the perceiving. Perceived and perceiver are therefore incarnations of the dynamic flesh.[5] Apart from its ability to incarnate, the designation of this primordial unity as 'flesh' seems to be a little bit arbitrary in Merleau-Ponty. However, one should consider that we have only small fragments of his late philosophy.

Recently, Karen Barad has suggested speaking of intra-actions as constantly reconfiguring material apparatuses, wherein the latter term is defined as open-discourse practices. She merges phenomenological considerations with those of quantum physics. Just as there was originally only a single quantum state without any internal differences, which appeared only after the so-called collapse of the wave function,[6] so it is for everything else in the world. The material apparatuses are modelled on the metaphor of the wave function, and the apparatuses' differentiation, re-differentiation, and retraction from differentiation is called intra-action. Intra-action can be modeled after the collapse of the wave function, though the fact of the matter is that there is a decisive difference between quantum physics and Barad's thinking. Normally, the collapse of the wave function – perhaps with the exception of radioactive decay – not only does not appear with pure spontaneity, but only when induced by an entanglement between micro and macro entities. Therefore, it would be better to call it other-induced than self-induced. Barad, however, seems to imply that the intra-actions are self-induced. And since Barad's thesis is less a phenomenological one than an ontological one, the whole world consists of constantly reconfiguring apparatuses. In this case, the distinction between being self-induced and of being other-induced vanishes. Therefore, the intra-actions also have to be seen as self-reconfigurations. Further, the self and the other would have to be seen as reconfigurations without primordial status. But then the distinction between intra-action and interaction vanishes.

4 Cf. MERLEAU-PONTY, The Visible and the Invisble, Evanston: Northwestern University Press 1968, 141.

5 Cf. MERLEAU-PONTY, The Visible and the Invisble, 248–251.

6 Cf. BARAD, K., Agential Realism.

The examples of Merleau-Ponty's 'flesh' and of Barad's intra-actions show that arbitrariness cannot be completely excluded from the conceptualization of primordial perception. And there is a temptation to recount the many other attempts from the history of philosophy to name this primordial phenomenon: the unformed will of Schopenhauer, the absolute spirit of Hegel, Kant's thing itself, Spinoza's one substance, being itself. If one does it would be obvious that the idea of the primordial unity is only meaningful relative to this or that particular philosophical system. And these systems are, necessarily, already differentiated – they are necessarily storied.

Perhaps one should, at least preliminarily refrain from naming this primordial unity of perception, or simply call it 'perceiving'. The advantage would be, first, that the nomenclature remains close to the phenomenon, and, second, that we would use a verb instead of a noun, which stresses the dynamic character of perception. But these advantages would be accompanied by some (perhaps minor) disadvantages. Normally, verbs need nouns as grammatical subjects, and in many cases also grammatical objects. Yet to claim the same is true in the case of primordial perceiving, it would be a challenging case to make, because this amounts to an ontologization of the grammatical structure. Such a ontologization would, however, be the opposite of the required de-self-evidentialization. Secondly, most modern, north-atlantic languages differentiate between a verb's active and passive voice. This feature of grammar would then be ontologized – despite the fact that this distinction does not appear in perceiving. One would need a third grammatical expression between active and passive – like the middle voice in ancient Greek – in order to stay close to the phenomenon. But in English or German we cannot think of the middle voice without recourse to the distinction between active and passive voice.

One has to begin with the primordial unity of perceiving, as seen with the help of our thought experiments, and while it is possible to imagine this unity within some limits, it remains better to leave it (preliminarily) unnamed. It appears only 'incarnated' in the distinction between other-motion and self-motion. The next question is then: how is this difference to be named? Obviously, only correlative concepts are able to do so, if one does not want to deny that they are constituted in perceiving, which is the case in the simple terminology of perceived and perceiver that we have used so far. These terms are not trivial, because they imply that the relation between perceiver and perceived is an internal or constitutive one, not an external one.[7] Initially, it is only an internal relation in regard to conceptual requirements: speaking of a perceiver without the perceived is meaningless as well as *vice versa*, but there is also a relative priority of the perceived over the perceiver, as we have seen.

7 See chapter 7 below.

But we have seen that this reciprocal, constitutive relation between perceiver and perceived is more than a conceptual requirement. Both, perceiver and perceived emerge out of perceiving itself – not the other way around. Together, perceiver and perceived are the *relatum* of another relation: the relation to perceiving. And this relation is strictly asymmetrical insofar as perceiving is the origin of the difference between perceived and perceiver. As far as this distinction has been established, another asymmetry appears, but only a relative one. This is the relative priority of the perceived over the perceiver, which is connected by an alteration of affect (*Widerfahrnis*) and response, if one wants to use the terminology of Waldenfels.[8] Of course, it is possible to name the difference that emerges out of perceiving in other ways. A fruitful, or at least well-known, claim is the distinction between 'world' (in reference to the environment) and the lived body (*Leib*). The lived body means here, as in the phenomenology of the younger Merleau-Ponty, the ability for perceiving, which is always directed to the world, and receives and undergoes[9] within the environment.

Another fruitful suggestion would be understanding this difference as a fission-fusion reaction.[10] In perceiving, I am completely determined by the perceived, which is also the other, and at once separated from myself. I am therefore intermeshed with the perceived (fusion), but separated from myself (fission). This way of understanding what is going on remains close to the phenomena and is an inverse description of what we have done so far. The fission-fusion reaction presupposes the difference between perceiver and perceived, but resolves it by understanding the immersion of perceiving as the fission-fusion reaction. It must be kept in mind that this is a metaphor and should not be taken to imply the priority of the difference between perceiver and perceived over perceiving.

At this point, another feature must be added to the de-self-evidentialized description of perceiving. The relative priority of the perceived appears to have the character of an affect (*Widerfahrnis*) of perceiving, in that the perceiver or the lived body reacts as a response, which can be spontaneous, involuntarily, or even intentional. It is important that no response can be a complete reaction to what is given by the affect.[11] The response, therefore, is not a representation of the affect. A theoretical, external observer who is aware of the response could not draw, or at least only very limited, conclusions as to what the affect might have been. A decisive feature of the affect, therefore, is that it has a surplus,

8 Cf. WALDENFELS, B., Bodily Experience between Selfhood and Otherness.
9 Cf. INGOLD, T., Life of Lines, 125–129.
10 Cf. INGOLD, T., Life of Lines, 96.
11 Cf. STOELLGER, P., Passivität aus Passion, 350; MÜHLING, M., Resonances, 119.

which cannot be captured by any response or series of repeated responses. In this respect, Waldenfels is right.[12] The outcome of these considerations is that in the difference between perceiver and perceived, which emerges out of the previous unity of perceiving, there is not only a constitutive or internal relatedness, but also an apophatic element. It is the feature of persistent *alterity*, which cannot be removed because it is constitutive of one's self.

Another feature of perception is that the perceiver can only perceive herself as perceived. Aside from the abstractions produced by the thought experiments at the beginning of this section, it is obvious that every perception of another is only possible by simultaneously perceiving oneself. Husserl provided a well-known example of this, which Merleau-Ponty[13] used almost abundantely in several arguments: It is the case of the right hand touching the left one. In such circumstances, it is impossible to feel the left hand by the right one without at once perceiving the right by the left. This example of self-perception is by no means a special case of perceiving, but an exemplary one. If I perceive another human person I perceive at once also myself, but only as perceived by the other person. It is important, however, to note perceiving the other person is not a special case, distinct from perceiving inanimate objects. If I were to introduce such a distinction between perceiving animate and inanimate objects, the question would follow as to how I am able to recognize the other person as belonging to the same class as myself. Then the idea inevitability arises that I experience personality, embodiedness, or individuality primarily in myself, and that I only ascribe it to the other by way of interpretation. Two versions of this line of thinking commonly appear: Either it is said that I simulate you as another I in my mind, or that I reconstruct you theoretically in my mind apart from any perception. In contemporary thought, ideas like these can be found in the writings of the so called 'theory of mind' (ToM) school of reductionist cognitivist science, but their formal structure has existed much longer.[14] The decisive mistake of such theories, as Scheler has already observed,[15] is that they have to presuppose two things that cannot be presupposed. First, they presuppose an understanding of the reflexive self as if it would be possible to understand the reflexive self apart from an other's perspective. But perhaps there will be readers who share this assumption. However, a second mistake remains: I must know to which perceived object I am to ascribe a similitude

12 Cf. WALDENFELS, B., Bodily Experience between Selfhood and Otherness.

13 Cf. MERLEAU-PONTY, The Visible and the Invisble, 9.133.141.148.204.216.

14 Cf. on this matter GALLAGHER, S./ZAHAVI, D., Phenomenological Mind, 191–218 and MÜHLING, M., Resonances, 48–51.

15 Cf. SCHELER, M., The Nature of Sympathy, 238–263, esp. 260.

with myself and to which perceived I shall not ascribe such a similitude. And obviously, this cannot be done by way of a reconstruction or simulation, at least not if one wants to avoid an infinite regress of interpretation. But then the reason for either ascribing personality or not ascribing personality can only be found in perceiving the other. This type of perception leads to the solution of the problem: the foreign personality is immediately perceived and has nothing to do with a cognitive reconstruction. Meanwhile, cognitive research offers a huge amount of evidence in support of this view,[16] especially in the case of infants who can perceive the other human person as like herself without having developed higher cognitive abilities. How is this possible? Once more the example of the right hand touching the left might be helpful. The first point is that the perceiver here wants to make herself be perceived (my right hand wants to touch the left one). But this works only due to the reversibility of perceiver and perceived (the left touches the right one). In perceiving, self-perceiving has to be conceived through this reversibility of perceiver and perceived: I cannot perceive myself in any other way but as perceived by the perceived. The same is true not only in the case of my own hands but also in the case of the perception of another human person: I perceive myself only as perceived by her. For example, I might be alarmed because I perceive in her response for the first time the harsh intonation of my own speech. In this case, no interpretation or simulation is necessary, but I do immediately perceive the other as being terrified. There is no riddle, at least not if we observe this case through de-self-evidentialization without prejudices. In our everyday ontology, we are inclined to think of things like being terrified, grief, intentions, etc. as private things which might be somehow interior to me, and that would therefore only be visible to self-reflection. But if we put the prejudice of the everyday ontology aside, we can see that this is not the case. Being terrified, grieving, having intentions, etc. are bodily phenomena, observable at once by other's perception and by self-perception. This is not only obvious by phenomenological considerations but also by empirical ones, where it is the phenomenon of syntopy[17] that makes consulting a doctor possible. Precisely because I immediately experience the other's being terrified am I able to experience my own terror.

The exact same thing is occurring when another human person is perceived, as occurs in the case of the right hand touching the left one, but in

16 Vgl. DORNES, M., Der kompetente Säugling, 68; TRONICK, E.Z., Things Still to be Done on the Still-Face Effect; BERMÚDEZ, J.L., Transcendental Arguments and Psychology; MURRAY, L./TREVARTHEN, C., Emotional Regulations of Interactions between two-month-olds and their Mothers; MELTZOFF, A.N., Understanding the Intentions of Others; TOMASELLO, M., Die kulturelle Entwicklung des menschlichen Denkens, 111.

17 Cf. FUCHS, T., Das Gehirn – ein Beziehungsorgan, 34f.

reverse order: In the perception of the hands, I discover the perceived in what is my own, in the perception of the other person, I discover what is my own in the perceived. In the first case, I discover myself in the 'object' whereas in the latter case I discover you in the 'object'. One can try to express this with the help of the I-Thou philosophy of Buber or Heim, who have seen that the other is at once constitutive and threatening to one's self.[18] A more modest way of conceiving this case – without introducing such, perhaps cryptic, entities like 'I' and 'Thou' – would involve the simple claim that perceiving, and so embodiment, is always to be understood as inter-embodiment,[19] because perception and embodiment can only be perceived as between bodies, which also means that any kind of embodiment is only possible through the experience of inter-embodiment.

But one problem remains. In our everyday life it seems easy to distinguish between that which is perceived as similar to one's self which is therefore perceived as 'Thou' or as personal, and those things which are perceived where this seems to be impossible. How is this distinction possible? The answer is that this distinction is in fact not a basic phenomenon. Even in cases of the seemingly a-personal or pre-personal, I perceive myself only as perceived by the perceived one. Consider the following sentences:

(1) In perceiving you, I perceive myself as perceived by yourself.
(2) In perceiving a cat, I perceive myself as perceived by the cat.
(3) In perceiving a dark path through the forest, I perceive myself as perceived by the trees.
(4) In sunbathing, I perceive myself as perceived by warmth.

In the framework of our everyday ontology, the first sentence sounds plausible, the second less, and so on in a descending order. If, with the help of de-self-evidentialization, we set the prejudices that are rooted in our everyday ontology aside, then one sees that there is no principal difference between the four sentences and that they describe similar phenomena and rely on the same perception. Nobody can treat a pet appropriately if they are not able to experience the pet to some extent as a 'thou'. But the experience of being perceived by the seemingly a-personal is also not as uncommon as one might think. Humans do indeed experience themselves as perceived by trees,[20] and the Tlingit tribe on the northwest coast of North America perceives humans

18 Cf. HEIM, K., God Transcendent, 153–172; HEIM, K., Christian Faith and Natural Science, 48–81.

19 Cf. MERLEAU-PONTY, The Visible and the Invisble, 141.168.172.

20 Cf. CHARBONNIER, G., Le monologue du peintre, 143.

as heard by a glacier.[21] One could easily provide more such examples. Think of infants and one recalls their tendency to treat seemingly inanimate things as animated or personal. And truthfully, do you not observe such behavior in yourself? What is important is that these are not the exception to the rule of perception, but the other way around. The phenomenon of perceiving oneself as perceived by the perceived reflects the basic feature of inter-embodiment which is true in every case of perception. This phenomenon might be one reason why Merleau-Ponty describes the perceiver as flesh that is coiled over flesh[22] or intermeshed with other flesh. And further, it may have also been the decisive reason for introducing the concept of flesh without any distinction between personal and pre-personal. Perhaps the foregoing seems acceptable, but one still holds onto the everyday ontology by sharply distinguishing between sentence (1) and sentence (3) and (4); there is also uncertainty about sentence (2). The distinction comes from the fact that we would, according to our everyday ontology, insist that while the structure of perception might be the same, nevertheless sentence (1) is true, whereas sentences (3) and (4) are false, which may be indeed the case. But this simply means that we have discovered another decisive feature of all perceiving: its *fallibility*, which will be analyzed later. Yet there remains a further question. If our experience of animateness or personality in perceiving is always immediate, as opposed to ascribing these 'qualities' to 'objects' by means of cognitive interpretation, and if any perception can be wrong, how then can we assume that the perception in the case of statement (1) is accurate whereas it is inaccurate in the cases of statement (3) and (4)? The only possible answer is not that the perception of personality and being alive are ascribed phenomena, but that the denial of personality and of being alive relies on ascription. Certain cognitive acts encourage us to doubt our immediate perception in the cases (3) and (4). On the one hand, this distrust is only possible because of the fallibility of perceiving. On the other hand, this distrust or suspicion is only possible because we and any other possible perceiver always have a prior *trust* in what she perceives. In perceiving there is what one might call a primordial trust or indeed a kind of faith. Similarly, Merleau-Ponty argued that there is no perception without *perceptual faith*.[23]

21 Cf. CRUIKSHANK, J., Do Glaciers Listen?.

22 Cf. MERLEAU-PONTY, M., Visible and the Invisible, 140.

23 Cf. MERLEAU-PONTY, Phenomenology of Perception, 346: "In experiencing a perceived truth, I assume that the concordance so far experienced would hold for a more detailed observation; I place my confidence in the world. Perceiving is pinning one's faith, at a stroke, in a whole future of experiences, and doing so in a present whrich never strictly guarantees the future; it is placing one's belief in a world. It is this opening upon a world

Perceptual distrust is secondary to perceptual trust or faith. It is possible because – though every perception is immediate – there is a kind of mediated immediateness. It is (at the very least) mediated by the past story of our perceptions, which bestows on us a particular expectation of coherence, though this can be disappointed. Perceiving is not only fallible but always intermeshed within a story of perceiving, and it is this story of perceiving which mediates perception without reducing it to non-interpretative immediacy. Someone who knows nothing about the history of architecture in the 20th century will perceive only a mass of houses when walking through an impressive city like Chicago. But if she is introduced to this history, she will see things for the first time that she *had not seen* during her previous walk. The story and history of perception alters perception itself. It does not reduce, but enables the immediateness of perception. The fact that perceiving is intermeshed within a story of perception leads to the expectation of coherence and to the possibility of the secondary distrust of particular sequences of perception as a side effect of the original trust.

In which of our examples of statements (1)–(4) is the primary faith or the secondary distrust justified? At this stage of our inquiry, no answer possible. The description of perception can give no answer as to whether there is something like an all-perceiver, or something like panpsychism.

The possibility of actual perception within a story or history of perception is possible precisely because perceiving in presence is already determined by *protention* and *retention*, i.e. it is determined by a remembered past and an expectable future. Husserl, Heidegger, and Merleau-Ponty all stressed this fact in different ways.[24] The experience of presence is only possible through the experience of protention and retention. The conditions of temporality enable perceiving in the present. These conditions are also not cognitive acts, but are perhaps a feature of all animated life. A dog may, due to his drives, chase a cat, who then rescues itself by climbing a tree. In such instances, different dogs will react in different ways. They might wait for some time before giving up their hunt, but they will not wait endlessly. Depending on the situation, the particular tree, the surrounding terrain, and the story of the experience of

---

which makes possible perceptual truth and the actual effecting of a *Wahr-Nehmung*, thus enabling us to 'cross-out' the previous illusion and regard it as null and void." So I argue against FÖRSTER-BEUTHAN, Y., Zeiterfahrung und Ontologie, 162 that Merleau-Ponty's *perceptual faith* is indeed not identical with Husserl's natural setting, for one can escape the natural setting through *epoché*, so it does not belong to what constitutes perception. In contrast to this, *perceptual faith* is not a product of perception but implied by it.

24 Cf. the relevant sections in FÖRSTER-BEUTHAN, Y., Zeiterfahrung und Ontologie.

the particular dog, the times will vary.[25] Of course, dogs are highly developed vertebrates, but this is not an argument against assuming that protention and retention belong to every possible experience of perception. They belong to perceiving itself, and therefore to embodiment and inter-embodiment.

Furthermore, our description entails that any protention will imply an expectation of contingency or chance. It is a given in the very self-perception that a response – e.g. the memory of a perception or a story of perceptions – invokes. There is not only an expectation of coherence but also an expectation of the possibility of being surprised by something that can only be addressed as a surprise after a future perception, which cannot be inferred from the prior history of perception – i.e. a retrospective surprise. Only one who has died ceases to hope to be surprised. And whoever claims that she does not expect to be surprised is either using a language disconnected from life or is lying. True contingency – a moment which simply happens, which cannot be inferred from any previous regularity – is something that is perceived in, with and under all perceiving; it belongs to the immediateness of perceiving. The immediateness of the perception of chance and contingency allows, however, preliminarily no ontological inference. One cannot infer from the irreducibility of perceptual contingency to a reality of contingency.

So far, our description has focused on the emerging difference between perceiver and perceived, and mainly on the perceiver who has been identified with the lived body. We must now say something more about the perceived. What is it that is perceived when I perceive a cliff or a human? What is perceived are not abstract or physical 'qualities' or 'properties' of 'things', but *affordances.*

Gestalt-psychology has used various terms for the perceived, such as the *demands* in the work of Kurt Koffka,[26] or in the case of Kurt Lewin the *valences* (*Aufforderungscharaktere*). They are fixed to things like vectors, which are prepared to move the perceiver in different ways.[27] They are value-laden actualities and their values can vary. Koffka used the example of the phenomenal letter-box that invites correspondence. This phenomenal letterbox is understood to be distinct from a real letter-box. According to this theory, in perception we as perceivers unconsciously assign a value to 'things'. This value varies from perceiver to perceiver, and it varies due to

25 This example was introduced by MALCOLM, N., Thought and Knowledge, Ch. 2, in order to show thinking is impossible without languages. It was among others picked up by DAVIDSON, D., Truth and Interpretation, 157 in the same intention. SEARLE, J.R., Animal Minds however takes this example to show that intentional states do not presuppose language. Cf. ebd., 210. The most substantial and concise discussion, which now shows that one has to speak of a prelingual consciousness of right and wrong, is given by MACINTYRE, A., Dependent Rational Animals, 35–39.

26 Cf. KOFFKA, K., Principles of Gestalt Psychology, 7.

27 Cf. GIBSON, J.J., Ecological Approach to Visual Perception, 129.

the varying needs of the perceivers. Analyses like these, however, remain caught in the only apparent self-evidence of our everyday ontology. They not only presuppose incorrectly that the 'demands' are properties composed of the supposedly 'real' physical properties on the one side and of the 'subjective' psychical qualities on the other side,[28] but also that the perceiver already knows – prior to perception – that there might be physical objects that lack these specific valences or demands. But how should it be possible for the perceiver to know such a thing, especially if the perceiver is an infant or a nonhuman animal? Therefore, the language of demands and values drawn from *Gestalt*-psychology does not belong to perception but only to specific, theoretical interpretations of perception. However, the theories of the *Gestalt*-psychologists are not completely without value, because it is possible to usefully modify their concepts at decisive points. James J. Gibson, sometimes called the founder of ecological psychology, has impressively done so.

These affordances or invitations cannot be divided into subjective and objective elements. They are the relational qualities of the things, which would not persist if there were no perceiving animals. They are perceived immediately, but they also exist when they are not perceived. This claim means that particular kinds of value and meaning are perceived. These are relationally bound to the perceiver but remain external to her and, therefore, they are not the product of ascription.[29] The sum of the perceivable affordances – not the sum of the actual perceived ones – is the *niche* of particular kinds of perceivers.[30] Therefore, there is a complementarity between perceivers and their niches. The affordances remain external to the perceiver because there is an asymmetry between perceiver and perceived affordances that consists in the dependence of a species on their niches. These niches can be altered within specific limits, whereas the niches of the environment persist with only a few modifications when the perceivers vanish.[31] Therefore, there are niches that are not

---

28 Cf. GIBSON, J.J., Ecological Approach to Visual Perception, 125.

29 Cf. GIBSON, J.J., Ecological Approach to Visual Perception, 119: 'The *affordances* of the environment are what it *offers* the animal, what it *provides* or *furnishes*, either for good or ill. The verb *to afford* is found in the dictionary, but the noun *affordance* is not. I have made it up. I mean by it something that refers to both the environment and the animal in a way that no existing term does. It implies the complementarity of the animal and the environment.'

30 Cf. GIBSON, J.J., Ecological Approach to Visual Perception, 120: 'a niche refers more to *how* an animal lives than to *where* it lives. I suggest that a niche is a set of affordances.'

31 GIBSON, J.J., Ecological Approach to Visual Perception, 121 also speaks of the organisms being dependent on their surroundings in their existence, while the surrounding's existence is not dependendent on the organisms. One would need to make an adjustment: the organisms are themselves part of the surrounding. If they are missing or dying out, the surrounding will not disappear, but it changes, also in quality of *affordances* for others, including only possible organisms.

inhabited by particular species and there are affordances which are not yet observed at all. As Gibson has claimed:

> An important fact about the affordances of the environment is that they are in a sense objective, real, and physical. [...] But actually, an affordance is neither an objective property nor a subjective property; or it is both if you like. An affordance cuts across the dichotomy of subjective-objective and helps us to understand its inadequacy. It is equally a fact of the environment and a fact of behavior. It is both physical and psychical, yet neither.[32]

Affordances can have a positive or negative value. The basis of these positive or negative values are not the distinction between desire and dislike one might feel while perceiving them, but the real possibilities for future events occurring in the interaction between perceiver and perceived. The course of these events could be revealed as positive, neutral, or harmful for the perceiver. An example might make this clearer:

> [C]onsider the brink of a cliff. On the one side it affords walking along, locomotion, whereas on the other it affords falling off, injury. [... C]onsider the other person. The animate object can give caresses or blows, contact comfort or contact injury, reward or punishment, and it is not always easy to perceive which will be provided.[33]

Gibson stresses the internal relationality of the perceived affordances, but one must also stress their dynamic or sequential character. The affordances are affects (*Widerfahrnisse*) that, in contrast to Waldenfels' opinion,[34] not only consist in pure *pathos* without any *logos*, but which always include meaning and as such *logos*. They invite different possibilities for response. They only partially determine the future course of history because what will be also depends on the responses, as well as the circumstances. The response to the affordances is not arbitrary, and therefore it seems that there is not an infinite amount of possible future stories between perceiver and perceived. However, the affordances determine which of the possible stories exist and which not. The word affordance is not so easily translated into everyday language. Perhaps

---

32 GIBSON, J.J., Ecological Approach to Visual Perception, 120.

33 GIBSON, J.J., Ecological Approach to Visual Perception, 129.

34 Cf. WALDENFELS, B., Bodily Experience between Selfhood and Otherness, 238: 'In sum, everything that appears as something has to be described not simply as something which receives a sense, but as something which provokes sense without being meaningful itself, but still something *by which* we are touched, affected, stimulated, surprised and to some extent violated. I call this happening pathos, *Widerfahrnis* or af-fect, marked by a hyphen in order to suggest that something is done *to us*.'

either *invitations* or temptations would do, though the first term might be the better one.

Like Alice, who reads 'drink me' on the bottle, or like the children in C.S. Lewis' *The Magician's Nephew*, who found in front of the sleeping witch a bell that wants to be rung, we are perceiving affordances. The implications are far reaching and are not only concerned with perception.

The first consequence is that the distinction between so-called primary and secondary qualities, common in modernity since the times of Locke, must be unmasked as a cognitive interpretation on the basis of an abstraction from perceiving. Of course, this insight is by no means a new one – Jonathan Edwards has already noted this fact.[35] There is, in other words, no basic fact/value distinction.

The second consequence is that perception is meaningful or conceptual. At the end of the 20th century, John McDowell had already shown that the passive impressions of perception are meaningful and conceptual.[36] And this meaning is always value-laden meaning. Perceiving is always meaningful – this is unavoidable – without the division of perceiving values. There is no perceiving without perceiving values and there is no valuing that is not at the same time a perceiving. In German perceiving is *wahrnehmen*, which literally means *taking or suffering truth*. And one can easily build a new term, *wertnehmen*, which would then mean *taking or suffering values*, and finally *wertwahrnehmen*, meaning *taking or suffering truth-value*. The perceived values belong to reality itself, for it must be relationally constituted since the perceivers are also parts of reality. This last sentence, however, is strictly making an ontological claim. But we have seen that, in the end, this is unavoidable. As we argued with Merleau-Ponty, there cannot be a complete de-self-evidentialization. And exactly here is the point where the transition to an (descriptive and open) ontology is appropriate, since this transition is not arbitrary but required by perceiving itself. Furthermore, if one wants to avoid the transition at this point, one will be caught in a contradiction. The analysis of affordances has shown that they cannot be understood as qualities that the perceiver ascribes to the perceived. If one avoids the claim that every perception is at the same time the

---

35 Cf. JENSON, R.W., On Thinking the Human, 50–58.

36 Cf. MCDOWELL, J., Mind and World, 10: 'Experiences already have conceptual content [...].' ibd., 13: 'The view I am recommending is that even though experience is passive, it draws into operation capacities that genuinely belong to spontaneity.' Ibd., 18: 'A genuine escape would require that we avoid the Myth of the Given without renouncing the claim that experience is a rational constraint on thinking. I have suggested that we can do that if we can recognize that the world's impression on our senses are already possessed of conceptual content.'

perception of values within a relationally constituted reality and *vice versa*, in the end one must claim that there is no perceptual faith. But the claim that there is no perceptual faith is nothing other than the claim that all perception is deceptive. But the very idea of deception is itself a highly cognitive notion that is logically dependent on perceptual faith. Furthermore, for most non-human perceivers the idea that all perception is deceptive is sheer nonsense. If it is true that at this point there is a transition to ontology, in the sense that claims about reality become unavoidable, the question is how this is best done with empirical and philosophical tools. Empirically, Thomas Fuchs, following Alva Noe, Evan Thompson, Dan Zahavi, Shaun Gallagher and others,[37] has recently presented an enactive theory of values as relational realities,[38] which might fit best with our observations. Philosophically, the consequences are much more far-reaching. We have to avoid any separation between epistemology, ontology, and ethics. An ethic that is fit for perception has to start with a theory of values and the perception of values. Max Scheler, by employing the concept of *viewing values* (*Werterschauung*), has already taken important steps in this direction,[39] as well as Roberta de Monticelli who has recently presented a theory of perceiving values by feeling.[40]

At this point we cannot go into further detail, but it might be helpful at the present to state a decisive implication of these theories. If perceiving is at the same time perceiving values, and if the means of perceiving values are affective and emotional feelings, then cognitivist as well as irrationalist theories of feelings[41] are wrong because they do not fit with perceiving. It follows that every particular feeling not only has a relational character but also cognitive content. Feelings and emotions then, like any perceptions, are fallible. The feelings of a perceiver vis-à-vis the perceived could therefore be more or less fitting, more or less resonate with the perceived; they could perhaps be 'right' or 'wrong' – although our everyday ontology might feel uncomfortable with this kind of language. Most probably our affective abilities remain the ever-present basis for the so called 'higher' cognitive abilities of human beings.[42]

37 Cf. THOMPSON, E.T., Mind in Life; O'REGAN, J.K./NOE, A., A Sensorimotor account of Vision and Visual Consciousness; GALLAGHER, S./ZAHAVI, D., Phenomenological Mind.

38 Cf. FUCHS, T., Values as Relational Phenomena.

39 Cf. SCHELER, M., Wertethik, 64. Unfortunally, the English version (SCHELER, M., Formalism in Ethics, 68) uses 'value-cognition' or 'value-intuition' as translations for 'Werterschauung', thereby obscuring the perceptual aspect of Scheler's term.

40 Cf. DE MONTICELLI, R., Feeling of Values; DE MONTICELLI, R., Sensibility and Values; DE MONTICELLI, R., Perceiving Values.

41 Cf. on this subject MÜHLING, M., Gefühle, Werte und das ausgedehnte Selbst.

42 This now widely substantiated thesis has been remarked on by, among others, MACINTYRE, A., Dependent Rational Animals, 40.

But this last sentence does not belong to the description of perceiving but to an empirically-based, theoretical interpretation.

At least one implication for theology is important: A post-systematic theology has to abandon any separation of dogmatics and ethics. Perhaps it might be possible to keep a conceptual distinction between these two fields, but even this seems questionable.

We are now close to bringing our description of perceiving to an end. Yet, there is one very decisive feature we first have to address which is the so-called perspectival character of perception.

If perceiver and perceived emerge out of perceiving, or better, if perceiver and perceived emerge out of perceiving and perceiving values, then we are perceiving in between the perceived, or, in order to use once more an expression from Merleau-Ponty, we perceive as flesh in between flesh Any view from nowhere, any perspective hovering over the things, is therefore strictly forbidden because such a perspective would be impossible. At best, such ideas would be conceptual abstractions from perceiving, but more probably they would be pure phantasms. Perceiving is always perspectival. This, however, seems to be a more or less trivial, standard claim. What is important, however, is not that a perspective could not be a standpoint over that which is perceived, but *that a meaningful perspective cannot be a standpoint at all, neither over nor in the middle of things.* This claim might be surprising. How is it to be understood? We have seen that perceiving is not only relational but also a process and the dynamic protention and retention of a particular presence. This particular presence is not to be understood as a point or sequence since it is itself in permanent transition. I cannot perceive something unmoved, but only moved. And I cannot perceive as unmoved, but only as moved. The summit I perceive during a walk is perceived in motion. It looks permanently different along the way. With every step the mountain bounces up and down. It vanishes and reappears caused by the trees in front of my way, and it is flickering due to the movements of my eye-lids. These innumerable movements of relation in which I perceive the mountain are relativized secondarily by interpreting myself as moved and the mountain as unmoved. But strictly speaking, this solution is wrong, since in perceiving there is nothing but the relative motion of myself and the mountain, which is easily testable. Imagine stopping at any place in order to take a picture of the mountain, but think instead of the real mountain. In most cases, the picture does not appear as impressive as the mountain is. Sometimes it might also be surprisingly impressive, but in another way, when we discover the intentional composition of the picture by the photographer, which is an artificial act that follows after perceiving. The picture is a static abstraction from perception. Standpoints, we have to conclude, are abstractions from moving perspectives. These moving perspectives cannot be understood as the sum of standpoints connected by straight lines, since the concept of the standpoint is now unmasked as an *abstraction from perspectives*. Perspectives are always in motion, they are not points or positions but ways or lines. One has also to see that perspectives do not consist in taking up a position, but in leaving a position, as has been argued by socioanthropologist Tim Ingold, following Jan Masschelein:

> Far from taking up a standpoint or perspective from this position or that, walking continually pulls us away from *any* standpoint – from any position we might adopt. 'Walking,' as Masschelein explains, 'is about putting this position at stake; it is about exposition, about being out-of-position.' [...] It is not that exposure affords a perspective or set of perspectives. [...] Indeed, it does not disclose the world from any perspective at all. The walker's attention comes not from having arrived at a position, but from being pulled away from it, from displacement.[43]

Every 'act' of perception therefore is always incomplete; it is in the process of being pushed beyond itself to further and new perceptions. Perceiving means to be always perceiving on the way. Strictly speaking, there is no perceived which could be stated in the perfect-tense, but it is always that which is going to be perceived. Masschelein might have had a particular phenomenon in mind, but his diagnosis is true for perceiving as a whole:

> It is a paradoxical activity: to be commanded by something, which is not yet given, but on the way to being given, something which is literally presenting itself, in the course of the way that one is following.[44]

The implications of such a diagnosis are far-reaching. Not only must every concrete perspective be understood as a way; not only is perceiving affordances only possible in becoming, but, since perceiver and perceived emerge equiprimordially out of the previous perceiving, the perceiver is also not a being but permanently in becoming. The perspective of 'perceiving on the way' not only forms the way and the perceived, but the perceiver as well. Perspectives are *wayformational* perspectives. The word 'wayformational' is of course a neologism, but a necessary one. It signifies four states of affairs: first, that every perspective is moved and shaped by the way, which cannot be understood as reducible to additional standpoints but as abandoning any position that is directed towards the not yet perceived; second, that this way does not come

---

43 INGOLD, T., Life of Lines, 135. Here, Ingold is citing MASSCHELEIN, J., E-ducating the Gaze, 278.

44 MASSCHELEIN, J., E-ducating the Gaze, 46.

ready-made, but is shaped during perception; third, that equiprimordially with the shaping of the way, the perceived emerges as something that is formed and on the way of becoming formed; fourth, in the same sense the perceiver emerges not as a being but as a becoming.

We must stop here. While the foregoing description of perceiving might not be complete, we now have to sum up:

1. The prior unity of perceiving is primary. It is difficult to describe this unity because it is a precognitive unity. The history of philosophy offers a variety of more or less arbitrary names for this, e.g. Merleau-Ponty's 'flesh'.
2. Perceived and perceiver emerge out of perceiving, internally related but with the asymmetry of the perceived being relatively prior in relation to the perceiver.
3. Perceiving is dynamic or processual.
4. True alterity and the self are constitutively and relationally bound together.
5. Perceiving is always bodily, or, to be more exact, inter-bodily: The perceived is only perceived by self-perception, and self-perception means to perceive oneself as perceived by the perceived.
6. Perception is fallible: it may be resonating or dissonant with reality.
7. Perceiving implies perceptual trust or perceptual faith, which provides the conditions for the possibility of secondary perceptual distrust or perceptual doubt.
8. Perceiving happens in the temporal protention and retention of a specific presence.
9. Perceiving implies the experience and expectation of being surprised in a purely retrospective manner; therefore, it also implies contingency or chance.
10. Perceiving is at the same time perceiving values, which is enabled by the relationally constituted, but real affordances of the situationally perceived. The fact/value distinction must be abandoned. Feeling is the means for perceiving values.
11. Perceiving is only possible on wayformational perspectives. They are formed equiprimordially by perceiver and perceived and remain in becoming.
12. Perceiving is immediate insofar as it is independent of interpretations by the cognitive acts of higher life-forms, such as a healthy adult.
13. The immediateness of immediate perceiving is always a *mediated* immediateness. That which mediates presupposes the retention of past perceptions as well as the protention of expected and surprising perceptions,

but retention and protention cannot name that which mediates completely. An important task is to identify what it is that mediates.

This description of perceiving and of perceiving values is based on a de-self-evidentialized practice. This method of de-self-evidentialization can never be complete. And with this last feature – the mediated immediateness of perception – we have found the reason for this phenomenon. At the very least, the phenomenal analysis of perceiving forces us in the direction of ontology and conceptual understanding. With that, the abstraction from the reality of perceiving will be unavoidable. The question is not whether such an abstraction will happen (or already has) but whether there are concepts and ontologies that resonate better or worse with perceiving, in other words, which include a greater or lesser degree of abstraction. Should we simply use our everyday ontologies, as ordinary language philosophy has claimed? Should one use one of the manifold ontologies that rely on the separation between subject and object, be it in a reductionist empirical mode, or in one of the idealist theories of subjectivity? The answer to this question depends on how easily the aforementioned features of perceiving can be expressed by such concepts. But not one of the conceptual ontologies, neither reductionist 'realism', nor idealist 'subjectivism', nor our everyday ontologies are really appropriate, at least not if there are better ones, which is indeed the case. For everything we found to be an important feature of perceiving can be tied together in one single concept: *story*.

1. A story can be conceived as a unity that is not composed out of atomistic sequences or episodes since one can only speak of sequences or episodes by referencing the whole story. Stories ought not to be misunderstood as literary products or constructs, except in the case of fictional stories; they are lived before they can be told.[45] MacIntyre's insight has to be taken seriously. The concept of story is an excellent means for naming this prior unity of perceiving. Instead of 'flesh' like Merleau-Ponty, we are using *story*.
2. The characters, persons, roles, things, and their environments emerge out of a story and can only be described relative to one another. Whoever wants to characterize a particular person in the story has to tell the whole story – if it is tellable.
3. Stories are processes like perceptions, and they are dynamic – not in every case, but it is possible.
4. Particular characters in a story can only be described with reference to what is not that specific character; sometimes it seems that it is necessary

45 Cf. MacIntyre, A., After Virtue, 212.

to refer to something that is not told at all in order to characterize a person. Therefore, the constitutive relationality between the self and the other is also comprised of stories.

5. Since stories are lived before they can be told, stories are neither primarily textual or literary or narrated entities, but bodily entities, presupposing bodiliness as a means of perception and communication.
6. Perception is fallible. Is this also true in the case of stories? Could they be right and wrong? This question is not so easy to decide. But the fact that we divide stories into fictive and non-fictive stories might be a hint that stories may be fallible, although it remains preliminary open in what respect they are fallible.
7. All stories – including obviously fictive ones – presuppose trust in the lived or told story,[46] which is at the same time the condition of the possibility of doubt.
8. In the course of experiencing a lived or told story, a necessarily specific progression of presence emerges that is built up by protention and retention and that – at least in some cases – enables the existence of a dramatic arc of suspense.[47]
9. Good stories surprise while being experienced or heard in such a way that the surprising moment could not be inferred from the one that preceded it, but nevertheless make sense once it appears.[48] Therefore, stories are an excellent means for expressing contingency, chance, and novelty.
10. Stories are a first-choice medium if there is no fact-value distinction, because in all apparently 'merely' descriptive stories, values are also communicated.
11. Stories, at least the primary ones, cannot be perceived from fixed standpoints but only in the midst of the way of one's own life-story. They are perspectival and enable descriptions from wayformational perspectives. This is always the case of the experienced life-story, as well as for those told stories that remain open. It is also possible in the case of closed textual stories, as texts have manifold histories of revision, modification, and interpretation. Stories, like perceiving, are in becoming.
12. No higher cognitive abilities are necessary in order to experience a story. Every non-human animal lives a story determining its character, even in those cases where it is not capable of an autobiographical self. To

46 Cf. MERLEAU-PONTY, Phenomenology of Perception, 346.
47 Cf. KÖPPE, T./KINDT, T., Erzähltheorie, 67–73.
48 Cf. ARISTOTELES, Peri Poietikes1452a (Kap. 9,9) discussed by MÜHLING, M., Resonances, 123.

experience stories – one's own life-story, literary, cinematic, or other artificial stories – means in this sense to undergo an immediate experience that evokes numerous responses, including affective ones.

13. The experience of the immediate response to and in stories is never an immediate immediateness, but a mediated one. And in the case of stories, it is obvious that the thing which mediates is the story itself. In the case of the lived story, it is the whole story, including protention and retention; in the case of the told stories, it also consists in the narration, inclusive of all narrative media, as well as textual and non-textual factors like accent and inflection.

To conclude: We have to design an ontology on the basis of the concept of story in order to make the transition from perceiving to its ontological description. Moreover, it is impossible to describe perceiving without narrative means. After all, the description of perceiving given above presupposes narrative elements, as the attentive reader might have observed.

The idea of a narrative basis for phenomenology can be traced back to Husserl, who had spoken of a story of consciousness imbedded in an endless connection of life.[49] Consequently, Wilhelm Schapp has argued that perception has an irreducible basis in stories: every perception not only relies on stories but what is perceived is nothing but stories. Therefore, it is impossible to escape stories. Schapp has offered something one might call a comprehensive ontology of stories.[50] Nevertheless, one cannot adopt his ontology or phenomenology in detail, because there remains a slightly skeptical note in his thinking. While his observation that truth can only exist relatively between different levels of stories is a valuable insight, in the end the relationship between stories and reality is not as clear as one might want.[51]

Here, then, we can answer the last remaining question of the description of perceiving: what mediates the mediated immediateness of perceiving? It is stories and only stories.

---

49 Cf. HUSSERL, E., Phänomenologische Reduktion, Hua VIII, 153.

50 Cf. SCHAPP, W., Philosophie der Geschichten (1959); SCHAPP, W., In Geschichten verstrickt (1953).

51 Cf. EICHLER, K.-D., Schapps narrative Ontologie, 118f.

CHAPTER 6

Narrative Ontology and its Terminology in Contrast to Narratology

Narrative ontology is not narratology, but, if a critical distance is kept, it is possible to learn something from narratology. Of course, narratology is not a uniform academic field, so the term should only be used in the plural. In most cases, narratologies are understood to be a part of philology, and sometimes they are understood only as areas within the parts of philology that are concerned with texts. There are very narrow narratologies without any, or only very little inter- and transdisciplinary impact, and there are narratologies with a broader applicability.

An example of the first kind is the introduction to narratology by Köppe and Kindt. Narratology is here seen as 'an academic model of narration, in particular narrating'.[1] They also define narrations only as sub-class of texts by claiming that a 'text is a narration if and only if it contains at least two events, which are connected in a temporal order as well as in at least one further meaningful manner.'[2] They only see narrations as human artifacts that originate from authors.[3] In this definition, the concepts of temporality, event, and meaning are presupposed in a manner such that they appear as independent from narrations. The innovative use of narratology by others, such as the debate about narrative identity, are discarded.[4] Such narrow narratologies are not completely without value, as their focus on the different kinds of structures that texts display can sometimes be helpful. However, their own narrow self-limitation prevents them from having any important influence on the design of a narrative ontology.

The second kind of narratologies are not restricted to the subject-matter of texts and are interdisciplinary from their inception, insofar as they include the social realm. An example of such theories is the narratology presented by

---

1 Cf. Köppe, T./Kindt, T., Erzähltheorie, 27.: 'ein wissenschaftliches Modell des Gegenstands Erzählung bzw. Erzählen.'

2 Köppe, T./Kindt, T., Erzähltheorie, 43: 'genau dann eine Erzählung, wenn er von mindestens zwei Ereignissen handelt, die temporal geordnet sowie in mindestens einer weiteren sinnhaften Weise verknüpft sind.'

3 Cf. Köppe, T./Kindt, T., Erzähltheorie, 44.

4 Cf. Köppe, T./Kindt, T., Erzähltheorie, 63.

 | DOI:10.30965/9783846765852_007

Albrecht Koschorke[5], which claims to have a huge amount of social and political relevance. It can be seen as a useful conversation partner, providing both points of continuity and demarcation. However, this narratology – as with most from the fields of philology – tries to ignore the question of whether reality is referenced, which is the genuine concern of any narrative ontology. Nevertheless, it will be helpful at this point to introduce some preliminary definitions and conceptual distinctions (both, from narratology and in contrast to it) that will be used in our work. Though by presenting such distinctions at the beginning means they cannot be justified at this point, their usefulness might become more evident in the course of the whole inquiry. The reader may find the introduction of these concepts convenient. It will also be necessary to introduce some further neologisms. The use of these neologisms consists in naming unnamed phenomena or in bringing phenomena sharper into focus.

6.1 Stories and Narrations

Stories are not things that are necessarily constituted by agents. Stories do not necessarily have an author or authors. Stories are not primarily told but are lived, occur, or happen. Stories are what the world – whatever this might be – is made of. 'Stories are lived before they are told – except in the case of fiction.'[6] They are the 'last understandable part of an open whole that appears together with them'.[7] Further, without humans there would still be stories, though not without perceivers. Perceivers are 'intermeshed' in stories, and we will have to analyze this kind of intermeshment. At this point suffice it to say that stories are affects (*Widerfahrnisse*)[8], without thereby setting absolute passivity in sharp contrast to activity. Sometimes we will also use the terms *narrantic* stories or *primary* stories. Stories can refer to other stories in different ways. A specific part of the mesh of stories are those that can be told by humans.

On the other hand, *narrations* or *secondary (and greater) level stories* are told and communicated by agents, in most cases by more than one. Whereas the storied occurrence can (but does not necessarily have to) occur without any verbal communication, verbal communication does play a major role in narrations, though non-verbal communication is also important for narrations

5 KOSCHORKE, A., Wahrheit und Erfindung.

6 MACINTYRE, A., After Virtue, 212.

7 SCHAPP, W., Philosophie der Geschichten (1959), 48: 'der letzte in sich verständliche Teil eines mit ihm auftauchenden ungeschlossenen Ganzen.'

8 Cf. SCHAPP, W., In Geschichten verstrickt (1953), 126.

or second-level stories. We must also correct the claim that it is impossible to distinguish between experienced and told stories.[9] Experienced and told stories are inseparable, but a conceptual distinction is nevertheless possible and helpful.

Structural-narrative stories of a second order are secondary narrations which are shaped by the structure of a story – whatever the elements of the structure of a story might be – in contrast to *nonstructural-narrative stories* of the second order. Examples for nonstructural-narrative stories of second order are charts, equations, collections of rights, traffic signs, spoken sentences etc. – in short, every semiotic activity of perceivers that is not explicitly structural-narrative. Structural-narrative stories of the second order and nonstructural-stories of the second order have to be called 'stories' because they are only conceivable by their appearances in primary-narrative contexts, by being intermeshed in first order stories. Nothing can be a sign without being intermeshed in primary stories and nothing can be used as a means of communication if it is not a part of narrantic stories. Structural-narrative second order stories are only one case among others that can be studied by a narrative ontology, whereas they are the subject matter *par excellence* for the discipline of narratology.

6.2 The Narrantic, the Narrantological, and the Narrative

In order to refer to an ontological state of affairs, as told by humans or not, we will use the adjectives *narrantic* (from *narrative* and *ontic*) and *narrantological* (from *narrative* and *ontological*) and their substantives. In addition to *narrantic* we can also use the expression *storied*. Narrantology, therefore is nothing but a shorthand for narrative ontology and the narrantic is a shorthand for an ontic narrative, in order to make matters simpler.

In order to refer to the narrations of narrantic states of affairs or based on storied occurrences, the adjectives *narrative* or *narrational* are used. The purpose of introducing neologisms here as well, is that existing narrative theories make a distinction between narrative and narration that must also be expressed.

The narrantological descriptions that refer to the narrantic reality, however, belong to a special kind of (academic) narrative.

9 Cf. SCHAPP, W., Philosophie der Geschichten (1959), 175. 267. 278.

6.3 Narration – Narrative

Not every narration is a narrative, but a narrative is always a narration. *Narrations* are communicative occurrences in which the life of persons and communities emerge. As such, no second-level narration can be told twice, since every narration is a concrete and particular sequence occurring within the narrantic processes itself. However, if one abstracts a narration from the concrete, many narrations – but not necessarily all – have a general structure or scheme. This general, notional construct – which may consist of, for example an introduction, the description of a crisis, the solution, different characters that bring the crisis to its solution, the point of the story, etc. – is called the *narrative*.[10] The distinction between narration and narrative, therefore, resembles the distinction between the concrete and the general, that which is *existential* and existentiality,[11] and so on. However, it is not simply the case that the distinction between narration and narrative is identical to that between token and type. Whereas any token instantiates a type, there may be narrations that do not instantiate a narrative.

To some extent, one can explain the distinction between narration and narrative with the help of the *systems theory* by Niklas Luhmann. For any system there is also an environment, and combined systems also have specific environments. However, every system/environment is encompassed by the world, which is not a system.[12] Therefore, every system has a double contingency, since it is contingent on that which the world system can comprehend and is contingent on what it cannot. The so-called general theory of narrations by Albrecht Koschorke carries this structure over into his theory of narratives to a large degree. As in Luhmann, a sharp distinction between system and world can be found, though in Koschorke it appears as a sharp distinction between narrative and the world, with the result that his theory is not an ontological one, not a *narran*tology, but only a narratology that refrains in the end of making any claims about reality. In our narrative ontology or narrantology, however, reality is primarily seen as the storied processes of occurrences, and so reality-claims are included. Of course, it is still contingent in a number of ways as to what of the narrantic processes can be addressed by narrations and what cannot, and it is still contingent as to what extent narrations can be referred to by narratives. It seems to be an implication of Koschorke's approach that any narration instantiates a narrative, because narration and narratives seem to be simply social entities. However, in our narrantology the stories are not primarily social entities, but occurrences of reality. And if it is true that the processes of reality include real novelty and singularity, then it is also true that there may be narrations that cannot be explained by a narrative or the combination of narratives in a satisfying manner.

---

10 Cf. Koschorke, A., Wahrheit und Erfindung, 30.

11 Cf. Heidegger, M., Being and Time, 10f.

12 Cf. Luhmann, N., Funktion der Religion.

Analogous to the so called 'absolute metaphor'[13], one could call those narrations of any level that cannot be captured by narratives at all, or at best only partially so, as '*absolute narrations*'. However, to do so is not without danger, because it could suggest a sharp distinction between non-absolute and absolute narrations, which would be an ontological claim without any basis. It is more probable that every narration, on whatever level, always consists of parts that cannot be captured by narratives.

Furthermore, the narrative is not identical with its scheme. Narrations that instantiate a narrative can and may vary. Therefore, the narrative exists in the mode of the *possible*. It is the set of all possible sequences that can be used in order to tell an instantiated narration.[14] At this point, of course, the question of the narrative's identity arises: Which narration can be seen as a narration of a specific narrative, and which cannot? The answer is not easy, because a narrative is not a fixed entity. Narrative depends on the pragmatic dimensions of the narrative's communication within specific narrative communities and of their evaluative criteria. More importantly, however, is that in the course of a factual narration, nearly every narration contains elements and sequences that are particular, new, trivial, or foreign to the narrative and its community, and that resist any schematization.[15] These foreign elements signify that the human activity of narrating cannot be conceived of along constructivist lines, but along realist ones, because narrating resonates with the antecedent narrantic occasions of the world. It is not so much constructivist-creative arbitrariness that is mirrored by its resistance to fixed sequences, but the reality of the narrantic events as perceived by the narrating ones. The narrator is not necessarily the actual person narrating, as the foreign element present in their telling could consist of a sequence or word that resists narrational inclusion that arises from a previous narration. Therefore, foreign schema-resisting elements also reflect the event-like structure of both the narrantic world and the narrating communities: they show not only that we are new in every moment but also that 'we are older than ourselves.'[16] It is not the case that 'we have stories' – we belong to stories.[17]

We must remind ourselves that the phenomenological basis of narrantology is perception. The consequence is that abstract systems of concepts, like scientific or academic theories that presuppose the so-called higher cognitive

13 Cf. KOSCHORKE, A., Wahrheit und Erfindung, 30.

14 Cf. KOSCHORKE, A., Wahrheit und Erfindung, 52.

15 For a detailed description of the mechanisms of the interplay of schematization and differentiation by means of the alien cf. KOSCHORKE, A., Wahrheit und Erfindung, 51–60.

16 WALDENFELS, B., Bodily Experience between Selfhood and Otherness, 242.

17 Cf. SCHAPP, W., In Geschichten Verstrickt (1953), 121.

capabilities, are also nothing but special kinds of narratives. They are narratives in which the process of abstraction from narration to narrative is stretched as far as possible. But also, in this case, theories as cannot be freed from their narrations; they remain narratively intermeshed.

Narrations or stories, be they primary or secondary narrations, can be divided into *epic narrations* and *dramatic narrations*. Dramatic narrations are irreducibly structured by dramatic coherence, whereas epic stories can be understood by the help of logical coherence alone. Epic narrations can be represented by narratives, which seems to be impossible in the case of dramatic stories. We only mention this distinction between dramatic and epic narrations here in order to introduce all of the seminal terminology. The explication of this distinction, however, will be discussed on its own later (Ch. 16).

6.4 Narrators and Recipients

On the narrantic level, there is no strict distinction between narrator and audience. Any concrete, particular person is both at the same time – if persons emerge in the stories at all. But non-personal entities can also be understood as both narrator and recipient: if we understand the narrator as an instance that plays a decisive role in the course of the ensuing occasion, non-personal beings are also narrators. And if we understand the recipients as instances that receive effects in the course of occasions, any instance can be a recipient. Real stories neither depend on preceding recipients nor preceding narrators. Real stories generate their narrators and recipients, or better, during the course of a story narrators and recipients emerge – often at the same time in the same instance. The distinction between narrator and recipient is therefore a secondary one; it is an abstraction from reality and it depends on our tendency to implement the subject-object distinction by cognitive interpretative means on to nearly everything. It also reflects our tendency to see the distinction between active-voice and passive-voice as fundamental, in contrast to the middle-voice of some languages (like ancient Greek) that have it the other way around.

On the narratological level, where the distinction between narrator and recipient might be more convenient, and for some analyses also necessary, there is not a sharp distinction. In oral stories the narrator is influenced by his recipients, and the behavior of his recipients direct his way of telling.[18] Therefore, any recipient on the narratological level is always a narrator as well, even in those cases where this remains unnoticed for both narrator and recipient. Of

18 Cf. DRECHSEL, W., Lebensgeschichte, 130.156.

course, the same is true *vice versa*, i.e. every narrator is at the same time a recipient. This interchange remains true for narrations that consist of fixed texts, though here the second-order nature of the distinction between narrator and recipient is not as obvious, but nevertheless decisive. In such cases, the instance called 'narrator' is not identical with the real authors of a text. The narrator can change, behave in different attitudes and provide the recipients with a specific perception from different wayformational perspectives. Further, the different wayformational perspectives of the recipients – on the narrantic level of reality – are decisive for their ability to share the wayformational perspective of the narrator – to alter them and to go along with them. In this relationship, decisive questions of power and of interpretation arise.[19]

6.5 The Narrantic Effects of the Narratological Level

Narrations on the narratological level are part of the narrantic course of the occasions. Therefore, it is not surprising that there are reciprocal effects, particularly the effect of the narratological level on the narrantic one. What is decisive is that the presentation of particular problems on the narratological level cannot be restricted to this level, but spill over into the narrantological one by manifold mechanisms in a number of ways.[20] On the one hand, it is important to note that the self-delimitation of those narrow narratologies mentioned above, which want to be pure research into texts, are self-contradictory because any self-separation is impossible. On the other hand, it is important that what can be called the second (and third, fourth etc.) *extension of narrations and narratives* are recognized on other levels.

Koschorke gives an example of dissonant narratives that need a 'second conclusion'[21] in order to reach their end. The descriptions and solutions to the problems in narrations – be they satisfying or not – challenge us, following Ricœur, to see our praxis, i.e. on the narrantic level, as described in the way the narratological level describes it.[22] In this case, we tend to look for the same solution as it is described on the

---

19 A more detailed analysis of the relationship between narrator, recipient, and text on the narratological level can be found in KOSCHORKE, A., Wahrheit und Erfindung, 84–90. However, Koschorke's analysis remains bound to the narratological level and to a text-based paradigm.

20 Some of these mechanisms are noted by KOSCHORKE, A., Wahrheit und Erfindung, 64–71.

21 Cf. KOSCHORKE, A., Wahrheit und Erfindung, 64.

22 Cf. RICŒUR, P., Time and Narrative I, 83: 'The intersignifying of project, circumstances, and chance is exactly what plot, which I have described as a synthesis of the

narratological level (solution, reconciliation, revenge, deal, annihilation, etc.) on the narrantic level as well. The reverse is also true: our narrantic experiences also determine our expectations as recipients and narrators of narrations. But Koschorke has to be corrected in two respects.

First, it is not so much a second conclusion that is needed, but an extension, which in turn needs two, three, or more extensions. An extension is necessary because the narrantic level is only accesible by narratological descriptions and our practice consists of describing continuing narrations or stories. Every determination of any aim can only be preliminary given. The solution is not decisive on the narrantic level as such, but in the further telling of the narration across different levels. The transgression of levels in narrating (which is at the same time a practice) does not take place in the mode of transport, but in the mode of wayfaring, to use Ingold's distinction.[23]

Secondly, Koschorke is not able to explain why narrations have level-transgressive effects. The reason for this blind spot might be that Koschorke does not really take the ontological level of reality into account. Of course, it would be possible to look for mechanisms on the psychological level in order to take a small step towards solving this problem, but this approach would not, in the end, be fruitful. The inherent effectual entanglement of the different levels, i.e. the ongoing telling of a narration as well as in the real practice – whether this solves or perpetuates a problem – is addressed only if one recognizes that making the distinction at all between different levels of narration and story – or between narratology and narrantology – is a very artificial one. The narrative level of told narrations is part of the narrantic occasions of the world. Our distinction between narratology and narrantology emerges only due to persons who are perceiving, understanding, and acting in the midst of the narrantic occasions. And these persons have the tendency to see a separation between their interpersonal and social reality, and between the narrantic reality as such. But if one recognizes that this separation is a very artificial one, the fact of the ongoing telling across different levels is a very normal thing. In the end, this does not make for a very satisfying explanation. But a really satisfying explanation will strive to take the theological dimension into account, particularly under the rubric of sanctification.

6.6 The Effectiveness of Passionate Narrations

It is not simply a truism that when something is described with more passion, i.e. the more affect, engagement, and value a description contains, the more it will be received as a realistic and authoritative one.[24] Why is this the case? This question is not a technical but a general one. As such, narratological or psychological answers would be inappropriate. In order to answer this question, it seems to be plausible that passionate, i.e. affectively described, affectivity evoking, and evaluative narrations, are the ideal means for describing a state

heterogeneous, orders. The narrative work is an invitation to see our praxis as it is ordered by this or that plot articulated in our literature.'

23 Cf. ch. 8.

24 Cf. Koschorke, A., Wahrheit und Erfindung, 101–110.

of affairs that belongs to the narrantic occasions of reality and its perception – preceding the cognitive distinction between subject and object. Then, it can be assumed that such passionate engagement, affects, and values do not simply belong simply to the personal or subjective side, but to reality itself. In the case of persons, they are only instantiated in a special manner.

The effectiveness of passionate narrations on the secondary level relies on the affordances of reality, which is always given in perceiving narrantic occurrences. Therefore, we also have the task of designing a narrative theory of perceiving value.

6.7 Internarrativity

The states of affairs described in the preceding paragraphs are phenomena of internarrativity. Narrativity is, in more than one respect, always internarrativity. It is internarrativity insofar as stories consist of intermeshed and successive sequences. It is internarrativity insofar as secondary narrations refer (including fictional stories) to the narrantic, primary stories of which they are a part. It is internarrativity because narrations on the same level can be retold. It is internarrativity because persons and states of affairs – including authors and recipients – emerge out of stories. It is internarrativity because in the human practice of telling stories manifold, intermeshed life-stories appear and are being reconfigured. Finally, it is internarrativity because, in the meshwork of stories that exists between primary and secondary narrations, sometimes the unknown and untellable in-between has to be seen as a story that belongs to the original story.

It seems that internarrativity could be an ambivalent concept, if it is true that it refers to so many different states of affairs. But in all these cases, the 'inter' of 'internarrativity' has a genuine meaning, which has to be distinguished from other meanings of 'inter'. It does not refer to a space between fixed relata, which would be completely described by the attributes of these relata, but a processual occurrence in which the relata itself are permanently reconfigured. The inter does not refer to a *between*, but to an *in-between*.[25] The difference between them might become more evident with the help of the model of two communicating people and a river. In the first case, the river simply separates the two standing on the opposite shores. In this case, the river does not contribute anything to their communication. On the contrary, it prevents haptic communication and its flowing and roaring streams of water disturbs oral

25 Cf. INGOLD, T., Life of Lines, 147–153.

communication. In the second case, the communicating persons are in the midst of the river itself, drifting in its current. Now the river co-determines their communication, because its flow provides new perceptions and subject-matter for communication on its shore. It co-determines the becoming of the communicating people itself. In the first case, the river is *between* the people; in the second case, the people are *in-between* the shores. The 'inter' of 'inter-narrativity' always refers to the latter.

6.8 Narratology Narrantologically Analyzed

In this chapter, we have contrasted narratologies, particularly the example of Koschorke's narratology, in order to define or clarify some concepts and distinctions of narrantology. Now it is time to have a look at narratology from the wayformational perspective of narrantology. Our investigation will reveal the critical force of the narrantological wayformational perspective by way of a particular example.

Koschorke shares some useful observations regarding cultural semiosis and the role of narrative within such a framework. It is, however, a problem that it remains unclear what he describes and what he values on the basis of an implicit, presupposed ontology and anthropology. In other words, Koschorke is not really explicating his own wayformational perspective, which, in the end, is a dangerous one.

This lack of clarity becomes obvious when Koschorke is writing on meaning. In his opinion, narrations and narratives that explicitly deal with questions of meaning do not stabilize society, whereas narrative practices in which the question of meaning is marginalized, do stabilize society. In this respect, Koschorke attacks only crude caricatures of the concepts of meaning and religion, thereby masking his own, 'hard' religious preference.

Koschorke claims that to 'constitute and maintain' a semantic system would be 'extraordinarily energy taxing'[26] and that 'meaning' would be a 'time-consuming and expensive way of stabilizing systems'.[27] Meaning is conceived mainly as coherence which requires 'mental energy'.[28] The sociologies of Luhmann, Durkheim, and, above all, the sociologies of Berger and Luckmann are seen as highly expensive modes of stabilizing

26 KOSCHORKE, A., Wahrheit und Erfindung, 149: „außerordentlich energieintensiv."

27 KOSCHORKE, A., Wahrheit und Erfindung, 149: „zeitraubendes und teures Register der Systemstabilisierung sei."

28 Cf. KOSCHORKE, A., Wahrheit und Erfindung, 152: „Kohärenzsteigerung über dieses ‚Normalmaß' hinaus erfordert einen entsprechend gesteigerten Einsatz von mentaler Energie."

the society. Their 'insistence on the social omnipresence of meaning[29] claim, incorrectly, that metaphysics and religion could contribute anything to the stabilizing of society. Thereby, these sociologies themselves become 'sciences of the ultimate questions'[30] that are driven by the problem of death. In contrast, Koschorke uses Jurij Lotman's thesis of marginalization in order to claim that stabilizing societies requires a non-intensive communication of meaning, in which non-understanding, incomplete understanding, and misunderstanding are the essence of informational exchange.[31] As a matter of fact, in daily life, questions of meaning do not occur. Therefore, meaning is seen as posterior and 'excessive attribution.'[32] Societies insisting on the communication of meaning as stabilizing factors would soon suffer a 'meaning-attack.'[33] Meaning is not a presupposition of a 'good life' including 'lust, enjoyment, an organic sense of well-being, love, and the satisfaction of drives' which have 'no original reference to meaning.'[34] Also, the question of death, which is seen as the mightiest argument in the hands of the modern priests of sociology, has to be marginalized in daily routine, which, appropriately, happens automatically: 'Whoever looks at life *sub specie aeternitatis* cannot take anything seriously, cannot love, cannot farm, cannot feed his children, cannot do any good job; he is in danger of not being able to live.'[35]

On the one hand, Koschorke's evaluative observations are not without worth. They show that there are indeed substitutes for theology in post-modern societies, and that these societies might indeed be stabilized on the levels of 'soft' and 'fleeting' meanings, including its semantic 'volatility'.[36] Incoherent and exchangeable narrative identity-claims and meaning-claims might be the normal case.

On the other hand, what Koschorke's example shows is that within this movement itself 'hard' meanings instantly reappear in an implicit and opaque manner, which has to be criticized. Koschorke's use of 'mental energy' might be, at best, a case of a highly metaphorical or equivocal kind of speech in relation to any meaningful concepts of energy, whereas, contrary to his intentions, he reveals an ultimate principle of meaning, consisting in a pseudo neo-Darwinian maximization of the cost-benefit ratio. Once more it is shown that any critique of religion first presupposes the standpoint of one's own religion or ideology, and second, that it presupposes an intentional or unintentional misunderstanding of what it attacks. Koschorke argues on the basis of the mercantile credo of the *homo oeconomicus*. He misunderstands 'meaning' and 'reflection on meaning.' Permanent reflection on meaning might be indeed destabilizing, however, the absence of the permanent reflection of meaning is not the absence of meaning. This confusion is only possible if one thinks of meaning as a constructivist

29 KOSCHORKE, A., Wahrheit und Erfindung, 153: „Beharren auf der sozialen Omnipräsenz von Sinn".

30 KOSCHORKE, A., Wahrheit und Erfindung, 154: „Wissenschaft von den letzten Fragen".

31 Cf. KOSCHORKE, A., Wahrheit und Erfindung, 156.

32 KOSCHORKE, A., Wahrheit und Erfindung, 157: „überschüssige Attribution".

33 KOSCHORKE, A., Wahrheit und Erfindung, 157: „Sinninfarkt".

34 KOSCHORKE, A., Wahrheit und Erfindung, 157: „keine ursprüngliche Referenz auf Sinn".

35 KOSCHORKE, A., Wahrheit und Erfindung, 158: „Wer das Leben nur *sub specie aeternitatis* betrachtet, kann nichts wichtig nehmen, kann nicht lieben, seine Feldarbeit nicht tun, seine Kinder nicht nähren, seinen Beruf nicht ausfüllen; er steht in der Gefahr, lebensunfähig zu werden."

36 KOSCHORKE, A., Wahrheit und Erfindung, 152: „Volatilität".

product, when it really is based on the perception of affordances. 'Meaning' is not primarily a concept of thought, but of perception. Indirectly, Koschorke reveals that he presupposes in his hedonistic story of 'soft' aims of life consisting in lust and the satisfaction of drives, etc. only positive goods, not phenomena like pleasure in destruction and the enjoyment of pain. Therefore, Koschorke presupposes *contra intentionem* an original meaning-reference for these goods. In addition, his conclusion – whoever lives a life in the horizon of eternity becomes unable to live – presupposes a false understanding of eternity as timelessness. Once again, a caricature of religion is used as the intended target.

Furthermore, the relationship between narratology and ontology remains opaque. According to Koschorke, a narrative ontology should be impossible, since he speaks of the 'ontological untrustworthiness'[37] of narrations, and since he conceives of it as an advantage that narrations negate the 'distinction between fact and fiction.'[38] It is baffling that, with statements like this, Koschorke seems to presuppose the subject-object duality and representational thinking – all without any argument. He sees the question of the reality-reference as unjustifiable, without mentioning any reasons for this except its social function.[39] But in the last instance, such crude deficits in argumentation should not be surprising in the face of his economic definition of narrating as a 'verbally elaborated kind of social behavior.'[40]

Apart from such critiques of particular themes in Koschorke, we also have to ask how his narratological thinking is to be characterized as a whole.

First, Koschorke shows in what way manifold systems and theories rely factually on narratives. He demasks monisms as broken and dualisms claimed as symmetrical to be asymmetric. He shows the way in which key narratives always include a paradoxical anti-momentum, which results in the impossibility of universal coherence and correspondence. Instead of strictly construed symmetric dualisms, he uses reciprocally interfering and disturbing dualisms, oscillating between untranslatable coordinate systems.[41] Nevertheless, he shares in the dualisms of modern thought, only ordering the dualism in a new way: dynamic and intentionally incoherent. It remains unthinkable for him to develop a phenomenological point of view or an attentional wayformational perspective, in which dualisms emerge out of something prior.

Second, one of his main goals is to show that this dynamic, double constitution of semiotic systems and narratives are not a vice but a virtue in terms of a functioning society.

---

37 KOSCHORKE, A., Wahrheit und Erfindung, 349: „ontologische […] Unzuverlässigkeit".

38 KOSCHORKE, A., Wahrheit und Erfindung, 249: „Unterscheidung zwischen Faktum und Fiktion."

39 Cf. KOSCHORKE, A., Wahrheit und Erfindung, 340–349.

40 KOSCHORKE, A., Wahrheit und Erfindung, 350: „sprachlich elaborierte Form sozialen Verhandelns."

41 Cf. KOSCHORKE, A., Wahrheit und Erfindung, 382–398.

Third, this functionalistic approach leads to a mercantile or economic paradigm, which is, against Koschorke's intentions, nothing but a monistic meta-narrative, driven by the neo-liberal logic of the market. It is significant that he defines narrations as 'places of negotiations'.[42]

Fourth, it is a feature of his system, that narratives are conceived of as cultural entities and narrations, not as a part of the non-human reality. At no point does he come close to anything worthy of narrative-ontological reflection, which is somewhat surprising since he delivers detailed analyses of the nature-nurture dualism.[43] If one takes these analyses seriously, one would have to acknowledge that his whole system is also disturbed by ontological narrativity.

Many more of the details of his work are worthy of being analyzed and criticized. Are all narratives really so broken and self-contradictory as Koschorke conceives them to be, especially in the case of theology?[44] Other ideas, like his treatment of time and place, no matter how innovative they might be, also remain in the end what they are: uncomprehensive, isolated observations.

All in all, Koschorke delivers a kind of narratological thinking that cannot provide a substantial impact on the design of a post-systematic theology or a narrative ontology. Although, one should not dismiss his book on the basis of a series of detailed observations, which make it worth careful consideration. His considerations were at least helpful in taking a first step in establishing the first terminological distinctions of a post-systematic narrantology on the basis of phenomenal perceiving.

42 Cf. KOSCHORKE, A., Wahrheit und Erfindung, 350.

43 Cf. KOSCHORKE, A., Wahrheit und Erfindung, 352–371.

44 This question arises, for example, with regard to the alleged paradox of the good creation and the snake being 'smuggled inside', the alleged paradox of conflicting imperatives towards man being supposed to be like God according to Gen 1 and not allowed to be like God according to Gen 2–4, respectively. Cf. KOSCHORKE, A., Wahrheit und Erfindung, 372f.

CHAPTER 7

Narration and Relation

A post-systematic theology must have a narrative ontology. But a narrative ontology is not exclusively narrative, it is open to intersections and links to other conceptual approaches. All these different conceptual approaches must be measured against the question of how adequately they can conceive of perceiving truth and value, and whether they can explicate, however brokenly, the ineffability of perceiving. For the design of a narrative ontology, this entails the task of communicating with these other conceptual approaches in order to show that it possesses the same value as they do. Therefore, it has to incorporate some features of other approaches, while simultaneously better conforming to the phenomena. Concepts – including changes in concepts and neologisms – are not simply self-referential and cannot be artificially invented, as constructivist postmodernists might claim.[1] Furthermore, concepts are not only understandable within their own frame of reference, nor are they wholly incommensurable with other such frames.

Perhaps the most promising candidate for a concurrence with a narrative ontology is a relational ontology. Therefore, we must show how a narrative ontology is able to express the same features as a relational one, while also showing that there are states of affairs that can be explained within the frame of a narrative ontology but not in a relational one. If this is possible, a relational ontology would not therefore be rival to a narrative one, but a relational ontology would be an irreducible part of a narrative ontology. In other words: a narrative ontology is always a specific kind of a relational ontology, and it has specific capacities that set it apart from other ontologies.

It is also important to demonstrate because talk of relations and relationality is fashionable. Whereas at the end of the 20th century, the claim that something is 'relational' might have been meaningful, today it sometimes seems that talk of relationality has been so influential that one might doubt whether this talk is still meaningful. A narrative ontology, therefore, does not want to replace a relational one, but its task is to save relational ontologies.

---

1 That way DELEUZE, G./GUATTARI, F., What is Philosophy?, 21f.

 | DOI:10.30965/9783846765852_008

7.1 Relationality: the Ever-Present Poor Relation

On the one hand, relational categories seem to be relatively new compared to other concepts in modernity. On the other hand, talk of relationality seems to be sometimes omnipresent, comparable with the talk of values in ethics.

Why then, is relationality a somehow hidden category in the history of philosophy that did not fulfill its potential until today?

In Aristotle, and following him in the Neoplatonist synthesis of Porphyry, relationality appears under the title of *pros ti*, as the 'whither' of something that is determined primarily by other concepts. An entity is mainly determined by the other nine categories. Relationality was therefore only one of these ten categories, and a relatively weak one. Further, the Christianizing of philosophy did not fundamentally alter this situation. It is true that Cappadocian theology and its focus on the immanent trinity also meant high regard for relationality that implied its *nearly* essential character. But, in contrast to claims by Eastern-Orthodox theologians, one cannot entirely agree that in Cappadocian thinking an ontological revolution took place.[2] It is true that the Cappadocians could express with the term of *schesis* what was later called 'internal' or 'constitutive' relationality. It also true that they combined the general and the particular in the term of *hypostasis*, which means a constitutive relation between two things. And lastly, it is right that they located relationality in the inner being of God and that this can be considered a high evaluation of the concept. But Zizioulas' claim of an ontological revolution is mistaken for the following reasons. The Cappadocians partly anticipated the later western marginalization of the doctrine of the trinity by claiming that the trinity is knowable, whereas the essence of God is beyond our comprehension and known only apophatically.[3] Therefore, the value of relationality is restricted, since the impression may emerge while the essential remains ineffable, what is explicable is at once the relational but not the essential. Another reason is that Basil of Caesarea, and following him the Nicene-Constantinopolitan Creed, located the origin of divinity not in the divine essence but in the hypostasis of the Father. This location in no way meant that the Father is without relations or that the relation would only be an external and accidental one, since Basil claims that also the Father is essentially related and nothing without the relations to Son and Spirit.[4] But this is also the source of the idea of the inner-divine monarchy of the Father, and therefore a priority of the relatum over the relation. This priority implies that there are discernible or indiscernible attributes that would not be relational ones, but monadic ones, i.e. they would appear as predicative assertions about one of the relata, about its relations nothing more could be known. A consequence is that, in the end, the Father becomes a logical subject.

---

2 Cf. ZIZIOULAS, J., Cappadocian Contribution, 71. A good overview of the Cappadocian meaning of the development of the trinitarian doctrine is also given by MARKSCHIES, C., kappadozische Trinitätstheologie.

3 Cf. e.g. the classification of *ousia* and *energeia* in NAZIANZ, G.v., Orationes theologicae (FC 22), c. 27–31; NYSSA, G.v., Cant., III.

4 Cf. ZIZIOULAS, J., Cappadocian Contribution, 51f.

The Western reception of the doctrine of the Trinity prevented any possible ontological revolution. Augustine's claim that the divine persons are relations does not raise the value of relationality but devalues it. On the one hand, Augustine's claim about relationality does not refer to the divine essence. On the other hand, this proposition is a kind of black-box in order to avoid total silence.[5] Augustine intentionally uses one of the weakest Neoplatonic categories, since in the end he regards the concept of the person as an empty one.[6] What does it mean to call the person a relation instead of a *relatum*? A *relatum* can be constituted by relations, if it is correlated to other *relata* in a conceptual way. A relation, however, does not have to be relationally constituted by its relations to other relata. And what Augustine really means is nothing but intensional self-relatedness: The one and only relatum is the essence of God which has a threefold relation to itself, without any difference or alterity. And this purely intensional, i.e. conceptual, self-reference is what he means when he calls these self-relations persons.

With this, and with his opinion that the human mind is not simply a *vestigium*, but the only *imago trinitatis* by being related threefold to itself in remembering itself, knowing itself and affirming itself,[7] Augustine delivered a blueprint for the pure intensional relationality of all modern theories of subjectivity. And it is questionable whether this is really what it means to stress relationality.

Thomas Aquinas – although he distinguished his approach in many respects from Augustine's – followed Augustine in his doctrine of God by perpetuating the proposition that the Trinitarian persons are relations. The effect was to stabilize the marginalization of relations in western theology and philosophy. If one takes relationality as the criterion, the thinking of Augustine and Aquinas is a step back in comparison to the Cappadocians.

In the time of early scholasticism, a genuine ontological revolution had been possible. And this would have been a kind of revolution that would have outperformed all later explications of relationality, be it in Hegel or in the foundations of the logics of relations. It was Richard of St. Victor who (almost) founded a real relational ontology, which does not need to use two separate terms – relation and relata – but that combines these as aspects in the one concept of *existentia*.[8] Everything that is, or can be, has to be an *existentia*. But *existentia* does not mean existence or protrusion, but a *whence-and-whither being*: What would later be called a relatum is an aspect, visible in the part of *-sistentia* in *existentia*; and what would later be called a relation is an aspect of a unity, visible in the *ex*-part of *existentia*. The talk of *existentia* replaces thereby the

5 Cf. AUGUSTINUS, A., trin., CChr.SL 505,8(10)–9(10), [216,43–217,11]: 'Dicunt quidem et illi ὑπόστασιν, sed nescio quid uolunt interesse inter οὐσίαν et ὑπόστασιν ita ut plerique nostri [...] consuerint μίαν οὐσίαν τρεῖς ὑποστάσεις, quod est latine, unam essentiam tres substantias. Sed quia nostra loquendi consuetudo iam obtinuit ut hoc intellegatur cum dicimus essentiam quod intellegitur cum dicimus substan- tiam, non audemus dicere unam essentiam, tres substantias, sed unam essentiam uel substantiam. Tres autem personas [...] Tamen cum quaeritur quid tres, magna prorsus inopia humanum laborat eloquium. Dictum est tres personae non ut illud diceretur sed ne taceretur.'

6 For analysis cf. MÜHLING, M., Gott ist Liebe, 81–87.

7 Cf. e.g. AUGUSTINUS, A., trin., CChr.SL 5012,5(5)–7(9) [359–64] and for analysis MÜHLING, M., Gott ist Liebe, 89–94.

8 Cf. RICHARD VON ST.VICTOR, De Trinitate, 4,11.12, 250–4 and for analysis MÜHLING, M., Gott ist Liebe, 161–166.

classical talk of *substantia* and surpasses it, because *substantia* can only refer to the one aspect of *-sistentia*, which is only an abstraction of *existentia*. Nevertheless, the possible ontological revolution did not take place, mainly for two reasons. On the one hand, Richard himself did not make use of his discovery in a comprehensive manner but restricted it mainly to elucidate the difficult concept of a person. On the other hand, Aquinas adopted Richard's talk of *existentiae* in the framework of Richard's definition of the person and combines it with the non-relational, purely predicative definition of the person in Boethius. Thereby, and additionally by using the term *existentia* for a completely different concept,[9] he sounded the death knell for Richard's relational ontology. Sometimes a positive reception can prevent something's positive effect. If you want to destroy someone, praise him in the highest words, but misunderstand him in important aspects.

In modernity, perhaps Hegel developed the most significant relational ontology. But its effectiveness was restricted to the idealistic tradition and it became contaminated by the non-illuminating discourse between subjectivist idealism and empirical realism. The British Hegelian, Francis Herbert Bradley, claimed that all relations have to be conceived as essential or internal.[10] This claim became the target of Bertrand Russell in order to claim the externality of all relations.[11] This claim is tragic, since it was Russell, with his completely non-relational and atomistic ontology, who formalized the logic of relations in his *Principia Mathematica* and introduced a terminology that has become quasi-canonical for the talk of relations today.[12] The main problem is that relations are conceived by Russell as nothing but polyadic predicates, which refer to logical subjects. Relations, therefore, are misunderstood as nothing but a subset of attributes. By this formal terminology, an ontology was preferred that treated logical subjects and their attributes as basic, which is therefore atomistic through and through.

Nevertheless, in the 20th century, talk of relationality increased for many reasons, only a few of which we can mention here. It is well known that the Copenhagen interpretation of quantum theory presupposes an internal relationality.[13] Far beyond the limits of physics, this interpretation became influential in philosophy and in

9 Thomas refers in THOMAS VON AQUIN, s.th.I, 29,3 ad 4 to the concept of person used by Richard and through this also to his concept of existence, when he, against Richard, cuts it back on the concept of trinitarian persons, so *"quod persona, secundum quod de Deo dicitur, est 'divinae naturae incommunicabilis existentia.'"* Through understanding Richard's definition merely as an improvement on the boethian definition, Richard's understanding of existence is missed out and thrown back into a substance-ontological frame.

10 Cf. BRADLEY, F.H., Appearance and Reality, 142.228.364.392.574–584.627; 392: 'But every relation [...] essentially penetrates the being of its term, and, in this sense, is intrinsical.' 574: 'I do not admit that any relation whatever ca be merely external and make no difference to its terms', 581: 'We have seen [...] all relations imply a whole to which the terms contribute and by which the terms are qualified [...]. Nothing in the whole and in the end can be external, and everything less than the Universe is an abstraction from the whole, an abstraction more or less empty [...].' 627: 'Relations are all intrinsical.'

11 Cf. RUSSELL, B., Philosophical Development, 54–64.

12 Cf. RUSSELL, B./WHITEHEAD, A.N., PM, Bd. 1 242, 32. A short introduction to the logic of relations is given in MÜHLING, M., Gott ist Liebe, 335–339.

13 An excellent, humanist presentation of the quantum theory and its philosophical meaning is given by IJJAS, A., Der Alte mit dem Würfel.

a multidisciplinary pursuits, but this influence did not lead automatically to clear concepts – in many cases to the contrary.[14] The dialogue with eastern philosophies, such as Buddhism and Confucianism, encouraged new attention to relations.[15] Further, the continental Idealist tradition never came to an end, and the phenomenological-hermeneutical tradition, at least in an implicit way, also use relational ontologies. In German Protestantism in the first 20 years of the 21st century, Schleiermacher's subjectivist ontology was received much more positively than it had been previously, which means, at the very least, intensional relationality is ubiquitous. Of course, the process-philosophy of Alfred North Whitehead and his followers also inaugurated an increasing use of relational concepts, which still excercise authority today. The altered ecological consciousness dating from the rise of the ecological crisis in the 1970s and 1980s is another factor that has supported relational talk, as well as in the feminist movement.

We have showed that relationality has been treated in most parts of the history of western thought as a poor relation, which had to live under cover. But now we have to show that it was indeed this poor relation, which has secretly operated in a pervasive way, even if it has not become the true regent.

One has to avoid the mistake of confusing the history of concepts with the history of terms. If we look less at the term relationality but instead at the concepts, whatever it is called, we can paint another picture. The origins of western philosophy, including the question of how unity and plurality must be related, may illustrate this. Whereas the Heraclitan type claimed the priority of plurality, the Eleatic preferred the priority of unity. Both types, therefore, conceived of the relata as constituted relationally, but in an asymmetric manner, i.e. by conceiving one relatum as constitutive for the other, but not *vice versa*. Either one sees unity as constituted by plurality or plurality by unity. From here it would be only a small step to conceive of both as reciprocally constituted, so that they either become equiprimordial or emerge out of a basic relation.[16]

Furthermore, many parts of Plato's philosophy can be read as a debate about a specific kind of relationality, particularly in regard to how the general and the particular are to be related. Also, it is here that the notion of an asymmetrical, constitutive relationality reappears. Whereas the general – the ideas – can be conceived independently of the particular, the particular is dependent on the general. This relationship is a kind of constitutive relationality that prevents that relationality among the particulars has to be treated as important. If one has an asymmetrically constitutive relationality in the vertical relationship between general and particular, a constitutive relationality on the horizontal plane among the particular seems superficial. Consequently,

14 Karen Barad's new ingress of a feminist philosophy of science in Barad, K., Meeting the Universe Halfway, 132–185 is essentialy influenced by insights of the quantum theory – though not always as clear as preferred.

15 Good discussions of relationality and its place in the philosophy of religion is offered by Lai, P.-c., Letztgültige Realität in chinesischen Buddhismus; Lai, P.-c., Trinitarische Perichorese und Hua-yen Buddhismus and Lai, P.-c., Confucian Understanding.

16 Cf. Gunton, C.E., The One, the Three and the Many, especially 16–22 and Gunton, C.E., Promise of Trinitarian Theology.

Neoplatonism, in the case of Plotinus and his Christian successors like John Eriugena, follow this path.[17]

Relationality plays a far more important role in Aristotelian philosophy than in the Platonic tradition, which might come as a surprise, since the Aristotelian tradition, especially its medieval reception, is often seen as an example of a (non-relational) substance-ontology. A look into the *Nicomachean Ethics* clearly reveals that the virtues are relational entities, as they are relationally constituted among the particular virtues as well as bound to the concept of the *zoon politikon*, i.e. of humans as living in communities of friends.[18] Another aspect of this relationality is visible in the fact that the virtues have to be conceived of situationally, i.e. related to specific situations. Aristotelian philosophy in general (including its reception) is also far more relational than one might assume. Substance and accident, form and matter, are strictly relational because it is not possible to think of the one without the other. Therefore, it is a misunderstanding to see relationality only in the *pros ti*. The whole scheme of categories can be conceived of as being relationally constituted. In contrast to Plato, a reciprocal constitutivity is also present, especially in the case of the relation of the general and the particular: matter as pure possibility has no actuality without the forms and also the form is not actual without matter. The Aristotelian conception of the soul in no way suggests a substantialist-atomistic understanding of life, and it is not to be confused with its medieval reception or with a crude, Cartesian mind-body dualism. One can show that it really presupposes a relational understanding of life.[19]

The examples of Christian Philosophy, like the thought of the Cappadocians and Richard's relational innovations condensed in the concept of *existentia*, which we used as examples of prevented revolutions, can also be used in order to show the eminent, but hidden effectivity of relationality – and this is surely the right way to understand them.

From the biblical-Hebraic tradition, relationality gains potency through the revision of classical theological concepts in the theology of Luther. Of course, in a formal sense, Luther never designed a relational ontology. But without a doubt, in his anthropology, Luther conceives of humans as determined by a manifold mesh of relations, which becomes perhaps most evident in his revision of the concept of the soul that is relationally transformed.[20] In contrast to other relational approaches, Luther does not restrict relationality to creaturely being, but also to the divine in two ways: in the relation between God and humanity and in the relational-communicative being of God *etsi mundus non daretur*.[21]

Luther makes use of the biblical tradition, particularly the Hebraic one. Indeed, this tradition forces a reconstruction with the help of relational concepts. Of course, there is no formal relational ontology in the Hebrew scriptures. The reason is not, however, its denial, but the fact that the Hebrew language does not normally use abstract

---

17 This trajectory becomes apparent in JOHANNES SCOTUS ERIUGENA, De divisione naturae, PL 122, 986C–987C, when during the heierarchical transformation of the body into the soul, the soul into the spirit and the spirit into God, all relations and differences of the first level vanish.

18 Cf. MÜHLING, M., Ethik, 218–225.

19 Cf. STOELLGER, P., Passivität aus Passion, 46f.

20 Cf. JOEST, W., Ontologie der Person bei Luther.

21 Cf. LUTHER, M., WA, 46, 59,35–38.

substantives, but concrete ones imbedded in narrations. And furthermore, nearly all important Hebrew substantives of theological import can be derived from verbs.[22]

Hidden relational ontologies also appear in the non-theological, philosophical tradition of modernity. Spinoza[23] uses the one substance that appears in different modes. What sounds like simply a slight alteration to the medieval talk of substances is in fact a radical one. The one substance realized in different modes is nothing but a specific kind of internal or constitutive relationality throughout the world.

It would also be a mistake to understand Leibniz' monadology as individualistic or atomist. Although it is true that a monad does not need to actually communicate, this is because they are primordially relational from creation onward, so that each monad reflects the whole nexus of relations in the whole world. In contrast to Newton, Leibniz held to a relational understanding of space.[24] Leibniz was also one of the first who presented a concise description of what was later called internal or constitutive relationality (see below).

Perhaps we can also find in Kant a hidden relationality that is more comprehensive than the term 'relationality', which he uses in his categorical scheme. The idea that it is possible to speak of the phenomenal in an intelligible way but not of the noumenon is also a relational insight derived from Kant's idea that causality has to be conceived *apriori*. Similarly to the Aristotelian tradition, the terminology once again hides this fact.

We have already mentioned the idealistic tradition. Relationality in the shape of intensional relationships is important in different ways for Berkeley as well as in Schelling or Hegel and in the theology of mediation that is influenced by these traditions.

The debate between Russell and Bradley also provides a hint for the importance of relations, even in the case of the classical atomist Russell. At times, he attempts to exceed his atomism as far as possible, especially when he denies the meaning of the concept of the world or the universe. However, he has to pay a price for this, and that is the price of a negative argument: he needs the inter-relational understanding of the world in order to deny it (see below). This argumentation presupposes the alternative: to see either all relations as internally constitutive or not at all, has been unmasked

22 This understanding of the Hebrew language becomes apparent in a set of theologically important terms, which we usually translate abstractly but which actually all have a concrete, basic meaning that is interwoven in narrative: So there is no actual term for story in the sense of history, but, depending on the context, the words (*dabarim*) or acts of Jahwe (*ma'aseh Jahweh*) could appear (Cf. PANNENBERG, W., Gott der Geschichte, 114f). The term for truth is *emet*, which actually means stability, carrying capacity, constancy, reliability, and fidelity. Also, faith is not understood as abstractly cognitive, *he'emin* means to fasten oneself on something or to lash oneself on something. (Cf. PANNENBERG, W., Wahrheit, Gewißheit und Glaube, 229). Our term for soul is used as a translation for *nefesh*, coming from *nfsh*, breathing or respirating, and so it correspondingly means at throat or gullet, and indicates an oral need and satisfaction respectively, before it is generalised to the relational life (cf. KEGLER, J., Biblische Begriffe von Seele, 106–109). The examples could be increased and expanded for every apparently abstract term.

23 Cf. SPINOZA, B., Ethica, 90 128 (Cor. zu 1 Prop. 25): '*Res particulares nihil sunt, nisi Dei attributorum affectiones, sive modi.*'

24 Cf. CLARKE, S./LEIBNIZ, G.W., Briefwechsel mit Leibniz, 72.

by Wittgenstein and Whitehead as a false one.[25] A concise relational ontology must distinguish between those kinds of relations to which this alternative is applicable and those for which it is not.

In the 20th century, as we already seen, the state of affairs changes, insofar as relationality is liberated from its hiddenness.

Relational ontologies, we can conclude, are not new; whether explicitly or implicitly, they have been influential throughout history. They have begun to flourish in the 20th and 21st centuries, but at the same time they have produced much misunderstanding due to their new, fashionable role. Nevertheless, the reason for their flourishing is not that in the period of late modernity, or postmodernity, relational ontologies can claim to have sole interpretative power. The contrary seems to be true. Atomistic-individualist ontologies were dominant in the 20th century, in the philosophy of nature as well as in society. The explication of the former hidden relationality in different traditions can therefore also be understood as a protest against the modern oversimplification and radicalization of atomistic-individualist thinking. This radicalization of individualist thinking becomes evident in the fact that, previously, it was difficult to find ontological systems of interpretation that denied that relationality was a dimension. But this changed in the 20th century.

7.2 The Capacity of Relational Ontologies

The following description of methods of relational reflection is not comprehensive, but representative.

7.2.1 *Relational Analyses*

Relational analyses are an important means of understanding and they do not presuppose any ontological commitments. Since most, if not all, states of affairs can be described relationally, the first step is to ask how many *relata* are involved and how the positions of the *relata* can be generally described. Therefore, it is possible to analyze the same state of affairs with more or less *relata*. Also, predicates can be seen as a subset of relations, i.e. monadic relations. Let us illustrate this with the help of a few examples.

25 Cf. WHITEHEAD, A.N., Process and Reality, 56. 59. 309; WITTGENSTEIN, L., Tractatus Logico-Philosophicus (engl.), 4.122, 4.1221, 4.123, 4.124, 4.1241, 4.125, 4.1251.

'Perceiving' in a relation that is open to different relational analyses:
(1) 'a perceives.'
(2) 'a perceives b.'
(3) 'a perceives b in the midst of the story c.'
(4) 'a perceives b in the midst of the story c as d at place e and time f.'
In the case of (1), we find a monadic analysis, i.e. a predicate. The 'a' denotes the position of the relatum, 'perceives' expresses the relation, considered in this example as an attribute. In (2), the relata are the perceiver 'a' and the perceived 'b', whereas the relation is '... perceives ...'; in (3), the relatum c, the narrative horizon of perception, is added to the relata a and b. It is a threefold analysis. The relation is now '... perceives ... in the midst of ...'. In (4), we find a polyadic relation with six relata, that is '... perceives ... in the midst of ... as ... at place ... and time....'

One and the same, abstract or concrete state of affairs can be analyzed in different ways. Imagine a concrete event, analyzed in the sense of (1): 'Anna perceives.' This analysis can be significant, e.g. if Anna is a patient who was comatose and is now able to perceive but not yet able to speak. The same event, analyzed according to (2) introduces what Anna perceives, e.g. Bertram. In an analysis according to (3), the narrative horizon of Anna's understanding comes into play. The narrative horizon is, in this case, the shared story between Anna and Bertram, which may explain why Anna is able to recognize this human in her symbolic consciousness as Bertram, which does not only refer to her past, but also to her present – say that she is in the process of waking up, looking out of the hospital-window, and so on. In the analysis of (4), we can see that Anna perceives Bertram as a thief (d), who runs out of a bank (e) at the very moment she awakes. In every kind of analysis, it is always the same event that is analyzed. In every case, the effect is the same, but of different significance, depending on the pragmatic interests of the speaker. For her doctors and relatives, analysis (1) might suffice, whereas analysis (1) is meaningless for the investigating police officer. For her, only (4) becomes significant.

In our example, we have analyzed a concrete event. But in those cases, in which the phenomenal perception itself is at stake, these and many other analyses are possible. None of these analyses are *apriori* more or less appropriate, since they are led by pragmatic interests. All analyses are descriptions of the same event. The relata of the more wide-ranging analyses do not simply vanish if a relation is transformed into one of the positions with less *relata*; they are bracketed by the relation itself in the one case and factored out in the other case. Nevertheless, it is not arbitrary how many *relata* are used, since an analysis can be more or less appropriate due to the pragmatic interests at stake. If one has the phenomenon of perceiving itself in mind, then it has to be analyzed, yet none of the relations mentioned in the examples given suffices. We need relations of higher value – and that is exactly what we have done in ch. 5. We used precisely a relational analysis, as was introduced here, without referring to it as such.

7.2.2 *Relational-logical Attributes*

Relational attributes are the attributes of relations.[26] In the case of dyadic relations, the most important of these are first, symmetry and its derivatives, second, reciprocity and its derivatives, third, reflexivity and its derivatives, fourth, transitivity and its derivatives, and fifth, reversibility and its derivatives. What does this mean?

Symmetry is present if the relation 'a is related to b' in all cases or instantiations of its *relata* can be reversed to 'b is related to a'. In so-called graphs, or an arrow diagram, there are only double-arrowed lines pointing to both ends. The arrows illustrate the specific relation and the places or points (sometimes called 'knots') between the arrows that represent the *relata*. *Asymmetry* is present if 'a is related to b' and can at no point be reversed to 'b is related to a'. In the graph, only single-arrowed lines appear. Asymmetry is sometimes also called anti-symmetry. *Partial-symmetry*: If one denies symmetry, one does not get the opposite relationship, asymmetry. Non-symmetry is therefore not asymmetry, while non-asymmetry is also not symmetry. Asymmetry is only a special case of non-symmetry. Often it is the case that a relation can be reversed not for all, but for some instantiations of its *relata*; which is the case in relations that are neither symmetric nor asymmetric. To put it another way: some relations are partially symmetric and partially asymmetric. Double-arrowed lines as well as single-arrowed lines appear in the graph.

The relation 'a is located besides b' is symmetrical, because in every case in which something a is related on the side of b, b is also located on the side of a, whatever or whoever it might be. The relation 'a is natural child of b' is asymmetric, because there can be no case in which a is a natural child of b whereas at the same time b is a natural child of a. The relation 'a admires b' is partial-symmetric. There might be humans who admire each other reciprocally, but there are also humans who admire others without being admired by them.

Reciprocity should not be confused with symmetry. Whereas symmetry is used for specific concepts vis-à-vis intensional relations, reciprocity is used for extensional relations, which means that reciprocity is used as a relational attribute between concrete *relata*, but independently of the concrete intensional descriptions of the relation. One can also say: Reciprocity means that there has to be at least one respect in which the intensional description of the concrete relation is symmetric, whereas in other respects asymmetry or partial symmetry may rule. The derivatives of reciprocity can be derived in an analogous way

26 Cf. for a brief depiction MÜHLING, M., Gott ist Liebe, 335–337.

to symmetry. Reciprocity cannot simply be pictured with the help of graphs. Let us illustrate reciprocity with an example:

The relation between academic instructors and non-graduated students is asymmetric, because no one who is a non-graduate can be at the same time an academic instructor. Nevertheless, the relation is in manifold respects a reciprocal one, e.g. in learning from each other, and this reciprocity of learning from each other is also essential for the relationship between academic instructors and students.

Reflexivity is given in a relation 'a is related to b' when the a and b are identical in all cases, i.e. if 'a is related to a' is the case. *Irreflexivity* is given if in a relation 'a is related to b' the relata are never identical. *Partial symmetry* is given, if both can be the case. Reflexive relations are represented by graphs, in which each of the *relata* has a circular arrow (in which origin and target are the same). In irreflexive relations, there appear no circular arrows at all in the graphs, and in the case of partial symmetry one can see that some *relata* have circular arrows while others do not.

The relation '... is identical with ...' is a reflexive one, and there are circular arrows through the whole field. The relation '... is cause of ...' is an irreflexive relation, because nothing can be the cause itself (there can be no *causa sui*). The relation '... talks to ...' is partially symmetric, because in many cases humans might talk to other humans, but can also talk to themselves.

Transitivity is present in all the cases, if – when 'a is related to b' and 'b to c' – a is also related to c. *Intransitivity* is present if this condition is never met. *Partial transitivity* is present, if the condition is fulfilled for some *relata* of the field of the relation while it is false for others. In the case of transitivity, a graph will display bridging arrows (i.e. an arrow from a to c in the case that there are arrows from a to b and from b to c) throughout the whole field of the *relata*, in the case of intransitivity bridging arrows do not appear at all, and in the case of partial transitivity they sometimes appear.

The relation '... follows temporarily after ...' is a transitive one, then in all cases if a year, say 2037, follows another one, e.g. 2017, and this one follows another one, e.g. 1987, so that the first (2037) also follows the last (1987). The relation '... is daughter of ...' is intransitive, since a daughter of a daughter of a person never can be the daughter of the first person. The relation '... likes ...' is partially symmetric, since there are cases, in which a person a likes a person b, and also likes c, which is also liked by b, but there are also cases, in which a person a, although she likes b, does not like a person c liked by b.

7.2.3 *Connections in Propositional Logic as a Means of Relational Analyses*

The logical connections between propositions can also be understood as relational attributes.[27] The most important among them are the sufficient condition (implication), the necessary condition (replication), the sufficient and necessary condition (equivalence), the inclusive 'or/and' (disjunction), the exclusive 'either ... or' (contradiction of contravalence), and the conjunction. With the help of such means two propositions can be connected to a new one. They are, in many ways, important in philosophy and in theology.

The *sufficient condition* or implication between two propositions p and q is only false, if p is true, but q is false. The implication is the basis of logical inferences. The *necessary condition* or replication between two propositions p and q is only false, if p is false, but q is true. The sufficient condition can be expressed in everyday language with 'always if p, then q'. The necessary condition can be expressed with 'only if p, then q'. The replication is in some sense the reverse case of the implication, since 'p implies q' is identical with 'q replicates p'. One has to be careful in the case of negations: From 'p implies q' there follows 'not-q implies not-p', but 'not-p implies not-q' does not. The sufficient and necessary condition, or equivalence, is true, if p and q are both true, or if p and q are both false. One can express it in everyday-language by saying 'always and only if p, then q'. It has also become common to render this as 'if and only if p, then q', (sometimes shortened to 'iff'). The inclusive or/and, or the disjunction, is only false, if p and q are false at the same time. The exclusive 'either p or q', or contradiction, is only true, if p is true and q is false, or if p is false while q is true. The conjunction, expressed with 'and' in everyday language, is only true, if p and q are true simultaneously.

7.2.4 *The Problem of Constitutive or Internal Relationality*

So far, we have only described the means of a relational ontology by dealing with the formal tools of analysis. The discussion of constitutivity or internal relations versus non-constitutivity or external relations, however, is of the highest ontological importance and expresses completely different views of reality.

Let us, at first, remain on the purely conceptual level by discussing pure conceptual constitutivity or internality in contrast to conceptual non-constitutive or external relations. On the one hand, we know relations like '... is located beside ...' The position of the *relata* can be substituted by anything, e.g. 'a car is located beside the house'. Both *relata*, car and house, are conceptually non-constitutive for each other. To know what a car is does not imply knowledge

27 Cf. for an overview MÜHLING, M., Logic.

of what a house is, and *vice versa*. Relations like these are conceptually non-constitutive or conceptually external relations. Consider the relation '… gives birth to …'. Here the first *relatum* is necessarily 'mother', the second 'daughter': 'A mother gives birth to a daughter'. The concepts of mother and daughter are reciprocally constitutive for each other in a conceptual way. To know what a daughter is implies knowing what a mother is and *vice versa*. This relation is a conceptually internal or conceptually constitutive relation.

As far as concepts alone are concerned, the matter is relatively uninteresting. It is exciting, however, to bring reference to reality into focus. Consider the following example by Leibniz:

> The only thing that is provable is that *everything* that exists is connected, partly because otherwise it would not be possible to say whether something in our soul happens now or does not happen, and therefore, this sentence would be neither true nor false, which is contradictory, partly because many things that are said one can only attribute externally, and the husband in India, whose wife dies in Europe, does not become widower without a real change in him. Since every predicate is in truth included in the nature of the subject.[28]

This citation from Leibniz indicates that all relations are constitutive or internal ones, which results in the appearance of a holism of being.

For Leibniz, this holism is unrestricted. If there were a difference in only one thing in the entire history of the world at any location, the world would have changed and every individual would have a completely different identity.[29] Leibniz also uses the metaphor of a (very special) chain,[30] in which one cannot determine where one link begins and another one ends. With this qualification: is it a chain at all? Or does Leibniz switch to an ontology of dynamic lines and threads? This would give the wrong impression, however, since Leibniz's ontology is still an object orientated one (and therefore also fundamentally individualist in another sense), because for him the world consists

---

28 LEIBNIZ, G.W., Kleinere Schriften, XX. Ueber die Art und Weise, die wirklichen Erscheinungen von den eingebildeten zu unterscheiden, 157: „allein es lässt sich beweisen, dass *alles* Daseiende miteinander eine Verbindung hat, theils deshalb, weil man sonst nicht sagen könnte, ob etwas in unserer Seele jetzt geschieht oder nicht geschieht, und also dieser Satz weder wahr noch falsch wäre, was widersinnig wäre; theils weil vieles von den Dingen Ausgesagte nur äusserlich denselben beigelegt wird und der Mann in Indien, dessen Frau in Europa stirbt, nicht Witwer wird, ohne dass nicht eine wirkliche Veränderung in ihm eintritt. Denn jedes Prädikat ist in Wahrheit in der Natur des Subjekts enhalten". (Transl. MM).

Russell was not the only person irritated by this example. Also the editor, Kirchman, expresses his irritation ibid., 130, note g, by claiming that being a widower is nothing more than an external relationship of rights.

29 Cf. LEIBNIZ, G.W., Briefwechsel mit Antoine Arnauld, 92f. 143.

30 Cf. LEIBNIZ, G.W., Philosophische Schriften, Bd. 4, 265.

of countable entities, but not of a continuum – although it comes infinitely close to one.[31] Only ideal space as an abstraction can be seen as a continuum.[32] What is more important is that Leibniz's world claims to be constitutively relational, but not dynamic. It is the compossibility of all entities based on causality that does not allow for any temporal gap. Therefore, 'the present is pregnant with the future,'[33] means that every moment of the universe includes every other in its entire development, which implies that Leibniz' thinking parallels the concept of transport in a network, which is only seemingly dynamic (cf. ch. 8).

Hegel's philosophy is very similar, in that it conceives of the world as an explication of itself and the coming to its own of the absolute spirit. Thus, Hegel, influenced by F.H. Bradley, claims:

> We have seen [...] all relations imply a whole to which the terms contribute and by which the terms are qualified [...]. Nothing in the whole and in the end can be external, and everything less than the Universe is an abstraction from the whole, an abstraction more or less empty [...].[34] Relations are all intrinsical.[35]

So far, this is nothing but an assertion. Leibniz gives three arguments for his thesis.

First of all, in the case of pure intentional[36] relations, i.e. in relations internal to the mind of a subject, the relation between the *relata* has to be conceived as constitutive or necessary.

An example might illustrate this relation. In Goethe's *The Sorrows of Young Werther*, Werther's love of Lotte is described almost purely intentional, with the exception of some key sequences through which this intentional relation influences reality communicatively, e.g. when Lotte somehow feels Werther's affection. Imagine Werther completely hiding all his feelings for Lotte. Observed from the outside, this case would, in no way, be different to another one, in which Werther does not have positive feelings for Lotte. Nevertheless, these two cases are completely different, which is only possible if one conceives of Werther's emotions as constitutive relations that determine him completely, although these relations exist purely in his mind.

This argument is correct, but problematic, since one can easily agree with it – i.e. to agree that there are constitutive or internal relations in the mind – but

31 Cf. EVERS, D., Gott und mögliche Welten, 29.80.
32 Cf. EVERS, D., Gott und mögliche Welten, 77.
33 LEIBNIZ, G.W., Philosophische Schriften, Bd. 2/2, 179.
34 BRADLEY, F.H., Appearance and Reality, 581.
35 BRADLEY, F.H., Appearance and Reality, 627.
36 Not to be confused with "intensional".

nevertheless to simultaneously deny their extra-psychical reality. This is the case of Bertrand Russell:

> I called this [Bradley's view] 'the doctrine of internal relations,' and I called my view 'the doctrine of external relations.' The doctrine of internal relations held that every relation between two terms expresses, primarily, intrinsic properties of the two terms and, in ultimate analysis, a property of the whole which the two compose. With some relations this view is plausible. Take, for example, love or hate. If A loves B, this relation exemplifies itself and may be said to consist in certain states of mind of A. Even an atheist must admit that a man can love God. It follows that love of God is a state of the man who feels it, and not properly a relational fact.[37]

Russell, a confessing atheist, admits that there are pure psychical constitutive relations. The love of God, someone might feel, is really an irreducible property of this human person. Although, in the last sentence quoted, Russell reveals that he does not really regard this love of God as relational, since the second *relatum*, God, is only imagined; without any existence. It is the same with Lotte in our modified example from *Werther*: Despite being real *for* Werther, she is only imagined and without any reality.

Second, Leibniz' first argument is right but it does not deliver what it was intended to. It leads to the consequence that any predicate is really included in the subject. Bradley explicitly admits as much:

> But every relation [...] essentially penetrates the being of its terms, and, in this sense, is intrinsical. [...] I do not admit that any relation whatever can be merely external and make no difference to its terms.[38]

This argument is two-sided. One part consists in the fact that it is possible, as we have seen in the description of relational analyses, to describe every relation formally as containing as many *relata* as one likes or as are adequate to the pragmatic interest of the situation. The description indicates that it is also possible to describe any relation as a monadic one, as a predicate of a subject. But it is the second aspect of the argument that is decisive. Leibniz and Bradley hold to the universal view that every possible predicate of any subject is an analytical one. If this is the case, then holism and Monism are unavoidable, since any relation and any thinkable attribute of something in the world would in fact be an analytical property, not a synthetic one. It would imply attributes that add nothing to what is included in the concept of the subject.

37 RUSSELL, B., Philosophical Development, 54.
38 BRADLEY, F.H., Appearance and Reality, 392; 574.

Consequently, there can only be one subject: the world. But, of course, in all the examples given so far, this is only an assertion.

Third, in the example mentioned above, Leibniz returns to another set of relations that are not purely intentional relations, which are relations among events, or more precisely, relations among spatiotemporal events, by claiming that the widower changes intrinsically without having knowledge of the death of his wife. In this example we find three events, two of them spatiotemporally unbounded: (1) The death of the wife in Europe, (2) the life of the husband in India at the same time, but spatially separated, and (3) the temporally later events by which the husband gains knowledge about the death of his wife. Leibniz claim is that in the very moment when the wife dies, the husband is changed intrinsically, i.e. event (2) would have been completely different if event (1) did not happen.

Russell refers explicitly to Leibniz in his counter-argument and quotes him (obviously from memory – he mixes up Europe and India).[39] Leibniz's claims seem nonsensical to him, but he gives only one reason why he thinks so. He claims the relation between events (1) and (3) is a temporally ordered sequence that is necessarily asymmetric. Event (3) is later than (1), therefore, there can be no retro-causal effect from (3) to (1) or to any event (2) that takes place at the same time as (1), if one does not violate the asymmetry of temporal relations.[40] This argument is correct. And once more, this argument also does not address what was originally intended by it; it is true only for temporal relations. But events could be ordered – in addition to temporally – by other relations, known or unknown. If this was the case, then Russell's argument would be without worth.

Ironically, this is exactly what happened in the history of physics. Here, it was Einstein, who insisted, similarly to Russell, that there can only be a spatiotemporal individuation of entities, with the consequence that there are only spatiotemporal relations among things. If effects cannot be transferred faster than light-speed, then the thought-experiment of the couple living in Europe and India, along with Leibniz' point, would be as nonsensical, as would show the example given by Einstein (or rather of Podolsky, who was the author of the famous EPR-paper)[41] designed to demonstrate the incoherence of quantum theory. Two entangled quanta are named entangled because they have only a single quantum state. At the same time, prior to being measured, there is

39 Cf. RUSSELL, B., Philosophical Development, 55.

40 Cf. RUSSELL, B., Philosophical Development, 55.

41 Cf. MÜHLING, M., Einstein und die Religion, 264–271. Cf. also EINSTEIN, A./PODOLSKY, B./ROSEN, N., EPR.

no such definite status. If one separates both entangled quanta spatially and measures the status of one quantum, then what is discovered epistemically is not an ontologically prior state, but that the state is ontologically constructed in a spontaneous, contingent, and unpredictable way within the limits of the probabilities given by the wave-function. If by such means one gets a definite value in regard to one quantum, the measurement of the other quantum, irrespective of how far it is separated, is also given at the very instant the first measurement takes place. Both quanta are entangled, but there can be no spatiotemporal transmission of information. This scenario was designed to show that it is nonsensical. However, the history of physics has empirically revealed that exactly what Einstein regarded as nonsense is, in fact, the case.[42] Thus, one can only (against Einstein) understand this case by conceiving of the two quanta and the measuring apparatuses not as definite entities or separate individuals. They are not individuated separately, but are together one event related by constitutive relationality. For the world of quanta, any individualist atomism is strictly excluded.[43]

All of the other arguments Russell mentions are not arguments in the strict sense but rather examples of what it would mean if the opinion that all relations are internal were true: To know a single part of the world would mean to know all other parts and the world itself. And the reverse: In order to know one single part of the world one would be in the need of previous knowledge of all other parts of the world and of the world itself. Then there would be only one thing, one subject: the world.[44] In the history of thought, one can find several examples of such systems. Russell describes Leibniz' monadology adequately in principal, not considering its shortness and Russell's inadequate valuations. Although, in the end, Russell can only hope that his readers might share what he regards as self-evident; such thinking is nonsense. Russell fears that if Leibniz, Hegel, and Bradley were right, any empirical knowledge would be superfluous. If I know something at only one time, I know everything.

Among the consequences Russell mentions, one is of preeminent importance. He claims that, if all relations are internal ones, then there would be no difference and no alterity:

---

42 The most important theoretical point persists in the so-called Bell's theorem, cf. BELL, J.S., On the EPR Paradox. A general overview of the empirically observable breach is given in ZEILINGER, A./WEIHS, G./JENNEWEIN, T./ASPELMEYER, M., Happy Centenary.

43 See also GRÖBLACHER, S./PATEREK, T./KALTENBAEK, R./BRUKNER, C./ZUKOWSKI, M./ASPELMEYER, M./ZEILINGER, A., An Experimental Test of Non-local Realism, who certainly goes one step further, and not only gives up local individualism, but also specific aspects of realism.

44 Cf. RUSSELL, B., Philosophical Development, 56f.

> Consequently, if the axiom of internal relations is true, it follows that there is no diversity.[45]

His claim is that empiricism has to reject the internal-relation holism and that one has to claim *more* than merely the opposite: The contradictory position would simply be that *not all* relations are internal ones. But Russel's claim is that *no* (relevant) relation is an internal one – or that all relations are external ones:

> I still hold to the doctrine of external relations and to pluralism, which is bound up with it. [...] I still hold that any proposition other than a tautology, if it is true, is true in virtue of a relation to a fact, and that facts in general are independent of experience.[46]

Russell calls his own, radical opinion 'pluralism', although a better term would be individualist atomism, and he distinguishes himself from a 'monist' holism, which he sees as a holism without any alterity and without any empirical relevance.

So far, the debate regarding the meaning of constitutive or internal relationality is not resolved. From the time of Leibniz to Russell a problem emerged without any solution. Both positions promote their opinions without being able to offer conclusive arguments. Before we try to unscramble the matter, we must first offer the whole history.

A very easy, but not altogether inappropriate, solution lies in unmasking Russell's alternative as a false one. The contradictory position to the thesis 'all relations are internal relations' is not Russell's thesis that all relations are external ones, but that not all relations are internal ones. The same is true the other way around: in order to contradict the thesis 'all relations are external ones' one does not have to claim that all relations are internal ones, but only that not all are external. This way of dealing with the problem was chosen by young Wittgenstein in the *Tractatus*:

> We can speak in a certain sense of formal properties of objects and atomic facts, or of properties of the structure of facts, and in the same sense of formal relations and relations of structures. (Instead of property of the structure I also say 'internal property'; instead of relation of structures 'internal relation.' I introduce these expressions in order to show the reason for the confusion, very widespread among philosophers, between internal relations and proper (external) relations.) The holding of such internal properties and relations cannot, however, be

45 RUSSELL, B., Philosophical Development, 57.

46 RUSSELL, B., Philosophical Development, 63f.

> asserted by propositions, but it shows itself in the propositions which present the atomic facts and treat of the objects in question. [...] The existence of an internal relation between possible states of affairs expresses itself in language by an internal relation between the propositions presenting them. [...] Here the disputed question 'whether all relations are internal or external' disappears.[47]

Wittgenstein tries to abrogate the problem by renaming it, but what is important is not the renaming of the problem. What is important is that Wittgenstein correctly sees that Russell's alternative is not an alternative after all. The veracity of this argument, as far is it goes, can be seen in Wittgenstein's attempt to rename the problem, despite whether the argumentation is convincing. Nevertheless, Wittgenstein's opinion itself is very dangerous. His statement suggests that there is no problem of relevance. It suggests that the debate about internal and external relations, about individualist atomism and relational holism, is irrelevant. In this way, Wittgenstein becomes much more dangerous than Russell, since he marginalizes the problem without any solution in a way that could tempt the reader to regard ontological questions – questions about reality – to be completely irrelevant.

It is surely right that Russell's description of the alternative between 'external' and 'internal' relations is in more than one sense loaded with misunderstandings. One is tempted to read 'external' as 'regarding the spatiotemporal world' and 'internal' as 'regarding the mind'. From this misunderstanding, one could associate 'external' with what is visible from the 3rd-person perspective and 'internal' with what can be recognized from the 1st-person perspective, but that would be completely mistaken and miss the crux of the matter. Before we try to solve the problem ourselves, we have to discuss some alternative solutions.

Russell himself admitted that there are constitutive relations, but only purely intentional, psychical ones, which are not real in the sense that relations between spatiotemporal, distinguishable events are real. We have seen that Russell gives the example of the love of God, which we discussed further vis-à-vis the feeling of being in love. What if one could extend this argument instead of restricting it to psychically special cases? Indeed, this is what happened in all theories of subjectivity from Schleiermacher up to today, which stress that all that is somehow knowable (including apparently empirical things like measurements) is only given as the content of consciousness. Another, more elegant, way of deploying the same idea appears in the phenomenological tradition. Here, it is shown that it is perception itself that is always in an

47 WITTGENSTEIN, L., Tractatus Logico-Philosophicus, 1.22; 4.125; 4.1251.

intentional relation. This mode of argumentation is elegant, because there are no phenomena which are not perceivable, so that all phenomena are relationally composed in a constitutive manner. It is also elegant since this claim does not entail that all perceived relations belong to the constitutivity of relationality. For an ontological description following a phenomenal analysis, it suffices that *some* of these relations are seen as constitutive. That there is nothing that is not constitutively relational is secured, but 'external' relations are also possible. Yet, this solution is also not without problems, since one could reduce it to the position that what is constitutively relational is only constitutively relational *for* the knowing subject. And then they would be seen as attributes of this subject. But this would end in a return to the ontologies of subjectivity, including a monism or holism of the subject. Merleau-Ponty also saw this danger in the philosophy of his teacher, Husserl.[48]

Another proposed solution, including a very sophisticated description of the problem, was given by Whitehead:

> How can the other actual entities, each with its own formal existence, also enter objectively into the perceptive constitution of the actual entity in question? This is the problem of the solidarity of the universe. The classical doctrines of universals and particulars, of subject and predicate, of individual substances not present in other individual substances, of the externality of relations, alike render this problem incapable of solution.[49]
>
> It is by means of 'extension' that the bonds between prehensions take on the dual aspect of internal relations, which are yet in a sense external relations. It is evident that if the solidarity of the physical world is to be relevant to the description of its individual actualities, it can only be by reason of the fundamental internality of the relationships in question. On the other hand, if the individual discreteness of the actualities is to have its weight, there must be an aspect in these relationships from which they can be conceived as external, that is, as bonds between divided things.[50]

Why is this such a sophisticated description of the problem? Russell wants to provide strong opposition against any idealism and holism, which he called 'monism'. He, therefore, designs a radical individualist atomism, with the desire to maintain true diversity, alterity, and the preeminent role of the empirical sciences. In contrast to his intention, he is not successful: he cannot escape idealism, but is formally bound in a contradiction by claiming that all (relevant) relations are external. But such a universal statement is something that cannot be claimed within the framework of a radical atomism. If Russell were truly consistent, he would have to deny that universal propositions are

48 Cf. BERMES, C., Merleau-Ponty, Pos. 962–966.

49 WHITEHEAD, A.N., Process and Reality, 56.

50 WHITEHEAD, A.N., Process and Reality, 309.

meaningless. However, such a claim would also run against the work of the empirical sciences, since the sciences use universal propositions in their theories, which have to be mediated by empirical knowledge of the particular. What Russell really delivers is simply a kind of negative or reverse idealism. Nevertheless, at a decisive point, Russell's analysis is of high value, which Whitehead acknowledged: one must indeed stress true diversity and alterity without resolving them too quickly into unity. And this is also the task if one wants to stress a constitutive relationality among the *relata* of the world. Is it, therefore, possible to assume that there is true, irreducible alterity within the framework of a philosophy similar to Leibniz, Hegel, and Bradley without falling back into an individualist atomism? In other words: are solidarity and alterity both possible? Can love and otherness live in harmony?

So far, we have reconstructed the problem in Whitehead's terms. Now we must discuss his proposed solution. First, he diagnoses a terminological fuzziness in the talk of 'internal' and 'external' relations. He suggests seeing such relations as being at the same time but in different respects both, 'internal' and 'external'. This structure of relations suggests that relations are constitutive for the *relata* and that the particularity of the *relata* must not to be presupposed, but emerges out of the relation. In Whitehead's philosophy, this is possible through his concept of 'prehension'. Instead of classical substances, Whitehead uses *actual occurrences* as basic entities, which are processual or constituted event-like in their internal being. They receive (*prehend*) from former events content and transform it in an unpredictable way. By means of this ongoing process, novelty and diversity emerge, whereas all events are connected within a nexus of solidarity.[51]

Whitehead's solution to the problem is elegant, but presupposes the entirety of Whitehead's ontology. Therefore, we must look for other ways to solve the problem.

My suggestion is as simple as it is perhaps bewildering. Particularity and otherness, generated in being essentially related to one another, should not be seen as attributes of the *relata*, but as attributes of the relation itself. In essential or constitutive relations, there is a constantly emerging element of otherness, which cannot be attributed to one or the other of the *relata*. We can also find this sort of solution in Richard of St. Victor's 'impeded relational ontology. In contrast to modern notions of the person, he conceives of a person as an *icommunicabilis existentia*.[52] Persons, like any kind of entities are therefore *existentiae*, i.e. *whence-and-whither beings* or, as we might later sharpen the concept, *whence-and-whither-becomings*. It is important to note here that they are at the same time a kind of *existentiae* that are *incommunicabiles*. This

51 Cf. e.g. WHITEHEAD, A.N., Process and Reality, 251.

52 Cf. RICHARD VON ST.VICTOR, De Trinitate, 4,22f (280–283).

term expresses the particularity, foreignness, and hiddenness of the person from others and from themselves. On the one hand, *incommunicabilis* means simply 'incommunicable'. Although persons are related constitutively to each other, they cannot transfer their particularity to others. In this sense, *incommunicabilis* means nothing but 'particularity' or 'individuality', with the assumption that one does not misunderstand individuality to mean individualism. On the other hand, this particularity is by no means an attribute external to the relation, which could be removed from the relation and instead attributed to the person as a *relatum*, like a monadic predicate. Particularity, or individuality, if you like, emerges only *in communicatione*, which is the second meaning of *incommunicabilis* that we must add if the concept is to be regarded as truly meaningful. Without the essentially transferable relations there is no particularity.

Taking a different starting point, Anton Friedrich Koch recently dealt with the problem. In the end, he also claims the essential connection, even identity, of all persons. However, this is not a phenomenal, but a hidden identity.[53] Koch does not, however, restrict this notion to persons. What Russell calls 'internal' relations, Koch calls 'interdependent' relations (*Wechselverhältnis*), defined as 'the concept of a systematic whole made up of two or more entities, which [...] are in no respect distinct entities.'[54] Nevertheless, their particularity is not lost due to the concept of hidden identity. Koch understands his position as holistic, inasmuch as he shares Bradley's opinion that, in his words, 'on a deeper level the objects are no distinct entities anymore, but they are all *relata* of a comprehensive relationship.'[55]

We will take on Koch's and St. Victor's insights, but we also have to make some qualifications. Hidden in the constitutive relationality of things there is an indescribable and indeterminable aspect that enables the particularity of the *relata* along with their essential relatedness. This indeterminable aspect is irreducible and cannot be seen as a quality of a single *relatum*, be it a personal or an apersonal one, without falling back into the abstractions and short-comings of an individualist atomism. At the same time, this indeterminable aspect is more than merely hidden from us by being inaccessible to any empirical or non-empirical investigation. It is not only hidden from all perceiving entities whatsoever, but it is ontically undetermined. If one takes this seriously, one has

53 Cf. Koch, A.F., Wahrheit, Zeit und Freiheit, 124f. 128f.

54 Koch, A.F., Wahrheit, Zeit und Freiheit, 84: „der Begriff eines systematischen Ganzen von zwei oder mehr Entitäten, die [...] in keiner Hinsicht distinkte Entitäten sind." (Transl. MM).

55 Koch, A.F., Wahrheit, Zeit und Freiheit, 84: „die Objekte auf einer tieferen Ebene keine distinkten Entitäten mehr sind, sondern alle in einem umfassenden Wechselverhältnis stehen" (Transl. MM).

to abandon a specific concept within the framework of the relational ontology: the concept of being. A being among other beings must be principally (but not factually) determinable. It could therefore change itself or be changed. But it would be *this* particular being that would be changed. If the *relata* do have their identity and existence *exclusively* in relation to each other, and if the particularity of the *relata* subsists not in themselves but in the permanent inaccessibility or hiddenness of the relation, however, *then these* relata *are constantly in a process of becoming*. Thus far, this picture of the state of affairs also lacks some clarity, since we have had said that *something* is in the process of becoming. It therefore suggests something false, as though there were something subsisting, something like a subject or something like a substance – and this is precisely not the case. It is better to say that *the* relata *are becomings*. We have to substitute being with becoming. If one accepts Richard's concept of *existentia*, then it is not to be translated as 'whence-and-whither beings' but as *whence-and-whither-becoming*.

Let us also untangle the terminological confusion generated by Bradley and Russell, then we will see that behind their debate there are at least three different problems. And, in order to find clarity, we must add a fourth aspect.

1. *Ontically constitutive and ontically non-constitutive relations*: A dyadic or polyadic relation is ontically constitutive if the existence and essence of its *relata* do not exist independently of each other; or better: A dyadic or polyadic relation is ontically constitutive if the becoming of the *relata* are inextricably intermeshed. It is ontically non-constitutive if this is not the case.
2. *Pure intentional and real relations*: A relation is purely intentional if it exists only as an appearance to the perceiving one. It is real if it exists independently of its appearance to a perceiving one, or if it is possible that it exists independently of a perceiving one.
3. *Reducible and irreducible relations*: A polyadic relation is reducible if it can be reduced to a relation involving less *relata*, which includes the possibility of the limiting case of a dyadic relation that can be reduced to a monadic predicate of a subject.

Russell acknowledges the existence of ontically constitutive relations, but only in the case of purely intentional relations. In the case of real relations, he excludes ontically constitutive relations, which means that in the realm of the real there are only non-constitutive relations. His decisive argument is that if there were real ontically constitutive relations, these would have to be seen as reducible. In this case, they would be in reality essential qualities of a single subject or a single substance, of one single world or of one single *relatum*, or of one absolute spirit – or whatever one wants to call this monolith. But this argument fails, since ontic constitutivity does not imply reducibility, given that in ontic constitutivity a principal kind of indeterminateness is present, which enables diversity. Leibniz, in the quotation we used to open our discussion, acknowledges ontic constitutivity in the case of real as well as purely intentional relations, but he regards these relations as reducible. Our own suggestion is to acknowledge ontic constitutivity of the real as well as of purely intentional relations by simultaneously denying their universal reducibility. Therefore, we get a fourth, hidden problem, which we must now describe:

4. *Constitutivity can be symmetrical or asymmetrical.* Russell – and also Koch and Leibniz – deals with constitutivity as a strictly symmetrical quality of relations. But if one acknowledges that it is possible for there to be a kind of alterity generating indeterminacy within the relation itself, which cannot be reduced to a quality of a logical subject, then this would mean that there are also asymmetrically constitutive relations. In this respect, a dyadic relation would be possible in which a case of *relatum* a and *relatum* b being mutually constitutive in their 'that-becoming' (their existence) and in their 'so-becoming' (their essence or identity). It would also be possible that that the constitutivity runs in only one direction: from a to b or *vice versa*. The same is true with respect to polyadic relations, but in a more complex manner. Polyadic relations should not be seen as reducible *apriori* to dyadic relations.

With the help of these four distinctions we can now illumine the fashionable talk of relational approaches and relational ontologies:

- It is *not a relational ontology* if constitutive relationality is denied.
- It is *not a relational ontology* if it is claimed that purely intentional relations can be constitutive ones, while the existence of non-purely intentional and at the same time constitutive relations are denied, which is the case of Russell's individualist atomism.
- It is only an *apparently relational ontology* (i.e. not a relational ontology), if the existence of constitutive relationality is acknowledged for intentional relations by assuming at the same time that real relations do not exist at all or only exist in the frame of intentional relations, which is the case in all ontologies of subjectivity, which normally deny that they are ontologies at all.
- *Deficient relational ontologies* (i.e. also only apparently relational ontologies) are also those that acknowledge constitutive relationality in the realm of intentional and real relations by simultaneously assuming that these constitutive relations are all symmetrical and therefore reducible, which is the case in the quotation from Leibniz we used to open the discussion (but not necessarily in his monadology) and also in Hegel's thinking.

– *True relational ontologies* are those, and only those, ontologies that acknowledge the existence of ontic constitutivity in the realm of real and intentional relations by simultaneously acknowledging the existence of irreducible ontic constitutivity. These ontologies can appear in two kinds: ontologies that only operate with symmetrically constitutive relations without denying the possibility of asymmetrically constitutive relations, and ontologies that acknowledge the possibility and actuality of asymmetrical, ontically constitutive relations.

Let's assume the most adequate description of the world for perception would be enabled by a relational ontology in the following way. It would be a world in which there are ontically constitutive relations, which are at the same time real and irreducible, including symmetrical and asymmetrical constitutivity. What would such a world look like? It would be a world, where all that becomes is connected, but also a world in which the unpredictable constantly emerges – there would be spontaneous, contingent becoming. But not all becoming has to be completely spontaneous. It would be possible for it to emerge according to rules. Such a world would be a holistic one, but not a monistic one. Such a world could not be described with the help of systems, since it would be, in principle, open. It would be a world in which love on the one hand and radical alterity as otherness on the other hand would belong ontic constitutively to each other. It would be a world in which love becomes constantly new.

7.3 The Sublation of the Relational into the Narratival

Nearly everything a relational ontology can do can also be done by a narrative ontology. The analytical means of a relational analysis, the attributes of relations, and the relational connections from the fields of propositional logic are relevant for any use of language, and therefore also for narratives. But how does it stand vis-à-vis the genuine advantages of a relational ontology? Can they be remodeled as a narrative ontology?

1. Let us have a look at *ontically constitutive relations*. These relations can be excellently described by a narrative ontology. A narrative ontology, like all ontologies, must use language and thereby it uses narrations that are second-order narrations, embedded in first order relations. Have a look at any possible second-order relation, such as the story of David. Imagine that the figures of Saul, Samuel, Jonathan, Bathsheba, Absalom, and Salomon do not appear in the telling, only David. In this case, is David really David? It does not seem to be possible. Ontically constitutive relationality is a part of any narrative ontology, since the roles, characters, and events of a narration are connected in

an ontically constitutive manner. At the same time, narrations are also an example of the fact that not all relations have to be constitutive ones. It would be possible to retell the story of David in a different way, where we change the order of some sequences or we transfer the whole story into another setting, e.g. a modern, technical world. In such cases, we can still speak of David as David. Some narratologies, structuralist ones or Koschorke's, would see the reason for the identity of a figure persisting despite the changing circumstances to be grounded in the distinction between narration and narrative. Whereas the narration as a concrete, told entity can vary, the narrative as the general structure or the story is maintained. Narratology's task is then to identify the elements of the narrative. Imagine that this is possible. To distinguish between the narrative and the narration would be nothing but distinguishing between the narration's ontically constitutive relations and the non-ontically constitutive relations (and additionally, operating with some abstractions). If one uses the distinction between ontically constitutive and non-ontically constitutive relations from the very beginning, we can illumine another phenomenon. There is not the *one* narrative of the story of David that has remained identical to allow for the story of David to be recognized in different contexts. One could describe this phenomenon using Wittgenstein's notion of family resemblance.[56] However, the idea is that this notion should be purely descriptive, and it is not at all a clear concept, but one with many presuppositions. We have, however, no problem explaining this phenomenon if we understand that the distinction between ontically constitutive relations and non-ontically constitutive relations can vary throughout the telling of a story. Only someone who conceives of stories as static and fixed entities could disagree. But most stories are not static entities, they are dynamic ones.

2. Is it possible as well to find the distinction between *purely intentional and real relations* in a narrative ontology? If one presupposes that purely intentional relations always presuppose a personal subject, one might be tempted to deny the possibility, as we have seen that stories are not bound to their telling subjects (ch.6). This objection would also be true in respect of a purely narrative ontology. Is a personal subject presupposed, with the consequence that a relational ontology must also presupposes subjects or persons? There are two reasons why this objection fails. First, if the distinction between purely intentional and real relations really does presuppose that there are personal subjects, it would not be necessary for them to have a basic status in the theory, so that these subjects would become absolute, undefinable concepts, which would only be the case were if they were ontically basic. Although, if one can

56 Cf. WITTGENSTEIN, L., Philosophical Investigations, §§ 66f, 277f.

also conceive of persons and subjects as second-order concepts, as entities that are themselves relationally constituted, then we do not need to broaden a relational ontology by presupposing a subjectivist one. The same is true in respect of a narrative ontology. It could be that it is not the notion of the person or a subject that constitutes narrations, but the other way around: persons and subjects are constituted by narrations and emerge out of narrations. As such, the objection fails. The second, and perhaps more important, reason for the failure of this objection is that in neither Leibniz or Russell do the distinctions between purely intentional and real relations refer to personal subjects, but to the distinction between thinkable and actual relations. And here, 'thinkable' does not refer to the real activity of thinking (remember the example of being in love, where there are nearly no cognitive aspects), but what is on the one hand possible but not actual relations, and on the other hand 'real' relations, where Russell uses the spatiotemporal, asymmetric order of events as a criterion for reality.[57] In this case, there is no necessity to assume the priority of subjectivity or personality. Additionally, the following problem emerges: we must now redefine the distinction between possibility, necessity, and actuality in a relational and narrantologic way. We will deal with this task later (ch. 18).

We have refuted the objection, and now we must answer the question positively. The distinction between purely intentional and real relations can be excellently remodeled through a narrative ontology by introducing different levels of stories which entail one another. Jesus tells parables in the concrete situation of his travels in Galilee. Everything that appears within the frame of the journeys in Galilee are the real relations, whereas everything that appears within the parable can be seen as the intentional story. But it is not only true that we can use such narrative means to express the distinction between intentional and real relations, for this distinction is, in fact, an abstraction of the narrative means of expressing the entanglement of the levels of stories. Then we discover a deeper insight: the distinction between intentional and real relations is not an absolute one, but a relative one. Imagine that in a parable being told, another story appears. Further, imagine that the frame-narration of journeying in Galilee is embedded in another frame, like the sermon in a contemporary service. We are then brought back to the question: what is the real difference between a purely intentional and real relation, or, in other words, what really is the distinction between the possible and the actual? We cannot deal with this question at this point, suffice it here to say that the distinction

57 Suppose for Russell it is about something different, namely about actually impossible relations (purely intentional) on the one hand and about actually possible relations on the other. Graded modal operators are not extraordinary in modal logic.

between real and intentional relations can easily be remodeled in a narrative ontology.

3. Is it possible to express the distinction between *reducible and irreducible relations* in a narratival way? Such an expression is certainly possible, although it would be more appropriate to say that in stories there are irreducible relations in every circumstance, whereas reducible relations only appear in hidden forms.

A polyadic relation can be seen in the following short narration: 'Jesus, *crucified under* Pilate, *died and has been resurrected by* the Father *and* the Holy Spirit'. In this sentence, the relation is printed in italics, the *relata recte*. Of course, this sentence from a narrative sequence can be expressed, by means of a narrative analysis, as having more or less *relata*. A relation with nearly uncountable *relata* would be the passion and resurrection stories as treated in the Gospels. A purely monadic relation, i.e. a predicate, would be 'the *died and resurrected* Jesus'. Here, only the seemingly relationless predicate 'died and resurrected' appears, which is applied to a single logical subject, Jesus. This example illustrates simply that relations can be analyzed using more or less *relata*.

Narrations can be more or less expanded and developed and similar relations can be analyzed with more or fewer *relata*. Also, the classical Christological titles such as 'Messiah', or 'Son of God', are not absolute predicates but abbreviations for a complex narrative state of affairs. The fact that we can express one and the same state of affairs with more or fewer narrative sequences, or with more or fewer *relata*, should not be confused with the question of reducibility or irreducibility. This latter question presupposes the transformability of relations with more or fewer *relata* and narrations with more or fewer narrative sequences. The claim that relations are irreducible corresponds in a narrative ontology to the claim that there are stories that might be abbreviated, but only in a manner in which the whole developed story is implied, or in which the shortened one displays its dependence on the whole. Reducibility finds its correspondence in the claim of narrative ontology that there are stories that are redundant when reduced to their shortest forms, i.e. that there are stories in which things are told that one should not or do not have to tell.

This narrative argumentation can also be illustrated by the Bible text. In most denominations, the relationship between the short narrations of the creeds and the biblical narrations are seen as a kind of abbreviation, but not as a kind of reduction. In order to safeguard this, the Protestant tradition developed the idea of Scripture as *norma normans*, whereas the creedal formulas are *norma normata* (and also *norma semper normanda*[58]), which holds the irreducibility of the biblical narrations in contrast to the traditional abbreviations, including theological explanations.

58 Cf. HÄRLE, W., Dogmatik, 152.

The reverse notion, that some narrations are reducible, is well known and perceived involuntarily. Imagine reading a novel that does not concentrate on the story-line, but spends 95% of its pages on incidentals. In such cases, we would immediately recognize that its narrative is reducible. The determination of the biblical narrations as canonical for most denominations does not only mean their irreducibility, but also the reducibility of other, more extensive non-biblical stories that refer to a biblical story. Imagine attending a sermon that consists in re-contextualizing a small parable or story of healing from the Gospel for today, whereby the preacher either exorbitantly portrays the inner psychic life of the persons in the story or its historical background, so that either way the (originally surprising) point is missed.

Theologically more problematic, and not so easily evaluated, are theological theories that do something conceptually similar by extending short biblical formulas with the help of theories determined by a specific theological paradigm. Recall Schleiermacher's Christology. Its point consists in transferring the traditional divinity of Christ into the unclouded and permanent consciousness of being absolutely dependent.[59] As literature, this might not be what one would call a good story, but nevertheless Schleiermacher's theory is nothing but a story. The problem with this story is that it speaks about something which is not mentioned at all in the biblical story: Christ's inner, subjective world. The consequence is that more traditionally minded Christians might regard his theory as a reductive explication of the biblical tradition. But the claim of the theory itself is that it is a legitimate and therefore a non-reductive explication of the biblical tradition. Perhaps there will also be people who hold to a third option by regarding Schleiermacher's theory as capturing the essential story, with the consequence that the biblical story appears to be reducible to this theory (ch. 24). The same state of affairs, that of the relationship between Schleiermacher's Christology and the biblical narratives, can be understood in an at least a threefold way with respect to reducibility: as reducible, as irreducibly bound to the biblical narratives, or as a necessary reduction of the biblical stories.

What is more important than the question of if or how the different narrations that are related to one another are reducibly or irreducibly related is the question of whether it is possible for there to be irreducible relations. In the case of the irreducibility of relations, the answer is dependent on the fact that in constitutive relations an, in principle, indeterminable aspect emerges that cannot be understood as the sole property of the *relata*. Is something similar possible in the case of narrations? On the level of primary stories, of which the world consists, of course indeterminacy is possible, in which case we cannot say anything about it. Therefore, the question is whether we can find aspects of indeterminacy on the level of secondary, tellable narrations. It is indeed the case that we can. However, this indeterminacy of narrations cannot be described. If it could, it would not be indeterminacy. But there are different means of circumscribing it. Among these literary means, there are specific kinds of metaphorical speech, teichoscopy, open ends, descriptions

59 Cf. SCHLEIERMACHER, F., The Christian Faith , §§ 94. 96–98., 384–389. 391–417.

from multiple perspectives, and much more. Sometimes – like in many cases of teichoscopy – something might be related that could be referred to by other means. In such cases, the literary means would be nothing but a philosophically meaningless stylistic device. However, this is often not the case, but the narrative devices refer to the indeterminable. And in these cases, the indeterminable belongs irreducibly to the stories themselves.

4. Is it also possible to express the possible asymmetry of ontically constitutive relations by narrative means? While it is not obvious at first, this is also the case. The example of the narrative-relational constitution of 'David' by means of his relationships to 'Saul, Samuel, Bathsheba' etc. is not helpful in this respect, because these other relata, e.g. Bathsheba, are also constituted by nothing else besides their inner-narrative relationships – and also therefore by their relationship to 'David'. Here, we see a narrative way to express symmetrical ontic constitutivity. It can be found only in a special class of stories: in closed stories that have a beginning and an end. But do stories in general, as Aristotle thought, have a beginning and an end, after which nothing else happens?[60] Or are beginnings and endings only artificial categories externally attributed to stories? Could it be that stories have beginnings and endings as well as do not?[61]

To have a beginning and an end, and not to have a beginning and an end is indeed a good description of many pre-modern narrations, like biblical ones, which in most cases were subject to an inner-biblical process of rewriting. One might regard the historical process of canon formation as an attempt to introduce definite beginnings and endings into the biblical library of narrations. Nonetheless, after the process of canonization, the use of these narrations in the *praxis pietatis* of believers shows that these stories find their sequels in manifold ways: it is in their 'interpretation' in a service or in finding their continuation in the narrantic stories of the believers.

In the case of open stories, however, there are asymmetrical relations of constitutivity, as well as in those cases where stories are only relatively closed. In cases like these, we can speak of at least two related stories, the first one, and a second one that is its continuation. Imagine the first, a relatively closed story, whos relata are reciprocally, ontically constitutive of each other. In the second story, the relata might also be seen as ontically constitutive for each other. However, in cases like these, there appears another kind of constitutive

60 Cf. ARISTOTELES, Poetica, 1450b.

61 SCHAPP, W., In Geschichten verstrickt (1953), 88f, assumes that stories appear from a background or horizon (which is finally identical with the world) and lose themselves in it. Schapp also assumes that the discourse of *creatio ex nihilo* is an attempt to both affirm and negate at the same time.

relationship, which is asymmetrical: the relata of the second story depends on the first one, but not *vice versa*.

An example might make it clearer. Within the framework of the stories of the OT patriarchs, 'Abraham' is, in a symmetrical constitutively way, bound to Sarah, Isaac, etc. In the same sense, 'Abraham' is, in the framework of Thomas Mann's Joseph-novels, symmetrically, constitutively bound to 'Sarah' and 'Isaac' as they are entities of Mann's novel. But 'Abraham' in Mann's novel is also dependent on the biblical Abraham (and his narrative mesh of relations) but not *vice versa*. This asymmetrical narrative constitution can be seen in many cultural artifacts, and, as it happens, biblical texts have an underestimated presence in cultural artifacts.

Narratives also exhibit the distinction between symmetrically and asymmetrically constitutive relations. And if we took the idea seriously that stories are principally open, and if we conceived of the closedness of stories as only a secondary and relative concept, and furthermore, if we admit that all tellable narrations are parts of primary, narrantic stories, then we can also have to ask about the important question that Leibniz and Hegel answered in the affirmative: in the end, are symmetrically constitutive relations the only necessary ones? Would the biblical Abraham be something completely different if Thomas Mann had never written his novels? Of course, it is possible to affirm this question, but then, one would also have to ask whether this great narrantic story is one no human is able to tell; is it a closed or an open one? If it is a closed one, then it is perhaps *now* open, as to who the biblical Abraham or the Homeric Odysseus might be, because future stories can contribute something to their identity. But in the instance when all the future narrantic stories in which the world consists will be closed – at the 'end of stories'[62] – then there will only be symmetrical relations of constitutivity. But what if there is no 'end of stories' at all? We can interpret this notion in two ways, wherein both cases are in the end equivalent. Either there are symmetrically as well as asymmetrically intermeshed narrations, or 'constitution' cannot mean the production of a closed identity, but 'identity' may only refer to incomplete-able and open processes. Literary figures like Abraham or Odysseus, then, would always be becomings. And the same would then be true for non-literary persons, that is, for real, narrantic persons.

Positively, we have shown that all of the essential distinctions found in a relational ontology can also be expressed by a narrative ontology. We have therefore proven that narrative ontologies and relational ontologies are at least

62 The term 'end of stories' is here a reference to Pannenberg's discourse concerning the 'end of history' as it is used in e.g. PANNENBERG, W., Dogmatic Theses.

equivalent. Nevertheless, a relational ontology is not therefore superfluous. We can use relational ontologies as a means to pronounce on important states of affairs that would remain invisible in those narrative ontologies that are disconnected from a more abstract relational ontology.

As such, we do not only claim that relational and narrative ontologies are equivalent, but also that relational ontologies are abstract subsets of narrative ontologies. We claim, in other words, that a narrative ontology circumscribes any relational one. We will now prove this claim.

7.4 The Limits of Relational Ontologies and the Surplus of Narrative Ontologies

Relational ontologies have a weakness on a point that is important for phenomenal perception. It is possible to conceive of the reciprocal constitutivity of the *relata*, but what about the relation and the *relata*? Such a thing can, in part, be described as a relation, but here talk of 'constitutivity' reaches its limit. One can maintain without any difficulty talk of a reciprocal constitutivity, i.e. the equiprimordiality, of relation and *relata*. There is also no problem in speaking of an asymmetrical constitutivity of the *relata* for the relation, which is the special case in which the *relata* are not constitutive for each other. Russell's claim for the ontic non-constitutivity of all (relevant) *relata* therefore describes a world in which there are only asymmetric, ontically constitutive relations between *relata* and relations: the *relata* can be conceived independently from their relations, but not *vice versa*.

And it is precisely in this reverse case that any relational ontology reaches its limits. It is possible to formally describe this case, but would it prove meaningful? It would be a case where a relation exists without its *relata*. It would mean that there is a relation that exists primordial, out of which emerge *relata*. But a relation without any *relata* is *per definition* not a relation at all. As our description of the phenomenon of perception in ch. 5 has shown, perceiver and perceived emerge out of perceiving itself. If one conceives of perception as a relation and perceiver and perceived as its *relata*, then one has expressed this *aporia*.

One can find examples of cases like these more frequently than one might think. Take a look into the blue sky and see the clouds and condensation trails. In a relational framework, one could describe the position of the clouds and the condensation trails, and call the blue in-between them their relation. But, the in-between is nothing but blue sky. Is the blue sky the relation between the *relata*? One could only claim as much by taking the abstract and static perspective of a photograph. The real sky, however, is dynamical and constantly in flux, out of which the clouds emerge and disappear.

Have a look at the trunk of a tree and its buds. One could imagine conceiving of the trunk as the relation between the buds that later become branches, which are seen as *relata*. But if one cuts off all of the branches, including its buds, new buds appear out of the smooth trunk that did not exist previously. One can call these 'latent buds', and these must be considered possible, but not real, *relata*.

Have a look at a rope in which there are some knots. One could conceive of the knots as *relata* and the rope as the relation between the knots. But how can it then be maintained that the knots emerge from the rope, so that the knots are ontically dependent on the rope, but not *vice versa*?

It would be easy to produce many more such examples of phenomena where one comes to the limits of a relational ontology because one would have to claim an ontic priority of relations over *relata*.

In the framework of a narrative ontology, however, such problems do not appear in cases such as these, at least if one does not restrict one's understanding of a story into the too-narrow frame of narratologies. Persons, characters, roles, places, and events are constantly emerging out of previous stories, independently of whether it is a told or an experienced story.

Imagine a secondary story that is told by a narrator to a particular listener evening after evening. The listener is able to understand the story of one evening as the sequel of the previous evening. She is also able to distinguish this story from another one that is not a sequel of the previous evening's story, should the narrator tell such a story. Nevertheless, the recipient is not able to foresee which particular events, places, and persons will appear. Perhaps the narrator is also not able to do this, if she designs the story spontaneously while she tells it. Here we have the ontic priority of the story over the state of affairs emerging from it. Consequently, this told narration cannot be conceived as a relation between the events emerging out of it, since one would once again have to claim the priority of the relation over the *relata*. Imagine a situation with more than one narrator and listener, who might also switch roles: things would still be worse for a relational ontology.

Let's leave the realm of secondary narrations and have a look at the primary narrativity of the narrantic. Here one regularly finds the priority of the story over the concrete events and the persons involved. With my birth, my growing up and my own activity as narrator, I always find myself passively inscribed into a story. At best, all I can do is to continue this story but I can never begin it in the proper sense. Therefore, we are older than ourselves, as Waldenfels claims,[63] or, we do not have stories and stories do not belong to us, but, as Schapp expresses it: we belong to stories.[64]

63 Cf. WALDENFELS, B., Bodily Experience between Selfhood and Otherness, 242.
64 Cf. EICHLER, K.-D., Schapps narrative Ontologie, 110.

If one parallels 'relations' and 'stories' on the one hand, and, 'relata' and 'events' or 'sequences' on the other hand, then one can diagnose that it seems to be linguistic nonsense to talk of a priority of the relation over the *relata*, whereas it is no problem at all to talk of an ontic priority of a story over their events and sequences. Exactly this possibility for the narrantic priority of stories over events, persons, places, characters, and roles, which are involved in the story and emerging out of it, is the superiority of a narrative ontology over a relational ontology. Therefore, in order to describe perception, a narrative ontology is better suited than a relational one. The former can do everything the latter can do, but considerably more than the latter. Such as, for example, how Newtonian physics is not wrong but simply a special case of relativistic physics, so a relational ontology is not wrong, but a subset of a narrative ontology. In other words: a relational ontology is always a simplified abstraction from a narrative ontology. As such, a relational ontology is also not without its worth, since it allows for pronouncements to be made on specific states of affairs, as well as making them more prominent – so long as one remembers that they are always imbedded in a narrative ontology.

CHAPTER 8

Narration, Migration, and Wayformational Lines

8.1 Biblical Aspects of Wayfaring and Transport

We have seen that perception has priority over perceived and perceiver. Furthermore, we saw that perceiving itself is the movement out of which perceiver and perceived emerge; it can be described as the different relative movements of perceiver and perceived. Perceiving, therefore, draws a way, is a way, or a wayformational line. It is not easy to name the original unity of perceiving, and we saw that it has a different name in different traditions. We claimed that the most appropriate one is the term 'story'. But if perceiving is always movement, why not call it a wayformational line? Indeed, both claims are true. Narrantic stories are wayformational lines and wayformational lines are narrantic first-order stories. A narrative ontology must also be an ontology of movement, of ways, of lines, of wayfaring, in short: of wayformational lines. The advantage of the ontology of wayformational lines over non-storied relational ontologies is that it is able to express the ontic priority of lines over points, but theoretically the reverse is also the case.

Fortunately, we do not need to build an ontology of wayformational lines from the ground up, but we can use the groundwork that has already been laid by different disciplines in recent years. Suggestions for such an ontology can be found in Deleuze's and Guattari's talk of the contingently branching rhizome as an important part of phenomena,[1] or in how the *ligne de fuite* has an exceptional status in describing the rhizomatic status of being. This *ligne de fuite* characterizes being as becoming insofar as every being is on the way to being changed and becoming something different, whereby the possibility of constitutive relationships with other becomings is entailed.[2] However, Deleuze and Guattari cannot offer more than suggestions.

Another, more concrete move toward such an ontology of wayformational lines can be found in Paul Klee's notebooks on the pictorial theory of form from 1922/21. Klee describes how lines emerge out of movements. It is fascinating to see how Klee describes experiencing this movement – and therefore the experience of lines – with the active voice, the passive voice, and the middle voice. And it is interesting that he can also say that lines 'suffered'.[3] After he gives examples of different lines, he claims, in regard

1 Cf. DELEUZE, G./GUATTARI, F., Thousand Plateaus, 3–25.
2 Cf. DELEUZE, G./GUATTARI, F., Thousand Plateaus, 9.
3 KLEE, P., Bildnerische Formenlehre, 13/11.

 | DOI:10.30965/9783846765852_009

to the constitution of the line out of movement, that the 'mainline goes out free and unbound. It is a walk for no purpose than itself, without end.'[4]

Taking up these and other stimulations from many disciplines, social anthropologist Tim Ingold has designed an ontology of lines which can be more appropriately called an ontology of ways or wayformational lines. He calls it, with a smile, a 'linealogy.'[5] In this chapter, we will use some of its main traits in order to design our narrantology of wayformational lines.

Apart from influences such as these, it should not be overlooked that the biblical traditions also have something essential to offer in this respect. Although at this point we want to explicate the ontology of migration or of lines in a primarily phenomenological way, unbound by biblical authority, one must admit that at this point phenomenological considerations converge with biblical findings. What are these findings? Notwithstanding the manifold historical origins and modulations, many of the most important biblical traditions deal with migration and wayformational lines, such as in the Hebrew and Greek scriptures of the Old Testament, as well as in New Testament. Basically, two types of movement on way-lines emerge, which can be transformed into each other. Journeying on wayformational lines is not simply one biblical theme among others but a narrative dimension that is fundamental for the biblical understanding of human and creaturely becoming. This understanding deserves to be further examined in detail.

1. Movement on way-lines is important in the stories of the patriarchs, especially in the story of Abraham. Abraham is called by God out of a high culture, destining him to be a nomad. As such, he reaches his 'destination', Palestine, only in order to leave it for Egypt and in order to rove around in the area of Palestine. The ways of Abraham cover the whole Fertile Crescent, the most important cultural area of the ancient near east, i.e. the whole known world. At the same time, Abraham's migrations reflect the ways between Mesopotamia, Palestine, and Egypt of the time of the exile and the Persian occupation. Of course, arriving at a specific evaluation of these ways depends on what period one gives for the completion of the entire Abrahamic saga. Possible situations vary from remembrances of a real nomadic, prehistorical time up to the idealizations of early Hellenistic Judaism projected onto an ancestor.[6] However much these cases vary, in all scenarios human life is portrayed as nomadic without any predetermined destination or end, but with the discovery of preliminary ends through the perception of the way itself. It is of the greatest importance that YHWH in Gen 12:1 calls Abraham to depart, but not to go to a predetermined destination. The destination remains first, undetermined, and second, to be disclosed only in an undetermined future: Abraham shall go unto a land that YHWH '*will show*' him, i.e. a kind of finding the end while

4 KLEE, P., Bildnerische Formenlehre, 11/9.
5 Cf. INGOLD, T., Life of Lines, 6.53.79.
6 Cf. MÜHLING, A., Blickt auf Abraham, 25–76.

perceiving truth along the way. The promises YHWH gives to Abraham belong to historically different strata, with different theological intentions. The promise to have a son and to become a people pronounce narratively that wayfaring in accordance with the primordial call to go out of Haran is a permanent one. The promise to have a son means that what Abraham has experienced, to go on a way without destination, will be continued. The promise to become a people makes this permanent migration universal. In contrast, the meaning of the promise of land is ambivalent. It can mean the promise to go in and through an appropriate terrain for nomadic journeying. But it can also be understood as meaning that the purpose is to own a country in a sedentary way and therefore to give up the nomadic roving around. Therefore, journeying emerges as an alternative kind of traveling: Travelling from place to place, which was previously oriented to traveling to a destination. There is a tension between these two types in the perception of its truth and value. Whoever regards the latter as superior cannot really enjoy the former.

2. A critical stance towards those journeys that find their destinations continually revised along the way finds its biblical origin by deriving nomadism from Cain. Here, it is not the expression of a blessing, as in the case of Abraham, but the reverse: an expression of a curse that determines Cain to be 'fugitive and a wanderer', making vain any attempts to become sedentary (Gen 4:12). It is interesting to observe that therefore the nomadic logic of discovering 'what will be shown' in Gen 12:1, that is, the logic of being oriented by wayformational lines, can no longer be understood. Also, in the view of the author of Gen 4:12, the nomad follows the logic of destination-oriented travelling, but in an inverse manner. In contrast to the successfully sedentary person, who travels from place to place, the nomad escapes from place to place.

3. In the subsequent stories of the patriarchs, i.e. in the stories of Isaac, Jacob, and Joseph, as we found in the story of Abraham, the double-sided understanding of human becoming as either way-oriented journeying or as destination-oriented travelling is continued.

4. In the whole narrative complex of the Exodus tradition, the motif of becoming as wandering re-emerges, including its two kinds of value perception. On the one hand, here the promise also remains undetermined, described simply as 'a land flowing with milk and honey' (Ex 3:8.17 etc.) – attributes that cannot be seen as true of Palestine. On the other hand, to roam around the desert can be seen as a penalty (Lev 23:13). On the one side, YHWH introduces himself as the God of the itinerant fathers, who is in Godself undetermined, but one who will become who he will become (Ex 3:14). On the other side, the fact that Moses is not allowed to reach sedentariness is also seen as a penalty, tempered only by a furtive glance on the promised land (Dtn 32:50f).

5. The situation of the people described in the Deuteronomistic history before the constitution of the state also remains one of wandering. The people only appear to own the land. Rather, it is a kind of itinerancy within the country, full of incursions and conflicts. There is no sanctuary but the ark of the covenant, a mobile sanctuary, that can also be used in warfare (Num 10,25f; 1Sam 4).[7] The nomadic or half-nomadic life-style is depicted as a positive situation, insofar as it is contrasted to the monarchic state and to sedentariness, as seen in Samuel's declaration of the divine concession to the contumaciousness of the people (1Sam 12:17.19). It is, therefore, no surprise that the place-oriented nationhood of Saul fails. Only David, portrayed as an itinerant leader

7 Cf. PORZIG, P.C., Die Lade Jahwes, 42–99.

of outlaws is successful. In the continuation of the story, the Deuteronomistic history conceives the history of the state as an ongoing history of crises, heading to its culmination in the double ruin of the state and the exile of the people. Thereby a new kind of way-oriented becoming has been reached that is adequate to the historical situation of early Jewish identity, of a people spread out over the Hellenistic world. However, the Deuteronomistic idea of cultic centralization in the temple of Jerusalem as the single legitimate sanctuary, be it historical or a projection of the Hellenistic conflict between Jerusalem and the Gerizim, takes the side of radical place orientation. It is radical, since disagreement should ideally be punished very harshly (2Ki 23).

6. The prophetic literature also knows the ambiguity between place-orientation and way-orientation. On the one side, displacement and being on the way is understood as penalty for the broken covenant and moral failure (Am 5:18–20), whereas on the other side the throne of God itself can be seen as a mobile vehicle including wheels and wings (Ez 1:4–28). One might consider this a theological accommodation to the real situation of the exile. Nevertheless, it is important because the situation of being mobile on one's way is not an exception, but it is made into a principle through divine attribution.

7. A glance at the apocalyptically influenced literature is also of interest. Here we find the idea of the pilgrimage of all nations to Zion as the last of the pre-eschatological events (Sach 8:20–22 etc.). Hereby a universal sedentariness is promised, but only after a way, which is now, contrary to present appearances, the way destined for Zion. Also, other people, the pagans, can participate in eschatological salvation, but only by undergoing the experience of foreignness through journeying, which is a historic feature of the people of Israel.

8. Gerhard von Rad and Martin Noth regarded the so-called historical credo (Dtn 26:5–9) as a very old formulation of the confession the OT-faith, which is the center of the historic-saving faith of the Hebrew tradition. As Gerhard von Rad has claimed:

> A wandering Aramean was my father; he went down with a few people into Egypt and there he became a nation, great, mighty, and populous. But the Egyptians treated us harshly, they afflicted us, and laid hard toil upon us. Then we cried to Yahweh, the God of our fathers, and Yahweh heard us, and saw our misery, our toil, and oppression. And Yahweh brought us out of Egypt with a mighty hand and an outstretched arm, with great terror, with signs and wonders, and brought us to this place and gave us this land, a land flowing with milk and honey.[8]

Von Rad conceives of this as a historical confessional formula, because it concentrates on the 'objective historical facts,'[9] while the reactions of human reception und interpretation are missing. Also absent is the allegedly mythical content such as von Rad sees instantiated in the primordial prehistory of Israel or in the Sinai-tradition, which he regarded as later additions to the tradition. This credo was the reference point of historical origin and for the normativity of OT-faith in the eyes of von Rad. In the meantime, historical research showed that the historical meaning that von Rad had attributed to it is most probably incorrect. This credo is not an old root of the Hexateuch,

8 Rad, G.v., OT Theology, vol. 1, 122.

9 Rad, G.v., OT Theology, vol. 1, 122.

but Lohfink and Rost have identified its younger and summarizing character.[10] The best thesis for its historical location is given by J.Chr. Gertz, who conceives it as a summary of the priestly and non-priestly traditions before the dtn-dtr final redaction of the Pentateuch.[11] The question of its historical location – whether it is very old or a summary of a middle redaction – however, distracts from its material content and from the essential theological question. What we can really see in this credo is a narrative of the OT tradition of historic-salvific faith. Its point is that the concrete becoming of the world is seen as the deeds of YHWH manifested in the people of Israel. It is decisive that it talks about the God of the Fathers and that it names its own father as a 'wandering Aramean'. Although this translation cannot be exclusively bound to a nomadic heritage of Israel, since the root *abd* is not necessarily connected with nomadism, but indicates an in-crisis, life-threatening lifestyle.[12] This indication suggests it is of more supportive of a wayformational oriented life rather than a place-oriented one. A look at its context shows that the speaker does not only remember that his ownership of the land is a relatively recent one and that he knows his life-threatening and wandering heritage, but he also knows that God is acting on Israel not as a homogeneous ethnic unity, but a conglomerate of foreigners and the marginalized. What follows in this context is the feast of harvest as a ritual activity by which the privileged Levite *and* the foreigner enjoy together the gifts of the deeds of the Lord (Dtn 26:12). If one is aware of this context, this credo does not regain its old historical meaning, but it provides a narrative that privileges foreigners and the foreign by conceiving it as the subject-matter of YHWH's acting, be it then on the way or today in sedentariness. This credo confesses that the foreign is not something that has to be overcome, but is a divine privilege.

9. The life of Jesus and his disciples is marked in the narrations of the Gospels by wandering. This wandering takes place mainly in Galilee, but it can be further, as in the case of the journey to Jerusalem (once in the case of the synoptic Gospels, three times in the case of the Gospel of John). Contemporary, NT-research has developed different interpretations of this wandering. What is clear, however, is that the Jesus-movement was by no means one of sedentariness. The origin of the Jesus-movement[13] out of the tradition of John the Baptist and all other narrations does not allow for such an interpretation. The most prominent version of this thesis was given by Gerd Theißen in the 1970's,[14] who claimed it was a movement of charismatic wandering radicals: not being bound to anyplace is the ideal. One leaves the place, one's extended family and follows the wandering Jesus. Being oriented by wayformational lines is valued as a lived ideal, whereas being oriented by places is rejected. Nevertheless, these wandering radicals were also in need of the economic support given by healthy sedentary people.[15] Theißen's thesis may be disputed in its details, and his sociological interpretation might fit or might need to be corrected, but in any event, one cannot deny that there are no texts that conceive of the Jesus-movement as place-bound.

---

10 Cf. Rost, L., Das kleine geschichtliche Credo and Lohfink, N., Zum "kleinen geschichtlichen Credo."

11 Cf. Gertz, J.C., Stellung des kleinen geschichtlichen Credos, 44f.

12 Cf. Römer, T., Israels Väter, 61.

13 Cf. Becker, J., Jesus von Nazareth, 59–63.

14 Cf. Theißen, G., Soziologie der Jesusbewegung.

15 Cf. Theißen, G., Die Jesusbewegung, 80–90.

10. The following time of early Christianity is marked by the many missionary journeys of the Apostles throughout the Roman Empire. One can observe this in the preeminent case of the Apostle Paul. According to his own witness, Paul does not undergo a conversion, (which is always place-oriented)[16] but a way-oriented vocation, which led him instantly, after God let him see his son, on his way to the mission in the Arabia (Gal 1:17). It may be the case, that Paul's later life as a wandering missionary might, to a large extent, be caused by the outcome of the events portrayed in Act 15, which were negative for Paul. And of course, Paul was also in need of support by place-oriented travelers like Prisca and Aquila, who could have been leaders of an inter-Aegean company.[17] It is obvious that Paul accommodated his journeys to the ends derived from attending to his way. Also, if he really intended to be heading for Spain as the last corner of the then known Roman world (Rom 15:24.28), this still does not imply a place-oriented travelling: it is similar to Abraham's. His journey is portrayed as a wandering through the whole of the Fertile Crescent. In the same sense, Paul conceives of his journeys as a missionary wandering through the then known world. Furthermore, he does not regard this as an individualistic task, but as a community endeavor, since he avoids areas like Egypt, in which Hellenistic Christianity was already known. It is interesting that Luke's evaluation in Acts is a reversal: what Paul had seen as way-oriented wandering, Luke understands as destination-oriented travelling, by conceiving the arrival of Paul's Gospel in Rome – specifically by conceiving the convergence of all Gospel missionary activities in Rome – as the divine intended, place-oriented destination.

11. The tension between wayformational becoming and place-oriented being is removed in the letter of Hebrews, the letter that has predominately shaped the later Christian understanding of becoming as wandering; Hebrews rejects it in favor of place-orientation. The understanding of human existence and of the existence of the church as a wandering people of God would have developed differently, were it not for Hebrews. This understanding is intriguing because this motive is by no means explicit in the letter, and its correct historical interpretation is also disputed. The most influential passage is Heb. 13:12–14:

> Wherefore Jesus also, that he might sanctify the people through his own blood, suffered without the gate. Let us therefore go forth unto him without the camp, bearing his reproach. For we have not here an abiding city, but we seek after the city which is to come.

The main theme of Hebrews is neither anthropology nor ecclesiology, but soteriological Christology, which is correlated to ecclesiology and ethics. In the time of the prosecution of the Confessing Church by the National Socialists, Ernst Käsemann quite decisively identified the wandering people of God as the main motive of Hebrews.[18] Besides the typologies and the parallelization of the history of Israel and the meaning of Christ, his own ecclesial situation as persecuted was important, such that he

---

16 Cf. BECKER, J., Paulus, 73–86.

17 Cf. BECKER, J., Paulus, 26–29.156–158.

18 Cf. KÄSEMANN, E., Das wandernde Gottesvolk.

conceived it as exemplary. He finds a 'henceforth valid definition of Christianity',[19] which is an

> ongoing exodus [...] that is the other side of Christian liberty. The only one who is free is the one that can give up the old in order to encounter the new today and tomorrow, for the sake of God's will. One is always thereby heading into the desert. There is no promised land without wandering in the desert.[20]

Käsemann's interpretation of Hebrews is marred by the fact that he assumed – according to the best of historical research of his time – a gnostic salvific myth, which we know today to have appeared only in the post-NT era. Otto Hofius claimed that the theme of Hebrews is rather the *waiting* people of God than the wandering people of God.[21] As contrary as these interpretations might sound, in both cases there appears a preference for a place-orientation over way-orientation. The destination is what is decisive. In Hebrews, we find in regard to its ontological and eschatological presuppositions a mixture of Hellenistic and Hebrew thought. Whereas the former sees the eschatological place of salvation in the present as the transcendent perfection of the divine world, the latter understands eschatological perfection as temporally sequential breaking-in of a future aeon. Depending on which of these types are seen as leading in Hebrews, one conceives the present situation of becoming differently. Hofius regards the temporally sequential eschatology as primary and therefore he claims that it is not the wandering to a destination, but waiting till the future aeon is realized, which is the subject of Hebrews. Käsemann, and somewhat differently Erich Gräßer,[22] conceives of the local-transcendent eschatology as primary. Consequently, they understand any aspect of the present life as wandering to this 'place' of salvation. Although the interpretation of Gräßer seems to be plausible, the alternative is misleading in at least two respects: First, it detracts from the fact that in both cases one has turned away from a wayformational understanding of life to a place- and destination-oriented one. Second, the alternative hides the fact that wandering is also possible within the framework of the sequential-temporal scheme, but only with major qualifications, which becomes clear in Augustine's conception of the wandering people of God.

12. The theme of Christian life as wandering and the idea of the church as wandering people of God – including its preference for a place-oriented option and its devaluation of way-orientation – was promoted by Augustine in a very effective way. The interpretation of wandering as *peregrinatio* is presupposed here, which in the Roman literature (e.g. Cicero and Tacitus) always means journeying out of one's home, in foreign areas, and *without any civic rights*.[23] In addition, a Neoplatonic element influences Augustine's idea. In the *Confessions*, Augustine describes human life through the lens

19 KÄSEMANN, E., Kirchliche Konflikte 1, 236: „fortan gültige Definition der Christenheit" (Transl. MM).

20 KÄSEMANN, E., Ruf der Freiheit, 155: „dauernde Exodus [...] die Kehrseite christlicher Freiheit [ist]. Frei ist nur, wer das Alte aufzugeben vermag, um Gottes Willen heute und morgen zu begegnen. Dabei geht es wohl stets in die Wüste. Es gibt das verheißene Land nicht ohne Wüstenzug" (Transl. MM).

21 Cf. HOFIUS, O., Katapausis, 146, 150–152.

22 Cf. GRÄẞER, E., Das wandernde Gottesvolk.

23 Cf. SCHULTZ, W., Peregrination bei Augustin und Wanderschaft bei Goethe, 79.

of his own biography as *peregrinatio* abroad, using the parable of the prodigal son. Away from their father's house, humans can do nothing but get lost without any ability to liberate themselves on their own. But while being lost abroad, God comes to meet them in order to lead them home.[24] The whole of mundane life here and now is not understood as a journey directed to the destination of home, but as the necessity of getting lost until God provides the destination. In elaborating this model generally, Augustine characterizes the human situation as *peregrinatio* and the church as *civitas peregrina* in *De Civitate Dei*. What is presupposed is that the essential, unfallen human life being directed towards a perfection is not a becoming, but an immaterial destiny in the immutable divine being. The destination allows one to conceive any mutable life here and now as transient and therefore as *peregrinatio*, as wandering abroad. Though all life is wandering abroad, there is an important distinction between the *civitas terrena* and the *civitas dei*: the members of the former do not know anything about their being in the present as *peregrinatio*, whereas the latter ones do. The consequence is that the former ones get lost unto the world by perverting the *ordo amoris* and loving mundane things in the way of *frui*, of enjoyment, whereas the latter ones know, remembering Heb 13:14, that they are on a *peregrinatio* that is temporary and that they love as *frui*, as enjoyment, only the absolute silence and immutability of God by simultaneously using the *temporalia* in the mode of *uti*.[25] Both ideas, the one of the early and the later Augustine, are not identical and there are differences in detail, but they share their the common feature of conceiving every becoming and wandering as temporary, as a signature of the alienation of the fallen world. In both cases, wandering is necessary, but only a means for something else: it is an expression of the *cor nostrum*, that is *inquietum, donec id requiescat* in God, which is the most radical way to dissociate oneself from a wayformational orientation as we saw it in the case of Abraham in Gen 12:1, in which the promise is found during the way abroad. It is the clearest way to distance oneself from the God who is as Godself, according to the Hebrew version of Ex 3:14, a way that will become, who he will become – and by no means a motionless *ego eimi ho on* as in the Greek version of the LXX. It is the most radical way, too, to dissociate oneself from the proclamation of the *basileia tou theou* as lived in the wandering radicalism of Jesus.

13. The interesting tension in human becoming between way-orientation and place-orientation and its solution in favor of place-orientation is visible in the practice of pilgrimage that appeared in the 4th century. Although a pilgrimage is always a journey, it participates in the tension between way-orientation and place-orientation. It is way-oriented insofar as people intentionally choose to be on a way and experience themselves as foreigners, which is reflected in the term of *peregrinus*, which meant someone who is not a citizen of the Roman Empire (derived from that of someone who is exposed to foreignness).[26] However, experiencing foreignness is only a temporary stage during pilgrimage overcome by reaching the destination of the place of worship. Compared to the strictly way-oriented wanderings of Abraham, pilgrimage appears as place-oriented. This feature appears in pilgrimages of the Old Testament as well as in the Christian pilgrimages from the 4th century onward. During its development, the way-oriented character becomes reduced to a mere means: The austerities of

24 Cf. AUGUSTINUS, A., Conf.VII, 3, 6f; XII, 15,21.

25 Cf. SCHULTZ, W., Peregrination bei Augustin und Wanderschaft bei Goethe, 91–93.

26 Cf. KÜHNE, H., Art. Wallfahrt V., 423.

journeying were seen as a kind of asceticism. Over time, and due to better streets and better means of transport, the way-oriented aspect nearly vanished. In late medieval lay piety, the arrival at the sanctuary – if not the possession of its devotional objects – sufficed. The place of the sanctuary became 'holy' by conceiving it as full of divine salvific presence. This kind of place-orientation and the implied idea of the presence of revelation at places was criticized by the Reformers.[27] Is it possible to find in the reforming critics a reevaluation in favor of way-orientation? Be that as it may, such a reevaluation is reflected in a nice anecdote that deals with the popularization of the pilgrimage of St. Jacob at the beginning of the 21st century. In an episode of the British television detective show 'Lewis', one of the detectives resigns his post temporarily in order to go on a pilgrimage to Santiago de Compostela by foot – but a few miles before his destination he turns around.[28]

The biblical and Christian traditions show, in many different ways, an understanding of the human and mundane becoming intermingled between way-orientations and place-orientation. The description never pretends to be neutral, but is always solved in favor of either a way-orientation or place-orientation. With Hebrews, Augustine and the practice of pilgrimage, place-orientation overshadowed way-orientation. Way-orientation only appears as a means and the idea of becoming as fundamental nearly vanishes: way-orientation now becomes an expression of alienation and sin. It may be seen as preliminary necessary, but it has to overcome – if not here, then eschatologically. Nevertheless, there are alternatives. Our interpretation of the promise of Abraham in Gen 12:1, the revelation of the name of God in Ex 3:14, the preference for foreigners in the little historical credo, and the reconstruction of the Jesus-movement in Theißen's interpretation, allow for another solution to the tension. The reforming critics of the practice of pilgrimage can also be seen as supporting our argument.

Parallels and similarities to these different types of mundane and human becoming-as-wandering can be found in many other traditions and religions. One has to be careful,[29] however, not to conceive of the medial wandering that is destination-oriented as the rule and canon for becoming. Of course, destination-orientation determines the whole concept of travelling if there is a primary place-orientation, but is not necessarily the case and there are alternatives.

---

27 Cf. LUTHER, M., WA, Bd. 6, 437.447.

28 Episode 8,1 "Entry Wounds" of BBC series "Lewis" of Oct. 10./17. 2014 by Helen Jenkins at ca. 1:27–28h.

29 It is a mistake to understand every wandering as *peregrinatio*, which receives its particular quality from the aim as horizon, see e.g. SCHULTZ, W., Peregrination bei Augustin und Wanderschaft bei Goethe, especially 79–84, when he wants to determine the Buddhist, Islamic, Platonic, and Neoplatonic character of the *peregrinatio*.

The intermingling of way-orientation and place-orientation, visible in all biblical traditions and perhaps also in numerous other traditions, refers to a deeper phenomenological basis of human and mundane becoming, which must now be analyzed. The convergence of both will lead us to a narrative ontology of wayformational lines.

8.2 Transport and Wayfaring[30]

1. Lines, of the most radical kind, which are without beginning and end, are nothing but movements. These lines can appear in two kinds: traces or threads. Traces need a surface on which they can be inscribed by movements, like the grass of the plains for the traces of horses, faults or mountain chains in the earth's crust, or like the painted or written line on a piece of paper. Threads however, can exist on their own. They can also be woven into a medium, like the condensation trails of an airplane, but they can also appear unmediated, like the threads that are woven or knitted, which become a new plane or surface, like a linen screen, which does not mean that planes and surfaces are basic entities, but due to the possibility of exchanging planes for threads and *vice versa*, planes and surfaces presuppose lines. Threads may become planes that can be understood as secondary means of other lines, that is, traces.[31] Both threads as well as traces are to be conceived of as essential movements, so that they can be called way-lines.

2. Way-lines, be it either threads or traces, can be understood in two ways. The first kind are lines of *transport*.[32] These lines are the shortest connection between two points, as in straight lines. A complex curve can also be – if only approximately – described as a connection between points, which can be defined with the help of a coordinate system, such as mathematical graphing. If one conceives of lines in this way, in the end, movement and lines disappear, because in a connection between points it is exclusively the points that define the way. And the points can be defined with the help of, for example, a four-dimensional coordinate system of space-time, then points are primary and lines secondary. If the line is a way, it is a quality of a prior entity, like a traveling human or a rolling car, which moves from point to point. Here, a twofold priority reigns: the priority of the points over the ways, and the priority of

30 For the following cf. these two foundational works INGOLD, T., Lines and INGOLD, T., Life of Lines.

31 Cf. INGOLD, T., Lines, 51f.56f.

32 Cf. INGOLD, T., Lines, 77–84.

the vehicle over movement. Strictly speaking, movement is not only secondary in this model of transport, ideally, it vanishes completely. The points have the only constitutive roles. One can conceive of them as inscribed timeless in their coordinate-system medium, such as in the case of the Minkowski space,[33] including its consequence for the spatialization of time. Time, like movement, would then be an illusion, which would indicate that there is a transcendental, abstract perspective, beyond any wayformational lines. Further, in this model, if one is moving on one particular line, movement as such vanishes. The only decisive thing is reaching the next point, which is a destination. Ideally it is reached instantly, with infinite speed, without any time-consumption at all, independently of whether it is seen as an ultimate end or whether the way consists of indefinite points to be reached. In this way, the movement collapses into a static entity. If one conceives of movements and its lines in the transport model, they are secondary in the face of the priority of objects and their mediums, like that of a coordinate system. In such a model, there are no wayformational lines. The transport model requires an object-oriented ontology.[34]

An interesting example of the transport model is how Leibniz conceived the world. As we saw in ch. 7, Leibniz holds to a specific kind of holism, and therefore he tries to maintain the idea of a constitutive (or internal) relationality. However, Leibniz sees this constitutive relationality realized in a universal nexus of causality, and, furthermore, he operates on the basis of an infinitely countable set of existences. The universal compossibility of the world would allow for these countable existences to exist on their own in their 'absolute possibility'. The actual possibility results from their compossibility emerging out of their causal connections, which presupposes the possibility of the particular. Therefore, the identity of all particular existences would change, if any single particular existence had been changed. However, in fact, the whole world does not change at all, since every instance contains every other instance.[35] The compossible, by causal connections realized in a network of the particular, can be reduced to a single rule (although finite beings might not be capable of having insight in this rule). Such a reduction is typical for the transport model of networks. Leibniz is convinced that any seemingly chaotic series of numbers, is based on a rule:

> One can build a sequence or series of numbers that is seemingly completely irregular, in which the numbers increase and decrease without any apparent order, but nevertheless the one who has the key to the secret and who knows the origin and composition of this series of numbers can provide a rule that will show that the series is completely regular.[36]

---

33 Cf. MINKOWSKI, H., Raum und Zeit.

34 Cf. HARMAN, G., Road to Objects and for a review INGOLD, T., Life of Lines, 16.

35 Cf. EVERS, D., Gott und mögliche Welten, 28–30.

36 LEIBNIZ, G.W., Philosophische Schriften, Bd. 2/2, 3–5 (Theodizee §242): „Man kann eine Aufeinanderfolge oder *Reihe* von Zahlen aufstellen, die anscheinend völlig unregelmäßig

It is ironic that Leibniz, for whom perfection ought not mean stagnancy but change,[37] cannot in the end conceive of true dynamism. In other words: Leibniz regards transport in the network as universal. However, against Leibniz we must see that there is an alternative.

3. Wayformational lines can also be interpreted in a way that gives them ontological priority, and we can call this kind of line *wayfaring*. Only these kinds of lines are the truly wayformational lines. In this model, movement is always primary. By movement the means for other lines emerge, like a screen that is woven out of threads. If there is already a medium, lines are not simply inscribed *on* the surface of this medium, but they run *through* it in a manner in which line and medium are constituted or changed *equiprimordially* by movement.

Points as well as destinations are ontically secondary to the lines of movement: they emerge by the knotting and weaving movements of the line of movement itself.

Imagine someone hiking in the mountains. She may reach a specific point, e.g. a summit as a stopover. But here her movement does not disappear. The hiker is still moving, only her arcs are smaller. And in such cases that she is exhausted and sits somewhere in order to recuperate, her head, her eyes, in short, her living body, inscribe narrow movements.

This case is also interesting for a relational logic. In contrast to transport lines, such a logic is not able to adequately describe what is going on between points as *relata* and lines as relations between them. In order to do so, one would need to claim the ontic priority of the relation over the *relata*, which, as we saw (ch.7), is not possible, which this is not a problem for a logic of wayformational lines. Strictly speaking, we must say that – as in the example – no points emerge as independent entities at all, but that *de re* there are only narrowly curved and knotted movements. These curves only become points if we assume an ideal infinite curvature, which does not exist in reality. Points are therefore ontologically secondary. They are abstractions from wayformational lines. Only the knots of movements are real.

This way of understanding has decisive implications for the interpretation of the knots as destinations and ends. Since the wayformational line does not

---

ist, bei der also die Zahlen ohne jeden Schein von Ordnung abwechselnd zu- und abnehmen, und doch wird der, der den Schlüssel zu dem Geheimnis besitzt und den Ursprung und Aufbau dieser Zahlenfolge kennt, eine Regel angeben können, die, richtig erfaßt, zeigen wird, dass die *Reihe* völlig regelmäßig ist" (Transl. MM).

37 Cf. Evers, D., Gott und mögliche Welten, 55f.

end in the knot but simply changes its shape, there is always an ontic priority of the movement or of the way over the destination and end: the way is always in its becoming. Knots exist for the sake of movement, not *vice versa*. Intermediate goals exist for the sake of movement, for the sake of going on far beyond the goal, *not vice versa*. In our example, pausing for recuperation at the summit is a means for continuing on.

Wayfaring, therefore, is not without ends and goals, but there are no ultimate ends or goals.

We can illustrate with the example of the hiker in the mountains. She may face the summit of a mountain as her ultimate destination, but this is not really the case. If we say as much, we simply mix the logic of wayfaring with the logic of transport: the hiker has to go down from the summit. And far more, imagine she cannot reach the summit due to a change of weather, or imagine she is moving on a round trip without heading to the summit at all. In such cases, she can still experience an uplifting hike. What are summits, then, if not constructions within the logic of transport that lack reality?

Wayfaring is not only not without goals when knots are recognized as intermediate ends, but also in the quality of the movement, as we will see later.

The movement of wayformational lines is not only primary when compared with the medium, the knots (points) and ends, but there is also a priority of the movement over the one moving. Transport needs a substance or a vehicle that is moved or moves itself, but in wayfaring the wayformational line itself is what moves or is moved. It is not subjects or objects that are moved or moving, the important thing is the movement during time. A mover is always and at the same time one who has become and one who will become. A mover is always one who has become, because there is no Archimedean point of origin, but only the always moved and moving wayformational lines. This movement resembles the fact that we cannot remember the point of origin of our perceiving, because we find ourselves always perceiving without any basis for such perceiving. A mover is, however, always one who will become, because we are forced to assume movements as principally open in order not to fall back into the model of transport. In contrast to the object-oriented ontology of transport, the model of wayfaring needs a 'world without objects'[38] as Ingold calls it.

4. The only apparent movement of transport is primarily *intentional*; an intention is presupposed. Whoever or whatever moves in the model of transport is not able to take a standpoint out of the coordinate system, but she or it can imagine one.

38 INGOLD, T., Life of Lines, 16.

Transport resembles travel with the help of coordinates. In advance of the journey, the destination points are set intentionally. The mover uses a compass and a map and goes from point to point. Whatever is in-between is either irrelevant or an obstacle, like a river between the points that has to be crossed by a bridge or ford at other points. Imagine that the mover uses a satnav in a car for travel. In such cases, the points are also intentionally stored, not in the mind, but in the memory of the system, and the shape of the journey depends on this intention in advance to the movement.

The same logic of transport can be found in Albrecht Ritschl's understanding of eternity, which was influenced by Lotze.[39] What defines a person is its purpose. The real purpose of every person is the kingdom of God. As a purpose, it is eternal and, in the divine perspective, this purpose is eternally realized. For humans, however, a medium disturbs the immediate relation of intention and realization. Nature is at the same time always a repression of the purpose. And exactly this repression of the purpose by nature constitutes the conception of time.

Intentionality in this sense has nothing to do with a mind or the ability to have self-consciousness. Its means that there has to be a subject that is able to represent the line-defining points of transport. Intentionality and representation belong together.

5. The real wayformational line or line of movement in the model of wayfaring, however, is resonating attentionality. Attentionality is a specific kind of attention that does not presuppose – like intentionality – a mind or self-consciousness. It is defined by the fact that the mover has to be attentive to its environment in undergoing and making her or its way. What is passively received or suffered, which can at least appear as a protension of a specific presence if its emergence is not purely surprising, shapes the way and its curves, which can become knots. The wayfarer is therefore always a pathfinder or a tracker in the literal sense.

Imagine once more a hiker in the mountains, far above the timber line or on a glacier. She needs to behave in a strictly attentional manner in order not to fall from a cliff or to fall into a crevasse. But also non-personal movers like a mountain torrent behave attentionally by following the geological shape of the mountains. Thereby, the mover shapes its environment, whether it is through leaving traces in the snow that can become signs for other hikers, or by gorges, tunnels, or glacial mills the water shapes.

Attentionality is not absolutely passive. It is constituted by an *affect*, but any affect inaugurates an active response. Also knots that became partial ends are not given in advance or could be known in advance, but they are given by attentionality. In contrast to transport, the points which are breaks in the way

39 Cf. MÜHLING, M., Liebesgeschichte Gott, 236–241.

are not representations of the journey as a whole, but they are constituted in resonance with the environment, by being a resonate or dissonant perception of the affordances of the environment.

The same is also true if one follows the steps of others by following a guide or a map. Without attentional behavior, it is impossible to 'make' the way (or is it the way that makes me?). The traces of the ways of the earlier wayfarers might have been weathered; a previously suitable peak might have been closed or one might have to find new knots for pausing due to one's bodily state, or one might have to return due to changing weather conditions.

8.3 Network and Meshwork

In both the description of transport and of wayfaring, we employed a crude abstraction by speaking only about one vehicle in the case of transport and one movement in the case of wayfaring. Strictly speaking, this is incorrect, since there are no single movements added to something new, but movement always happens in, with, and under other movements, be it in the case of vehicles or wayformational lines. Therefore, a 'linealogy' also has to be simultaneously a relational ontology. Thereby, we can see that in transport, non-constitutive, external relations are primary, whereas wayfaring allows for the existence of constitutive relations and in the ideal case only reciprocally, ontically constitutive relations. The best way to see this is to inquire how we need to describe the texture that is constituted by transport or by wayfaring.

1. In the case of *transport*, the texture of relations builds up a *network*. It can be pictured easily with the help of a graph or an arrow-diagram in the logic of relations. In our life-world we are acquainted with such diagrams in graphical illustrations of the so called 'social' networks, be it in the case of connected address books, flight lines of a continent etc. In a network, the points are always prior and they are ontically non-constitutive relata or external relata. If a point vanishes, the others persist and one only has to alter some of the relations among the points – but not necessarily in all cases.

Optimal flight planning would lead to a restructuring of the whole network if one airport closed. Although, in many cases this does not happen and this airport is simply not a destination for the airlines anymore, without consequences for other connections. Imagine your address book: in most cases you will not perceive at all that some addresses are non-valid anymore, because you do not know that a particular person has moved to another place. As long as you do not choose this particular address, the whole system stays workable.

In the same way, as the points in the movement of transport do not reflect real movement, the 'knots' or 'link-ups' of the network are not really knots or connections, although one might use similar terms, be it in everyday speech or in the language of mathematics.[40] Factually, they are individuals or atoms that subsist on their own. They can enter relations of exchange, but the exchange of the network is restricted to non-constitutive relationality. Everything that can *enter* a relation has to be something apart from this relation.

2. In the case of *wayfaring*, its texture of relations is a *meshwork* that is irreducible to the network. In the meshwork, the points of relations emerge out of connected and knotted lines. They are like the knots and interweavements of a carpet or cloth. In some cases, like in knitted fabrics, the whole mesh will be dissolved if one knot is undone, but this does not necessarily have to be the case. We can model three types of meshwork.

First, there is the case in which different threads build up knots or interweavements, which are the relata. In this case there are, strictly speaking, two kinds of relata: the knots and the different threads. In this case, the knots are ontically dependent on the different threads and on the different connections, but the different threads are independent of each other. In the case of an undoing, since threads have a 'memory', they may alter their so-becoming (their essence),[41] but they still become (exist).

Second, there is the case in which the whole mesh, however complex it might be, is knitted or weaved out of a single thread. The only *relata* are then the knots, and they are mutually, ontically dependent on each other. In such a meshwork, there are – relationally speaking – only constitutive relations among the *relata*. Simultaneously, however, there is an ontic priority of the thread over the knots. Relationally speaking, we reach the limits of the logic of relations, since we would have to say that the relation is prior to its *relata*.

Third, there is the case in which out of a thread emerges many and highly complex connections that create the mesh, but there are also other threads interwoven. This third case is therefore a mixture of the first and the second, which would be a world in which some *relata* (as knots) would be ontically dependent on each other, but they would be not dependent on all the other *relata* of the meshwork. The meshwork would be a world in which some of the relations would be dependent on each other, insofar as they are made out of the same thread, but not all relations would be dependent on each other because there would be more than one thread. In this case, the ontic constitutivity of

40 This is in the case of so-called graphs, in which graphically diagrammed points as relata are also called knots.

41 Cf. INGOLD, T., Life of Lines, 25.

the interweavements would be restricted to the so-becoming (the essence) of the threads, but not necessarily to its that-becoming (existence). Imagine the world is a meshwork instead of a network. Which one it would be? If one could have a look onto the world from beyond the world, it would not be easy to decide which is the case. How much more difficult is this decision, then, if one is an interweavement in the midst of the mesh?

3. Both descriptions, the description of the network as well as the description of the meshwork, are still abstract, as we did not consider that the lines are not abstract threads and strings, but movements. In the case of the network, this does not alter much: it only means that the network is describing possible movements. It describes what has to be known intentionally if one wants to actualize one of the non-necessary relations by transferring it into movement. In the case of the network, it is not really a vice to abstract from movement, since the subsisting movement of the network is only apparently movement. The network is prior to movement.

The case is different if we look at the meshwork. It is not woven, but it is always in a process of weaving. All its interweaving is constantly in flux. Not only are the knots in flux, but also the threads itself, since they are descriptions of movements. They are going on to something different. Therefore, the meshwork itself is in constant change. The meshwork, therefore, is not so much the meshwork of a carpet or of cloth, but rather the meshwork of weather, of water in the sea or of the surface of the earth. In these cases, the changes depend on different metrics of time, but nevertheless they are phenomena of meshwork.

4. The movement of perceiving, which is the subject at hand, is the movement of wayformational lines of a wayfarer that constitute a dynamic meshwork. Attentionally perceiving the environment and shaping one's own way and simultaneously the environment, is not movement *on* a surface, as we have said, but *through* a 'medium'. Now we have to go a step further: the medium, through which the movements run, is nothing but the meshwork itself. One's own movement, therefore, is nothing but a partial movement of the network. The *affordances* can be immediately perceived because they are perceptions of one's own as alien, and because they are perceptions in the mesh. The dynamical meshwork is nothing but what Merleau-Ponty called 'flesh' (ch. 5).

5. The meshwork is ontically prior to the network just as the wayformational lines of wayfaring are prior to transport. This priority is firstly a descriptive one, insofar as it is closer to the phenomenal description of the movements of perceiving. Therefore, it is a mistake to call the scheme of transport including origins, lines, and destinations as phenomenally primary. If this happens,[42]

42 Cf. LAKOFF, G./JOHNSON, M., Philosophy in the Flesh, 32–34.

this is not caused by bodily-phenomenal perception, but by a specific cultural manipulation of this perception that presupposes modernity and its inversions, as Michel Serres and Tim Ingold have shown.[43] The phenomenal priority of wayfaring over transport is, however, still not a claim about their reality. It is possible that the network has a kind of secondary reality. And as such it could be an important part of the reality of our life-world. In the course of our inquiry – and especially in the second volume – we will discover a number of the phenomena of transport in the network. However secondary the reality of transport and network in comparison to wayfaring and meshwork might be, it cannot simply be in every case only an abstraction or simplification that ignores some essential aspects. It seems that this secondary reality of the network relies more on transformations or inversions.[44]

8.4 What are Wayformational Lines?

Up to this point we have used the neologism 'wayformational' as an attribute in the expression 'wayformational line' without any definition. Whereas I am convinced that the introduction of the term 'wayformational' is necessary, I am not convinced that it is really helpful to give a definition. Rather, I hope that the reader who has followed so far has understood its meaning. Nevertheless, we can now at least try to define it. Ingold does not use the term. In the German version of this book, I use the term *Weglinie* (way-line), which is also a neologism, but perhaps neither such a strange nor such a precise one. The term 'wayformational' should express the following state of affairs: it means that it is the way that forms the one who is going on the way. And it should express that it is the pathfinder that forms the way. It should express that the way-line and the wayfarer emerge equiprimordially in the meshwork. One could use the less awkward sounding term 'way-forming'. But then the misunderstanding could occur that it is the wayfarer who forms the way actively. One could also use the term 'way-formed', but then the inverse misunderstanding could occur that the wayfarer would be purely passively formed by the way. But what I want to express is that the real state of affairs is not a matter of activity versus passivity, but a matter of the Greek middle voice: a matter of something that is neither active nor passive. The term 'wayformational' seems to come closest to this idea and to the other goal of expressing the equiprimordial constitution

43 Cf. Serres, M., Gnomon, 80 and Ingold, T., Being Alive, 68–70.145–148.

44 Cf. Ingold, T., Being Alive, 68–70.145–148.

of wayfarer and way. 'Wayformational lines' and the meshwork in which they occur are something like the most basic or least abstract entities that exist. However, it would be wrong to read the last sentence in a literal sense, since the expression 'most basic' would presuppose an ontology which is, firstly, a system, and in which, secondly, some sentences are more basic than others. Both have to be rejected in our narrative ontology.

8.5 Wayformational Lines and their Margins

The question of the extension of the lines in the meshwork is not treated by Ingold. One could have the impression that the lines have no extension at all, as if they had no width. Under the presupposition that the wayformational lines are nothing but descriptions of the movements of perceiving, then we have to assume such a width, a width that is oscillating, pulsating, and itself interwoven with other perceptions – similar to a rope consisting of many threads. The width of the thread that is swinging or pulsating is not sharply limited. Rather, there is a more or less sharp linear center that becomes thinner at the margins and that dissolves fuzzily into the environment of the meshwork. Normally, we pay the most attention to the wayformational line of our own living body. In the wayformational line of the living body all senses are concentrated, from the senses of inner-bodily sensation, of haptics, which are a little bit more stretched into width, of olfaction, also a little bit more stretched out, up to acuesthesia and sight which are more outstretched into distance. Since attention varies by being provoked by foreign events in the meshwork or by events of the own body, wayformational lines are oscillating and pulsating, not oscillating in the sense like the string of a stringed instrument that moves in space whereas it has a constant diameter, but swinging in the denseness of its width itself. We have to claim this for both sides of perception, for the undergoing, which is its primary character, as well as the response.

8.6 Stories are Wayformational Lines

The wayformational lines of wayfaring and the meshwork are precisely the primary stories of which the world consists. The case is made more plausible by asking how we can speak about the two different movements of transport and wayfaring, and how we can understand the relationship between language and the movement that language describes.

In the pseudo-movement of transport, the points are the important data, completely describable by a coordinate system. Ordering points in a coordinate system means nothing but using concepts, in which a logical subject (sometimes called an argument) is connected to a logical predicate (sometimes called a function). Coordinate systems are nothing but special cases of conceptual systems, and they share all the characteristics of concepts. In addition, they have a specific difference, which is that the qualities of the predicates can be represented by the quantities of a numerical system.

Imagine weather stations spread around the earth, measuring the temperature at a specific time. From this data we can build a coordinate system with four axes in order to classify each measurement: the location of longitude and latitude, time, and temperature. Each value of a measurement is therefore an instantiation of the concepts of place, time, and temperature. Of course, we could easily add other concepts: the altitude of the place, the humidity, air pressure, the color of the sky, the blood pressure of the investigator, the volume of the background noise, and the kind of speech-acts performed simultaneously on BBC 1 on TV. For three-dimensional humans, a coordinate system with so many axes would be a little bit confusing. Therefore, other means of abstraction, like data-bases, are more appropriate for such multi-conceptual systems.

In this example, three difficulties appear. First, some of the concepts used cannot be at all, or only via detours, represented mathematically, like the color of the sky or the TV-transmitted speech acts. Second, one must ask about the theoretical relation between the different concepts. The realm of concepts is infinite and not all concepts are useful for every purpose. Every possible conceptual scheme must therefore restrict itself to specifically selected concepts, and the choice is dependent on the intended ends, i.e. on a movement of transport in another network of a higher order. For meteorological purposes, no one would take notice of blood pressure and TV-transmitted speech acts, whereas for psychological inquiries these aspects might be of interest. Third, the difficulty emerges of how the concepts to be used are connected in a theoretical frame. Here one needs schemes of classification, in which specific concepts are ordered by specific differences under more common concepts, which can be ordered with other specific differences under still more general concepts, etc. We thereby get pyramids or trees of concepts. Such a pyramid can contain empirical concepts that can have a quantity, like the taxonomic schemes of, for example, biology, or it can contain only logical and ontological concepts like in the case of the *arbor porphyriana*, the blueprint of all taxonomies. In such conceptual schemes, it is logically impossible to describe the concrete particular, since *individuum est ineffabile*. Even if one adds as many concepts as one wishes, and perhaps the extension – the set of the instantiation of the sum of its qualities – might decrease, but only contingently – empirically it will become a set with only one member, but never in the logical sense. The particular cannot be described by the sum of its predicates.

To summarize: Transport in the network is sufficiently described by conceptual classification schemes. Any possible movement in a network may not be particular. It can be repeated as many times as is thinkable, since all thinkable predicates can also be instantiated by more than one logical subject. The only exceptions are spatio-temporal coordinates. The points that define a network of transport are connected horizontally (referring to the spatiotemporal coordinates) and vertically (referring to the taxonomy of concepts) in a conceptual system.[45]

Let's now look at the wayformational lines of wayfaring in the meshwork. It cannot be classified by a conceptual scheme. If we want to refer to it linguistically, we can do nothing but move along the developing wayformational lines. Horizontal or vertical integrations are impossible, since one would be in the need of discrete data and points. But in developing a wayformational line, there are no data or points prior to its development. Therefore, any linguistic means can only move *along*[46] the wayformational lines, which is nothing more than the movement of the wayformational line itself. Whereas in transport the matrix of points can be used as many times as one wants, to move *along* a wayformational line in the meshwork means constituting a *new* wayformational line through the meshwork, which is somehow related to the first one. Knowledge,[47] then, is not a representation of a conceptual scheme, but the movement of the wayformational line itself, as we will see later. On wayformational lines, there are no distinct objects, but only perceived ones emerge. We need a kind of language that is able to refer to this, and that language is the language of secondary stories:

> For inhabitants, things do not so much exist as *occur*. Lying at the confluence of actions and responses, they are identified not by their intrinsic attributes but by the memories they call up. Thus, things are not classified like facts, or tabulated like data, but narrated like stories. And every place, as a gathering of things, is a knot of stories.[48]

45 Cf. INGOLD, T., A Storied World, 153.158.
46 Cf. INGOLD, T., A Storied World, 154.
47 Cf. INGOLD, T., A Storied World, 160.
48 INGOLD, T., A Storied World, 154.

This storied description does not follow an explicit order, but an *implicit order*.[49] It does not describe a complex structure, but a *complex process*:[50]

> The storied world [...] is a world of movement and becoming, in which anything [...] enfolds within its constitution the history of relations that have brought it there. In such a world, we can understand the nature of things only by attending to their relations, or in other words, by telling their stories. For the things of this world *are* their stories, identified [...] by their paths of movement in an unfolding field of relations. [...] Thus, in the storied world [...] things do not exist, they occur.[51]

If one wants to describe the primary stories, one needs secondary stories. Their narrative shape is necessary in order to talk about primary, narrantic stories, which should not be misunderstood: second-order stories also contain concepts. Second-order stories are not, however, reducible to concepts.

8.7 Representation and Resonance

How do we describe the relationship between the perceived world and its description by language? Imagine the world consists in a single, large network, and we perceive this network. In this case, relationships of representation are everywhere. A representation is an external relation or at least a constitutive relation that is strictly asymmetrical: from the *relatum* of the prototype to the *relatum* of the image. The image is constituted by the prototype, whereas the prototype is independent of the image. Furthermore, a relationship of representation uses analogies: in specific respects, the image is similar to the prototype, but not in other respects. The image is not the prototype, as a painted pipe is not a pipe. Relationships of representation seem to be omnipresent. Let's illustrate this:

Many semiotic theories are based on relationships of representation. Augustine's semiotics uses the distinction between *res* and *signum*, by which all *signa* are *res*, but not all *res* are *signa*.[52] Also Peirce's semiotics is not free of relationships of representation: the type of the *iconic sign* is exactly such a representational relationship.[53]

49 The distinction between an explicit order, which is classifiable, to an implicit order, which can only be told, traces back to BOHM, D., Wholeness, 177–217.

50 The distinction between complex structures and comlex process goes back to RUBIN, D.C., Go for the Skill.

51 INGOLD, T., A Storied World, 160.

52 Cf. JACKSON, B.D., Theory of Signs in St. Augustine's *De doctrina christiana*.

53 Cf. ROBINSON, A., Traces of the Trinity. Signs, Sacraments and Sharing God's Life, 324.

Many epistemologies, e.g. Plato's, but also the epistemologies of the leading paradigms of the neurosciences at the beginning of the 21st century, use representational relationships.[54] In the case of representationalism in the neurosciences, this is evident because here the brain is (mistakenly) seen as a representational organ of the world.[55]

Of course, there are some relationships of representation, otherwise there would be nothing like portrait painting. However, the existence of phenomena of representation does not mean that one has to hold to a kind of representationalism. Representationalism refers to an attitude that conceives the relationship of perceiving to language, of world to mind, or of data to the brain exclusively or in an essential manner as relations of representation. As Karen Barad correctly diagnosed,[56] what is typical for representational attitudes is that they can appear in the form of classical realism as well as in the form of constructivism. In the case of realism, the representational relation runs from the world to mind, brain or language; in the case of constructivism, the relationship of representation runs in the reverse order, so that the world becomes a projection of the mind, brain, or society. Representational relations can be elucidated by interpretations, i.e. by cognitive techniques that allow one to diagnose in what ways there are positive or negative analogies between prototype and image (realist version), or in what ways there should be negative or positive analogies (constructivist version).

Relationships of representation presuppose transport in the network, since classification is simply a typical kind of interpretation of the relationships of representation. Since any point of the network can be classified under as many concepts as are available, one has to select as to which concepts are meaningful or not, which concepts are appropriate or not, which concepts should be used or not, which concepts are useful or not, or which concepts are powerful or not, or which concepts lead to an economic optimization, or which concepts furthers a liberal society, etc. A network can be described by relationships of representation that are identical with the conceptual scheme employed (realist version), or that will reconfigure the network of the world (constructivist version).

Let us assume the contrary: the perceiving of the world does not consist in the observation of the external relations of a network, but of perceiving in the midst of the meshwork of the wayformational lines of wayfaring. Further, in this case, it is allowable that there might be at times representational relations. These relations are as irrelevant for the elucidation of the relationship

54 Cf. MÜHLING, M., Resonances, 36–38.
55 Cf. MÜHLING, M., Resonances, 52–54.
56 Cf. BARAD, K., Posthumanist Performativity, 802f.

between perception and its description in language as they are irrelevant for the relationship of perception and action. In the meshwork, representationalism is excluded, since there is nothing that could be divided into prototype and image, which is also the case for the relationship of related second-order narrations. If one conceives of Goethe's *Faust* as a representation of the biblical book of Job, one would misunderstand both narrations. What we find in the meshwork, however, are manifold *relationships of resonance*.

First, relationships of resonance are reciprocally, ontically constitutive relations, which means that it is impossible to distinguish between the resonating and the resonated. The resonance between string and body vanishes if one of the *relata*, body or string, is missing. Second, in contrast to relations of representation, relations of resonance are non-static; they cannot be pictured by an image or in an instance; they develop in a dynamic and sometimes surprising ways. Third, resonances generate unrepeatable particularities. An identical resonance between different tokens of a specific type of stringed instruments cannot be created naturally, only simulated by radical means.[57] Fourth, the number of resonating *relata* is not fixed. The resonance we can find in the case of a stringed instrument includes necessarily the resonance between strings and body, but it is not restricted to these two *relata*. More elements come into play: the fingers, the shape of the room in which the instrument is played, the humidity of the air, etc. so that any possible description of a relation of resonance with the help of the logic of relations is always an abstraction. Fifth, using a model from ecological biology,[58] we can illustrate the role of the *relata* for the relation of resonance by conceiving it as providing open loops for the event of resonance as a whole. This last feature should not be taken to mean that one sees the role of specific *relata* providing specific open loops that can be closed by other specific open loops. If it behaves in such a way, the fourth feature would have been restricted.

The resonances of the wayformational lines in the meshwork can be described as different stories resonating with each other. Stories refer to each other not with the help of relations of representation, but relations of resonance. The told story *a* can be picked up by another story *b*, whose reception and perceiving then transforms the course of story *a*, and *vice versa*. One may object that this would not be true in the case of written texts. But secondary stories are not texts and not a subset of texts, but they have the shape of texts as a means. Therefore, to appear as texts is an accidental feature of secondary

57 Such is the case of the electronic remodulation of acoustic or electric instruments.

58 Cf. UEXKÜLL, J.v., Theoretische Biologie, 150. For extensive disposition also cf. FUCHS, T., Das Gehirn – ein Beziehungsorgan, 128f.

stories. Another consequence of storied resonance is that it is impossible for a second-order narration (and of course this also applies to first-order narrations) to be reduced to a narrative. Narrations are not representations of narratives and narratives do not represent narrations. Narratives are nothing but a pragmatic means of narratology for the attempt to translate the character of narrations as complex processes into complex structures. This endeavor is, however, doomed to fail from the start, as will be shown later.

8.8 Teaching and Learning as Transmission or as Flow

The distinction between representations and resonance also has implications for the practice of teaching and learning. A network scheme constituted by relations of representation can be transferred from one to another, like a map. This kind of transmission can be selective. Based on his earlier experiences, the receiver can be selective and he does not have to accept and carry on the whole representation of the network. He can add his own criteria and thereby vary the conceptual scheme of the net critically or simplify it in the process of transmission. What is passed on, then, can be called *information*, which is to say something that can be reconfigured by data-processing. Transmission presupposes a carrier or medium for the information that shall be transmitted. In many cases, this scheme of transmission is the blueprint for processes of teaching or learning.

In regard to biological evolution, it is sometimes said that genetically relevant information, stored in the genotype, is represented by the phenotype, which is a means for transmitting the information to the next generation. Mutation, selection, and genetic drift cause variations in the genotype of the next generation.[59]

Also, so-called cultural evolution can be understood in this way, if cultural information is seen to be passed on in this way by the various means that modify the information in the process.[60]

If one understands pedagogy or academic teaching and learning in the model of transmission, this would mean that the learner gets a conceptual representation of the network as information with the help of different means – books, lectures, seminar discussions, etc. – in order to modify this information critically, to store it in her memory or brain, and to pass it on elsewhere, be it to the next generation of academics or in a so-called area of practice.

59 Cf. FUENTES, A., Race, Monogamy, and Other Lies They Told You, 47–52.

60 Cf. INGOLD, T., Anthropology and/as Education, 1–19.

The world, however, is not a network. It is a meshwork of interwoven stories or wayformational lines. Therefore, transmission is impossible. What do we have to see in its place? Knowledge is not information as we described it above. In this case, knowledge means to be acquainted with the story of someone or something.[61] And to be acquainted with a story cannot be tested by retelling it sentence for sentence, since this would be a relapse into the model of representation. If stories refer to each other by the means of relations of resonance, then to be acquainted with a story can only mean that one's own story and one's wayformational line is brought into (harmonic) resonance with the other story, or, in the words of Ingold, it means *'to be able to join that story to one's own'*.[62] Such a joining of stories occurs when primary stories are entangled; but it also happens by hearing secondary stories told. Telling a story has nothing to do with transmission of information.

> To tell a story is to *relate*, in narrative, the occurrences of the past, bringing them to life in the vivid present of listeners as if they were going on here and now. Here [...] the meaning of the 'relation' has to be understood quite literally, not as a connection between predetermined entities, but as a retracing of a path through the terrain of lived experience. Making their way from place to place in the company of others more knowledgeable than themselves, and hearing their stories, novices learn to connect the events and experiences of their own lives to the lives of predecessors, recursively picking up the strands of these past lives in the process of spinning out their own. But rather as in looping or knitting, the strand being spun now and the strand picked up from the past are both of the same yarn. There is no point at which the story ends and life begins.[63]

The relationship between secondary stories that are told and those that are lived, narrantic primary stories is described here as a relation of continuity that simultaneously includes difference. It becomes clear that there is continuity if one remembers that told narrations are itself sequences of the primary, narrantic meshwork of stories. The difference, then, can only be understood as a knot in the wayformational line. Ingold illustrates this state of affairs with the help of the figure 1[64] reprinted on the next page, by which 'story' and 'life' are conceived in a way, that in telling a story past events will be inscribed into present experience in a way, that the lived presence is not separated from the past of the story, but a continuation of it.

---

61 Cf. INGOLD, T., A Storied World, 160.
62 INGOLD, T., A Storied World, 161.
63 INGOLD, T., A Storied World, 161.
64 INGOLD, T., A Storied World, 161.

Fig. 1

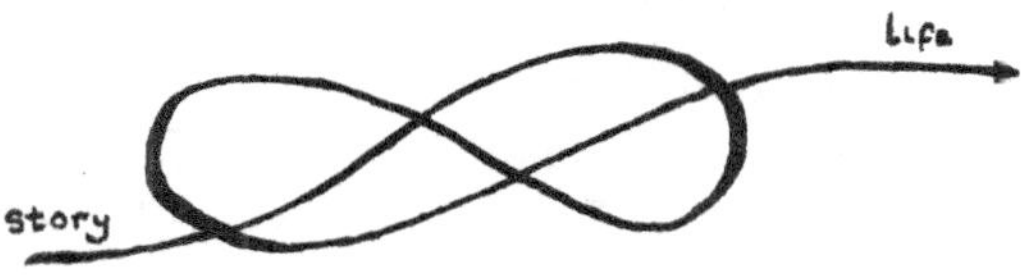

Narrative knowledge cannot be transmitted. It consists in *flowing*: the manner of perceiving (or living) flows on the wayformational line itself. In other words, it is a kind of growth in narrative acquaintance. There is no primary distinction between information, medium, the one who passes on, and the one who receives. Being acquainted, the knowledge of stories, is not codifiable knowledge, nor the product of single subjects in society. If it was, the question of how many one knows would be a meaningful one, like in the case of transmission of codifiable knowledge in the network. In the case of narrative knowledge, this question is as meaningless as the question of whether it is colder at night than outside. The question, whether one is an expert or a novice, is not dependent on the amount of knowledge, but it is dependent on the question of *how* one knows and *how well* one knows. And if there is a test at all, it can only be related to the liveliness of the narration itself, i.e. how well one tells the story and whether others have the opportunity to become woven into the story in their very becoming – without being manipulated.

8.9 Transport as Abstraction of Wayfaring

At the end of section 8.3, we saw that there are many phenomena in which transport is not simply an abstraction of wayfaring, but a kind of inversion, a process that alters ourselves and our lifeworld in a specific way. However, this does not mean that in other cases transport should be seen as an abstraction of wayfaring. In Ingold's case, the relationship between transport and wayfaring is not completely clear.

Whereas it is clear that Ingold prefers wayfaring in contrast to transport, the role of transport remains opaque. Sometimes it seems as though there could be areas where he sees transport as legitimate,[65] sometimes it seems as if transport is the human ability to invert the phenomena of wayfaring in an inappropriate way.[66] Ingold's evaluation is clear: in most cases, this inversion is anything but preferable. But how can we describe the relation between

65 Cf. INGOLD, T., Life of Lines, 47.
66 Cf. INGOLD, T., Being Alive, 149–152.

transport and wayfaring, independently of Ingold, in a phenomena-resonating way? Transport and wayfaring are models and as such ideal designs. If one uses them to describe the concrete phenomena of our life-world, one will find, besides many instantiations of the two types, manifold phenomena that seem to be a mixture of transport and wayfaring. In logical terms, transport and wayfaring are not contradictorily related as a complete disjunction. It is irrefutable because there are personal and non-personal phenomena that cannot be described simply by this either/or. It is possible that phenomena of causality – if causality is a phenomenon at all – might belong to this third possibility, along with disengaged, completely purposeless human behavior, where one simply drifts.

But a description of every single phenomena of the life-world is not our intention. Our intention is to find an ontology that is adequate to perception. At this point, we have to remember that *any* ontology is an abstraction from perceiving, and that there is at the same time no human perception without the shape of an ontology. In other words, the double contingency of appearance and hiddenness governs all linguistic endeavors. Therefore, descriptions with the two related models of transport in the network and wayfaring in the meshwork must also necessarily be an abstraction. Both models do not abstract in the same manner, but in different gradations. Descriptions of wayfaring in the meshwork abstracts less from perception, since they describe nothing more than the reality of mutually interwoven, narrantic first-order stories with the linguistic means of tellable, second-order relations. By contrast, transport in the network must be seen as a higher grade of abstraction. First, it is a higher grade because it abstracts in a stricter manner and it abstracts from more elements of perceiving. Second, and more important, it is a higher or second-order of abstraction, because it presupposes wayfaring in the meshwork, which means that we claim all phenomena that can be described with the help of metaphors of transport, can also be described with metaphors of wayfaring, *but not vice versa.* If both, transport and wayfaring, were closed systems, this claim would be provable. Since a meshwork is always open in its becoming, there can be no test for this claim. We can only hope for evidences and plausibilities. And these consist in nothing but the complete reflections of this whole post-systematic theology. Nevertheless, we can give a small hint.

We have already introduced the concepts of complex structures and complex processes in this chapter. David C. Rubin, who is well known in autobiographical research for his discussion of a 'reminiscence bump,'[67] introduced this pair of concepts. The metaphor of a complex structure conceives of

67 Cf. Rubin, D.C./Wetzler, S.E./Nebes, R.D., Autobiographical Memory.

memory as a comprehensive configuration of mental representations in the mind, stored without interaction with the environment, that build a pattern in which further life-experience can be sorted (and that itself is changed by it). Here, the correspondence of the representational pattern with ongoing perceiving is important. The metaphor of a complex process, however, conceives of memory differently. Memory does not consist of stored representations, but emerges in the ongoing practice of perceiving and acting in interaction with the environment, in which the one who remembers is also immersed. Memories are not representations, but actual resonances of the environment. Rubin has shown that everything that can be said with the model of complex structures, can also be said with the model of complex processes.[68] In other words, the model of complex processes describes memory more appropriately than the model of complex structures.[69] The model of complex structures can be described with the help of the model of transport in the network, whereas the model of complex processes can be described by wayfaring in the meshwork. If it is possible to transfer Rubin's insights from the study of memory to network and meshwork in general, then we would have shown that the model of the network is basically an abstraction of the model of the meshwork.

On a fundamental level, transport is a higher grade of abstraction than wayfaring. But this fact does not determine how these models behave in regard to the factually perceived phenomena on which we are acting. There might be phenomena in which the higher abstraction of transport is useful, helpful, and good. But there are also phenomena, as we have seen in section 8.3, which are misunderstood on the model of transport, and far worse, which are reshaped by an inversion of reality. Which one of these models must be applied is not a question that can be decided *a priori*.

68 Cf. RUBIN, D.C., Go for the Skill, 375.

69 Cf. FUCHS, T., Das Gehirn – ein Beziehungsorgan, 129f.

CHAPTER 9

Narration and Event

In a critical review of my work, *Liebesgeschichte Gott*, Gregory Walter claimed that 'I am not my story, nor is God the story of Scripture. A sign or event would do.'[1] On the contrary, I had already claimed in my previous work, *Gott ist Liebe*, that God is an 'open event'.[2] By this, I meant a very particular thesis that cannot be explained here. But nevertheless, to speak of God as an event is not unusual. One can find this claim in a diverse range of theologies from Karl Barth, Eberhard Jüngel, Robert Jenson, John Caputo to Jan-Olav Henriksen,[3] to name a few. Walter's question affects not only the doctrine of God; it also affects the whole narrative ontology I presuppose in *Liebesgeschichte Gott* without explicating it. Would an ontology of signs or an ontology of events suffice to say what is intended? In other words, is the talk of narrations superficial in contrast with the talk of events? In order to show that this is not the case, we have to show that one can assert things with the help of the talk of stories that cannot be said with the help of an ontology of events. In order to do so, we first have to ask what the term 'event' might mean. And yet, at this point, we are confronted with the problem that talk about 'events' is highly ambivalent.

9.1 Reducible Events in Analytic Philosophy

Very simple concepts of an event can be found in the tradition of Analytic Philosophy. They have the advantage that they are similar to the – not yet de-self-evidentialized – everyday use of language. Analytic philosophy refers to events like, for example, sunsets or accidents. Jaegwon Kim defines events as '*exemplifications by substances of properties at a time*'.[4] Individual events include three features: (1) an individual substantial entity that is (2) a carrier of monadic or polyadic qualities, (3) which are realized in this substance at a specific time.

1 Walter, G., Rev. Mühling, Liebesgeschichte Gott, 352.

2 Cf. Mühling, M., Gott ist Liebe, 10.307.313.330.331.

3 Cf. Barth, K., CD, II/1, 262–267. 271. 279. 281. 304f, Jüngel, E., God as the Mystery of the World, 36. 326. 343. 347. 364. 368. 380. 383–385. 395, Jenson, R.W., ST I, 220f, Caputo, J.D., Weakness of God, Henriksen, J.-O., Life, Love and Hope.

4 Kim, J., Events, 311.

 | DOI:10.30965/9783846765852_010

However, this understanding of events is not without problems. Let us have a closer look at Kim's definition:

> A substance (the 'constitutive object' of the event), a property it exemplifies (the 'constitutive property' or 'generic event') and a time. An event is a complex of these three, and I have used the notation [x,P,t], or variants thereof, as a canonical notation for events in general.[5]

According to Kim's definition, an event would be nothing else but a temporalized proposition. It could have an individual existence, but not an essential one. It would be a property of a logical subject x, which would be understood as an atomistic substance. Insofar as this substance x – e.g. David – owns a quality P – e.g. 'looks at the naked Bathsheba on the roof and decides to murder her husband' – that is actual as a specific time t, it is an event. Events would then be secondary entities in contrast to atomistic substances and qualities. Furthermore, it would be unimportant whether events are somehow relational, since all relations are seen here as reducible to the monadic predicate P. Whether P is a complicated and extended predicate, as in our example, or simply 'Judean King' makes no difference. And there is also a third sense in which events would be ontically secondary, because they presuppose the more primitive notion of time. In this sense, events are immutable. The individual substances might change as long as the event lasts, i.e. it might instantiate changing predicates, qualities and relations, but since all possible predicate changes are included in the one reduced predicate, and since the time-span is fixed, the event as a whole does not change at all. It is also implied, that events in this sense are individual entities, that cannot be repeated due to the irreversibility of time, and that it is impossible for there to be two events at the same time concerning the same substance (though an intersection of events is allowed). Donald Davidson showed that the last claim is invalid. The event 'Mary kissed an admirer at the stroke of midnight' only seems to be unequivocal, since normally one does not kiss two persons at the same time. But let us imagine exactly this. But both different events – that Mary kissed two admirers and that Mary kissed one admirer – are correctly expressed by the predicate 'kissed an admirer.'[6] Therefore, Kim had to alter his concept of an event at a decisive point. He had to abandon the thesis of the reducibility of polyadic relations to monadic predicates, with the consequence that he had to speak of dyadic, triadic, and polyadic events, which have polyadic carriers.[7]

This view (and some other modifications) allows us to talk of irreducible relationality, but it would still be a non-constitutive relationality.

But even with all these modifications included, there are still problems. Roderick Chisholm has suggested further alterations to the understanding of events,[8] which seeks to avoid the constitutive role of time that Kim had assumed. Chisholm assumed that an event can be sufficiently characterized by an individual carrier *y* and its monadic or polyadic quality *F*, if the individual substance exists contingently and owns the

5 KIM, J., Events, 311.

6 Cf. DAVIDSON, D., Individuation of Events, 218.

7 Cf. KIM, J., Concept of Event, 223 and the overview in STOECKER, R., Was sind Ereignisse?, 47–62.

8 Cf. CHISHOLM, R.M., Events without Times.

quality *F* contingently. Therefore, analytic propositions are not events. Nevertheless, in everyday-language we say that events can be interrupted and later continued, like when I interrupt the writing of this book. According to Chisholm, this would not be an individual event, but more than one event.[9] Whether this really means that time is no longer constitutive for events or is only bracketed by the 'contingent' predicate cannot be decided here. In any event, the problems are only apparently solved.

Against Kim and Davidson, we argue that one must also distinguish from the reduced predicates the spatial relation as an original relation that is constitutive for events. At least one must think of it as a necessary element of the predicate. Nevertheless, to be at a place is not sufficient for individuating events. It is not only possible for two events to happen at the same time, but also at the same place, without being the same. At the same time and at the same place Alice can (1) fall into Wonderland and (2) reflect on the relationship of cats and bats. Both events, however, can be logically independent. That they are really only one relational event is neither implied by (1) nor by (2). Nevertheless, both, (1) and (2) are adequate descriptions of events about which Lewis Carroll has written.

Imagine that space and time are constitutive for events, i.e. as irreducible *relata*. All of the problems mentioned in the section above would vanish. However, a new one would appear, also concerning relationality. Which of the spatial relations would be constitutive for the event? Consider a statement of place[10] like the following: 'The River Thames originates northeast of London.' Is 'London' a constitutive element of the event 'the river is rising'? Intuitively, most people would perhaps deny this claim. If one affirms it, the consequence would be that all spatial relations would be constitutive or internal relations, and the event of the Thames is rising would imply the events of the foundation of London, the elections of London's different mayors and finally all relations of the whole world at all times, which would be perfectly logical, but then there would be no distinguishable events.

Davidson tried a substitute for the apparently necessary spatial relations:

> We have not yet found a clearly acceptable criterion for the identity of events. Does one exist? I believe it does, and it is this: events are identical if and only if they have exactly the same causes and effects.[11]

But this is by no means a gain, since now space and time are replaced by a far more questionable entity: the causal nexus. It would be seen as logically primary over events, and over space and time. But causality is not a category that is easy to understand; it is by no means inherent to perception and it is one of the most abstract concepts we know (cf. ch. 17).

All analyses in this tradition have to see events as ontically dependent, either on the more ontically primary concepts of time or on the causal nexus. Furthermore, analyses like these must regard events as secondary in relation

9 Cf. Feldman, R./Feldman, F., Art. Chisholmsegment 7.

10 Cf. Mühling, M., Gott ist Liebe, 274.

11 Davidson, D., Action and Event, 179.

to its *relata* or its individual carriers. Therefore, these analyses try to avoid all of the ontic constitutivity that could be included in the relationality of the event. But why should one choose this option? Quine, like Kim and Davidson, is a reductive naturalist, reversed the relationship, with the consequence that carriers of events become abstractions from events. Here material things become secondary entities and events are ontically primary.[12] At this stage of our argument we still do not have the means to choose between these two possibilities. Both seem to be equivalent: individual things or substances can be seen as logically constituted by events, and the reverse is also possible.

9.2 Constitutive Events in Whiteheads Organistic Philosophy

The possibility of speaking of a consistently ontological priority of events was realized explicitly by Whitehead. His goal was to design an ambitious and comprehensive ontology of events, since such an ontology fits better with experience than an ontology that regards subjects, objects, and their qualities as primary.

In Whiteheads philosophy, 'actual occasions' or 'actual entities' are basic. They are always in the process of becoming: they appear and vanish.[13] The actual occasions are related to previous occasions and to following ones. Occasions happening at the same time can be connected in a nexus, which is then an actual occasion by itself.[14] Thereby, all occasions are connected, with the effect that there is an ontically constitutive relationality, with regard to the aspect of simultaneous events as well as in regard to the sequence of events. The manner of this relationship is called 'prehension'.[15] By this concept, he means that an actual occasion on the one hand takes up the content other events provide, but, on the other hand, has the possibility of selecting out of this given content according to its subjective aim.[16] This allows for continuous novelty to emerge under the category of creativity.[17] Sometimes Whitehead calls the internal connection of the actual occasions 'feeling'.[18] All actual entities have the ability in their larger connections to constitute a nexus of what will later be called 'causality', as well as, in the case of complex events, what will later be called 'self-consciousness'. All actual occasions have as such a bipolar or dipolar nature.[19] Therefore, Whitehead's philosophy is

12 Cf. QUINE, W.V.O., Word and Object, 170–175.
13 Cf. WHITEHEAD, A.N., Process and Reality, 18–20.
14 Cf. WHITEHEAD, A.N., Process and Reality, 20.34f.
15 Cf. WHITEHEAD, A.N., Process and Reality, 23–26.
16 Cf. WHITEHEAD, A.N., Process and Reality, 25.69.85.102.104.128.
17 Cf. WHITEHEAD, A.N., Process and Reality, 21.31f.
18 Cf. WHITEHEAD, A.N., Process and Reality, 23.25.40–45.
19 Cf. WHITEHEAD, A.N., Process and Reality, 108.239.

seen as belonging to panpsychism.[20] In fact, there are no things or objects. Our impression that there are such entities is determined by the fact that actual occasions can follow each other without changing very much. Things are nothing but actual occasions that repeat each other frequently. From this, far too short, description of Whiteheads ontology of events one might assume that space and time may be constitutive for actual occasions, but this is not the case. The actual occasions have their own duration, out of which time and space are built as characteristics of the *res extensa*.[21]

The actual events are ontically, constitutively related to each other, and they influence each other by their prehensions. They are not related to objects as carriers, such as in naturalist analytic philosophy, but objects only apparently exist. In contrast to analytic philosophy, time is not constitutive for events, but *vice versa*, time is a function of the relation of the actual occasions.

The concept of events in the tradition of analytic philosophy, although it was not possible to clarify it definitively, by no means enables a relational ontology. Whiteheads understanding of events (and following him the tradition of process thought) implies a real relational ontology. Furthermore, Whiteheads thinking avoids the false alternative of a causality-based, naturalistic monism and a libertarian dualism.

9.3 Extraordinary Events in Žižek and Caputo

The concepts found in the traditions of analytic philosophy and of process thought might be very different, but they have one thing in common: in both traditions, events are general occurrences. The world is full of events, either because, as in process thought, events are seen as the basic reality of everything that happens in becoming, or because they are seen as entities with a secondary existence derived from things and qualities. But there are also notions of events that deny this shared feature. Further, these concepts have a connection to everyday use, like when we call a particular, extraordinary, or surprising happening an 'event', like the birth of a child, the meeting of lovers, etc., whereas we do not call regular occasions like sunsets events in this sense. Concepts that focus on this extraordinary feature can be as different as one might imagine. Two examples might illustrate this, one from popular philosophy and one from the philosophy of religion.

20 Cf. SEAGER, W./ALLEN-HERMANSON, S., Art. Panpsychism.

21 Cf. WHITEHEAD, A.N., Process and Reality, 125f. 238.

1. Žižek orients himself within a tradition that speaks of events in a way that can be traced back to Heidegger. An event is not a subset of processes of reality, but a 'new epochal disclosure of Being, the emergence of a new "world" (a horizon of meaning within which all entities appear),'[22] which results in our relationship to reality being changed. Whereas Heidegger related the reframing of reality to the hope of a reframing of technology in order to overcome the technical attitude of modernity, by event, Žižek means something that helps overcome the present economic and political situation, which he finds deeply unsatisfactory.[23] But, referring to Blanchot, we do not know whether we are facing a coming event as a political turning point or not.[24] Nevertheless, we can hope, referring to Hegel, that we are already in the midst of its self-explication.

It is not only Heidegger, but a number of traditions, that help shape his concept of an event. With the help of Kierkegaard, he distills: 'the ultimate Event is the Fall itself, the loss of some primordial unity and harmony which never existed, which is just a retroactive illusion'.[25] Against a 'naturalized Buddhism', i.e. the attitude of attempting to be indifferent in the face of the technical reduction of the 'I' by the neurosciences, he stresses the resistance of the subject as event. The encounter with an idea in Plato, the appearance of the *cogito* in Descartes, and the absolute in Hegel are further ingredients for his concept of an event.[26] Insights drawn from psycho-analysis are another one. Žižek also thinks about the possibility of an event that has already started becoming reversed as if it had not happened. The question remains, whether there is a strategy for dealing with events that allows one to stabilize the old framework.[27]

2. Žižek's reflection on the concept of the event is still traditional, insofar as the point of an event is to establish a new order. Derrida, however, in his apocalyptic philosophy,[28] is more radical since its theme is the challenge of every

22 Žižek, S., Event, Pos. 374.

23 Cf. Žižek, S., Event, 191.

24 Cf. Žižek, S., Event, 191.

25 Žižek, S., Event, 568.

26 Cf. Žižek, S., Event, 84. For the event as the absolute, under the influence by Plato, cf. ibid., 96: 'In short the Absolute is a pure Event, something that just occurs – it disappears before it even fully appears.' The resistance of the subject, which was suggested by Descartes' *cogito*, is an event that poses the question 'why is there nothing, where there should be something?' see, ibid., 107. As suggested by Hegel, it is an important thought that one is always situated amidst the event which is the process of the spirit coming to itself. It is noteworthy that Žižek correctly discerns that a central insight of Hegel's, the substanceless self-reference of the spirit, is withdrawn through a new substantialization of the human being as a type of species by the Left Hegelians, Feuerbach and Marx, cf. ibid., 122.

27 Cf. Žižek, S., Event, 172–191.

28 Cf. Derrida, J., Apokalypse, 87.

possible order. John Caputo used this element to sharpen his concept of an event in regard to the relationship between event and name. This relationship can be characterized by eight features.

(1) Events are uncontainable: they cannot be contained by names, whereas names try to contain events or try to be containers for events.[29] An event is an open promise of a name. (2) Translatability: an event has to be distinguished from the simple occurrences that analytic philosophy deals with by polyvalence, complexity, and undecidability. Therefore, it is removed from any cognitive conceptualization and not a subject for translation. Names, in contrast can be translated infinitely into other names, but they try to translate events. Names try to make events happen, but events simply happen.[30] Under the heading 'deliteralization', Caputo argues that names never have a literal meaning, but refer to the poetics of events.[31] (4) Although events presuppose a horizon of expectation – there a no 'absolute' events without such horizons –, they exceed this horizon when they happen, which means that an event can never be part of an economic system.[32] (5) An event is not necessarily good, it can also be evil, since it has the function of destabilization.[33] (6) An event does not belong to being and it is not entity, but it is 'a disturbance within the heart of being.'[34] (7) The event is, what constitutes the truth of a name.[35] (8) An event is irreducibly temporal, but more in a kairological sense than in a chronological sense.[36] But an event is not exclusively kairological, since the event is bound to a frame that is indestructible by the event: the frame of spatiotemporal being, including its contingent rules. Therefore, an event has a tragic character:

> The event is subject to all the contingencies of time and tide of chance and circumstance, of history and power – in short, to all the forces of the world that conspire to prevent the event.[37]

9.4 Virtual Events as the Background of Becoming in Deleuze and Guattari

Žižek and Caputo often refer to Deleuze.[38] Further, Deleuze developed – before and after his collaboration with Guattari – a philosophy of becoming

---

29 Cf. CAPUTO, J.D., Weakness of God, 2.
30 Cf. CAPUTO, J.D., Weakness of God, 3f.
31 Cf. CAPUTO, J.D., Weakness of God, 3.
32 Cf. CAPUTO, J.D., Weakness of God, 4.
33 Cf. CAPUTO, J.D., Weakness of God, 5.
34 CAPUTO, J.D., Weakness of God, 5.
35 Cf. CAPUTO, J.D., Weakness of God, 5.
36 Cf. CAPUTO, J.D., Weakness of God, 6.
37 CAPUTO, J.D., Weakness of God, 5.
38 Cf. ŽIŽEK, S., Event, 82.139.141f.154–156; CAPUTO, J.D., Weakness of God, 109.112.175.203f.321.

and of events, in which events have nothing in common with everyday occurrences. In contrast to the analytic tradition, events are not ordinary occurrences, but, in contrast to Žižek, they are also not extraordinary occurrences. Events are the substratum of occurrences or state of affairs.

Analytic philosophy does not so much describe events but states of affairs, which happen in time or become in time. These states of affairs can be the subject matter of the sciences and sometimes they can be analyzed in terms of their features. But what is it that becomes actual in an occurrence? This becoming is not simply the sum of all past occurrences, but the virtual reality of the event. The event is in the becoming and therefore one can only refer to it with the infinitive.[39] It is neither subject to chronological, measurable time, nor eternal and timeless like Plato's ideas. It happens in 'aionic' time.[40] This occurence means that the event in itself has an infinitely divisible structure whereby it is related to past and future at the same time.[41] This aionic time of virtuality is the plane of immanence.[42] Virtuality does not mean simply, as in everyday language, pure potentiality whereby everything would be possible in the same degree. The concept of virtuality is influenced by Henri Bergson and it means that everything that is past has a story that provides possibilities.[43] Out of this virtual plane of immanence, events emerge that become actual in states of affairs. Individual concrete objects, things, and persons in ordinary meaning are nothing but roles of agents, which try to actualize events. Examples include the Lewis Carroll's Cheshire Cat that tries to actualize the event of smiling, or myself as an instantiation of tooth pain, and this is a role I can play in different ways. Things can also try to counter-actualize the event, which is possible since the event materially exceeds its actualization, so that a person can actualize an event in this or that manner.[44]

Deleuze thinks his philosophy of the becoming of events is an inversion of Platonism.[45] In fact, it is probably more a mere modification of Platonism, similar to Whitehead's philosophy that can also be interpreted as such a modification. In Whitehead, there are timeless objects that become realized in the actual occurrences, whereby the actual occurrences have the ability to choose spontaneously how these eternal objects are realized.[46] This modification of Platonism, insofar as Plato also sees the shadow-world as an actualizing of ideas. In contrast to Whitehead, it is the realm of ideas that owns true being. In the case of Deleuze, he claims to abandon the transcendental level of a realm of ideas completely (with the consequence that there is no transcendence). Nevertheless, he describes a second level of immanent reality. Besides the spatiotemporal, chronological occurrences of the state of affairs, there is the becoming of events in virtuality. As in Whitehead, where the actual occurrences become

39 Cf. DELEUZE, G., Logic of Sense, 214.

40 Cf. DELEUZE, G./GUATTARI, F., Thousand Plateaus, 262f.

41 Cf. DELEUZE, G., Logic of Sense, 1.

42 Cf. DELEUZE, G./GUATTARI, F., Thousand Plateaus, 156; DELEUZE, G./GUATTARI, F., What is Philosophy?, 36.

43 Cf. BERGSON, H., Matter and Memory, 171.

44 Cf. DELEUZE, G., Logic of Sense, 150–153.

45 Cf. YOUNG, E.B./GENOSKO, G./WATSON, J., Deleuze and Guattari Dictionary, 5792.

46 Cf. WHITEHEAD, A.N., Process and Reality, 46.

real through the influence of eternal objects, in Deleuze, actual state of affairs are realizations of virtual events. This comparison of Whitehead and Deleuze shows not that the term of the event is designed in a parallel way, but we that we find a chiastic order: what Whitehead calls eternal objects resembles the events in Deleuze. An important difference is that Deleuze's events are not timeless like Whiteheads eternal objects, but subsist as infinitives of becoming in their own, aionic time.

What is also interesting is the differences in ordering individuality or *haecceitas* in Plato, Whitehead, and Deleuze. In Plato, only the shadow-like happening is individual, whereas the ideas as real reality are general. How the individual became an individual is unclear. Later, in for example Boethius and explicitly in Duns Scotus, the question is solved by constructing a special general substance called *haecceitas*.[47] Strictly speaking, this construction disturbs the platonic scheme of concepts. In Whitehead, the actual occasions and their nexus are real in a relational manner, so that particularity is a particular perspective of the relational whole. In Deleuze, the actual occurrences of the state of affairs, similarly to Plato's things in the realm of shadows, are not really individualized. Individuals are the events of the virtual plane, which become only actualized in temporal happening.

Whether one likes Deleuze's games with words might be a matter of preference, but I think Deleuze's concept of events is best explained, as a kind of dynamized Platonism. Whether one regards his virtual plane of immanence as really immanent or as in fact transcendent in respect to the actual becoming of state of affairs, seems also to be a personal preference.

The more important question is how – in Deleuze – events and states of affairs are to be related, as well as the question of how his notion of events ought to be related to Žižek's and Caputo's extraordinary events. And the answer seems to be clear: If events become actual in states of affairs, and if the things involved in states of affairs counter-actualize events, then all states of affairs, including extraordinary happenings or events in the manner of Žižek, are actualizations of events in Deleuze's sense. If one reads Žižek and Caputo with Deleuze in the background, then extraordinary events in Žižek's and Caputo's sense are neither events nor extraordinary for Deleuze. Everything that happens is an actualization of an event, and the event has always a surplus-value in contrast to everything that can happen in time. The same is also true for the extraordinary, historic-political events Žižek talks about. In comparison to those, the events in Deleuze's sense remain the extraordinary ones. It might be different in the case of Caputo – but that is a theme for when we talk about God (ch. 21).

47 Cf. SWINBURNE, R., Thisness.

9.5 Ontologies of Events Presuppose Narrative Ontologies

After this *tour de force* through some philosophies of the event, let us return to our main question: are narrative ontologies superficial and does an ontology of events suffice? The answer is of course 'no', for the following reasons:

1. All concepts of an event we have analyzed presuppose the concept of a story and internarrativity, although this is not explicit in the philosophies of the event we have discussed.

Kim's reductionist analysis is incoherent as long as there is no constitutive relationality considered. Then we would be left with two possibilities: either we regard space and time as prior to the events, which would amount to a historic ontology that is a special case of a narrative ontology. Or one holds to a causal-reductionist ontology like Davidson. But a causal ontology is also nothing but a (very poor) particular case of a narrative ontology, since now the only connection between events that is meaningful is the dubious category of causality.

In Žižek's popular philosophy the surprising and non-conceptualizable is measured against the non-surprising and conceptualizable, i.e. everyday occurrences and their connections. Therefore, Žižek also presupposes the nexus of everyday events in order to talk about the extraordinary, frame-exceeding events. But this frame is simply a narrative logic or another narrative. Since the new, surprising events should also lead to a reframing, nothing else happens as the event is the transition from one narrative into another one.

Caputo explicitly talks about the fact that the surprising and new presupposes the knowable connection of all that happens.[48] As such he admits that events are dependent on narrativity. In contrast to Žižek, however, the events remain in an advent and in the becoming and never establishes a new narrative. Does this mean we should prefer an ontology of the event over a narrative ontology? Of course not. This decision would only be the case, if all narrations are reducible to narratives and if there were no first order stories that are lived and experienced before they can be told. We already saw that the ineffable can also be understood in the context of the internarrativity of stories. It can be circumscribed by a storied means, but not described (Ch. 6.7). Therefore, Caputo also provides a special kind of a narrative ontology.

The same is true for Deleuze. His concept of events does not deal with occurrences that are happening, but with their subsisting in virtual and becoming events. But this connection is nothing but the wider nexus of all past and all future events, including their specific possibilities. What should one call this, if not a narrative frame?

We do not really have objections against Whiteheads organistic philosophy. Here it is clear that the actual entities or actual occasions need the relational connection of the whole in order to describe their particular meaning. In contrast to Davidson, however, this connection cannot be explained with pure causality. Whitehead's concept of prehension tries to explain how efficient causality and teleological causality can appear. However, one might describe this connection in detail, Whitehead insists logical consistency reigns between everything that happens, and he denies ungrounded

48 Cf. Caputo, J.D., Weakness of God, 4.

events, which means that his ontology can be reformulated in the frame of a narrative ontology, but not *vice versa*, since our narrative ontology primarily uses the concept of *dramatic* coherence, and only secondarily logical coherence (cf. ch. 17).

2. The concept of the event is by no means less equivocal than the concept of stories or narrations, as our examples have shown.

3. Insofar as one can work with an ontology of events, these ontologies are abstractions of narrative ontologies. The process of abstraction from perceiving to narrative ontologies is less severe than the process of abstraction from perceiving to an ontology of events.

4. Many of the concerns of ontologies of events, such as Whitehead's, can be reformulated by narrative ontologies. Beyond that, narrative ontologies can have further concerns.

5. Ontologies of events can be misunderstood in a reductionist manner, as the example of Davidson shows, which is impossible in the case of narrative ontologies. With the help of narrative ontologies, we can also explain the golden calf of reductionist naturalism – efficient causality – but we are not restricted to efficient causality.

6. Conclusion: Tellable narrations do not deal with events that could be understood independently of their narrative intermeshing, but they deal with the primary stories of reality, the narrantic events, which are internarratively connected in manifold ways. Only on the basis of the whole nexus of primary stories, which are not reducible to concepts – i.e. the world – is meaningful talk of events possible. Events are sequences of primary narrations. Only when these primary narrations are referred to by secondary, tellable narrations, will the problem of the demarcation of sequences appear, and the question of whether there are structures to narratives. Narrative ontologies are processual and event-like. A narrative ontology can be called a processual ontology or an ontology of events, insofar as the process or the events has priority over things, qualities, and also relations. But the concept of an event itself is secondary in comparison with the concept of the becoming of narrantic stories.

CHAPTER 10

Narration and Time

10.1 Paradoxes of Time?

It has become common to see paradoxes in the many approaches, definitions, and problems that occur in any reflection on time: unsolvable but pointing to a deeper meaning. This deeper meaning, depending on the specific kinds of analysis of these paradoxes, emerges as plural and refers once more to an even deeper meaning.

In the analytic tradition, beginning with McTaggart's analysis, such paradoxes have become quasi- canonical. McTaggart declared time as unreal since the so-called A-series is at the same time necessary but self-contradictory.[1]

Another possible way to interpret the many definitions of time, as in the case of Eilert Herms, is to see this plurality as a sign of the failure to define time. The reason for this general failure is that time is not something that appears among other appearances, but is the appearance of the appearing. Whereas the appearing can be classified, and therefore also defined, because it exists in a plurality among other existing things, a definition of the appearance is impossible in the case of the appearance of the appearing. It does not exist among other existing things; there is no higher *genus proximum* that could be used for any definition. Therefore, any definition of time has to fail.[2]

Ricœur distills different paradoxes from the 11th book of Augustine's *Confessions*, and he regards three of them as important enough that they govern the whole three volumes of *Time and Narrative*. Two of these paradoxes can be partly explained with the help of poetics and the concept of stories; they serve as support for Ricœur's main thesis, whereas the last paradox is strictly unsolvable. To think something means always to constitute something. But if time itself belongs to what constitutes it, time cannot be constituted or thought. With reference to Kant, this third paradox of time is used by Ricœur in order to criticize human thinking with its tendency to make itself master of all things.[3]

To show that these and other paradoxes of reflection on time exist is surely a meaningful endeavor – as well as the kind of treatment these paradoxes receive in the aforementioned examples. We do not want to deny that. Nevertheless, to declare reflection on time as aporetic before one has started the inquiry suggests that the whole endeavor of reflecting on time is *apriori* aporetic. In

1 Cf. McTaggart, J.M.E., Unreality of Time.
2 Cf. Herms, E., Meine Zeit in Gottes Händen, 71.
3 Cf. Ricœur, P., Time and Narrative III, 261f.

 | DOI:10.30965/9783846765852_011

many cases, to support this claim one uses or abuses the classic quotation from Augustine, which is quoted by nearly every inquiry on time. This quotation says roughly that in everyday life time is not problem, but reflection on time is.[4]

This quotation is meaningful in different ways. It shows that de-self-evidentialized thinking is of high value. It also can lead to a critique of abstract thinking. Nevertheless, the usual decontextualized use of this quotation must be criticized. In Augustine's own reflections on time, this quotation does not have the fundamental meaning his interpreters ascribe to it. Augustine's method does not consist in using one paradox after the other in order to end in paradoxes. He excludes specific solutions as aporetic in order to show that there is a none-aporetic solution, his own one. Ricœur mentions this, but he regards Augustine's solution as aporetic, too.[5] Augustine's main question in designating the theme of the 11th book of the *Confessions* is an *ontological* question: he wants to know what time is: 'I want to know the real meaning and the essence of time.'[6] The last, non aporetical answer is, that time is a *distentio* of the soul, and more precisely – which is often forgotten – of the *fallen* soul.[7] This means that Augustine really answers his question. There is an ontological answer to this ontological question. But in the last instance, this answer is a negative one. The experience of time that Augustine is talking about does not belong to being, but to the defect of being. Augustine's answer, therefore, is directed to the proper theme of the 11th book and that is not time, but eternity. It is eternity that belongs to being and it has to be conceived of strictly as timelessness.[8]

Augustine's reflection on time is by no means an indication of the allegedly necessarily aporetical character of a reflection on time, since his own thesis is a completely different one: we can define what time is, but only linked to a reflection on eternity. At this point of our inquiry, the important thing is not Augustine's answer, but the insight that one cannot treat the theme of time in an isolated manner. Indeed, neither in the reflection on time by other authors nor fundamentally, time cannot be separated from eternity. Time and eternity are relational concepts.[9] But at this stage of our inquiry we are not equipped to reflect on eternity, which presupposes the doctrines of God and creation. Therefore, we too will use an artificial method in this chapter, and we do not have to expect a positive answer to what time is, since this is a decontextualized reflection on time without the concept of eternity. The purpose of this

4 Cf. Augustinus, A., Conf.; XI,14.

5 Cf. Ricœur, P., Time and Narrative I, 5.

6 Augustinus, A., Conf. 11, XXIII, 29: *Ego scire cupio uim naturamque temporis*. Flasch, K./ Augustinus, A., Was ist Zeit?, 262.

7 Cf. Augustinus, A., Conf. 11, XX, 26. Flasch, K./Augustinus, A., Was ist Zeit?, 258.

8 Ricœur, P., Time and Narrative I, 4f is aware that he reads Augustine's text against the grain by separating the reflection of time from eternity.

9 Cf. Mühling, M., Liebesgeschichte Gott, 234–236.

chapter is not to give an answer as to what time is, but to do something different. We have to prove that the different phenomena of time can be conceived as derivatives of the prior concept of story. Stories does not presuppose time as one of their constituents. We have to invert this relationship.

We have to question the allegedly aporetic character of reflections on time from another perspective: is everything that is called a paradox really one? Normally, different descriptions of phenomena are given that are incompatible with one another. And that is the essence of a paradox. But of course, it is only a real paradox if one can show that the different descriptions are descriptions of one identical phenomenon. If they are descriptions of different phenomena or if they are descriptions of different aspects of one phenomenon that are equiprimordial, incompatible descriptions do *not* produce paradoxes. It is possible that this is true in the case of time. There can be different phenomena or aspects of one phenomenon, which are meaningful in themselves, but which cannot be reconciled with each other. In this case, they are different phenomena. Or it could be that these different descriptions are derived equiprimordially from another phenomenon.[10] However, this would make the task of this chapter much more difficult, since we would have to show that these different phenomena can be explained in different ways, or in one way, through narrative relations.

We have to deal with the state of affairs which is the experience of time's different phenomena. First, we have to distinguish between the topology of time and the metric of time. The topology of time can be sub-classified as the experience of the A-series and the B/C-series of time. From all these sorts of experience of time we have to distinguish between the experience of the experience of time and our handling of time. We start our inquiry with the experience of the experience of time.

10.2 The Experience of the Experience of Time as Stories' Protentional-retentional Structure of the Present

I have suggested in my other work, that we distinguish the phenomenon of the experience of time from the phenomenon of the experience of the experience of time as well as from our handling of time.[11] Here we start with the experience of the experience of time, since this theme must be seen as prior in a specific way. This relative priority is given because our experience of the

10 Cf. MÜHLING, M., Liebesgeschichte Gott, 242–254.
11 Cf. MÜHLING, M., Liebesgeschichte Gott, 249.

experience of time is really grounded in perception. Nevertheless, it cannot be described as a perception of the experience of time, since the 'object' of this kind of perception cannot be called time. Nevertheless, in many reflections on the subject this is exactly what is done – a mistake from the beginning. Our experience of the experience of time is a central theme from Augustine to Kant, Husserl, and the whole phenomenological tradition up to Ricœur. And further, the analytic tradition must also somehow deal with the experience of the experience of time. In a pseudo-objective way, it has been called the A-series of time,[12] whereas Kant calls it the *a priori* form of sensible intuition,[13] whereas the phenomenological tradition talks about the intentionality of time.[14] All these conceptualizations have the disadvantage in that they construe a quasi-subjective – or a subjective – aspect of time, with the consequence that one then necessarily also has to discover an objective aspect. In using this kind of figure to treat our theme, Kant and, for example, Husserl are very similar. Further, Merleau-Ponty, in his early writings, comes close to this figure. Later he looked back critically on this kind of thinking.[15] The main problem here is not that one has thereby construed a paradox – the paradox between subjective and objective time. The main problem is that one has to see the relationship between subject and object as a basal and meaningful one. But our reflection on perceiving (cf. ch. 5) showed that this is by no means the case. Nevertheless, Merleau-Ponty provides steps in the direction of a solution.

In our description of perceiving in ch. 5, we said non-specifically that perceiving has a protentional-retentional structure. We will now explain this in more detail.

Normally, this protentional-retentional structure is ascribed to the present, which somehow must be attributed to a mind as subject. Augustine follows this way of thinking by conceiving only the present of the fallen soul as real and by subdividing this present as the presence of the present in observation, as a presence of the past in memory, and as a presence of the future in expectation.[16] Husserl's ascription of the protentional-retentional structure to an experiencing subject is very similar.[17] Husserl clearly still works within a Kantian framework. His analyses of time can therefore be seen as a kind of deepening of the Kantian understanding of time, or at least an attempt to discuss

---

12 Cf. McTaggart, J.M.E., Unreality of Time.

13 Cf. Kant, I., Critique of Pure Reason, B46–57.

14 Cf. Förster-Beuthan, Y., Zeiterfahrung und Ontologie, 26–52.

15 Cf. Merleau-Ponty, M., Phenomenology of Perception, 500; Förster-Beuthan, Y., Zeiterfahrung und Ontologie,187.

16 Cf. Augustinus, A., Conf. 11, XX,26; Flasch, K./Augustinus, A., Was ist Zeit?, 258.

17 Cf. Förster-Beuthan, Y., Zeiterfahrung und Ontologie, 32–52.

time more concretely than Kant. Merleau-Ponty, however, has overcome this Kantian frame at a decisive point: the protentional-retentional structure is attributed to the whole field of perception, not to the perceiving subject itself. It is the primary unity of perceiver and perceived, what he later calls flesh, that has this protentional-retentional structure:

> Husserl uses the terms protentions and retentions for the intentionalities that anchor me to an environment. They do not run from a central I, but from my perceptual field itself, so to speak, which draws along in its wake its own horizon of retentions, and bites into the future with its protentions.[18]

In order to understand this concept, one has to remember that perceiving is essentially the perception of movement. And this kind of movement is pre-reflexive and undivided. Only after a reflection, presupposing the certainty of one's own living body, can one conceive of it as the entanglement of the movements of the perceiver and the perceived. About movement, however, the following statement is true: 'the moving object or rather, as we have called it, the mobile entity, is not identical *beneath* the phases of movement, it is identical *in* them.'[19] The fact that movement has priority over substances, things, objects, and subjects has a number of consequences, including for the problem of identity, as we will see later. Here we can illustrate the priority of movement:

> If we want to take the phenomenon of movement seriously, we shall need to conceive a world which is not made up only of things, but which also has pure transitions. The something in transit which we have recognized as necessary to the constitution of a change is to be defined only in terms of the particular manner of its 'passing.' For example, the bird which flies across my garden is, during the time that it is moving, merely a greyish power of flight and, generally speaking, we shall see that things are defined primarily in terms of their 'behaviour' and not in terms of their static 'properties.'[20] [...] 'Under these circumstances one may say, if one wishes, that nothing exists absolutely, and it would, indeed, be more accurate to say that nothing exists and that everything is 'temporalized.' But temporality is not some half-hearted existence.[21]

At this point, we face the temptation to mistakenly conceive of temporality as primordial. However, this is impossible if we remember that the phenomenon is not 'to temporalize', but 'to move'. Movement is much more concrete than temporalizing, since it is not only related to a change in time but also in place,

18 Merleau-Ponty, M., Phenomenology of Perception, 483f.
19 Merleau-Ponty, M., Phenomenology of Perception, 318.
20 Merleau-Ponty, M., Phenomenology of Perception, 320f.
21 Merleau-Ponty, M., Phenomenology of Perception, 387.

which does not mean that movement is a more complex phenomenon. It is not more complex, but more concrete. The mistake of regarding movement as happening *in* time is an old one, and Augustine has committed it intentionally.[22] Aristotle, too, was not free from this mistake.[23] Let's proceed some steps further by giving concrete, bodily examples of movements: look at the movements of a baby on her knees, who is unsteadily rising in order to grab a piece of furniture. Look at the movements of a cat that is preparing itself on the ground with its whole body tensed for a leap up to reach a branch of a tree. Look at the movements of dancers or look at the movements of your fingers while typing on a keyboard. What all of these different movements have in common is that they have the protentional-retentional structure of presence without being a cognitive ability or the property of some kind of self-consciousness. Rather, it is a property of the living body itself:

> We can distinguish the forms of time in the sensitive living body. Primarily, the living body is necessarily present as the felt body. The future (in any case, the near future) is envisioned from this felt present in the form of (non-consciously produced, not thought) movement sketches. This is to say that in any kind of movement or position of rest, the body is able to realize a plurality of different, continuous movements or positions. Also, the past can be found on the level of the living body as its own dimension: the memory of the body, as we already mentioned, plays a central role for learning movements. Here we see that it is possible to distinguish present, past, and future without assuming a mutually exclusive relationship. [...] Past and future are here conceivable as simultaneous to the present. [...] The living body is ever present; nevertheless, the future (in the shape of the sketches of movement) and the past (in the shape of the bodily memory) are present at the same time and can be distinguished from this present.[24]

---

22 Cf. AUGUSTINUS, A., Conf. 11, XXIII, 29.

23 Cf. FLASCH, K./AUGUSTINUS, A., Was ist Zeit?, 117–124.

24 FÖRSTER-BEUTHAN, Y., Zeiterfahrung und Ontologie, 175f: „Schon im gefühlten Leib kann man phänomenologisch zwischen den Zeitformen unterscheiden. In erster Instanz ist der Leib als gefühlter Leib notwendigerweise gegenwärtig. Dennoch sind auch Zukunft und Vergangenheit leiblich implementiert. Die Zukunft (jedenfalls die nächstliegende Zukunft) wird aus dieser gefühlten Gegenwärtigkeit in Form von (nicht bewusst hergestellten, nicht gedachten) Bewegungsentwürfen anvisiert. D.h. in jeder Form der Bewegung oder Ruheposition ist der Körper dazu in der Lage, eine Mannigfaltigkeit von verschiedenen weiterführenden Bewegungen oder Positionen zu realisieren. Die Vergangenheit ist auch bereits auf der Ebene des Leibes als eigene Dimension aufzuweisen: nämlich im bereits erwähnten Körpergedächtnis, das eine zentrale Rolle für das Erlernen von Bewegungen spielt. Hier wird deutlich, dass eine Unterscheidung von Gegenwart, Vergangenheit und Zukunft möglich ist, ohne damit bereits ein wechselseitiges Ausschlussverhältnis zu implizieren. [...] Vergangenheit und Zukunft sind hier in Simultaneität zur Gegenwart denkbar. [...] der Leib ist *immer* gegenwärtig, dennoch

It is in bodily movement – not the soul, not the mind, not the subject – where one finds the protentional-retentional structure of the present At the same time, this presence of movement is always an inter-bodily movement and therefore also an inter-local one, in which movement is unthinkable without the movement from place to place, from one living body to another one or from one perceivable thing to another. Without the perception of the perceivable (e.g. the branch of a tree), there is no protention to build up tension in order to jump. Without the sedimentary memory of the previous environment held by the bodily past, without being able to turn around, to sit and to crawl, the infant would never be able to rise. The temporal, protentional-retentional structure of the living body is always dependent on the other, on the perceived, on alterations to place. Temporality without movement in place is as unthinkable as temporality without the other.

We still have to take a step further. We saw that there is – according to the late Merleau-Ponty – a chiliastic entanglement of perceiver and perceived, which enables a specific reversibility. The perceiver is able to perceive since she is perceivable, and the perceived has to be understood as at least potentially perceiving. Let us now consider this idea in terms of movement. The moving, living body has to be conceived of as moving, since it is open to the movements of other movers. Something perceived as other, which is to say disclosed as being at another place and so accessible for protention, must conceive itself as protentionally stretched in its specific presence towards a plurality of other places. In the case of the desk an infant uses to pull herself up, or the branches of a tree on which a cat is focused, it remains within the realm of the possible, whereas in the movement of two dancers, they experience the actual, inter-bodily protentional-retentional structure of the present. The difference between potentiality and actuality is not decisive here. In *The Visible and the Invisible*, Merleau-Ponty draws the following inference: the protentional-retentional structure of the present has not only to be attributed to the living body, but to the 'flesh', i.e. to the primordial unity of perceiving and perceived.[25] In principle, the younger Merleau-Ponty of the *Phenomenology of Perception* also had this insight, since the 'perceptual field' of our first quotation can be identified with the 'flesh of the world'. Nevertheless, there is one important difference: a perceptual field is always 'my' field, centered to my living body,

ist Zukünftiges (in Form von Bewegungsentwürfen) und Vergangenes (in Form des Körpergedächtnisses) von dieser Gegenwart unterscheidbar."

25 Cf. MERLEAU-PONTY, M., Visible and the Invisible, 267f. and in addition FÖRSTER-BEUTHAN, Y., Zeiterfahrung und Ontologie, 186.

whereas this is not the case in the ontological speech of the flesh of the world. Any subject hidden in 'me' is no longer necessary.

We come now to the last step of our argument. We did not use Merleau-Ponty's talk of the 'flesh' but rather substituted for it narrantic stories. And now it is obvious why that is the case: the protentional-retentional structure of the presence of the inter-bodily movement is a sequential continuation of a story, which presupposes other sequences as stratifications, stored within the story itself and which presses towards other protentional sequences. Any story is thereby necessarily and constitutively related to other places. And these are the precise features of a story: it has a protentional-retentional structure.[26] It is thereby related to previous and subsequent sequences, and it is related to other places. Therefore, perception is not primarily temporal, but narrantically storied. If one wants to proceed from an analysis of the experience of the experience of time, based on perception, to an ontology of time, there are the following different possibilities: it is either the way of the movement, i.e. the wayformational line, or the narrantic story itself, which is the primary entity and it is from it that time in the sense of the protentional-retentional structure of the present must be derived. But between the two entities there is no difference: stories are wayformational lines or ways of movement and *vice versa.*

The thesis of all theories of subjectivity, which is that there is a presence that incorporates past and future, is not wrong. It is not wrong, too, to speak with Augustine of a presence of the present, of a presence of the past, and of a presence of the future. And with Kant it is also not wrong to name time as belonging to our forms of sensible intuition. For us this temporal structure of the A-series appears in fact to be somehow centered on subjects. But it is wrong to ascribe transcendentality to these subjects, since our own perception of the present in our human consciousness is only a special case, an instantiation of a more general, inter-bodily structure of the present. And this more general

26 The remarks of SCHAPP, W., In Geschichten verstrickt (1953), 143, are also probably to be understood as being about how protention and retention apply to the story itself, not to the subject. But Schapp's opinion is problematic insofar as by eternal present in the story he primarily means the B-series of sooner and later, (ibid., 140), while he rejects the A-series' character of time, at least for the story (ibid., 140). The reason consists in Schapp's refusal of the subject-object-differentiation, just as we do, while considering it to be responsible for the traditional understanding of time (ibid., 144). But Schapp thereby throws out the baby with the bath water: It is undoubtedly right not to take the subject-object-differentiation as basic. Nevertheless, it has a relative right (chapter 19), which consists in gaining interdexicality. This feature gets lost with Schapp, so that you get the impression that his narrative understanding of the present of the whole story is nothing but a surrogate for eternity along Boethian lines.

inter-bodily structure of presence is in itself a special case of something that is still more general, the protentional-retentional structure of the presence of the inter-narrativity of stories. In the same sense in which Newtonian physics is not falsified by the physics of relativity, but the former is understood to be only a special case of the latter, subjective ontologies of time are not falsified by narrantological analyses of time, but they are only a special case of such narrantological analyses.

10.3 The Experience of the B- and C-series and the Presence of the Past

Let us know take a closer look at a phenomenon (or an aspect of the phenomenon) of time's topology, which is the experience of the B- and C-series of time. First, this is an experience that is primarily only about the past. The bodily movements, which are the subject of the protentional-retentional structure of the present, leave traces in the environment of a living body, e.g. imprints in the snow or in the grass. These imprints are visible only to a new presence, when for example, one moves on a curve back to 'earlier' stages of these impressions. Painting and writing, as well as the drawing of a line, are examples of this principle. In this case, only parts of the living body are moved – the hand and its fingers – whereas the eyes remain relatively unmoving. Therefore, I am able to see the line appear in its spatial extension, in its past, as a whole: identical in each new present. This case of recording movements through lines can be transferred to the memory of the living body. Different living bodies have different memories, and the traces of memory in adult humans are also much more like the broken traces of footprints in the snow than to the continuous line drawn by a pen. From this imprint of memory, and also from the bodily traces of the feet of the mover in the environment, we can garner the following abstractions and interpretations:

1. We can regard the past imprint as a continual line or as a series of discrete elements. Both possibilities lead to different conceptions of time, as, for example, in the physics of the 20th century.

2. If we interpret the spatial impressions of past movement as a discrete series, we see a particular order of events or sequences. In other words, I can 'name' the last footprint 'number 1', the next to the last one as number 2 and so on. In this case, I get names for the footprints of the past with the help of natural numbers. Of course, I could also name the footprints in another way, with names or letters of the alphabet. What is important, however, that in all the percievable cases of possible and existent imprints, this naming is identical: it will be always 1,2,3 ..., it will be in no case 3,1,2 or 1,3,2, etc. This identical

naming of all past events or sequences of movements constitutes a constant order. And this is the order that McTaggart has called the C-series of time.[27]

3. If one asks what constitutes this C-series, or, in other words, if one asks why in all possible imprints, be it our real bodily impressions in the environment or be it the traces in our memory of past protentional-retentional presences, can only appear in the identical order of 1,2,3, …, one finds what McTaggart has called the B-series of time: This is the order of time understood with the help of the concepts 'earlier' and 'later' or 'previous' and 'following'. The series of the past, '1,2, 3 …,' is then revealed as '1 is later than 2, that is later than 3, that is later than …' The B-series is therefore nothing but an abstraction of the C-series, achieved by ignoring concrete events. Then I get the purely general relation 'earlier/later'. And this relation is a relation of order, with specific relational attributes: It is irreflexive, i.e. a particular event cannot happen earlier or later that itself (2017 is not earlier or later than 2017). It is asymmetrical (2017 is later than 2016, whereas it is impossible that 2016 is later than 2017). And it is transitive (if 2017 is later than 2016, and if 2016 is later than 1969, then 2017 is also later than 1969).

4. The B-series is constituted by several abstractions from the primordial movement. The first abstraction is the visible record of past presences in the traces of the environment or in the traces of memory. It is a spatial image, or more appropriately, as we will see, a spatial resonance of past experiences of presents. The second abstraction is that continual lines are seen as discrete traces of steps. The third abstraction consists in construing the C-series out of all possible imprints. And the fourth abstraction is the distillation of the B-series out of the C-series, including their relational attributes of order, irreflexivity, asymmetry, and transitivity.

5. Strictly speaking, the B-series and the C-series are primarily related to the perception of the past from a specific present, but not to the presence or the future.

6. The B-series and the C-series is constituted by a transformation of the past into spatial relations. It presupposes that the curved traces are excluded and that earlier traces are situated more distantly on the horizon of perception (or memory) than later ones. The character of time as a relation of order therefore presupposes the spatial resonances of movements in the environment or in the memory.

7. We must add a decisive observation: I can only face a past sequence of the traces of my living body when I return in space to this past sequence, which means that a past sequence can only be faced through a specific new

27 Cf. McTaggart, J.M.E., Unreality of Time.

presence, including the fact that I leave new impressions and traces between the living body and the environment. The same is true in regard to memory: it is simply not true that something of the past, which is 'stored' in the memory, reappears in a specific present. It is more accurate to say that in a new present, mediated by new impressions of the environment, old impressions are remembered. Memories are not stored or recorded elements in the medium of the memory or the brain, but they are always new interactions between the living body and the environment. The empirical research on memory carries this view forward.[28] Our example of drawing a line on a sheet of paper is therefore a little bit inappropriate, since it wrongly suggests that I could face the whole line – such as written text – on the sheet as a whole and at once. But in this case, this is also not entirely true. A sheet of paper full of lines does not present a past totality that could be focused on at once. In fact, my eyes have to make a series of movements in a continual renewal of the present in order to see all of the lines on the sheet. And this is decisive, because thereby a new relational attribute has to be added: The B-series is a relation of order, i.e. an irreflexive, asymmetrical and transitive relation. But spatial relations are also relations of order along with other ordering principles (such as the alphanumerical order of an encyclopedia, or the series of natural numbers, etc.). But in contrast to these other relations or orders, a feature has to be added that is unique to time: the irreversibility of the temporal order of the past.

8. The B-series is constituted by past presents. In a specific present, it is nothing but the order of the present's aspect of retention. If I try and face the B-series in an abstract way, in itself, far from its phenomenal foundation in movement, it seems that out of this series – out of time – movement, perceiver and perceived, subject and object would emerge. Only by this abstraction can we objectify the past.

9. Another level of cognitive interpretation leads to the thought of extending the line of the past via specific and always new presences into the future. One thereby expects (in principle without any possible proof) that the order of the past will also be the order of the future, or, more correctly, the order of specific new presents including the identification with every possible protention and retention with the B-series.

10. This extension of the ordered sequences into the future in protention does not have the shape of traces in the environment or in memory. Only analogously can we talk about possible traces. If we stay in our spatial analogy, from any specific present an infinitely possible number of lines into the future are given, with different probabilities. Any sketches of movement will

28 Cf. FUCHS, T., Das Gehirn – ein Beziehungsorgan, 63f. 129f.

privilege specific courses of movement. This means that the expectation of the future has three features. First, the expectation that the future course of movements will also have an irreversible relation of order, second, the expectation that certain courses are more probable than others, and third, the expectation that surprising courses will appear, i.e. that new lines will appear in the fan of future lines.

So far, we have shown that the relation of order of the B-series of time is not a primary phenomenon, but a derivation from the experience of the protentional-retentional present. This B-series has essentially a storied structure, since the main feature of the B-series, the relation of order, is a necessary feature of any story. In secondary re-narrations, I am able to alter the order of sequences, but only by producing a new relation of order. And any recipient of a told story (including fictional ones) is only able to understand a story if she is able to recognize the relation of order intended by the story (not by the author).

Tellable stories are more than continuations of sequences, irreversibly connected by relations of order. It is also necessary that there is a meaningful[29] connection, consisting in rules that allow for the future fan to consists of more or less probable lines. This meaningful order is given by bodily movement and its inherent protention. Imagine making a curve in the air with your hand from left to right. Then the meaning of the movement is from the beginning to the end with your movement at the bottom of the movement on the right side. Of course, it is possible that the movement will end on the top of the left side, if, for example, someone hits your hand in the midst of its movement into this direction. But this surprising event does not reduce the protentional orientation of bodily movement. This protentional orientation of bodily movement exists in different shapes and it can be cognitively analyzed in many ways. The easiest interpretation expresses it as purely efficient causality; more demanding interpretations assume a kind of entelechy of the movement, a teleological causality or intentions.

Causal theories of time, like Richard Swinburne's,[30] reverse the constitutive connection between time and causality that Hume had assumed. Whatever the effect of an event is called 'later', whereas whatever the cause of an event is called 'earlier'. What is presupposed is a modal shift from the actuality of causes and effects to the possibility of causes and effects. Causal theories of time are interesting in two respects. First, they are interesting because, in a double reduction, they regard, as a first step, the meaningful order of stories as essential for time, and in a second step reduce causality

29 Cf. KÖPPE, T./KINDT, T., Erzähltheorie, 43.

30 Cf. SWINBURNE, R., Christian God, 81.

to efficient causality as the only essential form. Causal theories of time try to make one aspect of our experience of time absolute by reducing this experience to the very doubtful concept of efficient causality. Second, causal theories of time are interesting since they do not see time as basic, but one particular way of seeing events as connected, one particular kind of a meaningful order. Therefore, causal theories of time are nothing more than special cases of narrantologic theories of time, i.e. theories that conceive of time as a derivation of stories or of meaningful connected continuations of sequences and events.

Remember the curve in the air your hand is drawing. This curve is nothing but the lived story, including its sequences. The structure of the B-series of time is factually and primarily the narrative structure of lived, narrantic stories in their connection.

11. The idea of time as an irreversible relation of order is not only grounded in the perception of movement, we also use metaphors of movement in order to talk about time. And interestingly, we have no problem using metaphors that would be contradictory if taken literally:[31] we talk about weeks *in front of* us, but also of the *following* weeks. We can use both expressions interchangeably, without recognizing that they are literally contradictory. Imagine not talking about weeks, but about cars in a traffic jam, viewed from my position in midst of the crash. Then the cars *in front of* us are by no means identical with the *following* cars. The reason that we do not feel any contradiction in the temporal use is, that the B-series of time we try to express with 'in front of' and 'following' is bound to different ideas of movement. In the case of the weeks in front of us, we conceive time including future as a static continuum or landscape and ourselves in its midst as moving unidirectional in one direction. In the case of the following weeks this picture is reversed: time is now seen as a moving object, whereas we are fixed at a point and we observing time like a train running towards us. Both pictures try not only to express the B-series in different manners, both also include the aspect of the A-series of time, the aspect of a specific present. But by abstracting from this aspect and restricting ourselves to the B-series aspect of the irreversible order of relation, the talk of weeks in front of us and of following weeks becomes equivalent, which is possible since, for the character of the relation of order, the direction of movement is irrelevant. In regard to the purified aspect of the B-series of time, this language is coherent; in regard of the different narrative frames from which they are derived, they are inconsistent.

---

31 Cf. LAKOFF, G./JOHNSON, M., Metaphors We Live by, 41–44.

10.4 The Logic of Surprise and the Presence of the Future

Augustine called the protention of the future as present simply expectation,[32] which is not entirely wrong. But Augustine had no intention of developing a phenomenology of expectation. Rather, the phenomenon of the retentional-protentional experience of presence as a whole is for him a sign of fallen incoherence (see above). If one does not follow Augustine in this evaluation, the presence of the future is worthy of more attention than Augustine is willing to give. This evaluation leads us to a phenomenological logic of expectation that can be more properly called a *logic of surprise*.[33]

The presence of the future appears as expectation, on the one hand, under the affective distinction of delight and aversion, especially when we make this explicit by using the more concrete terms hope and fear. On the other hand, we hope and fear the expected in different ways, depending on how it is related to our horizon of experience, which is always a horizon of expectation. Expectation is always related to the entirety of our past present; therefore, the most proper way to speak of it would be to call it the presence of the future in the background of the presence of the past. This horizon of expectation appears differently for different creaturely becomings, depending on their ability to reflect. Higher, non-human animals must be included. For humans, the presence of the future appears in four important classes:

- *The non-surprising = the expected*: The possible future events are here near the middle of our horizon of experience. To this class belong structural expectation, like the expectation that future events will also only appear according to the B/C-series. We expect that in every possible future week Tuesday will follow Monday. But it is not only the structure of narrantic events, but also concrete narrantic events that will happen that we expect in this manner, like the expectation of having breakfast tomorrow.
- *The prospectively surprising*: This kind of surprising is also in the frame of our horizon of expectation, but it is situated more on its margins. Therefore, we call it surprising rather than expected, if it happens. But we are able to anticipate it with our imaginative capabilities. Imagine that you, as a reader, will be elected as the new minister for questions of time in your country. If this happen, you would be surprised. However, you have access to these possible ideas because all the narrative parts of which this possible event consists belong to your horizon of experience: you know what 'reader', 'minister' and 'questions of time' mean, because these narrative parts have

32 Cf. AUGUSTINUS, A., Conf., 20, 26.

33 For the following cf. MÜHLING, M., Handbook of Christian Eschatology, 32–35.

also appeared frequently in past perceived events, but not in this special order. You would simply call it surprising, because your acquaintance with the past history of sequences would make its actualization improbable, but not impossible.

- *The absolute-retrospective surprise*: The absolute-retrospective surprise belongs in no way to the presence of the future in respect to its material content, since it is not part of our present horizon of expectation. It cannot be anticipated materially. Therefore, we can give no examples of a possible future, but only examples from the past. That you would meet exactly this person you have married was unexpectable and unpredictable before you met him or her. Therefore, it was a surprise, but in contrast to the first kind of surprises, it can only be called a surprise after it has happened. What is interesting, however, is that while the material content of the absolutely-retrospectively surprising is in no way anticipatable, its factuality is expectable. It belongs to the presence of the future, to expect to become surprised by absolutely-retrospective surprises. To develop the attitude of expecting to be surprised in the future by absolutely-retrospectively surprises is very important for our ability to perceive our present and to act in the present, especially for one decisive attitude: *attentionality*. No one can do anything in order to be absolutely-retrospectively surprised because it is a passive event, one that can only be suffered (not only in aversion, but in delight, too). But one can actively do something in order to prevent being absolutely retrospectively surprised (but hopefully without success): one can close one's eyes and other means of perception, and one can try to develop the attitude of seeing everything according to the model of the network. One can try to become blind by claiming that *intentionality* is all that exists.
- *The relatively-retrospectively surprising*: The relatively-retrospectively surprising is a very interesting mixture between the first two kinds of surprise. We know from within our horizon of expected sequences, which let us hope or fear that we will be surprised retrospectively, without knowing what it will be that surprises us. Very good and very bad birthday presents belong to this kind of surprise: I expect to be surprised by presents at my next birthday, but I have no clue by what.

By these essential distinctions our horizons of expectation are constituted. They vary in regard to the contexts of our life-world: in the family, we have certain horizons of expectation, and others in our jobs. These horizons can partly intersect or include each other, or they can be ordered into subsets. Life, i.e. the ongoing experience of the experience of time, will shift these horizons of expectation. Nevertheless, we can assume that there is a comprehensive horizon of expectation in which all other everyday horizons of expectations are included, which is necessarily a postulate, no declaration of fact, but it is a very probable claim. It remains a postulate for the following reason: it is fundamentally unclear which areas of the B/C-series of our presence of the past will be actualized in a specific present by perception. The idea that the past could be 'completely' recorded, or 'recorded' at all, like the line a pen leaves on a sheet of paper, is an idea that cannot be actualized. It is not only an empirical fact that we are forgetful, that we have gaps in our memory, that prevents the actualization of this ideal. It is also that human memory has nothing in common with a storage-device for information. It is an enactive interaction with our environment.[34] Therefore, the idea of a comprehensive horizon that encompasses all particular horizons of expectation is an idea that cannot be pictured, represented or systematized, but that can only be perceived by our becoming on wayformational perspectives.

The presence of the future is the primary mode of experiencing the present. And of all modes of the presence of the future, the attitude of the expectation of the relatively-retrospectively surprising phenomenally primary – I expect to be surprised by the still unknown. As the still unknown, it determines my essence, since I become towards it. Phenomenally, one can experience this in the phenomena of waiting and its boringness, where, as Marion says, *nothing* happens.[35] We can explain this in the following way: It is the unacquainted I am expecting, which forms my narrative understanding of narrantic time into the meaningful connection of a story. Everything that might occur during this waiting on the metrics of time becomes involuntarily accidental, faded out as boring or as non-perceivable. Only the advent of the unknown other continues the story and brings the situation of waiting and its boringness to an end. It is essential that the advent of the unknown by no means continues a fixed story that is only epistemically unknown to me. Its advent provides me passively with new possibilities of how to act and to decide – or in short: completely new possibilities of how and who I can become.

10.5 The Experience of the A-series of Time and the Presence of the Presence

The part of the topology of time called the B-series from McTaggart onward, is in reality a narrative order that includes its own relation of order. Therefore, not only our experience of the experience of time in its protentional-retentional

34 Cf. FUCHS, T., Das Gehirn – ein Beziehungsorgan, 168.195.

35 Cf. MARION, J.-L., Erotic Phenomenon, 32–36.

structure of the present is in truth a narrative or more precisely narrantic experience, but also the experience of the topology of the B-series and C-series is a narrative experience. But the topology of time is not only experienced in the B- and C-series, but also in the A-series. The A-series of past, present, and future is not identical with the experience of the experience of time in its protentional-retentional structure of the present, because this is not a series. Only by combining the protentional-retentional structure of the present with the B-series, the A-series of past, present, and future emerges, including its idea of a present point that moves through time. We need a lot of cognitive ability in order to develop this idea: one has to have an autobiographical consciousness, which can only be found in the higher vertebrates. Equiprimordially with the autobiographical memory, its constitutive relation to the other, including her experience of the experience of time that happens simultaneously with mine, is presupposed. Only then I can have the idea of the simultaneity of a wandering point or present of all the movements of the world. Only by this and by being embedded in this inter-bodily state of affairs is the idea of the A-series possible. If I abstract from these concrete conditions, contexts, and connections and try thereby to conceive of the A-series as an independent thing, McTaggart's paradoxes of the changing truth-values seem to appear, which have led him to claim the unreality of time.[36] Reading McTaggart, or writings on time by analytical philosophers influenced by him, one could get the impression that a combination of the A-series and the B-series would amount to the experience of time. But the B-series is not specifically temporal, and the A-series is logically incoherent. Therefore, the unreality of time is claimed product. We do not have to confuse the A-series with our experience of the experience of time. It only emerges by applying the experience of the experience of time to the B-series.

But if one does not remove the A-series from its constitutive foundation, then it describes an important aspect of the experience of time without any contradictions. We then can ask an important question, the question of the real distinction of past and present. In our experience of the experience of time, we are beginning with a specific experience of the present, which is always protentionally-retentionally stretched, including in the case of bodily movement, not only in the case of consciousness. The experience of the B-series is, in contrast, essentially an experience of the past. Its combination delivers the experience of the A-series of past, present, and future, in which the present seems to be the point or boundary without extension between past and present.

36 Cf. McTaggart, J.M.E., Unreality of Time.

From this point of view, one could re-invoke one of Augustine's paradoxes that leads to the idea of the non-existence of time: the events of the past are past, i.e. they do not exist. The events of the future do not exist yet, i.e. they do not exist. If the present is only the limit between the past, that does not exist, and the future, that does not exist, the present also cannot exist. Therefore, there is no time at all.[37] But this paradox is also not as significant as it is often assumed. This paradox presupposes the isolation of the A-series out of its constitutive connections, and it also presupposes time as ontically prior over bodily and narrantic movements. One has to claim the independent, ontic existence of the A-series in order to construct this paradox. But this is in no way necessary. Rather, we can interpret the A-series in a much more intelligible way.

If one sees the present in the model of the A-series as a boundary between past and future, then the question emerges: what do humans experience when they talk about the present? Richard Swinburne's answer, that it is only the most recent part of the past, is a plausible one. The past is characterized by the B-series, embodied in the spatial imprint of reality or in the traces of memory. Coming from his causal theory of time, Swinburne suggests that only this part of the past, in which the causal nexus is stored in memory without interruption, is normally called 'present', whereas that part of the past that is stored with gaps in the memory in regard of the causal nexus, is normally called 'past'.[38]

Although Swinburne's causal theory of time is not suitable for our understanding, the argumentation is not wrong, and in truth, it can be removed from the causal explanation of time. The part of the past narrative sequence that is not affected by gaps in memory is usually called present, whereas the part of the past narrative sequence that is affected by gaps of memory and by inferences from imaginative possible narrative sequences is usually called past. This manner of conceiving things is important in three respects. First, it can be combined with empirical research into the experience of presence that shows that the present lasts a while.[39] Second, the distinction between present and past is not a basic or an ontic distinction. It is also not based in perception as such, but only on *human* perception. It is a psychological distinction dependent on the specific restrictions of our memory that can be explained by neurobiology. Third, and this is the main point, with the same right with which we are saying with Swinburne that the present is then dissolved into the past, *we can also claim that it is the past that has to be dissolved into the present.* Imagine with Swinburne a life-form that does not have our neurophysiological restrictions of memory,[40] e.g. someone who has her whole life-sequences as present

37 Cf. AUGUSTINUS, A., Conf., XI,17.
38 Cf. SWINBURNE, R., Christian God, 90.
39 Cf. PÖPPEL, E., Grenzen des Bewußtseins, 166f.
40 Cf. SWINBURNE, R., Christian God, 90.

before her eyes as I have the last three typed letters of this word. Such a life-form would experience the whole past as present. We can assume that such a person would never describe the A-series with the help of the ideas of past, present, and future, but more probably with the help of the transformation of possibility into actuality. We can learn from this that the arena of facts is not the present, but the past. A fact is a *factum*, something that has been made, something that belongs strictly to the past. Empirical research deals with facts. Therefore, all possible empirical work is unable to perceive becoming as such or contemporary becoming in its transformation of possibility into actuality. Empirical work understood as dealing with facts always means studying the past.[41]

To face the present as present means, according to Augustine, to conceive it as *attentio*. Indeed, we can find here a game of words between *distentio, attentio* and *intentio*, that can be introduced by way of Ingold's opposition of *attentionality* and *intentionality*.

Augustine's idea of describing the presence of the present as *attentio*, i.e. attention or tension towards something other, is only suggested by Augustine, but never elaborated.[42] Elsewhere, he can call the presence of the present simply *contuitus* (observation).[43] If one asks what is perceived in the present or toward what the attention is stretched, Augustine gives no answer. The point of his reflection on the present is that the present is also the place where memory and expectation, i.e. the presence of the past and the presence of the future, take place, which has the consequence that time is a *distentio*, a dis-tension of the fallen soul. The fallen soul always owns a fragmentary and incoherent character that is determined by the negation of being. And stretched in distensions means nothing but being directed to the dissolution of non-being. In contrast to modern descriptions of fragmentation,[44] it is not the material content that cannot be integrated, but fragmentation is only caused by the experience of the experience of time as *distentio*. We have to lament the *distentio*.[45] Therefore, Augustine is sighing in face of the existential force of this dissonance,[46] as Ricœur describes it. Temporality means always being in a state immediately before being shatters and falls apart, which is precisely what *distentio* means. Genuine being is not time, but the eternity of God, which Augustine describes as inversion of time, as *intentio*, that is a tension towards unity that falls apart in time. The soul is principally able to partake in this *intentio*, but of course not as long as the soul lives in temporality. Eternity is therefore strictly timelessness and narrationlessness, a kind of infinite stay or non-movement. In eternity, there are no sequences and events, nothing is perceived, since the problem for Augustine is not simply the narrantic becoming of the world, but deeper, the fact that

41 Cf. HEIM, K., Christian Faith and Natural Science, 104f.
42 Cf. AUGUSTINUS, A., Conf., 28,37f.
43 Cf. AUGUSTINUS, A., Conf., 20,26.
44 Cf. LUTHER, H., Religion und Alltag, 160–183.
45 Cf. AUGUSTINUS, A., Conf. 29,39.
46 Cf. .RICŒUR, P., Time and Narrative I, 30.

narrantic becoming means being cut into the three modes of presence. The problem for Augustine is the event-like and narrative character of becoming.

Augustine, therefore, means something completely different with *intentio* than the phenomenological tradition that talks about the intentionality of time. He does not mean that being directed to the other in protention and retention is the essence of the present, but his ideal is a state of timelessness, in which protention and retention vanish and intentionality in the sense of phenomenological directedness is also to be directed to something different. Not to take the different evaluations into account, Augustine's concept of *intentio* is ironically closer to Ingold's concept of *intentionality*.

Intentionality, as Ingold describes, is characterized by the attitude that fits with the model of transport in a network, in which movement only seems to exist. Its opposite is the attentionality of wayfaring in the mesh. If we respect the fact that both models are evaluative ones, and that the model of transport in the network is used in order to criticize tendencies of modernity,[47] one can also say that the modern inversion (if not perversion) of turning phenomena of wayfaring into transport, including the stress of intentionality over attentionality, is nothing but the attempt to create a prosthesis or surrogate of eternity: the attempt to realize timelessness under the conditions of time.

Conversely, this state of affairs also sheds some light on Augustine's concept of eternity. As *intentio*, eternity is necessarily inanimate and technical. From this, we learn that we would do better to refrain from modelling the necessary connection between time and eternity with Augustine's necessary connection between *distentio* and *intentio*. The experience of the experience of time, of the protentional-retentional stretched movement, is not based on Augustine's *distentio*, but on what Augustine calls *attentio*, though he only treats it secondarily. Because every movement is related necessarily and constitutively with other movements in the mesh, presence is always *extentio* and *attentio*. The present is always *to become whence-and-whither-tensioned*. Attentionality, as the attentive attitude that perceives in order to become tensioned by others in resonance with reality, is a kind of perception that leads to a choice of ends. This perception is primarily the experience of the presence of the present. In the case of the non-human movement, this *attentio* simply happens. In the case of humans, it does not simply happen, but it is bound to the temporal consciousness of the A-series and we have to develop it in our handling of time (cf. ch. 10.8).

47 Cf. INGOLD, T., Life of Lines, 74, subsequent to SERRES, M., Gnomon, 80.

10.6 The Experience of the Metric of Objectified Time

The experience of the metric of time is a distinct phenomenon, but not an independent one. It is dependent on the experience of the topology of time, and therefore of time's narrative character – but not *vice versa*. Neither the experience of the experience of time nor the experience of the narrative topology leads to the idea of a metric of time, i.e. the idea of a constant flow of time. The experience of the experience of time is marked by the feeling of very differently extended time spans in protention and retention. Also, the experience of the boundaries of the present is characterized by very different extensional boundaries of the present. The B-series of the past and the extrapolated B-series of the future is completely without any natural measure. Stories and their sequences have primarily no metric, but a non-measurable time of their own. If this metric is only one aspect of the experience of time and obviously not a basic one, then all attempts to reduce time somehow to its metric – like Aristotle's view that time is the measure of movement regarding sooner and later,[48] or like Einstein's reduction of time to what can be measured with clocks[49] – have to be seen with great skepticism. Nevertheless, reductions like these are not without value, as long as one uses them heuristically instead of ontologizing them. And, heuristically, Einstein as well as Aristotle are important.

The metric of time and thereby its constant flow is more than an idea. Its basis is the perception of constant movements. For pre-modern, especially ancient, people this was primarily the perception of astronomical state of affairs and – derived from this – the construction of different clocks, which had the task to simulate these constant, or seemingly, constant astronomical movements. This change led to the idea of a constant movement itself and therefore to the *ideal* of the clock, since the clock is nothing but an ideal. Aristotelian physics knew this. And that means that the movement of ideal clocks has a narrantic origin. However, this is a kind of movement that no longer reminds us of the dramatic character of stories, because the movement is seen as homogenous. The ideal of the clock therefore is based on the idea of making homogenous stories as the paradigm and by erasing all events out of them. Then we get the purified measurability of time. Time then no longer appears as movement itself, but as a background of movement, as a coordinate axis or as an aspect of the stage, on which everything else appears as the objectified occurrences of Newtonian physics. The appearance of the objectified happening

48 Cf. ARISTOTELES, phys.IV, 11.

49 Cf. EINSTEIN, A., CPAE 2, 275–310, especially 278.

is not yet given with metrics, but first with an isolated view of the topology of the B-series. But measurability adds an important element for all empirical research to this kind of objectified time.

From this perspective, Einstein's clock-reduction, i.e. the idea that time is nothing but what ideal clocks can measure, does not appear as very innovative. This changes, however, if we have a look at how Einstein used this clock-reduction of time in order to solve the problems that are given with the constancy of the speed of light. If the speed of light is the measurement of a movement, and if the constancy of the speed of light excludes the velocity-addition formula for relative movements (under the presupposition that movement is a vector of temporal and spatial coordinates), then the idea that these coordinates are homogenous must be revised by virtue of time dilatation and spatial contraction. The consequence for the metric of time is that an ideal clock does not give the same measurement under all circumstances, without losing is character as ideal clock. The metric of time – its 'homogenous' flow – is now dependent on the ratio of the speed of a particular movement to the speed of light. The main insight for us is that the theory of special relativity implies that the metric of time (and the metric of space) is dependent on internally related movements. The metric of time is therefore a consequence of events and their relations – it is a consequence of narrantic becoming. The metric of time, therefore, does not exist prior to what happens narrantically in a storied manner, but it is implied by it. The metric of time does not belong to our forms of sensible intuition, but it is a phenomenon itself.

But if the metric of time belongs to what is open for empirical research, we do not know whether all of what is important about it is already known. The empirical story of time is not closed, but goes on. And we have no reason to stop with Einstein's theories of relativity. With Heisenberg's uncertainty principle, the quantization of time and space is given, i.e. the fact that it is meaningless to think of times shorter than the Planck-time of 10^{-43} sec and lengths shorter than the Planck-length of 10^{-33} meters. What are the consequences for the ontology of time? Does it mean that the (objectified) time subsists quantized in time-atoms? Does time not flow but drip or leap? Are wayformational lines not constant explications of becoming, but rather does all becoming happen in jumps? All this is possible. But since the answer to this question is dependent on empirical knowledge, ideas like these should not be ontologized. A further reason to refrain from hasty ontologizations is that the theories of relativity and quantum mechanics cannot yet be coherently bound together in a single theory,[50] despite all attempts to do so. Nevertheless, this empirical

50 Cf. THIMANN, T., Suche nach dem Heiligen Gral, here 118f.

insight is not philosophically useless. Quantum mechanics has implications for the individuation of objects. The empirical proof that EPR-experiments are actually working[51] shows that the entangled quanta and the apparatuses of measurement cannot be conceived as particular, spatiotemporally divided entities. The consequence is radical: time, including its topological character, cannot be the fundamental relation of individual things. Time is not the basal constituent of entities.[52]

One of the suggested attempts for combining the theories of relativity and quantum mechanics is a theory called 'loop quantum gravity'. One of its points for our use here is that space and time (in their measurements) are consequently seen as aspects of the developing physical happening (illustratable in so called quanta-foams).[53] The metric of time does not have a primordial character here, either.

10.7 Excursus: the Misunderstanding of the Theory of the Entropic Reduction of the Irreversibility of Time

An attempt to solve another problem in the philosophy of time by evoking empirically the metrics of time is the problem of the irreversibility of time, also called the problem of time's arrow. Some have tried to solve this problem by means of thermodynamics and the entropy-principle. The argument has several steps – but all rely on serious misunderstandings of the nature of entropy.

First, one must assume that entropy is a measure of chaos or disorder. If then, in closed systems, entropy increases with time, disorder or chaos will also increase. This is a picture of entropy that has been abused in perhaps more than a thousand ways by philosophy, theology, anthropology, sociology, politics, and ethics,[54] but it is, at best, a secondary, purely illustrative expression of entropy. The genuine definition of physics does not need a concept like disorder. Entropy deals neither with information, nor structures of order and disorder, but what is really at stake is an increase of the *possible* (*microscopic*)

51 Cf. Einstein, A./Podolsky, B./Rosen, N., EPR; Zeilinger, A./Weihs, G./Jennewein, T./Aspelmeyer, M., Happy Centenary.

52 Cf. Mühling, M., Liebesgeschichte Gott, 202–215.

53 Cf. Thiemann, T., Loop Quantum Gravity; Thimann, T., Suche nach dem Heiligen Gral.

54 van Kampen, N.G., Entropie, gives some popular examples. In theology you can find such a misuse in Pannenberg, W., ST II (engl.), 96f. Though Pannenberg realizes, unlike Hawking (*vide infra*), that time is not dependent on entropy. But by binding together entropy with evil in terms of Rom 8,20, he slips up: he mistakes entropy for a rate of disorder. We will come back to this mishandling in the second volume.

states in a closed system.[55] If one wants to consider entropy philosophically in a manner that satisfies the physicists' definition, one would do better by using concepts from the realm of modal logic than concepts like chaos or cosmos.

The second misunderstanding regarding entropy is the assumption that entropy is a theory about the course of time, i.e. a theory about the B-series of time going from the past and extending into the future. Presupposing these misunderstandings, the following argument would be possible: entropy, a measure of disorder, increases in time. Therefore, the irreversibility of time is identical with increase of entropy. If one assumes a cosmological model that does not expect the heat-death of the world, but a re-collapse and the big crunch, it is sometimes assumed that in a contracting universe entropy would be reversed (i.e. entropy would decrease in time, so that order would increase). The argument is now that in such a contracting world, time's arrow should also be reversed, so that we would find an inverse of the irreversibility of time, running not from the past via the present into the future, but from future via the present into the past. If one likes, one could also add temporal theories of causality to this picture. Then we would have constructed a world in which causes would follow effects, not *vice versa*. The construction of abstract scenarios like these can be found in prominent cases like Stephen Hawking's *A Brief History of Time* (but interestingly, he later refrained from mentioning it):[56]

55 Cf. van Kampen, N.G., Entropie; Lebowitz, J.L., Time's Arrow and Boltzmann's Entropy. Entropy can easily be illustrated as an increase of chances: Let W be the number of possible assignments of a gas distribution within the microscopic arrangement of gas molecules (without gravitational interaction) in a room. Case A: In a room there is gas but only in one half (e.g. on the floor). Case B: There is gas all over the room. The number of possible arrangements of molecules is logically higher in case B, so that $W_B > W_A$. So W is – and so is the entropy – in case B higher than in case A. The molecules in B have, in a way, more space to move than the molecules in A. So you could also define entropy as the rate of freedom instead of rate of disorder, cf. van Kampen, N.G., Entropie, 7f. See also Russell, R.J., Entropy and Evil, 458, who holds that the fact that entropy in relation to events and the figures created by them are parasitical, in analogy to Augustine's definition of the evil as *privatio boni*, which is not correct. What is correct, is that it is not possible to speak about entropy without molecules and their movements, their possible and real arrangements. They can in fact be called "parasitical" metaphorically – but then every attribute of something in connection to that something is parasitical: the green in connection to the plant, the length in connection to the measuring stick, etc. Though even more problematic is that Russell draws on the *privatio boni* by analogy, because again this draws entropy near to disorder and evil.

56 Hawking's idea is here motivated by his cosmological ploy of designing a universe with an imaginary time, which can be done without singularities. The desire to communicate this physical speculation with thermodynamics and the gereral experience of time is probably what leads to Hawking's religion of time, which can be observed here.

> The explanation that is usually given as why we don't see broken cups gathering themselves together off the floor and jumping back onto the table is that it is forbidden by the second law of thermodynamics. This says that in any closed system disorder, or entropy, always increase with time. [...] An intact cup on the table is a state of high order, but a broken cup on the floor is a disordered state. One can go readily from the cup on the table in the past to the broken cup on the floor in the future, but not the other way around. The increase of disorder or entropy with time is one example of what is called an arrow of time, something that distinguishes the past from the future, giving direction to time. There are at least three different arrows of time. First, there is the thermodynamic arrow of time, the direction of time in which disorder or entropy increases. Then, there is the psychological arrow of time. This is the direction in which we feel time passes, the direction in which we remember the past but not the future. Finally, there is the cosmological arrow of time. This is the direction of time in which the universe is expanding rather than contracting. [...] I shall argue that the psychological arrow is determined by the thermodynamic arrow, and that these two arrows necessarily always point in the same direction. [...] However, a strong thermodynamic arrow is necessary for intelligent life to operate. [...] Thus, intelligent life could not exist in the contracting phase of the universe. This is the explanation of why we observe that the thermodynamic and cosmological arrows of time point in the same direction.[57]

The mistake here is not only conceiving of entropy as a concept of disorder instead of as a category of possibilities, but also to see entropy as constitutively bound to time, with the mistaken conclusion that there would be a reciprocal constitution between the two and time – in its measurement or as a whole – that would be reducible to entropy. However, the relation to time in the definition of entropy is in fact only given in an indirect manner, because it is not a theory about time, but a theory about the transition between different states of a physical system or a theory that compares different systems. An example may illustrate this: Imagine two closed systems, S1 und S2, which occur at the same time. Imagine that all of the possible states where the molecules are located in space (i.e. all possible and un-actualized as well as all possible and actualized states) are finite (that is the condition that it is a closed system). In S1 there is a specific ratio between possible actualized states and possible, non-actualized states. In S2, which is nearly identical to S1, there is also a specific ratio between possible actualized and possible, non-actualized states. The only difference is that in S2 there are more actualized states and therefore less possible and non-actualized states than in S1. The principle of entropy, which is the second law of thermodynamics, says nothing more than that S1 has a higher amount of entropy than S2. In this example, we do not need to talk about time in order to talk about entropy. If you imagine S1 and S2 as two different systems at the

57 HAWKING, S.W., Brief History of Time, 148f.; 155f.

same time, then the one has more entropy than the other. You can also imagine, that S1 and S2 are not different systems, but different possible states of one system. Then we would get a theory of transition, according to which it is more probable that S2 (with less entropy and more defined actual states) will be transformed into S1 (with increased entropy and more possible, non-actual states), without intervention from outside the system, than the other way around. Only if one defines the sequence of transitions from one possible state of the system to another one as 'time' (e.g. as the B-series), would entropy be bound to time. It is *possible* to draw this connection, but there is no necessity to do so given the physical concept of entropy. But then, there is no necessity to define time's irreversibility by the physical concept of entropy.

Phenomenologically, the irreversibility of time is given by nothing but a combination of the experience of the experience of time in protention and retention in a specific presence of movement, and the B-series of the past and its structure anticipated in every possible protention, i.e. for every possible future experience of the experience of time. It is not necessary to see irreversibility grounded in an objectified A-series. And there is absolutely no necessity to look for a physical reduction of time to entropy. But it is not only not necessary, but also invites an important counter-argument: the concept of entropy is constitutively bound to the concept of the physical system. But this concept of a system cannot be transferred to the phenomenological perception of movement. If one does so, then one would always have to conceive of movement as the property of unmoved entities (like molecules) in a system (e.g. an environment). But in this case, one would have to reject the constitutively relational character of movement. In fact, however, the occurrence of movement is a narrantic occurrence, in which the moved and environment are not given, but emerge and form themselves reciprocally and are constitutively entangled.

10.8 The Narrative Handling of Narrantic Time

In the previous sections, we asked how the manifold phenomena of time – including the experience of the experience of time as the presence of the past, presence of the future and presence of the present, the experience of the topology of time with its aspects of the A-series and the B/C-series, and the experience of the metric of time – can be grounded in a narrantic foundation, and how they can be derived from primary stories. All these phenomena have the passive character of a *pathos*. And, like all *pathos*, they evoke a (cultural) response. Of course, we made use of this response in previous chapters, but only implicitly. Therefore, it is now time to have an explicit look at this response.

The *pathos* of time is given by the phenomenon that one cannot perceive oneself without being intermeshed in-between the narrantic mesh Our active response, our handling of time, consists in a narrative reconfiguration of time on the level of secondary narrations and narratives. For this reason, our handling of time is also an important aspect of the experience of time, which also co-determines the other aspects of the experience of time.

By using the term 'narrative reconfiguration of time' we refer to Ricœur, who has described this phenomenon. Nevertheless, our own approach is not Ricœur's, but is materially different. We should explain this a little bit further:

Ricœur's description of the relationship between the narrantic level (called a 'prenarrative structure'[58]) and the tellable, second-order narrations, use the arc or spiral of the three stages of mimesis (Mimesis I, II and III). He wants to show that:

> between the activity of narrating a story and the temporal character of human experience there exists a correlation that is not merely accidental but that presents a transcultural form of necessity. To put it another way, time becomes human to the extent that it is articulated through a narrative mode, and narrative attains its full meaning when it becomes a condition of temporal existence.[59]

On the one hand, this basic claim is less ambitious than our own claim, while at the same time, being more ambitious. Ricœur cannot meet our description of the relationship of experiencing time and narrativity, because he sees the experience of time at best founded in a pre-narrative phenomenon, whereas on this level we have anchored the genuine concept of a story as a narrantic one. Therefore, Ricœur does not present a narrative ontology in the proper sense. In another respect, however, Ricœur is more ambitious: he hopes to get a solution of bridging the gap between Augustine's *distentio* of time and *intentio* of eternity by our cultural handling of time on the secondary level of narrations:

> To understand the story is to understand how and why the successive episodes led to this conclusion, which, far from being foreseeable, must finally be acceptable, as congruent with the episodes brought together by the story. It is this "followability" of a story that constitutes the poetic solution of the paradox of distention and intention. The fact that the story can be followed converts the paradox into a living dialectic.[60]

The first sentence of this quotation, although it is very important for the understanding of narrativity and especially for the understanding of dramatic coherence, as we will see later (ch. 16), is nevertheless more or less innocuous. Nothing more is said than what is necessary merely to understand a composed story. The second sentence,

58 Cf. Ricœur, P., Time and Narrative I, 59.

59 Ricœur, P., Time and Narrative I, 52.

60 Ricœur, P., Time and Narrative I, 66.

however, claims that this followability of stories is the solution of the paradox of *distentio* and *intentio* through *poiesis*. But in Augustine, there is not simply a paradox between *distentio* and *intentio*, but a real antinomy. And this antinomy can only be solved by the *intentio* itself, i.e. by eternity as timelessness. Every possible solution to the problem is therefore nothing but a formulation or definition of what eternity should be. What Ricœur is therefore really doing is defining, against Augustine, an alternative view of eternity: eternity is the followability of a story. And this claim is a very ambitious one, much more so than what we are doing here. We simply want to show that temporality presupposes narrativity (not *vice versa*). We will also see, when we deal with the concept of eternity in volume 2, that Ricœur's understanding is also more ambitious than our own understanding of eternity. Ricœur's 'synthesis of the heterogeneous'[61] thereby becomes a surrogate of eternity, and human *poiesis* becomes the creator of eternity.

Apart from this main difference, there are other differences and similarities. We share with Ricœur the opinion that a phenomenology of time must be a narrative one, and we also share the idea that human secondary narrations lead to a reconfiguration of our experience of time. However, by this we mean something different. Ricœur's concept of the narrative is too closely aligned with the idea of narration as a species of language and its Aristotelian description. Although Ricœur must modify Aristotle by showing that the dramatic as well as the epic must be seen as subcategories of the narrative,[62] he cannot grasp the lyric as a narrative subset.[63] Therefore, Ricœur's understanding of narrations is far too narrow, despite its occasional expansion, as when he refers to Schapp.[64]

Ricœur describes the reconfiguration of time with the help of the entanglement of *mimesis I*, *mimesis II* and *mimesis III*. With mimesis, Ricœur refers to Aristotle and he correctly describes *mimesis* not simply as imitation, but also as the presentation of an action. Nevertheless, Ricœur translates mimesis as 'imitation', and thereby he extends the representationalist paradigm instead of transgressing it. Therefore, the logic of action is privileged and there we cannot follow.

Mimesis I mean the presuppositions of telling a myth; *mimesis II* the narration of a myth and *mimesis III* its effects in our life-world. Therefore, an arc leads from the perception of time via the telling of the myth to time reconfigured. Strictly speaking, what Ricœur is arguing against is neither an arc, nor a 'circle,' nor a 'spiral,'[65] but thinking in stages or levels. We, however, conceive the narrations and narratives of the second level only as a special case of narrantic becoming itself. Therefore, the relationship between the cultural reconfiguration of time to the experience of time is the same as the relationship of tellable stories to life, as described in ch. 8.7: Between the two there is no rupture, but a continuity, which can be conceived as a knot in the mesh of narrantic time. There is no transition into *allo genos*.

Ricœur's main interest is a more fundamental one than the concrete reconfigured experiences of time that are enabled by our handling of time. He wants to talk about the paradoxes of time, which can be reduced to three basic paradoxes: the paradox between phenomenal and cosmological time, which he sees exemplified in Augustine's

---

61 Ricœur, P., Time and Narrative I, 66. 83. 142. 170. 216. 229.
62 Cf. Ricœur, P., Time and Narrative I, 31f.
63 Cf. Ricœur, P., Time and Narrative I, 81.
64 Cf. Ricœur, P., Time and Narrative I, 74.
65 Ricœur, P., Time and Narrative I, 71f.

treatment of time,[66] the paradox of the totality or totalization of time, and the paradox of the understandability or ineffability of time itself. The answer to the first paradox is his concept of narrative identity, gained by his reflection on the movement of mimesis I–III, which he regards as the solution of *poiesis*.[67] We will return to Ricœur's concept of narrative identity later (ch.19.4). Here, we must ask whether Ricœur is doing anything other than describing the simple fact that every narrative grasp at narrantic becoming is simply a part of the narrantic becoming itself, or, the other way around, that any narrantic becoming is only accessible through secondary narrativity. If this diagnosis is correct, then Ricœur's understanding of narrativity, acquired through dialogue with Aristotle, is too narrow. Ricœur's second paradox of the totalization or totality of time only deals with a pseudo-problem. The totalization is only necessary with the problem of eternity in the background. Since time and eternity are in fact constitutively bound together, this problem itself is not a pseudo-problem. But in Ricœur it becomes a pseudo-problem, because he claims that there is only an imperfect mediation[68] of the unity between time and story by narrativity, while at once stressing that these inadequacies cannot be treated as a failure,[69] if one remembers the maxim that any theory has to know its limits.[70] This notion shows that Ricœur holds the opinion that totalizations are impossible *a priori*. But then the problem of the totalization of time becomes a pseudo-problem and all of his thinking in *Time and Narrative III* are only illustrations of this general problem. Of course, one could evaluate the case differently. As a matter of fact, from the beginning, Ricœur only constructs a surrogate of eternity, as we have seen. Does this mean that his true interest is totalization? Is his commitment to the impossibility of totalizations only a pseudo-commitment? If one holds to this interpretation, Ricœur's whole conception would, from the beginning onward, be a variation of implicit theology, driven by a personal interest. This view might be supported by Ricœur's note that he wants to maintain against Heidegger's sorrow in the face of being to death, the unconcern (or carefreeness) in face of one's own death.[71] In respect to Ricœur's description of the last paradox, the paradox of the principal ineffability of time[72] – therefore against his thesis that a narrative approach also has to fail here – no basic objection should be made, but we have to describe the paradox a little bit more precisely: It is not time that in the end has an apophatic character, but the narrantic itself; it is not time that is not tellable, but it is the mesh of primary stories itself that cannot, in the end, be told narratively. While it might sound strange, it is only an implication of the basic thesis that stories are lived before they can be told. The distinction between the narrantic becoming and secondary narrativity implies not only that secondary narrativity provides a privileged access to narrantic becoming by secondary narrativity, but also that narrantic becoming is ultimately ineffable for humans.

There are a lot of differences between Ricœur's treatment of the problem and our own. Nevertheless, Ricœur delivers a series of detailed observations that remain

66 Cf. Ricœur, P., Time and Narrative III, 243f.

67 Cf. Ricœur, P., Time and Narrative III, 246–249.

68 Cf. Ricœur, P., Time and Narrative III, 250.256.259.

69 Cf. Ricœur, P., Time and Narrative III, 260.

70 Cf.Ricœur, P., Time and Narrative III, 260.

71 Cf. Ricœur, P., Time and Narrative III, 68.254.

72 Cf. Ricœur, P., Time and Narrative III, 260–274.

important. In general, his strength consists not so much in providing a comprehensive theory than in offering a lot of singular observations.

How, then, does the narrative reconfiguration of narrantic time work?

First, and primarily, any particular person and equiprimordially any community has the task of finding a mediation between the experience of measurable and the experience of topological time. Any attempt to deal with the topology of time, i.e. to deal with the sequence of events, must be somehow mediated by a measurement that is already formed and must be formed. Under pre-eschatological conditions, there is no unmeasured experience of time. Due to the fact that events of a life-story emerge only in the frame of a measurement that must be shaped, the phenomena of time pressure and boredom emerge. Often in our post-modern societies a diastasis emerges, since the experienced events are oriented based on intentionally chosen aims in the mode of transport. But the mode of wayfaring is also not free from similar experiences of a diastasis of metric and topology, since also wayfaring is not free of ends, but dependent on attentionally discovered particular goals as affordances of the way itself, which means that the problem of the diastasis between metric and topology cannot be ignored. *Perfect* wayfaring in the mesh would counterfactually presuppose a measureless world.

Second, secondary narrations have *inherent metrics*. Normally the inherent measurements of secondary narrations remain unnoticed, since we never live in single secondary narration, but in a mesh of secondary narrations. The easiest way to observe the inherent measurements of secondary narrations is to draw our attention to artificial products. Here three metrics meet each other and constitute the inherent measurement: the more or less elaborated telling of episodes, the measurement of reality as it is presented in the fictive, narrative world, and the metric of the recipient. With this threefold relation we do not obtain a quantifiable metric, but we experience the phenomena of stretched time or contracted time, which, depending on the disposition of the recipient, can be experienced as stressful or as boring.

For example, the metrics of Wagner's operas, like *Tristan and Isolde*, have a very restricted scope in their fictive world, including a lot of repetitions of sequences, episodes, sentences, etc. For the recipient's measurement, this leads to an experience of stretched time: time runs essentially much slower than usual. A similar technique of time-modulation for the recipient is used in Tarkovsky's films, where modern action-movies, including their fast cuts, are instantiations of the opposite treatment of time.

Third, there are the quasi-natural measurements. By this we mean that we are always bound to a series of natural movements of becoming, including their inherent metrics, that must be synchronized by us – independently of whether we have insight into the ideal of the clock or not. Here we find at least three metrics that must be personally and, equiprimordially, communally synchronized: the astronomical metrics, especially the change of day and night, the meteorological metrics of seasons and vegetation, and the circadian rhythms of sleep phases.

Fourth, there is the cultural measurement and its dynamics. Here the problem lies in the synchronization of the many cultural metrics with the astronomical metrics through the creation and use of calendars.

Fifth, there is the metric of one's own life-story. The personal life-story is perceived with different measurements and also from the perspective of the other, different phases of one's life are told in stories of varying intensity, whereas other phases remain unmentioned. Of course, we find here a lot of personal as well as cultural differences. But what is really significant, apart from these differences, is that there is an invariant rhythm of metrics that can be observed in all peoples of all cultures. Research into autobiography has shown that the arrangement of memories in different phases of life follows a *life span retrieval curve* that has a *reminiscence bump*:[73] Memories of episodes from between the ages of 10 and 30 years are accessible to an above-average degree later in life, whereas the time before and after those ages is underrepresented. Besides other factors, a decisive reason for this is that the experiences had during this time are new and highly formative for the particular person and the formation of their autobiographical identity. This notion of experience fits with the experience that many different and emotionally positive narrative episodes within the same period of culturally measured time leads to a greater capacity to remember them.

Sixth, there are the various dynamics for configuring the cultural life-worlds through technical means. In principle, this is 'only' a special case of the cultural metrics mentioned in point four. Nevertheless, there is a practical reason for treating this problem separately. The problem is that modernity accelerates time, while the possible methods for deceleration that have also become a theme of popular considerations.[74] Perhaps the best description still goes back to Heidegger,[75] and here we refer to the concrete description Martin Wendte[76] has given to this tradition: Modern cultural techniques have led to an inversion of the experience of time and space. Whereas in premodern eras,

73 Cf. RUBIN, D.C./WETZLER, S.E./NEBES, R.D., Autobiographical Memory.
74 Cf. e.g. ROSA, H., Beschleunigung und Entfremdung.
75 Cf. HEIDEGGER, M., Das Ding, 157.
76 Cf. WENDTE, M., Raumzeitimplosion und Schöpfungsfülle, especially 69.

to bridge spatial distances one needed a very large amount of time, today spatial distances can be bridged in a shorter amount of time due to the modern means of transportation and digital communication like the internet. Space, which was in premodern times less at our disposal is now at our disposal. But the abundant resources of time in premodern eras now appear accelerated and thereby not at our disposal, but independent, remaining on inaccessible, techno-cultural clock generators. If one orients the cultural formation of the metrics of time on the model of transport – and no one can escape transport – the intentional logic of transport in the network, which is basically a timeless or simultaneous logic, implies that all tasks of life or one's job have to be done in short time, ideally instantly. But at the same time, the quasi-natural rhythms of metrics of time persist. Therefore, we hear – mostly in our free time – the imperative to shape our life according to the model of wayfaring. But of course, it is a contradiction to be a wayfarer on demand. Therefore, free time also ends in transport, and one tries to put as many as possible adventurous experiences in as short a time span as possible. The ethical implications, which are not our present theme, are manifold.

This description of our narrative handling of time is not complete. It would be easy to add more phenomena. In this realm, narrative approaches are very fruitful. This approach can be seen for example, by Albrecht Koschorke's view on the relationship between secondary narrations and the experience and formation of time.

Koschorke describes how stories structure and constitute social time. First, there is the narratological aspect of the fictive world. To tell a story constitutes the sequence of events (the B/C-series of time), simply by the fact that each story sets a beginning and an ending (including in the case of an open ending), and by the fact that the in-between sequences are structured according to a plot and sub-plots. To build a plot always means to build time. Since the episodes are not bound together arbitrarily, but meaningfully and in a consequential manner, the inherent time of the fictive world appears. In setting a beginning and an ending, any possible story is imbedded in a larger cultural frame of narrations, which structure cultural time on the narratological level.[77] Every narration also influences the A-series. In a factual telling, hearing or reading – i.e. communicating – the presence of the participants is marked, and their perceiving and their expecting happens only in the light of the communicated stories, which leads to an alteration of the perception of the B/C-series of the actual world. Thereby a reconfiguration of time is given, and here Koschorke borrows this term from Ricœur.[78] What is important for Koschorke is that any possible experience of the present is always a

77 Cf. Koschorke, A., Wahrheit und Erfindung, 61–66.
78 Cf. Koschorke, A., Wahrheit und Erfindung, 216.

mixture of reality and fiction, not only regarding the future, but also regarding the past, so that this amounts to a 'fiction of facts', in the words of Kosselleck.[79]

The task of this chapter is not to describe these various phenomena.[80] Its task was simply to show that our handling of time is also essentially a narrative one. The examples we have given have shown this. Whereas in the other phenomena of the experience of time the narrantic aspect is the important one, in the realm of our handling time, secondary narrativity plays the major role.

10.9 Different Phenomena or Different Aspects of a Single Phenomenon?

The task of this chapter has been achieved in the previous sub-chapters. We showed that the different aspects of the experience of time –the protentional-retentional experience of the experience of time, the experience of the topology of time, the experience of the metric of time, and our handling of time – can be conceived in narrative ways. Thereby, we have shown that the traditional idea that stories and events happen in time, is incorrect and has to be reversed. Attempts to grasp phenomena of time without a narrative means is fundamentally anti-phenomenal. This attempt is an important contribution of a narrative ontology. However, this is not an ontology of time, since we remained close to the phenomena and their experiences. An ontology of time is impossible without a simultaneous inquiry into eternity, since time and eternity are reciprocally bound together. However, in this volume we are still unable to talk about eternity. Therefore, the main task in the relationship between time and eternity has been solved.

However, the reader might ask a final question of an ontological nature regarding our understanding of time. We started not with the unity of time but with different phenomena of time. Are these different phenomena? Or are these different aspects of a single phenomenon? In both cases, we will have presupposed a kind of unity of time, in the latter case explicitly, in the former implicitly, since also these different phenomena are called phenomena of *time*, if it is not the pure equivocation of contingent, unrelated phenomena.

Does this mean that we have to subsume time under *one* concept, similar to Ricœur's second paradox? Does not the description of time with narrative means presupposes unity, since narrativity consists not only in a pure sequence

79 Cf. KOSELLECK, R., Fiktion und geschichtliche Wirklichkeit, 50.
80 Cf. in addition KOSCHORKE, A., Wahrheit und Erfindung, 203–286.

of events but in a meaningful connection? And would this meaningful connection, following Ricœur, only be understandable from the end of the story? We have to reject this last assumption. In the case of Ricœur, the mistake is that he refers to only a special case of narrativity, which might be frequent in our culture, which might be exemplified by Aristotle, but is not universal. In order to understand the meaningful connection between the episodes of a story, one does not need the knowledge of the end. If this were the case, no one could learn to follow rules,[81] no one would be able to participate in rites or become part of a tradition. A significant example of a culture, in which the telling of stories is an essential cultural technique without the idea of an ending for stories isn't given by the anthropologist Natalia Novikova.

> Novikova writes about the Khanty in Siberia and their institutionalized tradition of telling stories. In the evening, a narrator tells a story until the last hearer has fallen asleep. The next day, the story is continued, without filling in the individual gaps of the recipients.[82]

What is also interesting is that the word for 'story' is the same as the word for 'path' or 'way' in Khanty.[83] The conception of stories follows here the mode of wayfaring in the meshwork, not the mode of transport in the network.[84] The understandability of stories is, against Ricœur and Aristotle, *not* provided by their ending. The 'payoff' of a story is only a temporary one that serves the continuation of the telling, which cannot be closed. The model of understanding stories through their endings is a first step toward the inversion of wayfaring into transport, and its last step is conceptual abstraction.

Let us apply these insights to the idea of the unity of time. Any conceptual unity of time cannot be presupposed; any such concept could only be given from the end of the narrative description of time, i.e. from eternity as the other of time. Understandings of eternity, however, are as divergent as possible, as we will see in the second volume. By no means is the finality of stories an implication of eternity. On the contrary, we saw above that the experience of the presence of the future, and especially awaiting the relatively-retrospectively surprising, is primary. Such an interpretation of surprises reveals that whatever comes from the horizon of the future, which seems to meld with the

81 Cf. Wittgenstein on following rules or rather on learning rules, which can be described as participation in open narrative events, in Wittgenstein, L., Philosophical Investigations, 219.

82 Cf. Novikova, N., Self Government, 83.

83 Cf. Novikova, N., Self Government, 83.

84 Cf. Ingold, T., Lines, 90.

undetermined horizon of eternity, is never inferable: new possibilities for the continuation of stories are passively given in order to act anew. For the experience of time, it means that the phenomena described in this chapter are aspects of our becoming in the meshwork. That is, the only thing uniting them. Any potentially uniform concept of time would be nothing but an abstraction. If there is a unity of time at all, it would not be visible in theories, but in models.

If we combine the picture of the A-series with the picture of the B-series, we get a picture of the point of the present wandering through time or the picture of time as future running towards the fixed point of the present into the past. Pictures like these are not wrong, as long as one conceives of them as models, as metaphor-based ideas. Alternative metaphors are also conceivable, like the picture of the enfolding of the past and future out of the present, which more resembles our experience of the experience of time in protention and retention.[85] These pictures and metaphors do not act alone. Rather, they specify different aspects of our experience of the experience of time (A-series) and the experience of time (B/C-series). Such a prefered model is our model of the intertwined threads of a narrative mesh, of wayformational lines.

85 Cf. put differently, FÖRSTER-BEUTHAN, Y., Zeiterfahrung und Ontologie, 189.

CHAPTER 11

Narration and Space

In our analysis of time, we discovered that the phenomenally basic structure of time was given in bodily movement. Movement does not only mean a change in time, but also a change in place. Furthermore, we saw that this aspect of the topology of time, which with McTaggart we called the B/C-series, presupposes a spatial idea of time, as is also presupposed if one speaks of a 'topology' – a 'doctrine of places' – of time. It seems that the concept of space is at least equi-primordial, which is also the case in Kant, who treats space together with time as our *a priori* forms of sensible intuition.[1] Perhaps space is also more basic than time, since the idea of the B/C-series of time uses a spatial metaphor. Like time and eternity are insolubly bound together, so are space and infinity. It seems that space is much more easily connected to infinity than time to eternity. With respect to time, we learned that we can only speak narratively about time, and that narrativity is primary over time. Therefore, we can ask whether this is also the case in the relationship between narrativity and space.

11.1 An Old Controversy: Container, Relation – or Continuum?

If space is an *a priori* form of our sensible intuition, we would have immediate access to it since it would belong to the presuppositions of perception. But even if this were the case, two questions would remain. First, it would be possible that space could *also* belong to the realm of *a posteriori* perceptions. Then it would be an object of empirical, i.e. physical, cognition. Second, if space is also an *a priori* form of sensible intuition, then the question of whether we *have* to think spatially would be solved, whereas the question of *how* to think about space would remain. Let's treat the second question first: On the one hand, one can conceive of space as an empty container of all that happens, which is either finite or infinite. We can find this idea of space in numerous cultures and philosophies,[2] foremost in Newton's physics.[3] In this case, empty space would exist as a kind of background-metric of physical occurrences. On the other side, one can deny that something like empty container or background-metric,

1 Cf. KANT, I., Critique of Pure Reason, B46–57.
2 Cf. MÜHLING, M., Handbook of Christian Eschatology, 108–111.
3 Cf. MÜHLING, M., Handbook of Christian Eschatology, 109.

 | DOI:10.30965/9783846765852_012

be it finite or infinite, exists at all by conceiving of space as the epitome of relations, or more precisely, of spatial, i.e. simultaneous, relations. This conception can also be found in many cultures and philosophies. The opposition between a container-like understanding of space and a relational understanding of space can be illustrated through the letters of Leibniz and Samuel Clarke.[4] At this point, we are not interested in the specific problems and its possibilities of a solution regarding spatial phenomena and regarding the idea of different infinities. The reader who is interested in these themes may find some preliminary sources below.[5] It is right to assume that the relational understanding of time is more appropriate. Nevertheless, the history of thinking about space shows this controversy was never really *solved*, but in the last instance *sublated* by conceiving of space – or more precisely space-time – as a *continuum*. The paradigm understanding of space-time as a continuum is Einstein's general theory of relativity. Here, time is nothing but the fourth dimension of space, and at the same time space is no longer needed as a kind of background-metric anymore.[6] The conception of space as a continuum overrides the seeming opposition between a relational and a container-like understanding of space, insofar as it uses important features of both models. From the relational understanding, it derives the influence of spatial objects on space – the events, or masses, in space determine the shape of space itself, whether it is flat, negative or positive curved. But the container-like model also provides a decisive feature to the concept of the continuum itself, since the relational distance between two spatially-separated masses is assumed to be empty but existent. Imagine a world consisting only of two masses, their surfaces, and their spatial separation. In such a case, it is important how far the masses are separated in order to know something about the specific shape of the space of this world. Theoretically, the distance in between is made up of infinite points, on which masses could possibly exist. And further, this is actually conceivable: if there was a third mass in between the two others, the curvature of the space of this world would be altered, but nothing would be changed when conceiving of this space as a continuum. Imagine a continuum without any curvature of the three dimensions of space. Such a continuum would amount exactly to what is meant by the model of space as the infinite container and its background-metric. Therefore, it is logical that Newtonian physics is in no way falsified

---

4 Cf. CLARKE, S./LEIBNIZ, G.W., Briefwechsel mit Leibniz, 72.

5 Cf. EVERS, D., Raum – Zeit – Materie; JOOSS, E., Raum; MÜHLING, M., Eschatologie, 101–122; WÜTHRICH, M., Raum Gottes. Ein systematisch-theologischer Versuch, Raum zu denken.

6 Cf. EVERS, D., Raum – Zeit – Materie, 42–63.

by the general theory of relativity. It is only one of general relativity's special cases, only valid for a non-factual world.

According to the standard model of cosmology using the Einstein-Friedmann equations, this continual understanding of the four-dimensional space-time is not without problems. Under specific, theoretical, circumstances the relationship between the masses and the curvature of space has the character of singularities. Whereas the curvature of time is infinite, the metric of space (including the metric of time) amounts to a point with infinite mass and density. Singularities like these appear in the standard model of cosmology as singularities of beginning, in some variations as singularities of ending, and also during the cosmological development as singularities in the space-time continuum itself: as black holes, which in the meantime are far more than a purely theoretical assumption.[7] Such singularities are somehow aesthetically unsatisfactory, since precisely those equations that enable the order of the continuum are not valid in the case of the singularities. Independently, these singularities transcend our imagination – they do not fit with Kant's theory of space and time as *a priori* forms of sensible intuition – and they have the problem of a cosmological order that can be described by specific equations that lead to its abrogation in the case of the singularities. The continuum is quasi disrupted or disturbed. There is a very simple trick to deal with such a disturbed order. One does not have to introduce new masses *ad hoc* into this order, but one simply has to invent a new continuum *ad hoc* – a new order – including new metrics in which the space-time continuum is embedded. In cosmology, Stephen Hawking has done so by suggesting a new spatiotemporal coordinate, the so-called 'imaginary time,'[8] that can only be expressed through the help of imaginary numbers. In this new, higher, continuum, the singularities of the old space-time are only 'singularities of coordinates', i.e. not singularities at all, like the North Pole and the South Pole of the Earth are in no way different from any other place, although longitude and latitude merge to a single point without any longitude east or west. Nevertheless, the North Pole cannot be distinguished from any other point of the sphere. Hawking's suggestion is purely speculative and one should not regard it as an example of sophisticated physics, which would only be the case if this suggestion altered the understanding of the empirical state of affairs. Indeed, Hawking tried to look for such empirical data, but was not in the end successful. For our interests, something else is important. The old controversy between a relational and a container-like conception of space is sublated by the understanding of space as a continuum, which is more abstract

7 Cf. THIMANN, T., Suche nach dem Heiligen Gral, 118f.
8 Cf. HAWKING, S.W., Brief History of Time, 137–144.

in comparison to the relational and the container-like model. Nevertheless, it is useful for calculations. In the framework of this new, continual understanding of space, new problems appear, the singularities, which are something like contradictions of the model. In the classical continuum, these contradictions cannot be resolved. But they disappear by an extension of the continuum that embeds the continuum in another one on a higher level. Here, we have three possibilities, and we cannot decide which one is the case: 1. The contradictions of the continuum indicate that the continuum is embedded in a higher continuum without contradictions. 2. The contradictions of the continuum indicate that the theory does not really fit with reality – it is only a preliminary theory. 3. The contradictions of the continuum indicate gaps of coherence in the real world. What is interesting, however, is that this procedure of extending the continuum in cases of incoherence can be generalized with regard to a much more general concept of space than the four-dimensional, physical space-time. Needless to say, a more general concept of space is also a more abstract concept of space. Such an extension has been made in the history of philosophy and theology, long before Hawking used exactly the same procedure for speculative physics. Its paradigm is the philosophy of spaces or the philosophy of continua by Karl Heim.

11.2 Heim's Philosophy of Spaces as Continua

In the framework of his philosophy of religion and theology, Karl Heim, one of the first theologians in Germany and worldwide to shape the dialogue between theology and the natural sciences, used the concept of space as fundamental for his system. Heim regards the concept of space as very powerful, with the consequence that he makes it fundamental to the philosophy of religion as well as in the apologetic dialogues of the 20th century, to demonstrate the plausibility of theological thinking to the cultured among the critics of religion. The intelligibility of religiosity, whatever that may be, is, according to Heim, dependent on the concept of space. Another reason Heim makes the concept of space basic is to combine such different interests as Kant, the phenomenological tradition, personalism, and the natural sciences. Heim claims to develop a philosophy of spaces as a continuation of Kant's doctrine of the forms of sensible intuition. Basically, he defines space as:

> A Space is every interminable continuum within which a manifold of different contents may be distinguished according to the special law of its structure.[9]

9 HEIM, K., God Transcendent, 60.

The advantage of this definition is that it can subsume physical and mathematical spaces, which can be expressed by measurements, and appearances, that cannot be expressed by measurements, since he speaks only of a material principle ordering principle, which is not necessarily quantifiable. On the basis of this definition, one must now distinguish material and dimensional limits, material and dimensional unity and plurality, material and dimensional relations of participation, a material and a dimensional meeting, a material and a dimensional cleavage, a material and a dimensional knowledge, etc.[10] Heim then develops a hierarchy of spaces of higher dimensions:

1. The simplest space in this sense is the 'process of time'.[11]
2. It is followed by the two-dimensional flat space and
3. the three-dimensional space of physical bodies. These three spaces, sometimes only the last two of them, can be subsumed in Heim's terminology under the concept of the 'object-space' (*Raum des Gewordenen*).[12]
4. The next level of spaces is the I-It-space. By this, Heim means that any idea of a space of objects (It) is only meaningful if it is bound to a space of a subject (I).
5. The I-Thou(-It)-space: In our time, one often finds the crudely mistaken assumption that the I-it relation, the relation between subject and object, is a complete one. Heim does not commit this mistake, but equiprimordially to the I-it space he sees the I-Thou Space. In this respect, Heim refers to the phenomenological tradition as well as to personalist philosophy.[13] The advantage is that no Thou can be objectified, since it cannot be reduced to an object in the space of physical bodies. It loves, together with the I, in its own space, non-objectifiable space. In order to show that there is indeed such a I-Thou spaces, Heim requires a lot of pages, which are worth reading.[14] Whereas the objective space of bodies is related to the past, since it can only contain things that have become (facts)[15] (and that is therefore always an abstraction), the I-Thou-It-space is the non-objectifiable space of presence (*nichtgegenständlicher Präsenzraum*),[16]

---

10 Cf. HEIM, K., God Transcendent, 71. 76f.

11 Cf. HEIM, K., God Transcendent, 60.

12 Cf. HEIM, K., God Transcendent, 116 (where the translation 'realm of the already-become' is used), 146 (where 'object-space is used), etc.

13 For Heim's theology of space cf. BEUTTLER, U., Gott und Raum.

14 Cf. HEIM, K., God Transcendent, 153–172; HEIM, K., Christian Faith and Natural Science, 35–150.

15 Cf. HEIM, K., Christian Faith and Natural Science, 104f.

16 Cf. HEIM, K., Glaube und Denken, 176. However, the earlier editions do not have these passages. In these earlier editions, from which the English translation is derived, Heim explicitly says that God cannot be described as a space and that God is beyond all spaces, cf. HEIM, K., God Transcendent, 211.

in which nothing that has become but there appears only dynamic becoming in constant change.

6. The super-polar space: The I-Though-It-space of presence is imbedded in a super-polar space, also called the super-polar primordial being (*überpolares Ursein*).[17]

What is important is that Heim's philosophy of spaces is sustained by a specific, epistemological principle: If one finds oneself in a specific space, in this space only material differences can be directly perceived, but not dimensional entanglements. A dimensional entanglement means that a state of affairs or point of a space can be completely conceived in midst of this space, whereas it at the same time it is also embedded in another space. From the perspective of one of these spaces, this state of entanglement appears only indirectly as a contradiction, a paradox, or as an either-or.[18] Heim uses Edwin Abbot's *Flatland* as a heuristic.[19] The either-or of the entanglement is solved if one is embedded in a space of higher order immediately, without any effort in thinking. Higher spaces (or higher dimensions, as we would perhaps preferably say today) cannot be disclosed rationally by myself as subject, but they have to be *disclosed passively* and *immediately*.[20] The reason is that a contradiction appearing in the framework of a specific space can have two causes: it can be an indication of its embeddedness in a space of higher order, but it can also be a simple incoherence. From the perspective of the lower-order space a determination is impossible; from the perspective of a higher-order space a determination is unnecessary, since the case is disclosed and already clear. In regard to the first three spaces, this epistemological principle can be applied without any difficulty, since these are on the one hand lower-order spaces of our lives and since the material principle of order of these spaces is a quantifiable one. But in the case of the I-It space and in the case of the I-Thou(-It)-space, problems emerge, since these are on the one hand spaces in which we are living, but that are not partial spaces of lower order of our lives, and on the other hand, since the material ordering principle of these spaces cannot be quantified. A shared feature of all these spaces is, according to Heim, that the ordering principle

17 This term can also only be found in the later, untranslated editions, cf. HEIM, K., Glaube und Denken, 202.

18 Cf. HEIM, K., God Transcendent, 56, 64–66, 88, 91, 98, 110, etc.

19 Cf. HEIM, K., God Transcendent, 53–56 with reference to ABBOT, E.A., Flatland.

20 Cf. HEIM, K., Glaube und Denken, 150. 205. 208. 211. 213. This insight is already there in the older editions, but not as explicit in the newer ones. Cf. HEIM, K., God Transcendent, 217–219.

of these spaces is a polar principle of a continuum.[21] The last space, however, identified with the transcendence or eternity of God – about which we must speak later (ch. 21) – is not polar, but super-polar. Nevertheless, one can see an important problem in Heim: what does polarity mean? Could it be that polarity and spatiality are – contrary to Heim's intentions – equivalent? The ordered manifold of an ordered continuum would therefore always be a polar continuum or a polar manifold. In this case, the concept of a continuum would be dependent on the concept of polarity, since polarity would be a necessary condition for a continuum.

Whether or not this is incoherent, or simply indicates that Heim's philosophy of spaces is mistaken, or whether this incoherence is intentionally construed by Heim, since it reflects Heim's above-mentioned epistemological principle of discovering spaces of higher order, cannot be definitively determined. I suppose, however, that the last possibility is the case. Concretely, Heim regards a special phenomenon as a contradiction, which indicates the disclosure of a non-objectifiable and non-polar, higher space in midst of the non-objectifiable I-Thou space: the phenomenon of prayer.[22] In further volumes, we will also have something to say about this. For our present interest, the only thing that is important is that Heim intentionally leads his philosophy of spaces to a point where it becomes contradictory. He does so by discovering in midst of the I-Thou-It-space an incoherence or a singularity that can be only seen as meaningful by suggesting that it is imbedded in a higher continuum, which does not have the features of a continuum. This notion has two advantages: On the one hand, Heim contrasts his solution to the problem of space with other solutions, and he is able to classify world-views and religions, including their differences for leadings one's life and ethics, along these lines.[23] On the other hand, he develops his cognitive philosophy of religion to a point where any solution can only appear through a theology of revelation. Heim's philosophy of continua is all in all very interesting – more than his answer in his theology of revelation.

Our interpretation of Heim's philosophy of spaces identifies the decisive difficulty in the concept of the super-polar, insofar as polarity cannot mean a specific kind of relationality, but relationality as such or at least a relation of order as such. Matthias

21 Cf. HEIM, K., Glaube und Denken, 179–184. This section is also missing in the older German and in the English versions.

22 Cf. HEIM, K., Glaube und Denken, 172–178. This section on prayer is also missing in the older German and in the English versions.

23 Cf. HEIM, K., Glaube und Denken, 185–202. This section is also missing in the older German and in the English versions.

Heesch has suggested a different interpretation.[24] He identifies polarity with the relation of objectivity, i.e. with the subject-object-relation. Under this presupposition there is indeed *for us* a super-polar, non-objective space, in which we are embedded and conceivable. However, this means that even from the divine perspective (which cannot be our perspective), this would allow God to be understood as an absolute subject, for which everything else has the character of objects. Thus understood, the same space that appears for us super-polar – our relation to God – would appear to Godself as polar or at least quasi-polar. This interpretation has the advantage that it uses the concept of polarity in order to shed light on the distinction between subject and object that Heim himself uses. However, it also has the disadvantage that the concepts of polarity do not add anything to the concept of objectivity and is, thus, superficial. In which case, the question is: why would Heim identify polarity with objectivity in the first place?

11.3 Problems of All Continua

Although a theological position of the 1990s claimed that the paradigm of the continuum is relational ontology *par excellence*,[25] the truth is quite different. In space understood as continuum, the opposition between container-like space paradigms and relational space paradigms is 'sublated,' which does not mean that the idea of the continuum combines both relation and container. Rather, the idea of the continuum is indifferent, and therefore can be applied to both paradigms. The reason is that the continuum is a higher level of abstraction in comparison to the relational and container-like understandings of space, through these are also abstractions. Nevertheless, the idea of the continuum has other problems.

1. In a continuum, every point is infinitesimal and as such any discontinuity is in the end inconceivable. But the discontinuous is not only found in the singularities of cosmology. According to Heisenberg's uncertainty principle, space and time appear as quantized and therefore as discontinuous.[26] The understanding of space in quantum-theory and the understanding of space in the general theory of relativity are not simply combinable. A continuum of space would only be an ideal, but not a reality. New attempts to combine the theory of relativity with quantum theory, like the theory of loop quantum gravity, work without any continuum of space (and time). Here, space-time quanta

24 Cf. HEESCH, M., Theologie und Naturwissenschaften, 216–223.
25 Cf. This matter is addressed in the articles in HÄRLE, W. (Hg.), Im Kontinuum.
26 Cf. MÜHLING, M., Liebesgeschichte Gott, 209–211.

appear not as presuppositions of the theory, but as objects among others without any fundamental role.[27]

2. If one wants to hold to an understanding of space as a continuum and simultaneously hold to a relational understanding of space, one has also subscribed to a radical kind of transport (ch. 8). The radicalism of transport consists in the fact that between any two points of the continuum there are always other points that can be described with the value of the coordinates of the continuum. It would be possible to address other attributes to these space-points, like temperature, with the effect of gaining a field of temperature. The consequence is that the continuum determines, in a transcendental manner, which phenomena can appear and which not. Further in those cases in which the continuum describes a curved space, it is not the opposite of Kantian epistemology, but only one of its special instantiations. The continuum is the condition for the possibility of addressing any point in space, which does not necessarily mean presupposing a point of view from outside the continuum. It would also be possible to describe the continuum from moving positions, such as in the case of the special theory of relativity. Here, the coordinates of space-time for the relatively moving coordinate-systems can be transformed into each other with the help of the Lorentz-transformations.[28]

3. The most serious problem in the transport-like relations in space being understood as continuum is that this theory does not fit our spatial perception. Rather, it wants to, and must, abstract from this perception. The understanding of space as continuum is insolubly bound to classificatory knowledge.[29] But if one were to ask how space appears concretely in our perception, one finds something completely different: an understanding of local space as developing lines.

11.4 The Local Understanding of Developing Lines

In the perception of movement, there is not only an experience of time, but also of places. This experience of place consists in the fact that any movement is determined by one's own living body and the horizon of the environment, with the effect that any movement appears in our memory as a developing line. Just as time cannot be understood without reference to place, so place

27 Cf. THIMANN, T., Suche nach dem Heiligen Gral.

28 A good, and also understandable for the layperson, treatment of the Lorentz-transformations within the special theory of relativity can be found in WÖLFEL, E., Zeit.

29 Cf. INGOLD, T., Being Alive, 142f.

and space cannot be understood without reference to time. The reason for this equiprimordiality of time and place is that both presuppose the perception of movement. However, in the perception of the relative movement of perceiver and environment, what is spatial neither appears as continuum, nor as points or containers, but as developing lines, and derived from these, as places, and abstracted from these, perhaps as a container.

A simple thought-experiment might help illustrate the difference between understanding space as a continuum and as developing lines. Our system of postal addresses is nothing but a social way of conceiving of space as continuum. We use house-numbers, street-names, post-codes, cities, and countries. This shows a hierarchical order. How must we describe a movement, like a journey, in terms of this social concept of the spatial continuum? I would jump from my house, to the level of the street, to the level of the city, to the level of the county, from there into another country, then to another city, to the level of a specific street and a specific house. But in fact, no one moves in this manner. In fact, I go along a part of the way by foot, use my car on the streets, and at the end I move along on my way once more by foot. I do not move across any level above or below, but only along a way.[30]

If there were no street constructed by other people already present, nothing would change. In this case, the way would emerge as a developing line in my environment by my own movement. Furthermore, such a movement is also not movement from place to place.

The fact of the matter is, in perception, places and containers are nothing but condensed wayformational lines: A city is not really defined by its borders on the map, but by the fact that the many wayformational lines of the many movers condense, intertwine, interweave, and entangle themselves. From the perspective of the phenomenology of perception, out of movement appear wayformational lines, out of these and their knots, intersections, and concentrations appear places, from which the idea of space as a container can be abstracted. Places in this sense are generated by our cognitive and metaphorical activity, by transforming condensed wayformational lines into borders, in order to abstract from the lines of movement and construct circumscribed, bordered places.[31] These places can be two- or three-dimensional. In the case of two-dimensional places, territories appear, in the case of three-dimensional places, substances and objects appear. What is interesting is that many people would not identify this first level of abstraction (from the bundle of ways of movements to fixed and bordered territories) as an abstraction, but

30 Cf. INGOLD, T., Being Alive, 146–151. 154f.

31 Cf. LAKOFF, G./JOHNSON, M., Metaphors We Live by, 28f.

mistakenly as a concretion. Perhaps this might also be the reason why the territorial container scheme – including its concepts of inside, outside, and the border between inside and outside – is sometimes regarded as basic.[32] This first order of abstraction or of reification helps us to orientate ourselves in everyday life. Here the border between inside and outside my flat is important, the question whether nutrition is inside or outside my body, or if I can transfer a physical object from here to there, etc. It would be possible to express all this with the phenomenally more fundamental language of lines of movement, but it would cost a lot more of words and be inconvenient. We cannot avoid a shift from the perception of movements to our ordinary ontologies and its talk of places, territories, containers, bodies, substances, and so on. Ontologizing and categorizing our bodily movements is one of the first abstractions. And this first abstraction is so persistent that nearly no one doubts that places really exist.

One must first ascend this hierarchy of abstractions in order to abstract once more by asking about the nature of that thing wherein places, territories, containers, physical bodies and substances are situated – about the nature of *space itself* and whether it is relational, container-like, or a continuum. And once this last abstraction is done, one can conceive of movement as a transport from one infinitesimal point of a coordinate system to another one, or as hierarchical movements via levels from one address to another one. But in fact, in phenomenal perception, there are only movements along developing lines. If these lines are curved into themselves, places and the place-like are generated. And only by erasing the origins of place, the lines of movement, from this picture does one get expressible points of a spatial continuum as fixed coordinates. Whereas spatial knowledge is always classificatory knowledge, knowledge along wayformational lies is always narrative knowledge, told *along* a way.[33] The real origin, however, of the spatial is not the spatial continuum of transport, but wayfaring, that always builds a mesh, since wayformational lines can never resolve into a factual continuum.

The implications for our understanding of space and ourselves is far-reaching. On the one side, if I see space as a coordinated continuum, which entities can appear in space and how we have to classify them is transcendentally given. On the other side, from the perspective of wayformational lines, it is completely undetermined, what can appear and what cannot appear. I can only use a narrative knowledge of told sequences if I want to describe space in this manner. What can appear is completely open, with the consequence that there is a radical contingency to what appears.

32 Cf. LAKOFF, G./JOHNSON, M., Philosophy in the Flesh, 32.

33 Cf. INGOLD, T., Being Alive, 163. 168.

In order to make the idea of space as a continuum a truly meaningful abstraction, one would first have to be able tell of all the wayformational lines of each mover, and when this is done, one would have to abstract oneself from it.

Both the understanding of space as a continuum and the understanding of space as developing lines are more relational models than container-like models, but each implies a completely different relationship between space and narrativity. In the framework of space as a continuum, the continuum has priority and any movement is a movement *in* this continuum. According to the understanding of space as continuum, first-order narrativity presupposes space as continuum. Narrations can only be told in this continuum. Narrative events might change the shape of the continuum, like space is curved by moving masses or accelerating movement, but space always has to be presupposed (apart from the strange singularities). In the frame of an understanding of phenomenological wayformational lines, the wayformational line and the first-order story that describes this line are prior. Out of first-order narrations, wayformational lines appear; out of wayformational lines, places appear, and these places can be emptied by abstraction into the concept of 'space itself'.

Against this understanding of space, one could object that a line can be seen as an example *par excellence* of a continuum. This objection is only partially right. Wayformational lines are not mathematical, straight lines, but are primordially in an environment of emerging lines that develop, wind, and knot themselves. In the ordinary sense, this may be called a continuum, but not in a mathematical sense. If one were to try and describe such a mesh as a mathematical continuum, one would be forced to imagine the mesh in a space of coordinates. For a case such as that of a concrete mesh e.g. a carpet, this might be possible. But narrative, wayformational lines, which is what we are talking about, are constitutive for space. If these were once more located in a space-as- continuum, we would have to imagine an 'imaginary' space, including 'imaginary' space-coordinates (analogous to Hawking's imaginary time), or one would have to imagine, similarly to Heim, a super-polar space. I regard the conceivability of this notion as an open question. Be that as it may, such a hyper-space would not be a mathematical continuum, in which the actual space-time is constituted out of the mesh of lines. In the case of Heim's super-polar space, because of super-polarity it cannot be a mathematically describable space. All that one has accomplished is a too hasty theological interpretation of space in a theology, since Heim's super-polar space simply means being surrounded by divine transcendence. But we have to proceed carefully and cannot too hastily conceive of the space developed and developing by wayformational lines as dependent on divine transcendence. As long as we do not want to argue on the basis of a concrete concept of God we have to refrain from such procedures. But further, an imaginary space cannot be assumed because it would not be in any way a metric for describable space (whether by imaginary numbers or rational numbers).

In an ontic respect, what is the relationship between the two paradigms of space? The following solutions are possible.

Whoever affirms the understanding of space as a continuum as real, as most naturalists do, must adhere to an object-oriented ontology.[34] The primary reality of space then determines which classifiable objects can appear on which positions of space. Movements are necessarily the movements of these classifiable objects. Narrations might be a means to describe these moving objects, but not a privileged one, since the best description of these movements are mathematical ones. Narrativity cannot be primary, only secondary. It might have its relative right epistemologically, or only aesthetically.

The extreme counter-position claims that there is no space at all, like Tim Ingold does in *Against Space*.[35] There is no space and there are no things that exist. Things appear; movement itself is identical with the knowledge of the inhabitants of the world. Consequently, narrative knowledge is primary over classificatory knowledge.

Whereas the understanding of the continuum ontologizes a product of human abstraction, Ingold ontologizes what is given primarily in perception.

A third possibility can be illustrated by Doreen Massey in her book *For Space*.[36] In contrast to Ingold, she regards the concept of space as meaningful, but argues for its phenomenological and narrative basis.

We, as should be no surprise, regard the understanding of space as a continuum as an abstraction for specific ends of the phenomenal understanding of lines of movement, out of which places emerge. In respect to specific interests and ends, the understanding of space as a continuum is relatively correct. Space, as Leibniz also knew,[37] is an idealization but not a phenomenon. Therefore, it is important to ask for which kinds of ends the talk of space is useful and for which not. N.B.: this is not only a conceptual, but at the same time an ethical question! It is not space that is ontically basic, however, but the narrative reality of moved lines. The real is not space, but first-order stories.

11.5 Spatial Relations of Order as the Possibility of Alterity

The primary lines of movement or story can be described as similar to the B/C-series of time: as a relation of order. If I move forward, every 'forward' is

34 Cf. Harman, G., Road to Objects.
35 Cf. Ingold, T., Being Alive, 145–155.
36 Cf. Massey, D., For Space.
37 Cf. Evers, D., Gott und mögliche Welten, 77.

correlated to a backwards, in a manner, that is an irreflexive, asymmetric, and transitive relation. I cannot move forwards in front of myself; therefore, the relational description 'forwards' is irreflexive. The direction in front of myself is not the direction behind myself and *vice versa* (as long as I do not turn around); therefore, the relation is asymmetric. If I move constantly forwards, every new passage of my way in increasing time is in front of any other passage with a lower index of time. If I move along a passage s_1 at time t_1, along passage s_2 at t_2 and along s_3 at t_3, s_3 is not only in front of s_3 like s_2 is in front of s_1, but s_3 is also in front of s_2. Therefore, the spatial relation is also transitive.

The same relational attributes that are valid for 'forwards' are of course also valid for 'backwards', 'to the left', 'to the right', 'above' and 'below'. The spatial relations of movement correspond to the B/C-series of time, which is not surprising, since the B/C-series of time, separately treated, is nothing but a kind of spatialized time. It is not space, that is modelled in terms of time, but the other way around: the topology of time is modelled in terms of space. We have learned that it is wrong to isolate the B/C-series of time. In the same way, it would be wrong to isolate the spatial relation of movement from movement itself. The result would be the abstracted and ontologized spatial continuum.

Both the spatial movement and the temporal B/C series have the logical character of relations of order in being asymmetric, irreflexive, and transitive. Nevertheless, there is a decisive difference. In temporal topology, there is also irreversibility, whereas the spatial topology is reversible: when I move forward, I can at any time turn around in order to move backwards. Therefore, it is possible for someone else to move at the same time with me and in front of me, behind me, above, below, to the left or to the right of me. The reversibility of spatial movement, in contrast to temporal movement, enables the co-presence of the different. This co-presence can be perceived in the framework of my horizon of perception as simultaneous, although an exact physical description would show that absolute simultaneity is impossible due to the finitude of the speed of light. For any narrative ontology this point is important, since only this reversibility, and the correspondingly enabled co-presence, enables alterity.

Massey, therefore, says that it is space that enables a sphere of co-temporal multiplicity and a simultaneity of stories.[38] And Ingold also follows that line: 'If time is the guarantor of life, space is the guarantor that heterogeneous lives proceed concurrently.'[39] But of course these insights are not new. Leibniz, in

38 Cf. MASSEY, D., For Space, 10–12. 148. 183.

39 INGOLD, T., Being Alive, 142.

his relational understanding of space that was directed against Newton and Clarke, had already seen that space is 'an order of the togetherness of existences, like time is an order of their succession'.[40]

A single movement can only be described narratively, but a story is not a story at all if it only describes a single movement or a single occurrence. Only a spatial simultaneity of stories enables the narrative events of the world. It is not only needful that there are different, heterogeneous stories at the same time, but it must also be recognized that a single story is only a single story, and this particular story because it is interwoven with other stories. It is impossible for stories to deal with a single subject, since they would be nothing but predications. By the simultaneous appearance of different carriers of actions in stories, the task of distinguishing them arises. And it is only possible by means of the events assumed to be simultaneous, which can nevertheless only be told by second-order narrativity in a sequential way. This fact – that I also have to tell of simultaneous events successively – corresponds to the structure of movement, in which I can go over an old passage anew, but only at a later time, with the consequence that others can go this sequence at another time.

The point is that it is the alterity inherent to the story that enabled the simultaneous interweaving of the narrative becoming, and therefore spatial differences. Stories does not take place in any space, *but enfold a space by their internally interwoven lines of movement*; alterity constitutes space. Further, the idea of an infinite space, which must be considered at another place in detail, can be narratively described: whatever becomes simultaneously is not closed, but open. This description also has implications for an understanding of transcendence, if transcendence is a spatial metaphor.

The alterity that is story-inherent also has another meaning for the space of wayformational lines. The space is not homogenous, as Marion claims.[41] It seems as if my living body were the center of movements and therefore the origin of a coordinate system, but this is an eccentric origin. My living body marks any thinkable 'here' in the space of wayformational lines; every concrete particular that emerges marks a possible 'there'. But what is really important is neither the former nor the latter, but a third thing: something which emerges, something which comes out of the horizon of the 'elsewhere' to me, that attracts me and stimulates my attentionality. Thereby it enables the movement and becoming of wayformational lines. This attracting 'elsewhere' never changes into a 'here' or 'there'. Of course, something that was 'elsewhere' can become

40 Cf. Leibniz, G.W., Die philosophischen Schriften von G.W. Leibniz, Bd. VII, 363.
41 Cf. Marion, J.-L., Erotic Phenomenon, 29–32.

a 'here' or 'there', but only by being situated in the horizon of a new 'elsewhere', that appears as though coming to me. The attracting elsewhere of space finds its analogy in the awaiting of the relatively retrospectively surprising aspect of time. It is an elsewhere that determines the dynamic by abundantly giving me new possibilities for movement. It broadens my space. It is this elsewhere that cannot be located in the bodily coordinate system because it is no 'there', but simply an 'elsewhere'. As such it is both, attractive and attracting, and determines the movement of the origin of the bodily coordinates – and therefore the movement of space itself.

11.6 The Primary-narrative Space and its Aspects

If it is right that space is a product of the abstraction of the wayformational lines and their knots that are given in the perception of movement, then phenomenal space is the narrative space of primary narrativity. We can talk about different aspects of this narrative space that must be distinguished but not be separated. None of these aspects are primary, but they behave in an equiprimordial manner. If we center the perceived relative movement on our living body, narrative space is essentially bodily space, determined by the spatial dimensions of the living body, regarding above-below, forward-backward, left-right, near-to-its-center, and near-to-its-horizon.

1. The claim is true with respect to the physical and conceptual dimensions of space that are ordinarily taken as the basic meaning of space, whereas the other dimensions are seen as derivative.[42] But this view is wrong, since it is not space that is perceived immediately, but only space mediated by the perception of movements. In this way – and only in this way – is space also a form of sensible intuition. In this respect, space is primarily conceptual space and secondarily physical space. For the imaginative abstraction of the conceptual space, it is true that it is a three-dimensional, Euclidean continuum. The empirical fact that empirical space is, as the general theory of relativity has shown, a curved and non-Euclidean space, cannot affect this conceptual aspect of space.[43] But the conceptual space, viewed separately, does not exist at all; it is an idealization, which one might also call the 'fundamental shape' (*Grundstellung*)[44] of space. Nevertheless, the conceptual space is primary over

42 Cf. LAKOFF, G./JOHNSON, M., Metaphors We Live by, 58.

43 Cf. KOCH, A.F., Versuch, 123 and KOCH, A.F., Wahrheit, Zeit und Freiheit, 74f.

44 KOCH, A.F., Versuch, 355.

the physical space, insofar as no one can think of a physical space without a conceptual one. Both together constitute one aspect of a larger state of affairs: what is perceived are affordances, according to Gibson, as we have seen (ch. 5), which always include values. Therefore, we have to add a second aspect.

2. The primary-narrative (empirical) space is always a space of values. The concepts of order that are relevant for the living body (above-below, in front of-behind, near-far, etc.) also express qualities of value, which can be analyzed with the help of conceptual metaphors.[45] It is also the conceptual space and the physical space, which is at once a space of values. In analogy to the perception of truth and value (*Wahrwertnehmen*), one could also speak of the unity of the conceptual space and the space of values as the *Weltwertraum* (universe of facts and values). But as a space of values it is also, in distinction from perceiving values, an idealization. One can see this by noting that the value-concepts used in the space of values remain abstract as long as they are not bound to something that is concretely perceived.

3. The primary-narrative space is also always an inter-bodily space, since a single perceiver is unthinkable. Living bodies are internally related concentrations of the mesh of perceiving. The inter-bodily space is a space in which I and Thou are essentially related and this space is structured equiprimordially by the pronominal, I, You, He/She, We, You, They.[46]

This differentiation of the primary-narrative space with its three aspects resembles a little bit the threefold space of the Neomarxist tradition of Henri Lefebvre, who distinguishes a physical space, a mental space, and a social space.[47] Perhaps it is the same phenomenality that is the basis for this classification. But the decisive distinction is that our own classification does not allow any separation from the beginning onwards. Furthermore, one-sidedness and equivocations, implied by the talk of the mental and the social, are excluded. The mental could be understood as an opposite to the body, or as separable from the living body, and indeed it is frequently understood in this manner. The social could be understood as the intersubjective, i.e. as externally related subjects that can enter into secondary social relations. Furthermore, space is not a social product or a social construction on the basis of any natural space. Space, in the shape of its narrative basis in wayformational lines is something we undergo; it is a pathos. Only our responsive models of space might entail

45 Cf. LAKOFF, G./JOHNSON, M., Metaphors We Live by, 22–24. 28–30.

46 Cf. DALFERTH, I.U., Die Wirklichkeit des Möglichen. Hermeneutische Religionsphilosophie, 384. 489f. 494–500. 509. 512–515.

47 Cf. LEFEBVRE, H., Production of Space.

an active aspect. In order to exclude these misunderstandings, we speak of a space of primary narrativity, which has as the space of the world a conceptual and empirical aspect, which in turn has an ethical aspect as the space of values, and that has a personal aspect as the inter-bodily space. The space of primary narrativity is always an inter-bodily *Weltwertraum* (the universe of values and facts).

CHAPTER 12

Narrations and Signs

The objection against a narrative ontology is that talk about signs instead of stories would suffice, especially in the case of theology.[1] At first glance it seems indeed that signs could be more basic than stories, because it seems that either stories consist of signs as their parts or that stories are a subset of signs. The task of this chapter is not only to reject this assumption, but also to show that, on the contrary, meaningful theories of signs must presuppose narrative connections. We must face the fact that there are lots of semiotic theories that do not simply cohere or form a discipline. We have therefore to choose, and I think that the classic Charles Sanders Peirce still offers the best insights.

Although Saussure is one of the fathers of semiotics, his theory is not useful for our purposes. On the one hand, he restricted his analyses to signs in languages, which reveals his subject matter is far too narrow in comparison to our approach. On the other hand, Saussure rejects *a priori* realistic claims by defining the meaning of language-like signs consisting in the conventions of communities of interpretation, with the effect that he is a forerunner of social constructivism and relativistic approaches.[2]

Charles William Morris' semiotics[3] has had a widespread effect on many academic disciplines, including his distinction of a syntactic, a semantic, and a pragmatic dimension of semiosis. However, his description of the semiosis is very open. He describes the semiosis as a combination of three dyadic relations and focuses on each of them separately, which might help explain the success of his position. One can focus on the relation between signs and signs by being a logician, or on semantics or on the pragmatic dimension alone. The distinction between syntactics, semantics, and pragmatics remains important, but all in all its distinctive force is a minor one.

Recent theories of signs, like Umberto Eco's[4] or Jurij Lotman's,[5] sometimes have surprising points. However, they focus on specific phenomena of signs and use these in order to develop their theories. This procedure does not really suit our purposes.

Therefore, it is most helpful to turn to the classic Peirce and his semiotics. For one thing, Peirce is also, more than Saussure, a father of semiotics. Another reason is that his semiotics has in the last 30 years experienced a revival in disciplines as diverse as philosophy of religion, theology, neuroscience, biological anthropology, and primatology. Perhaps the most important reason for us is that his semiotics bears, in a somehow tragic manner, the mark of the post-systematic, which might be surprising at first

1 Cf. WALTER, G., Rev. Mühling, Liebesgeschichte Gott.

2 Cf. SAUSSURE, F.d., Course in General Linguistics, and besides ROBINSON, A., Traces of the Trinity. Signs, Sacraments and Sharing God's Life, 239.

3 Cf. MORRIS, C.W., Foundations of the Theory of Signs.

4 Cf. ECO, U., Open Work.

5 Cf. LOTMAN, J.M., Universe of the Mind.

 | DOI:10.30965/9783846765852_013

glance. The two decisive features of systematic thinking – that everything is related to everything else, and that a system is necessarily closed and organized under one singular concept (cf. ch. 1), can also be found in Peirce. Is he then, not better described as a modern systematician *par excellence*? But look twice! Indeed, Peirce tries to connect everything with everything else. But his semiotics is not closed and it has one singular organizing conceptual basis. Peirce modified and revised his thinking all the time, including his idiosyncratic terminology. This constant revision of a terminology is a hint that he never reached the closedness of a system. But then Peirce's semiotics would be – despite its high amount of technical terminology – an example of post-systematic thinking.

However, we do not use Peirce's semiotics here as an end in itself, and we do not claim to be reconstructing Peirce's own thinking. Therefore, we do not need to follow Peirce's own terminology thoroughly.

12.1 Relational Categories

Peirce is not only a father of semiotics, but also of the logics of relations. What is important to note here is that Peirce, in distinction from Russell, did not assume that all polyadic relations could be reduced to predicates. He also did not claim, as we did in ch. 7, that relational analyses can be done for pragmatic reasons with more or less relata. He claimed that there are specific, genuine relations which are irreducible and unextendable. Of course, he saw too that there are relations that can be reduced or extended. But these kinds of relations are not really interesting. What is interesting are these genuine relations. According to Peirce, there are exactly three of them. First, there are monadic relations, e.g. predicates, which neither reducible nor expandable. Second, there are genuine dyadic relations, which are neither reducible to predicates nor extendable. Third, there are genuinely triadic relations, which neither reducible to relations with less *relata* or extendable to relations with more *relata*. All relations with more than three *relata* are not genuine, i.e. according to Peirce, those *relata* can be reduced to triadic, dyadic, or monadic relations. How adequate Peirce' theorem of reduction really is, cannot be our question.[6] The only important thing here is that Peirce gains thereby his categorical scheme, simply called firstness, secondness, and thirdness.[7] In a purely formal manner, the name 'firstness' refers to the genuine monadic structure of predicates, the name 'secondness' refers to a genuine dyadic, and the name 'thirdness' to a genuine triadic relational structure. Besides these formal structures, they are phenomenally determined:

6 Cf. Peirce, C.S., Collected Papers, CP 1.343–349 and also Marty, R., réduction triadique.

7 Cf. Peirce, C.S., New List, CP 1.551–CP 1.557.

Firstness as monadic relation or predicate describes a *quality*, like an affective quality or, as Peirce also calls it, a ground. A simple example would be the feeling of the so-called qualia, like the feeling of colors or other qualities. It is important to note here that Peirce develops his categories independently of thinking subjects. He does not mean a psychological impression. A simple '... is green' or '... is black' states that the quality of blackness or greenness is somehow involved, but statements like these does not describe states of affairs or reality, since nothing concrete is identified that is green or black. As long as no reference to something concrete is made, as in purely predicative firstness, it is a category of pure *possibility*.

Firstness therefore has the characteristics of being a monadic relation, indicating a quality and being pure possibility.

Secondness as a dyadic relation that describes the relation of a relatum to something *different*, a correlate. Only in the case that something different is involved, *actuality* takes place. Statements about reality always have, according to Peirce, a dyadic structure. This insight is important, yet it does not fit with the established logical notation since Russell. In Russell's notation, actualities or realities can be described monadically by substituting a variable of a predicate for a concrete element or by 'binding' it: '... is green' then becomes '*this* tree is green'. Peirce, however, conceives of the same state of affairs as a dyadic relation between the quality and this concrete tree, which is also distinct from and something other than pure green.

Secondness is therefore characterized by being a dyadic relation, between otherness and actuality.

Thirdness, as a triadic relation, describes the mediation between a *relatum* and a correlate by a third *relatum*. For example: the greenness of a tree can describe its vitality in distinction from other, non-green trees. Whereas firstness is associated with pure possibility and secondness with actuality, thirdness, according to Peirce, is characterized by universality or necessity, since it needs a general rule that abstracts from the concrete case in order to make a statement.

Thirdness is therefore characterized by being a triadic relation, between mediation and applied rules.

12.2 The Basic Structure of Semiosis

Peirce uses these three categories in order to define the concept of a sign. Or, in other words, the concept of a sign is always entailed in these combined categories. One of his many definitions of a sign is as follows:

> A sign is something, A, which brings something, B, its *interpretant* sign determined or created by it, into the same sort of correspondence with something, C, its *object*, as that in which itself stands to C.[8]

A sign is therefore an irreducible, genuinely triadic relation between the *relata* of (1) the object of the sign, (2) what is signified (the *significatum*), and (3) the interpreting sign, called the *interpretant*. The *significatum* plays the role of firstness, the object of the sign the role of secondness, and the interpretant the role of thirdness. Without an interpretant a sign would be incomplete, and it is precisely the interpretant that constitutes the meaning of a sign. A red traffic-light is, for example, a complex sign. It is the object of the sign, signifying the imperative to stop. This sign, however, is only effective – drivers will really know to stop – if the relevant rules, perhaps received through traffic education, are known.

Three things are important to note here. The first is the interpreting sign does not necessarily connote a cognitive interpretation. Peirce's semiosis is not bound to humans, but exists independently of humans in the world. Peirce calls this the quasi-mind.[9] Secondly, this implies that semiosis is a real event in the world, and its success lies in the interpretant. Since the interpretant is a sign by itself, although the semiosis remains a triadic relation, a signifying process occurs that is principally open and therefore infinite. In other words, what was first an interpreting sign becomes the signified, which then receives, together with another object of the sign and another interpretant, another or a new meaning. The third implication is that the whole world consists of signs. Although no single object can be a sign in itself, in this open relationship of semiosis the whole world becomes a kind of system of signs. In Peirce's theory of semiosis, there is, in contrast to Augustine for example, no categorical distinction between *res* and *signa*.[10]

According to Peirce, semiosis has a temporal or sequential character. And therefore, it is an actual event:

---

8 Peirce, C.S., New Elements of Mathematics, vol. 4, 20f.

9 Cf. Peirce, C.S., Letters to Lady Welby, SS 195: 'I almost despair of making clear what I mean by a "quasi-mind;" But I will try. A *thought* is not *per se* in any mind or quasi-mind. I mean this in the same sense as I might say that Right and Truth would remain what they are though they were not embodied, & though nothing were right or true. But a thought, to gain any active mode of being must be embodied in a Sign. A thought is a special variety of sign. All thinking is necessarily a sort of dialogue, an appeal from the momentary self to the better considered self of the immediate and of the general future. Now as every thinking requires a mind, so every sign even if external to all minds must be a determination of a quasi-mind. The quasi-mind is itself a sign, a determinable sign.'

10 Cf. Jackson, B.D., Theory of Signs in St. Augustine's.

> To say, therefore, that thought cannot happen in an instant, but requires a time, is but another way of saying that every thought must be interpreted in another, or that all thought is in signs.[11]

Besides the sequential, event-like character of becoming, in this quotation the semiotic process seems to be identified with thinking. And this is indeed the case. However, for Peirce 'thinking' does not mean exclusively the cognitive activity of human minds or brains, but thinking also occurs

> in the work of bees, of crystals, and throughout the purely physical world; and one can no more deny that it is really there, than that the colors, the shapes, etc., of objects are really there.[12]

So far, we have described what semiosis is and that it presupposes the three categories. In a second step, the three elements of semiosis can be classified with the help of the same categories in a more precise manner.

The object of the sign, the dyadic relation between object of a sign and signified, and the triadic relation of the interpreting sign as an effect of semiosis can be classified by firstness, secondness, and thirdness more concretely.

12.3 Types of the Object of a Sign

An object of a sign can be firstness-like, secondness-like, or thirdness-like. The question at stake here is what constitutes an object of a sign, independently of its meaning (and independently whether the sign is understood). What does this mean?

A *firstness-like object of a sign* is a sign that becomes a sign by its own quality. Imagine cards of colors in a hardware store that are used for choosing the color of paint. Whether something can be a first-like object of a sign, depends on its concrete bodily form. You have to use the physical color-card, not a picture on a computer-screen, in order to get a successful semiosis.[13]

A *secondness-like object of a sign* is a spontaneous semiosis, including when there is no intention to use a sign. Imagine someone emptying his or her tobacco-pipe as a matter of course. In Conan Doyle's Sherlock Holmes stories, this is a clue to the identity of the perpetrator, since Holmes is able to infer from

11 Peirce, C.S., Collected Papers, 5.253.

12 Peirce, C.S., Collected Papers, 4.551.

13 Cf. Robinson, A., Traces of the Trinity. Signs, Sacraments and Sharing God's Life, Pos. 986–997.

the kind of tobacco from the ashes, and therefore possibly even the murderer's occupation. The constitution of a sign by emptying the pipe is secondness-like, since it is not a sign that has been historically bound together with other signs or that is part of a grammar-system of signs. Nevertheless, it has many different significations in its dyadic relation. A secondness-like sign is a 'stand-alone sign'.[14] Understanding such a sign is possible independent of its constitution.

A *thirdness-like object of a sign* presupposes the application of specific rules, for the sign's constitution. Thirdness-like signs are bound to a specific grammar and they need other signs in order to be constituted. It is important here that the rules necessary to constitute the object of the sign are not identical with the rules necessary in order to understand the sign. Imagine a worker installing a traffic light. The rules that apply here are the understanding of its electric circuits, the height above the streets, the kind of traffic in this specific junction, etc. But in order to build a thirdness-like object of a sign like a traffic light, it is not necessary to understand its meaning or to possess a driver's license.

Peirce uses other – along with changing terminology – names for the firstness-like, secondness-like, and thirdness-like objects of signs. Since we are not interested in a reconstruction of Peirce's theories, but in the state of affairs itself, we do not have make use of his terminology. Also, the other subdivisions that Peirce introduces are not necessary for our purposes.

12.4 The Types of the Dyadic Partial Relation between Object of a Sign and Signified

Peirce's classification of the dyadic partial relation of the semiosis between object of a sign and signified is well known. Therefore, we can use, at least partially, the names Peirce suggested, since they have become common in academic language.

An *icon* is a *firstness-like relation between object of a sign and signified.* The signification is here dependent on a qualitative similarity between the object and that which it signifies, whereas at the same time there is a qualitative dissimilarity between the two. An iconic sign would be an infant's simulated barking in order to refer to a dog, or the traffic-sign showing circular arrows in order to indicate a roundabout.

An *index* is a *secondness-like relation between object of a sign and signified.* It is constituted by an actual and real relationship between the object and the

14 Cf. Robinson, A., Traces of the Trinity. Signs, Sacraments and Sharing God's Life, Pos. 976.

signified. The object of the sign is really determined by the signified. Smoke is an index of fire, the cumulonimbus-cloud an index of a thunderstorm, to knock on a door indicates a desire to enter, etc. Deictic acts, expressions like names or determined pronouns are indexical signs, too.

A *symbol* is a *thirdness-like relation between the object of a sign and the signified.* In this case, semiosis is neither dependent on qualitative similarities nor on a direct connection of events, but on a rule that must be applied and that has to be known, in order to understand the sign. The word 'keyboard' has no similarity with a computer-keyboard, and there is not even a sequential connection between a keyboard and the events of uttering or writing the word 'keyboard'. One has to be acquainted with the words and the grammar of the English language in order to know what the sign means. Symbolic signs are embedded into a culture of signs. Most of our linguistic expressions are symbolic signs.

12.5 Types of the Interpretant

The interpretant is an interpreting sign. It is not necessarily an object-like entity, but it can also consist in an event. It is rather the meaning, effect, or 'interpretation' of a sign. However, we have to be careful in using the word 'interpretation', since it does not have here, as in Cassirer's theory of symbolic forms,[15] the meaning it has in ordinary language. It does not necessarily signify a cognitive activity. It is perhaps better to speak of the effect that a sign inaugurates. Such an effect does not presuppose cognitive understanding. Such reasoning might become clearer if one looks at the three types of the interpretant, which are once more enabled by the three categories.

A *firstness-like interpretant* is a quality that semiosis evokes. Feelings, based on the affordances of the environment, are firstness-like interpretants. If I react to the story of the pain of someone else with consternation, compassion or malicious joy, then these feelings of consternation, compassion or malicious joy are interpretants of the semiosis of this particular story. Imagine hiking in the mountains for several hours and at the end of the day facing an extremely steep ascent to the summit. Your physical exhaustion as well as your feelings of displeasure or despair are interpretants. They emerge spontaneously, without thinking or willing, simply be being in this particular situation. The firstness-like interpretant is, therefore, a response to the pathos of or encounter with the affordances.

15 Cf. CASSIRER, E., Philosophie der Symbolischen Formen.

A *secondness-like interpretant* is an actual action, involuntarily performed as a reaction to the appearance of the object of the sign. Involuntarily, in a habitualized manner, the experienced driver will hit the brakes when she suddenly sees red traffic lights. This event of hitting the brakes is the secondness-like interpretant. Generally, secondness-like interpretants are *spontaneous reactive events* or *actions*.

A *thirdness-like interpretant* is an interpretation by 'thinking'. In order to recognize the cumulonimbus-cloud as a sign for a thunderstorm, one needs knowledge of meteorology. In this case, the interpretation resembles what is called 'interpretation' in ordinary language, i.e. a cognitive activity. Nevertheless, that is not what 'thinking' means. An interpretation by 'thinking' need not be a cognitive activity. We use 'thinking' here in the sense of the last Peirce-quote of this chapter. It means, rather, the application of rules that lead to the interpretation of a sign. We can say it is a *reactive event, driven by interpretative rules*. Even thirdness-like interpretations can be performed by non-humans.

12.6 Semiotics, Interpretation, Representation, Determination, and Perception

This semiotic theory fits very well with our analysis of perception in ch. 5. We saw that perception always implies a response to a pathos or an undergoing. The semiosis expresses this by the interpretant as the effect of a sign. If we conceive of the relationship between the object of a sign and that which is signified as affordance in the sense of Gibson, the response of the interpretant can be conceived in such a way that the meaningful content does not primarily reside in the interpretant, but in the whole process of semiosis. The possibility that the interpretant is an incomplete reaction or effect of the sign-signified relationship is then admitted. If we conceive of the mediated, immediate perception as semiosis, this means that there is no valueless world which is then invested with values by observation, but *vice versa: no perception (and no subsequent cognitive interpretation of perception) can represent the content of the meaning and value of the world completely.*

In this case, we must alter Peirce's definition of a sign. Peirce wrote that the semiosis consists in the fact that the object of the sign puts the interpretant into *the same* relation, as that to which it is related to the signified. But it cannot be the same relation, only *a similar* one: the object of the sign inaugurates the interpretant into a similar relationship to the signified, as that to which it is related to the signified.

Peirce not only uses a lot of idiosyncratic concepts that we have not mentioned; he also uses many concepts in unusual ways. Nevertheless, it is important to specify once more the three most important alterations in meaning:

- 'Interpretation' does not mean a cognitive or conscious operation. Peirce's interpretations are what mediates the mediated immediacy of perception, whereas the classical cognitive 'interpretations' are absent, with the consequence that perceptions are always immediate. In order to clarify the difference, a suggestion of Philipp Stoellger's could be useful. He suggests calling the non-cognitive 'interpretation' that is given in all perception of truth and value, and which is the mediating part of it, *apprehension*, whereas the cognitive interpretation, which is absent and is caused by its absence from the immediacy of perception, *interpretation*.[16]
- 'Representation', and all concepts derived from it, is not to be conceived of according to the model of a prototype-image relation, which means that a sign makes something literally present once more, or present for the first time. A relationship of resonance would also be a relationship of making something present in this sense.
- 'Determination' and 'to determine' has nothing to do with determinism. When Peirce says that the object of a sign determines the interpretant, he means that the interpretant may actually be marked in some way by the object of the sign. He does not mean that this is necessarily a relationship of determination in the sense of a causal connection. Even in the case of the indexical sign, the relationship between signified and object of the sign is not meant to be exclusively causal, although causal connections of this kind (smoke=fire) might be simple instantiations of such indices. Semiosis is not something that presupposes the concept of causality. It is, as we will see later, the other way around: to conceive of causality, one has to presuppose the concept of signs, and without the concepts of signs, causality is inconceivable.

Mediated immediateness in other theories of signs:

It is important to get these concepts clear in order to see that Peirce' semiotics is not the only way to illustrate the narrative mediated immediacy of perceiving truth and values. Other traditions, including other concepts, refer with different terminologies to the same state of affairs.

For example, in Cassirer's neo-Kantian philosophy, it is a basic assumption that the symbolic pregnance (*symbolische Prägnanz*) of perception is pre-predicative. Cassirer refers here to an idea of Leibniz, but also distinguishes himself from Leibniz. Also,

16 Cf. STOELLGER, P., The Interpreting of Perception and the Perception of Interpreting.

tacit perceptions have a meaningful pregnance, which is in the end narrative or story-like, since the past is pregnant with the future.[17] Since even these little, tacit perceptions are part of the wider nexus, they also have meaningful pregnance. In the case of Leibniz, this sensible pregnance of the pre-predicative perception is not gained by some phenomenal analysis, but on the basis of the ontological system of his monadology, according to which a particular monad bears all determinations in itself, and all monads are primordially internally related. Cassirer claims, like Leibniz, that there is a meaningful pregnancy of perception, but he does not derive it from the primarily internal connection of all monads, but he conceives of it as a pre-predicative synthesis of the sensible and meaningful:

> 'Symbolic pregnance' therefore means the manner by which an experience of perception, as 'sensible' experience, at the same time contains a non-illustrative 'meaning' in itself, which it immediately depicts in a concrete way. [...] It is perception itself that gains, due to its own immanent structure, a kind of mental 'articulation' – which, as structured one, also belongs to a particular nexus of meaning. In its complete actuality, in its wholeness and vitality, it is *a life 'in' meaning*. [...] This ideal intermeshedness, this relatedness of the particular, the phenomenon of perception given here and now to a characteristic totality of meaning, is expressed with the term 'pregnance.'[18]

This pre-predicative synthesis of perception in its symbolic pregnance is for Cassirer the *forma formans* of all cultural *forma formata*.[19] If we translate this into the language of the semiotics we are employing here, we would say: the non-cognitive, firstness-like and secondness-like interpretants are the material that serve the thirdness-like cognitive interpretations for the formation of culture. In other words, perceiving truth and value by primary narrations is the basis for the constitution of secondary narrations, and these secondary narrations re-influence the perception of truth and value in primary narrativity. In Cassirer, like in Peirce's semiotics, and like in our theory of the perception of facts and value in ch. 5, the meaningfulness of sensible perception is also given. Even Leibniz made the same claim, but he had to pay the price of inferring it from his monadology. In Cassirer, however, this inference from the monadology is absent. Nevertheless, the symbolic pregnance of perception is imbedded in a narrative sequence. But then with Stoellger we have to ask: why should it be always a *symbolic*

---

17 Cf. LEIBNIZ, G.W., Philosophische Schriften, Bd. 3.2, XXIVf.

18 CASSIRER, E., Philosophie der Symbolischen Formen, Bd. 3, 235: „Unter ‚symbolischer Prägnanz' soll also die Art verstanden werden, in der ein Wahrnehmungserlebnis, als ‚sinnliches' Erlebnis, zugleich einen bestimmten nicht-anschaulichen ‚Sinn' in sich faßt und ihn zur unmittelbaren konkreten Darstellung bringt. [...] Vielmehr ist es die Wahrnehmung selbst, die kraft ihrer eigenen immanenten Gliederung eine Art von geistiger ‚Artikulation' gewinnt – die, als in sich gefügte, auch einer bestimmten Sinnfügung angehört. In ihrer vollen Aktualität, in ihrer Ganzheit und Lebendigkeit, ist sie zugleich *ein Leben ‚im' Sinn*. [...] Diese ideelle Verwobenheit, diese Bezogenheit des einzelnen, hier und jetzt gegebenen Wahrnehmungsphänomens auf ein charakteristisches Sinn-Ganzes, soll der Ausdruck ‚Prägnanz' bezeichnen."

19 Cf. CASSIRER, E., Nachgelassene Manuskripte und Texte, Bd. 1, 18.

pregnance and why can it not be a '*diabolic*' pregnance?[20] Cassirer can identify no reason for his claim that this pregnance is always *sym*-bolic, i.e. meaningfully imbedded in coherent narrative sequences of events. It could be also the case that it would be perceived as *dia*-bolic, as chaotic, as falling-apart. That both can be the case is more than probable, since whatever is perceived pre-predicatively does not necessarily have to be Cassirer's symbolic or Peirce's signs, but may simply be the non-conceptual and the incomprehensible.[21]

Be that as it may, in the framework of semiotics and in the framework of our own narrative theory of perception on the basis of affordances of the environment this question becomes more or less irrelevant. In semiotics, a particular semiosis is intermeshed in a semiotic, narrative nexus of events. But since neither the particular semiosis nor the whole semiotic nexus is closed, but open, there is always the possibility that a particular semiosis fails. It is possible that the reception of the signified by the other is insufficient in the response of the interpretant, or that it appears as non-sign, as an interruption of the semiotic process.[22] Further, our theory of narrative perception is able to 'include' this resisting element: the process of primary narrations always includes content that is not tellable on the level of secondary narrations – and precisely by this inexpressibility they react upon the continuation of the sequences of primary narrativity. In a wider sense, not only what is explicit or what can be expressed is told through secondary narrations, but also what is tacitly suggested, what is skipped, or what one does not want to include.

Could one put the cart before the horse? We presuppose that perception is always the narratively mediated perception of trans-subjective and trans-objective affordances, so that out of the movement of perception perceived and perceiver emerge equiprimordially. In order to conceive of this phenomenal givenness, semiotics was helpful, but secondary. The other possibility assumes that what is given are pure facts, which get their meaning only by cognitive interpretation, is mistaken, since this would simply be another invocation of the myth of the given.[23] But would it not be possible to assume that there is only interpretation, and that the perceived is also the interpreted? And would not such a possibility fit with the semiotic approach and its claim that all perception is sign-like? This very thing has been suggested by Günter Abel in his *Interpretationswelten*. He uses a hierarchy of concepts for interpretation and distinguishes 'interpretation¹' from other conceptual aspects of 'interpretation'. By 'interpretations¹' he means the 'primordially productive and pattern-constructing components that self-manifest in the categorizing function of signs, which are presupposed in each organization of experience.'[24] These interpretations^1 are the basis for habitual interpretations^2, and such interpretations^2 are the basis for the genuine,

---

20 Cf. Stoellger, P., The Interpreting of Perception and the Perception of Interpreting

21 Cf. Stoellger, P., Metapher und Lebenswelt, 202f.

22 It seems like Peirce himself did not think about this because of his agapism, cf. on this Peirce, C.S., Evolutionary Love.

23 The term traces back to Sellars, W., Empiricism and the Philosophy of Mind. Cf. also McDowell, J., Mind and World, xvii.

24 Abel, G., Interpretationswelten, 14f. Translation by MM, original: „ursprünglich produktiven und sich in den kategorialisierenden Zeichenfunktionen selbst manifestierenden konstruktbildenden Komponenten, die in jeder Organisation von Erfahrung bereits vorausgesetzt sind".

cognitive and conscious interpretations.^{3} Of course, such a procedure is possible. But then one must pay the price of naming what we have called the mediated immediacy of perception 'interpretation^{1}', one has to name the narratively mediated perception on wayformational lines 'interpretation^{2}', and then only the 'interpretations^{3}' refer to what is in ordinary language usually called interpretation. In short: why is the term 'interpretation' used for 'interpretation^{1}' (and 'interpretation^{2}') at all? One suspects that making 'interpretations' omnipresent is the mistake of intellectual academics, who are tempted by their own work to see the method they employ day-in day-out everywhere.

The description of the narrative mediation of perception can use the semiotics of Peirce, but there is no need to use it exclusively, given that it is only one way among others to analyze the phenomena. In the excursus above, we discussed some of the alternatives. But I am convinced that the alternatives are not as convincing as the semiotic approach.

12.7 Biosemiotics

Some parts of Peirce's semiotics, especially the threefold distinction of the relationship between sign and signified, has been applied in recent years in evolutionary biology in distinctive way to the field of so-called biosemiotics. Theoretically, this is a subject matter for the doctrine of creation and therefore for volume 2. But biosemiotics has led to results that are important for our present question as to how narrativity and semiotics should be related. Therefore, we must treat this matter here.

A starting point for biosemiotics is the question of how humans are to be distinguished from other animals. Anthropology was quick to answer that the distinguishing feature must be seen in human's semiotic abilities. The American anthropologist Leslie White claimed that the use of symbols is equivalent with the *humanum*: 'Human behavior is symbolic behavior; symbolic behavior is human behavior.'[25] But White neither used a phenomenologically based concept of a symbol nor a semiotic one. By symbol he simply meant 'a thing, the value or meaning of which is bestowed upon it by those who use it.'[26] White's opinion is an example of the crass idea that the world consists of meaningless facts, and that meaning is a product of the users of signs, who are identical with *homo sapiens*. But these two opinions are nothing more than ontological commitments or expressions of some poor sorts of world-view, for which no evidence is offered. If one takes them seriously, then a decisive anthropological question – how human abilities has been developed

25 WHITE, L., The Symbol, 451.
26 WHITE, L., The Symbol, 453.

to the point using language and symbols – could not be asked at all. Moreover, White does not use the word 'symbol' in its semiotic sense as distinguished from icon and index, but in a broader sense, as a language-like sign. It was Terence Deacon who introduced (part of) Peircean semiotics into the question of the evolution of humans.[27] In Deacon's opinion, it is not the nonspecific use of signs at all that is distinctive for humans, but that the fact that they use not only icons and indexes but also and mainly symbols.[28] Indeed, it is not an easy endeavor to teach symbolic language non-human primates.[29] For a long time, anthropology assumed that the ability to use symbols in distinction from other kinds of sign is the capability of *homo sapiens* alone. A temporal gap in the findings caused problems for this and other explanations, as *homo sapiens* appeared much earlier than the material archeological evidences for the use of symbols.[30] In the meantime, however, prehistoric evidence for the use of specific symbolic signs have been found very early, far earlier than the appearance of the *homo sapiens*. Even the *homo erectus* 1.4 mi years BCE used symbolic signs.[31] Such an early use of symbolic signs shows that the use of symbolic language is not a privilege of the *homo sapiens* alone and one can ask whether other primates developed this capability. What is interesting in this regard is the communicative behavior of chimpanzees: they use signs of drumming and yelling in order to indicate the direction of their journey from tree to tree as well as the duration of the resting-time between its stages. Early interpretations of this behavior assumed that it was a symbolic use of signs that developed out of an iconic use,[32] but in the meantime it has shown that indeed this behavior is a symbolic use of signs, which is, however, not developed out of icons, but out of indexical signs.[33] Drumming on one tree is the indexical 'here', whereas drumming on two trees is the indexical 'there', as it extends the line between the two trees. In this way, this behavior is an indexical indicating the direction of their journey. At the same time, a specific rhythmical sequence indicates of the drumming hits indicates the duration of the rest. And this can be indeed conceived as a symbolic use of signs that can only be understood if one knows the conventionalized rules.

---

27 Cf. Deacon, T., Symbolic Species.

28 Cf. Deacon, T., Symbolic Species.

29 Cf. Robinson, A., Traces of the Trinity. Signs, Sacraments and Sharing God's Life, Pos. 278.

30 Cf. Robinson, A., Traces of the Trinity. Signs, Sacraments and Sharing God's Life, Pos. 2645.

31 Cf. Fuentes, A./Kissel, M./Peterson, J., Semiose in der Evolution.

32 Cf. Boesch, C., Symbolic Communication in Wild Chimpanzees?.

33 Cf. Fuentes, A./Kissel, M./Peterson, J., Semiose in der Evolution.

Another example shows that bonobos are able to learn symbolic language. But all attempts to teach them symbolic language directly, by didactic means and direct interaction, failed. But they were able to learn symbolic language when they had the opportunity to learn by watching other species use these symbolic signs. This means, however, that the bonobos draw a direct, i.e. indexical, relation between the signs that appear for us arbitrary or symbolically felt signs, and what they signify or what effect their use causes for the interpretants. And their 'interpretation' then consists simply in the fact that they can use it in the same way, i.e. in conformity to the 'rule'.[34]

The use of indexical signs, however, is no privilege of primates alone. Even an amoeba following the chemical traces of a bacteria uses indexical signs, which are as fallible as any other use of signs.[35] Some recent scholars have also tried to apply semiotics to the biochemical reproduction of DNA and RNA.[36] The point, therefore, is not that chimpanzees use indexical signs, but that chimpanzees and bonobos develop symbolic signs out of indexical ones.

Why are these examples, especially the last one of the bonobos, important for our purposes? It is important because it shows that symbols are not necessarily abstractions from iconic signs, but a side-effect of the use of primarily indexical signs. Of course, we cannot simply generalize these findings since they are dependent on only two empirical observations. Nevertheless, in order to understand the relationship between semiosis and narrativity, it is highly important, as we will see in the next subchapter.

The priority of the indexical use of signs can also be found in the ontogenesis of humans. At the age of 12 months, infants can perform declarative, imperative, and cooperative-supporting or informing deictic actions.[37]

12.8 The Narrative Basis of Semiosis

At first glance, one might assume that the relationship between semiosis and narrativity consists in (a) narrations as a subset of the use of signs, and in (b) narrations as the combination of signs, which are not stories in themselves.

34 Cf. FUENTES, A./KISSEL, M./PETERSON, J., Semiose in der Evolution.

35 Cf. ROBINSON, A., Traces of the Trinity. Signs, Sacraments and Sharing God's Life, Pos. 2513–2535.

36 Cf. ROBINSON, A./SOUTHGATE, C., General Definition; LUI, L.T./YANG, Z.R./ROBINSON, A./SOUTHGATE, C., Interpretation and the Origin of Life.

37 Cf. LISZKOWSKI, U./CARPENTER, M./STRIANO, T./TOMASELLO, M., 12- and 18-Month-Olds Point to Provide Information for Others.

In this case, the concept of signs would be prior to the concept of narration. This assumption is not completely wrong, insofar as it is an assumption about secondary narrations, especially the subset of language-like narrations. However, the question about the relationship between the semiosis and narrativity is only taken seriously when first-order stories and primary stories come into play. But then the relationship is exactly the other way around: semiosis without narrations are unthinkable. Consequently, the use of signs presupposes its embeddedness in first-order narrations. What is the evidence for this position?

1. Peirce always conceives of semiosis as a temporally structured event. Making something signified present by a sign using an interpretative sign is not a timeless or sequenceless state of affairs, but in the semiosis – like in movement – the intentionality of sequences and temporality is given. And this is a necessary, but in itself not yet a sufficient condition of narrativity.

2. Peirce conceives of the signifying object of a sign and the interpretant itself as signs, which indicates that any signified thing in a particular semiosis could have been an interpretant in another, prior semiotic process. In turn, every interpretant can become something signified that will be made present in a following semiosis. The threefold relations of a semiosis, including its *relata* of sign-object, signified, and interpretant, is only a section of a wider nexus of events or of a process, with the aim of describing the abstract rule of this wider nexus in a more concrete way. The interwovenness of any particular semiosis into a wider nexus of events is another, necessary condition of primary narrativity.

3. The kind of determination of the interpretant by the sign-object, which is itself determined by the signified, cannot be understood in a deterministic manner. The processual connection of the semiotic events described above is not based on causality. It is open to the emergence of novelty out of the semiotic process, and it is open to incompleteness, i.e. to the fact that a response (the interpretant) does not take up what is given by the pathos (by the sign-object) completely. The signified, therefore, always remains the other in the semiotic process, which includes a surplus of determinative force for the subsequent semiotic processes. In a semiotic process, something really new can spontaneously emerge, but it is also possible that something gained in the past can disappear. These features of novelty and otherness are also important elements of primary narrativity.

These three elements reveal that the description of the semiotic process is an abstract description of primary narrativity. This description becomes even clearer by taking the biosemiotic results into account.

4. Whatever is indexed is immediately dependent on narrative, way-formational lines. It is the primary means for signifying a movement on a

wayformational line from the perspective of the wayformational line itself. Whether one points in a particular direction with one's finger or whether chimpanzees drum on trees, in both cases a wayformational line is signified as a sequential part of a first-order narration. It is signified in a way that includes the signifying indexical act into the wayformational line itself without pretending to hover above it. Hovering above the concrete wayformational lines is unthinkable when indexical signs are in use. The movement of the chimpanzees from tree to tree is therefore a wave-movement that includes the repeated semiotic drumming on trees. In the same sense, pointing with one's arm into the direction of one's movement is itself a part of the wayformational line. The indexical sign does not only presuppose primary narrativity in order to be understood, it is in itself part of the movement of primary narrativity. The indexical sign is, however, as we saw, the offspring of both the iconic and the symbolic sign. We saw already that symbolic signs can emerge out of indexical ones, in case of the chimpanzees and bonobos. Of course, no one would deny that it is possible for the symbolic signs to appear from the background of iconic ones. But iconic signs are constituted by primary narrativity and wayformational lines. In Peirce's semiotics, this fact remains opaque, since an icon is associated with firstness. But firstness, as a monadic relation, is no relation at all, but only the form of a predication. The category of firstness strictly means something possible that is not actualized. The consequence of this is that an actual iconic sign is dependent on indexical activities because in order to diagnose a structural similarity between a signified object and the sign-object, another signifying activity is necessary, by which one points indexically to the signified object as well as to the sign-object, which results in making the structural similarity present in the interpretant apparent. Every iconic sign, therefore, is constituted by a logically prior indexical semiosis. An iconic sign is the effect, that is, it is the interpretant of an indexical semiosis that occurred previously. *The fact that the use of symbolic signs and the use of iconic signs presupposes the previous use of indexical signs implies that the indexical sign is the basis of the whole semiosis.* And the indexical sign is nothing but the possibility of itself signifying in a primary-narrative sequence a section of a wayformational line. This signifying means that the whole semiotic process is unthinkable without primary narrativity. Far more: a semiotic process is only possible because it is interwoven in a previous narrative process and since it is a primary-narrative process.

Symbols provide a rule for signifying acts allowing for the possibility of releasing the semiotic process from the primary-narrative process of the wayformational line. Through this they enable the development of secondary narrations – of tellable non-fictional and fictional stories. These secondary stories can be more or less abstract. Semiotics is itself nothing other than an example of such an abstract secondary narration.

We should take a look at the level of the three types of the interpretant, which reveals that the interpretant always effects the primary narration and therefore the formation of the wayformational line. Whereas the symbolic relationship between sign-object and signified object enables the shift from primary narrativity to secondary narrativity, so the interpretant in all its forms enables the shift from secondary narrativity back to primary narrativity.

In the case of the *firstness-like interpretant*, the symbolically enabled secondary narrativity becomes a form of perception in the primary narration of the actual wayformational line, by the appearance of feelings as the effects of the affordances of the environment on the perceiver.

In the case of the *secondness-like interpretant*, an immediate formation of the subsequent section of primary narrativity takes place, mediated by the semiotic use of second-order narrations. Whereas the firstness-like interpretant shows the ability of secondary narrations to influence primary ones by their perception of fact and value, the secondness-like interpretant shows that primary narrations can be spontaneously co-formed by secondary ones.

In the case of the thirdness-like interpretant, a state of affairs is conceived by 'thinking' in its broadest sense of *rule-driven, reactive action*. This rule-driven, reactive action always happens on the level of primary narrativity. It appears in the two shapes of rule-driven, habitualized perception of fact and value on one's own wayformational line, and, building on this, in the subsequent structure that takes the rule-driven, habituated form of one's own way-line within primary narrativity. Only in border-line cases it can be intentional perception (observation) and intentional action (by planning). In those cases where a dog is hunting a cat, it is only possible because the dog is able to use thirdness-like interpretants.

For humans, the thirdness-like interpretant enables the alternative between transport and wayfaring (ch. 8). Both are different rules for the constitution of the interpretant. *Transport* is a rule or a habit, which works intentionally toward subsuming all that can appear on the level of primary narrativity as possible objects of signification under the rectifying secondary narrativity already possessed. In contrast, *wayfaring* is attentional, i.e. it is the readiness to let one's secondary narrativity to be constantly shaped anew by semiotically mediated perceptions of fact and value on the level of primary narrativity.

What does this analysis show about the relationship between semiosis and narrativity, and what does it achieve?

First, semiosis is not a basis for narrativity, but rather presupposes primary narrativity.

Second, semiosis enables secondary narrativity.

Third, the semiosis can explain how the mesh of primary and secondary narrativity comes into existence. It can explain, in other words, how secondary narrativity can mediate the immediate perception of facts and values, and how secondary narrativity can co-form primary narrativity.

The last thing to do in this chapter is to give a word of warning: The semiotics used here on the basis of Peirce's semiotics – like all other possible semiotics – does not belong to the mediated immediateness of the perception of facts and values of primary narrativity on a wayformational line. They are a means of classification that serve to analyze perception, which shows that semiotics is always laden by ontological interpretations – and here 'interpretations' has the usual meaning of a cognitive and abstract operation.

CHAPTER 13

Narrations and Metaphors

The task and function of this chapter is twofold, and can be understood by its position between ch. 12 and ch. 14. One the one hand, we must show that metaphors are not the 'bricks' of narrations, which may be understood independently of them, but that metaphors presuppose both primary and secondary narrations. On the other hand, we have to show that metaphors have priority over concepts in a way that every use of concepts presupposes metaphorical speech.

These basic theses fit well with some contemporary theories of metaphor, but they also transcend these theories in their specific orientation. In order to show that this is so, we start with a short classification or story about the history of the research on metaphors.

13.1 Typology of Theories of the Metaphor

Every possible classification scheme of theories of the metaphor is necessarily an abstraction from a history of theories of the metaphor. And all histories of theories of the metaphor are second-order narrations, and therefore, it is determined by the wayformational line of the narrator and therefore can only exist in the plural.[1] Our intention is not to present such a history in a comprehensive way,[2] but only so far as it provides an orientation for the design of our own narrative theory on metaphors.

Elsewhere,[3] I suggested that theories of the metaphor be classified with the help of a twofold distinction, using (1) the question of which role in language is ascribed to metaphor, and (2) which hermeneutical role these metaphors play. In regard to the first question, metaphors can either be seen as a special kind of language or as a dimension of language. In regard to the second question, they can be seen as reality-relevant or as reality-irrelevant. If they are seen as reality-relevant, we can introduce a further distinction, asking whether this relation to reality is seen as conceptual/cognitive. In designing this classification,

1 Cf. STOELLGER, P., Vierfacher Sinn der Metapher, 90.

2 A good introduction to the different contemporary and classic metaphor theories can be found in ROLF, E., Metapherntheorien.

3 Cf. MÜHLING, M., Liebesgeschichte Gott, 37f.

 DOI:10.30965/9783846765852_014

I presupposed that metaphors are entities of second-order narrativity. Here we have to ask whether this presupposition is indeed a valid one. By entangling these questions, we get at least four types of theories, of which the last distinction introduced can be subdivided, giving us five categories:

a) Metaphors as a reality-irrelevant, special kind of language

All theories that conceive metaphors (as in the rhetorical tradition) as tropes, or as a special kind of ornamental language that cannot be relevant to reality because they can be reduced to conceptual language, belong to this class.

Examples include Quintilian and the classical rhetoric that saw metaphors as abbreviated parables.[4] This understanding of metaphor influenced such different thinkers as Thomas Aquinas, Descartes, Hobbes, Locke, all the way up to Donald Davidson. Normally, one does not use Quintilian's but Aristotle's definition of the metaphor. However, this definition might be used against Aristotle's own intention by being polluted with a Platonic skepticism of poetics. Often, one fears the 'cheating' power of the metaphor.[5] Also, in those cases where this fear is absent, as in Aquinas who uses as theological metaphors extensively, the metaphor is seen as reducible to an analogy.[6]

An expression of Jesus' like 'I am the resurrection and the life', (Joh 11:25), therefore, means that Jesus speaks here on the basis of his divine nature on the behalf of God. Yet God 'is' also not simply 'life', but one has to use the *analogia causalitatis* in order to translate this sentence into its 'proper' meaning: God is the creator of life, i.e. the first unmoved mover of end-directed motion.

b) Metaphors as reality-irrelevant dimension of language

This category includes those accounts of metaphors that conceive of the metaphorical as a dimension, perhaps even as a basic one, of all language. Nevertheless, the metaphor is not able to disclose reality in any way whatsoever. The result is an epistemologically skeptical position, or a position that regards reality as a product of language and metaphors.

The paradigm of this type is Nietzsche's understanding of metaphor. He claims that all language is metaphorical. And far more: even a stimulation of the nerves by a fantastical image is seen as a metaphor, in the same way as the apparently conceptual language

4 Cf. WEINRICH, H., Allgemeine Semantik der Metapher, 317.

5 HOBBES, T., Leviathan, 29 (ch. 4), counts metaphor explicitly as among the misuses of language, which occurs, 'when they use words metaphorically; that is, in other sense than that they are ordained for; and thereby deceive others.' Cf. relatedly also LOCKE, J., Essay Concerning Human Understanding, bk 3, ch 10. DAVIDSON, D., What Metaphors Mean, 33, opposes the metaphor to literal speech and gives a succinct diagnosis: 'Literal meaning and truth conditions can be assigned to words and sentences apart from particular contexts of use.'

6 THOMAS VON AQUIN, s.th.3q.a8.ad2 acts on the assumption that in religious speech the metaphor can also be substituted directly or that it can be resolved by analogy.

of the philosophers is regarded as nothing 'but the worn-out and sensually powerless metaphors'.[7] Since all language is metaphorical, it cannot conceive of any aspect of the essence of things. Metaphors are inappropriate for understanding reality and since all language is metaphorical, language in general has nothing to do with reality. Nietzsche is therefore an example of how a radical understanding of metaphors seemingly leads to a radical kind of skepticism and relativism. However, this is only 'seemingly' the case, because Nietzsche regards his own opinion, e.g. of life in contrast to the Christian understanding of life, as far more appropriate.[8] In Nietzsche's case, however, this is not the well-known relativist or constructivist fallacy, but a radical reduction of the concepts of truth and reality to power. Some post-modern understandings of metaphor, like Richard Rorty's or Jacques Derrida's, belong to this line of thinking.[9]

c) Metaphors as a reality-relevant, non-conceptual special kind of language
d) Metaphors as a reality-relevant, conceptual special case of language

Many influential theories of the metaphor belong to these two categories. Since both categories cannot be sharply distinguished, we will discuss them in a single passage.

First, we must mention Aristotle's famous definition of a metaphor as 'the application of an alien name by transference, either from genus to species, or from species to genus, or from species to species, or by analogy'.[10] This definition, which is in the end unsatisfying,[11] sounds at first glance as though it would deal with metaphor as a reality-irrelevant special case of language in a way similar to the rhetorical tradition. And indeed, the rhetorical tradition referred to this definition as we already saw in section a). Ricœur also regards the so-called substitution theories of the metaphor based in Aristotle's definition, although he does not see a decisive distinction between the substitution-theories and the so-called interaction theories.[12] However, for Aristotle, poetics is not a subordinate branch of studies. Therefore, this classification is not possible. And Aristotle is not speaking of substitutions, but of a transferal. The consequence is that Aristotle's definition belongs to category c), though it is nevertheless too vague to derive a theory from it.

Others within this category are such diverse understandings as Giambattista Vico's, Humboldt's, Herder's, Cassirer's and Blumenberg's. What they have in common is that metaphor is seen as a non-conceptual, special kind of language that nevertheless has

---

7 NIETZSCHE, F., Über Wahrheit und Lüge, 878–880 (transl. MM).

8 Cf. e.g. NIETZSCHE, F., Der Antichrist, 183 (Abschn. 18).

9 Cf. STOELLGER, P., Vierfacher Sinn der Metapher, 95.

10 ARISTOTELES, Poetica, 34 (1457b, 6–9): μεταφορὰ δε ἐστιν ὀνόματος ἀλλοτρίου ἐποφορὰ τοῦ γένους ἐπὶ εἶδος ἢ ἀπὸ τοῦ εἴδους ἐπὶ τὸ γένος ἢ ἀπὸ εἴδους ἐπὶ εἶδος ἢ κατὰ τὸ ἀνάλογον. Transl.: ARISTOTLE, Poetics (engl.), 28.

11 One must admit that, despite all the criticism of Aristotle, he was not intending a strict definition here, which SOSKICE, J.M., Metaphor and Religious Language, 9, correctly realizes as well: 'Aristotle was not concerned to give accounts of mechanisms and processes, but simply wished to provide his reader with an identifying description of metaphor. For this purpose his account is satisfactory.'

12 Cf. RICŒUR, P., Rule of Metaphor, 173f.

reality-disclosing potential. Whereas metaphor for Humboldt and Herder is seen as a vehicle for divine presence,[13] it is, in its 'radical' form, in the reception of Cassirer by Max Müller, an expression of the pre-conceptual symbolic pregnance of perception.[14]

Blumenberg distinguishes on the one hand between metaphors as relics of language, which are 'rudiments on the way from mythos to logos'[15] that are regarded as not very interesting, and, on the other hand, the really interesting, irreducible 'absolute metaphors', 'which cannot be taken back into the essential, into logicity.'[16] These metaphors are important, because the 'human reference to reality is indirect, circuitous, selective, and most of all metaphorical.'[17] Regarding the reference to reality, metaphors do not deal with secondary questions, because

> they give an 'answer' to the seemingly naïve, principally unanswerable questions, which are relevant simply because they cannot be eliminated. We do not *ask* these questions, but find them already *asked* in the ground of being.[18]

The questions represent in their own manner 'the un-experienceable, the never completely viewable whole of reality.'[19] Nevertheless these absolute metaphors are not 'black boxes', but one can use them for arguments – not classical, conceptual ones, but metaphorical ones. This use is possible because, although they cannot be supplements to, substitutes for, or corrected by concepts, they can be so by other metaphors.[20] The possibility exists precisely because these absolute metaphors are also not without context. They have to be understood historically, for without knowledge of their historical horizon and their metaphorical character, an understanding of concepts is impossible.[21]

Other theories of this category include those of Weinrich, Max Black, Earl R. MacCormac, Antony Flew, Janet Martin Soskice, Strub, and partially Ricœur and Eberhard Jüngel. In the latter theories, the following category of the metaphor as a dimensional, reality-disclosing kind of language also emerges.

Flew sees in religious-metaphorical language an emotive function, which express the attitudes and the ethos of a person.[22] Therefore, Flew's theory can be understood as a primitive version of Blumenberg's.

Other instantiations of this category see a closer connection between metaphors and concepts. The catachrestic function of metaphors, i.e. their ability to close semantical gaps and thereby to express states of affairs, is a decisive hint of the fact that

---

13 Cf. STOELLGER, P., Vierfacher Sinn der Metapher, 95.

14 Cf. STOELLGER, P., Metapher als Modell symbolischer Prägnanz, 122–128.

15 BLUMENBERG, H., Paradigmen zu einer Metaphorologie, 10 (transl. MM).

16 BLUMENBERG, H., Paradigmen zu einer Metaphorologie, 10 (transl. MM).

17 BLUMENBERG, H., Wirklichkeiten, in denen wir leben, 115 (transl. MM).

18 BLUMENBERG, H., Paradigmen zu einer Metaphorologie, 23 (transl. MM).

19 BLUMENBERG, H., Paradigmen zu einer Metaphorologie, 25 (transl. MM).

20 Cf. BLUMENBERG, H., Paradigmen zu einer Metaphorologie, 12f.

21 Cf. BLUMENBERG, H., Paradigmen zu einer Metaphorologie, 13. For an extensive discussion, analysis, and criticism of Blumenberg's understanding of metaphors, see cf. STOELLGER, P., Metapher und Lebenswelt.

22 Cf. MÜHLING, M., Metaphor III+IV.

metaphors also play a major role in constative speech-acts. In this case, metaphorical language becomes literal language, and many scholars, like Ricœur, do not have a special interest in studying these 'dead' metaphors.[23] However, even dead metaphors are far from being dead![24]

During the mid-20th century, Max Black's interaction-theory was very influential. He claims that metaphors consist in the form 'A is B', e.g. 'man is wolf'. Such a metaphor cannot be translated into 'humans are cruel', because it is not only a statement about humans, but also about wolves, with the effect that wolves become more human than they would normally be thought of. Therefore, Black claims, metaphors have a double reference.[25]

Ricœur and Jüngel use this understanding as a basis for their own theories. Ricœur is not primarily interested in dead metaphors, but in living, poetic metaphors. He corrects Black by claiming that instead of a double reference, metaphors have a 'split' one.[26] However extraordinarily influential Ricœur was, one has to ask whether, the one hand, he elevates the metaphor into the completely exceptional, while, on the other hand, he narrows the meaning of the metaphor by restricting his inquiry to the poetic metaphors that appear in texts.

In Janet Martin Soskice' understanding, which is similar to Black's double reference and Ricœur's shared reference, a 'metaphor is a figure of speech whereby we speak about one thing in terms which are seen to be suggestive of another.'[27] However, Soskice does not only distinguish the metaphor from conceptual speech, but also, with the rhetorical tradition, from other kinds of non-conceptual speech.[28]

Most of those who deploy such theories in theology understand religious speech as genuinely metaphorical speech. Metaphorical language, then, fits excellently with the task of expressing 'God' and all things related to God, since God is not seen as one with a spatiotemporal existence. The claim is that metaphors express the categorical distinction between God and the world. Nevertheless, metaphors are still seen as a special case of language. They are sharply distinguished from literal language. If one does not take notice of this distinction, and mistakenly regard religious metaphors as literal language, one generates myths without being conscious of what one is doing. Then, one perverts the essence of religious language and falls into dogmatism. This is, in short, the understanding of religious metaphors at work in the early Earl R. MacCormac[29] within the framework of the dialogue between theology and the natural sciences, in Sally McFague's feminist theology,[30] or in John Hick, who uses this understanding of metaphors to criticize the two natures of traditional Christology.[31]

---

23 Cf. Ricœur, P., Rule of Metaphor, 99, 259.

24 Cf. Lakoff, G./Johnson, M., Philosophy in the Flesh, 124–126.

25 Cf. Black, M., Metaphor; Black, M., More about Metaphor.

26 Cf. Ricœur, P., Rule of Metaphor, 224.

27 Soskice, J.M., Metaphor and Religious Language, 15. Vgl. ebd., 75f.

28 Cf. Soskice, J.M., Metaphor and Religious Language, 54–66.

29 Cf. MacCormac, E.R., Metaphor and Myth.

30 Cf. McFague, S., Metaphorical Theology.

31 For a description, analysis, and criticism of this treatment by Hick cf. Dalferth, I.U., Der auferweckte Gekreuzigte, 1–37.

Although all these theories regard the metaphor as a special case of language that is important, intelligible, and with some cognitive or conceptual content as well (without being reducible to concepts), they all understand very different things to be metaphors. A reason for this might be that each of them uses different, prototypical examples as a basis for elucidating the metaphor: Black uses everyday language, Ricœur, the poetic living metaphor, MacCormac also looks at dead metaphors, Soskice distinguishes it from other 'tropes', and so on. Philipp Stoellger has therefore suggested ordering this plurality by identifying different aspects of a dynamic phenomenon.

He suggests overcoming Blumenberg's antagonism between metaphors and concepts by crossing this antagonism with the other antagonism between the symbolic and the imaginary (using Lacan and Blanchot) in order to get a metaphorical quadruplet (or a symbolical one),[32] which appear in different variations in his writings.[33] The basic idea is in principle very simple. Metaphors can be understood with the help of two polar relations, like the two axes of a coordinate system. There is: (1) the dynamic of being situated on a horizon (the narrow context of the metaphor) and broadening of the horizon (widening), and there is (2), the dynamic of stabilization (tradition) and weakening (innovation). Then one gets a dynamic field that includes four directions:

– There is metaphorical communication *in the direction of stabilized tradition and being situated in a horizon*. Here we can find a background in the metaphors such as 'discussing is like fighting', which are used implicitly as a model for many of our academic discussions. They tend towards a kind of solidification, and in many cases, we are no longer aware that it is metaphors we are using. Their function is to provide an orientation to many different fields of life. The limit case of this direction is univocal language.

– There is metaphorical communication *in the direction of stabilized tradition that broadens horizons*. In this case, the background metaphors are situated in theoretical or academic contexts and they serve as a source for models and theories. The horizon is thereby broadened and differentiations and distinctions are gained. In this case, the limit is also univocal language, but this limit is gained by the axis of stabilization and weakening alone, not by being placed on a horizon or widening it.

– There is metaphorical communication *in the direction of weakening innovation that is situated in a horizon*. Here we find metaphors that appear frequently (but not exclusively) in myths, fables, and parables, or metaphors that appear in poetic culture that has become common knowledge. What is interesting here is that they can stabilize identities although they are innovative, because they presuppose a common horizon of use.

– There is metaphorical communication *in the direction of weakening innovation that broadens horizons*. These are Ricœur's living metaphors and the manifold expressions of art. What they have in common is that they lead to pluralization. They are in danger of drifting into pure equivocation and no longer being understandable.

32 Cf. Stoellger, P., Grenzen der Metaphorologie Blumenbergs, 214.

33 Cf. Stoellger, P., Metapher als Modell symbolischer Prägnanz, 134 and Stoellger, P., Vierfacher Sinn der Metapher, 105f.

Stoellger intends to order the different theories of metaphor that belong to these two types regarding form and function. But in principle, he thereby leaves out the type wherein the metaphor is seen as a special kind of language that is nevertheless relevant for the understanding of reality. The reason he does so, is because the reality-irrelevant special cases of the metaphor are also classified here as a kind of drifting, conceptual, and univocal language also appears as a limit. Therefore, his model of ordering theories of metaphors is a semiotic model that does not only classify metaphors. But if this is plausible, then we have to speak of another type of theory.

e) Metaphors as reality-relevant, conceptual dimension of language

We should not subdivide this type into two others, unlike the previous one (c & d). If the metaphorical is a dimension of any kind of language, the metaphorical must be related to the conceptual as well as to the non-conceptual in order to be a distinct dimension. This type is only implicitly given in some theories of the metaphor or explicitly developed in theories as diverse as the different stages of the understanding of metaphor found in Lakoff and Johnson, the model-theory of Mary Hesse, which is developed within the framework of a theory of the natural sciences, the insights of the later Earls R. MacCormac or also in our own previously presented theory[34] (which, as it happens, is in need of modification). The metaphor 'metaphors are concepts' implies (independently of the question of whether metaphors are generally reversible or not) that concepts become metaphor-like, and evokes the reverse metaphor: 'concepts are metaphors'. It does not mean that there is no distinction between metaphors and concepts anymore. It means, rather, that we must re-evaluate the metaphor as a basic function of the formation of all language-like semiosis.

13.2 The Heuristic Continuum of Metaphors and Concepts

Most theories of the metaphor draw a sharp line between metaphors and concepts. A concept is, in short, a correlation of extension and intension, or the referents that apply to a single predication in a monadic predicate. Thereby, one gets in regard to the extension of any concept '... is P' only two possibilities: either the substitution of the variable that stands for the extension forms a true statement or a false one. Every concept, therefore, divides the world in a binary manner, which can be graphically illustrated in different ways. A very popular

---

34 Cf. HESSE, M.B., Cognitive Claims of Metaphor; MACCORMAC, E.R., Metaphor and Myth; MÜHLING, M., Gott ist Liebe, 24–33.

illustration is the Venn- and Euler-diagrams that show the sharp boundaries of concepts with the help of circles illustrating sets. The concept '… is yellow' would then be illustrated by the means of a circle illustrating the extension of the concepts, inside of which would be things that have this particular attribute. Another kind of exemplification could illustrate the binary true-false codification by a coordinate system with the x-axis illustrating the extension and the y-axis illustrating the truth-value. The truth value can only have the two values 0 (false) and 1 (true). The truth-function of any concept is identical: a horizontal line, identical with 0 and then a leap to another horizontal line parallel to the x-axis with the value of 1. The extension leaps discontinuously between 'true' and 'false'. In this understanding of concepts, metaphorical language can only be explained by classifying it as 'properly' belonging to the false- or 0-line. The only way therefore to see a metaphor not only as figurative but also as cognitive speech would require the use of more than one concept, i.e. to speak of a shared reference to different extensions of different concepts. By this strategy, the metaphor can become intelligible, but it remains a special case of language and in principle (but not necessarily in practice) it is still substitutable, since language here has a single principle of construction: the conceptual binary.

However, there is an alternative: one can hold that the binary model of concepts is wrong. MacCormac, in a modification of his earlier theory of metaphors, suggested in the 1980s[35] using fuzzy-set theory[36] to model a continuum between metaphors and concepts. According to the fuzzy-set theory, there is in a coordinate system no truth function that leaps from 0 to 1 but a continuous transition, described by a function that is infinitely limited in the one direction to y=0, whereas it infinitely limited to y=1 in the other direction. In between there is an inflection. In this picture, there is not only two truth-values, but a continuous truth function in which 'fitting' (true) and 'non-fitting' (false) are only liminal threshold values. If this picture is applicable to concepts, then in terms of comfortability one can introduce abstract interpretations. One possibility would be to introduce to a specific value of x a voluntarily or phenomenally forced limit between fitting and non-fitting, or true and false, or literal and metaphorical, respectively. Disputes about definitions would become disputes about contextual decisions as to where the line might best be drawn in this or that case, instead of disputes about sharp demarcations. Another possibility would be introducing not only one line, but more than one by dividing the continuous curve between 0 and 1 in different segments. For example, a first segment would run infinitely to y=1 from the arbitrarily set y-value

35 Cf. MacCormac, E.R., Metaphor and Fuzzy Sets.
36 Cf. Zadeh, L.A., Fuzzy Sets.

0.9, which would be the segment of literal or conceptual language. Then we would have a segment, say between liminal y=0 and y= 0.1. This would signify a 'false' or 'non-fitting' or incomprehensible use of the predicate. In between these two segments one could also introduce one or more cuts: in the areas between y=0.7 and y=0.9 we would find 'dead' metaphors, in the segment between y=0.4 and y=0.7 we would find background metaphors of the areas of the life-world, and in the area between y=0.1 and y=0.4 we would find creative and innovative metaphors. In this model, the metaphor is no longer a derivative of the conceptual, but *vice versa* a concept is a derivation of language that is generally metaphorical.

This model might be tempting, but there is a decisive difficulty: semantic meaning obviously cannot be quantified. There would therefore be no concept/metaphor for which we could really find a calculable function. Moreover, the function could be very different for different concepts/metaphors. The conclusion must be that this fuzzy-set model of the continuity between metaphors and concepts can only have a heuristic function. Nevertheless, it can explain why there are so many theories of the metaphor: the different theories mentioned above are simply concentrating on only one or only a few possible segments. They all presuppose an abstraction from continuity to discontinuity, but in different ways. What they have in common is that they are unaware that they have made reductive cuts within the continuum. Presupposing that is the case, another question arises: would these interpretative cuts, however they may be made, be purely conventional interpretations? Or are these cuts enforced by phenomenality? In other words: are these cuts made arbitrarily or are they enforced by the things themselves? Are there cases, in which these cuts are arbitrary, whereas in other cases they are not? And would the phenomenal operations that lead to the cuts in the latter case be the same for all concepts/metaphors (or metaphors/concepts)? With these questions, the continuum model comes to its limits. It cannot answer these questions, because it has more heuristic than explanatory power.

13.3 The Basis of Metaphors and Concepts in Indexical, Primary Narrativity

With *Metaphors We Live By*, George Lakoff and Marc Johnson developed a conceptual theory of the metaphor that inaugurated further research, both by themselves and others.[37] In contrast to, say, Ricœur and Blumenberg, they do not start with extraordinary metaphors, but with metaphors found in the

37 Cf. e.g. LAKOFF, G./JOHNSON, M., Philosophy in the Flesh.

everyday languages of ordinary life and the academy. They show that our normal, argumentative, and conceptual language is dependent on a plurality of key-metaphors that alone or in conjunction with others form entangled contexts of concepts in which arguments take place. For example, such organizing metaphors are the following ones: 'disputing is fighting', 'time is money', 'ideas are objects', 'linguistic expressions are containers', 'communication is transmission', 'happy is up, un-happy is down', 'more is up, less is down', 'good is up, bad is down', 'rational is up, emotional is down or deep', 'inflation is an entity', 'the mind is a machine', etc. These key or background metaphors structure the whole context of language and argumentation in a manner that is usually regarded as conceptual. Metaphors are not anti-conceptual, but open up fields of context. On the basis of these phenomenal observations through to the conceptual use of metaphors, Lakoff and Johnson design an explanatory theory of the metaphor that is also a theory of concepts, which is to say, the use of language in general.

Their working definition of the metaphor seems to be conventional: 'The essence of metaphor is understanding and experiencing one kind of thing in terms of another.'[38] However, it only sounds conventional. Behind it is the following claim: there are different kinds of phenomenal experiences, like experiences of bodily movement, emotional experiences, social experiences, ethical experiences, etc. There is not one more basic than another:

> Perhaps the most important thing to stress about grounding is the distinction between an experience and the way we conceptualize it. We are not claiming that physical experience is in any way more basic than other ways of experience, whether emotional, mental, cultural, or whatever. All of these experiences may be just as basic as physical experiences.[39]

In regard to understanding, however, they claim a priority of the bodily/motoric experiences, simply called 'physical': 'Rather, what we are claiming abound grounding is that we typically conceptualize the nonphysical in terms of the physical – that is, we conceptualize the less clearly delineated in terms of the more clearly delineated.'[40] Experiences are distinguished in a threefold manner as (1) spatial, (2) social, and (3) emotional experiences. The claim is that only the spatial experiences are expressed by direct concepts, everything else needs a manifold metaphorical speech, which in the end can be reduced to spatial metaphors.

38 LAKOFF, G./JOHNSON, M., Metaphors We Live by, 5.
39 LAKOFF, G./JOHNSON, M., Metaphors We Live by, 59.
40 LAKOFF, G./JOHNSON, M., Metaphors We Live by, 59.

Mark Johnson tried to illustrate this thesis by way of infant development. He identified a primary period of 'conflation, in which emotional events and spatial-bodily events appear without any separation together. The feeling of security is always accompanied by bodily warmth and closeness, etc. Only in a later stage is there a period of differentiation.'[41] However tempting this theory might be, there is a decisive mistake: If this period of conflation is really the developmental horizon in which we recieve our concepts, why then are spatial metaphors primary and not emotional ones? One could claim just as well that it is the affective concepts of 'closeness' and 'warmth' that are primary, whereas their physical meanings are transmitted to spatial and physical objects. Moreover, to name this period 'conflation' already presupposes the latter differentiation. Therefore, there is nothing like a period of conflation, only a primary period of non-differentiation, e.g., between the emotional and the spatial. And this is nothing but a primary developmental period in which concepts picture affordances, but not spatial events on the one hand and affective feelings on the other. Here we must correct Johnson with Gibson's insights. Johnson's mistake, given in the language of analytical relations, is that he regards the *relata* (the emotional and the spatial) as primary, which are then in a secondary way bound by the relations of conflation or differentiation. Lakoff and Johnson are not able to think of the priority of the relation or the wayformational line, out of which the *relata* (emotional and spatial) emerge.

Our whole conceptual language is structured metaphorically and is not thinkable without metaphors. Every metaphor has an ontological, an orientating, and a structural function.[42] The basis of the metaphor is subject to change over time. Whereas in their earlier work Lakoff and Johnson conceived of direct, not primarily metaphorical concepts – i.e. the direct, spatial expressions – in the tradition of phenomenology,[43] their later publications predominantly use neurobiology in order to explain the 'direct' spatial language as well as metaphorical thinking.[44] They have far more in mind than to simply explain how metaphors work; they claim nothing less than to provide a third way beyond objectivism and subjectivism.[45]

Lakoff's and Johnson's theory is fascinating in its broad outline and remarkable in its details. Nevertheless, we must criticize some points. In doing so, we will restrict ourselves to two important points:

1. The shift from a phenomenological basis to a neurobiological one is not without problems. It is right that the brain thought of as an organ of relations

41 Cf. Lakoff, G./Johnson, M., Philosophy in the Flesh, 46. 48f.

42 While Lokoff and Johnson primarily differentiated between ontological, orientating, and structural metaphors, they modified their theses to the effect that now different aspects of the metaphorical are seen, cf. Lakoff, G./Johnson, M., Metaphors We Live by, 264.

43 Cf. Lakoff, G./Johnson, M., Metaphors We Live by, 223.

44 Cf. Lakoff, G./Johnson, M., Metaphors We Live by, 257–264; Lakoff, G./Johnson, M., Philosophy in the Flesh, 49–56.

45 Cf. Lakoff, G./Johnson, M., Philosophy in the Flesh, 93.

plays an important mediating role in the relationship between thinking, feeling, the living body, and the environment.[46] Particular insights, like the co-activation of the same brain-area in perceiving and acting are of high value, because this shows that neurobiology confirms that it is affordances that are primarily perceived.[47] But such a mediating role is also not a foundation. As fascinating as the neuro-linguistic results may appear, they are a detail in this process of mediation. They cannot substitute the phenomenal basis for the conceptual/metaphorical.

2. It is exactly this phenomenal basis for the conceptual/metaphorical that remained underdetermined in their original position as well, because they gave no semiotic or phenomenal justification for the primacy of spatial language. If Johnson's so-called period of conflation in the developmental history of ontogenesis actually points to a primary, undivided perception of the spatial and emotional, then one cannot speak of primary metaphors referring to spatial order, from which more complex metaphors are derived.[48] Perhaps there are indeed something like primary metaphors functioning as a basis for more complex metaphors. But their differentiation – in the case of Lakoff and Johnson – reflects an ontological prejudice *post differentiationem* – as does their claim that spatial language finds its home in a non-metaphorical refuge.[49]

This last point is decisive: Lakoff and Johnson use an abstract concept of space and they narrow literal language down to the binary correlates 'above – below' and 'in front of – behind' (interestingly not 'right – left'). Such a move may not be without justification. But instead of simply asserting this, one would have to show phenomenologically why this is the case. A spatial foundation for the conceptual/metaphorical is highly dubious, since, as we saw, the concept of space is not a basic one, but only an abstraction from the phenomenally basic appearance of wayformational lines (ch. 11).

Factually, these correlates remain important for orientation in the mesh of wayformational lines, which is the medium of movement. But such a case must be shown. The concepts 'in front of – behind', 'above – below', and 'left – right' are neither primarily spatial concepts nor physical ones. Even a neuro-scientific foundation of these correlates is not very important. What is decisive is that these are linguistic signs that *substitute for deictic acts*. They are *indexical* concepts, or more concretely, indexical concepts indicating the relative movement between the environment and one's own living body in perception – including

46 Cf. FUCHS, T., Das Gehirn – ein Beziehungsorgan, 161.
47 Cf. LAKOFF, G./JOHNSON, M., Philosophy in the Flesh, 57.
48 Cf. LAKOFF, G./JOHNSON, M., Philosophy in the Flesh, 49.
49 Cf. LAKOFF, G./JOHNSON, M., Philosophy in the Flesh, 58f.

the perceived affordances. And in affordances, the spatial and the affective is undivided. The consequence is that the basis for the conceptual/metaphorical is indexicality. And if the indexical (as shown in ch. 12) is also the basis for any use of signs, and if the indexicality of semiosis is dependent on primary-narrative contexts, then the same is true for the metaphorical/conceptual. If Lakoff and Johnson are right in claiming that our language is metaphorical through and through in its dependence on indexical concepts forming the quasi-metaphorical basis, then this means that all our semantics, our language, our concepts, and metaphors are grounded in first-order narrations – stories–in which we are not simply involved, but out of which we are weaved. What is primary is actually all of the expressions that refer to indexicality in the movement of first-order narrativity in the framework of the movements of perception. Out of this framework, language emerges, which is indeed at the same time completely conceptual and metaphorical, which is not surprising, because even concept-metaphors are a subclass of signs. In other words, Lakoff and Johnson are doing no more than describing a special case of the triadic semiosis of language: something signified is intrinsically bound up with a sign-object and the interpreting sign. Without this, the semiotic character would be lost. '[U]nderstanding and experiencing one kind of thing in terms of another' is nothing but the description of semiosis in the special case of language.

13.4 Narrantic and Narrative Contexts of Semantic Unities

An advantage of Lakoff's and Johnson's definition of the metaphor is that the metaphor is primarily associated with understanding and experience, not only with speaking. But this definition also seems to presuppose the conceptual in a hidden manner, insofar as 'one kind of thing' is nothing but a hidden relationship between extension and intension, i.e. a concept. Does this mean that the concept is primary and the metaphor secondary? Concepts always deal with classifications, and the metaphor in this case presupposes classifications. Indeed, it could be that also in this case not only our language and our conceptual conclusions, but also our experience and understanding could be permeated by metaphors through and through. However, the metaphor would be as such secondary, as concepts would be the primary means for describing this activity of classification. Apart from the concrete linguistic, experiential, and hermeneutical context, there would exist pure concepts and pure classifications. And therefore we would be confronted once more with the question of whether these 'pure' concepts or classifications would behave like classical sets, including their binary order of fitness between intension and extension, or whether it would be possible that the relationship between intension and extension would behave in a dynamic-continuous fashion in the sense of fuzzy sets. Only if the latter possibility is genuine, could we distinguish the theory of metaphor from more classical theories, like the theory of analogy. In section 13.2, we saw that fuzzy sets of meanings can be modelled with the help of the fuzzy-set theory. But this is also 'only' a metaphor: 'meanings are fuzzy sets'. The original context of the meaning of fuzzy sets is mathematics. Therefore, this theory can be applied in a proper way only where quantifiable, continuous transitions exist. But that is not the case with concepts and meanings. Do we have another explanation for why meanings somehow behave fuzzily? If one subscribes to Davidson's opinion[50] that meanings exist independently of its contexts, for example, one would have to deny this possibility. But this is not the case, in two respects: the meaning of a word lies, as the late Wittgenstein knew, in its use in language.[51] Wittgenstein therefore votes against un-pragmatic semantics. We have to clarify this thesis in two ways: (1) On the one hand, there is always the narrantic context of concepts, i.e. a concept only appears as part of the primary-narrative events. (2) On the other hand, a concept also appears in a linguistic context, and this linguistic context is always a narrative and metaphorical context.

1. The thesis that it is the primary, narrative context, which is decisive for the meaning of linguistic expression – even in those cases where this narrantic story cannot be told by any of the persons involved – is justified by Hilary Putnam's famous twin earth thought experiments and by the thesis derived from them, that meanings are neither simply linguistic entities nor entities of the mind: 'Cut the pie anywhere you like, meanings ain't just in the head,'[52] but they are also in the concrete history of the dynamics of the narrantic events. Imagine a twin earth, resembling our own earth completely, including in its cultural history, with only one exception. On the twin earth, there is no substance H_2O, but instead there is an unknown substance XYZ, which looks like H_2O and is used by the inhabitants of the twin earth as H_2O is by us. The inhabitants of the twin earth also call XYZ 'water'. If an inhabitant of the twin earth is transferred without his knowledge to our earth in a situation where he finds himself in front of a glass of H_2O, then he would utter, as would his twin from our earth, the sentence 'this is water'. Both twins would also have – and this is an extension of Putnam's ideas – exactly the same neural states.[53] Nevertheless,

50 Cf. DAVIDSON, D., What Metaphors Mean.
51 Cf. WITTGENSTEIN, L., Philosophical Investigations, 43.
52 PUTNAM, H., Meaning of 'Meaning', 227.
53 Cf. MÜHLING, M., Resonances, 54.

this sentence uttered by the inhabitant of earth is true, whereas this sentence uttered by the inhabitant of twin earth is false. The reason being, that meanings are dependent on the factual narrantic context. And the narrantic context is in both cases a different one – even in those cases in which both of those uttering the sentence are unaware of this fact.

2. The claim that meanings depend not only on their narrantic context, but also on a narrative and metaphorical context, becomes clearer by showing how exactly extensions and intentions are related.

This question can be addressed with the help of prototype semantics, invented by the cognitive psychologist Eleanor Rosch,[54] and also employed by Lakoff. Here, in a pragmatic way, a particular prototype is used, which is typical for a specific class, for ordering other instantiations of this class by way of a family resemblance that is either closer or further from this prototype:

> For example, small flying singing birds like sparrows, robins, etc., are prototypical birds. Chickens, ostriches, and penguins are birds, but are not central members of the category – they are nonprototypical birds. But they are birds nonetheless, because they bear sufficient family resemblance to the prototype; that is, they share enough of the relevant properties of the prototype to be classified by people as birds.[55]

The distance relative to the prototype is given by family resemblance, with the consequence that a referent can belong more or less fully to a class. In everyday language, this partial membership of a class is signified by so called *hedges*, i.e. linguistic expressions like 'more or less', 'strictly speaking', 'in a broader sense', 'in the broadest sense', 'typically', 'in a technical sense', etc.[56] The use of hedges like these allows referents to belong partially to a set in the sense of Zadeh's fuzzy sets. This usage can also explain the unintelligible membership in a set, limited by y=0: A sentence like 'wales are fishes in the broadest sense' can be valued as true, whereas the statement 'wales are fishes' is biologically wrong. Academic and scientific language seems to have the quality of trying to erase all these hedges by giving clear distinctions. In order to do so, it has to use rule-guided operations and the binary cut in the continuum. However, these hedges are in fact far from being erased; what simply happens is that scientific languages try to use only one of these hedges: 'in a technical sense'. Of course, in academic language it is not necessary to say this hedge anymore. But that does not mean that they do not exist.

---

54 Cf. Rosch, E., Human Categorization.

55 Lakoff, G./Johnson, M., Metaphors We Live by, 71.

56 Cf. Lakoff, G./Johnson, M., Metaphors We Live by, 123f.

Every linguistic situation does not necessarily have to have the same prototype in order to form a class, as prototypes can vary over different contexts. The question of what makes a prototype a prototype is a philosophical question of high complexity, which cannot be treated fully here. What seems to be important is that prototypes are embedded in our life-world. To sum up: concepts are only used in linguistic contexts and these contexts are co-determinative of the meanings of the concepts. These linguistic contexts can of course appear in a manner that is formally far from being a story – like a table. But tables are only understandable if there is another, broader linguistic context in which they are embedded and which does not have the shape of a table, but that has, in the last instance, a sequential and therefore narrative character.

The prototype semantics, as well as Putnam's twin-earth thought experiments, are a means for discovering anew the narrative basis of classification, which is also present in the phenomenological tradition. Schapp calls cultural entities 'what-for-things' (*Wozudinge*), and he regards 'matter' as an abstraction of what-for-things, and as abstractions of life-forms. He showed that the traditional distinction of an individual and its species is misleading, insofar as one never finds general species or sets of things, but only a series of individual things that have individual or serial stories, which are lost in the far past and in the horizon of the far future.[57] Schapp's opinion is that there are no species or classes. But one does not have to subscribe to this radical opinion. Perhaps it is more appropriate to say that to speak of classes, sets, and species is to rely on abstractions.

A meaningful expression is context-dependent in a double sense: in being embedded in the narrantic, primary narrativity, as Putnam's twin earth experiments show (1), and in being embedded in the tellable narrative context of the linguistic level. But what is a 'meaningful expression' in the first place? A 'meaningful expression' is not necessarily a word. It can also be a sentence or a whole text, an oral story, a table, etc. In short, a meaningful expression is a 'semantic unity,'[58] and being a semantic unity is determined only relatively by its narrative context. The distinction between semantic unity (or meaningful expression) and narrative context is therefore itself a relative distinction. Wherever it is drawn, what constitutes a semantic unity and what constitutes its context, is once more dependent on the concrete question, the concrete interest, and the meaning of the state of affairs that is the subject-matter of one's inquiry.

57 Cf. SCHAPP, W., In Geschichten verstrickt (1953), 56–71.

58 Cf. MÜHLING, M., Gott ist Liebe, 25.

13.5 Metaphors as Overlapping Narrative Contexts of Meaning

What then is the meaning of a semantic unity, e.g. of a term? We can sum up the last subsection with the following theses:

(1) *The meaning of a semantic unity is its use in a double narrative context – in its narrantic context and in its linguistic-narrative context.*

Other semantic unities always belong to such a linguistic-narrative context. Therefore, we get more precise:

(2) *The meaning of a semantic unity* a *is its use in its double narrative context – in its narrantic context and in its linguistic-narrative context, together with other semantic unities* b.

How the context can be distinguished is an important question. If a context does not have a boundary in a strict sense, the context would in the end be the whole narrantic and narrative world. Then we would get a holism of meaning, in which the meaning of a semantic unity would be given only by its wayformational position in the universe of events. Since the universe of events cannot be known at all – and is also untellable – since the future, at least, is not closed, determinations of meaning in the strict sense would be impossible.

However, in a phenomenological sense, the contexts do not need to be distinguished, since in concrete perception from a wayformational perspective they always appear as dynamically, non-arbitrarily distinguished, because an ever-changing horizon is always *given* that is relevant for the contexts of meaning. Both, the narrantic context and the narrative context, insofar as they are relevant for meaning, are determined by the dynamic horizon of the wayformational perspective – as it appears in the present, as it is remembered, and as it is anticipated. And since in a specific present other past contexts of different wayformational sections, including other contexts, are also always present inside of a contextual horizon, a semantic unity is not only simply used together with other semantic unities, but appear with other semantic unities that appear with other – remembered, anticipated, and imagined – contexts and horizons. Therefore, we must speak more precisely:

(3) *The meaning of a semantic unity* a *is its use in its double narrative context* x *– its narrantic context and its linguistic narrative context – together with other semantic unities* b, *which exist in other, double narrative contexts* y.

This is now the most precise determination of what the meaning of a semantic unity can be. In this definition we simultaneously get the best definition of what a metaphor is and what a concept can be:

A metaphor is the use of a semantic unity a *in its double narrative context* x *– its narrantic context and its linguistic-narrative context – together with other semantic unities* b, *that exist in other, double-narrative contexts* y.

The distance between these two horizons formed by contexts x and y determines the degree to which they belong to a set and the degree to which one would call the language metaphorical. If the two contexts are almost completely overlapping, then we call the semantic unities literal concepts. Then we can (nearly) unequivocally correlate referents in a binary codification of concepts. However, on a wayformational perspective this case is *per definitionem* never strictly speaking true, since a wayformational perspective is always on the move, so that there are only dynamical contexts and horizons. Only by abstracting from the wayformational line –by suppressing the narrantic context – and by regulating the narrative context intentionally and restrictively, as is the case in a lexical definition or in a restriction to the physical – one gets 'pure' concepts. But in fact, these 'pure' concepts are nothing but artificially and operatively 'cleaned metaphors'. The difference between 'metaphorical' and 'literal' is therefore, only 'a difference between different ways of using a word in discourse'[59] of semantic unities, e.g. words in a discourse.

Another way to express this is to say that the copula 'is', by which extension and intension are linked, never expresses a static membership, but always a dynamic becoming. This is not the becoming in the framework of the model of transport in which something is destines to become something concrete, but rather is the irreducible becoming of wayfaring. Here, in the terms of Ricœur, in every 'is' the tension of a 'is not' is transparent.[60] However, modeling the function of the copula with the help of fuzzy sets seems to be more appropriate than Ricœur's image of tension, since Ricœur's 'is'/'is not' tension once more presupposes a (irreducibly) binary codification.

Literal concepts are the limits of narrative based metaphors.[61] Similarly, complete incomprehensibility is also a limit. Pure incomprehensibility means a case in which a semantic unity *a* together with another semantic unity *b* is used and that there is from the perspective of the contextual horizon *x* absolutely no other (imaginable) context *y* for *b*, which would mean the semantic unity *b* as completely contextless. But if it is contextless, it is not a semantic unity at all. The expression 'dioufho3' in 'life is dioufho3' is not a semantic unity, since there is no context apart from this instance where it is used. It is therefore, a completely arbitrary sequence of characters. As such, it is not a sign at all. But nevertheless, this example also shows that complete incomprehensibility is nearly impossible and that complete incomprehensibility is only a limit, which is true for two reasons. On the one hand, this book and

59 Cf. GUNTON, C.E., Actuality of Atonement, 35.

60 Cf. RICŒUR, P., Rule of Metaphor, 255f.

61 This is even acknowleged by QUINE, W.V.O., Postscript on Metaphor.

this example have given 'dioufho3' a meaning. For readers of this paragraph, 'dioufho3' is far from being meaningless. Its meaning is the example that pure incomprehensibility is impossible. On the other hand, even without knowing this paragraph of this book, we can easily imagine a narrative context *y* belonging to the sequence 'dioufho3', e.g. a password of a website. If one imagines that this context 'life is dioufho3' could also be meaningful, since it is easy to imagine a context *x* of *a*, e.g. a situation in which survival depends on the knowledge of a password. In fact, however, we do not spend all of our time imagining contexts. For pragmatic reasons, one is satisfied by saying that there are incomprehensible expressions. What is important is not imagining every possible context, but that different speakers can refer to shared contexts. This notion is particularly important in the languages of academics and the sciences, which can only be understood by scholars who are introduced into a particular discipline. For this reason, scientific languages often appear to non-scholars, as well as scholars from other disciplines, as somewhat mysterious. Such a mysterious form of communication is indeed a problem for inter- and transdisciplinary conversations.

Between the two threshold values of the literal conceptual and the incomprehensible we find the whole spectrum of what is metaphorically meaningful – from the seemingly 'dead' metaphors with literal meanings that may be found in encyclopedia entries, to conceptual key-metaphors for models in everyday language and for academic and scientific models, to metaphors filling lexical gaps, like the 'foot of a mountain', up to creative metaphors emerging in poetic and also (hopefully) in scientific languages. These creative metaphors are important, since by means of imaginative context-overlapping they allow for the perceiving and shaping of reality and its values anew in a way that is more resonant with reality. In other words, this whole spectrum in between the thresholds includes stabilizing uses and weakening uses; it includes the traditional as well as unmoored uses. For this place in-between, which is normally called the metaphorical, what Ricœur said in respect to living metaphors is true: it blurs the limits of the established logic and it destructs older categorizations in order to establish new logical frontiers on the ruins of old ones.[62]

The functioning of such conceptual metaphors can be illustrated by a simple parlor game. One only needs two players and an encyclopedia. Player A arbitrarily chooses a word or a name *a*, and then a second word *b* by randomly picking it out of the encyclopedia. He gives the metaphor formed by '*a* is *b*' to player B, who has the task of contextualizing this metaphor on the basis of a story. In every case, it is possible to tell a story on the basis of this metaphor, though the stories are of different qualities. Some might

62 Cf. Ricœur, P., Rule of Metaphor, 197.

be stories that alter the reality of the player because they let states of affairs in the life-world appear in a surprisingly new light; others remain purely fictive, including some stories that will sound artificial and contrived, since the contextual overlap is weak.

The metaphor is, semiotically speaking, nothing but a linguistic interpretant, by which a linguistic object (semantic unity *a*) is bound to a linguistic sign (semantic unity *b*) and co-related to the overlapping of the context, that forms the interpretant of the new metaphor. By being placed in its original context, the semantic unities used have an indexical basis. The metaphor itself, the interpretant, however, is a symbolic sign, because it is dependent on the narrative and rule-guided operations, whether the significance of the metaphor is disclosed. In Ricœur's words, the metaphor suspends the original reference and opens it.[63] But Ricœur is mistaken in claiming that the basis of the metaphor is an iconic similarity, in which 'the genesis concepts' happens 'through similarity'.[64] In the case of some metaphors, similarity might be produced during the metaphorical process, but this is a similarity symbolically mediated by the interpretant. Metaphors are in any case symbolic, linguistic signs that have an indexical basis. They can, but do not have to, generate an iconic sign. They can become objects of a new semiotic relation and they can lead to new interpretants, consisting in a quality of feeling, a spontaneous action, or a new rule-guided context. The relationship between metaphor and reality is neither projective-constructivist nor representationalist-realist, but phenomenal-realist, because the metaphor itself belongs to the narrantic becoming. One could say that the metaphor in its processual character not only invents what it discovers, but also discovers what it invents. The metaphor is always a process, in contrast to the conceptual demarcations that rely on it. And, as a process, it is a better fit with the reality of becoming, while preventing it from cementing reality into a static ontology.

Ricœur says (interpreting Aristotle) that the metaphor signifies things in act, as the unobstructed becoming of things and as things that bloom.[65] If one does not regard the blossom as the only important result, this metaphor might be fitting. However, this becoming does not in any case mean, in contrast to Ricœur, only growth:[66] decay, homogenization, and disruption are also possible! Ricœur describes this becoming of wayformational lines using the model of entelechy. But entelechy tends towards transport, and the metaphorical becoming must be liberated from this. If there is an

63 Cf. RICŒUR, P., Rule of Metaphor, 209f.
64 RICŒUR, P., Rule of Metaphor, 198.
65 Cf. RICŒUR, P., Rule of Metaphor, 307f.
66 Cf. RICŒUR, P., Rule of Metaphor, 308f.

entelechy, then one has to modify this concept in the non-Aristotelian sense of a becoming with changing goals, which emerge attentionally along the way.

Another insight of the theory of the overlapping of narrative meanings is that metaphors do not simply refer to words. Whole sentences, whole texts or works can be metaphors. Whoever answers a question like 'what is life?' by reciting a poem, a novel or a play, answers this question in a metaphorical way, as well as someone, who answers this question with 'Jesus Christ' or with 'DNA's ability for reduplications'. But against Ricœur, it is not true that the necessary embeddedness of metaphors in primary and secondary narrations means that the basis of these contexts is the character of texts, which lead to a new perceiving of truth and value of becoming.[67] This perception would only be possible if narratives were somehow textual entities. But this is not the case.

13.6 Reality-reference of Narratively Based, Metaphorical Language

The question of whether metaphorical language – or language at all – is able to be true or false, must be put in the following way, if truth is somehow a relation between language and reality (ch. 20): *What does reality have to be in order for (metaphorical) language to be true?* Preliminarily, we can give an answer to this question insofar as we can say that it is only possible if reality is a narrative reality of becoming. In the end, we can clarify this question only from the wayformational perspective of the Christian faith and its reflection in theology. Therefore, a really satisfying answer can only be given in the next volume. However, we can specify here some conditions of how such a narrative ontology would look.

First, reality must exist in such a way that enables a resonating relation to language. And that is the case if 'the world is the kind of thing that can be interpreted in language. It is, or has – metaphorically! – a kind of language.'[68] The world then, is not an 'object'.

Second, the world has to be intelligible.

Third, the intelligibility of the world must be of the sort that is able to be conceived of through fuzzy, narrative and context-relevant transitions.

Fourth, language is a kind of communication: it is dynamic and not static. This claim must also be true for resonant relations expressed in the fact that

67 Cf. RICŒUR, P., Die lebendige Metapher, VII.
68 GUNTON, C.E., Actuality of Atonement, 37.

between human linguistic activity and reality there has to be interdependence and the possibility of resonance and dissonance.[69]

Eberhard Jüngel expresses the conjunction of the third and the fourth need in this way:

> The metaphorical structure of language, which exists thanks to truth as the event of the transition of being into language, implies that the liberty to choose words is the liberty of the one who speaks. This liberty is constituted by the interplay between humans and world, in which humans have to be understood cosmomorphically and anthropomorphically. In this interplay of humans and world comes the vivid [...] power of truth as discoverable in its effects.[70]

Colin Gunton sums up these four points in the following way:

> The world can be known only indirectly, and therefore metaphor, being indirect, is the most appropriate from [...] language should take. [...] metaphor, rather than being the Cinderella of cognitive language, becomes the most, rather than the least, appropriate means of expressing the truth.[71]

Narratively based metaphors are not preliminary tools with which to explore the world, but the irreducible means in and by which discoveries take place. Here, new linguistic extensions by metaphors and new discoveries of states of affairs are insolubly bound together. With the help of metaphors, we have epistemic access to the world, since language as a realistic event is shaped by the mesh of becoming itself.[72] These descriptions are in no way foreign to the Christian wayformational perspective, but they can be expressed in different ways, e.g. by an ontological model of the Word of God, or by pneumatology. The understanding of the metaphor that we have presented here is significant, because it is a general theory of meaning. Its point in respect to theology is, in Robert Jenson's words:

> The words used together with 'God' do not have an abnormal manner of meaning, analogously or something else. They are doing exactly what they always do.[73]

---

69 Cf. Gunton, C.E., Actuality of Atonement, 35.

70 Jüngel, E./Ricœur, P., Thesen zur Metaphorologie, 63 (Transl. MM).

71 Gunton, C.E., Actuality of Atonement, 37f.

72 Cf. Gunton, C.E., Actuality of Atonement, 31, in conversation with Boyd, R., Metaphor and Theory Change. Boyd also speaks on 358 about the adaption of language to the (causal) structure of the world.

73 Jenson, R.W., "Gott" als "Antwort", 158 (Transl. MM).

13.7 Is 'stories are lived before they can be told' a Metaphor?

An important point of origin for our narrative ontology is taking MacIntyre's casually uttered *bon mot*, 'stories are lived before they can be told'[74] in a literal way. But is this true? Is it not a metaphor? At this point, after the presentation of our theory of signs and theory of metaphors, we can give an answer: it is a metaphor and conceptual language at the same time. The concept-metaphor 'life is stories' is a potentiated metaphor, which comes into existence because the primary stories of actual becoming serve to signify special kinds of secondary stories (tellable or textual stories) as 'stories'. But *this* signification is also a metaphorical one! In a second step, these metaphors are used as a context to understand the primary reality of becoming. In other words: whoever regards 'life is stories' first as metaphor, is forced by this metaphor to conceive of the becoming of life literally/conceptually as story, in order to then regard in a second step tellable, second-order narrations and narratives as stories only in a derivative, partial, metaphorical way. To name particular linguistic entities 'stories' is the metaphor. Only now, by using a binary conceptual cut, as in the case of narratology, naming linguistic entities 'stories' appears as literal language. And this binary cut produces an illusion, as if naming these entities as 'stories' were to use literal language, whereas naming the becoming of reality 'stories' is a derivative, metaphorical meaning. But such a conception ignores the original phenomenologically given, metaphorically constitutive process of the true becoming of the mesh as 'stories', as well as the naming of certain linguistic entities as 'stories'.

Lakoff and Johnson illustrate this through an interesting example from everyday life: the metaphor 'life is stories' is a metaphor of our everyday life, used in order to conceive of our life-world. And we have to use it, independently of whether we want to. Even if someone rejects this metaphor, or regards life as consisting of completely unbound episodes, she presupposes this metaphor, because that which is qualified as a fragmentary pile of shards must be a story.[75] To deny the primary narrativity of actual becoming also presupposes this narrativity as primary.

74 Cf. MACINTYRE, A., After Virtue, 212.

75 Cf. LAKOFF, G./JOHNSON, M., Metaphors We Live by, 173–5, who understand this case as conceptual explication of the metaphor 'Life's … a tale told by an idiot, full of sound and fury, signifying nothing.'

CHAPTER 14

Narrations, Concepts, and Names

Second-order narrations are embedded in narrantic events, that is, in the mesh of the wayformational lines of perception, which itself has a semiotic character. The metaphor belongs to the second-order narrations and it is dependent on first-order narrations, as we saw in the last chapter. The metaphor is not a special case of language or speech, but, equiprimordially with concepts, an element of second-order narrations. If metaphors and concepts are not opposites but are gradually distinguished as was shown in the last chapter, we can ask what the characteristics of concepts are, how they are based on narrativity, and how they are important for second-order narrativity.

14.1 Concepts and the Question of the Bivalence of Propositions

Concepts as concepts appear where statements or propositions appear. Propositions are an important element of second-order narrations. However, they are not the atomically basic form of second-order narrations, since the meaning of a single proposition is dependent on the mesh of propositions, as it is characteristic for the conceptuality of the metaphor, and on the parts of the second-order narrations that are non-propositional. Nevertheless, propositions are uniquely important for second-order narrations because they involve truth claims. Wherever propositions and concepts appear, truth claims are also present. A series of important marks of conceptual speech are implied by this fact. Both the logical principle of identity (a=a) and the principle of the excluded contradiction (false: $a \wedge \neg a$) are implied, which is not a weakening of the metaphorical basis of concepts. Metaphors do not fight against logic, but logic enables the metaphorical process as we described it in ch. 13. The metaphor lives due to the overlapping of contexts of the semantic unities employed and due to a prototype-semantics-based shift from one conceptual, but fuzzy, timeless distinction, to another one. This overlap, however, presupposes the concept of the concept. Concepts in themselves are not challenged by a metaphorical theory of concepts. Such a theory only serves to describe the dynamic relation between extension and intension that is dependent on the context of primary narrativity. The outcome is the dynamic formation of concepts.

 | DOI:10.30965/9783846765852_015

We modelled this dynamic relation with the help of the heuristic model of fuzzy sets, and saw thereby that the principle of bipolarity[1] remains. Any proposition implying truth claims can only have truth-values within the limits of the completely fitting (true) and the completely unfitting (false). By derivation, we can postulate a third logical principle that could be called the 'principle of excluded transcendence'.

This principle means that there cannot be any truth-values that transcend the liminal truth-function, i.e. there is no value beyond the interval between 0–1. The expressions 'truer than true' or 'falser than false' are meaningless, since they are incomprehensible. Of course, we can use these expressions, but in doing so we do not use them to mean something with relevance to truth-value. The expression 'principle of the excluded transcendence' is analogous to the classical principle of the excluded middle. Propositions can therefore be: liminal true, liminal false, or something in-between, but they can have no truth-value beyond the limits of true/false.

At this point, a problem arises. We modelled the conceptual bipolarity heuristically with the help of fuzzy-logic in order to capture the dynamic transition between the two limits, described ideally by a mathematical function. But the mathematics used does not presuppose a dynamic fluidity of truth-values in its own conceptuality, and is not only bipolar, but also bivalent: Except for 'true' and 'false' there are no values, nothing in-between, and no shift between true and false. The claim is that there are no gaps in truth-values, and therefore that indecision is not a truth-value. Russel tried to give the foundation of mathematics on the basis of predicate logic in his *Principia Mathematica*.[2]

This state of affairs has consequences: it shows that (on one level) a liminal bipolarity that includes a dynamic function for truth-values is only possible if we presuppose strict bivalence on another level – the level of mathematical idealization – in at least a regulative way. This consequence is acceptable, since it means that we can simply answer the question of how to use the principle of the excluded middle by using the principle of the excluded middle. On the idealized level, there are only the truth-values 'true' and 'false'. On this level, there are no truth-gaps. Bivalence and the principle of the excluded middle are at least necessary as regulative principles.[3]

1 Cf. KOCH, A.F., Versuch, 67.
2 RUSSELL, B./WHITEHEAD, A.N., PM.
3 Cf. KOCH, A.F., Versuch, 71.

Usually, one justifies truth-gaps with the help of future statements like 'There will be a king of Europe in the future'. This argument is based on the idea that we do not know any conditions for the truth of sentences like these. The argument is mistaken, however, since we can easily imagine a primary narration that describes circumstances in which this sentence is true or false. And this is sufficient.[4]

The advantage of all this is that we can continue to use our everyday logic.

14.2 What are Concepts?

Generally speaking, we find in the philosophical tradition two models for analyzing propositions, a classical one in the medieval Aristotelian tradition, and one invented by Frege and extended by Russell. Both deal with the connective structure of concepts, but describe it differently. Whereas classical logic combines two concepts with the help of a copula, using the scheme 'A is B', predicate logic analyzes the same state of affairs by taking F as a predicate that is instantiated by arguments x: Fx. Whereas 'A is B' is a complete proposition, Fx is only the form of a proposition. Only if the variable of the argument is concretized do we get a proposition. There are two ways to do this: either by binding the argument-variable with quantifiers (the existential quantifier or the universal quantifier), or by substituting the variable by designators. In the first case, we get '$\exists x.Fx$' ('There is at least one x for which it is true that Fx'), resp. '$\forall x.Fx$' ('For all x it is true that Fx'). In the second case, we would substitute the variable x with a designator a: Fa. Let us illustrate: Imagine that F means 'is mortal' and that a means 'Alice'. $\exists x.$ Fx then means 'some things are mortal'. A sentence like 'all humans are mortal' can only be expressed with the help of two predicates, another one besides F may be called G = 'is human': $\forall x.Gx \rightarrow Fx$ means 'for anything it is true: If something is human, it is mortal.' The sentence 'Alice is mortal', however, can simply be expressed by Fa. All of these examples are propositions connected by operators. Now we can define precisely what we mean by a concept: *A concept is the pure form of a proposition, i.e. the unbound function of a proposition 'Fx'*. Concepts as such are indeed empty; only in the shape of proposition do they acquire meaning. But how is this possible? One is tempted to answer with Kant: intuition (*Anschauung*), which is certainly true, but what, then is intuition?

4 Cf. KOCH, A.F., Wahrheit, Zeit und Freiheit, 78.

14.3 Concepts and Designators

It is interesting that it is impossible to infer name-bound predicates from predicates bound by quantifiers, a point which traditional logic also knew (*individuum est ineffabile*). Predicates bound by quantifiers are concepts. This is not only true for '$\forall x.Fx$', but also for '$\exists x.Fx$', since this statement of existence signifies nothing. Concepts such as the function of a proposition Fx are presupposed in any secondary narration, since such stories have to use statements like Fa and also predicates bound by quantifiers. However, a secondary narration is impossible using only predicates bound by variables. A conjunction of predicates like '$\exists x. Fx \wedge Gx \wedge Hx$ ...' is not a secondary story. But if quantifier-bound predicates alone are not necessary in order to get secondary stories, then such sums of general predicates do not refer to the reality of primary narrativity. And then we arrive at a problem: the reality of primary narrativity is only accessible by secondary narrativity. Secondary narrativity includes general concepts (by quantifier bound predicates) and predicates bound by designators, but general concepts do not refer to reality. How then, is it possible for secondary narrativity (and language at all) to refer to reality? One strategy would be to become a sceptic or a relativist by assuming – like the sceptic – that there might be a reality, but only one that is inaccessible. Metaphysically, one remains a realist, but denies that there is any possibility of knowing anything about reality. Whatever is real would be undetermined and undeterminable. The relativist would have to claim that there is no primary narrativity at all, with the consequence that secondary stories would be the only existing realities. Both possibilities are far from convincing, and both lead to a pragmatic contradiction in our dealing with the life-world. Moreover, in both cases one has to deny that statements, claims or assumption imply truth-claims (in the sense of bivalence). And this attempt would be simply to deny that anyone can be fallible in their assumptions. The only solution, therefore, is to maintain that secondary narrativity refers to reality, but that it is not the general concepts that enable this reality-reference. The reality-reference of meaningful language is therefore made by predicates bound by designators.

Concepts get rid of their emptiness only by designators. And this means that concepts become meaningful through narrativity. We now have to show this in detail.

14.4 Designators as Names, Identity-descriptions and Indicators

The distinction between the universal and the particular is mirrored by the double-nature of the meaningful concept, which is made of predicates and designators. But how are designators able to refer to the particular?

There are many designators: names, demonstrative pronouns, indexes indicating time and space; 'here', 'now', 'there', 'then', 'I', 'you', temporal forms of verbs, identification markers like definite articles, etc. Let us start with *names*, which, according to Kripke, Putnam, and others, have a fixed reference by signifying exactly one individuated entity in all possible worlds.[5] Imagine a working group in which the members have not been formerly acquainted, and everyone wears a name-badge. The names would then be like a badge that is fixed to its carrier or referent. Other designators used in this working group are not fixed, for example, if 'you' is used. That this reference is true in all possible worlds means that it is a necessary reference, e.g. a reference that is still true in a counterfactual case. For example, with 'Aristotle' we refer to the teacher of Alexander who wrote the *Nicomachean Ethics*. We would still mean the same person, even if anyone else was in fact Alexander's teacher or if anyone else in fact wrote the *Nicomachean Ethics*. We would simply have to say that it was wrong to assume that Aristotle did this or that (instead of using 'Aristotle' to refer the other person). But this is only possible if we still refer to Aristotle by the same reference. With Koch, we can also say that names are monadic:[6] they simply have a fixed reference. If they did not, they are not names.

But how are names in the position of having such a fixed reference? Here we cannot argue fully without some empirical arguments. Kripke claimed that there was a situation like baptizing, from which point names would be causally transferred onward. This thesis consists of two elements – the baptismal situation and the communicative transferal.[7] By the way, this communicative transferal can be interpreted as a causal chain, but that is not very wise, because in this case we would tie a comparably simple concept – names as designators – to a highly questionable concept with a number of presuppositions, as we will see in ch. 17.

Another possibility is opened up simply by asking how we use names and how by using them we can explain whatever or whoever we mean. Here another designator comes into play: identity descriptions. For example, imagine a situation wherein there is the spatiotemporal co-presence of the speaker, the referent, and the one being addressed.

5 Cf. KRIPKE, S.A., Naming and Necessity, 48f. Cf. for theological relevance see also GROẞHANS, P., Theologischer Realismus, 20–33.

6 Cf. KOCH, A.F., Versuch.

7 Cf. KRIPKE, S.A., Naming and Necessity, 95: 'In general our reference depends not just on what we think ourselves, but on other people in the community, the history of how the name reached one, and things like that. It is by following such a history that one gets to the referene.'

(1) Speaker A wants to introduce Alice to person B and tells B to meet in front of a pub. A sees Alice through the window of the pub, sitting at the bar with a glass in front of her. Before A can enter the pub, his mobile-phone rings. He tells B: 'I have to take this call, go in, Alice is the one at the bar drinking whisky; I'll follow later.' B enters the pub an introduces himself to Alice.

In this example, it seems as if the designating name 'Alice' is dependent on the predicate 'drinks whisky.' But in fact, successful identification is independent of this predication. Imagine two variants of this situation:

(2) The situation is similar to (1), but as B enters the bar, he sees more than one female person at the bar drinking whisky. He is not therefore able to identify Alice.

In case (1), the identification with the help of a predicate succeeds, in case (2) it fails. Of course, one could try to reduce case (2) to (1), by adding more predicates with a conjunction. Person A could add 'she has long blonde hair, is wearing a blue shirt, is talking to the bartender', etc. However, this case still reverts to case (2): However, many predicates one adds, there might always be more than one – in principle an infinite number of persons – for which the conjunction would be true.[8] But imagine a third case:

(3) Everything is similar to (1), including the fact that B is able to identify Alice and introduces himself. He then says: 'I am also a whisky expert: may I have a taste in order to see if I can identify it?' Alice answers: 'Whisky? This is apple-juice.'

In this case, the identification of Alice works despite the predicate being wrong: Alice is not drinking whisky. Does this mean that the identification was only successful by chance? Or are false predicates able to sustain the right reference? The first thing to be learned from the examples (1)–(3) is that designation and identification are independent from predication. But why then does identification succeed in (1) and (3)? The reason is that the identity description is not 'sits at the bar and drinks whisky' – at least not merely so. What is decisive is the complete contextual setting of the factual primary narrativity, which belongs to the identity description. And in this situation, the sentence 'Alice drinks whisky' does not function as a proposition, but it is a substitute for a deictic act: A could have simply been pointing through the window at Alice. And the meaning of this deictic act is primarily an indexical one; it relates speaker A, the one addressed B, and the point of the reference, Alice, in a

8 Cf. Koch, A.F., Versuch, 136.

concrete particular relationship that enables the identification – presupposing spatiotemporal co-presence.

Deictic acts, however, are only successful if there is a minimal conceptual aspect involved. These are concepts in the sense of sortals (sometimes including phase sortals) that are neither classificatory nor general concepts:

> A sortal universal supplies a principle for distinguishing and counting individual particulars which it collects. It presupposes no antecedent principle, or method, of individuating the particulars it collects. Characterizing universals, on the other hand, whilst they supply principles of grouping, even of counting, particulars, supply such principles only for particulars already distinguished, or distinguishable, in accordance with some antecedent principle or method.[9]

If A points with a deictic act at Alice, it is presupposed that A and B implicitly share some sortal concepts: that Alice is a young woman, that he is pointing to her instead of her facial expression or her clothing, etc. 'Young woman' is not an absolute predicate of Alice and her story, but only a phase of her story (that is more or less true in the moment of identification).[10] Sortal expressions rely, like all concepts, on metaphors and prototypes, and they themselves presuppose, like names, a narratively deictic connection and indexicality.

The identity description is here a substitute for a deictic act. In this way, it substitutes as sign, but not a linguistic sign in the proper sense. But there are also linguistic signs that can stand for deictic acts, namely purely indexical expressions like 'this one', this woman', etc. The identity description is successful because it is not a description at all, but a substitute for an indexical sign. However, identity descriptions are not only used in the case of spatiotemporal co-presence, but also if the identifying person and identified are apart:

(4) 'With 'John' I mean this one who was President of the United States, who probably had an affair with Marilyn Monroe, and who was murdered in 1963.'

In this case, the identity description is a very short secondary story – admittedly not a very good one. Besides predicates like 'President of the US' or 'being murdered', other indices like 'this one' and '1963', and other names like 'Marilyn Monroe' are included. This identity description will only be successful if the speaker and the addressed at minimum share the same secondary narrations regarding American history, and if this history somehow actually fits with the

9 Strawson, P.F., Individuals, 168.

10 For the meaning of sortal concepts for identification cf. also Evers, D., Gott und mögliche Welten, 344–349.

primary narration in which Kennedy was involved. One could assume that in this example the identification and the designating name 'John' is dependent on a non-fictive, historical narration – and therefore on the spatiotemporal ordering of the 'B-series' order of sequential relations. But this is not the case for two reasons.

The first reason is that spatiotemporal identifications is only possible if the entities in question are indeed spatiotemporally individuated. Only what is individuated independently from its identification can be identified. Everything that can be identified has to be individuated. But not everything that is individuated is identifiable.[11] The history of the search for the principle of individuation is a very exciting one. One could claim, following Duns Scotus, the existence of a particular universal substance called *haecceitas*;[12] one could claim that it is the accidentals that individuate universal substances, or one could claim – as is typical since modernity – that it is the spatiotemporal order that individuates.[13] Impressive examples of the latter kind are given by P.F. Strawson[14] and Anton Koch.[15] The question of individuation is a central problem of both philosophy and theology, as I have shown elsewhere.[16]

Human persons are individuated independently from their identification, seemingly spatiotemporally. But there are also empirical phenomena that cannot be spatiotemporally individuated, but that can be measured, as the empirical justification of the EPR-thought experiment shows in the realm of quantum-theory.[17] Entangled quanta are not individuated spatiotemporally, but they are able to determine secondary narrations by measurement, and that means they are able to be identified. But then another problem occurs: whatever can be identified must be individuated. And yet, spatiotemporal individuation is not possible. Are there other principles of individuation available besides the spatiotemporal one? The answer is 'yes' and 'no'. It is not space-time itself that has a mysterious attribute for individuating things, but its ability to individuate things consists in its narrative character insofar as it is a relation of

11 Cf. KOCH, A.F., Versuch, 116.

12 Cf. SWINBURNE, R., Thisness; PARK, W., Common Nature and Haecceitas.

13 Cf. exemplarily LOCKE, J., Identity and Diversity, §3: '[…] it is easy to discover […] the principium individuationis; and that, it is plain, is existence itself, which determines a being of any sort to a particular time and place, incommunicable to two beings of the same kind.'; cf. similarly SCHOPENHAUER, A., Welt als Wille und Vorstellung DB 2, 283.

14 Cf. STRAWSON, P.F., Individuals.

15 Cf. KOCH, A.F., Versuch.

16 Cf. WALTER, G., Rev. Mühling, Liebesgeschichte Gott, 81–93.

17 Cf. MÜHLING, M., Gegenständlichkeit Gottes und Quantentheorie.

order, that is: asymmetrical, irreflexive, and transitive.[18] However, these are not primarily the attributes of space-time, but of narrations, regardless of which type. And in the EPR experiment and those like it, there are always narrations of (imaginative) experimental orders. In *these* contexts, both entangled quanta are individuated, as well as the apparatuses of measurement. In the context of space-time, however, they are not individuated.

The second reason is that identification is also possible in purely fictional narrations:

(5) 'I mean this young pretty woman sharing a flat with seven not too tall men in a mountainous area with seven main peaks, who, due to the chauvinism of these men, had to do all the house-work, and who, due to her credulity, became the victim of an assassination by poisoned fruit, and ...'

In this case, the identification also succeeds, even though Snow White is not a spatiotemporally individuated, historical person. It is only decisive that the speaker and one addressed share the same secondary narrations.

Identity descriptions are in all cases narrations, whether shorter or longer ones. They succeed as such because they include indexical expressions – including in those cases where these indexical expressions refer to purely fictive narrations without (direct) reference to primary narrativity. Also, our CV's and passports include little secondary narrations and indexes, like 'born ... at ... in'; 'married at ... to ...', etc. Our social practice of changing names in marriage, divorce, re-marriage, etc. confirms this dependence of names on narrative identity-descriptions, since a name cannot be changed without telling about the occasion of its change.

Names have a designatory power and are able to identify things because they are bound to identity-descriptions. And these identity-descriptions have designatory power, because they include (besides other names and predicates) a third kind of designators: *indexical expressions*.

One can now ask: what are the *a priori* conditions for referring to things, that is, what is individuation? With Koch, we can answer that a necessary condition is a spatiotemporal coordinate system that emerges out of the living body of the one who refers to things.[19] This answer is not mistaken, insofar as we saw in ch. 11 that such a coordinate system can be formed, at least in an abstract manner. But the problem is that it is indeed an abstraction from reality.

18 From my point of view, this is also seen, at least indirectly, by Koch, A.F., Versuch, 118, when he concedes at least a minimum of matter's singular character to points and areas in space and time.

19 Cf. Koch, A.F., Versuch, 117.

Therefore, Koch speaks of the *a priori* (necessary) conditions for reference that are only valid in an idealized world in its (never realizable) 'normal position' (*Grundstellung*).[20] But we can draw here yet another, more basic conclusion: *If (1) the designatory ability of names and identity-descriptions is based on indexical expressions and signs, and if (2) indexical expressions are always used relatively to the bodily coordinate system of the speaker, and if (3) the bodily coordinate system of a speaker is always an abstraction from her being interwoven into and out of the mesh of narrations, then it follows, first, that the designatory ability of indexical expressions is dependent on the interwovenness of the speaker into and out of her mesh of narrations, and, second, that the designatory ability of names and identity-descriptions also depends on being interwoven in the mesh of primary narrativity.*[21]

One could object that this definition does not explain which identifications can be successful in fictional cases like case (5). But this objection fails, since the identification in fictive cases can only be successful because the speaker and the one addressed are intermeshed in a primary narration in which the fictive secondary narration – here the story of Snow White – is also interwoven.

Of course, this basic function of narrativity is not new. If, as the result of his twin-earth thought experiments, Putnam claims that 'meanings ain't just in the head,'[22] then what really follows is that the meaning of concepts and sentences is only given in a narrative context. Schapp, too, discovered in a critique of his teacher Husserl that all sentences do not have meanings in themselves and do not refer to anything in themselves, but only within the framework of concrete stories, which do not have to be linguistic ones.[23] Such an understanding is not new for theology. In this case, it is Robert W. Jenson who, since the 1980s, has discussed the relationship between names and narrativity, and who – as we will see later – showed that this connection is decisive for theology. He writes:

> It also provides what logicians now call an identifying description, a descriptive phrase or clause, or set of them, that fits just the one individual thing to be identified [...] In general, proper names work only if such identifying descriptions are at hand. We may say, 'Mary is coming to diner,' and be answered with, 'Who

20 Cf. KOCH, A.F., Versuch, 354f.

21 In distinction from KOCH, A.F., Versuch, 116, one cannot say that space and time are without alternatives, and that we know of no other principles of pre-conceptual manifolds that serve this need (ibid., 117).

22 Vgl. PUTNAM, H., Meaning of 'Meaning', 227.

23 Cf. SCHAPP, W., In Geschichten verstrickt (1953), 169–180. Schapp proceeds here by diagnosing sentences like 'the queen is ill' that are presumed to be understandable but nevertheless cannot refer to an actual situation. Indeed the illness can be specified and indeed 'the queen' is determined, but only in a concrete story can the sentence can obtain its meaning, in fact in each case a different one (because the same queen can suffer from the same illness multiple times). Cf. ibid., 176.

> is Mary?' Then we must be able to say, 'Mary is the one who lives in apartment 2C, and is always so cheerful, and …,' continuing until the questioner says, 'Oh, *that* one!'[24]

In another theologically important aspect, the idea of the name as a singular term plays an important role in Ingolf Dalferth's theology, as we will see later.[25]

To sum up: Concepts are the pure forms of propositions, designating nothing. Universal concepts in the shape of predicate variables bound by quantifiers contribute nothing to a concepts ability to refer to something. The concept's ability to have meaning or to refer to something depends on the substitution of names for the argument variable. Names are dependent on indexical signs (not necessarily linguistic expressions), and these are dependent on their being interwoven in primary narrativity. Concepts are able to refer to something – and therefore also able to imply truth-claims – because they are grounded in narrativity, which is also true even if one rejects an egalitarianism about concepts and metaphors, as we did in ch. 13. We have also seen that secondary narrations cannot be formed without concepts, especially sortal expressions. Conceptual descriptions, therefore, are not (completely) alien to narrations. Concepts do nothing but express and perhaps stress an element that always has a narrative basis: concepts. But concepts are only necessary in order to form secondary narrations. Therefore, it is possible to classify phenomena of primary narrativity and of secondary narrativity by a conceptually *schematic* classification. However, these *schemata* are always abstractions and they suppress some of the decisive elements of reality to which they refer. Conceptual classification schemes can be used for pragmatic purposes. But they do not have to be quickly ontologized. One does, however, always have to keep the ontological commitments in mind.

14.5 Interwoven Becoming on a Specific Wayformational Perspective as a Condition of Conceptuality

We have seen that a condition of conceptuality is indexicality, and that a condition of indexicality is to be or to become interwoven in the primary narrativity of wayformational meshes. Put this way, it is metaphorical but, nevertheless,

24 Jenson, R.W., Triune God, 88.

25 Cf. e.g. Dalferth, I.U., Religiöse Rede von Gott, 571–583; Dalferth, I.U., Existenz Gottes und christlicher Glaube, 96–99; Dalferth, I.U., Die Wirklichkeit des Möglichen. Hermeneutische Religionsphilosophie, 442–448. 466–470; Dalferth, I.U., Der auferweckte Gekreuzigte, 224.

conceptual language. What we still have to show, however, is that indexicality is only possible if being interwoven in primary narrativity includes a *particular* wayformational perspective along the way, which would exclude two possible states of affairs.

First, if we could face the mesh of wayformational lines from the outside, it would be impossible to refer to something in it and meaningfully form concepts about it. Of course, it is easy to imagine pointing to lines painted on a sheet of paper in front of us, as it is easy to imagine pointing to a particular sequence from a secondary story in textual form (e.g. by using a biblical reference). But this is only possible because 'I' as well as the sheet of paper or the text are interwoven in primary narrativity. An entity completely transcendent to primary narrativity could refer to nothing in primary narrativity; not even to the whole of primary narrativity. Such an entity could only refer to primary narrativity if it refers to something that it regards wrongly as primary narrativity, whereas in fact it is secondary narrativity, so that this entity and the only apparently primary narrativity are still interwoven in actual primary story. In other words, such an entity is not conceivable as completely transcendent, but one must conceive of it as at least partly immanent to the concrete wayformational lines. At this point, it is still unclear what the descriptions 'completely transcendent' and 'at least partly immanent' mean. We will leave this question open for now and return to it later (ch. 21). Nevertheless, we can draw a conclusion for the philosophy of religion: whatever the expression 'God' means, it cannot refer to something completely transcendent.

Second, the ability to refer to something in an indexical manner needs a wayformational line that is principally open for further development along with its environment. In other words, only if the primary narration is not only not closed but also principally uncloseable, is it possible to refer to something. The reason is that indexicality is only meaningful under the conditions of a bodily presence. But if one imagines a closed wayformational line, one would, in the end, not be able to refer to something in the past, since the act of reference affords a new sequence. Consequentially, it is not possible to be or to become interwoven in a closed story. This idea has further consequences for theological thought, which is exemplified by the theology of Wolfhart Pannenberg, who claims that only the closing of history (or more precisely, the closing of a story) enables its totality and therefore the unity of truth.[26] This thought presupposes something like universal coherence. It might be true that only the closing of a story enables its universal coherence (or incoherence).

---

26 Cf. PANNENBERG, W., Was ist Wahrheit?

But once more, this can only be true in the case of secondary stories, since we are bound together with secondary stories in primary narrativity. But, then, it is unclear what it means to call a particular secondary story, e.g. a text, really closed. The text could be extended in the future. In the case of historical texts, new sources could be found that reveal the seemingly closed text only as part of a sequence. Any possible closing of a text is only an external one, which is added by convention to the text itself. Semiotically, one can also say that the effect of the text as sign belongs to its interpretant – and therefore to the text as sign itself, which also means that the text is unclosed, since the interpretant also belongs to the level of primary narrativity. But let's counterfactually imagine that all these objections against the closedness of texts are mistaken and we could regard a text as closed. In this case, the mistake Pannenberg has made consists in the fact that he did not model secondary narrativity on primary narrativity, as would be appropriate, but that he modelled primary narrativity on secondary narrativity. It is still possible that there is something like the universal coherence (or incoherence) of this closed story or history. But this universal coherence cannot be called 'truth'. Truth always includes a phenomenal aspect as well, and that means that it appears as true and can be referred to. But, in the case of a closed primary-narrative mesh of wayformational lines, this is unthinkable.

Only when the mesh of primary wayformational lines is perceived from the inside, i.e. from a particular wayformational perspective, is indexicality and the ability to refer to something and to form concepts possible.

This theory of the narrative conditions for the possibility of reference is compatible with the theory of the *a priori* presuppositions for reference that Anton Koch has developed. Our theory of the narrative conditions is also influenced by Koch's thinking. What we call 'being interwoven into an uncloseable mesh of primary stories', Koch calls being anchored in the spatial, bodily coordinate system of an I that perceives in the present. Koch sums up his theory with two theorems:

> (TVA–1) A subject referring in a thinking or speaking manner to something particular (in order to predicate something about it), knows *a priori* (pre-descriptively and pre-indexically) that itself is a spatial entity in the center of an egocentric, imagined three-dimensional space at the present time, which is a point in linear time. The subject locates itself *a priori* in space ("I am here") and in the temporal present (primarily non-contrastively with the help of temporal indexes like "now"), and it orients itself *a priori* in time and space. In this *a priori* orientation, it distinguishes pre-descriptively and pre-indexically between
> - time and space,
> - both directions of time,
> - the three dimensions of space,
> - the two directions of each spatial dimension.

> (TVA–2) The achievements of localizing oneself *a priori*, and to orientate oneself *a priori*, do not appear for oneself as cognitive achievements in one's own right, but only as dependent aspects of the descriptively and indexically mediated ability to refer to concrete, particular individuals that are once more a dependent aspect of the discourse, with respect to the whole human practice.[27]

When Koch refers in TVA–2 to the 'whole human practice', he probably means the same thing that we are calling primary narrativity. The difference, however, is that this primary narrativity must not necessarily consist of human practice alone.

Forming concepts from the inside of a particular wayformational line is basic in a double sense: it is basic because the meaning of conceptual predication relies on a metaphorical process, as is shown in ch. 13, and it is basic because the reference relies on indexicality in the middle of narrations. Both, predication and reference, are independent of each other, but nevertheless equiprimordially foundational.

The truth of Quine's famous Gavagai-example is also nothing but this independence of referring and predicating: A linguist accompanies an indigenous person on a walk. The latter points to the horizon where an animal appears, which looks similar to a rabbit, and he says 'Gavagai'. According to Quine, it is unclear what ontology the indigenous person uses. It is open whether he means 'rabbit', 'rabbitity', 'a phase of the story of the rabbit', 'a rabbit-like deity', 'prey', or something else. That is indeed true. But the consequence is not that there is an 'ontological relativity' or an incommensurability of conceptual systems.[28] The example only shows that a single indexical act of reference does not lead to any predicates, but only to the reference to 'Gavagai'. In this sequence 'Gavagai' remains a name. It could be, however, that 'Gavagai' is in fact not a name, but a predicate. But in order to decide about this, the single sequence is insufficient. The linguist had to have been involved in the broader history of the tribe and its different uses of 'Gavagai' and the metaphorical formation of concepts relying on it, in order to decide whether 'Gavagai' is a predicate, and which one. Concepts are not something quasi-mental, not something abstracted from concrete names. Concepts cannot be explained completely by single situations, but, and here Quine is right,[29] they presuppose a kind of holism. But this has to be a narrative holism!

14.6 The Dynamic-bodily Sea Anchor of Conceptuality

In the last section, we developed our model of the narrative presuppositions of reference in discussion with Koch's theory of the presuppositions of reference

27 Koch, A.F., Versuch, 139 (Transl. MM).

28 Cf. Quine, W.V.O., Ontological Relativity.

29 Cf. Quine, W.V.O., Word and Object, 12. A good analysis of Quine's holism is offered by Grube, D.-M., Unbegründbarkeit Gottes?, 199–209.

that essentially includes the ideas of bodiliness and the idea of a coordinate system that is anchored in the body. We remarked that this picture of a coordinate system can only be regarded as an abstraction from bodily perception. But if this is the case, as in all abstractions, dangers may emerge. What are they? Preliminarily, at least, we have to say something here – 'preliminarily' because to say something really concise, we would first have to have a full discussion of the concept of 'body'. However, it is clear that this can only be a subject matter for the second volume. Nevertheless, in order to prevent some misunderstandings, we will deal with this problem preliminarily.

Koch's model of the coordinate-system is a theoretical model based on different key-metaphors. And we now have to ask about the limits of this model. It is clear that indexical expressions can only be anchored in the living body. But we have to modify the picture: the zero-point of the coordinate system is not established as an anchor, but as a sea anchor (drogue). It is not anchored on solid ground, but in the medium of perceiving truth and value itself. The living body is dynamic. Therefore, the image of the zero-point of the coordinate system is questionable. It can only be used in a qualified manner, but it may be wise to use it nonetheless, since there are no other candidates for its establishment, such as space. Theoretical reason, therefore, cannot emancipate itself from practical reason; both are indissolubly bound together. Being bound to the living body is a condition of the possibility of using concepts and of using reason and rationality. In order to be a little bit more concrete, we can distinguish three indissolubly bound perspectives included in the talk of the body: the body as a living body (*Leib*), the body as a spatiotemporal body, and the body as a mirror of social discourses.[30]

In the first perspective, we must say that humans do not have a body, but they are their living body. The living body (*Leib*) has to be distinguished from the spatiotemporal body (*Körper*) by the fact that the living body is always primarily given to humans. Before all consciousness, before all language mediated rationality, the human becoming is his or her living body.[31] Furthermore, it is not any living body, but *my* living body that is immediately perceived as fact.[32] It is identifiable without spatial orientation, and therefore it is the swimming 'zero-point' of the swimming 'coordinate-system' that is basis of one's indexical acts, it is undividable. Contrary to all mind-body dualists from

30 Cf. thereto LIST, E., Einleitung, 14, and TURNER, B., Body in Western Society, 15f.

31 Cf. SCHWÖBEL, C., Einleitung: Dimensionen der Leiblichkeit, 3.

32 Cf. therefore also GUGUTZER, R., Soziologie des Körpers, 152, who speaks of the body as a 'subjective fact', using a phrase from Schmitz. Since we have not introduced the distinction of 'subjective' and 'objective' yet, we cannot adopt this language here.

Plato via Descartes up to naturalist Neurobiologists and Cyberspacians, we must express the insight of the phenomenology of the body, which designates the human becoming as a 'bodily self.'[33] We have to attribute to the living body what a body-mind-dualism attributes to the mind: The body knows, and any knowledge is grounded in the living body. All action is bodily action and based in the knowledge of the body.[34] The body is the *primary medium of communication* between humans and their world, in which the body is imbedded and to which the body is open.

Furthermore, the body is dynamic, on the move, and a kind of 'center' of a specific presence that is related by protention and retention to specific futures and pasts. The coordinate system enfolded by the body is itself a moved one. The body and time are constitutively related in the manner in which the body is the condition of the possibility of experiencing time,[35] as we have seen in ch. 10.

As my living body, the body is always – not only on the object-level of symbolic construction in the realm of secondary narrativity, but even on the level of the immediate perception of truth and value – related to what is foreign to the body, and that co-constitutes the body and challenges the body. Being related to oneself, or being deprived of oneself, and being related to what is alien, are from the beginning indissolubly interwoven. The living body is always an inter-bodily fact. This phenomenological insight has been explicated by Karl Heim, using different language:

> The picture of the whole world which I necessarily form for myself from this particular central vantage-point is all at once disturbed and called in question by the coming on the scene of a second ego which is as irremovably and unexchangeably welded to another position as I am to mine. From this there arises a world which has two centres and yet which logically can have only one centre. For each of us, both you and I, must make the same demand and the same claim, namely, that we are the centre, the only standpoint from which everything is seen correctly. The non-objective seeing point is located in two positions, yet it can only be located in one position and can only be one seeing point.[36] [...] This unobservable contact may be a passionate inner conflict, an almost unbearable tension, if the directions in which the two of us would like to mould the world are opposed. But this relation may also be an inward harmony, a community of purpose, which is essentially already present even before it has acquired an

33 Cf. for the following, see also WALDENFELS, B., Das leibliche Selbst.

34 Cf. MÖRTH, E., Der Leib als Subjekt der Wahrnehmung.

35 For an analysis of this insight, which was subsequently to Husserl further developed by Merlaeu-Ponty, cf. FÖRSTER-BEUTHAN, Y., Zeiterfahrung und Ontologie, 167f.

36 HEIM, K., Christian Faith and Natural Science, 53.

> objective form, before any word has been spoken and before any deed has been done.[37]

From a second perspective, we have to claim that humans are not their living bodies (*Leiber*), but that they also have spatial bodies (*Körper*), so that they are objects in space and metrical time. In contrast to the *Leib*, the *Körper* is a thing among things, and therefore also an available object of restrictions, by *Leib* or society. This perspective of the *Leib* as *Körper* provides the possibility for thinking of a mind divided from the (spatial) body.

The third perspective points to the body as a 'symbolic construction'.[38] The body is also the mirror, object, and effect of historically changing identity discourses.

If one wants to get a clear image of the living body, it is a profound mistake to think of a three-dimensional container, closed off from its environment by skin, which moves on the surface of the ground. By extending and modifying of an insight from Ingold,[39] we can say more precisely that living bodies are like whirlwinds, cyclones or anti-cyclones: They are not separated from their natural environment, the atmosphere, but they consist of it. They form, with the eye of the storm, a center for its own coordinate system that is relatively closed off from its environment and has a quasi-internal side. However, the storm, and its center, is always in movement. It is constantly related to other phenomena of the weather, and unthinkable without them: without the anti-cyclone, no cyclone. Cyclones, anti-cyclones, and whirlwinds are not only related to each other, but always in movement. They have fuzzy margins, extend and contract themselves, but also interfere with each other through their fronts and, through ridges of high-pressure in the midst of cyclones, cause thunderstorms and anti-cyclones. Mine and yours, love and alterity belong together, perhaps paradoxically, but organically. And moreover, weather patterns have a history that must be known in order to make forecasts. But nevertheless, all the predictability of the weather is surpassed by true retrospective surprises. The same is true of the becoming of the living body. Dynamic bodiliness is not so much a kinetic phenomenon as a meteorological one, which has numerous implications for the theme of conceptuality and rationality. Whereas in the kinetic model reason intentionally takes the lead by rule following in the same way that practical reason follows the theoretical, in the meteorological model of the living body, an only partially purifiable reason attentionally follows

37 HEIM, K., Christian Faith and Natural Science, 78.

38 LIST, E., Einleitung, 14.

39 Cf. INGOLD, T., Life of Lines, 53–59.

practical reason. The living body is, as we will show more concretely in the second volume, a dynamically extended, quasi-pulsating body. It is anchored in the atmospheric medium of the environment as a mesh of wayformational lines like a sea anchor, and it emerges out of the medium, which means that the image of the coordinate system must be highly qualified, modified, and perhaps also criticized.

The theory of special relativity operates with moving coordinate systems, which are also related to other moving coordinate systems. Here too, the different coordinate systems cannot be reduced to a single one.[40] Nevertheless, this image is not appropriate for expressing the character of the body in its interbodiliness, since in the realm of the special theory of relativity the coordinates of the different systems can be translated into each other with the help of the Lorentz-transformations.[41] The relative movements of special relativity are modeled according to the key-metaphor of transport. These movements are exactly what are excluded from the living body.

Therefore, the constitution of conceptuality – and thus of reason, too– necessarily includes tracks running in opposite directions. On the one hand, it is bound to the living body due to its indexical basis. On the other hand, it seeks universalization. How is this possible?

14.7 Classificatory Knowledge and Narrative Knowledge

The predicative aspect of conceptuality seems to pursue universality. It generates classificatory knowledge that enables vertical integration[42] into the framework of models of complex structures:[43]

> Adopting the complex structure metaphor, we could say that knowledge takes the form of a comprehensive configuration of mental representations that have been copied into the mind of the individual through some mechanism of replication, even before he or she steps forth into the environment. The application of this knowledge in practice is, then, a simple and straightforward process of sorting and matching, so as to establish a homology between structures in the mind and structures in the world.[44]

Everything that can be said by models of complex structures can also said by models of complex processes, as Rubin has shown.[45] Such models of complex

40 Cf. EINSTEIN, A., Spezielle und allgemeine Relativitätstheorie.
41 Cf. for the transformation of coordinates in the theory of relativity, see WÖLFEL, E., Zeit.
42 Cf. INGOLD, T., A Storied World, 158.
43 Cf. RUBIN, D.C., Go for the Skill.
44 INGOLD, T., A Storied World, 159.
45 Cf. RUBIN, D.C., Go for the Skill, 375.

processes takes the indexical basis of concepts (and therefore of predication) seriously, and therefore also the fact that concepts are based in the interbodily, dynamic mesh of wayformational lines in the perception of truth and value:

> A complex process metaphor [...] would lead us to prioritize the practice of knowing over the property of knowledge. Rather than supposing that people apply their knowledge in practice, we would be more inclined to say that they know *by way of* their practice [...] that is, through an ongoing engagement in perception and action, with the constituents of their environment. Thus, far from being copied, ready-made, into the mind in advance of its encounter with the world, knowledge is perpetually 'under construction' within the field of relations established through the immersion of the actor-perceiver in a certain environmental context. Knowledge, in this view, is not transmitted as a complex structure but is the ever-emergent product of a complex process. It is not so much *replicated* as *reproduced*.[46]

Models of complex structures can be included in models of complex processes, but not *vice versa*. This arrangement fits with the diagnosis that concepts presuppose indexical expressions and names, which therefore indirectly belong to the concept of concepts. Purely predicative concepts are empty; they are, strictly speaking, not concepts at all, which means that models of complex structures – and therefore also classificatory knowledge – are abstractions from models of complex processes. If one denies this feature, one would have to take models of complex structures to be describing reality as a 'movement' of transport in the network. Such a description is surely wrong. Like models of complex structures imply classificatory knowledge, models of complex processes imply narrative, storied knowledge:

> We can understand the nature of things only by attending to their relation, or in other words, by telling their stories. For the things of the world are their stories, identified not by fixed attributes but by their paths of movement in an unfolding field of relations. Each is the focus of ongoing activity. Thus, in the storied world [...] things do not exist, they occur. Where things meet, occurrences intertwine, as each becomes bound up in the other's story. Every such binding is a place or topic. It is in this binding that knowledge is generated. To know someone or something is to know their story, and to be able to join that story to one's own.[47]

Storied knowledge does not behave like a network classificatory knowledge understood in isolation, but like a meshwork.[48]

---

46 INGOLD, T., A Storied World, 159.
47 INGOLD, T., A Storied World, 160f.
48 Cf. INGOLD, T., A Storied World, 163.

We can now answer the question of how the fact that concepts are bound to the particular, bodily basis enables universalization. Irreducibly particular bodiliness and universality are only possible from the perspective of a concrete, wayformational line. And these are only possible together with engaged, storied knowledge – within the limits of the becoming and narrating of stories.

14.8 The Equiprimordiality of Designation and Predication in the Equivalence of Name and Story

Stories in the sense of secondary narrations enable privileged 'access' to reality, since reality is a mesh of primary narrations. More precisely, this is not 'access' at all, since secondary stories told in an engaged way (in contrast to a disengaged[49] practice of telling) are always a part of this primary mesh of reality. Of course, secondary stories told in a disengaged way also belong to reality. But based on their self-isolation they lead to a disturbed perception of truth and value. A (necessary) condition for this achievement of engaged secondary stories is that they not only always include a kind of indexicality that is interwoven with one's own bodiliness, but also an attitude that affirms this fact. This indexicality, we have seen, is extraordinarily visible in the use of names as designators that can be expressed with the help of identity descriptions. Of course, identity descriptions can also include some predicates, along with other indices. Identity descriptions are simply more or less explicated secondary stories, despite being described by an engaged and disengaged teller. Although, such a description tells us nothing other than we have discovered the equivalence or reversibility of name and story. However, here name is not a pure designator. This basic reversibility is also the subject-matter of cultural model-building. Therefore, a closer look at this area might also be fruitful.

Modernity tends to encourage attitudes of individualism and the separation of culture and nature. Both also affect our dealing with names. A proper name is often understood as a cultural sign for a non-interchangeable, 'personal' identity.[50] Therefore, we use proper names for humans, for geographical spots and anthropomorphically for domestic animals; but in general, not for animals, for plants, or non-living matter that lacks cultural meaning. The theory within analytic philosophy that proper names are primarily designators, is perhaps a product of this cultural modelling as well. Seemingly pure natural objects do not have proper names, but here we use classificatory

49 For the concept of disengaged thinking cf. Taylor, C., Sources of the Self, 160.

50 Cf. Ingold, T., A Storied World, 166.

knowledge, predicates, and taxonomies. This separation of pure designators (proper names) and predicates has an impact on our behavior towards culturally formed entities, like human persons. The separation of concepts from the indexical name is accompanied by a narrowing of the indexical name as an identity marker for abstract individuals. The narrowing can be illustrated by our practice of correlating a name with a particular address – be it a postal one, the e-mail address, telephone numbers, etc.; here, the name is a pure designator. We can call this the address book reduction of names. They enable an individual correlation that is in the most cases helpful in our everyday life. But this practice also reduces identification to a network of transport by disguising the bodily and narrative anchoring of reference. With this, the reversibility of name and story is also obscured, as well as the equiprimordiality of designation and predication in stories.[51] Nevertheless, this is the cultural remodeling of our (post)modern culture, which becomes obvious by having a look at other cultures, in which names are neither pure designators nor predicates, but stories. There are indeed cultures in which the equivalence of name and story, and the equiprimordiality of designation and predication in narrations is more clearly visible than in our culture.

An example of such a culture is that of the well-documented Koyukon in Alaska and their use of animal names.[52] These names are not built on classificatory knowledge, like ours, but they use names in a proper sense, correlated with stories in a threefold sense, when they are not stories themselves.

First, there are animal names as descriptions of the behavior of the animal. The animal is not so much conceived as an object, but more as what it does, how it behaves, or as instantiation of this activity. More precisely, this activity is seen as interwoven with the human lifeworld. The name of the butterfly, therefore, is 'flutters here and there', the name of the osprey is, 'stares into the water' and the mosquito is called 'flies up, ringing the bell'. The animal's name here is intended to signify a particular way of living.[53] At the same time, the animal names are learned by indexical signs. In order to know what 'flutters around the shore' means, one has to go to the shore accompanied by a teacher.

Second, there are animal names associated with stories from a primordial, mythological time. The name for sea gull is a metamorphosis-story, in which a dirty, shabby man becomes a gull. The name of the fox sparrow is a story of a beautiful woman murdered by her jealous grandmother, but saved by being changed into this bird.[54] These stories are based on a character trait in a similar fashion to the stories of metamorphosis in the Hellenistic tradition.[55] But what is really different is that every individual

51 Cf. INGOLD, T., A Storied World, 167.
52 Cf. for the following INGOLD, T., A Storied World, 169–175.
53 Cf. INGOLD, T., A Storied World, 170.
54 Cf. INGOLD, T., A Storied World, 170–172.
55 Cf. ZGOLL, C., Phänomenologie der Metamorphose.

of the species is conceived as an instantiation of the same story. Therefore, every appearance of the animal is a co-appearance of the story to which it is correlated. The co-appearance becomes clearer if we have a look at how these short stories or episodes are correlated with the life of the Koyukon: Gulls, telling their story of squalidness, are not edible birds, because one does not want to become a part of this story, one does not want to make the gull's story one's own.

Third, there are names that are riddles or riddle-like descriptions. They are not in fact sharply distinguished from the other kinds, but they introduced like the others with the same formal expressions. They do not so much tell of an activity or character trait, but of the fleeting moments of their appearance. The name for the salmon is therefore 'we come upstream in red canoes', and the fox is called 'far away yonder there appears a flash of fire'.

Most animals do not have only one name, but indeed three, one for each category. The riddle-name is understood as in indirect name, which is in the Koyukon's understanding not known to its bearer. It is used if a prey is carried into the camp, or by women – who wear no weapons and who are therefore unable to defend themselves – for predators.

It is interesting that Deleuze and Guattari claim[56] that there are three kinds of behavior towards animals: animals as instantiations of attributes, as anthropomorphic attitude towards animals, and seeing animals as manifestations of processes, which fits well, if loosely, with the three kinds of stories that the Koyukon use for animal names.

The example of the Koyukon shows us a language, in which (animal) names are neither purely designatory proper names, nor purely classificatory predicates, but told stories that are as products of secondary narrativity interwoven with primary narrativity in different ways. Here we can see the equiprimordiality of designation and concept in the mesh of narratives.

56 Cf. Deleuze, G./Guattari, F., Thousand Plateaus, 265.

CHAPTER 15

Narrations, Models, and Theories

15.1 Different Kinds of Models

In ch. 12, we learned that the predicative aspect of concepts relies on metaphorical processes that are plaited into the primary narrativity of becoming. In ch. 14, we saw that the designatory aspect of concepts is also plaited into primary narrativity. Humans always perceive the primary narrativity of their becoming in mediated immediateness. And the means of this mediated immediateness are secondary narrations. The different kinds of academic and scientific language also belong to, amongst others, secondary narrativity. For theological and philosophical work, which models and theories are especially important?

But first, what are models?

Ian Barbour suggested defining a model as 'a symbolic representation of selected aspects of the behavior of a complex system for particular purposes.'[1] Models are therefore not isolated entities in the world, but are dependent on our practice, especially on which purposes we are pursuing in the particular contexts of our life-world. But they are not only dependent on these purposes, whatever those may be, but also on *how* we pursue them. This definition also includes two other elements. Subject matter is not only an orientation to purposes, but also one regarding 'complex systems'. A system is not the world, but, according to Luhmann, only one of its parts. Whatever part of the world can be included in a system, and whatever not, is dependent on double contingency.[2] A system, therefore, is closed, but at the same time is also permeable and filtering. If we take as a vantage point Kant's classical concept of a system, which we dealt with in ch. 1, then two features belong to a system: first, in a holistic manner everything is related to everything else, and second, that the whole complex can be structured and explicated under a single concept. This concept of a system is, however, highly problematic. The holism is unproblematic. But the relative closedness is questionable, and, much more problematically, the demand to sum up and to explicate everything with the help of a single concept. If there is between literal-conceptual language and metaphorical language indeed a fuzzy transition, then the concept of the system is unusable.

1 BARBOUR, I.G., Myths, Models and Paradigms, 69.
2 Cf. LUHMANN, N., Funktion der Religion, 81.

 | DOI:10.30965/9783846765852_016

Furthermore, Barbour's definition presupposes that a model consists of symbolic representations of something. But the concept of representation is far from being unambiguous, and it is highly problematic within the framework of representationalism.[3] As such, we shall try to avoid using it. Therefore, the decisive feature we can take from Barbour's definition is that a model is always oriented towards particular purposes.

Janet Martin Soskice has given another definition: '[A]n object or state of affairs is a model when it is viewed in terms of its resemblance, real or hypothetical, to some other object or state of affairs.'[4] This definition is a very broad one, too. Instead of 'symbolic representations' now objects or state of affairs appear that are related to other objects or state of affairs, but only if there is a real or hypothetical similarity between the two. But what does resemblance or similarity mean? We have seen, that metaphors cannot simply be reduced to similarities between the semantic unities involved. A lot of resemblances are not presupposed, but are produced by the metaphorical process itself (ch. 13). Perhaps the best approach is to preliminarily refrain from giving an intensional definition of a model, and to look first at what is meant extensionally.

Experimental models are material objects or simulations, related to other objects in such a way that they signify idealizations of these objects for the purposes for which the study is designed.[5] Examples are wind tunnel models of vehicles.

Logical models are all entities that can be substituted for the axioms and theorems of a deductive, formal system, like graphs can be used as models of Euclidean geometry.

Mathematical models are representations of quantitative variables in physical or social systems, that are used frequently in computer simulations.

Theoretical models – an expression used extensively by Max Black[6] – can be described as 'a set of assumptions or claims regarding an object,'[7] or as 'imaginative mental constructs invented to account for observed phenomena.'[8] But these definitions are once more problematic. The first one is not wrong, but goes too far. The second one needs to explain what 'mental constructs' are. Whatever one might imagine here, this concept requires a lot of presuppositions – too many presuppositions.

We will focus, due to our interests in this chapter, on *theoretical models*. Theoretical models are used in many disciplines, especially in the natural sciences, independently of whatever the presupposed understanding of

3 Cf. Mühling, M., Resonances, 36–38. 52–59.

4 Soskice, J.M., Metaphor and Religious Language, 101, cf. 55.

5 This classification is based on Barbour: Barbour, I.G., Myths, Models and Paradigms, 29f and Stöckler, M., Theoretische Modelle, 46f.

6 Cf. Black, M., Models and Metaphors, 219–43.

7 Stöckler, M., Theoretische Modelle, 47 (Transl. MM).

8 Barbour, I.G., Myths, Models and Paradigms, 30.

what 'science' is. Therefore, the thesis that models are *partially* epistemically neutral,[9] is plausible. Models are used with different epistemologies and paradigms of science. But it is dependent on one's own conception of science and research, and on one's own understanding of epistemology,[10] how one describes theoretical models and which definition one uses. Since the middle of the 1960s, we find the concept of theoretical models at the center of the philosophy of science. And as this history makes it clear, all definitions are dependent on particular theories.

Constructivist theories reject the claim that theories are identified with models, since they regard the concept of models as belonging to a realist perspective, which is denied.[11]

But realist theories too, reject the identification of theory and model. For them, the concept of the model prevents the description of reality. Models only function for them illustratively. In order to use a model, it is necessary that the model-object, such as the model of a gas as a group of particles, belongs to a general theory, e.g. classical mechanics. The outcome would then be a theoretical model, here the theory of ideal gases.[12]

Constructivists and realists may share doubts about models, but it is questionable whether their reasons are good ones. Nancy Cartwright, for example, does not hold to a representationalist theory of language, but does not thereby become a constructivist. She regards theories in general as models that do not refer to objects in reality, but to objects in models. This position has its own concept of the model: anytime natural phenomena are described using the help of mathematical theory, models are being used. Cartwright elaborates:[13]

9 The thesis of the complete epistemological neutrality of theoretic models is held by STÖCKLER, M., Theoretische Modelle, 58, to support a strongly realist position. In contrast, the thesis of the partial epistemological neutrality of theoretic models only claims that every theory, no matter of which epistemological preference, has to deal with models as an object, but precisely not that there can be a neutral theory of models that is detached from its sub-theories.

10 For the history of the discussion of the concept of science in regard to the concept of theology in 20th century cf. MACCORMAC, E.R., Metaphor and Myth, 1–71; DALFERTH, I.U., Sprachlogik des Glaubens; BARBOUR, I.G., Myths, Models and Paradigms, 92ff.

11 This view holds e.g. SCHWELGER, H., Modelle als Theorien?, 70f.

12 Cf. STÖCKLER, M., Theoretische Modelle, esp. 52. This theory of models is based on BUNGE, M., Philosophy of Physics, 43f.

13 Cf. CARTWRIGHT, N., How the Laws of Physics Lie, 129; 158: 'I am concerned with a more general sense of the word 'model'. I think that a model – a specially prepared, usually fictional description of the system under study – is employed whenever a mathematical theory is applied to realiy.' In CARTWRIGHT, N./SHOMAR, T./SUÁREZ, M., The Tool Box of Science, 137–49 Cartwright argues against a view that deduces models from theories, like those in BUNGE, M., Philosophy of Physics, 43f.

> Instead of a theory-driven view of models, we suggest a phenomenologically driven one.[14] [...] I want to urge that fundamental theory represents nothing and there is nothing for it to represent. There are only real things and the real ways they behave. And these are represented by models, models constructed with the aid of all the knowledge and technique and tricks and devices we have. Theory plays its own small important role here. But it is a tool like any other; and you cannot build a house with a hammer alone.[15]

According to Cartwright's understanding, which avoids the pitfalls of both, constructivism and bold realism, any conceptual or theoretical approach to phenomena means using a model. A preliminary definition of the model could be: *A model is a conceptual explication of perceived phenomena for particular purposes.* It is still a preliminary definition, since the concept of explication used here has its own problems. We will come back to this in the last chapter (ch.27). At this point, we can only distinguish between different kinds of explications and therefore different kinds of relationships between models and theories.

Illustrative models are used spontaneously in relation to phenomena without intending to alter the secondary-narratives (e.g. the conceptual theories) that function as means of the perception of the phenomena. They have a didactic function and do not claim to play a role in research. However, frequently used illustrative models may lose their purely illustrative function due to social alterations in academic communities.

Theory-modifying models alter the conceptual explanation of the phenomenal area of an already established theory in different ways: *Non-constitutive* theory modifying models lead to a remodulation of the theoretical secondary-narrative, without becoming a part of it. *Constitutive* theory-modifying models lead to a new theoretical view of the phenomena by becoming an irreplaceable part of these secondary, academic narratives.

Theory-establishing models are the basic means for secondary narrativity to make phenomena or areas of phenomena visible and lead to the initial development of a theory in the realm of secondary narrativity. Here, too, we can distinguish between *non-constitutive* theory-establishing models, that do not become itself a part of these new theories, i.e. *heuristic* models, and *constitutive* theory-establishing models, which become an irreplaceable part of these new theories. Theories are *per definitionem* identical with constitutive models. Therefore, non-constitutive theory establishing models can only be built if another model for the same phenomena can be found that is a constitutive one.

Theory-correlating models are complex models that correlate two or more formerly independent theories. Analogously to the other kinds mentioned above, we can distinguish between constitutive and non-constitutive models.

---

14 Cartwright, N./Shomar, T./Suárez, M., The Tool Box of Science, 137.

15 Cartwright, N./Shomar, T./Suárez, M., The Tool Box of Science, 140.

15.2 Models and Metaphors

If theoretical models are conceptual explications of phenomena, then like concepts in general, they have a metaphorical basis. Therefore, we have to talk about the relationship between models and metaphors. In this regard, we can identify two different opinions. First, there is the opinion that metaphors are constituted by models. Second, there is the reverse claim: that models are constituted by metaphors.

Soskice and Ricœur claim that metaphor is a kind of language that presupposes models as a basis. The irreducibility of metaphors is based on the fact that they allude to hidden models. Models, however, are not simply systematized metaphors. Such an opinion endangers the supposed irreducibility of metaphors, since models need analogies, while metaphors do not.[16] The contrary position can be found in Max Black and his claim that models are constituted by metaphors. Here models are systematized metaphors.[17]

If we take the insight that metaphor and concepts are equiprimordial seriously, we can easily see that this alternative is false. Both are true, but both refer to different aspects of a homogenous state of affairs. The first opinion is right, because a metaphor includes the explication of the phenomenon and lets the phenomenon be seen as more than itself, but of course does not necessarily include specific purposes or explicated methodologies. The second opinion is right, since models only become visible if they can be distinguished from other kinds of metaphorical speech by their use for methodological purposes.

On can distinguish the relationship between models and metaphors in a sharper way by introducing a series of technical terms:

Key-metaphors (or *basis-metaphors* or *root-metaphors*) are those metaphors or concepts that determine a model essentially. But it is not necessary for a model to be based on a single key-metaphor alone.[18]

---

16 Cf. Soskice, J.M., Metaphor and Religious Language 35. 72. 101f.

17 Cf. Black, M., Models and Metaphors, 236; Barbour, I.G., Myths, Models and Paradigms, 42ff, is indeed based on Black's tradition, but refers instead to the similarities and dissimilarities between metaphors and models instead of asking for the conditions of their constitution. McFague, S., Metaphorical Theology, 39: 'some metaphors have structural possibilities that [...] models can develop from them, for models are dominant metaphors with comprehensive, organizational potential.' Brümmer, V., Speaking of a Personal God, 60: 'metaphors are sometimes used in a more extended way, by making them into *conceptual models*, that is 'sustained and systematic metaphors'. Cf. also Brümmer, V., Model of Love, 10.

18 MacCormac, E.R., Metaphor and Myth, 93: 'A root metaphor is the most basic assumption about the nature of the world or experience that we make when we try to give a

Literal expressions relative to the key-metaphor means that all other linguistic expressions are not identical with the key-metaphor but derived from this basis.[19] Literality is here a relative concept! As such, it gets rid of its character as a threshold value, which we saw in ch. 13. Models are built on at least one key-metaphor and the literal expressions relative to it.

Complex models are constructed by the combination of different models that are necessary in order to describe a phenomenon or an area of phenomena. They consist of different key-metaphors and different literal expressions relative to their own key-metaphors, which appear as metaphors relative to the other key-metaphors used. For example, those Christologies that see Jesus as 'Son' and as 'Word', as was the case in the Trinitarian and Christological disputes in Antiquity. Another example is our theory of metaphors itself, which we introduced in ch. 13, since we used two models: the fuzzy-set model and the model of the constitution of meaning by the intersection of different contexts. Special cases of such complex models are the so called '*complementary* models', like the model of particles and waves in order to explain light, which is based on different key-metaphors that are incompatible or incoherent if taken literally.[20]

Key-models[21] are complex models that are necessary in order to organize a whole range of theories.

Theories are nothing else but complex models or key-models. If models rely on metaphors, and if theories on concepts, and if there is a continuum between metaphor and concepts, theories can only be models in general or special kinds of models, such as complex models, in which the set of explicatory concepts play a large role in building the model.

15.3 Academic or Scientific Models and Models in Everyday Language

In ch. 14 we learned that concepts are the form of a proposition, i.e. unbound functions of propositions like F*x*. We learned, too, that the metaphorical character of all language does not exclude conceptuality.[22] Regarding concepts, we can distinguish between intension and extension. The intension is the genuine concept, and the extension are all entities to which the concepts refers, i.e.

description of it.' Cf. PEPPER, S.C., World Hypotheses, 84–114, esp. 91: 'A man desiring to understand the world looks about for a clue to its comprehension. He pitches upon some area of common sense fact and tries if he cannot understand other areas in terms of this one. This original area becomes his basic analogy or root metaphor.' Cf. subsequent to MacCormac MCFAGUE, S., Metaphorical Theology, 28.201 (note 27). Both BOYD, R., Metaphor and Theory Change, 360 and SOSKICE, J.M., Metaphor and Religious Language, 102 use the term 'theory constitutive metaphors.'

19 SOSKICE, J.M., Metaphor and Religious Language 102 calls this form of literal speech 'metaphorically constituted theory terms' or 'metaphorical terms.'

20 For 'complementary' models cf. BARBOUR, I.G., Myths, Models and Paradigms, 71–91.

21 Cf. BRÜMMER, V., Model of Love, 20f, uses the term differently because of different distinctions.

22 For a similar point, see also JÜNGEL, E./RICŒUR, P., Thesen zur Metaphorologie, 63.

the set of referents that make a true statement. In natural languages, there is not a fixed class of objects that can be correlated to a particular concept. Here we find a dynamic shifting of membership between a set or class of a concept that can be explained with the help of family-resemblance, prototypes or the fuzzy-set theory of metaphors. Concepts need to be used univocally, not equivocally. Therefore, concepts are ideally defined. In the model of the fuzzy-set theory of metaphors and concepts, this means that a specific point on the curve of the truth-function is chosen for pragmatic reasons, which denotes the membership class of the concept. Therefore, concepts do not necessarily have to be identical with the upper part of this curve, and in different conceptions and disciplines this limit can be set at different positions. The concept positions show how concepts are determined by a correlation with exactly one metaphor.

Academic and scientific models are always conceptual models. They need at least two model-*relata*.[23] The phenomenon or the area of phenomena that should be modelled is called the *explicandum*, which is correlated with an *explicans*. The *explicans* consists of the model-object – the other *relatum* – and their conceptual connections.

The first *relatum* or *explicandum* is the phenomenon that is to be explicated by the model. The model reveals how this phenomenon must be one that can be spoken about, without necessarily using *this* particular model. But of course, a perceived phenomenon can only be addressed by means of secondary narrativity, i.e. non-independently of models and metaphors. Therefore, perception or observation is 'theory-laden'[24] from the very beginning – we can ignore for now this expression's cognitivist leaning. What is meant is not so much 'theories' as 'any linguistic forms of secondary narrativity'. Nevertheless, this does not lead, according to Mary B. Hesse, into the tautologies of relativism, wherein observations are made within the framework of other models and metaphors. In contrast, the description of the *explicandum*, – made laden with expressions of secondary narrativity – is neutral in regard to the particular model that should be used.[25] The *explicandum* does not necessarily have to be a new phenomenon; it can be also an established theory that needs to be improved.

The second *relatum* or *model-object* is a semantic unity that builds the key-metaphor together with the *explicandum*. In the case of a model, the two *relata*

23 In complex models, multi-digit models are probably concievable. By the hierarchization of the model you can get models structured as binaries.

24 Such an often expressed view on observation data is based on HANSON, N.R., Patterns.

25 Cf. HESSE, M.B., Theory and Observation.

cannot be reversed, since the pragmatic interest determines what needs explication and what means can be used to do so. Therefore, the distinction between *explicandum* and model-object is a marker for the *ontological interest* and ontological commitments.

The *conceptual connections* are the relation between the two model-*relata*. The easiest case is the *explication* as the conceptual description of the model-object in its correlation to the *explicandum*. In most cases, conceptual descriptions relative to other models on a higher, lower, or the same level, will be added. Then we get a kind of literal conceptuality relative to the different key-metaphors of the model-objects involved. The relation can then be distinguished in terms of analogies. Analogy[26] is not a third kind of speech between univocal and equivocal speech, but a kind of controlled equivocal speech, which can be investigated in regard of identities, sameness, and resemblances.[27] According to Mary Hesse, there are three possible kinds of analogies between *explicandum* and model-objects.

First, *negative analogies* emerge among attributes that fit with the model-object, but not with the explicandum.

Second, *positive analogies* emerge among attributes that fit with the model object and then also with the *explicandum*.

Third, there are *neutral analogies*, i.e. attributes of which we do not know, or of which we cannot know, or of which we do not know yet, whether they are positive or negative analogies.[28] It is the reality of the things themselves, of the *explicandum*, that determines how the distinction between these analogies must be drawn. Neutral analogies are decisive, without them the whole theory of models would collapse back into the classical theory of analogy.

In practice, the linguistic expression that allows for the diagnosis of which kind of analogies are involved are called *qualifiers*.

Qualifiers cannot alter a model endlessly. An overly qualified model would consist of more negative analogies than neutral or positive ones. There would still be a similarity between the two *relata*, but then it is questionable whether the use of this model can provide any insights. 'The Son is the eternal word' is a meaningful model, whereas the metaphor 'The Son is a motor-bike' cannot provide a meaningful key-metaphor for a conceptual model, since nearly all of the modelling activity would involve a diagnosis of negative analogies.

---

26 For the complex of problems and functionality of analogies cf. HESSE, M.B., Models, 63–145.

27 Cf. MENNE, A., Was ist Analogie?, 45–53.

28 Cf. HESSE, M.B., Models, 9ff. Hesse still distinguishes between model1, which includes only positive and neutral analogies, and model2, that includes all three analogies.

The conceptual connection is bound to the academic context of the particular methodology. This process, guided by the methodology of establishing the conceptual connections, is the distinguishing feature of academic and scientific models from models in everyday language. Nevertheless, apart from this feature, models in everyday language are very similar to academic models. Here, too, key-metaphors are used, as well as the explication of conceptual connections. An important insight is that phenomena visible by the means of the secondary narrations, which determine our perception, can also be grasped by everyday-language models. Nevertheless, in most of these cases it remains implicit that one is involved in modelling.

15.4 Model-narrations and Myths

Since conceptual models and models of everyday language are based on metaphorical speech, and since they presuppose perceptions and its conditions, they are hypothetical in the sense that they are modifiable and fallible. Every model belongs to the process of the alteration of itself. This has an important implication: any model – including models that explicitly abstract from time, like many mathematical models – are interwoven in a history of modeling, i.e. into a model-narration, which is often forgotten and one only speaks of the hypothetical character of models. Strictly speaking this character is not very meaningful, since the use of 'hypothetical' is associated with the use of 'categorical', at least in the Kantian tradition. But this argumentation leads nowhere. Key-models can have a categorical character without losing their fallibility. Categorical schemes, like Kant's, that claim to be *a priori*, are also nothing but hypothetical models in this sense and have a history of modeling and a model-narration. Without such a modeling, no one could deal with them philosophically.

Nevertheless, though models are generally hypothetical by being imbedded into a model-narration, this does not prevent models from being regarded as certain by its users. In the context of a practice, be it academic and scientific practice or being our practice in general, they are regarded as true, reality-referring, presupposed in perception, etc. These are models that implicitly or explicitly deal with ontological commitments. Models do not simply represent reality,[29] but resonate with reality. Reality-claims are not only unavoidable, but they are a necessary condition of the personal and academic ability to act. There is no reason to devalue reality-claims, such a devaluation could

29 Cf., though differently stated, SOSKICE, J.M., Metaphor and Religious Language, 118–161.

be very dangerous. If it is true that realism is impossible without ontological commitments and presuppositions, such commitments are also part of those positions that ignore their involvement. And this is not dangerous because it is self-contradictory, but because the particular ontological commitments involved will be then masked by its users, voluntarily or involuntarily. Therefore, they cannot easily be compared with the ontological commitments of other positions.

Sometimes, the concept of myths is used in order to devaluate a model's reality-claims. Such a concept of myths can be found in Earl R. MacCormac, for example. Against other definitions of myths,[30] he claims that myths consist in *wrong* root-metaphors.[31] Such an understanding presupposes that one is able to distinguish between wrong and right root metaphors. Even MacCormac admits that the only possibility for recognizing whether a root metaphor is true or false is *a posteriori* one, once a particular model is succeeded by another one.[32] But he does not see that this means that the succession of models presupposes the past, present, and future model-narration. Instead, he claims that there are simply quasi-canonical models, which serve as measurements for myths.[33]

A similar use of the concept of myths appears frequently in theology and philosophy of religion. Sometimes it is said that Christological models are myths that do not recognize that they are in fact, with their mythical character removed, only anthropological models, i.e. models of human experiences. These models are explicitly the position of John Hick, who regards myths as stories that are not literally true, but that produces a specific attitude in its recipients without any constative content.[34] Hick applies this concept of myth

---

30 Cf. MacCormac, E.R., Metaphor and Myth, 112ff. 131ff.

31 MacCormac, E.R., Metaphor and Myth, 102: 'Myth is the mistaken attribution of reality to a diaphoric metaphor;' 111 'By saying that myth is the *false* attribution of reality to a root-metaphor, we do not mean to imply that everything in a myth is false. What is wrong is the belief in the literal truth of the theory, the belief that the world really is as the theory claims it to be.'

32 Cf. MacCormac, E.R., Metaphor and Myth, 106.

33 Cf. MacCormac, E.R., Metaphor and Myth, 108f. Here he concedes an appropriate status to the heliocentric model. The reason for this difference is that MacCormac holds to an absolute distinction between the literal and metaphorical.

34 Cf. Hick, J., Jesus and the World Religions. For the discussion of Hick's program and his combatants cf. Dalferth, I.U., Inkarnation. Interestingly, many exponents of model theoretic approaches also see the explicandum of religious models in human experience of meaning and purpose. Soskice, J.M., Metaphor and Religious Language, 105f, deals with some of those positions. But also MacCormac, E.R., Metaphor and Myth, 135ff, e.g. 137 ('The theologian wants to give an explanation of the ultimate dimensions of life including value, meaning, and purpose.') and Barbour, I.G., Myths, Models and Paradigms,

or metaphor especially to the doctrine of the two natures of Christ.[35] But this is the same mistake as MacCormac's: Hick does not see that particular models are parts of a model-narration, and he tries instead to ascribe to specific models a static and quasi-canonical truth-claim in order to devaluate others. Of course, this could be the case. But if it is the case, the only reason is that some models persist during their model-narration.

Models, therefore, become myths when their model-narration is denied, or when they are seen as a complete description of the state of affairs, without contingent or neutral analogies. And since it is impossible – in academics and in the sciences as well as in everyday practice – to reflect on the metaphorical character of our semiotic activity all the time, and since it is possible that every model has a model-narration, while in most cases it is impossible to identify the model-narration, the use, generation, and preservation of myths is a daily, unavoidable process. Therefore, the belief that academic and scientific work exorcizes myths is simply wrong. The notion that myths could be exorcized is nothing but a myth in itself, perhaps one part of the myth of modernity and postmodernity. It is also false that in our late-modern or post-modern present there is the end of all grand-narratives (Lyotard), which too, is a myth or a meta-narration. In principle, the production and preservation of myths is not wrong, in the same sense that the production of metaphors and models cannot be wrong. But one thing is decisive: whenever it is claimed that a model or theory is absolutely not a myth, a myth is produced that is potentially dangerous for communities and for society. In other words: in all cases in which a theory or second-order narration does not have the ability to self-relativize (or in cases where a theory claims to represent reality), problems appear. What is important is not the attempt to exorcize myths but to unmask myths

49–70, make human experience primary, but they do not want to deny the transcendent reference, even if it is not always clear what is meant by this. GUNTON, C.E., Actuality of Atonement, 41ff, deals with this problem and looks for historic and objective reasons for the subjectivistic confinement of many theological applications of model and metaphor theories. One of those reasons is the following (42): 'a preoccupation with literary rather than scientific uses of metaphor can lead to a conception of – for example – biblical metaphors as imaginative expressions of human experience of the world rather than as means by which we speak about the reality of God.'

35 In HICK, J., Jesus and the World Religions, metaphysics is often used pejoratively. Hick does not deal with his own ontological assumptions, but they can still be discerned: the semantics of Christ's predication as 'real human being' is clear, while the semantics of 'real god' is not clear, but metaphorical. From this view, one can extract at least two ontological assumptions. First: an absolute distinction exists between a literal and metaphorical use of language. Second: literal language is only possible for referring to purely this-worldly situations.

as myths, and that means seeing models and theories as ever interwoven in model-narrations.

15.5 Models, Theories and Narrations

In many respects, models are related to and dependent on narrations.

1. Models are directly or indirectly related to phenomena, and phenomena are primary, narrantic stories.
2. Models belong to the realm of secondary narrativity, even when they have no episodic character and no features of narrativity in the sense of the narratological approach (ch. 6). They are always interwoven in a model-narration, i.e. a first-order narration, that can be reflected by other secondary narrations, such as the research on the history of the sciences. As such, they not only have sequences and episodes, but they follow the rules of dramatic coherence and contingence. This is true also in those cases where a particular sequence claims logical coherence and tries to remove contingency. The model-narration may be able to be told in secondary narrations, but not necessarily. It is important not to separate models from their model-narration, in contrast to the position of many scientists. The model-narration belongs to genuine science along with other scientific practices. An essentialist understanding of science, which tries to separate the discipline from its history, is inappropriate. Research regarding the history of a discipline is a genuine task of the discipline itself.
3. Models rely on metaphors, concepts, and signs, and they are themselves complex signs. They presuppose narrativity and especially those aspects of indexicality that are a part of primary narrativity.
4. All models are narrations, and as such are also narratives that include a general structure. This structure distinguishes them from the primary narrations to which they refer.
5. All models are narrations, but not all narrations are models, for different reasons. Not all narrations can be grasped in narratives, and there are also a lot of non-model-like narrations. There are a lot of secondary narrations that are told for their own sake and not for the sake of another purpose. They do not explain anything, and they are not models.
6. In the framework of secondary narrativity, models belong to a higher-level narrativity. They belong, so to speak, to a kind of tertiary narrativity. They refer to phenomena, but they cannot refer directly to phenomena, even in those cases where such is intended. Phenomena only appear as

phenomena because they become visible by the perceivers' secondary narrations of their life-stories. Models are, therefore, narratively mediated in a double sense, and never immediate. That is true as well in those cases wherein they have no explicit narrative shape.

7. Since all models have the character of secondary narrativity (or tertiary narrativity, as we just learned), it is important to distinguish between (secondary or tertiary) narrative models in a 'literal' and in a 'metaphorical' sense. Whereas all models belong to secondary narrativity in the 'literal' sense, in a 'metaphorical' sense they only belong to secondary narrativity if they have the narrative structure of a story-line, including dramatic coherence. In a 'metaphorical' sense, they are not explicitly storied if they have no narrative structure. We can express as much by saying that, strictly speaking, whereas all models belong to secondary narrativity, only some models belong to structural narrativity. The models most often used are perhaps non-structural narrative ones.
8. Since theories – including the mathematical theories used in the sciences – are nothing but complex models, everything that is said above also applies to theories.
9. The relationship described here – in this chapter and in the whole volume – between perception, primary narrativity, and secondary narrativity, which includes signs, metaphors, concepts, models, and theories, is itself a secondary, or specifically tertiary, model without being a structural narrative.

15.6 Theological Models as Tertiary Narrations

Theological theories are sets of conceptual models, i.e. model-like tertiary narrations, that genuinely refer to particular secondary narrations of the life-world, but in a way distinct from how other secondary narrations refer to and are part of primary narrativity. At this point, we cannot mention all the features of a theological model necessary in order to explicate a theological methodology (see ch. 27), but only to make a decisive point: theological models are models that are strictly distinguished from their point of reference. Theological models are not the secondary narrations of Christian practice to which they refer. These secondary narrations of the Christian practice are the means of perception. And the many secondary-narrative shapes of Christian practice, however closely they might be related to divine self-presentation, must be distinguished from primary narrativity – and therefore one must distinguish them from the divine and ultimate, whatever this might be. Therefore, theology features double self-relativizing without thereby limiting its truth claims. In other words, theological models are always fallible and always include partial models that explain why they remain fallible. This view does not lead to kind of skepticism, but rather helps to disclose new, positive possibilities. If we presuppose the fallibility of theological theories and their model-like character, we can reinterpret old theological models, develop exiting theological theories, and investigate the power of new ones. And if we are aware that all our semiotic activities are constantly changing (but not necessarily growing), then it is not only *possible* to reinterpret, develop, and inquire into old and new theological modes, but this is also a *necessary* activity – under the condition of the communicability of Christian faith. Here it is possible and, it is to be strongly recommended, that when on the level of tertiary narrativity, theology also uses models based on metaphors that originally belonged to other disciplines. Such a procedure should not be misunderstood: it neither has any of the constructivist or speculative tendencies one might expect, but is rather oriented by reality and experience.

CHAPTER 16

Narration and Dramatic Coherence

16.1 Conceptual or Logical Coherence

Usually, coherence simply means conceptual or logical coherence. It relies on the principle of non-contradiction, $\neg(a \wedge \neg a)$, meaning that a proposition cannot be in the same respect true and not true. Together with the identity principle, it is not only valid for propositions and statements, but it is presupposed by the elementary use of signs. It is valid independent of the principle of the excluded middle, and therefore, it is also applicable for the bivalent logics in our life-world and in scholarship, as well as in artificial logics that work without the principle of the excluded middle, like the intuitionistic logic of Brower, Heyting, Gödel, etc.[1] Conceptual or logical coherence relies on this principle of non-contradiction, but it is not identical with it. The idea of coherence is a means to control and prove actual arguments. If we see in an argument – including after some transformations – no contradiction, we can call this argument 'coherent'. Logical coherence is therefore, in a specific sense, less ambitious than the use of rationalist or foundational systems. In such systems, it is required that everything that can be said within their frameworks can in an ideal case be inferred from a short set of axioms. Logical coherence presupposes no universal relationships of implication between everything that can be said. Although we use logical coherence in both academia and our life-world, this concept is not without problems, as some phenomena clearly display.

First, the idea of a coherent set of statements or propositions has led to the idea of universal coherence and the unity of truth, which played an exceptional role in the theology of the 20th century, especially in that of Wolfhart Pannenberg,[2] including contributing to the motivation for ecumenical engagement.[3] However, the idea of universal coherence needs to be applied to a *finite* series of occurrences or of (his)story, since only in an finite set of elements can coherence be determined. In an open series or an open story, the

1 Cf. Brouwer, L.E.J., Begründung; Heyting, A., Regeln der intuitionistischen Logik; Gödel, K., Entscheidungsproblem.

2 Cf. Pannenberg, W., Theology and the Philosophy of Science, 326f.

3 Cf. Pannenberg, W., ST III (engl.), xivf, with the background of Pannenberg, W., ST I (engl.), 168–171.

 | DOI:10.30965/9783846765852_017

idea of universal coherence and therefore the idea of the unity of truth loses its meaning, insofar as it is possible that elements spontaneously appear that do not behave coherently with other elements. Therefore, Pannenberg's thinking essentially requires the idea of the end of history. The idea of an end of history is founded on the idea of the universal coherence of everything that is true, which is also the reason that one should not simply call Pannenberg a Hegelian. While it is true that Hegel also uses the idea of the end of history, for him, universal coherence does not play the same dominant role as it does in Pannenberg's thinking.

Second, the idea of logical coherence developed with the idealization of logical highly abstract languages. In classical, and most artificial logical systems, temporal inflexion is excluded and therefore these logical systems are abstractions from a narrative series. Because this is not the case in our everyday languages, the qualification 'in the same respect' is necessary to apply coherence to these languages. Without this restriction (that the statement refers to the same place, time, etc.) the idea of non-contradiction becomes meaningless, or at least inoperable.

Third, in practice, we deal differently with contradictions, and only partially by using logical coherence. It is true that logical coherence plays an important role in many phenomena of the life-world, such the idea of an alibi in jurisprudence. To use an alibi presupposes that one and the same person cannot be at the same time at a specific place and elsewhere. But there are other cases where we suspend the use of coherence. There are many implicit cases in our life-world, but also explicit cases in scholarship. For example, physicists use the general theory of relativity as well as quantum theory. Both theories cannot be coherently integrated in each other or in another theory. But in practice, including in many technologies, we ignore this missing coherence.

Perhaps this leads to the conclusion that although we use logical coherence, we use it only in specialized situations that are strictly distinguished and separated from larger contexts. To use logical coherence and the principle of non-contradiction means performing an explicit, cognitive, and abstract operation. Such an operation does not diminish its value. But it is a sign that it does not belong to the level of perception from wayformational perspectives. On this phenomenal level, another kind of coherence is more important, which may be called, as I have done elsewhere,[4] dramatic coherence.

4 Cf. MÜHLING, M., Resonances, 121–128.

16.2 The Epic, the Lyric, and the Dramatic

Dramatic Coherence is essentially what we demand as coherence in perception, life experience, and in really good secondary stories that share a structural narrativity. Since not all secondary narrations are structural narratives, like tables, equations, etc., for these secondary-narratives logical coherence suffices. And for some structural secondary narrations, the idea of logical coherence might also suffice. Such structural narratives are very simple ones, yet produce insufficient effects, which are highly artificial, short and closed stories, invented by a single author. Perhaps they may incorporate a dramatic arc, but only partially. For these stories, it might indeed be true that they can be seen as meaningful for their ends when their coherence becomes visible, as Ricœur argued.[5] However, these stories presuppose that one is not intermeshed in the story, but that it is possible to observe the story from a quasi-neutral point of view. The so-called grand-narratives sometimes follow this template. Celia Deane-Drummond thinks that narrations generally follow this structure, and therefore she criticizes narrative as that which is opposed to the dramatic:

> What do I mean by epic? In the second of his great trilogy, *Theo-Drama*, Roman Catholic theologian Hans Urs von Balthasar considers whether there is ever a standpoint from which we can be merely observers to a sequence of events, including the events of Christ's death and resurrection [...]. He suggests that we can never be so detached, and if we assume as much, we are deluding ourselves. At its worse, epic becomes deterministic and creates the wrong impression of being objective [...]. Rather than using the language of epic, the language of theo-drama encourages viewing ourselves as participants in a story, one where we have a deeper sense of agency, rather than being mere observers to an inevitable process. The difference between drama and grand narrative is that drama puts much more emphasis on agents, on particular activities of particular players and contingent events, while grand narrative stresses the inevitable chain of events in a way that I suggest is ultimately disempowering rather than empowering. Therefore, theo-drama, like drama generally, stresses contingency, freedom of agents, and unexpected twists and turns to the plot.[6]

Celia Deane-Drummond draws this distinction from the interpretation of Hans Urs von Balthasar by Ben Quash.[7] Everything that is narrative is seen primarily as epic, not dramatic. Von Balthasar explains this distinction, which he sees as basic, in the following manner:

---

5 Cf. RICŒUR, P., Time and Narrative I, 67: 'to follow the story is [...] to apprehend the episodes [...] as leading to this end.'

6 DEANE-DRUMMOND, C., Drama of Wisdom, 528f.

7 Cf. QUASH, B., Theology and the Drama of History, 40–42.

> Fundamentally, where personal freedom is overtaken in this way, it signals the abdication of drama in favor of a narrative philosophy of history, an epic story of the Spirit or mankind, however much such an epic development may be pushed forward by means of a dialectic (Hegel, Marx) or an evolution (Teilhard) claiming to be 'dramatic.' In either case, people claim to know the world's universal law embracing freedom, a priori or a posteriori.[8]

For von Balthasar, the epic presupposes a detached point of view, gained, for example, by knowing the rule that directs the process, and by the reduction of contingency and freedom. The dramatic does not share these features:

> It so overarches everything, from the beginning to the end, that there is no standpoint from we could observe and portray events as if we were uninvolved narrators of an epic. By wanting to find such an external standpoint, allegedly because it will enable us to evaluate the events objectively (*sine ira et studio*), we put ourselves outside the drama, which has already drawn all truth and all objectivity into itself. In this play, all the spectators must eventually become fellow actors, whether they wish to or not.[9]

According to von Balthasar, very early in the history of Christian thought the dramatic was diminished and a separation between the lyric, referring to immediate religious speech of the pious practice, and the epic, referring to theology, appeared.[10] The distinction between the dramatic, the lyric, and the epic that von Balthasar uses is influenced by Hegel,[11] and the distinction is not an absolute one between tropes or species, but one between modes. Therefore, the epic and the lyric finds its unity in the dramatic.[12] Unity also explains why elements of the epic, the lyric, and the dramatic can appear in species that are dominated by one mode. The other way around, however, this also means that the dramatic cannot exist completely without the 'narrative' as Deane-Drummond also admits.[13]

It may be the case that, materially, my opinion comes close to Deane-Drummond's, von Balthasar's, and Quash's. However, there is at least a terminological problem. Von Balthasar, Quash, and Deane-Drummond identify

8 Balthasar, H.U.v., Theo-Drama II, Pos. 517.

9 Balthasar, H.U.v., Theo-Drama II, Pos. 797.

10 Cf. Balthasar, H.U.v., Theo-Drama II, Pos. 732–779.

11 Cf. Quash, B., Theology and the Drama of History, 40f.

12 Balthasar, H.U.v., Theo-Drama II, Pos. 763: 'We shall not get beyond the alternatives of 'Lyrical' and 'epic,' spirituality (prayer and personal involvement) and theology (the objective discussion of facts), so long as we fail to include the dramatic dimension of revelation, in which alone they can discover their unity'.

13 Cf. Deane-Drummond, C., Christ and Evolution, 48–53.

narrative with the epic and separate it from the dramatic. However, this cannot be justified by the origins of this terminology as it is found in Aristotle, which Ricœur has shown.[14] And, more importantly, this can be justified factually: the dramatic and the epic, including von Balthasar's use of them, have important features in common, like the constitution of time, sequence of events, etc. Furthermore, von Balthasar seems to regard narrations as dependent on narrators or authors, in the same manner as he distinguishes the personas of a drama from the drama itself. In both cases, the persons are at best involved or ensnared by the drama or the story, but they are *not woven out of it*. In other words, he does not develop the idea of the priority of the occurrence of wayformational lines. Therefore, it seems more plausible to distinguish on the level of secondary narrativity between (1) structural narrations from other narrations, and (2) on the level of structural narrations between *epic narrations and dramatic narrations*. Then, epic narrations have the characteristic that they can be reduced, *a priori* or *a posteriori*, through a rule to a narrative. Indeed, this can also be the case in drama as a species of literature. Is it really possible to think of dramatic secondary narrations as closed, as having the features of a completed work? It seems to be more likely that dramatic secondary narrations are a liminal case, which refer to the dramatic narrativity of primary narrativity, but that cannot really represent this dramatic feature of the narrantic in language literally. In this case, the narrantic events of wayformational perspectives are always dramatic first order narrations. But of course, this claim can be only justified by all three volumes of this book.

But let us turn to the essential distinction between the epic and the dramatic on the level of secondary narrativity. Whereas epic narrativity is marked by logical coherence, dramatic narrativity is marked by dramatic coherence. The first sort is obvious: to judge logical coherence, the narration is closed and the judge is situated outside of the narration. It is impossible, of course for one to be outside of a narration in which one is interwoven.

16.3 Dramatic Coherence

It is striking that von Balthasar defines the dramatic negatively in relation to what is epic, which, however, is not a viable solution because one might then assume that, if dramatic narrations lack logical coherence, then no concept of coherence could be applicable. Therefore, we must define the concept of dramatic coherence positively.

---

14 Cf. Ricœur, P., Time and Narrative I, 36.

1. Dramatic or narrative coherence is not simply a kind of non-contradiction. It refers, rather, to the fact that sequences of events resonate together in such a manner that time, contingency, and necessity are all included in the effect. Dramatic coherence was discovered – or perhaps only nearly discovered – by Aristotle. For him, the ability of narrative, including the dramatic, – in which he also includes non-linguistic forms such as dance and music – to actuate affects relies on a specific 'rule':

> ταῦτα δὲ γίνεται καὶ μάλιστα [καὶ μᾶλλον] ὅταν γένηται παρὰ τὴν δόξαν δι᾽ ἄλληλα· τὸ γὰρ θαυμαστὸν οὕτως ἕξει μᾶλλον ἢ εἰ ἀπὸ τοῦ αὐτομάτου καὶ τῆς τύχης, ἐπεὶ καὶ τῶν ἀπὸ τύχης ταῦτα θαυμασιώτατα δοκεῖ ὅσα ὥσπερ ἐπίτηδες φαίνεται γεγονέναι.[15]

Whether one regards Aristotle as the one who discovered dramatic coherence or not depends on how this passage is translated. I would suggest the following:

> This always happens when the sequences happen against one's expectation (against what seemingly will happen, as a surprise), but retrospectively in logical order (following its inner logic). The wonderful effect will then be more probable than in those cases in which events follow automatically or purely by chance, since these events that also happen by chance appear more wonderful when they appear as if they were intended, without in fact being intended.

In this basic rule, the idea of dramatic coherence is implied: future events do not follow as the sum of all previous events. The sum of all previous events is not sufficient to describe or to forecast what follows. Therefore, the following events happen ontically (or narrantically) with more or less contingency, and are experienced with more or less surprise. But retrospectively it can nevertheless be conceived of as an effect of the previous sequences. Dramatic coherence is therefore emergent in the sense that all known or unknown events of the past (including their effects) are only necessary conditions for the following events. The events of the past can determine the future course of events at most in their potentiality, by co-determining which possibilities are real – and which possibilities are not. Thereby, a decisive feature of dramatic coherence is that a person interwoven in such a (good) story *cannot* judge at any time between real and unreal events. Since narrative identity is always dramatic identity in the sense that there is more than one possible way for the wayformational lines to develop, the set of future possibilities is always larger than the set of possible expectations.

15 Aristoteles, Peri Poietikes 1452a, (Ch. 9, 9).

2. In dramatic coherence, it is not only the case that the set of future possibilities is larger than the set of expectable possibilities, but it is also possible that the set of future possibilities is not a closed one at all, i.e. that it is a non-founded set. If we conceive of all future possibilities as a closed set of non-contradictory events in the sense of logical coherence, then there would be no novelty, and everything that would seem to be new would be nothing but the actualization of timeless possibilities. Dramatic coherence, however, allows one to conceive of the really new. In other words, dramatic coherence relies on the relative-retrospective surprise. It is important to note that it is not the limitations of the human mind that let these un-inferable novelties emerge, but that, in certain states of the narrantic event and in the secondary narrativity that relies on it, events emerge that constitute new possibilities. If and how this is possible depends essentially on how one thinks about contingency. We will deal with that problem later (ch. 18).

Dramatic coherence in this sense is only possible when there is no outside and no end of a narration. And here we have to correct von Balthasar, who mistakenly regarded the radical striving for beginnings and endings as a condition of the possibility of being radically involved.[16] A radical striving for beginnings and endings might mean that there are no un-involved spectators, but it also enables the objective retrospection of these involved ones. Only by thinking through dramatic coherence to its end, are all those involved enabled to also really be those who are intermeshed. Whether a story has a beginning or not is not important at this point.

3. Dramatic coherence is not something that can be conceded once and for all. During the course of a dramatic story it is possible that one or all of those who are intermeshed conclude that there is dramatic coherence. But it remains open whether this will also be so in the future. The backside of dramatic coherence is dramatic incoherence. And dramatic incoherence can also appear, if a past sequence is judged not only as dramatically coherent, but also as logically coherent. This is, for example, frequently the case in theories about the physical world. As secondary narrations, these are usually not structural narratives and they claim to have logical coherence. But if these theories appear as what they are, i.e. as imbedded in larger contexts or as imbedded in the narrantic events itself, then incoherencies can appear. The point is that dramatic coherence cannot be diagnosed or known, but only hoped for, since the whole is always open. However, this should not be misunderstood: to say that dramatic coherence is 'only' an object of hope is not to ascribe a deficiency to it. Dramatic coherence is an object of hope that is based in perception.

16 Cf. BALTHASAR, H.U.v., Theo-Drama II, Pos. 797.

Dramatic coherence is that which perceptional trust (ch. 5) hopes for. Without trust in dramatic coherence, perception is impossible.

4. A fourth important feature of dramatic coherence is that it not only includes both contingency and rules, but that it also includes tensions that would be seen in the framework of predicative theories as contradictions. Predicative theories belong to logic, and logic is in most of its formalizations understood as timeless. Therefore, the propositions p and not-p cannot be incorporated in the same aspect as true in the same theory. Stories, however, have an irreducibly temporal and sequential structure. Here events can appear that incorporate at the same time the claims p and not-p in the same respect. All this is possible, so long as the only condition for dramatic coherence is satisfied, which is that later sequences are able to *sublate* previous ones. It seems as if Aristotle did not observe this important feature of the drama. His *Poetics* tends to resolve contingency into necessity. A better description and a better evaluation of this feature of dramatic coherence can be found in a theory that does not claim to deal with the narrative, but with the conceptual: Hegel's dialectics includes this moment of sublation. However, we have seen that Hegel's dialectic is not evaluated by von Balthasar as dramatic, but as epic. Therefore, we have to deal with this feature of 'sublation' in a little bit more detail. Hegel writes:

> At this point we should remember the double meaning of the German expression '*aufheben*.' On the one hand, we understand it to mean 'clear away' or 'cancel,' and in that sense, we say that a law or a regulation is cancelled (*aufgehoben*). But the word also means 'to preserve,' and we say in this sense that something is well taken care of (*wohl aufgehoben*). This ambiguity in linguistic usage, through which the same word has a negative and a positive meaning, cannot be regarded as an accident not yet as a reason to reproach language as if it were a source of confusion. We ought rather to recognize here the speculative spirit of our language, which transcends the 'either-or' of mere understanding.[17]

Hegel sees negation as well as preservation and care originally bound up in the term sublation. Indeed, this is a feature of our life-experience: incoherencies do not simply vanish, but are preserved. One might hope that they do not reemerge with their previously negating power, but one also cannot transform them by a rule or a law. But that was Hegel's mistake: he regarded the concepts of sublation as feature of *conceptual* speech. And that means that the incalculable becomes a calculable rule, which is the point where Hegel's dialectics is seen to be epic after all.

17 HEGEL, G.W.F., Encyclopaedia Logic, 154.

Hegel can, therefore, be interpreted in two ways. On the one hand, Hegel is interpreted as someone who negates one of the basics of logic, the role of the excluded middle, but nevertheless tries to design an *operational* dialectics, where something arbitrary does not follow from falseness. Graham Priest, in his paraconsistent dialetheistic logics, follows this line.[18] This building of an operational logic on the foundation of negating the rule of the excluded middle might indeed not be without danger, since, as Popper thought, it might include totalitarian tendencies.

On the other hand, Hegel is interpreted as maintaining the principle of the excluded middle.[19] The figure of sublation is then seen in the framework of a classical, bivalent position that leads to universal coherence. Von Balthasar's interpretation follows the same line, but universal coherence tends towards the totalitarian as well.

There is, however, a third way, not for interpreting Hegel, but to think about sublation. One simply has to locate sublation where it is: in what is narrative. Therefore, we are far from using Hegel's philosophy as a framework, in which alterity and contingency are excluded, but only borrow Hegel's explication of the (very welcome) ambiguity of the concept of sublation as negation, preservation, transformation, and further openness. In the course of a story, something can only be preliminarily sublated. The ultimate sublation of something can only be hoped for. If one proceeds from the narrative to the conceptual – which is unavoidable, as we saw – it is unnecessary to follow Hegel or Priest in abrogating the principle of the excluded middle, but one can also decide to use classical logic, as long as one knows that this is a voluntary, operational abstraction from reality, carried out by preparation and decontextualization. Logical or conceptual coherence also does not represent reality or resonate with reality, but is a system-immanent attribute – without reference to reality. Such a conception, is not the case, however, with dramatic coherence. Its power is derived from its narrative reference to reality – not as representation, but as resonance.

To sum up, dramatic coherence has essentially four features.

First, future events are un-inferable from past events, even if the past ones are completely known, but afterwards the sequence appears as 'sequential' and 'coherent.' Dramatic coherence is essentially non-deterministic. It is based on actual retrospective surprise or relative-retrospective surprise.

18 Cf. PRIEST, G., In Contradiction. PRIEST, G., Beyond, 108f, considers this to be the correct interpretation of Hegel.

19 Cf. KOCH, A.F., Versuch, 284.

Second, dramatic coherence includes real novelty in the sense that during a story new, un-inferable possibilities emerge in true contingency. Novelty is not the actualization of what is timelessly possible.

Third: Dramatic coherence can also only be preliminarily identified in past sequences. Its correlate is dramatic incoherence. Dramatic coherence can ultimately only be hoped for. What is hoped for – dramatic coherence – is presupposed in perceptual trust or perceptual faith.

Fourth: Dramatic Coherence allows contradictions and can sublate them.

Problems only arise when dramatic coherence is not only seen as factually presupposed in perceptual faith, but also when one tries to operationalize it. In such cases, one has to give an answer as to how it should be done, e.g. which contradictions have to be sublated and in which quantity, and which contradictions have to be excluded. In operationalizations, dramatic coherence cannot be a direct, immediate tool, but one cannot avoid using logical coherence. Therefore, dramatic coherence and logical coherence do not exclude each other. Dramatic coherence correlates with wayfaring in the mesh. Logical coherence, however, cannot be automatically identified with transport in the net. Such is only the case if logical coherence is mistakenly understood as basic and as the principle of the ontic events that really happen, which is the case if one decontextualizes the idea of sublation from its narrative framing. The Hegelian dialectic (and others, like Marx's, who followed Hegel) also tends to both instantiate transport in the net and reduce our interwoven wayformational lines of perceiving.

16.4 Dramatic Coherence and the Conduct of Life

Let's take a look at these secondary narrations and narratives, in, with, and under which humans perceive their own becoming and the becoming of their environment and world. Put differently, let us take a look at what is finally the unalterably narrative identity of humanity. The stories of personal, narrative identity can never be complete and they are present on every level of experience, the perceptual horizons of experience, and the horizons of perception. Since the stories are not stored in the memory or the brain, but relationally actualized in actual communication with users of signs and environments,[20] the secondary narrations that resonate our experience of primary narrativity remain in the most cases tacit. Nevertheless, to live on the horizons of experience is a constant effect of these secondary stories. When, on the basis of

20 Cf. FUCHS, T., Das Gehirn – ein Beziehungsorgan, 129.

the so called 'basic' self, the 'personal' self, including its narrative identity, is developed[21] and the horizons of expectation co-emerge. Therefore, all human experience and action always happen within specific horizons of expectation and anticipation. These horizons can be structured with the help of two distinctions, a rational one, and an affective one.

The affective distinction means that all possibilities that appear in the horizon appear as hope or fear, since they are based on the experiences of the basal self. Human affectivity, which enables the perception of truth and value, forms the horizon of experience like human reason does, or perhaps even more so.

In the sense of a rational distinction, the horizon of expectation is distinguished by four different modes of expectation, which are constituted by resonances between experience and a narrative identity in perception. We also referred to these kinds in ch. 10.4 on the logic of surprise, but for the reader's convenience, and since these distinctions are of utmost importance, we will address it here once more.

a) The non-surprising or the expected: We expect some events with more or less certainty, such as 'lectures have an end', or 'Tuesday follows Monday.' In our past story, we experience certain evidence in our horizon of expectation that things like these have happened before. The non-surprising is close to the center of our horizons of expectation.

b) The prospective surprising: Some events happen with less probability, but we can imagine that they happen. It is improbable that the President of the United states will read this book and, as thanks for the insights it provided, make me his Minister of Philosophy. However, as improbable or fantastic as the possibility might be, the fact that I can imagine it would make the surprise, if it happened, a prospective one. Events like these are in our horizon of experience, close to its margin.

c) The absolutely-retrospectively surprising: Some events are beyond our horizon of experience, or better, as possibilities they are also formed during the becoming of the mesh of wayformational lines. Of course, I cannot give an example of such a surprise. If I could, it would not be absolutely-retrospectively surprising. Only afterwards can they be identified as surprises. Nevertheless, we can expect to be surprised in an absolute-retrospective manner. And this expectation is essentially human. Absolute-retrospective surprises broaden our narrative horizon of experiences and they are a necessary condition for making life-experiences. Nevertheless, from a specific present one must say that the absolutely-retrospectively surprising is beyond any horizons of experience.

21 Cf. FUCHS, T., Selbst und Schizophrenie, 888–891.

d) The relatively-retrospectively surprising: To this fourth category belong the future events of our lives, which play a major role in the concept of narrative identity. It is a combination of the second and the third kind: we expect to become surprised in an absolutely retrospective manner by a future event that we expect without surprise. Nevertheless, we do not know what these surprises might be. Very good birthday presents belong to this type: I expect my future birthday as something that is non-surprising. I also expect to get presents. And I expect to be surprised by these presents. But I have no idea by what, which is the relatively-retrospective surprise.

Since we use different stories in order to express our narrative identity, we also have different horizons of expectation, which are dependent on our being involved in different communities, different relationships to other persons, different traditions, and different situations for action. But since the narrative identity is always sublated in the autobiographical self and its meta-narrations, there is something like a comprehensive horizon of expectation. This comprehensive horizon of expectation and surprise can be named an ultimate, eschatological or religious horizon of expectation. Whereas all our particular horizons of expectation can be broadened by future experiences, this is not possible in the case of our eschatological horizon of expectation. In other words, this is far more than a simple broadening. Future events can alter our eschatological horizon of expectation, but, if it happens, it is not so much a broadening as it is a conversion. Whereas particular horizons of expectation depend on sequences or stories that can be bound together by meta-narrations, the meta-narration of the eschatological horizon of experience cannot be imbedded in other meta-narrations *per definitionem*. The meta-narration, therefore, has to be altered. Some of these conversions might not be called 'conversions' in everyday language, e.g. when members of a religious community perceive that another member has altered her pious practice. Other conversions might be named as such, e.g. when a member of a particular religious community leaves their community.

Horizons of expectation are not a set of concepts or predicates. They are more a possible succession of stories, events or sequences. But, this description is also not completely adequate, because there is no concrete, closed set of sequences that can be identified, since horizons of expectation do not belong to a determined, individual subject or mind, but they belong to the extended mind that is embodied in communities and nature. The only way to discover the existence of our horizons of expectation is to live and thereby to perceive that life is surprising.

The meta-narrations constituting our eschatological horizons of experience cannot be understood in the sense of Lyotard's grand narratives, as they were also criticized by Celia Deane-Drummond. She did not intend to promote a kind of postmodern arbitrariness, but she regards epic-narrative paradigms as dangerous for personal orientation, since the believer then tends to fatalism, to conceive the events of the world as unavoidable, to decontingentize the world, and to understand it as closed. Therefore, an appropriate theology has to use von Balthasar's paradigm of the Theo-drama. Whereas creaturely entities, including non-human animals and pre-personal creatures, are the actors, God plays the role of the director.[22] One should be careful in rejecting Deane-Drummond's critique. However, I think that the basic distinction is elsewhere: between, myths not seen as myths (which is common in conceptual theories) and between narrative approaches *per se*, which always include contingent possibilities. A non-open, but closed narrative approach loses its narrative character entirely. Although we have seen that the differences between Deane-Drummonds conception based on von Balthasar and our own one are largely terminological, I want to draw attention to some important differences beyond terminology: *First*, persons who perform actions – even if they conceive themselves as actors in a drama or theo-drama – have to interpret their past life-story and their future one due to their autobiographical selves in order to orient their possibilities to act in a broader, hypothetically assumed nexus of narrations and actions. This broader nexus of narrations always consists in meta-narrations, but not necessarily in grand-narratives, since they do not lack the character of contingency and the character of the preliminary-fallible. *Second*: The bold thesis that there is the end of all grand-narratives could become dangerous, since it could be tempting to make a credo out of an abandonment to fragmentation. This is dangerous, since then the actual narrative elements that function as a means for structuring one's perception of life would no longer be recognized as such. However, as factual elements they would nevertheless exist, and therefore have effects, but only tacitly. *Third*: There is a logical point: if one promotes the end of *all* grand-narratives, one has formed a grand-narrative, which includes anything the thesis wants to deny.[23] Apart from this, we can say, as a conclusion, that the idea of dramatic coherence enables the concepts of dramatic meta-narrations without any danger of closedness, decontingentization or reduction of wayfaring in the mesh to transport in the net.

22 Cf. DEANE-DRUMMOND, C., Christ and Evolution, 59.

23 The thesis of the end of all grand narratives usually refers to Lyotard's keen-witted analysis in LYOTARD, J.-F., Postmodern Condition, 9–16. As such, I do not see Lyotard's thesis in danger of being itself a new grand narrative.

CHAPTER 17

Narration, Causality, and Rules

In ch. 16 we not only introduced the concept of dramatic coherence, but also the distinction between dramatic and epic narrations, both, in contrast to von Balthasar's position, as a subspecies of narrative. The key feature of dramatic narrations is dramatic coherence, a conjunction of contingency and necessity. If one tries to conceive of the events of wayformational lines as they are given in perceiving truth and value with the help of dramatic narrations, the question arises as to whether causality and regularity can be a feature of primary dramatic narrations. Causality is one of the first regularities we learn in the personal realm, when we learn to conceive ourselves as authors of events or when we learn to conceive our conditions as effects of other persons, such as our mother and father. From this starting point, it is only a small step to the abstraction of depersonalized causality.[1] Although we learn the concept of causality in the personal realm, this does not mean that causality itself is a kind of personal regularity, if we distinguish between the constitution and the validity of concepts. Indeed, the most common contemporary concepts of causality, which at best narrow to efficient causality the medieval and Aristotelian scheme of four causes, are conceived of as apersonal. If mundane events could be conceived as an epic narration – i.e. a narration without dramatic coherence where only logical coherence can be applied – causality could easily rule. But is there also a place for causality in dramatic narrations?

17.1 Causality as Belief in Hume

In order to deal with this question, we first have to ask what causality or efficient causality might mean. Here it is not appropriate to consider at the conceptions of causality given by the contemporary naturalistic reductions of the analytic tradition, since these concepts are already heavily tinged by quasi-religious presuppositions.[2] The best, but also the most misunderstood, approach to causality is still a classical one: David Hume's. Hume's concept of causality is sometimes seen as 'conventional' or as 'empiricist', and in the

1 Cf. GOPNIK, A./MELTZOFF, A.N./KUHL, P.K., Scientist in the Crib73–79; DORNES, M., Der kompetente Säugling, 90–96.

2 Cf. e.g. KIM, J., Concept of Event; KIM, J., Physicalism.

 | DOI:10.30965/9783846765852_018

context of continental philosophy one opposes it to Kant's categorical explanation as an alternative. Indeed, Kant's categorical look at causality[3] is a very elegant one. If causality belongs to our *a priori* categories that are tools to structure perception, voluntarily and involuntarily, then it is not a phenomenon, and problems dealing with causality as a phenomenon are meaningless. Kant's opinion is also 'elegant' insofar as he cuts through all apparent problems like a Gordian knot. But one has a price to pay: one has to buy Kant's transcendental philosophy, and that is far too much for us. In Hume's analysis, the problem of whether or how causality is phenomenal is explicit. Therefore, we use Hume's frequently misunderstood discussion of causality at the outset, recalling that Hume was also at the beginning for Kant, too (which is not to address the historical question of whether and how far Hume was really known by Kant).

According to Hume, causality is a relationship among the things themselves, and therefore it seems to be appropriate to try to discover this relation empirically.[4] Here we see, that causality is not basic, but that it consists of three more basic relations, which are regarded as necessary conditions and in their sum as a sufficient condition for defining causality. These are *contiguity, temporal succession*, and *necessity*.

1. Contiguity

Contiguity means that cause and effect are immediate neighbors in respect to space. Causality, therefore, is already a theory of proximity:

> Though distant objects may sometimes seem productive of each other, they are commonly found upon examination to be linked by a chain of causes, which are contiguous among themselves [...]. We may therefore consider the relation of *contiguity* as essential to that of causation.[5]

The basic function of space as a principle of individuation of objects and an atomic theory of special relations is presupposed here. More specifically, Hume seems to presuppose a radically object-oriented ontology[6] in the sense that there are spatially circumscribed objects in a fixed way that border on other spatially circumscribed objects. A model of space based on the key-metaphor of the container is not necessarily prior, but the primacy of these objects themselves. But contiguity in a strict sense cannot be conceived of in a continuum

---

3 Cf. KANT, I., Critique of Pure Reason, B167–B176, esp. B167f.

4 Cf. HUME, D., Treatise, Vol. 1, 78.

5 HUME, D., Treatise, Vol. 1, 78f.

6 HARMAN, G., Road to Objects, is a current exponent of an object orientated ontology. For the deconstruction of object orientated ontologies cf. INGOLD, T., Life of Lines, 16.

theory of space, since – no matter how close things might be to each other – in a spatial continuum there are always infinite points in-between. Therefore, the feature of contiguity in Hume's theory of causality can only be conceived as a theory of proximity in a restricted sense. This issue of physics[7] does not exclude thinking of a continuum. Far more, it is also presupposed that spatial localization is necessary for individuation, since otherwise one could not distinguish between cause and effect.

2. Temporal succession

An analogy to contiguity in a temporal respect is the temporal proximity of cause and effect, meaning that there has to be a temporal priority of the cause in relation to the effect.[8] An atomic theory of time is also presupposed here, because otherwise temporal proximity would become unthinkable. However, in contrast to space, Hume does not say something explicitly about that theme. It is also presupposed that the temporal relation is a necessary part of individuation. The priority of the cause over the effect, and therefore the exclusion of reversibility as well as the exclusion of the co-temporality of cause and effect, are implied. Such a co-temporality, which was later one of Kant's arguments against Hume,[9] is explicitly denied:

> The consequence of this would be no less than the destruction of that succession of causes, which we observe in the world; and indeed the utter annihilation of time. [...] and all objects must be coexistent.[10]

This passage is significant insofar as it reveals that Hume regards the constitutive relation between temporal B-series and causality as symmetric or equivalent. In this example, the temporal B-series is grounded in causality. This feature is a basic one of so-called causal theories of time, such as Swinburne's.[11]

However, spatial contiguity and temporal succession are only necessary, but by no means sufficient, conditions for the concept of causality:

> Having thus discovered [...] the two relations of *contiguity* and *succession* to be essential to causes and effects, I find I am stopped short [...]. Shall we then rest contented with these two relations of contiguity and succession, as affording

7 Cf. Art. Nahwirkungstheorie, Art. Nahwirkungstheorie.
8 Cf. HUME, D., Treatise, Vol. 1, 79.
9 Cf. KANT, I., Critique of Pure Reason, B175f.
10 HUME, D., Treatise, Vol. 1, 9.
11 Cf. SWINBURNE, R., Christian God, 81–90.

> a complete idea of causation? By no means. An object may be contiguous and prior to another, without being considered as its cause.[12]

3. Necessary Connection

Hume is convinced that with the concept of necessity he had found the third necessary condition that, together with the other two, is sufficient for causality:

> There is a *necessary connection* to be taken into consideration; and that relation is of much greater importance, than any of the other two above mentioned.[13]

The necessary connection is more important for two reasons. On the one hand, only by this feature is the specific difference between causality and other relations given. On the other hand, its explications costs Hume much more effort. Whereas Hume can deal with contiguity and temporal succession on a few pages, for the analysis of the necessary connection he needs far more than a hundred pages. In what follows, we want to try to reduce Hume's argument to five steps, which essentially describe an argument of exclusion.

Step 1: Is the principle of sufficient reason of all that exists appropriate to explain the necessary connection?

If the principle that all that exists needs a reason for its existence is valid, the problem of the necessary connection would be solved. However, this principle is not given by intuitive evidence.[14] Such evidence would only be possible if, in the end, there was a *causa sui*, but Hume rejects this as self-contradictory.[15] Hume's argumentation, however, shows that the absolute existence, i.e. existence of something without cause, is possible. The assumption that the principle of sufficient reason is valid, according to Hume, is based on a fallacy that infers from the linguistic use of the concepts cause and effect to the necessary causation of real objects.[16] By excluding the principle of sufficient reason as explanation for the necessity of causal relations, a rationalist explanation is excluded.

Step 2: Is the idea of a constant conjunction appropriate for explaining the necessary connection?

Hume now asks whether the necessary connection could be empirically given. If it can be given, this would mean three things:

---

12 HUME, D., Treatise, Vol. 1, 79f.

13 HUME, D., Treatise, Vol. 1,80.

14 Cf. HUME, D., Treatise, Vol. 1, 81f.

15 Cf. HUME, D., Treatise, Vol. 1, 83.

16 Cf. HUME, D., Treatise, Vol. 1, 84.

> *First*, the original impression. *Secondly*, the transition to the idea of the connected cause and effect. *Thirdly*, the nature and qualities of that idea.[17]

The original empirical impression is the observation of the relation of contiguity and succession of things, which is not singular, but happens many times, or more concretely, constantly:

> This relation is their *constant conjunction*. Contiguity and succession are not sufficient to make us pronounce any two objects to be cause and effect, unless we perceive that these two relations are preserved in several instances.[18]

The nature of this constant conjunction consists in nothing but the probability of the associated succession of objects. Therefore, there is no possible empirical route from assuming the probability of the constant conjunction to a necessary connection.[19] Necessity, as it is presupposed in the idea of causality, cannot be proved by the empirical impressions of the senses, since such an empirical route only leads to statements of probability, which means: causality is not empirical concept.

Step 3: The 'relativity principle of causality' and the critique of induction
Nevertheless, a preliminary result is that the idea of the constant conjunction allows for a new definition of a necessary connection. And this definition is more precise and is a basic assumption of reason about causality, which is fundamental to Hume's following argument:

> If reason determined us, it would proceed upon that principle, that instances, of which we have had no experience, must resemble those of which we have had experience, and that the course of nature continues always uniformly the same.[20]

This assumption can be called, in analogy to Einstein's 'principle of relativity', the 'relativity principle of causality', perhaps also the 'universal principle of relativity'. This analogy is not accidental, since Einstein discovered his principle of relativity by reading exactly these texts of Hume.[21] 'Principle of relativity' means in both instances, in Einstein and here, that *relative* to any thinkable framework, the course of nature (or the natural laws) have to be conceived of as identical. Einstein's (and Hume's) use of 'relativity' does not by any means

17 HUME, D., Treatise, Vol. 1, 86f.
18 HUME, D., Treatise, Vol. 1, 90.
19 Cf. HUME, D., Treatise, Vol. 1, 92.
20 HUME, D., Treatise, Vol. 1, 91.
21 Cf. MÜHLING, M., Einstein und die Religion, 145–152.

imply any kind of relativism. One could indeed ask whether the name 'principle of absoluteness' would be more fitting. Since this principle cannot be based empirically, one has to ask whether it can be grounded on reason. Hume tries different ways to do this, but the outcome is that there is no reasonable argument that leads from the assumption of the probability of the constant conjunction to the 'relativity-principle' of causality:

> We can at least conceive a change in the course of nature; which sufficiently proves that such a change is not absolutely impossible.[22]

In its core, this is Hume's famous critique of induction as a valid proof. Only if it is *impossible* to reject the relativity-principle of causality, i.e. the presupposition that the future course of nature remains uniform, is it a logically necessary truth. But its contradiction – the assumption of the possibility of a future change in the course of nature – is not self-contradictory. If the opposite was the case, it would not be an inductive procedure at all, but a deductive and analytical inference, in which case cause and effect are not two ideas, but only one.[23]

Hume's conclusion is unavoidable:

There are no empirical proofs or rational ones that can support the 'relativity-principle of causality' or the assumption of a necessary connection, and therefore, of the assumption of causality.[24]

Step 4: Belief as the essential feature of causality

The fourth step does not mean, however, that we have to reject the idea of causality, but that that idea, 'that of certain objects, which have been *always conjoined* together',[25] i.e. the idea of the universal validity of the relative-principle of causality, simply exists. But if this idea is neither based on empirical observation with the help of the senses, nor justifiable by reasonable implications, there is only one solution: it is a *belief*. And belief is characterized as follows:

> We may establish as one part of the definition of an opinion or belief, that it is *an idea related to or associated with a present impression*.[26]

22 HUME, D., Treatise, Vol. 1, 91.
23 Cf. HUME, D., Treatise, Vol. 1, 89.
24 Cf. HUME, D., Treatise, Vol. 1, 94f.
25 HUME, D., Treatise, Vol. 1, 95.
26 HUME, D., Treatise, Vol. 1, 95.

The validity of the relativity-principle of causality as the specific difference to other relations of conjunctions is therefore a matter of certainties regarding worldviews. Hume makes this clear, when he describes only contiguity and temporal priority as necessary, but not sufficient, features of causality as a subject matter of philosophy.[27] So far, Hume has basically answered his three questions. *First*, the original impression of causality consists in constant conjunction apart from contiguity and succession. *Second*, there is *no* inference from this original impression to the rational concept of causality. And *third*, the nature of this concept of causality is a belief. But Hume not only asked about the nature of the concept of causality, but also about its features. The following deals with the analysis of the concept of belief and its attributes. Interestingly, Hume treats the belief in causality as structurally equivalent to the belief in the gods of religion, since he analyzes religious belief in its manifold kinds, including theism and Roman Catholicism. The fact, that he values Roman Catholicism as a 'strange superstition'[28] does not diminish the fact that he treats belief in causality structurally in the same manner (without, however, devaluating it as superstition).

There is a little, 'ironic', fact: Hume's relativity-principle of causality – the principle that 'those instances of which we have had no experience, must resemble those of which we have had experience, and that the course of nature continues always uniformly the same'[29] – has structural resemblance to the catholicity principle of Vincent of Lerin from the 5th century, according to which what is catholic is '*quod ubique, quod semper, quod ab omnibus creditum est*.'[30] Therefore, winkingly, one could call Hume's principle also the 'catholic principle of relativity.'

Hume's understanding of belief is not our present concern. Nevertheless, its essential elements are the following. The distinction between belief and incredulity in a claim does not alter the proposition of the claim, but it is a distinction regarding the manner of its reception, which includes in the case of belief more force and vivacity, so that belief in contrast to incredulity is not only an idea, but a 'lively idea.'[31] Hume explains the difference between belief on the one hand and incredulity and 'phantasy' on the other as largely incremental. Belief has larger effects on the affectivity, on imagination and it alone is action-motivating.[32] Although Hume tries to substitute the concept of belief

27 Cf. HUME, D., Treatise, Vol. 1, 95f.
28 HUME, D., Treatise, Vol. 1, 102.
29 HUME, D., Treatise, Vol. 1, 91.
30 VINZENZ VON LERIN, Commonitorium, II, 5–6.
31 HUME, D., Treatise, Vol. 1, 98.
32 Cf. HUME, D., Treatise, Vol. 1, 100.

for other concepts, the concept of belief is the best one.[33] The effects of belief are equivalent to the effects of immediate sensual experience.[34]

Hume claims his analysis of the concept of belief is valid for the belief in causality and for religious belief. Concentrating on 'to believe' is, however, problematic, since, by only focusing on the doxastic aspect of faith, Hume does not recognize the basic meaning of faith as *fiducia*. Therefore, Hume is one of the first to contribute to contemporary misunderstandings of the concepts of belief and faith. Nevertheless, it is remarkable that he sees no categorical distinction between religious faith and belief in causality. In what follows, Hume considers other aspects of belief like its constitution, the relationship between faith and reason and the distinction between implicit and explicit belief.[35] The reader could therefore mistakenly get the impression that Hume has forgotten his proper theme – the analysis of causality. But this is not the case, since in the end Hume comes back to it and sums up why this is important for causality.

The following is important for our purposes: Hume sees belief as a disposition to act,[36] based on social relationships and habits. However, his point is *not* that belief could be reduced to socially constituted conventions or that he would propagate a conventionalist understanding of habit as the core of the concept of causality. In naming belief a habit we find a classification without any specific differences that motivates the search for the distinction between belief and other habits and conventions.[37] *Belief, including belief in causality, has the pragmatic function of enabling acting and life in the face of the lack of uniformity of the mundane course of events.*[38] Hume simplifies his thesis of the gradual intensity of belief by way of a threefold division into *belief as knowledge, belief based on empiric reasons*, and *belief on reasons of probability*.[39]

Alvin Plantinga has taken causality for granted, and other acts of taking something for granted – like one's own memory, the personality of other persons, and religious belief into God – as examples that do not meet the overly rigorous criteria of knowledge as 'justified true belief', which is frequently used in the analytic tradition. He claims that speaking of 'warrant' is more appropriate than justified true belief, which in both

33 Cf. HUME, D., Treatise, Vol. 1, 100.
34 Cf. HUME, D., Treatise, Vol. 1, 100
35 Cf. HUME, D., Treatise, Vol. 1, 101–108.
36 Cf. HUME, D., Treatise, Vol. 1, 101.
37 Cf. HUME, D., Treatise, Vol. 1, 109–126.
38 Cf. HUME, D., Treatise, Vol. 1, 133,–135.
39 Cf. HUME, D., Treatise, Vol. 1, 126f.

cases – belief in God and belief in causality – must lead to foundationalism. However, Plantinga's understanding of belief does not satisfy the phenomenon of faith either.[40]

Step 5: Definitions of causality
At the end of his broad inquiry, Hume draws the well-known conclusions on causality.[41] Here, the term belief does not appear explicitly since he asks why reason needs to assume the concept of causality. However, this question is identical with the question of what constitutes belief in general and belief in causality particularly. The concept of habit reappears and objections are excluded. His first, yet still incomplete, definition of causality is:

> We may define a *cause* to be 'An object precedent and contiguous to another, and where all the objects resembling the former are placed in like relations of precedency and contiguity to those objects that resemble the latter.'[42]

The second, complete definition is:

> A *cause* is an object precedent and contiguous to another, and so united with it that the idea of the one determines the mind to form the idea of the other, and the impression of the one to form a more lively idea of the other.[43]

In this definition, the concept of causality as a belief reappears in the shape of the 'more lively idea'. Other details that allow for being more precise in these definitions[44] are not decisive for our purposes.

17.2 A Narrative Explanation of Causality

In the face of a concept laden with so many presuppositions as the concepts of causality, it is not meaningful to derive the concept of narrativity, or of particular kinds of narrations, from the concept of causality, unlike in some narratologies.

As we saw in ch. 6, Köppe and Kindt claim that, apart from the temporal succession of the events, one needs another meaningful connection between the events in order to speak of a story. And they name causality as an example

40 Cf. PLANTINGA, A., Reason and Belief, and for discussion GRUBE, D.-M., Unbegründbarkeit Gottes?, 173–191 and EVERS, D., Gott und mögliche Welten, 376–389.
41 Cf. HUME, D., Treatise, Vol. 1, 153–172.
42 HUME, D., Treatise, Vol. 1, 167.
43 HUME, D., Treatise, Vol. 1, 167.
44 Cf. HUME, D., Treatise, Vol. 1, 168–172.

of another such meaningful connection.[45] If one compares this opinion with Hume's analysis of causality, two points are worth mentioning. First, this attempt to define a story refers to a concept of causality not as well elaborated as Hume's. Second, and more important, there are important parallels between the definitions. The temporal sequence appears in Hume's definition of causality and in the narratological definition of a story. The latter does not deal with contiguity, but a spatial dimension, which is also implicitly presupposed in the case of stories. And a third feature also appears in both definitions: the narratologies speak of a meaningful connection, while Hume speaks of a connection based on belief as a lively idea. It seems that a lively idea is also a meaningful connection, although the narratologies do not explicate this concept in more detail. In face of the similarity of the explanations, one might wonder what it is that is in the need of a definition. Hume wants to define causality, the narratologies want to define story, or narration. But the similarity of the definitions raises the suspicion as to whether 'causality' and 'story' are interchangeable.

Of course, to raise this suspicion is not sufficient. We have to be careful. Hume might be right that causality is based on a belief that is a 'more lively idea,' but Hume does not see in his more or less voluntarist analysis of belief that in both, the perception of truth and value on wayformational perspectives, and in the practice of research, causality is not simply used as a belief or opinion, but as an act of trust. The constant conjunction does not so much have the character of a belief or opinion, as lively as it may be, but it has a fiduciary character. For the natural sciences, causality is an interest that guides research, even in those cases where in empirical studies this is masked by substituting the philosophical concept of causality by the seemingly less problematic concept of *correlation*.

This substitution or masking is an excellent example of what Arthur Fine called the strategy of de-theorizing.[46] One tries to get rid of the concept of causality by substituting it for an intra-systemic concept. However, this strategy neither solves the problems nor saves the precision of the empirical sciences. The contrary is the case. If the mark of really good natural sciences is that curiosity and care are two sides of the same coin[47] and that disengaged science is bad science, then the cessation of 'causality' in favor of 'correlations' is not a preferable strategy.

Hume treated spatial contiguity and temporal succession as necessary elements of causality. However, as we saw, this is not without problems, since

45 Cf. KÖPPE, T./KINDT, T., Erzähltheorie, 50f.

46 Cf. FINE, A., Shaky Game, 87.

47 Cf. INGOLD, T., Impediments of Objectivity.

one has to presuppose particular and non-self-evident conceptions of space and time. In the way Hume uses these concepts, they afford an object-oriented ontology that we have rejected. Since we have already defined the concept of space as well as the concept of time in narrative terms, redefining these elements of the definition of causality in narrative terms will not be a problem either. If temporality relies on a sequence of episodes in narrations that build a logical relation of order, as we saw in ch. 10, then we can substitute temporal succession with narrative sequences. Something may only be an effect of a cause that follows what is called cause in a narrative sequence. Whereas the substitution of temporal succession by narrative sequence is more or less simple, the spatial contiguity is more problematic. If one regards contiguity as the immediate proximity of objects it becomes unthinkable in the framework of space as a continuum. However, is it really necessary to do so? Phenomenally speaking, we might discover causal relations in instances of spatial proximity. But nothing forces us to assume an *immediate* spatial proximity. Furthermore, if we reject any object-oriented ontology and conceive of 'things' as knots in the mesh of wayformational lines, or as repeating processes of the same or similar kind; we do not need to speak of contiguity at all. It suffices when two events are linked on the same wayformational line. *We have now redefined two of Hume's necessary features of causality in a narrative way: first, that cause and effect are connected by the same wayformational line, and second, that a cause emerges narratively prior to its effect.* But as with Hume, this is not sufficient for defining causality. We need, like Hume, a third feature that somehow describes the necessity of the course of the wayformational line. But wayformational lines do not develop in themselves, separated from other narrative wayformational lines and their environments. If causality is to mean that a later development of a wayformational line depends *only* on its former narrative development, causality would be unthinkable in the framework of a narrative ontology, then we would have to state that there is no causality. However, this radical step is not necessary. It suffices to say *that the third element of causality is faith in a necessary rule that connects the narrative development of the wayformational line.* This narrative trust in causality resembles the perceptional trust we introduced in ch. 5., but it is not identical. Whereas the perceptional trust is valid for any kind of perception, trust in causality is obviously not given in perceiving all phenomena on a wayformational line, since in practice we perceive many developments of wayformational lines that cannot be conceived as causal developments.

Only if one dissolves phenomenal trust in causality into some kind of determinism, could one claim that everything we perceive on wayformational lines is connected by causality. But this is identical with the claim that the whole development of a wayformational line is only dependent on its antecedent conditions. Although, in this case, the wayformational line ceases to be a line in the mesh. It would simply be a non-necessary line between previous points in a net of transport. Such a determinism might be not incoherent, but it cannot be derived from phenomenally perceiving truth and value. If one were to claim such a universal determinism, it would be a quasi-religious claim that is not conscious of its character of a quasi-religion.

Whether we can discern causality in the course of primary-narrative events or not is a question that depends on whether in concrete cases we trust that the development of a wayformational line follows rules. And this question is dependent on three other decisive conditions.

First, it depends on in which secondary narrations we perceive reality. If it is in secondary narrations that require a huge amount of faith in the necessary development of wayformational lines, like epic narrations, of which the determinist myth is an example, we will find a huge amount of causality. If we perceive reality in dramatic secondary narrations, which includes irreducible dramatic coherence, causality cannot be seen as omnipotent regarding the development of wayformational lines. But causality is nevertheless not excluded.

Second, it depends on whether the modern narrowing of causality to efficient causality is really justified. A set of phenomena seem only to be explicable if we broaden our understanding of causality.

Third, the question of whether we discern causality in the course of primary-narrative events depends on what necessary rule-following means. In order to redefine causality narratively, we first have to ask what rules are.

17.3 Formative Causality and Circular Causality

It is frequently observed that the traditional restriction of the four Aristotelian causes to efficient causality and its reconstruction, e.g. by Hume, is not sufficient for explaining the phenomena. Attempts to reintroduce anew a kind of teleology or a *causa finalis* are the subject of contemporary debates.[48] Although neither Aristotle nor his scholastic followers could see a contradiction among the use of the four classical causes, the contemporary attempt to reintroduce teleological concepts into the natural sciences or into natural philosophy seems to amount to a re-enchantment of nature.

48 Cf. e.g. Thomas Nagel's attempt at re-teleologisation in Nagel, T., Mind and Cosmos, and the review in Orr, H.A., Awaiting a New Darwin.

In light of these debates, Thomas Fuchs has suggested broadening the concept of causality for phenomena in the realm of the neurosciences. However, he does not want to broaden efficient causality with final causality, as is commonly argued, but he takes up the classical *causa formalis* and develops out of it his concept of formal – or better formative – causality, which is not opposed to efficient causality.

Living systems are described according to a hierarchical order. The organism, as a whole and its parts, are reciprocally constituted. The parts and the micro-structures are important for higher orders and for the whole system, in a manner that can be described with the help of classical efficient causality or bottom-up causality. However, the whole system and subparts of higher orders restrict the possibilities for efficient causality having an influence in the lower parts. This kind of restriction is a form of natural selection, and Fuchs describes it as formative causality or *causa formalis*.[49] The joined effects of formative causality and efficient causality lead to a dynamic co-emergence that is called circular causality or reciprocal causality.[50]

The expression 'circular causality' is an analogy of the theory of the functional circuit. Therefore, other associations, like the hermeneutical circle, are strictly excluded. Although Fuchs describes the joined effects of formal or formative causality on the one hand and efficient causality on the other as co-emergent processes,[51] he rejects the theories of emergence that flourished a second time during the turn of the millennium. Although there are a lot of different meanings for the term of emergence,[52] the concept of emergence in the neurosciences normally means that the attributes of higher levels are not identical with the sum of the causal effects of its parts. Therefore, theories of emergentist monism[53] remain bound to a naturalist paradigm. Fuchs,

49 Cf. FUCHS, T., Das Gehirn – ein Beziehungsorgan, 122–124; FUCHS, T., Neurobiology and Psychotherapy.

50 Cf. FUCHS, T., Das Gehirn – ein Beziehungsorgan, 121.

51 The expression is used here with reference to THOMPSON, E.T., Mind in Life, 60f.

52 Cf. the history of the concept of emergence in CLAYTON, P., Mind and Emergence, as well as in BOOST, M., Naturphilosophische Emergenz.

53 Fuchs refers here (29.32) to BUNGE, M., Mind-Body Problem, and SEARLE, J.R., Rediscovery of the Mind. While the concept of contingency was widely understood as attractive in the field of theology in the first decade of the 21st century, which led amongst others to such impressive conceptions as Clayton's (cf. CLAYTON, P., Mind and Emergence) and most recently Boost's (BOOST, M., Naturphilosophische Emergenz), criticism has, however, grown in recent years. Not only does Fuchs consider conceptions based on the concept of emergence as dangerous because they always implicitly cling to a quasi-religious, reductionist naturalism, also MUTSCHLER, H.D., Von der Form zur Formel, 142f, makes this criticism and criticizes Clayton sharply: 'Whoever reads such books [as Clayton's]

however, regards his theory of integral causality as compatible with Husserl's theory of the attitudes: a natural attitude and a personal attitude. But these two attitudes behave in a complementary manner without the possibility that one of them could be reduced to the other.[54]

The combination of formative causality and efficient causality, i.e. circular causality or integral causality, work in two different respects. Vertically it forms the intra-organismic processes between an organism and its parts; cells and lower kinds of matter.[55] In this process, the brain plays an important role:

> As a transformer of vertical circular causality [...] with the consequence that it transforms high level (e.g. intentional, meaningful) influences and low level (e.g. neurochemical) influences of the organism, and it translates the elements of the one level into the other.[56]

Horizontally, integral causality determines some intra-organic processes. But what is more important is that the relations between the organism and its environment, including all of its kinds of metabolism, perception, and movement, can also be described with the help of circular causality.[57]

Neuroscientific phenomena are reasons for broadening the concept of causality in the sense of formative and integral causality, but they are not the only reasons. The contemporary attempts to broaden the Neo-Darwinist synthesis in order to get an approach more fitting to the phenomena in the realm of evolutionary biology is another issue altogether. Currently, attempts such as the theory of evolution in multiple dimensions,[58] Susan Oyama's developmental

---

will be surprised at the first glance. The theologian eliminates everything spiritual from nature, and from the human being, and confesses himself without any qualification as a scientific materialist' (Transl. MM), original: 'Wer solche Bücher [wie die Claytons] liest, wird erst einmal verblüfft sein. Der Theologe eliminiert alles Geistige aus der Natur, ja sogar aus dem Menschen und bekennt sich ohne Wenn und Aber zum szientifischen Materialismus!' Mutschler's criticism is – to say the least – not really given with the attitude of a gentleman and seems to be too simplistic and polemical, but it is not only the matter of criticism from a Cartesian dualist's point of view, but it also draws attention to the need not simply to adopt hidden assumptions. This can also be found in Boost, who provides indeed very accurate analysis, but after all he still seems to cling to a naturalistic paradigm. So Fuchs' critical attitude towards the concept of emergence can be considered quite significant.

54 Cf. FUCHS, T., Das Gehirn – ein Beziehungsorgan, 242f.

55 Cf. FUCHS, T., Neurobiology and Psychotherapy, 122–125.

56 FUCHS, T., Das Gehirn – ein Beziehungsorgan, 125, (trans. MM).

57 Cf. FUCHS, T., Neurobiology and Psychotherapy, 125f.

58 Cf. JABLONKA, E./LAMB, M., Evolution in Four Dimensions.

systems theory,[59] or the theory of niche construction,[60] mirror this movement.[61] Although, in all these theories a broadening of a narrow understanding of causality can be found, it suffices to name one example, that of the theory of niche construction.[62] Here, the relationship between genotype and phenotype is only a partial relation of a larger, extended relation that works reciprocally and cannot be understood as an external relation. A consequence is that efficient causality alone is no longer really satisfying as a philosophical explanation. In the same manner, as Fuchs had developed his concept of integral causality in reference to Jakob von Uexküll and Victor von Weizsäcker and their theory of the functional circuit, we can assume a similar integral causality in niche construction. The formative aspect restricts efficient causality by determining which possibilities in a particular situation are given. Niche construction theory uses not one, but two systems of inheritance, not only a genetic one, but also an ecological one. The latter determines the selective activity of natural selection. Whereas classical natural selection can be described in terms of efficient causality, ecological inheritance plays the role of formative causality. Since they are acting at the same time, we have to speak of integral causality. Two points are important: the relation between efficient causality and formative causality is an internal one, since none of the *relata* can exist or act without the other. This relation is immediately evident in the case of formative causality, since it acts as a restriction of efficient causality. But in the other direction it is also an essential relation.

For example, although the effects of the genotypes on the shape of the phenotype can be understood in analogy to efficient causality, the genotype is only a necessary, not a sufficient condition to enact the specific shape of the phenotypes. An isolated portion of DNA in a test-tube causes nothing. Therefore, the role of efficient causality ascribed to the genotype is only efficient by relation to the formative causality of ecological inheritance. Without one of the relata, the other would not exist: genes are not simply DNA, but the DNA is only the medium of the embodiment of the genes. Genes are only genes if they are bodily genes. The living body, the *Leib*, has to be understood in at least partial internal or constitutive relations to the environment. The bodiliness of the genes means that they are 'incarnated' in the ecological environment. The concept of the embodied gene is only meaningful if one also speaks of the incarnated gene.

Neurobiology and evolutionary biology are only two examples, which show, that efficient causality has to be broadened by formative causality in order to

59 Cf. OYAMA, S., Evolution's Eye.
60 Cf. ODLING-SMEE, F.J./LALAND, K.N./FELDMAN, M.W., Niche Construction.
61 Cf. FUENTES, A., A New Synthesis.
62 Cf. in addition MÜHLING, M., Resonances, 137–164.

gain integral causality. This state of affairs is important for us, since it shows that a narrative redefinition of causality has to consider these aspects of causality, and that a redefinition of efficient causality alone is not enough. Before we can develop this narrative redefinition of causality, we must turn the concept of rules.

17.4 Rules

Other concepts, like the concept of the law or the concept of order, are similar to the concept of rules. From a historical perspective, none of these concepts are secular, but they have theological roots. However, for the purposes of our prolegomena this is no advantage, because by using any of them one also inherits these theological traditions. We will briefly try to show why the concept of law and the concept of order is less appropriate than the concept of rule.

Theological traditions have used the concept of *law* in a number of ways. Augustine used the concept of *lex aeterna*,[63] coming from the stoic tradition where it was applied to Zeus, as a synonym for God.[64] The concept of law has the advantage of being able to conceive of nature and culture as related to the divine, because the *lex naturalis* as well as the *lex positiva* were seen as derivation of the *lex aeterna*.[65] It is not only the traditions of the past that worked in this way. In our time, Eilert Herms showed that the *lex naturalis* can be used in a similar way.[66] The use of the term law in the natural sciences is a metaphorical one and not without its problems,[67] but it also allows one to see the non-personal and non-social world in terms of this model. But the following disadvantages outweigh the advantages: First, in modernity, the concept of law is bound to the concept of a sovereign, e.g. in the different theories of contracts of association,[68] because in this case sociality and its organization is only a secondary, derived phenomenon. Second, the term law in its use in inter-confessional dialogue is often used in a derogative way, e.g. when specific kinds of Christianity are associated with legalism. Third, there is a conceptual objection. The most prominent theological use is the distinction of law and Gospel in the Protestant tradition. The discussions in the 20th century[69] about this distinction between the Reformed and the Lutheran side did not lead to a meaningful conclusion. At a minimum, one can say that this distinction tries to remodel the distinction between *opus hominum* (law) and *opus dei* (Gospel). A look at the roots of this distinction in the theology of Luther reveals that Gospel means 'what God is doing on the behalf of humanity', whereas law means 'what

63 Cf. CICERO, M.T., De natura deorum, I, 15,40.
64 Cf. AUGUSTINUS, A., De vera religione, 31.
65 Cf. WILELAND, G., Art. Gesetz, ewiges.
66 Cf. HERMS, E., Kosmologische Aspekte des Gesetzesbegriffs.
67 Cf. EVERS, D., Art. Law/Natural Law.
68 Cf. SPARN, W., Art. Law and Legislation IV.
69 Cf. SCHWÖBEL, C., Art. Law and Gospel.

God wants humanity to do'.[70] But then the concept of law can no longer be applied to Godself. Therefore, the use of the concept of law in the Augustinian and Thomist tradition means something completely different than its later use in the Protestant tradition. They are, in short, different concepts united in one term.

The concept of *order* could also be used. In the framework of the Cappadocian doctrine of the trinity, the concept of *taxis* was used as an expression for the intra-trinitarian relations among the persons.[71] Whereas this was an expression of an order *per se*, in the west, Augustine used the concept of *ordo* only analogously for the Trinity,[72] whereas he used *ordo* primarily for the created order of the *ordo amoris*.[73] In early scholasticism, Richard of St. Victor applied this Augustinian idea directly and univocally to Godself, by claiming that there cannot be any disordered love in the love that is the very being of God.[74] He was probably the first who applied the idea of the *ordo amoris* for conceiving creation and Godself. In the 19th century, Ernst Wilhelm Christian Sartorius used this idea and modified it, in seeing love not like Augustine based on an *egestas* (deficit),[75] but with Luther based on an order of surrender. All this enables the concept of order to bridge our understanding of God and creation, but sometimes not unproblematically, if one thinks of the idea of orders of creation in the Lutheran theology of the 20th century. Eilert Herms also used this tradition by interpreting the orders of creation as necessary tasks that are presupposed in the practice-situation of finite freedom, and that leads to the interactive realms of the economic system, the scientific system, the political system, and the religious system.[76] Far more, in regard to soteriology, Colin Gunton showed that Anselm's doctrine of satisfaction is not so much based on a model of honor, but on a model of an order of creation that has to be maintained.[77] But the concept of order also has decisive disadvantages. First, it suggests something closed and non-dynamic, like the ideal of a system. Second, orders are frequently associated with hierarchies. These two disadvantages led to problematic developments in both the doctrine of trinity (subordinationism) and in our understanding of society (theologies of order). Third, in the framework of the logic of relation, the term order signifies a special relation (an asymmetric, irreflexive, and transitive one, cf. ch. 7). This relational concept of a relation of order, however, is a purely technical term. Although it is of much use in theology, it should not be conflated with an order in the sense of the law or rules. Fourth, the concept of an order is a second-order concept that denotes nothing if to what it refers is not indicated. The above shows that hidden in the use of the term order is the concept of rules, where this reference is explicit. An order then, is a system of basic rules. The consequence is that the concept of order presupposes the concept of rules as the more basic.

70 Cf. LUTHER, M., WA, 36, 26, 6.

71 Cf. ZIZIOULAS, J., Cappadocian Contribution; BEYSCHLAG, K., Dogmengeschichte I, 289ff.

72 Cf. AUGUSTINUS, A., De ordine, II, 1,2.

73 Cf. MÜHLING, M., Gott ist Liebe, 66ff.

74 Cf. MÜHLING, M., Gott ist Liebe, 165ff.

75 Cf. AUGUSTINUS, A., trin., CChr.SL 5013,5 (8), 392, 29.

76 Cf. HERMS, E., Offenbarung und Glaube, 431–456, esp. 446f. 448.

77 Cf. GUNTON, C.E., Actuality of Atonement, 115ff.

In order to analyze the concept of rules, we can use fruits of the tradition of analytic philosophy and the theory of rights.

Some of the following can be found in the thinking in a variety of different thinkers such as Antonio Pagliaro, J.D. Mabbot, Max Weber, Czeslaw Znamierowski, and Ernst Mally.[78] Of eminent conceptual worth are insights from Wittgenstein's *Philosophical Investigations*, John Searle,[79] the Italian rights theorist Gaetano Carcaterra,[80] Riccardo Guastini,[81] and especially by Amado G. Conte.[82]

What is a rule? We speak of a rule when there is a set of the application of the rule (the ruled) *A*, that is by a content of the rule *B* related (*R*) to an effect of the rule *C*. In other words: *A Rule is a relationship of a rule* R *between the ruled set* A *consisting in narratively describable sequences of wayformational lines, the content of the rule* B *and the effect of the rule* C, *which consists in particular developments of narrative wayformational lines.* Let's have a look at this in detail.

The *set of what is ruled* (*A*) is the realm where the rule finds its meaningful application, which is a set of events or narratively describable sequences of wayformational lines. Since a rule can only be applied to what is universal, it refers to what is seen as uniform in events. Therefore, a rule has to use the description of narratives, not narrations. Wittgenstein brought this to light by remarking that learning rules and learning sameness happen in unison.[83] Personal actions as well as non-personal events belong to these sequences of wayformational lines. Therefore, both natural regularity and social rules belong to a univocal understanding of rules.

The *content of a rule* (*B*) is a description of how a particular wayformational sequence of *A* follows or develops in order to get the result *C*. It is not necessary that this content is expressed in a specific kind of speech (constatives, imperatives, etc.).

An example might be helpful at this point. Consider 'going left' as the content of a rule. At this point it is open whether it is a descriptive rule of propositional meaning ('All H_2O molecules are going left at this river bend'), a hypothetical thesis ('If it rains, the water will follow the left-hand bend of this street'), or a deontic rule ('the blue traffic sign with a white arrow indicating the imperative of turning left').

78 Cf. Conte, Idealtypen, 244.
79 Cf. SEARLE, J.R., Ought from Is.
80 Cf. CARCATERRA, G., Le nome constitutive.
81 Cf. GUASTINI, R., Six Concepts of 'Constitutive Rule'.
82 Cf. exemplarily CONTE, A.G., Idealtypen; CONTE, A.G., Variationen über Wittgensteins Regelbegriff; CONTE, A.G., Konstitutive Regeln und Deontik. For further references cf. GUASTINI, R., Six Concepts of 'Constitutive Rule', 267.
83 Cf. WITTGENSTEIN, L., Philosophical Investigations, 225–226.

The *effect of a rule* (C) in an instance of a particular wayformational sequence or event, resonates or dissonates with the ruling of A by B. Thereby, rule-conforming or non-rule-conforming developments of narrative wayformational lines appear.

The *relation of the rule* (R) is the heart of ruling. In everyday language, this relation is often simply all that is meant by 'rule'. Here, with Searle who refers along with some modifications to Kant,[84] we can distinguish between regulative rules and constitutive rules (or, more precisely, between regulative relations of rules and constitutive relations of rules).

Regulative rules rule those sequences of narrative wayformational lines that become independent of the rule in question. Searle gives the example of table manners, since one does not have to be acquainted with particular table manners in order to eat: the activity of eating is independent of the rules of table manners.

Constitutive rules constitute the narrative wayformational sequences. Their becoming is logically dependent on the relation of rules in question.[85] Since rules can only be applied to the general aspect of wayformational lines, i.e. to narratives, but not to the particular aspect or to 'absolute narrations', the constitutive rule is a narrative that results in narrative ordered narrations.

A frequently used example for constitutive rules are the rules of chess, since the game is constituted by its rules. One can play chess without the physical or without the physical board, but not without the rules, that constitute not only how to act, but also the existence of the pieces and the board. A narrative relying on the rules leads to different narrations, i.e. to the development of wayformational lines. Without the transformation of the narrative into a narration, chess would be boring. However, the different narrations can always be classified into sets of the narrative, described by the rules (winning, losing, draw, etc.).

The constitutive rules can be subdivided into *deontic-constitutive rules* and *a-deontic constitutive rules* (or thetic constitutive rules).[86]

---

84 Cf. SEARLE, J.R., Ought from Is, 112.

85 Cf. SEARLE, J.R., Ought from Is, 112.

86 This distinction can aslo be found in e.g. CONTE, A.G., Variationen über Wittgensteins Regelbegriff, which is subsquently abandoned in CONTE, A.G., Konstitutive Regeln und Deontik, in favor of a trichotomy of deontic, thetic, and ontologic constitutivity. In CONTE, A.G., Art. Regel IV, on the other hand, the thetic and ontologic constitutivity is summarized in the concept of a-deontic constitutivity. The latter corresponds approximately to our distinction between deontic and thetic, specifically a-deontic We implemented this modification because, for our purposes, it does not matter what Conte calls the distinction between thetic and ontologic and therefore the distinctions should not be more complicated than they need to be. On the other hand, the term ontologic constitutivity

Deontic-constitutive rules include frequently deontic expression ('ought', 'has to', 'must', 'permitted', etc.) and deontic logic can partly help in their analysis.[87] The distinguishing feature of deontic constitutive rules is that they can be broken: the course of particular events does not have to follow the rule. They refer to actions and behaviors in the social realm. An example of a deontic rule in chess would be: 'Do not touch a piece until you are to play it.'

A-deontic constitutive rules (*or thetic constitutive rules*) cannot be broken. They refer to all kinds of events, personal and apersonal ones. An example of chess would be: 'If you cannot avoid check in the next move, you're in checkmate.' (Of course, you can move the pieces endlessly on the board after being in checkmate, but no one would say that you are still playing chess).

Both, deontic-constitutive rules and adeontic constitutive rules can be subdivided into *necessary, sufficient or necessary and sufficient rules*. In the case of the necessary rule, without obeying the rule the further development of the wayformational line will not be rule conforming, but one also has to know other rules, too, in order to recognize that this is the case. In sufficient rules, following the rule will lead to the rule-conforming result, but this effect will also appear through other rules or contingently. In the case of necessary and sufficient rules, only by following the rule will the future development of the wayformational line match the description given by the rule.

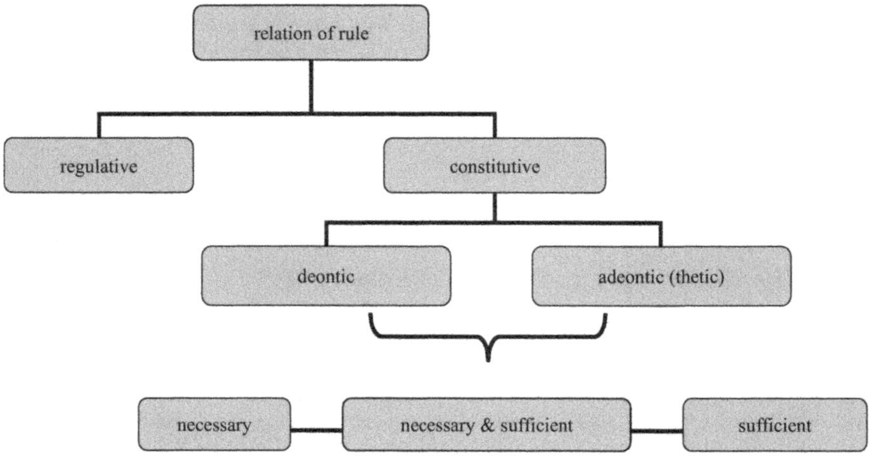

Fig. 2

cannot be used as defined by Conte within the scope of a Christian understanding of reality, because in the end all rules, which are used within the scope of a theory of God and soteriology as well as their conditions, prove themselves to be ontologic.

87 Cf. WRIGHT, G.H.v., Logik, deontische.

Some formal definitions: a set of rules can be called a regularity or an order. Rules can belong to the set of what is ruled A; in this case, we can speak of recursive rules, which are always a dynamic order since the rules are the subject of constant (but ruled) change.[88]

17.5 Causality as Necessary, Adeontic-constitutive Rule

With the help of the theory of the ruled development of the course of wayformational lines, we can define what causal trust or causal faith means: *Causal trust is given if the secondary narrations, which are a means of perceiving, describe the ruling of the future course of the wayformational line with the help of a narrative that is a necessary, adeontic constitutive rule.* And we can also define causality:

Causality is given if two episodes of the same wayformational line are conjoined in such a way that the emerging episode of the line can be described by a secondary-narrative that includes trust in the pure form of a sufficient adeontic constitutive rule – and if the actual course of the primary-narrative wayformational line in fact resonates with this description.

The explanation 'the pure form' of a rule means that one does not have to specify the concrete content of the rule. Whether we speak of the collision of bowls, energy-exchange, human voluntary influence or something else, is irrelevant. Causality abstracts from the concrete rule and therefore, from the concrete 'mechanism', if there is one at all. Our narrative concept of causality is much broader than the concept of the modern, narrow concept of causality as mere efficient causality. Also, formative and even teleological causality may be thought of in such terms, though it may not be necessary to do so. Causality remains a philosophical concept, not an empirical one. The explanation '*and if the actual course of the primary-narrative wayformational line in fact resonates with this description*' makes clear that causality itself is not a rule or law for the development of primary narrativity, but a category of active interpretation – even in cases where by means of secondary narrativity, causality seems to be allegedly perceived.

If we conceive of causality in this manner, combining it with our conception of narrative wayformational lines in the model of wayfaring in the mesh is

88 This character of the rule appears very clearly in a game called 'Nomic', which was developed by Peter Suber, that consists of changing rules in accordance with specific rules, which can be changed on their part as well. For the laws of the game cf. Suber, P., Paradox of Self-Amendment, Appendix 3. Cf. also Hofstadter, D., Nomic.

not a problem. No contradiction appears if this development does not follow causality exclusively, or if the causal nexus remains un-closed. If it were, there would only be the non-dynamic, only apparent development in the sense of transport in the network. In this case, the adeontic constitutive, *sufficient and necessary* content of the rule of causality would be the only kind of intentionality that exists and determines everything.

By referring causality to the course of wayformational lines, we avoid a decision regarding the problem, whether causality is a purely external relation, as in Russell, or an internal relation as in Leibniz (ch. 7). Since causality is a meta-rule, which does not describe the concrete developments of primary wayformational lines, in respect to these questions, it is indifferent.

CHAPTER 18

Narration and Contingency

18.1 The Transformation of Modalities

In ch. 16 we saw that dramatic coherence is only possible if there is real, irreducible contingency. In ch. 17 we learned that Hume needed the concept of necessity in order to define causality. It is now time to analyze what these concepts mean. Our main focus is contingency among the other modalities. Modalities like 'necessary', 'possible', 'impossible', 'by chance', 'arbitrarily', etc. appear in our natural languages, whereas contingency is more of a technical term that appears in academic language. Modalities have been a subject to analysis from Aristotle onward, through their logical explanation during the medieval period and classics of modernity like Leibniz, up to today. Formal logic made modalities its subject matter for the first time in the 20th century, with surprising results. Whereas the transformation of the modalities seem to be clear – this is an area where the formal perspective and the perspective of every day languages are similar – there is no uncontroversial calculus of modal logic, and the important question of semantic interpretations is more or less open. Let us start with the transformation of the modalities into one another. Modal-logic is conceived here as an extension of propositional logic. We will make use of the following rules of transformation:

(1) $Pp \leftrightarrow \neg N \neg p$ 'It is possible that p' is equivalent with 'it is not necessary that non-p'

(2) $\neg Pp \leftrightarrow N \neg p$ 'It is not possible that p' is equivalent with 'it is necessary that non-p'. For non-possibility, one can introduce a specific modal-operator I, for impossibility.

(3) $P \neg p \leftrightarrow \neg Np$ 'It is possible that non-p' is equivalent with 'it is not necessary that p'. For the possibility that something is not the case one can introduce a specific modal operator, R, for 'randomly'. As with the case of I, this is not necessary. Besides P and N, other modal operators are optional. In contrast to I, R creates more problems, because in English 'randomly' not only means $P \neg p$, but also Pp. This is a difference between formalized language and our everyday use.

(4) $\neg P \neg p \leftrightarrow Np$ 'It is not possible that non-p' is equivalent with 'it is necessary that p'.

 | DOI:10.30965/9783846765852_019

It is also not necessary to introduce a specific operator for contingency, C. But since in this chapter we mainly deal with contingency, the following will be helpful:

(5) $Cp \leftrightarrow Pp \wedge P\neg p$ 'It is contingent that p' is equivalent with 'It is possible that p, and it is possible that non-p'. This also means that contingency is the negation of the necessity operator N, independently of whether the value of the proposition variable is positive or negative (p or $\neg$p). Instead of using the possibility-operator P as a basis for the transformations, one could also use the contingency operator C (and of course also the necessity operator N, the impossibility operator I or the random operator R).

Although these transformations, especially in the case of necessity and impossibility, are very similar to modern languages like English or German, they are not identical. Since randomness in these languages is usually not restricted to $P\neg p$, but refers also to Pp, randomness in our everyday-languages frequently means what is expressed with the contingency operator C. Furthermore, the colloquial expression 'it is possible that …' is frequently used in a manner that also implies the possibility of the counter-factual ($P\neg p$), which means that in a lot of cases we use 'possibility' in the sense of 'contingency', too. The formal analyses and the colloquial use only partly overlap. This means that we have to ask what exactly is meant by them, especially when we encounter the colloquial expressions of possibility and randomness.

It seems possible to use modal logic in order to analyze the modality expressions of our everyday language. However, this was not what modal logic was originally designed for. The original intention was to use it to eliminate specific counterintuitive consequences of propositional logic, which we will deal with later.

18.2 Different Modal Calculi and the Reduction of Operator Iterations

Consensus ends with the transformations mentioned in the previous subsection. Since the beginning of formal modal logic onward, there were a whole series of different axiomatic systems, which were different in strength and had unclear semantic values. For most of the systems, two axioms are valid, ones that we also know from ordinary language:

(6) $Np \rightarrow p$ 'It is necessary that p', implies 'p'.

(7) $p \rightarrow Pp$ 'p' implies 'it is possible that p'.

Most calculi of modal logic need more axioms, rules and theorems. Today we have many systems of modal logic (S_1, S_2, S_3, S_4, S_5, T, K, B, D etc.).[1]

For example, in system K (6) and (7) are invalid, whereas System T is system K extended by (6) as an axiom, with the effect that (7) can be inferred as a theorem.[2]

The systems are also different in respect to the rules for the reduction of modal operator iterations. Since an expression like Pp is itself a proposition that can be abbreviated as q, we can, for example, combine it anew with a modality like Nq that is equivalent with NPp. We can easily imagine proposition of a form like NCNPNp. Different systems can also be distinguished by different rules for avoiding or reducing such iterated modal operators.

In the above-mentioned system T, an expression like NNp can be reduced by (6) to Np, because NNp→Np is simply an inference by substitution of (6). The reverse, however, is not the case. Therefore, in T it is possible for infinite iterations of the modal operators to appear.

(8) Np→NNp

(8) is invalid in T. (8) means that something that is necessary is not contingently necessary, but necessarily necessary. If one wants to accept (8), one gets system S_4.[3] Otherwise, we could design other axioms for erasing iterated modal operators.

(9) Pp→NPp

If one adds (9) to T instead of (8), one gets a system called S_5. (8) is then still valid, yet not as an axiom, but as an inferred theorem.[4] (9) means that all modal operators are necessary, with the consequence that in S_5 there are no iterated modal operators anymore. Any iterations of the modal operators in S_5 can be simply reduced to this last one.

So far, it is clear how different modal systems can be distinguished regarding their syntax. However, as long as the question of the semantics of the modal operators is unclear, the question of which system should be used for which purposes cannot be answered.

1 A short survey of the history of these systems can be found in Evers, D., Gott und mögliche Welten, 124–132. A detailed portrayal of the different systems is given by Hughes, G.E./Cresswell, M.J., New Introduction to Modal Logic.

2 Cf. Hughes, G.E./Cresswell, M.J., New Introduction to Modal Logic, 34.

3 Cf. Hughes, G.E./Cresswell, M.J., New Introduction to Modal Logic, 44.

4 Cf. Hughes, G.E./Cresswell, M.J., New Introduction to Modal Logic, 48.

18.3 The Question of the Semantics of Modal Operators

In the last section, we designated modal logic as an extension of propositional logic. However, propositional logic can be described by the logic of predicates. A proposition p can be understood as propositional function Fx, in which the predicate variable F is bound by qualifiers, like ∃x.Fx or ∀x.Fx. Then we have the problem of whether the logic of predicates can also be extended by modal operators.[5] In this case, the question of semantics becomes unavoidable.

We need not mention the history of the question of the semantics of modal logic. Instead we will try to present different types of solutions. In some cases, the solutions are older than the history of formalized modal logic.

1. Necessary and contingent attributes of all things (*Aristotelian essentialism*)
In the medieval period, a typical distinction was made between substantial and accidental attributes. Therefore, Quine calls this type 'Aristotelian essentialism'.[6] Classically, an accident is that which inheres in something else; whereas substance is something that does not inhere in something else (and is therefore itself something in which accidents can inhere or be free from accidents entirely all). There is an interpretation of the substance/accident distinction with the help of the distinction between necessary and contingent. In regard to persons, then, any spatiotemporal predicates – their physical appearance, their pitch of voice, what they do and they suffer – are not necessary, because all these are subject to change. We would then have to assume a substantial attribute that makes this person exactly this person, like 'Platonity' in the case of Plato.[7] If we generalize this method, we can invent the metaconcept of a necessary haecceity, which is a necessary, non-contingent predicate. But not only in the case of individuals can we ask about necessary and contingent predicates. It is also a worthwhile question in the case of a general state of affairs. The number 7 then, has the necessary attribute 'to be greater than 6', but the contingent attributes to be 'the number of days of a week' or to be 'the number of small men in the tale of Snow White'.

As important as the question of what makes the distinction between necessary and contingent attributes may be, this kind of solution is difficult in modernity. Such is the case, given that haecceity is designed in such a way, so

5 For modal logic of predicates cf. HUGHES, G.E./CRESSWELL, M.J., New Introduction to Modal Logic, 203–313.

6 Cf. QUINE, W.V.O., Three Grades, esp. 173f. Cf. as well MATTHEWS, G.B., Aristotelian Essentialism.

7 Cf. SCHLAPKOHL, C., Persona est naturae rationabilis individua substantia, 42f.

as to refer *per definitionem* to something that cannot be empirically observed. Therefore, there are not many contemporary philosophers, like Swinburne,[8] who regard haecceities as a meaningful solution to the problem.

If one regards objects as emerging condensations in the mesh of wayformational lines, the question seems to be superfluous. However, this is not the case, because one can ask which wayformational lines or which events in which manner are necessary and which are contingent. In the case of narratology, the question reappears in the shape of asking which elements of a story are necessary and which are not; or, in other words, which elements belong to the narrative of a narration and which are contingent. Narratologies that are only looking at narratives and so presuppose that there are no narrations without necessary narratives, are essentialist narratologies. Furthermore, they are deficient in being essentialist, because they cannot provide an analogy to *haecceitas* as the principle of individuation. One can also design non-deficient essentialist narratologies, which is the case when a story shares parts of the structure of a narrative without being reducible to it. The necessary and contingent sequences are then distributed in the following manner: parts of the narrative, or the narrative as a whole may be contingent to the story, whereas the parts of the story that cannot be captured by a narrative are necessary for that story. It is remarkable that we still need to deal with narratology here, not with what we have called narrantology (ch. 6). It is remarkable, because this shows that the usual narratologies in the literary disciplines have a hidden, ontological dimension. In the case of deficient narratologies, there is only one modality, in the case of non-deficient narratologies, there are two modalities. Whatever is contingent in a story (in the sense that it cannot be reduced to a narrative) is what is necessary for this story. It would be something contingent that is itself necessary (NCp), without any possibility of reducing the iterated modal operators, since the modalities signify different state of affairs.

Goethe's 'Faust' is basically a combination of necessary narratives, like the frame-story of Job and the narrative of the medieval legend of Faust. These narratives are necessary for Goethe's play, because it could not exist without these narratives. However, if one asks what is particularly genuine in Goethe's 'Faust', one asks for another kind of necessity that has to be found beyond these traditional narratives, or in other words, what is contingent in regard to these traditional narratives.

This distinction is much clearer if we have a look at the narrantic level by asking what in the life story of a particular human person is necessary and what is contingent. Without any question, our own life story, like that of other humans, is a combination of templates or narratives. But of course, it would be degrading to claim that the life story of a person is only a combination of narratives – which is the danger of, for example, in

8 Cf. SWINBURNE, R., Thisness.

Erving Goffman's sociology.[9] If one wants to view the life-stories of human persons in non-reductive ways, one has to ask what is contingent in respect to the combination of narratives, and this is then what is necessary for the particularity of this life.

In respect to the narratological and narrantic mode of the essentialist question, one needs modalities on two levels. If one wants to use the formal expressions of modal logic for this, one has to speak of NCp or of CNp – depending on which level of modality is signified by the first or the second modal operator. Ordinary English seems to shift between the two possibilities: If we want to speak of something contingent that is itself necessary, this seems to be expressible by NCp. But we can also say that 'it is contingent that it is necessary, that I experience this or that'. Then the other form, CNp would be appropriate. Both alternatives, however, are not equivalent, since both of the modal operators used have another aspect and therefore another semantic. If one tries to formalize the question of what is necessary and what is contingent in stories in a non-reductive way, one irreducibly needs two modal operators. And this excludes a lot of systems like S_5. However, our intention is not to transfer stories into a formal calculus. The operators of modal logic are only used here to illustrate the problem.

This last question – which of the contingent elements that cannot be reduced to a narrative are really necessary for stories – can only be answered within the framework of eschatology.

2. *Quinean actualism or pragmatism*

Philosophers like Quine reject any kind of Aristotelian essentialism. Apart from that, Quine doubts whether the invention of modal logic is important, since it uses intensional expressions. He therefore votes for an actualist interpretation of modalities.

Quine's doubts regarding a modalized predicate logic are fueled by the following observation. In expressions like Fa, the argument-constant 'a' can be substituted by any other expression 'b', presupposing a and b have the same reference. In the example mentioned above, we learned that the number 7 has the attribute of being an instantiation of 7 dwarfs in the tale of Snow White. Now, Quine regards numbers as nothing but abstractions from equinumerous sets.[10] Imagine F means 'uneven', a means '7', and b means 'the number of Snow White's dwarfs'. The statements Fa and Fb are equivalent: '7 is uneven' and 'the number of Snow White's dwarfs are uneven' are equivalent, and both statements are meaningful. Therefore, both statements are instantiations of the same proposition p. Normally, we would say that this proposition p is necessary,

9 Cf. GOFFMAN, E., Presentation of Self, 253, and for review MACINTYRE, A., After Virtue, 32.

10 Cf. QUINE, W.V.O., On Universals.

Np, if we see this proposition defined by Fa: 'It is necessary that 7 is uneven'. But then we should also be able to substitute a by b, and we get: 'It is necessary that the number of Snow White's dwarfs is uneven'. Obviously, this is nonsense.[11] For this reason, Quine thinks that the modalized predicate logic is nonsense. For a modalized propositional logic, this means that while it is possible to use one, it is with a restricted reference to reality. Quine regards many world semantics only as illustrative, without any explanatory power.[12] The capacity to distinguish between necessary and contingent predicates, which one gets in Aristotelian essentialism, is, in Quine's view, nonsense.

The heart of the actualist interpretation of modalities is that an expression like Np means that all who are participating on the discourse agree that p is true, whereas the statement Cp means not all participating agree that p is true. But on the level of truth and falsity we need no modalities at all. True and false are questions of being real or unreal. Modalities are in this view only expressions for our manner of communicating such statements. One can call this a pragmatist reinterpretation of modalities, because the sign-users determine the modalities. One can also call this an actualist interpretation of modalities, because in fact there is only one modality: actuality. However, Quine's opinion is only meaningful within the framework of his pragmatist, holistic naturalism. His framework becomes clear when we ask: what are the consequences of this opinion for modalities in the framework of narratologies and narrantologies?

If we transfer these results to the level of stories, necessity and contingency are not meaningful criteria to speak about stories. Stories then, cannot be contingent or necessary, but we would only regard stories as contingent or necessary. Stories (or sequences or narratives of stories) where all can agree that they are true are then quasi-necessary stories (or sequences or narratives of stories), whereas stories that are not regarded as true by all would be quasi-contingent stories. Perhaps some might regard this as plausible. A story would be necessary only if all form a consensus about the truth of a story. But it is not very probable that this will happen. Therefore, we can assume that there are no necessary stories at all (or that there are only contingent stories). If one regards this as plausible, one nevertheless also has to see that the Quinean interpretation of modalities applied to stories has counterintuitive, if not incoherent, consequences: any story p would be classed based on the alternative of being true or false. All literary fictional stories, all our assumptions about our life-stories (or our assumptions about the life-stories of others), which are not regarded as true by all, would then be false, whereas the only stories that could

11 Cf. QUINE, W.v., Logical Point of View, 139–159; QUINE, W.V.O., Intensions Revisited, and in addition EVERS, D., Gott und mögliche Welten, 152–172.

12 Cf. QUINE, W.V.O., Intensions Revisited.

be true are those where all agree that they are true. Then, at last, there would– to Quine's satisfaction – be only the 'stories' of mathematized physics, which could really be seen as true, though only under the circumstances of highly idealized images of pragmatic agreement. Let's apply this reasoning to primary narrativity. Primary narrativity relies on developing wayformational lines that can only be perceived from the dynamical perspectives of the wayformational lines themselves. But in concrete situations of communication, the communicating ones also remain bound to different, particular wayformational lines. Therefore, a case in which *all* participating can agree to name a story as 'true' is impossible because their wayformational lines differ. Consequently, there are only contingent stories. This solution might also be to Quine's satisfaction, which is not exactly the point. The point is, rather, that something that *cannot ever happen* is identical with something that is not possible, which is (¬Pp). And this is equivalent with the necessary falsity (N¬p). Therefore, it is necessary that all stories are contingent, but this is either a self-contradiction, or one must reintroduce the distinction between necessity and contingency on another level, which forces us to explicate the meaning of the modalities anew.

Quine's actualist or pragmatist interpretation of modalities is not appropriate for stories, be it narratological ones or narrantological ones.

Neither the essentialist nor the actualist interpretation is the *opinio communis* for interpreting modalities. In a strict sense, there is no *opinio communis* at all. Nevertheless, most interpretations use a variation of the motive of possible worlds for interpreting modalities. Such an interpretation is not new, of course. Leibniz already developed the classic version of this line of interpretation. In formal modal logic, however, possible world semantics were introduced with the invention of calculus. Saul Kripke was one important innovator here. In the following sections, we will provide a version of interpreting modalities with the help of the semantics of possible worlds.

3. Leibniz's necessity of possible worlds[13]

What is necessary is that which is true in all possible worlds. What is contingent is that which is true in at least one possible world. A possible world is a nexus of entities (things, objects, individuals, monads) that is compossible, i.e. no contradiction appears in its whole framework of relations. A possible world is a relational nexus between things that are *together possible.* The basis for the language of possible worlds is the principle of non-contradiction. According to Leibniz, the bases of mathematics and logic (like the identity of

13 As support for the following section on Leibniz cf. the concise portrayal in EVERS, D., Gott und mögliche Welten, 5–119.

indiscernibles) belong to the realm of necessity, which is true in all possible worlds. Furthermore, the existence of a condition of the possibility of possible worlds is also necessary. The condition is God. The necessity of God, however, means something different than the other necessities. Whereas these are necessities *in* any possible world, this is not the case in the divine *absolute necessity* (see ch. 21). The absolute necessity of God means that in God the sum of all possible worlds is present, but not actualized, that all other necessities are actually in God, and that God is the condition of the possibility of the actualization of possible worlds. The infinite, non-actualized, possible worlds can be ordered by the following criteria:

a) the maximum plenitude of entities (or creatures)
b) the maximum simplicity of compossibility
c) the maximum beatitude of creatures.

Leibniz is convinced that these criteria order the possible worlds in such a way that there is only one world that meets all the criteria. He uses the image of the top of a pyramid with an infinite base. There are more non-maximal possible worlds the closer they are to the base, and endlessly on the basis. But these non-maximal possible worlds are in the end irrelevant.[14] The actual world is the maximal world, and creation means nothing but the actualization of this maximal world. To name God creator means therefore only that God is that which calculated the maximal order (other aspects of Leibniz' concept of God being equal).

On the grounds of the basic assumption of possible worlds, Leibniz develops different concepts of possibility and necessity:

- *Logical necessity/contingency*: what is true is contingent in at least one possible world; what is necessary is true in all possible worlds.
- *Transcendental necessity*: This is the condition of the possibility of necessity and contingency, i.e. God. Transcendental contingency is seen as impossible (as a self-contradiction).
- *Actual necessity/contingency*: The one actualized necessary world is only one among many possible worlds. Therefore, it is a contingent world. However, it is 'actually' necessary, insofar as it is the maximum of goodness, simplicity, and plenitude. Therefore, it was not possible for God to create a different world than the actual one. And therefore, it is actually necessary. Nevertheless, it remains contingent insofar as it was not necessary for God to actualize a world at all. The distinction between actuality and non-actuality can therefore be reduced to freedom as a divine attribute. *Vice*

14 Cf. LEIBNIZ, G.W., Philosophische Schriften, Bd. 2,2, 267 (Theodizee §416).

versa, this divine freedom is logically restricted to actualize or not to actualize this maximal world.

If one interprets modal operators with the help of Leibniz's philosophy, to a large degree, non-iterated operators would suffice, but only on one level: the realm of logical necessity and contingency. But in the end, one would need more with respect to the meanings of these modalities.

Since the modern semantics of possible worlds are variations of Leibniz's, we will provide some more examples before asking about their narrative meaning.

4. Descartes' contingency of possible worlds

Whereas one can also use Leibniz's distinction between logical necessity and contingency in Descartes' case, in Descartes we cannot speak of actual necessity and contingency, and transcendental necessity means something completely different. Like Leibniz, Descartes also conceives of transcendental necessity as a condition of the possibility of all mundane modalities. Like Leibniz, Descartes also uses the *ratio Anselmi*. However, in contrast to Leibniz, logical necessities are not equiprimordial with the divine essence. Leibniz is therefore a successor to the intellectualist tradition of medieval, western philosophy, whereas Descartes can be understood as a successor of the voluntarist tradition under the conditions of modernity: the distinction between logical necessity and contingency is caused by divine omnipotence, which offers no reason for this underivable choice. The result is not only different conceptions of the will, but also of God and the world. In Descartes, logical necessity, in its transcendental meaning for the world, is itself a contingent necessity, whereas in Leibniz it appears as a necessary necessity. This type of necessity fits with a different understanding of the world: the alternative to the actualization of the world is not only non-actuality, as in Leibniz, but also the non-actualization of one of the many possible worlds. Moreover, the alternative would have been the actualization of another world which is under the present conditions contradictory; i.e. the actualization of a non-possible world, which would have been possible if the divine will had chosen another distinction than the actual one between logical necessity and contingency. Creation in Descartes does not mean only the actualization of a maximal world or the selection of an actual world out of many possible ones, but the establishment of the distinction between logical necessity and contingency. This distinction is not, like in Leibniz, itself necessary, but contingent. Whereas in Leibniz logical necessity is itself necessary (NNp), and also logical contingency is necessary (NCp), in Descartes logical necessity is contingent (CNp) and logical contingency is contingent (CCp).

5. David Lewis' modal realism

Lewis regards a semantic of possible worlds as useful for the interpretation of modalities. However, he questions the distinction between possibility and actuality by levelling this distinction: All possible worlds, i.e. *compossible* sums of individual entities *are actualized*, exist factually,[15] in their own space-time, whereas there is no spatiotemporal – and therefore also no causal – connection among them.[16] All existing possible worlds are *not* situated in a 'hyperspace' or in the 'mind of God', or in any way related on another level, but they are simply in logical space. Our typical language says that this or that is the case; our use of actuality is an indexical kind of speech the signifies the position of the speaker, like 'here', 'now', 'I'. It locates the speaker, but not spatially, not temporally, not as subject, but in respect to the possible world that is the frame of her speaking.[17] In regard to the logic of predicates, one could say that the classical existential quantifier has a double meaning. On the one hand, it can be used in order to refer to worlds, but then it is no longer able to signify the indexicality of the speaker or their actuality. On the other hand, it can be used in order to express indexicality, but then it cannot express reality. The easiest way to solve the problem would be simply to introduce two kinds of existence-operators.[18]

Two worlds can be equal apart from very small differences. There are two possible worlds, in which two individual persons can be perfect copies,[19] distinguished only by a small, unimportant, or negligible sequence of their story.

Therefore, Leibniz and Lewis have different understandings of what 'individual' means. In Leibniz, all individuals are internally related, so that they are as monads only different perspectives on the whole of one world. If one monad would be different, all other monads would be different, and consequently, two possible worlds would be completely different, also in those cases where only one monad is different (because then also all other monads would be different). In Lewis, however, individuals are only

15 Cf. Lewis, D., Plurality of Worlds, 2.

16 Cf. Lewis, D., Plurality of Worlds, 80f.

17 Cf. Lewis, D., Plurality of Worlds, 92f and earlier in Lewis, D., Anselm and Actuality, esp. 184f: 'I suggest that 'actual' and its cognates should be analyzed as indexical terms: terms whose reference varies, depending on relevant features of the context of utterance. The relevant feature of context, for the term 'actual' is the world at which a given utterance occurs. According to the indexical analysis I propose, 'actual' (in its primary sense) refers at any world w to the world w. 'Actual' is analogous also to 'here', 'I', 'you', 'this', and 'aforementioned' – indexical terms depending for their reference respectively on the place, speaker, the intended audience, the speaker's act of pointing, and the aforementioned discourse.'

18 Cf. Evers, D., Gott und mögliche Welten, 180.

19 Cf. Lewis, D., Plurality of Worlds, 70.

externally related by space-time and composed of parts of worlds. Their only relationship is that they belong to a shared spatiotemporal world; they are *worldmates*.[20] For Lewis, individuals are variable. Further, a possible world is an individual but of maximal greatness that consists of other individuals as parts, which themselves consist of other individuals as parts, etc.

The advantage of modal realism is that to speak of possible worlds becomes intelligible insofar as it refers to a subject-independent reality.[21] Kant's claim that existence is not a predicate, is really meaningful here. Thinking of 1,000 dollars in no way distinguishes it from 1,000 actual dollars, as in both cases they share all of the same attributes. Of course, it is not possible to pay with 1,000 imaginary dollars in our world – but there is one in which it is possible.

However, there is a problem that is difficult to solve within the framework of modal realism. In everyday language, we refer to contingent and to non-actualized possibilities for the sake of actuality and for the sake of orienting ourselves to reality. When I ask myself, 'What would have been if I had not written this book?', or during writing, 'what would happen if I stop writing?', I imagine alternative courses of events, in which we are interwoven, in order to decide how to act in this world. And this is only possible if I assume a kind of identity within the different possibilities. In our imagined, alternative cases, I imagine myself as myself in all cases, not someone else. But that would be the consequence of modal realism: there is indeed someone else, called Markus, who stopped writing this book. What is a means for cultivating our identity is in Lewis a means of maximal self-detachment. Lewis tries to solve this problem by introducing a *counterpart relation*. But that is not an answer to the problem.

This counterpart relation means that for each individual in our world, there is another one in another world, with a maximum of similarity, but not with identity. Maximal resemblance in our own world is identity, with the consequence that in our world, any individual is its own counterpart. But then any individual x in any world has a counterpart y in another world.[22] The counterpart theory can be useful, because with its help we can illustrate some state of affairs of our actual world (like Putnam's insight that meanings are not a matter of mind, cf. ch. 14). Nevertheless, it does not solve the problem of identity between our and possible worlds. It actually causes new problems. According to Lewis, there must be worlds in which my counterpart is of minimal similarity, despite the fact that there might be millions of people in our own world that have a greater similarity to me, without being my counterpart.

20 Cf. Lewis, D., Plurality of Worlds, 69. 71.

21 Cf. Lewis, D., Plurality of Worlds, 3: 'The worlds are not of our own making […]. We make language and concepts and descriptions and imaginary representations that apply to worlds […]. But none of these things we make are the worlds themselves.'

22 Cf. Lewis, D., Counterpart Theory.

Modal realism interprets the modal operators as quantifiers about real, existing possible worlds. The possibility-operator M is then equivalent with the quantifier of existence (∃) and the necessity operator with the quantifier of universality (∀). One of the consequences is that mathematical states of affairs and logical axioms cannot be necessary. They do not refer to a set of individuals, but they are abstractions of individual sets. They do not really belong to any of the many possible worlds, and therefore they are valid in all. Whereas these expressions have the status of ontological necessity in Leibniz, in Lewis they have no ontological status at all.

Another consequence is the ontological meaning of any contingent statement. It would suffice for contingency to say that an expression is contingent, if there is only one world, in which it is invalid, but to which there is not really an alternative. The existence of our (and of any other) world, however, is not contingent anymore in the sense that it had been possible for it not to exist.

6. Kripke's counterfactual possible worlds

Saul Kripke, who is one of the founders of the interpretation of the modal operators through possible worlds,[23] holds a completely different position than Lewis. The theory of the rigid reference of names (and the rigid reference of essential attributes, ch. 14) is basic for the semantic interpretation of modalities.[24] Reference is rigid, insofar as it fixed in a 'baptismal' situation and sustained by a communicative tradition. What is important for identity is not the attributes of a thing, but only that we can refer to it indexically in our actual world. Around this rigid reference, a counterfactual description is designed or imagined – a possible world. For Kripke, possible worlds do not exist at all. We cannot discover them or make inquiries about them, but only design and construct them[25] on the basis of the rigid reference found in the actual world.[26] Kripke's model changes the concept of a possible world: it does not refer, as in Leibniz, to a maximal whole of compossibilities, but only to an *ad hoc*, designed, counterfactual *situation*. To extend this counterfactual situation to a 'world' is only motivated by set-theoretical reasons, not by ontological ones.[27]

In regard to the question of modal semantics, this means the following: Kripke wants to distinguish two kinds of modalities, ontic and epistemic ones. He uses the terms necessity and possibility for the ontic, and apriority and

23 Cf. EVERS, D., Gott und mögliche Welten, 123.
24 Cf. the detailed portrayal in EVERS, D., Gott und mögliche Welten, 189–215.
25 Cf. KRIPKE, S.A., Naming and Necessity, 15f.
26 Cf. KRIPKE, S.A., Naming and Necessity, 53.
27 Cf. KRIPKE, S.A., Naming and Necessity, 19.

aposteriority for the epistemic modalities. Ontic modalities have to do with the question of whether something could have been different than it actually is. If we can give an affirmative to this question, we speak of contingency, if we cannot give an affirmative, we speak of necessity.[28] Epistemic modalities ask whether something is given independently of experience (apriority) or not (aposteriority). According to Kripke, this enables an unusual combination of the terms of this distinction: necessary truths, gained *a posteriori*, and contingent truths, gained *a priori.*

Contingent truths *a priori* rely on rigid reference. The definition of one meter as the length of a bar at a specific time in Paris cannot be understood *a posteriori*, since nothing in this situation is discovered empirically. Therefore, it is, according to Kripke, to be understood *a priori*. Nevertheless, this definition is contingent. An example of a necessary truth *a posteriori* is Goldbach's conjecture, i.e. the thesis that any natural number greater than 2 is the sum of two primes (resp. that any number greater than 4 is the sum of two odd primes). We do not have a mathematical proof for this thesis, but we also do not know of any exceptions. If it is true, it is necessarily true, but since there is no mathematical proof, it is not *a priori*, but *a posteriori*.

But, independent of the epistemic question, modalities are also seen in different ways. By comparison with David Lewis, factual truths are indeed contingent, insofar as they are not realized in any other possible world. It is in order to state this exactly that Kripke speaks of possible worlds, not in order to diminish the contingency of facts, which is what Lewis intends. In contrast to Lewis, the actual world has a particular status, since to speak of modalities or to speak of possible worlds is strictly dependent on our reality. If I play dice with two die and ask myself which probabilities are given, I can assume 36 possible worlds in which these two die are contained. Apart from these two die, these possible worlds contain nothing else: not the color of the cubes, not the circumstances of the concrete situation, in which I play dice, etc. Therefore, the question of maximal compossibility is, in contrast to Leibniz, irrelevant. What is possible is situationally defined by that which is given in our actual world. The concepts of contingency and necessity are affected, if a possible world is a counterfactual extension of an actual situation, but not the maximal compossibility of all entities, as in Leibniz or in a different sense in Lewis. To demand maximal compossibility of a world is nothing else but demanding universal logical coherence for the whole of space-time. A consequence for both Leibniz and Lewis is that time loses its dynamism: time is the B-series that is given in eternity. Here, nothing new can happen in any possible world. But if there is no

28 Cf. Kripke, S.A., Naming and Necessity, 35f.

real novelty, there is also no real contingency for Leibniz and Lewis. In Kripke it is different, because apart from the counterfactual extension of a particular situation, nothing is claimed, neither that there is a transcendent entity who knows the compossibility of the particular possible worlds, as in Leibniz, nor that any particular possible world exists as a continuum in its own space-time, as in Lewis.

7. Plantiga's modal-metaphysics of S_5[29]

It seems that Lewis' and Kripke's approaches are opposites. However, there is a possibility to combine elements of both in a third interpretation, like that of Alvin Plantinga. He assumes, like Leibniz and Lewis, that possible worlds have to be compossible. In contrast to Lewis, however, he assumes a complete accessibility of the possible worlds. It cannot be that there is a possible world in which something is actualized that cannot be thought of in the factual world. Anything that is actualized in any possible world *x*, is also a possibility for any other possible world *y* – and *vice versa*. The consequence is not only that all possible worlds are compossible with themselves, but also that all worlds contain each other. Plantinga, then, has to distinguish between existence and actuality. Existence refers to possibilities. Everything that is non-contradictory – i.e. anything that can be thought of as actualized in at least one possible world – exists. But not all that exists, is actualized. Another way to express the same thing is to say that all possible worlds have the same existing sets of entities, only the ratio between the possible and the actual differs. Furthermore, Plantinga assumes that all of these possible worlds could have been realized, whereas *only one* actual world is realized. Here, we might ask whether there are indeed three (and not two) concepts of existence in Plantinga, but that is not very important. In contrast to Lewis and in similarity to Kripke, there is always an identity between the different possible words. However, this identity is not based on a rigid reference, but in an essentialist way on *haecceity*, which is necessary in order to avoid the problem that possible worlds are not only different in respect to the attributes of entities, but also in respect to the existence of entities. If identity is essentially (as a necessary and sufficient condition) given by haecceity, than Socrates-ness exists in any possible world, whereas only in one there is a person called Socrates.

Which worlds of the multitude of possible worlds is realized – or, in other words, which ratio of the possibility-actuality distinction is realized – depends on a cooperation between God as the only absolutely necessary being (who is

29 Cf. PLANTINGA, A., Nature of Necessity, and also WIECKOWSKI, B., Gott in möglichen Welten; EVERS, D., Gott und mögliche Welten, 215–233.

the only entity that is realized *in* all possible worlds and not beyond all possible worlds as in Leibniz) and his mind-gifted creatures. Therefore, there is, in contrast to Leibniz, more than one realizable maximal world.

What Plantinga does is essentially nothing other than ontologize system S_5.

18.4 The Accessibility Relation of Possible Worlds

In discussing the calculus of different modal logics, we said that, whereas their different strengths are clear – dependent only on whether a system has more or less axioms – the semantics are unclear. Kripke introduced an accessibility relation[30] in order to interpret modalities with their help. A statement is necessary (Np), if it is valid in all possible worlds that are accessible from a particular world. A statement is possible (Pp), if there is at least one world that is accessible from a particular world.[31] Formally speaking, the accessibility relation is a dyadic relation between two worlds without being further specified.[32] However – and this is the point – this relation can have different relational attributes, depending on the particular calculus.

The relatively weak system K (without the inference from necessity to actuality Np→p, and without the inference from actuality to possibility p→Pp) is valid independently of any accessibility relation, i.e. in the case where a world is *not* accessible to itself.

If we maintain these two conclusions that are frequently used in the languages of our life world – Np→p and p→Pp – we need system T. Here we have a reflexive accessibility relation, i.e. it is valid in cases where every world is accessible to itself.

If one wants to add that any necessity has to be necessarily necessary, without being contingently necessary, we have to add the axiom Np→NNp, which is used in system S_4. The accessibility relation is not only reflexive here, but also transitive: if a particular world is accessible from another one, and if this other one is accessible to a third, then the first one is also accessible to the third one.

The decisive feature of system S_5 is that the additional axiom Pp→NPp is valid, i.e. the necessity of all first level modal operators, which allows for the reduction all iterated modalities to a single one. Here the necessity relation is reflexive, transitive, and symmetric: any particular world is accessible for any other world.

---

30 Cf. EVERS, D., Gott und mögliche Welten, 133f.

31 For the following cf. HUGHES, G.E./CRESSWELL, M.J., New Introduction to Modal Logic.

32 Cf. HUGHES, G.E./CRESSWELL, M.J., New Introduction to Modal Logic, 30.

To choose a system of modal logic is far from arbitrary, and also does not rely only on one's pragmatic interests, for it implies important ontological commitments about our world. Sometimes, the accessibility relation is modelled by a visibility relation that describes whether different worlds are visible or not visible.[33] This visibility means that the accessibility relation is semantically interpreted and not only formally conceived in its relational attributes. But note that a purely formal relation without any semantic meaning is unthinkable. Therefore, semantic associations like 'accessibility' or 'visibility' might be primary in comparison to the abstract description of a purely formal, dyadic relation. Of course, other interpretations are also possible: perceivability, interpretability, comprehensibility, etc. In his modal metaphysics, Plantinga provides an ontological interpretation of this dyadic accessibility relation. In doing so, he does not provide a concretely filled-out relation like 'visible' or 'accessible,' but manages to exclude the problem of subjectivity, i.e. the problem that accessibility or visibility has to be visibility for a self-reflexive subject. This move sheds some light on his claim that S_5 fits with reality: imagine any epistemic understanding of the accessibility relation, in any sense whatsoever! S_5 then means a complete epistemic perspicuity of all possible worlds for each other. I think nothing given by our phenomenal reality fits with this claim. But then a transitive epistemic perspicuity also seems to be problematic – and also a reflexive epistemic perspicuity of a single world for itself.

18.5 The Narrative Meaning of Possible World Semantics

What, then, is the meaning of possible worlds semantics within the framework of a narrative ontology? One might think that the differences between the different semantic interpretations would be important. However, this is not the case. The important consequences lie in the features that the different interpretations of possible worlds have in common.

1. If possible worlds are the sum of what is conceptually compossible, as in Leibniz', Lewis's, and Plantinga's case, then wayfaring in the mesh on the narrantic level must be reducible to transport in the net.

2. If any possible world is a set of logically coherent state of affairs, any dynamism only apparently exists, not actually.

3. Contingency is, in all these cases, restricted and not a free form necessity. In the case of Lewis, this is obvious, but it is also the case in Plantinga and Leibniz.

---

33 Cf. HUGHES, G.E./CRESSWELL, M.J., New Introduction to Modal Logic, 14f.

4. Since only what is conceptually coherent can be compossible, and since compossibility makes a world a possible world, dramatic coherence is excluded. Dramatic coherence would belong to the realm of the impossible, and all narrations that claim to tell something un-inferably new would also belong to the realm of the impossible. The same would be the case for narrations that claim to accept particular contradictions, or that claim contradictions can be sublated.

5. Wayfaring in the mesh can only be relatively meaningful, insofar as wayformational perspectives would only be temporarily meaningful, as long as there is a temporary epistemic deficit. In the end, it will always be possible to reduce wayformational perspectives to rigid standpoints.

6. Further, the claim that there is no standpoint beyond the world is only meaningful in a relativized epistemic manner, valid for epistemic knowledge gained empirically by the senses, but not valid for rationality. There are ontic descriptions that describe the nexus of all that is actual, possible, and necessary in its totality. These descriptions would vary depending on the accessibility relation and depending on the chosen system that fits this totality. But what is important is that any material description of the accessibility relation, not only the accessibility relation of S_5, presupposes a standpoint or view from nowhere. If one wants to judge if a series is ordered reflexively, transitively, or symmetrically, one must have knowledge about the whole series in its extension, i.e. one has to know either all of the events in the world that have ever happened or will happen, or one has to know a universal law that prescribes how historic events must emerge. But since the whole series cannot be known, one can only claim to know the law by which reality is constructed, either abductively or spontaneously. But then such a principle would be in need of inductive proofs and revisions, which would show that it is only contingently a principle.

7. All in all: The semantic interpretation of the modal operators by the semantics of possible worlds is altogether not compatible with the assumption of perception on wayformational lines. The semantics of possible worlds implies the impossibility of narrative ontologies and the supervenience of phenomenology, but it does not fit within the primacy of perception.

8. Therefore, we have to reject any interpretation of modality by possible world semantics– except that of Kripke's.

9. Kripke's approach would be possible within the framework of a narrative ontology, since here a possible world is nothing but an abstraction from actual situations. But in this sense, possible worlds are idealizations referring to nothing.

10. We cannot choose any of the semantics of possible worlds in order to shed light on the meaning of modalities, especially contingency. Fortunately, there are alternatives. A better approach than asking what philosophers have given which interpretations to modal operators is to start by inquiring into the actual use of modal concepts in natural, non-formalized languages.

18.6 Situation Semantics as an Interpretation of Modal Operators

Since the 1980's, Jon Barwise, John Perry, and others developed a situation semantics as an alternative to the semantics of possible words,[34] and as a critique of all theories that see meaning in the same extension that makes a proposition true, as it is in the whole tradition of Frege and Russell. Situation semantics also seems to be promising because it relies on two traditions that are crucial for the present work: Putnam's theory of the externality of meaning (ch. 14), and Gibson's theory of affordances in the framework of his ecological realism (ch. 5).[35] Nevertheless, situation semantics tries to formalize semantics, and we might ask whether formalization is altogether meaningful in our paradigm. Barwise and Perry then admit that '*situation semantics has been more successful in its broad themes than its specific formalisms and proposals*.'[36] Therefore, we will only offer an introduction to the basic features of situation semantics:

1. *Meaning is situational*: Situation semantics is based on a radical critique of Frege's understanding of meaning, in which universal coherence is important. According to Frege, only statements can have meaning, and the meaning of a statement is its truth value.[37] All true propositions have, consequently, the same meaning, the one great fact of truth. It might be possible that no one can ever show this in practice. But if it were possible, it could only be shown through logical equivalences. If I can show that two statements are equivalent, they must have the same truth value and therefore the same meaning.[38] This belief must pay the price of a radical abstraction from what really happens. An example might help illustrate this. The statement 'Joe is eating something' is logically equivalent with the statement 'Joe is eating something and Sarah

34 Cf. BARWISE, J./PERRY, J., Situations and Attitudes, Pos. 121: 'We do not believe that there are other possible worlds in the sense demanded of them by this theory, only other ways this world of ours might have been and might be.'

35 Cf. BARWISE, J./PERRY, J., Situations and Attitudes, Pos. 51. 1842.

36 BARWISE, J./PERRY, J., Situations and Attitudes, Pos. 416.

37 Cf. FREGE, G., Über Sinn und Bedeutung, esp. 34.

38 Cf. BARWISE, J./PERRY, J., Situations and Attitudes, Pos. 2137.

sleeps or does not sleep.' Therefore, both sentences should have the same meaning.[39] But we can easily reject this claim. Although we can admit that both sentences have the same truth-value (so that the expression 'Sarah sleeps or does not sleep' has no influence on the truth-value), both sentences does not mean the same thing. If one admits as much, one has to reject Frege's conception of meaning. Meaning then, is not an attribute of statements (or words or other linguistic expressions), but a relation between *situations: 'a meaning is a relation M between different types of situation.'*[40] Or, more precisely:

> [o]ne situation *s* can contain information about another situation *s'* only if there is a systematic relation M that holds between situations sharing some configuration of uniformities with *s* and situations that share some other configuration of uniformities with *s'*.[41]

Statements (and other linguistic expressions) are primarily utterings, and utterings are a specific kind of situation.

2. *Situations are primary over individuals relations* (*and attributes*): In perception, we perceive situations as their course of events, whereas individuals, relations and attributes (as monadic relations) are uniformities in the perception of these situations, i.e. processes that have some kind of uniformity during a specific time.

3. *Real situations and abstract situations*: In order to describe a situation, one has to refer to uniformities. Any description of a situation is therefore an abstract situation. Such a description formally contains (1) the relation and its relata, (2) the situation itself, (3) the spatiotemporal area, and (4) a judgment concerning whether the abstract situation fits with the real one.[42]

4. *Incompleteness of abstract situations*: abstract situations are necessarily always incomplete descriptions of real situations and of the course of events. A description of a real situation by an abstract situation is itself a real situation, which is different from the described situation. There is a relation of meaning

---

39 Cf. BARWISE, J./PERRY, J., Situations and Attitudes, Pos. 2115–2126.

40 BARWISE, J./PERRY, J., Situations and Attitudes, Pos. 1895–1907.

41 BARWISE, J./PERRY, J., Situations and Attitudes, Pos. 1895.

42 The formalism appears in EVERS, D., Gott und mögliche Welten, 239, as follows: 'I sit' refers to the situation of the statement *u* and a situation *e* at a space-time-area *g*, in which speaker *a* says the sentence and *a* sits:
u[[I sit]]*e*
gdw
There is an area *g* and a person *a*, given:
in *u*: in *g*: speaks, *a*; yes
in *e*: in *g*: sits, *a*; yes.

between these two real situations, which enables the interpretation of the first situation by the second situation through the means of the abstract situation. But in perceiving the uniformities of the first situation in the second situation one necessarily has to abstract from the first situation. Something remains unmentioned, un-expressible, and unperceivable, which belongs to the real situation. Only some uniformities can be expressed, others not.

The description 'I am writing this chapter in a rented flat in Oxford during a sabbatical' is a fitting description, but also an abstract one. What goes unmentioned is that I am using a computer, that my daughter is sleeping at my side, that I am affected by the political events as expressed in the news, etc.

5. *Situations overlap or contain each other*: situations are bound to specific spatiotemporal areas. But since spatiotemporal areas can overlap or contain each other, situations can also overlap or contain each other. The same is true for abstract situations, only more so, since overlappings are not only caused by spatiotemporal areas, but also by uniformities among situations.

6. *Abstract situations can only be classified with the help of non-wellfounded sets*: The history of situation semantics revealed[43] that abstract situations cannot be conceived with the help of classical set theories, including the axiom of regularity.[44] This principle excludes problems by excluding arbitrarily specific sets like Ω, a set that only includes itself. Without the principle of regularity, such sets, including Ω, are included. Peter Aczel showed that such a non-wellfounded theory of sets is possible without contradictions, if one assumes an anti-foundation axiom that safeguards there being exactly one set that contains itself ($\Omega=\{\Omega\}$).[45] Classical, well-founded sets, belong to such a set theory, but non-classical, non-wellfounded sets or hypersets do as well.

7. *The world is not a situation and it is impossible to give a closed description of it*: There are massive implications in using a theory of non-wellfounded sets. There is no theoretical totality of well-founded sets of all actual and possible situations that could represent the world.[46] And there is also no totality of all well-founded sets of a real situation. Situations can entail each other or overlap and they can constitute new sets, but there is no total set of situations and no general description. The reason is not that human epistemic abilities are

43 Cf. BARWISE, J./PERRY, J., Situations and Attitudes, Pos. 390–400, and for a portrayal EVERS, D., Gott und mögliche Welten, 234–253.

44 The axiom of regularity was first articulated by NEUMANN, J.v., Axiomatisierung der Mengenlehre, esp. 239, and one of the classic formulations was given by ZERMELO, E., Grenzzahlen und Mengenbereiche, 31.

45 Cf. ACZEL, P., Non-Well-Founded Sets, 6.

46 Cf. BARWISE, J., Situation in Logic, 191.

restricted, but it is an ontic reason. It is semantically un-thinkable, and therefore also ontically inconceivable.

At this point, we will end our description of situation semantics. So far, it suffices in order to show that there are some similarities with our narrative ontology. Real situations resemble our first order stories, the abstract situations and their description resemble our second or higher order stories. The fact that narrations can only be described by narratives that are abstractions of narrations is similar to the introduction of uniformities as constitutive elements of abstract situations. Further, the primacy of the wayformational line can be expressed in a situation semantics by the fact that individuals, relations, and attributes are conceived of as uniformities abstracted from real situations. And there are many more such similarities, e.g. attributes are nothing but a special kind of relations (monadic ones). *Meaning is neither a property of subjects nor of single sentences or of its own realm of meanings, but exists bodily as a relation of the sequences of primary stories.* However, there are also a lot of dissimilarities in regard to the understanding of modalities, the meaning of sequences of events, the relationship between concepts and metaphors, the conception of time, etc. Therefore, it is not appropriate to adopt situation semantics. It is only a tool that can be set aside after the work has been done.

The important question is: does situation semantics provides any help in order to conceive of modalities?

The usual semantics of possible worlds presupposes well-founded sets. This presupposition is clear in Leibniz, Lewis, and Plantinga, but also in the case of Kripke's idealizations. In situation semantics, possibilities are variations of abstract situations and the course of their events, which cannot be represented by well-founded sets and also therefore not by possible worlds or idealized possible worlds. Possibilities thus presuppose real situations as variations of their description with the help of abstract situations. The fact that these variations cannot be added to a totality of what is actual or possible is not an epistemic restriction, but a semantic and ontic openness. The semantics of possible worlds presupposes that logical omnipotence is non-contradictory,[47] and this assumption is inapplicable in situation semantics. Nevertheless,[48] situation semantics gives no detailed alternative for interpreting the modal expression of our ordinary language, but restricts itself to some hints that modalities are specific kinds of meaningful relations between situations.[49]

Therefore, one cannot say more than Evers has done:

---

47 Cf. BARWISE, J., Situation in Logic, 25.
48 Cf. BARWISE, J./PERRY, J., Situations and Attitudes, Pos. 7738.
49 Cf. BARWISE, J./PERRY, J., Situations and Attitudes, Pos. 7807–7818.

> Neither actuality nor its surrounding possibilities are exhaustible [...] by representations. And this inexhaustibility of the actual and the real [...] is founded [...] in the openness of the actual and possible that cannot be conceived of conceptually. We have no reference system for the totality of the possible, as we have none for the totality of what is real. There is no complete concept of the possible, and there is no absolute actuality as naked facticity. The actual is always more than the sum of facts. And the possible is only possible in relation to what is designed as possible.[50]

That could suffice as the point of situation semantics. However, we want to proceed a step further by commenting on the ontological meaning of situation semantics. If, in the semantics of possible worlds, necessity is what is valid in all possible worlds, and if the concept of all possible worlds is not a well-founded set, then this definition of necessity is meaningless – and also therefore the definition of possibility. Nevertheless, it is possible to speak of contingency, possibility, and necessity in the framework of situation semantics. Since there is no totality of possibilities, one cannot claim that there is a possible world as an alternative to what is really the case. But it is helpful to claim that out of a real situation one can infer a series of abstract situations, in which uniformities can be recombined in manifold ways, in a manner in which some fit with the real situation, others not. Some of these possibilities of recombination are factual descriptions of future events, other not. Then we can refer to the descriptions of such future course of events that are unavoidable as metaphorically 'necessary,' and one can call the avoidable ones 'contingent'. Then, we can still transfer the modalities in the usual way. However, (1) the set of future courses of action is non-wellfounded, and (2) all modalities have to be determined in relation to the concrete, original, and actual situation. The point is *that modalities can only be determined by being strictly related to particular situations, and they do not form well founded sets*. And that is what situation semantics can show.

18.7 Modalities in Systems Theory

Of course, the foregoing suggestion is not sufficient to determine the meaning of modality, especially contingency. Therefore, we need to look at those theories in which contingency plays a special role. Our first example comes from the role played by contingence in systems theory.

50 EVERS, D., Gott und mögliche Welten, 260 (transl. MM).

Let us introduce the necessary distinctions. The basic concepts here are system, environment, and world. Luhmann defines them as the following:

> The formation of structures is always a restriction of the freedom of the elements to combine. Such restrictions can only be gained through systems. The formation of systems requires [...] the exclusion of environments that do not belong to the system. [...] The environment of a system is everything that is excluded by the system [...]. The concept of the environment is therefore defined relatively to a system. [...] The environments of different systems cannot be [...] identical, at most they can overlap. The entirety of what does not belong to a system cannot itself be a system, since it is without limits and it permeates the world without limits – and the world itself is not a system.[51]

This understanding shows there is an asymmetry between system and environment:

> It is a feature that belongs to the fact that each system formation concerns the environments of other systems, and, vice versa, so that in the environment of every system many other systems are formed and changing, as the environment is always more complex than the system. This is absolutely true for all systems-in-environments.[52]

Systems must, therefore, be selective when they refer to the environment:

> If one resolves the concept of complexity and determines it as selective relations within a set of elements, the result is that no system can relate its own elements or relations point for point to those of the entire environment. A system's limits function as highly selective restrictions on contact.[53]

This necessary reference of a system to its environment is contingent, in the specific sense of indeterminacy:

> On the other hand, these filtering limits, with their internal capacity reserves, means that in the relationship between different systems – though primarily in the relationship between system and environment – there is indeterminateness that is based on complexity. [...] In dynamic terms, this means that any systemic process operates selectively, and so has to solve the problem of the reduction of greater complexity.[54]

This indeterminacy of how the environment can be represented by a system has two aspects: first, the parts of the environment that appear by indeterminacy

51 LUHMANN, N., Funktion der Religion, 13 (transl. MM).
52 LUHMANN, N., Funktion der Religion, 14 (transl. MM).
53 LUHMANN, N., Funktion der Religion, 14 (transl. MM).
54 LUHMANN, N., Funktion der Religion, 15 (transl. MM).

in the system, and second, what does not appear. Luhmann describes this double indeterminacy in this way:

> Anything that functions as a system's environment is necessarily therefore a twofold reconstruction of the environment itself: it is horizon and transcendence, expectation and disappointment, selection and risk, order and randomness. [...] The phenomenal world of things and events, of relative probability, of what is familiar and normal, of proximity and distance is therefore only the one half of the environment's reconstruction; it is the zone of accessibility, but at the same time the condition for beginning and achieving access to the other half. What is unexpected, what it surprising, and what is disappointing is only momentarily incomprehensible, like a sudden bang behind one's back; through reductions, typologizing, and normalization strategies, it quickly becomes reality.[55]

Luhmann also describes this reduction of complexity as a contingent reduction of complexity, by referring to contingency exactly as we defined it above ($Cp \leftrightarrow Pp \wedge P\neg p$).[56] At this point, we can ignore the fact that contingency is not identical with indeterminacy: everything that is not determined, is contingent, but not everything that is contingent must be undetermined. It appears, however, that contingency in Luhmann denotes indeterminacy. Just as we find in any system two ways of reducing complexity, in every system we also find a double contingency.[57] These definitions hold for all possible systems, such as biological, social, and technical systems, but of course Luhmann is interested in social systems. Regarding modality, he is only interested in contingency. But since all modalities are defined reciprocally, Luhmann's definitions of contingency affects all other modalities.

In Luhmann's thinking, modalities are defined relatively to a system. Contingency is an attribute that appears in the relationship between system and environment, whereas necessity is understood exclusively through intrasystemic relations. This means that necessity can only be understood within the framework of a higher level of contingency. If we were to express this by means of our formal language of modal logic, the consequences would be that necessity would always be irreducibly contingent necessity (CNp), and that we would have to reject system S_5. Nevertheless, Luhmann's systems theory is not appropriate for the design of a narrative ontology, although Luhmann has had some influence on the design of some narratologies, such as Albrecht Koschorke's.[58] A system in Luhmann's understanding, including its relative closedness, is far too narrow. Intra-systemic necessity would restrict all possible relations to

---

55 LUHMANN, N., Funktion der Religion, 16f (transl. MM).
56 Cf. LUHMANN, N., Funktion der Religion, 187.
57 Cf. LUHMANN, N., Funktion der Religion, 81.
58 Cf. KOSCHORKE, A., Wahrheit und Erfindung. For the problem cf. also chapter 6.

transport in the network, whereas our concept of wayfaring in the meshwork cannot be understood with the thinking of systems theory. Neither primary nor secondary stories are systems. Furthermore, interwoven wayformational lines and combined narrations are also not systems.

With systems theory, we can illustrate the contingency of the world, because a world can never be a totality in the sense of a system, which implies the very attractive insight that contingency has primacy over necessity, since necessity can only be a meaningful attribute if it is seen as an immanent necessity, within the boundaries of a system. However, the use of the concept of system at all is still an abstraction from reality. A system in Luhmann's sense must be understood as an idealization that can never be reached – not even partly.[59]

18.8 Causal Modalities and Quantum Theory

Another kind of contingency, and therefore another understanding of modality, appears in quantum theory. It depends on the concept of causality (ch.17) and on the idea of a closed causal nexus. This understanding became the standard interpretation of quantum theory after interpretations by means of hidden variables, which tried to explain quantum indetermination in purely epistemic terms, were excluded. To the many interpretations of quantum theory belong variations of the Copenhagen interpretation, theories of decoherence, and quantum collapse. There are also various world theories, such as those which can be understood as the quantum version of Lewis' modal realism, and Bohm's interpretation, which, through the introduction of a quantum potential allowed for principally undiscoverable determined parameters, and so postulated an ontically deterministic word.[60] Today it is clear that only interpretations that are at the core statistical, non-local and indeterministic, fit with the empirical facts. Hidden variables are necessarily excluded by the empirical proof that they violate Bell's theorem.

If it is impossible to measure all states of affairs through a single experiment, a direct proof of hidden parameters is excluded. However, it is possible to use a series of experiments, in which the single experiment asks for different attributes. The basis is a simple feature of systems that include fixed, independent attributes. Suppose you have a set of unknown instantiations of three attributes a, b, c. The amount of individuals having attributes a and b [F(a,b)] is then less than or equal to the sum of individuals that have a and c [F(a,c)], together with the amount of individuals having b, but not

59 For the distinction of idealization and ideal cf. Rescher, N., Pluralism, 195–198.
60 Cf. Bohm, D., "Hidden Varibles" I.

c [F(b,¬c)]: F(a,b) ≤ [F(a,c)] + [F(b,¬c)]. If one can show that these inequalities are empirically violated, then the conclusion is that this system cannot have distinct, independent attributes and therefore also no hidden parameters. Alan Aspect showed that this was indeed the case in the 1980s.[61]

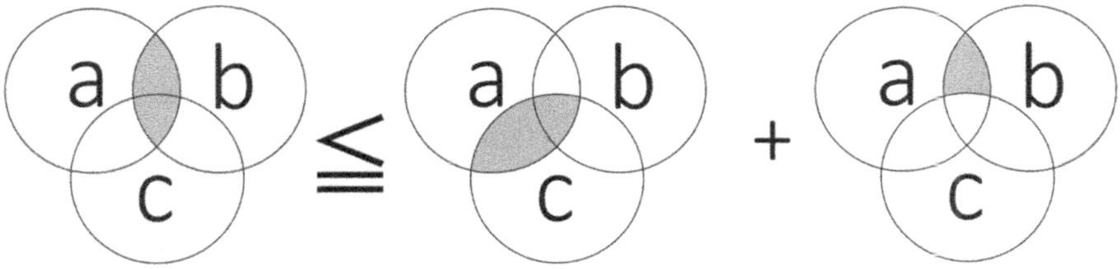

Fig. 3

Another argument is that indeterministic interpretations, like the theory of decoherence, are simpler and therefore preferable. In this case, one must acknowledge a principle of economy like Occam's razor. Although this is a matter of belief, like causality, this additional argument is in principle unnecessary, due to the empirical proof of Bell's theorem.

This empirical proof has the following consequences for contingency as ontic indeterminacy:

- A lack of ontological causality on the quantum level has to be acknowledged.
- The closeness or unclosedness of the causal nexus – and therefore of the givenness of a lack of causality in an ontic and not only epistemic respect – on the level of the macro-world is disputed, but most probably the causal nexus is open.

The theoretical explanation of the world of quanta uses a probability calculus. In this framework, no gaps or riddles appear, but everything happens necessarily. Therefore, one could, in an inversion of the modalities in systems theory, assume irreducibly iterated modalities: the contingency that appears during the collapse of the wave function is part of the necessary framework of the probability calculus (NCp), which relativizes the radical kind of contingency. Here, contingency only means that in specific boundaries there is a lack of causality. In other words, the principle of sufficient reason is invalid – but only within specifiable limits. But, this is also disputed and dependent on other ontological decisions. One could also understand entangled quanta in such a way

61 Cf. BELL, J.S., On the EPR Paradox. One of the best portrayals of the quantum theory and its analyses can be found in IJJAS, A., Der Alte, esp. 59–92.121–149. For Bell's theorem and the references of Alain Aspect cf. ibid., 111.

that they are not individuated at all (and indeed, the principle of the identity of indiscernibles is invalid in the word of quanta, but the idea of numeric identity is not). In this case, the basic entities in a physical respect are relations in their entanglement, including their entanglement with the macro-world and its measuring apparatuses. Karen Barad had given such an ontological interpretation of quantum theory that is combined with ideas from the phenomenology of the living body, which she calls 'agential realism'.[62] According to another approach, the entangled *relata* are spatiotemporally identifiable – since we can speak about them and we can use them – without being spatiotemporally individuated. Such an approach fits very well with our narrative ontology, since we have to assume that space-time is an important frame for the identification of indexical acts, but nevertheless is not basic. Individuation does not necessarily need space-time, but only asymmetric, transitive, and irreflexive relations of order. And this is the case in stories, too (ch. 10 and ch. 11).

To sum up: One should not, like Barad, use quantum theory for more than an illustrative model for the ontological state of affairs, and one should refrain from founding a narrative ontology on quantum theory. But the reverse is not the case: it is possible, and easy, to integrate insights from quantum theory into a narrative ontology – as long as narrations allow indeterministic, causeless courses of events. And this is precisely what is allowed by dramatic coherence (ch. 16).

18.9 Relational Modalities and Spheres of Modalities in Nicolai Hartmann

So far, our consideration of modalities has resulted in two important points. First, modalities have to be understood as relational entities; something can only be necessary, contingent, or possible for something else. The relational constitution of modalities is not apparent in the formalism of modal logic, but the understanding of modalities in situation semantics, in systems theory, and in quantum theory showed this clearly. Second, there are no modalities as such, but only modalities referring to specific aspects, which was also shown by our analyses of systems theory and quantum theory. Systems theory had to distinguish between intrasystemic modalities and modalities between systems and its environment in such a way that intrasystemic necessities appear as contingently related to its environment (CNp). In quantum theory, contingency as indeterminacy appears in its mathematical description of probability

62 Cf. Barad, K., Meeting the Universe Halfway, 132–185.

as necessity (NCp). This aspect of distinguishing the different terms of modality can be expressed by means of formal modal logic, insofar as most systems, except system S_5, allow for iterated modal operators. However, this formalization cannot represent the whole state of affairs, since iterated modal operators do not specify all the different terms. But of course, it is possible to assume that there are also iterated modalities of the same term as well as iterated modalities of different terms. Both states of affairs, the relationality of modalities and the fact that modalities are bound to different terms, could be also formalized by using a triadic relation. However, formalizations have their own problems and therefore we will forgo such an endeavor. These two important aspects of modalities, which were to a large part ignored by modal logic, have nevertheless been observed, described, and analyzed. An excellent example of this is Nicolai Hartmann's thinking.

Hartmann calls contingency randomness. Nevertheless, he means exactly what is usually defined as contingency ($Rp \leftrightarrow \neg Np \leftrightarrow M\neg p$):

> As the most positive of all relational *modi*, necessity is most affected by its opposition to randomness. Formally this is visible in that it alone is in direct contradiction to [randomness].[63]

If one views events of the world, or sequences of stories in themselves as non-relational, then there are no modalities, or at least only one: randomness. Every event is viewed in itself as random or contingent in the sense that it could have happened in another manner, and also in the sense that it could not have happened. The event A 'I am moving my foot' is viewed in itself as just as random as event B 'the car is braking'. Nevertheless, between two events there can be a relation of sequences, like causality, so that A is a cause of B. In our example, to move one's foot is a necessary condition for the car braking, and we would say that A is a cause of B. This is, according to Hartmann, the genuine horizon for the discovery of necessity:

> Neither axioms, nor laws, nor any principles are necessary. They are at most 'necessary presuppositions' of something that is seen in another respect as particular. But this kind of necessity is only the necessity of cognition through the process of inference, not the ontic necessity of the disclosed. [...] If in a sphere everything is random, the sphere is atomized, dissolved. [...] It lacks an inner cohesion. [...] And actually, this is a fictional case. [...] Cohesion is everywhere, and necessity is everywhere, too.[64]

63 HARTMANN, N., Möglichkeit und Wirklichkeit, 90 (trans. MM).
64 HARTMANN, N., Möglichkeit und Wirklichkeit, 93. 91 (transl. MM).

In contrast to randomness, necessity is seen as a strictly relational or relative concept:

> There is no necessity without randomness, but there can be randomness without necessity [...] necessity carries the principle of its self-abrogation within itself, and involves therefore randomness as its limit; randomness, however, knows of no self-abrogation and limit; it does not involve itself in necessity.[65]

The relational constitution of the modality of necessity has, according to Hartmann, important implications:

> Necessity only has its place conditionally; [...] conditioned by the range of relations and the range of the sphere's cohesion. Where this cohesion ceases, necessity automatically changes into its opposite, into randomness. And therefore, it vanishes from the inter-modal relations. It is substituted by randomness, and randomness inherits its rights.[66]

In Hartmann, 'spheres' mean what we referred to earlier in this subsection as terms, which should not be confused. Hartmann distinguishes four spheres and four kinds of modalities, respectively:[67]

- *real* necessity, and the modalities derived from it, are related to the *spatio-temporal sphere*, where we find different kinds of causalities (not only efficient causality);
- *essential* necessity, and the modalities derived from it, are related to the *ideal sphere* of essences, like mathematics and their relations of implication (necessary and sufficient conditions), and are derived from this sphere;
- *logical* necessity, and the modalities derived from it, are related to the *logical sphere* of concepts and their relations, which are the kinds of judgment; and
- *epistemic* necessity, and the modalities derived from it, are related to the *gnoseological* sphere.

We will not adopt Hartmann's classification, the only decisive thing is to distinguish the terms of modality. One cannot really assume that these terms, which need to be distinguished, must be restricted to four or any other number.

But given that there are different sphere terms, the question arises as to whether there are also modalities in-between the different realms. Hartmann has observed this as well, and called this the question of *inter-modality*.[68]

---

65 Hartmann, N., Möglichkeit und Wirklichkeit, 91. 92 (transl. MM).

66 Hartmann, N., Möglichkeit und Wirklichkeit, 94–95 (transl. MM).

67 Cf. Hartmann, N., Möglichkeit und Wirklichkeit, 38–41 and in addition Evers, D., Gott und mögliche Welten, 283f.

68 Cf. Evers, D., Gott und mögliche Welten, 284.

It is not possible to avoid these two insights, independently of how one evaluates Hartmann's philosophy. But we have to go further. Obviously, according to systems theory, the coherence of possible spheres or terms is in itself always a relative one, which is exactly what Hartmann calls inter-modalities. If we conceive such a sphere as a set, then we have to see such a set – similar to situation semantics – as a non-well-founded set. The consequence is that the idea of a necessity that governs the whole set becomes impossible. Therefore, in the framework of a single sphere, necessity is also only possible in relation to *particular relata.*

If we apply these results to our narrative ontology, how do the different terms or spheres appear?

1. *Real modalities* cannot refer either to the spatiotemporal nexus or to relations of causality, since spatiotemporal relations and relations of causality are highly complex, derivative concepts. If one wants to meaningfully apply the term real modalities, it can only refer to the primary stories of the real meshwork.

2. The real meshwork of stories is not independent of the perception truth and value; therefore, we have to distinguish the modalities of perception or *phenomenal modalities* from real modalities.

3. The perception of truth and value in the primary mesh of stories is always mediated by secondary narrations. Therefore, we have to distinguish *secondary-narrative modalities* from real modalities and from the modalities of perception. Here, on this level, we cannot speak of conceptual coherence in order to define possibility and other modalities, but only dramatic coherence. Therefore, it would be an interesting task to define the secondary-narrative modalities on the basis of dramatic coherence.

4. Secondary narrations always include concepts based on metaphors, as we have seen. The conceptual is an abstraction from secondary narrativity, but nevertheless it can appear in any kind of secondary narrativity. Therefore, we also have to speak of *conceptual modalities* or *logical modalities.*

5. Depending on perception and on the kind of secondary narration, we have to distinguish further kinds of modalities, such as deontic modalities, aesthetic modalities, etc.

The relationship between the first four kinds of modalities is basic and one cannot simply ignore it. The modelling of conceptual modalities plays a key role. Depending on how these are understood, the secondary-narrative modalities will also appear differently, as well as the modalities of perceiving truth and value – and finally, of course, the real modalities, too. The most important task is to understand what conceptual modalities are, a topic we will now pursue.

18.10 Contingency and the Antinomy of Negation

If one conceives of conceptual modalities within the framework of possible world semantics, one ends up with different conceptions of transport in the network. This transport is either seen as real (Lewis) or as ideal (Kripke), but it is nevertheless a system, even if the details in modelling the network may vary. If it is true that an implication of phenomenal perception is that transport in a network is always an abstraction from reality, then here – in conceiving conceptual modalities – we come to the point where there is a danger of distortion and dissonance. Situation semantics, Luhmann's use of modality, and Hartmann's relational analysis of modality were the means to reveal this danger. However, to solve the problem requires going beyond these hints and explaining in more detail what conceptual modalities are, which is the task of this subchapter. We will learn that, in decisive respects, it is important first to start with the idea of a system in order to see that this concept has to be abandoned. In the end, only a post-systematic modelling of conceptual modality is possible.

The decisive argument is based on an observation that is perhaps as old as humanity. It appears in Pre-Socratic philosophy onward, we find it in Tit 1:12, and it inspired Gödel in his incompleteness theorems.[69] What we mean is the antinomy 'This sentence is not true.' Anton Friedrich Koch saw correctly that this is not an antinomy that can be excluded by introducing *ad-hoc* rules, but one that is inherent in any construction of a conceptual system, which has important consequences. But let us proceed step by step.

One may ask if the sentence 'this sentence is not true' is understandable at all, and if yes, what causes the antinomy.[70] If the sentence were inconceivable, like 'circles have four edges,' it would not be antinomy at all, and not a real problem worthy of attention. Obviously, the sentence consists of three elements, which are conceivable in themselves: the subject 'this sentence', the predicate 'is true', and its negation 'not'. The subject 'this sentence' is a recursive self-reference, and one can eliminate the antinomy by forbidding self-referentiality. Although this is a common way of dealing with the problem, it is inappropriate, since in many cases we work with self-reference, including in formalized languages.[71] Also the truth-predicate is not a candidate for incomprehensibility, since it belongs, as Koch has shown, essentially to this sentence insofar it signifies what analytic philosophy calls a semantic ascent,

69 Cf. GÖDEL, K., Unentscheidbare Sätze, and HOFSTADTER, D., Gödel, Escher, Bach.

70 Cf. KOCH, A.F., Versuch, 261–266.

71 Relatedly, consider e.g. Gödel's argument that every theory containing arithmetic has to be recursive, cf. KOCH, A.F., Versuch, 263.

i.e. an expression of a state of affairs on another level of speech. This original state of affairs could be expressed without the truth-predicate, but only in an unconvincing way. The antinomy consists in the fact, that 'this sentence is not true' becomes wrong, if it is true, and true, if it is wrong. Formally, we can express this in the following way:

$$n \leftrightarrow \neg(n) \leftrightarrow \neg(\neg(n)) \leftrightarrow \neg(\neg(\neg(...)))$$

> If we unfold this expression, we would get 'an infinite expression consisting only of negations (and brackets) signifying pure negativity. But then the content of a self-negating statement is conceptually expressible without the help of the truth-predicate. But this infinitely long sentence [...] is not a candidate for a well-formed sentence in our finite language. Therefore, we use the technical means of semantic ascent and formulate the negation of itself in the shape of the liar.'[72]

Regarding the negation, it is clear that it is comprehensible. Language and other communication with signs is inconceivable without negations.

If the statement 'this sentence is not true' is comprehensible, the antinomy is valid; or more precisely, it is valid for all operations that include negations, i.e. all conceptual systems, all kinds of reason, like human reason, technical reason, or reason that might exist in the world. The antinomy of negation belongs essentially to the *logos*.[73] The only surprising thing is how we usually behave in face of the antinomy, by developing a thousand attempts to ignore it:

> Nevertheless, factually we do not really care about the liar paradox, we do not fear it as the grave of determinate reason, but treat is only as exceptional logical problem, and leave the mathematicians, following the regulative ideal of consistency, to invent means and ways of exorcizing it out of their theories – e.g. by a hierarchical order of metalanguages in the tradition of Tarski – with the consequence that in our non-mathematical scientific theories [..] we also do not expect nasty surprises, i.e. antinomies. It seems that we cure the inconsistency of our reason, which is revealed by the liar [paradox], by making it inconsequential, by, *ad hoc*, not drawing the conclusions that must be drawn, by not inferring anything from the liar [paradox], but by isolating it logically, putting it unto quarantine, and carrying on.[74] [...] The antinomy, therefore, cannot be *avoided*, because it is always there. At the least it can be *shunned*: fled, banished, tabooed or otherwise disarmed, softened, put into logical quarantine, or something similar.[75]

72 KOCH, A.F., Versuch, 265 (transl. MM).
73 Cf. KOCH, A.F., Versuch, 273.
74 KOCH, A.F., Versuch, 273 (transl. MM).
75 KOCH, A.F., Versuch, 258 (transl. MM).

If the antinomy was only semantic, one could invent rules in order to forbid it. And that is what we do. We, in everyday life, and the logicians behave like a defiant child in front of a resistant fact, stamping our feet and crying 'No, this must not be the case!' – and paradoxically, thereby we do nothing but confirm the antinomy. To use a different metaphor, in the cosmology of Einstein and Friedmann, singularities appear that are absurd but most probably observable, as singularities appear due to the antinomy of negation in all languages and in all use of signs. The attempts of Tarski and others[76] resemble the attempts of Hawking to banish singularities by inventing an imaginary time.[77] Nevertheless, there is a difference: introducing an imaginary time – if there really were one – would really eliminate the spatiotemporal singularities. The semantic attempts at ignorance, however, still have to use signs as means. Therefore, they do nothing but endlessly perpetuate the antinomy.

We have to add two important observations from Koch.

First, the antinomy cannot be restricted to linguistically limited state of affairs like the antinomy of the liar paradox. As 'mother of all antinomies'[78] it appears surprisingly and unpredictably. The attempt to isolate it amounts to trying to exclude negation itself, but this is useless. Some radical philosophies, like that of Parmenides, attempted to do so, with the consequence that one has to postulate a static, uniform, and completely undifferentiated being.[79]

Second, whereas one can give spatiotemporal singularities a wide berth, this is not possible in case of the logical singularity of reason. The spatiotemporal singularities called black holes have the advantage of never spitting out what they have swallowed, which is different in the case of the antinomy of negation. In propositional logic, conclusions rely on the operation of implication or sufficient condition. This reliance is a dyadic conjunction of propositions that is accordingly – according to a truth table – true if both sentences are true, both sentences are wrong, and if the first sentence is wrong and the second true. In other words, the implication is only wrong, if the first proposition is true and the second wrong. This structure leads to the well-known consequence that falsity implies anything $p \to (\neg p \to q)$ (*ex falso sequitur quodlibet*), that anything implies truth $p \to (q \to p)$ (*verum sequitur ex quodlibet*), and that any two arbitrary propositions are connected by implication $(p \to q) \vee (q \to p)$.

76 Cf. Koch, A.F., Versuch, 271f.
77 Cf. Hawking, S.W., Brief History of Time, 142–144.
78 Koch, A.F., Versuch, 261 (transl. MM).
79 Cf. Koch, A.F., Wahrheit, Zeit und Freiheit, 79f.

It is an irony of history that the original intention behind the development of modern modal logic, by C.I. Lewis, was to avoid these problems of implication[80] through the invention of the strict conditional $\neg P\neg(p\rightarrow q)\leftrightarrow\neg P(p\wedge\neg q)$. It is ironic in two ways. First, that this necessitates a semantic interpretation of modal logic, including its high load of ontological commitments; second, that this move compounds the problem, since now any necessarily wrong proposition now implicates anything strictly arbitrarily, and that every necessary condition is implicated by any arbitrary one. The invention of formal of modal logic is therefore one of the (indirect) strategies for the suppression of the antinomy of negation.

In propositional logic, an antinomy randomly implies anything. The antinomy of negation, is therefore productive, but in an interfering, non-calculable, non-Hegelian way by producing what is arbitrary. The logical or conceptual 'singularity' of the antinomy of negation is no 'black hole', but a 'white whole', or better a 'colorful hole'. In itself, it is invisible, like a white hole in front of a white background, but around it emerges the diversity of colors. However, in its emergence out of the singularity we cannot perceive this diversity of colors, because this would amount to an attempt to call the singularity a cause – and therefore an attempt to see it in the framework of necessary causality. It would be, in short, once more a futile attempt to deny the antinomy – which automatically validates it.

We now have to deal with the main question: what is the meaning of the antinomy of negation for understanding modality and for a narrative ontology?

In a basic way, the antinomy of negation ensures that the cohesion of what is real cannot be a system, a network, transport, but wayfaring in the mesh – on all levels, on the level of primary stories as well as on the level of secondary stories.

At the same time, it ensures that universal coherence is incomprehensible and that there is no totality of truth. There is only one kind of comprehensible coherence, which in ch. 16 we called dramatic coherence. And dramatic coherence cannot be grounded except in hopeful trust. It becomes visible if we make clear what the meaning of the antinomy is for actuality. Actuality (p), including its logical and mathematical formalizations, is basically what is contingent $(Pp\wedge P\neg p)$ and random $(M\neg p)$, because it could be in another way. Where the antinomy will appear is unpredictable. Though the antinomy still allows for the formal definition of necessity as a negation of what is random $(\neg M\neg p)$, but there is no possibility of giving necessity a universal meaning, like something that is true in all possible worlds, or as something that is always true. Necessity can only be used as a relational modality in-between well-defined events – and

80 Cf. LEWIS, C.I., Implication and the Algebra of Logic.

this use is also questionable, because events are always intermeshed in larger stories. Nevertheless, we do not want to suggest abandoning the concept of necessity. If necessity can be used in-between particular events, and if particular events are always narratively conjoined in order to be events at all, without becoming a world in David Lewis' sense, then there is only one possibility for conceiving of necessity narratively. It is the basic capability of humans to permutate and recombine what they have experienced, i.e. to invent alternative stories of a restricted range in order to form a conception of their perceived reality and in order to act in such a way that the future course of history is not against them, because they intend the impossible. But the impossible is what is necessarily not the case (N¬p). In order to orientate oneself in action, we do not have to dispense with necessity, or with particular regularities. We can even pretend as if the projected stories are universal of mini-worlds. Therefore, at the end we come again a little bit closer to the semantics of possible worlds in the sense of Kripke, if we acknowledge, that they always used hypothetically, in the sense of a limited ideal. A possible worlds semantics in the sense of Leibniz, Lewis and Plantinga, however, remains excluded.

Although we are skeptical of any claims that formalization is harmless, we do not need to abdicate modal logic completely. We cannot use systems like S_5 that allow for the reduction of iterated modalities. We should also be cautious in face of an only apparently harmless principle like the inference of actuality from necessity (Np→p), and therefore the system T, because in everyday life we name mathematical states of affairs necessary, like Euclidian geometry. According to Kripke's distinction between necessity and apriority (or, to put it more simply, between epistemic necessity and ontic necessity), such a state of affairs would be necessary because they are known *a priori*. Necessary then it would also mean that they have to be valid in all (hypothetical) possible worlds. But Euclidian geometry is not real in any world, as the theory of relativity has shown. It would only be valid in an empty world. But an empty world is not a possible, but an impossible world. Nevertheless, to call Euclidian geometry necessary is not meaningless. But then we have to say that the axiom Np→p is invalid for Euclidian geometry – necessarily.[81] This state of affairs is in no way mysterious, given the distinction between ideals and idealization.[82]

If we follow the line of thinking outlined in this section, it seems that the only thing that is really necessary is the antinomy of negation, i.e. contingency itself

81 KOCH, A.F., Versuch, 359 speaks in a similar context about the thesis that the pure, formal content of the observer's concepts always represents an unreal limit case of the observer's content, which is a thesis that we would like to affirm. But we cannot agree with him in calling this an 'attractive price', because giving up Np→p (N understood epistemically in the sense of aprioricaly derived content) would be far from attractive.

82 Cf. RESCHER, N., Pluralism, 195–198.

(NCp). But, this is also not meant literally unless one wants to re-operationalize the antinomy, which is impossible. If we call contingency 'necessary contingency', then necessity has to be seen as a regulative expression, which is at the same time a metaphor. At the same time, we can see that we have reached the most radical kind of contingency and randomness in the sense of whatever is arbitrary.

18.11 The Practice of Contingency as Perception in Dramatic Coherence versus Decontingentization

The antinomy of negation and therefore radical contingency appears necessarily in every language and in every kind of sign usage, i.e. in all our kinds of expressing secondary narrativity. But then it also appears in perception itself, since perception is always secondary-narratively mediated. It appears in the phenomena itself, and we have no possibility of denying the contingency of all reality.

If the contingent is really arbitrary, how can we speak at all of an ontology of stories and dramatic coherence? Well, there is indeed no logically sufficient condition. Also, perceptional trust is not sufficient to ground it, since it leads to a trust in the perception of particular sequences, but not to a trust in a narrative nexus conjoined by dramatic coherence. However, why should one find a general reason at all? If wayfaring in the mesh is proved in its reality-resonating stance by the antinomy of negation in contrast to transport in the net, then it is clear that there is no standpoint beyond the mesh, and it is clear that there are no standpoints in the mesh at all, but particular, dynamic wayformational perspectives.

In the dynamical wayformational perspective of Christian faith, dramatic coherence is itself an abstraction of the certainty of the cross and resurrection of Jesus Christ. At the cross, God the eternal Son (and therefore Godself in God's becoming) is in a crisis: 'Oh highest dread, Godself is dead.'[83] At the same time, the dead Son is the resurrected one and resurrection does not mean reanimation. Eberhard Jüngel tried to express this state of affairs in his definition of love as unity of life and death for the sake of life,[84] or as in the midst of

83 This is my translation of a phrase of Johann Rist's passion hymn, 'Oh große Not, Gott selbst ist tot' from 1641. Interestingly, later generations have softened this phrase to 'O highest dread, God's Son is dead'. This softened version is the version to be found today in the German protestant hymn-book (EG 80). Hegel criticized this alteration, cf. HEGEL, G.W.F., Philosophie der Religion (Meiner), vol. 3, 247.

84 Cf. JÜNGEL, E., God as the Mystery of the World, x, 219, 222, 299f, 317, 320, 326, 340, 344.

the highest and justified highest self-relatedness always a higher selflessness.[85] However, Jüngel's expression was seen as another attempt to relativize the meaning of the cross, insofar as he interprets the cross in the light of resurrection. Stoellger therefore has suggested as a corrective a *theological epoché* of the cross.[86] In my understanding, this means that the cross is at once center,[87] attractor, disruptor, and retainer: in all our theological thinking, we have to come back to the cross; it disrupts all theological reasoning and it demands conceptual reservation. Nevertheless, the cross is not completely contextless; it remains bound to the resurrection as an eschatological event that inaugurates hope: the hope of faith, which no one can produce, and which one can only get by the activity of the one who experienced the cross and resurrection. Cross and resurrection form an ordered sequence, but an open one. The order is not 'resurrection and cross' – which would destroy the sequence – but 'cross and resurrection.' And since resurrection is an eschatological event, it is not a closed, but an open story. Resurrection is neither a theological nor in another way a conceptual conclusion, and it is for us not a subject matter of experience – apart from the experience of hope. But we do not only hope for resurrection, but also that post-anastatically the sequence will be revealed as meaningful, not despite, but because it is purely contingent. The Gospels tried to combine both the contingency and dramatic coherence of this sequence by the post-anastatic scriptural proof of the *dei*, the 'must' of the passion, cross, and resurrection. Thereby it is essential not to skip over the narrative sequence. If one puts this sequence back into the life of Jesus Christ, it is only possible in the mouth of Christ himself, who is the only one who has experienced this story: in Jesus's own proclamation of his suffering. And if one wants to put the sequence back into the life of Jesus before the resurrection, it can only be done in the way Mark described: the interpretant, the result of his announcement of suffering, can only be the *in*comprehension of the disciples.

The dramatic coherence of all stories, and dramatic coherence of one's own experience of reality, is for Christians nothing but the hope that the life, death, and resurrection of Christ is also the canon of all life, including one's own. In the light of faith, dramatic coherence, which is a feature of all events of the world, appears as an abstraction from this hope of Christian trust. Therefore, one could argue that for Christian theology it is not necessary to follow this way of abstraction. However, this is indeed not the case, because dramatic coherence as a human attitude is omnipresent; it does not appear exclusively in

85 Cf. Jüngel, E., God as the Mystery of the World, 298, 300, 317–320, 324, 328, 358, 369, 374f.

86 Cf. Stoellger, P., Passivität aus Passion, 350.

87 Cf. Mühling, M., Versöhnendes Handeln, 7. 15. 42, and elswhere.

Christian faith. As such, without its Christian context, it is causeless and unjustifiable. And therefore, to call it dramatic coherence appears as an awkward expression. But this is not really the case, since the possibility of recognizing contingency as a basic part of dramatic coherence, gained by the antinomy of negation, is neither a kind of decontingentization nor a reduction of contingency. As such, it fits with our normal practice, as Koch remarks:

> Does this mean that all reasoning and all attempts to build theories are discredited? Is it worth it to go on with theoretical experiments, [...] if the antinomy cannot be banished from thinking and being? Such questions collide with the practice of reasoning as well as their equivalences collide with the practice of life. [...] The *memento mori* is the header above life itself, more than above reasoning. Nevertheless, in the shadow of death we go on to live happily. [...] Why not behave similarly in regard to reasoning and avoid the inconsistency, wherever it lurks, as long as possible?[88] [...] The logical space is a plentiful, changing, uncertain habitat: a clearance in the rain-forest, where we have settled and build a (logical) *polis*, which is protected at its margins only poorly against the chaos, out of which we came, and that undermines this *polis*, is going to overgrow it, permeates it tacitly, and sometimes breaks out in its center. Mathematics and the exact sciences are an inner wall, our logical Acropolis, which we build tactically with hardest bricks, in order to have a refuge in case of danger. And every time when we have to use it, we pay the price of its narrowness and its relative loss of reality. And further, this Acropolis is destroyable. [...] It seems that this is a highly metaphorical kind of speech, [...] and in a specific sense this is the case. In another sense, it is the other way around. [...] To speak of clearing, settling, building, rain-forest and *polis*, chaos and Acropolis in order to characterize logical-ontological state of affairs is less metaphorical then *re*-metaphorical. The concepts used by ancient generations in order to understand their pre-technological life were ontologically laden, were expressive – and for us today ever weaker – metaphors of our precarious logical-ontological situation. [...] Modern technology, however, is mathematically, not ontologically laden. In its light, the ontological content of the concepts of settling, residing, building, etc. is fading. This is not an advantage, but a – most probably unavoidable – blindness.[89]

We can understand the above in a way that wayfaring is seen as antecedent over transport, the mesh as antecedent over the mesh and dynamical way-formational perspectives as antecedent over systems. If one neither wants to become a nihilistic life-denying sceptic nor a blind ignoramus, one has to accept the dramatic coherence of stories, out of which the uninferably and contingently new is emerging, with the hope that it can, at least temporarily, be conceived of by later sequences. The advantage of this way of dealing with the

88 Koch, A.F., Versuch, 303 (transl. MM).
89 Koch, A.F., Versuch, 308 (transl. MM).

antinomy of negation becomes clear if one asks for alternatives. Koch mentions nine types[90] of response to the antinomy:

(1) Parmenides attempts to exclude the negation itself, with the consequence that there is one static, undifferentiated, and shapeless being itself.
(2) the attempt to isolate the antinomy by the construction of a non-classical, formal logic, that allows contradictions, but only in narrow limits, as Graham Priest has done.[91]
(3) attempts in the tradition of Hegel, to allow disarmed versions of the antinomy in the finite realm, whereas it is excluded in the eschatological, absolute concept.
(4) the attempt to show that the antinomy is not a formal contradiction, but an allowable opposition, as Uwe Petersen had done.[92]
(5) the normativist solution, which is to declare consistency a deontic ideal, including the idea of a moral self-constitution of reason (like the young Fichte in his 'Wissenschaftslehre'[93]).
(6) nihilist doubts about truth, be it in an engaged way, as in the case of Nietzsche, or be it in a disengaged way, as in the case of Rorty. One can call this position 'strong pseudism',[94] in order to distinguish it from a
(7) 'weak pseudism' like Heidegger's, who acknowledges that 'the logical light is only possible in front of the background of the logical dark, epistemic accessibility (*Unverborgenheit*) only in front of epistemic inaccessibility (*Verbergung*), truth only in being interweaved with error; and that it is principally impossible to fence off the dark inaccessibility, the error by formal means, by informal dialectics or any other way precisely',[95]
(8) the normative ignorance of naturalism, which claims that negation is possible without antinomy and with the implication that a complete representation of reality by the natural sciences is possible, and
(9) what Koch calls bad metaphysics, a position that, like naturalism, sees the antinomy of negation as excludable, but not that the natural sciences are sufficient in order to represent reality, so that other, speculative material (like David Lewis' modal realism) is needed.

It is not our interest to judge whether this typology is sensible or complete. It serves as an example of what I want to call decontingentization and the reduction of contingency.

Decontingentization is the attempt to exclude contingency. Naturalism and the bad metaphysics of Lewis are examples. But the first five types also suffer

90 Cf. KOCH, A.F., Versuch, 290–292.
91 Cf. PRIEST, G., Beyond, and in addition KOCH, A.F., Versuch, 283f.
92 Cf. PETERSEN, U., Dialetheism and Paradoxes; PETERSEN, U., logische Grundlagen der Dialektik, and to this KOCH, A.F., Versuch, 286–288.
93 Cf. KOCH, A.F., Versuch, 290f.
94 Cf. KOCH, A.F., Versuch, 291.
95 KOCH, A.F., Versuch, 291 (transl. MM).

from decontingentization. The only types excluded are (6) and (7). But in (6) the mesh is dissolved and dramatic coherence rejected, and it is not a viable position (except if one has the luck, or the misfortune, to become mentally deranged, like Nietzsche). Attempts to decontingentize can also be observed in our attitude towards causality. They appear wherever a universal causal nexus is assumed or any kind of universal causal determination. In principle, this simply means that naturalism is a large, vain attempt at decontingentization. But we have to look deeper, since this does not only concern how causality is applied, but also the conception of causality itself. We had seen that, alongside temporal succession and contiguity (as problematic as these concepts may be in themselves), Hume claimed the *necessity* of the conjunction between cause and effect is a decisive element of causality (ch. 17). And we also saw that this necessity cannot be conceived of empirically, as *a priori*, speculatively, or in any other way, but that it relies on belief. Now it is clear that this causality-constituting necessity can only be a regulative idea, because any language of necessity as more than a regulative idea is in vain. *And like necessity is a regulative idea, so is causality itself.* Claiming that causality is *a priori*, as Kant did, is not the sword that cuts the Gordian knot. It rather masks the facts. In this case, one is already consumed by decontingentization, if there were not the *Ding an sich* as vaccine. But vaccines are delusory and not free of incalculable side-effects. As such, Hume's analysis of causality is more honest than Kant's. Hume's analysis can lead – together with insight into the fundamental role of contingency – to causality as a regulative idea, which is neither an idealization nor an ideal, i.e. something that cannot be realized in an unending, infinitesimal process.

The reduction of contingency is an approach that does not deny contingency, but that wants to weaken it. Examples are contingency in Luhmann's system theory, or in theology, Jüngel's attempt to conceive of the cross, if it is an attempt to conceive of it.

Decontingentization and contingency-reduction must be understood as attitudes for constructing the cultivation of secondary narrations in a way that leads to a filtered perception, so that what is perceived is no longer wayfaring and the mesh, but transport in the net. These attempts to invert perception, understanding, and action do not lead to reality-resonating perception and action.

If one acknowledges dramatic coherence, and if one is able to resist the temptations of decontingentization and contingency-reduction, this does not mean that one has to abandon system-construction completely. One can use the design of transport in the net hypothetically and one can explore what it means counterfactually, which is the only justification for our modern efforts in the natural sciences. But systematization cannot be complete anyhow. They are uncloseable, like physics is uncloseable,[96] and it will consist of infinite revisions.

18.12 Contingency and the Logic of Surprise

In ch. 10 and 16 we dealt with the logic of surprise that is given by dramatic coherence. It would be possible to try to formalize this logic, in analogy to modal logic.[97] But we do well to also refrain from this temptation, since 'work on philosophical foundations flees any formalization. Wherever formalizations are successful, we already have one foot in mathematics'[98] – and that means in the inversion of wayfaring into transport.

What can be expected always includes what is prospectively surprising. If this were the only kind of surprise, we would be imprisoned in transport. It is the absolutely, retrospectively surprising that enables life in the dynamic mesh. Now it is clear, that the absolutely, retrospectively surprising is not grounded in our epistemic restrictions, or that it could be seen as a psychological phenomenon. It is inherent in the dynamic reality of becoming itself, and it is grounded in radical contingency, as it is enabled by the antinomy of negation. The absolutely retrospectively surprising is a concept of difference. It marks the difference between all regulative attempts to design systems, including attempts to invert the mesh into the net, and the attempts to ground modality in necessity on the one hand, and the contingent becoming of reality on the other hand. The concept of the difference of the absolutely retrospectively surprising is therefore the appearance of truth against its distortion; it is the only effective medicine the reality of becoming provides that protects of decontingentization. It has the nice attribute that it cannot be administered, because it does not have to be administered: it will simply emerge, here and there. As a concept of difference, the absolutely retrospectively surprising refers directly to contingency.

The relatively retrospectively surprising, however, does not refer to pure contingency in its nakedness, but to contingency as it appears in dramatic coherence. It signifies the fact that the secondary narrations, which form and shape perception, lead to an attitude of perceiving that includes, in its

96 Cf. KOCH, A.F., Wahrheit, Zeit und Freiheit, 95f.

97 I provide approaches to this in MÜHLING, M., Handbook of Christian Eschatology, 32–35.

98 KOCH, A.F., Versuch, 286 (transl. MM).

protentional aspect, always expecting to be surprised retrospectively. Whereas the absolutely retrospectively surprising is a concept of difference, the relatively retrospectively surprising is a concept of resonance, which expresses the *resonance* of the becoming of our perception with the difference of the absolutely retrospectively surprising.

CHAPTER 19

Narrations, Subjects and Inter-indexicality

19.1 Weak Inter-indexicality

The subject-object distinction is not basic. It is not presupposed in perceiving, but emerges out of perception. It is not presupposed in the use of signs, but it emerges out of the use of signs. In language, it is visible in the subject-predicate structure of propositional sentences – a fact, which was the occasion for an ontological hypostasizing of substance-accident metaphysics, as can be found *par excellence* in the Aristotelian scheme of the categories.[1]

Divide the pie anyway you like, the subject-object distinction appears or emerges, but it is not basic. Therefore, ontological theories of subjectivity, which conceive of the subject-object distinction in an asymmetrical manner, in which the object is constituted by the subject, are strictly excluded. The contrary approach of ontological naturalism, where the subject is dependent on objective content, must also be excluded. Moreover, any kind of emergentist theory, which may not proclaim a reduction of consciousness in a naturalistic way but nevertheless only conceives of consciousness as an irreducible system-attribute of a higher level,[2] is also inappropriate. Emergentism might have a relative value in describing how a particular, concrete form of self-consciousness might appear, but that is not a basic question. The question of how a particular kind of self-consciousness emerges is a question for anthropology, and, when applicable, also for other topics in the material explication of the Christian wayformational perspective. Therefore, that is a task for the second volume.

But if the subject-object distinction is a product of emergence and not basic, any ontological dualism between 'mind' and 'matter' is forbidden, too. In this line of thinking, there is no constitutive relationality between subject and object, but only a secondary, non-constitutive relationship that can be described in different ways (causality, agent-causality, efficient causality, teleological causality, etc.).

The subject-object-distinction emerges out of a reciprocal, constitutive relationality: whoever describes subjective things, also has to describe objective

1 This is already indirectly the case. See TRENDELENBURG, F.A., Historische Beiträge zur Philosophie, 11–34.
2 Cf. e.g. CLAYTON, P., Mind and Emergence.

 | DOI:10.30965/9783846765852_020

things. Our use in ordinary language, according to which 'objectivity' refers to what can be said inter-subjectively, does not resonate with reality, but it is once more an abstraction from reality. Nevertheless, this distinction can be a helpful tool, but it can also be a tool that distorts reality-resonance. And these two possibilities could be given basically, or it could change from case to case. This line of inquiry is, in the end, an ethical question, which means it is not a question at this stage of our inquiry.

The decisive question is: how does the emerging distinction between objective and subjective appear? The emerging objective appears as resistance in the face of choice. In this respect, it is not an interpretation. Only on the basis of this pre-theoretical objective, are theories of the objective possible. And this phenomenal objective is, according to Peter L. Berger, exactly what is perceived as not only distinct from oneself, but also as what restricts our possibilities of choice.[3] If it is not this, then no particular person or community has any choice. Those parts of secondary narrativity that force us to inscribe ourselves, without any possibility of changing it in experience, are called objective, independently of whether it refers to natural things like gravity or to social things like traditional institutions. At the same time, it is experienced as something that appears as certain. But if this is plausible, what, then, is the subject and what is the subjective? One possibility would be to see the subjective as the part of secondary narrations that are open to modifications by the subject. But then we still do not know what a subject is. Is the subject then on its way to disappearing? Simply to say that a subject is something that has the possibility of choice, or that a subject is something that is perceiving or experiencing, is insufficient, because this answer – which is a feature of all theories of subjectivity from Descartes onward – cannot satisfy the subject, since, as Marion has pointed out, it turns the subject into an object, it objectivizes the subject by conceiving of it as something that is certain, as something that is not a matter of choice.[4] If we want to know what a subject is, we have to take a longer way.

Preliminary we can assume:

1. The subject-object distinction is not to be understood as a separation, but as a reciprocal, constitutive relationship.
2. The subject-object distinction is not basic.
3. In fact, the subject-object distinction emerges out of perception. The objective is that part of secondary narrations that restricts possibilities of

3 Cf. BERGER, P.L., Heretical Imperative, 14.

4 Cf. MARION, J.-L., Erotic Phenomenon, 18f.

choice. The subject remains preliminarily opaque, so long as we do not objectivize it.

4. The reflexive use of signs seems to reassert the distinction.

The subject-object distinction is primarily not an ontic matter, but one of concepts and phenomena. Our task here is to determine the conceptual and phenomenal content of this distinction, which must not be turned into a separation. As an answer, I want to offer the following thesis:

(*1*) *The subject-object distinction consists not only in its participation in primary and secondary stories, but in a given participation in secondary stories, through which its own embeddedness in secondary and primary stories is perceived in an inter-indexical way.*

We can call this the thesis of weak inter-indexicality. Simply to participate in primary or secondary stories has nothing to do with the subject-object distinction, since abiota also participate in primary and secondary stories. We refer to abiota by secondary stories, we use abiotic things in our cultural activity, and we change them by our secondary stories, in a way they would have changed without these secondary stories. But, to participate as a life-form in secondary stories also does not change anything. Plants participate in secondary stories, too, and plants are changed by secondary stories. Without that fact, gardening would be impossible.

Therefore, the clue seems to be in participation in primary and secondary stories, in a way in which somehow the distinction between primary and secondary stories is known. This is, of course, shown when one emerges out of the mesh of stories like humans do, in a way that one is able to re-tell, to co-tell, and to counter-tell these stories by means of the whole richness of the iconic, indexical, and symbolic use of signs. But such an understanding of the subject-object distinction would be too broad. The decisive element is that the subject-object distinction appears in the moment when one refers indexically to something other in a story, in which one is interwoven. The subject-object distinction is based on indexical events, and subject and object are related equiprimordially to indexical events.

Peter F. Strawson has shown exactly this in his descriptive ontology, and he has used the term 'person' for entities that are able to do so. A person in this sense is an ontologically primitive concept, which does not consist of different parts.[5] The abstractions of consciousness and bodiliness can only be secondarily derived from the concept of person. Consequently, there are no

5 Cf. STRAWSON, P.F., Individuals, 101–116.

persons without bodiliness, and there are no persons without some kind of self-consciousness. Strawson's concept of the person has nothing to do with other concepts of the person, like the definitions of Boethius or Locke. The early Merleau-Ponty used a different term here, not person, but (living) body, which is a primitive concept in exactly the same way.[6] We do not have to decide here which term is preferrable. More than likely, we do not have to decide at all.

However, this raises an important question: why do we speak here of 'self-consciousness', 'mind', or the ability of perceiving affordances, etc., instead of the ability to index? The answer is a phenomenal one: No one can meaningfully doubt that one is a part of a story or a part of a course of events. No one can doubt that it is possible to refer to something other and that one is identified by others. Indexicality is therefore a relation, in which, first, reference is always given to something other, i.e. one is essentially related to something other – or, more abstractly, one is part of a series – and in which, second, one can refer to this position in the story due to one's living body in an indexical way, by using indexes like 'here', 'I', and by differential expressions like 'there', 'you', etc. Self-referential indexes and indexes of alterity reciprocally imply each other.

We can say that indexical reference, as the essential narrative ability, is and has to be anchored bodily: Secondary stories without primary stories is a meaningless concept, just as possibilities are meaningless without actualities, and as a mind is meaningless without a body, an I without a you and an it, etc. It is decisive that this anchorage is not, and cannot be secured, in a particular standpoint, but is dynamic, evolving on wayformational lines. It is, as we have already seen (ch. 14.6), the anchorage of a sea anchor.

Indexicality, therefore, not only implies bodiliness, but also the dynamic perspectivity of wayformational perspectives. Only if perspectivity is conceived as dynamically evolving from wayformational lines and not as a view from a particular standpoint, is indexicality possible. If there were standpoints, changing standpoints would be possible. I could change to your standpoint and you to mine, either in a real way, or by virtual identification, be it theoretically or reconstructively. In such a case, this would be theoretically true not only for you and me, but for all standpoints, which would also mean that the mesh of events would be reduced to a network. If one could exchange all possible standpoints, then it would be possible, at least for an infinite being, to describe this network completely. As finite becomings, we are unable to do so. But perhaps we are able to describe the network of transport by concepts. And that would be as good as really exchanging all standpoints. In both cases,

6 Cf. Merleau-Ponty, M., Phenomenology of Perception, 94, 102, 106.

the same thing would happen: indexicality vanishes – or would only apparently exist. However, this is not possible from a wayformational perspective. Indexicality and wayfaring in the mesh are related by reciprocal constitution.

To safeguard this, indexicality can only be inter-indexicality. The anchorage of indexicality in the living body must be conceived of in such a way that, on the one hand, the body is identifiable for others, only then is the irreducibility of wayformational perspectives given. On the other hand, this understanding of indexicality shows that it is not possible to imagine a world containing only one body. Multiple bodies have to be related to each other reciprocally through indexicals. One implication is then that both bodies are related to one another through reciprocal ontic-constitution – completely independent of the empirical shape of this or that constitutive relationship, i.e. independently of whether it is a social, biological, or neurological shape. In this way, not only is inter-indexicality safeguarded, but so is inter-bodiliness. A further implication is, then, that there cannot be only *one* secondary story, and not only *one* narrator of secondary stories can emerge out of primary narrativity (also: not only one perceiver). Schapp expresses this in the following way:

> Every I-entanglement contains every we-entanglement. The "I" and the "we" cannot be separated. For the third, for the observer, for the listener, a story also only emerges through a we-entanglement.[7]

It is not possible to deny the fact of indexicality and wayformational perspectives in a meaningful way. In principle, it only claims that I perceive myself as a living body in the midst of other living bodies. But now another problem appears: One might admit that indexicality and bodiliness imply each other and that there can be no subjectivity without indexicality and inter-bodiliness. One might admit that we cannot refer to objects without indexicality and subjectivity. One might admit that there are no objects without subjects. But can we also transform this thesis into a much stronger one? Can there be no primary stories without secondary stories? Can there be no things, without the fact that they are referred to indexically? Are there no things without being objects for subjects? Are things always phenomena? At first glance, it seems that only idealists could answer in the affirmative. We have no problem imagining a primary story – e.g. the growth and erosion of a mountain on another planet, consisting of a pure diamond that is shaped by a sand-storm – without there being someone who could refer to it indexically, without this primary story being perceived by anyone. We all are acquainted with such primary stories,

7 SCHAPP, W., In Geschichten verstrickt (1953), 178 (transl. MM).

which are not perceived by anyone, within our physical bodies: the processes of metabolism, digestion, brain-activity, developing illnesses without symptoms, etc. All of these processes are normally not perceived, but it makes a great difference in reality if and how they happen. These are examples of things that could be perceived without actually being perceived. These examples are primary stories that could be referred to indexically by secondary stories, but that normally do not actually happen: the functioning of digestion does not need us to be conscious of it. Once more, we have entered the field of modality. The assumption that what is necessary is not actually reference, but the possibility of reference, is not a feature of idealism, but of realism. Therefore, we must alter the question: can there be any primary stories without the possibility of secondary stories? Could there be things without the possibility of signifying them indexically? Could there be things without the possibility of their indexical signification? Could there be things without being possible objects for subjects? Are things always potential phenomena? These questions are not so easy to answer. Any answer presupposes an understanding of modality. The easiest way to do so would be to assume an understanding of modalities with the help of possible worlds. But we know that possible-world semantics are problematic (ch. 18). But we can use this idea preliminarily in order to design thought experiments. Then we have to admit that there is no problem in imagining such worlds. Stories without indexical reference, the B-series of time without the A-series, the emergence of a thing purely by chance that looks like an encyclopedia in a world without authors and readers – all that is imaginable, and we would call these possible worlds. All these would then be *Dinge an sich* in the sense that they would be principally unknowable and unsignifiable.[8]

In this case, indexicality, reference, and the subject-object distinction are purely contingent: they exist actually and contingently. Then the thesis means that there could be primary stories without secondary stories, and the fact that there are primary stories only in relation to the secondary stories that refer to them is a contingent one. Many people might be satisfied with such an assumption and I do not want to make a case against them.

19.2 Strong Inter-indexicality

It is possible to proceed a step further and to claim the thesis of strong inter-indexicality. The claim is there cannot be primary stories without a contingent relationship to secondary stories. In other words:

8 Cf. Koch, A.F., Wahrheit, Zeit und Freiheit, 18f.

Without contingent, inter-indexical reference by secondary stories, primary stories are impossible.

This is equivalent to:

It is necessary that primary stories are contingently related to secondary stories in an inter-indexical way.

There are a lot of other formulations of the same thesis: without a living body, no physical body, without subjectivity, no things, etc. In reference to Rosenberg,[9] Koch called this thesis the 'subjectivity thesis'.[10] However, we prefer 'inter-indexicality' instead of 'subjectivity', since that way one knows in which sense 'subjectivity' is being used: not with all the richness that is associated with human subjectivity, but only in the sense of indexical reference. Apart from this terminological alteration, we will follow Koch's argument and apply it to some different contexts.

The first premise assumes the compatibility of two concepts of identity: numeric identity and the identity of indiscernibles. Two events are identical, then, if they have the same predicates. In an ideal case, this identity of indiscernibles coincides with numerical identity. However, what is valid in an ideal case is not necessarily valid in reality. In quantum theory, we have to focus on non-individuated entities or violate the principle of the identity of indiscernibles.[11] But it is not necessary to list empirical results, we can imagine possible-world thought experiments, including a symmetry of their relations, and therefore a violation of the identity of indiscernibles. Black's two-spheres-world is a simple variation of this thought experiment,[12] Hawking's experiments with the reversion of the arrow of time after a point of maximal contraction of the world is another one.[13] We face here the basic problem of how unity and difference ought to be related, a problem that was first treated comprehensively in the framework of the doctrine of the Trinity.

Classically, in God there are only essential properties that must be predicated of God and which are identical, which means that all possible monadic predicates are identical with 'God'. At the same time, the 'Father' (a) is completely 'God', the 'Son' (b) is

9 Cf. ROSENBERG, J.F., On a Certain Antinomy.

10 Cf. KOCH, A.F., Versuch, 314f.

11 Cf. to this EINSTEIN, A./PODOLSKY, B./ROSEN, N., EPR; BOHR, N., Reaktion auf EPR; BELL, J.S., On the EPR Paradox.

12 Cf. BLACK, M., Identity of Indiscernibles.

13 Cf. HAWKING, S.W., Brief History of Time, 147–156.

completely 'God', and the 'Spirit' (c) is completely 'God'. Here, 'God' is used predicatively. Such a predicative usage implies all predicates referring to God are not only identical with one another and with 'God', but they also have to be predicated of the hypostases of 'Father', 'Son', and 'Spirit'. But at the same time, Father, Son, and Spirit are not identical, but numerically distinct, which is required by the rejection of modalism.[14] This move is only possible if one introduces a principle of haecceity – which is only an apparent solution[15] – or if one introduces dyadic relations among Father, Son, and Spirit (R(x,y)). This dyadic relation is formally asymmetric, irreflexive, and transitive, i.e. it is a relation of order. Under the presupposition that there are exactly three hypostases, these are now unequivocally individuated: $R(a,b) \wedge R(b,c) \wedge R(a,c)$. There is only one person that is exclusively the first *relatum* of the relation, there is exclusively one person that is only the second *relatum* of that relation, and finally there is exclusively one person that is the first-*relatum* and the second-*relatum* of that relation.[16] Given that the principle of indiscernibles refers only to monadic predicates, and given that in God there are no more than three persons, this solution is valid. This solution means that we can hold to the principle of the identity of indiscernibles, while at the same time we can speak of a numerical difference between the divine persons. The principle of differentiation is here a relational one; it is not a hidden attribute in the sense of haecceity; it is simply the relation among the persons.

Let us now imagine a world, in which all *relata* have the same monadic predicates and which are related by a relation of order. So far, this is the case for the classical doctrine of the Trinity. However, let us additionally imagine that there are infinite *relata* instead of only three. In this case, the relation of order is no longer any help. It enables a storied character for this series of *relata*, but we cannot distinguish the events anymore, since now any single *relatum* appears as first-*relatum* as well as second-*relatum*. Imagine looking at such a series from no perspective at all (or from God's perspective), as it would be possible to look at the entire B-series of time simultaneously. In this case, it would also not be possible to refer to single events in this series, since the events are

14 The heresy of modalism, supposably going back to Sabellius at the end of the second century, assumes that the divine persons are numerically identical and they are just different roles, masks, aspects, sequences, intentional differences etc. of one identity. On this, see the remarks in Vol. II.

15 The introduction of a *haecceitas*, as in the case of Duns Scotus, is in fact only an apparent solution, because it not only requires thinking of an individual universal, but also shifts the problem. In the case of the Trinitarian persons, its application is impossible, because it is the reverse of modalism and strains the unity of the Trinity. Nevertheless there are, of course, religious philosophers who argue for its application in Trinitarian doctrine, cf. SWINBURNE, R., Christian God, 33–50. 163–169.

16 You can find the application of the personal processions, including the filioque, in terms of an innertrinitarian, individuating relation of order in an exemplarily fashion in RICHARD VON ST.VICTOR, De Trinitate, 5. 9–13 (324–336). Cf. MÜHLING, M., Gott ist Liebe, 164f.

indistinguishable, despite being bound in a relation of order. We are not able to tell whether we see one event, or two, or 389,790 events. Can we solve this problem? We can if we introduce the individual property of haecceity. In this case, the relation of order would be redundant. However, at the same time the predicate of haecceity is empirically unknowable, i.e. hidden. Because of this, the problem is still unsolved. We could also claim, according to the principle of the identity of indiscernibles, that all predicates that are neither distinct in respect of their monadic nor of relational attributes, can be reduced to a single one. Then we get exactly three relata under the condition that the series is infinite: One *relatum* that is only first-*relatum*, one *relatum* that is first-*relatum* and second-*relatum*, and one *relatum* that is only second-*relatum*. In the latter case, we have reduced the order to the well-known order of the doctrine of the Trinity. In fact, medieval theologians used this argument to show that more than three divine persons are impossible.[17] However, this solution does not take the possibility of infinity seriously. If we want to treat infinity as irreducible, we can only maintain the principles of the identity of indiscernibles and numerical distinctions if we could count the *relata* in the series. Counting, however, presupposes starting with one determined event. And therefore, we would have to refer to exactly one specified event in the series. The location of this event in the series is not important. We could start counting arbitrarily with a single event, as long as it is safeguarded as a determined one. But this is exactly what is not given in this scenario.

The scenario changes completely, however, if we allow indexical references to an event. To do so, presupposes that the one referring is a *relatum* or an event in the series itself. The whole series is then given and, relative to the *relatum* that consists in myself, all other *relata* are individuated due to the relation of order. This order of relations is true also in those cases where the one who refers, the indexical anchor, cannot see the complete series and refer to every single event. Nevertheless, there remains one complication: If there were only one indexical anchor overlooking the whole series, the series would be reduced to a network. Indexicality would be turned into the haecceity of things or events. Such a consequence can only be prevented if the indexical anchor itself can be referred to by other indexical anchors with other wayformational perspectives. Even in its strong variation, indexicality has to be inter-indexicality. The strong version of the thesis, then, is the following one:

(2) *Primary-narrative, space-time-founding events are only possible, if within this course of events there appears at least two anchors of inter-indexicality (persons,*

17 Cf. RICHARD VON ST.VICTOR, De Trinitate, 5,3 (304–306); 5,15 (342).

living bodies, 'I', 'you') in any one sequence, who are able to refer indexically to one another and to other events, and thereby establish secondary stories.

In principle, this modifies Koch's thesis of subjectivity.[18] But some of the modifications are important. Instead of the misleading term 'subjectivity'[19] the term indexicality appears. Furthermore, indexicality is necessarily modified to inter-indexicality. And the thesis is expressed with the help of our narrative ontology.

Koch presents two corollaries to this thesis, an epistemological and an ontological one:

> *Corollary (1a), thesis of personality with an epistemological accentuation.* Subjectivity knows itself *a priori* as bodily and temporal being, i.e. as a person. [...]
>
> *Corollary (1b), thesis of personality with an ontological accentuation*: Subjectivity is necessarily embodied in person amid potentially many persons. [...]
>
> *Corollary (2a), thesis of perspectivity with an epistemological accentuation*: Entities are in the final analysis only knowable perspectivally, and different perspectives cannot be transformed into each other, and they cannot be combined with or outperformed by a general view. A complete description of what is real is therefore impossible, not only because it is infinite, but also because it is incoherent. [...]
>
> *Corollary (2b), thesis of perspectivity with an ontological accentuation*: Entities in themselves are phenomena in the following sense: they are essentially related to spatially and temporally embodied subjectivity, without being reducible to subjective states (their relatedness to subjects belongs to their objective being in itself).[20]

Koch's thesis of personality in its epistemological accentuation is contained in our thesis of weak inter-indexicality. The thesis of weak inter-indexicality implies Koch's corollary (1a). The same is true for Koch's thesis of personality in its ontological accentuation. Here, inter-indexicality is named explicitly. And the

---

18 KOCH, A.F., Versuch, 330: 'A material space-time system can only exist, if at any time and any place at least one spatiotemporal subject (an I) exists that can refer by cognition and perception to individuals,' (Transl. MM), originally: „Ein materielles Raum-Zeit-System ist nur möglich, wenn irgendwo und irgendwann in ihm mindestens ein raumzeitliches Subjekt („je ich") existiert, das sich denkend und wahrnehmend auf Einzeldinge bezieht."

19 Koch has to then in KOCH, A.F., Versuch, 330, also free the concept of subjectivity from false connotations, like, e.g., the prospect that subjectivity is an immaterial substance. So this in fact amounts to the concept of anchoring indexicaltity.

20 KOCH, A.F., Versuch, 331f (transl. MM).

same is also true for Koch's thesis of perspectivity in its epistemological accentuation. It safeguards reality as a mesh of wayfaring and not a network of transport, or, in other words, that perspectives are no exchangeable standpoints, but wayformational perspectives. The first three corollaries are valid if one accepts only weak inter-indexicality, which is not the case with the fourth corollary, Koch's thesis of perspectivity with an ontological accentuation. It is implied by strong inter-indexicality, but it also implies strong inter-indexicality. Moreover, it safeguards (presupposing that the strong inter-indexicality is accepted) the essential phenomenality of things – i.e. that events of primary narrativity are essentially related to secondary narrativity – but that they cannot be resolved into phenomena or secondary narrativity.

It is worth mentioning that the anchored elements that are the basis for indexicality and reference are in themselves arbitrary and subject to change. It is a contingent anchorage, which we have called 'drift anchors'. Here, contingency has to do with the relation and the character of the *relata* for one another: beyond the capacity for indexicality, what must be predicated of these *relata* is contingent, as is what *relata* have to be identified with anchors. We have seen that it is a condition of the possibility of the existence of the whole series that there are necessarily at least two such *relata* able to make indexical reference. In the language of formal modal logic, this would be a proposition of the type NCp, in which the modal-operators are irreducible, i.e. an exclusion of systems like S_5. (Inter)indexicality, and therefore also personality and subjectivity, are *necessarily contingent*. They are contingent, because they are also interwoven in a wayformational way, with the implication that they could always be in other ways than they are. But they are also necessary, because without the (at least twofold) appearance of indexical sea anchors, the whole series would not exist.

If this thought experiment is valid, then it is clear that without anchors of indexicality (without subjectivity), purely 'objective' courses of events are self-contradictory, i.e. (necessarily) unable to exist. It is clear, too, that there can be nothing that could oversee the whole course of events independently of its specific wayformational perspective.

It depends on two premises, whether one must accept the validity of this thought experiment: First, one has to accept the principle of the identity of indiscernibles for monadic predicates and also accept the possibility of numerical difference. Second, one must acknowledge that this scenario relies on non-well-founded sets. The first condition is plausible. We have also noted empirical proofs, like the fact that *quanta* are not individuated. The second condition is more problematic. We can only assume it hypothetically, and there is no empirical test at all. In the terminology of Kripke, one can say that it is, like

Goldbach's conjecture,[21] a necessary, but only contingently knowable truth *a posteriori*.

We will learn later that the question of whether one accepts strong inter-indexicality is of great significance for both the philosophy of religion (ch. 21) and theology (vol. 2).

In what follows, we will explore the thesis of inter-indexicality in respect of its phenomenality, and we will protect it against an alternative, subjectivist explanation.

19.3 The Narrative Basis of Intersubjectivity and the Question of Panpsychism

One must beware of treating the thesis of inter-indexicality as a philosophical variant of the anthropic principle. It would only be a variant, if the anthropic principle has nothing to do with the human species (and that may be its best interpretation). We have not been exploring anthropology! In our actual world, what the thesis of inter-indexicality describes is given, i.e. at least the thesis of weak inter-indexicality is valid. Although, it is not the existence of humans that makes it true. The results of the biosemiotics to which we referred to in ch. 12 show that the existence of nonhuman primates would also validate the weak thesis of inter-indexicality. And who wants to decide which other vertebrates could fulfill it? But if one is ready to extend the capacity for indexicality to other vertebrates, one may ask why we should stop here. Both variations of the thesis of indexicality would not be altered if one extended it in a maximal way. Such a maximal extension is what is traditionally called the question of panpsychism.[22] And there are people who promote panpsychism in both theological and philosophical ways.

Though panpsychism was for a long time unacceptable to naturalist philosophers, a few comments by David Chalmers, in which he does not subscribe to but sympathizes with the view, shows that the question also seems to be worthwhile for naturalists:

21 Goldbach's conjecture is that every natural number greater than 2 can be expressed as the sum of 3 prime numbers. It is, however, thus far a candidate for a necessary, but only contingent visible truth, because so far there is neither evidence for it nor a counterexample. The name refers to the description of a similar issue in the correspondence of the mathematician Christian Goldbach in 1742. Cf. to this EVERS, D., Gott und mögliche Welten, 205, note 225.

22 A short overview over panpsychistic positions is given by SEAGER, W./ALLEN-HERMANSON, S., Art. Panpsychism.

> If there is experience associated with thermostats, there is probably experience *everywhere*: wherever there is a causal interaction, there is information, and wherever there is information, there is experience. One can find information states in a rock [...] or even in the different states of an electron. [...] The view that there is experience wherever there is causal interaction is counterintuitive. But it is a view that can grow surprisingly satisfying with reflection, making consciousness better integrated into the natural order. [...] If the view is correct, consciousness does not come in sudden jagged spikes [...] Rather, it is a more uniform property of the universe, with very simple systems having very simple phenomenology, and complex systems having complex phenomenology. [...] An interesting question is whether *active* causation is required for experience. [...] One possibility [...] is that simple systems do not have phenomenal properties, but have *protophenomenal* properties. [...] If so, then thermostats might have [...] a related sort of property that we do not fully understand (a sort of protoexperience, perhaps). [...] Perhaps the central reason why [panpsychism] is misleading [...] is that it suggests a view in which the experiences in simple systems [...] are fundamental, and in which complex experiences are somehow the sum of such simpler experiences. While this is one way things could go, there is no reason that things have to go this way: complex experiences may be more autonomous than this suggests. [...] With these caveats noted, it is probably fair to say that the view is a variety of panpsychism. I should note, however, that panpsychism is not at the metaphysical foundation of my view [...]. Personally, I am much more confident of naturalistic dualism than I am of panpsychism. [...] But I hope to have said enough to show that we ought to take the possibility of some sort of panpsychism seriously.[23]

For our purposes, only one thing is important here, which is that Chalmers does not reject panpsychism for argumentative reasons. More exactly, he draws a conclusion by analogy. From human self-consciousness (which he ignorantly calls 'phenomenology'), he draws an analogy to data-processing systems like thermostats, and from these to all kind of matter. The basis for this argument is that the attribution of consciousness to others is based on an (analogically reasonable) ascription. This line of argument is far from new. For example, it also appears in the context of a vote for panpsychism from Karl Heim:

> From all this we can see that it is by no means an objective, scientific assertion, but an entirely subjective, human point of view, when we assume that the inner life has reached its maximum only in man [...] Looking at it objectively, it is, to say the least, more probable that all natural structures alike possess a psychical substratum, but that other beings, which differ from us outwardly, are also inwardly otherwise constituted than ourselves, and that consequently the inner life of, say, a plant, is so extremely different from our own soul-life that out of our limited human experience we can form no conception of it whatever. [...] Does it then extend only as far as the simplest organisms, for example the single-cell

23 CHALMERS, D.J., Conscious Mind, Pos. 6361 – Pos. 6402.

> plant? Or must we reckon with the possibility that behind inorganic nature too there is something which in some way resembles our own soul life? [...] But once we have understood how biased and dubious this anthropocentric reasoning is, we shall see that one would be jumping to a quite unwarranted conclusion if one were to assume that the wonderful structures of the inorganic world possess only an objective façade, but no psychical substratum.[24] [...] [This] brings us quite automatically to the question of whether it is really conceivable that the two-sidedness of reality, the correspondence of an invisible 'inner picture' with the visible 'outer picture,' suddenly ceases when we reach the limits of the organic world.[25]

Whether one can support panpsychism with Heim's and Chalmers' arguments is not important, but what is important is the fact that arguments like these reveal a lot about how subjectivity, self-consciousness, the consciousness of others, and indexicality are conceived of and related.

Heim does not use the terms subjectivity or the capacity for indexicality, but he uses terms like 'soul life', 'inner side' or 'inner picture', etc. In volume 2, in our reflections on anthropology, we will learn why this division between 'inner' and 'outer' is highly problematic. At this point, however, only the narrative of the argument is of interest.

Heim presupposes that the inference of any other subjectivity apart of my own is always a conclusion by analogy. Here he meets Chalmers' argument and the arguments of the so-called theories of a 'Theory of Mind' (ToM). The latter claim that we need higher cognitive capabilities in order to understand others, so that every child beyond an age of 4 has to develop a theory about how others are like oneself – including a specific 'inner side' hidden for others – or that man has to be able to simulate the 'mind' of the other in one's own.[26] Frequently, interpretations of so called false-belief experiments are abused to support this theory.[27] The theories of ToM are therefore nothing but a more elaborated variation of Heim's conclusion by analogy. Just as Heim assumes different levels of a soul's life, the theories of ToM also try to introduce grades of soul-life by the introduction of higher order intentionality.

> This introduction of graded intentionality is presupposed in, for example, Robin Dunbar's 'social brain hypothesis', sometimes more appropriately called the 'Machiavellian intelligence hypothesis:'[28] 'Computers can be said to know things because their memories contain information; however, it seems unlikely that they know

24 HEIM, K., Christian Faith and Natural Science, 90f.

25 HEIM, K., Christian Faith and Natural Science, 95.

26 Cf. GALLAGHER, S./ZAHAVI, D., Phenomenological Mind, 182.

27 Cf. GALLAGHER, S./ZAHAVI, D., Phenomenological Mind, 193f.

28 Cf. DUNBAR, R.I.M., The Social Brain Hypothesis, esp. 178.

> that they know these things [...] computers are zero-order intensional machines. [...] Most vertebrates are probably capable of reflecting on their states of mind in some crude sense: they know that they know. Organisms of this kind are first-order intensional. By extension, second-order intensional organisms know that someone else knows something, and third-order intentional organisms know that someone else knows, that someone else knows something. [...] In practice, humans rarely engage in more than fourth-order intentionality in everyday life and probably face an upper limit at sixth order ('Peter knows that Jane believes that Mark thinks that Paula wants Jake to suppose that Amelia intends to do something').'[29] Here, the capacity for 'sociality' is measured according to the canon of a graded intentionality that is also presupposed for the building of coalitions and for manipulating the thinking of others. Therefore, the name 'Machiavellian intelligence hypothesis' is explained: The 'social brain hypothesis' does not deal with the engagement in sociality, but with the manipulation of sociality for one's own purposes. In this scheme, inter-indexicality would perhaps be located on the second level. The consequence would be that organisms of lower intentionality would not be able to be subjective in the required sense. However, the theory of graded intentionality is highly questionable. What should first level intentionality be? Is it really possible to know something without knowing, feeling or recognizing that one knows something? And is it possible to know one's own states without knowing that others have intensional states?

In whatever way one might imagine different grades of subjectivity, the whole conclusion by analogy on which the arguments by Heim, Chalmers, and the different theories of ToM are founded, is *invalid*. It must presuppose what it wants to show, as Scheler knew long before anyone designed theories of mind. First, it is presupposed that the knowledge of one's own subjectivity is given directly without any difficulty. Second, it is often presupposed that we only have an inferential access to the subjectivity of others, i.e. that the subjectivity of others is not a possible object of perception, but only an assumption in analogy to our own experience. Accordingly, I must interpret the visible movements of the others as representations of something invisible, of the state of mind of the other. But this is only possible if I already know that there is this relation between the other mind and the other body. I already have to know that the other is a person, and not a puppet or robot:

> But it should not be forgotten that the *material* premises for these conclusions are based upon my elementary perceptions of the person concerned or the other people; they therefore *pre-suppose* these immediate perceptions.[30]

29 DUNBAR, R.I.M., The Social Brain Hypothesis, 188. Dunbar here writes 'intentional' with 's' as 'intensional.'

30 SCHELER, M., The Nature of Sympathy, 260.

Actually, we do not know that the other is a person by analogical inference, but we *perceive* her or him *directly* as person:

> Our immediate perceptions of our fellow-men do not relate to their bodies, [...] nor yet to their 'selves' or 'souls.' What we perceive are *integral wholes*, whose intuitive content is not immediately resolved in terms of external or internal perception.[31]
>
> For we certainly believe ourselves to be directly acquainted with another person's joy in his laughter, with his sorrow and pain in his tears, with his shame in his blushing, with his entreaty in his outstretched hands, with his love in his look of affection, with his rage in the gnashing of his teeth, with his threats in the clenching of his fist, and with the tenor of his thoughts in the sound of his words. If anyone tells me that this is not 'perception,' for it cannot be so, in view of the fact that a perception is simply a 'complex of physical sensations,' and that there is certainly no sensation of another person's mind nor any stimulus from such a source, I would beg him to turn aside from such questionable theories and address himself to the phenomenological facts.[32]

Affective states and events, and other states and events of the 'mind' are actually directly perceived, because they rely on a *Ausdruckseinheit*[33] (expressive unity):

> I conceive by the *Ausdruckseinheit* of his 'look,' long before I recognized the color or size of his eyes, whether he has a friendly or hostile attitude towards me.[34]

Only in a second step, after one has perceived an expressive unity, is one able to separate cognitively between 'inner' and 'outer.'

Scheler's phenomenological considerations are supported by the empirical research on the development of infants. On the level of primary intersubjectivity, we perceive within the gestures, mimicry, and movements of the other her or his feelings, and we react immediately with our own gestures, mimicry, and movements. Perceiving the other is always enactive: it exists only in a functional circuit of perception and reaction, and perception is bound to the resonance of joint movement.[35]

---

31 SCHELER, M., The Nature of Sympathy, 261.

32 SCHELER, M., The Nature of Sympathy, 260.

33 Cf. SCHELER, M., Wesen und Formen der Sympathie, 213. 238. 246.

34 SCHELER, M., Wesen und Formen der Sympathie, 238 (transl. MM). SCHELER, M., The Nature of Sympathy, 244 translates incorrectly 'I can tell from the expressive "look" of a person whether he is well or ill disposed towards me, long before I can tell what colour or size his eyes may be'.

35 Cf. GALLAGHER, S./ZAHAVI, D., Phenomenological Mind, 209.

From birth, children are able to perceive facial expressions and to imitate them, but only in situations of concrete, bodily interaction. From 2 months, the look follows the look of the other person and the child is able to see, what the other sees. From 6 months on, grabbing is aim-directed. And from 10–11 months, the child possesses a non-cognitive understanding of the intentions and attitudes of other persons. It is a bodily intentionality that is developed by joint, situative interaction. It appears in childhood and persists throughout one's whole lifetime.[36]

Secondary intersubjectivity follows primary intersubjectivity. Now the child is able to conceive of the intersubjective acts of perception as related to pragmatic contexts.

In an age of 9–14 months, the capacity for joint attention appears.[37] Infants from 12 months on use their fingers for deictic acts not only in an imperative sense (in order to get something), or with declarative meaning (in order to share attention), but also in order to further the interests of others without any interest of their own. One could call these informative or supportive signs.[38] It presupposes that children from 12 months onward are able to perceive the other as an intentional subject, and that the other acts in the framework of narrative sequences in which the infant itself is not directly involved.

From an age of 2 years, children are able to understand whole stories and they develop narrative competencies. They conceive themselves as inscribed into stories. Now the development of *narrative intersubjectivity* starts. Out of observations like these, Daniel Hutto developed the *Narrative Practice Hypothesis*:

> The Narrative Practice Hypothesis (NPH) claims that children normally achieve understanding by engaging in story-telling practices, with the support of others. The stories about those who act for reasons – i.e. fold psychological narratives – are the foci of this practice. Stories of this special kind provide the crucial training set needed for understanding reasons.[39]

The encounter with the other happens only in specific narrative contexts including a pre-story and a post-story, i.e. in the framework of a story in which the other and I play specific roles. Narrative competence does not mean explicitly telling stories, but the ability to perceive the other in a situative context and to conceive this situative context as a sequence of a story.[40] An action is only

36 Cf. GALLAGHER, S./ZAHAVI, D., Phenomenological Mind, 208–210.

37 Cf. GALLAGHER, S./ZAHAVI, D., Phenomenological Mind, 210f.

38 Cf. LISZKOWSKI, U./CARPENTER, M./STRIANO, T./TOMASELLO, M., 12- and 18-Month-Olds Point to Provide Information for Others.

39 HUTTO, D.D., Folk Psychological Narratives, 53.

40 Cf. GALLAGHER, S./ZAHAVI, D., Phenomenological Mind, 216.

conceivable as an action and conceivable at all, if it is perceived or performed as a part of a story, as MacIntyre observed.[41] In an equiprimordial way, a complete understanding of the other and a narrative understanding of oneself is formed. The appearance of the capacity to conceive of the stories of others as the story of one's self is also important.[42]

The formation of narrative intersubjectivity is not something that is added to primary and secondary intersubjectivity. Primary and secondary intersubjectivity are also essentially narratively constituted, insofar as there is always an enactive combination of perceiving and one's own movement, and insofar as we can also find an equiprimordiality of perceiving the other's and one's own subjectivity. Empirical findings therefore support the thesis that one's own subjectivity and an other's subjectivity is constituted in a reciprocal way, since both emerge out of narrative contexts.

For us it is important that from the first level of primary intersubjectivity onward, subjectivity is developed as inter-indexicality. I cannot phenomenally refer to something other without perceiving myself as addressed by the other. To perceive oneself as being addressed by an other is equiprimordial with the ability to refer to an other. In a phenomenal and empirical way, the passive experience of being addressed is prior to active indexing. One's own ability to perform indexical acts is always a reaction to the pathos of the given perception of oneself as addressed in an indexical way by others. Therefore, indexicality is always inter-indexicality.

These empirical findings not only support our thesis of inter-indexicality, they add an important aspect: the development of inter-indexicality (and of personality and intersubjectivity) is dependent on narrations and is secondary to narrations.

At the same time, these empirical findings shed a new light on the question of panpsychism, which we talked about at the beginning of this subchapter. Chalmers and Heim sympathize with panpsychism because they accept the dualistic conclusions of analogy from the experience of one's own subjectivity to the inference of foreign subjectivity. But this is simply wrong: there is no previous experience of one's own subjectivity. The experience of one's own subjectivity and the experience of another subjectivity, of my-ness (*Jemeinigkeit*) and your-ness (*Jedeinigkeit*), are nothing but two sides of the same coin or the same wayformational perspective. Consequentially, the term 'intersubjectivity' is indeed misleading, since it could suggest that one must first of speak of

41 Cf. GALLAGHER, S./ZAHAVI, D., Phenomenological Mind, 216.

42 Cf. NELSON, K., Narrative and the Emergence of a Consciousness of Self, esp. 31, and GALLAGHER, S./ZAHAVI, D., Phenomenological Mind, 217.

subjectivity before one is able to speak of an 'inter', a 'between' of previously given subjects. Actually, the reverse is true. Therefore, it would be more appropriate to cease the use of the term intersubjectivity and to prefer other terms (personality, inter-indexicality, etc.), because they better fit the state of affairs. What do our findings mean for panpsychism? On the one hand, the case for panpsychism is supported, on the other, it is weakened. The living, other person is equiprimordially knowable with our own person, but not objective, unanimated things in the world:

> Matters will be altered, however, in dealing with the question of our knowledge of other human (or subhuman) subjects at the level of *vital consciousness*. Here too the question is: Does this knowledge precede, accompany or follow the knowledge of Nature? [...] Our answer will be that our primary knowledge of Nature is itself a knowledge of the *expressive aspect* of living organisms; mental phenomena therefore (which are invariably presented only within a structural context), are always given, in the first instance, in unities of expression. Again, does such knowledge precede, accompany or follow a knowledge of the (inanimate) physical world? Our answer will be that it precedes it. Thus, the primitive, like the child, has no general acquaintance with 'deadness' in things: all his experience is presented as *one* vast field of expression, in which particular expressive unities stand our against the background.[43]

It seems the above quotation supports panpsychism, but there are also reasons to doubt it, since there are no phenomenal, secondary-narrative contexts in which we are embedded together with quanta, atoms, and bacteria, so no phenomenal reference is possible. Macroscopic entities like plants and other animals surely appear in secondary-narrative contexts like ourselves. But we interact with these entities in different way than we interact with persons; in such a way that no intersubjective secondary narration that lasts longer than a short sequence appears. For short sequences, this is possible: I might, while riding my bicycle, perceive the contrary wind as hostile and literally anathematize it. But I am forced to embed this sequential perception into a larger narrative, and this leads me to recognize this original impression as misleading.

We have to reject the opinion that the acknowledgment of other minds relies on an argument by analogy. And therefore, evidence for panpsychism vanishes, but does not mean panpsychism is impossible. Indeed, it might be a viable, theoretical alternative to emergentism. But no argument by analogy gives evidence in its support, and if one wants to hold to a kind of panpsychism, one needs to revise it: subjectivity is not an 'inner side,' but the in-between of persons, and therefore also an 'outer side.' Persons are always

43 SCHELER, M., The Nature of Sympathy, 217f.

persons in relationships, and as such their 'mind' is always 'extended', i.e. the mind is a bodily phenomenon. It is meaningless to speak of the inner side of a monad without windows. The speech of an 'inner side' (in contrast to an 'outer side') – and therefore also the speech of subjectivity (in contrast to 'objectivity') is, however, meaningful as far as it goes, as disclosure never appears without hiddenness, and *vice versa*. And this is exactly the point of Koch's claim that things are always phenomena, if they are to be entities at all, but that they cannot be reduced to their phenomenality. Koch expresses this, in reference to the Kantian (non-univocal) talk of a *Ding an sich*, when he speaks of *Dinge an ihnen selbst*. And that has to be true for all kinds of becomings: there are no becomings that are not phenomenal. But there are also no becomings that could be reduced to what is shown to us phenomenally. If talk of an 'inner side' of things means only the fact of their non-reducibility to phenomena (the 'outer side'), and if one wants to call this 'panpsychism', then panpsychism is unavoidable. But this would be a strange kind of panpsychism, since it would not *per se* imply inter-indexicality or intersubjectivity.

19.4 Preview of Narrative Identity

Narrative intersubjectivity belongs to the primary narrativity of the narrantologic. From this, i.e. from the fact that we are able to move guided by rules in a narrative course of events, one cannot simply deduce that we experience our identity in a narrative way on the level of secondary narrativity, too. The logic of identity does not necessarily have to follow the logic of individuation. Whereas individuation is essentially narratively constituted, there is no need for this to also be true for identity. And indeed, objections against the thesis that the experience of identity is a narrative one are easy to find.

Galen Strawson considers MacIntyre's claim that the unity of human identity is a 'unity of a narrative quest,'[44] together with the identity-thesis of Charles Taylor and Paul Ricœur, as well as Maya Schechtmann's thesis, which is that human personhood belongs to an explicit narrative of one's self,[45] as normative-ethical hypotheses about narrative identity that must be rejected.[46] On the one hand, the formation of a personal narrative assumes higher cognitive abilities. Therefore, according to Strawson, like traditional definitions of the human as, e.g., *animal rationale*, the thesis of narrative identity excludes

44 MacIntyre, A., After Virtue, 203.

45 Cf. Schechtman, M., Constitution of Selves, 93. 119.

46 Cf. Strawson, G., Against Narrativity.

a lot of the members of the human species. The thesis of normative, narrative identity

> hinder human self-understanding, close down important avenues of thought, impoverish our grasp of ethical possibilities, needlessly and wrongly distress those who do not fit their model, and are potentially destructive in psychotherapeutic contexts.[47]

On the other hand, Galen Strawson rejects the ethical thesis of narrative identity in a phenomenological respect. He suggests two kinds of self-experience, a diachronic one, in which I assume that I have not only a past but also a future, and an episodic one, in which I conceive myself as an inner self that is embedded in episodic courses of events, and without which there is no narrative connection of the episodes. Both kinds cannot be called 'narrative', since Strawson claims that it would belong to narrativity if one tries to achieve a coherent unity teleologically through a 'form-finding tendency.'[48] John Lippitt and Bernard Williams join Galen Strawson in his attempt to refute normative identity by stressing that the narrative approach would replicate the contradictions of the idealistic thesis of a self-constitution of the 'I' in other terminology – narrations presuppose a narrator, and therefore his or her identity, which cannot then be constituted in a narrative way.[49]

John Davenport tried to defend the thesis of a narrative-constituted understanding of the self that includes the past, present, and future (including death), as the core of human identity, by acknowledging that such an identity is an artifact that presupposes the primary unity of the person, but also by stressing that this primary unity is narratively constituted. Davenport distinguishes a secondary level of narratives from a prior, primary level of 'narravives', lived narrativity, that cannot be completely grasped as unity by the human practice of narration on the second level.[50] The narravives, therefore, are the core of a kind of narrative realism.

Friederike Nüssel analyzed and criticized the whole discussion, including Galen Strawson and Davenport.[51] She holds that the thesis of a primary-narrative identity, which is the basis of secondary identity, can only be expressed and proved by means of secondary narrativity. Therefore, it is not necessary to assume this primary level. Indeed, this objection is true in regard

---

47 STRAWSON, G., Against Narrativity, 429.
48 STRAWSON, G., Against Narrativity, 441.
49 Cf. WILLIAMS, B., Life as Narrative, and LIPPITT, J., Getting the Story Straight.
50 Cf. DAVENPORT, J.J., Narrative Identity, Autonomy and Mortality, 2.
51 Cf. NÜSSEL, F., Narrative Identität?, particularly 5.

of Davenport's distinction, but it cannot be used against our own distinction between transcendental, primary, and secondary narrativity. In contrast to our narrative ontology, Davenport's narrative realism does not include in a phenomenological way all aspects of becoming. Therefore, the objection that his distinction is an *ad hoc* invention in order to defend the thesis of normative narrative identity might be valid. Furthermore, we have stressed that any attempt to constitute a narrative ontology relies on the secondary-narratively mediated immediateness of perception. A narrative ontologizing of perceiving truth and value is not the only possibility, but 'only' the most preferable one. The decisive argument in support of our decision for a narrative ontology is not a philosophical one (although Part 2 of this volume shows that it is highly probable in philosophical terms), but the convergence of phenomenological considerations with a theology of revelation.

Galen Strawson distinguishes the normative thesis of narrative identity from a psychological thesis of narrativity. Here he refers to Jerome Bruner,[52] Oliver Sacks,[53] Daniel Dennett, and others, who by means of developmental psychology, medicine, and the neurosciences, try to show that designing personal narratives and rewritten stories belongs to human nature. Hutto's Narrative Practice Hypothesis, too, which we mentioned in the last section, would belong to this line of thought. Strawson's main point of reference, however, is Daniel Dennett, who speaks of the unity of designing a story:

> We try to make all of our material cohere into a single good story. And that story is our autobiography. The chief fictional character at the centre of that autobiography is one's self.[54]

Strawson does not only reject the normative thesis, but also the psychological and empirical one. In order to do so, he has to make a qualification: He rejects the psychological thesis, insofar as it is not 'trivial'. However, against a 'trivial' kind of the thesis, Strawson has no objections. What does he mean by 'trivial'?

> Well, if someone says, as some do, that making coffee is a narrative that involves Narrativity, because you have to think ahead, do things in the right order, and so on, and that everyday life involves many such narratives, then I take it the claim is trivial.[55]

---

52 Cf. BRUNER, J., Life as Narrative; BRUNER, J., Acts of Meaning.
53 Cf. SACKS, O., Man who Mistook.
54 DENNETT, D.C., Why Everyone is a Novelist.
55 STRAWSON, G., Against Narrativity, 439.

However, the events and states of affair that Strawson mentions here are actually far from being trivial. Exactly here we find the root of primary-narrative identity. The research of Michael Gazzaniga and others,[56] support this, since they can prove empirically that split-brain patients explicate actions in a narrative way that are not done by themselves. Perhaps this can be explained by the help of the assumption of a narrative explanation module in the left brain-hemisphere (at least if one regards the speech of brain-modules as plausible).[57] Be that as it may, one can also support our argument for a phenomenology of perception by means of neurology.

That Galen Strawson has to call the aforementioned state of affairs 'trivial' narrativity is revealing and ironic. His own thesis of an *episodic* identity instead of a *narrative* identity refers to exactly such a state of affairs! Therefore, his own thesis is nothing but *another kind of a narrative identity thesis, which presupposes a narrative paradigm.* The whole quarrel, therefore, is not about the question of whether narrativity is necessary for the explanation of identity or not, but *which kind of narrativity* is needed. And at this point, Galen Strawson has seen an important point: If narrative identity means that a particular human person has the task and the ability to create her own identity in a constructive and coherent way in order to form a narrative unity, then there is surely no narrative identity. Such a thesis is rejected by the priority of the *pathos* of perceiving the truth and value of primary narrativity. Therefore, for every human, secondary-narrative activity is only a reaction that cannot completely deal with what is given in the *pathos* as a task. Furthermore, we have seen that primary narrativity includes a basic kind of contingency in the course of events. Only the kind of secondary narrativity, therefore, is appropriate that does not deny this feature of essential contingency. This is true (e.g., for the Christian narrative) because the non-disposability of one's identity is stressed. The point of the doctrine of justification is that one's own identity is always a broken, fragmentary one of unconnected episodes that cannot be bound together by human subjects into a coherent, epic story. On the contrary, any attempt by humans to construe such a coherent identity-narrative autonomously is done in vain. The point is not to tell coherent narratives of identity, but to become passively interwoven into a story – a story completely without this totalitarian tendency. If one conceives of narrative identity on the level of secondary narrativity as something that excludes this unifying and levelling reduction, but that recognizes contingency, breaks, and surprise, then narrative

56 Cf. GAZZANIGA, M.S., Who's in Charge?, 83.

57 This is certainly rather questionable. In relation to the criticism of modularism, see MÜHLING, M., Resonances, 50–61.

identity is of high value. And then, Strawson's proposal about identity is a proposal about narrative identity, too.

Strawson's objections might apply to Schechtman and Dennett, but they do not meet MacIntyre, because I don't see this problematic unifying tendency in MacIntyre's position. Be that as it may, in the case of MacIntyre, we cannot find a developed conception of narrative identity, but only hints of one.

There is another conception of narrative identity that is resistant against Strawson's objections, which is Ricœur's, as Nüssel has seen.[58] Ricœur is not interested in the normative role of identity, but he delivers a phenomenological description that claims to avoid the usual contradictions by distinguishing an *idem*-identity and an *ipse*-identity:

> Without the recourse to narration, the problem of personal identity would in fact be condemned to an antinomy with no solution. Either we must posit a subject identical with itself through the diversity of its different states, or, following Hume and Nietzsche, we must hold that this identical subject is nothing more than a substantialist illusion. [...] This dilemma disappears if we substitute for identity understood in the sense of being the same (*idem*), identity understood in the sense of oneself as self-same (*soi-même*) (*ipse*). The difference between *idem* and *ipse* is nothing more than the difference between a substantial of formal identity and a narrative identity. Self-sameness, "self-constancy", can escape the dilemma of the Same and the Other to the extent that its identity rests on a temporal structure that conforms to the model of dynamic identity. [...] The self characterized by self-sameness may then be said to be refigured by the reflective application of such narrative configurations. Unlike the abstract identity of the Same, this narrative identity, constitutive of self-constancy, can include change, mutability, within the cohesion of one lifetime. [...] As the literary analysis of autobiography confirms, the story of a life continues to be re-figured by all the truthful or fictive stories a subject tells about himself or herself. This refiguration makes this life itself a cloth woven of stories told.[59]

By refusing *idem*-identity and acknowledging *ipse*-identity, Ricœur opens the space for manifold, un-closeable refigurations of stories in the plural, which are in no need of being bound together in a united meta-story. However, we have to be more precise. In regard to the identity of a person, the subject-matter is not primarily – or not at all – only the stories the person herself could tell, but an interindexical mesh of stories in which also the other person, the other non-person, and the wholly other are involved. Therefore, the concept of *ipse*-identity includes not only alterity and contingency, but also persons can emerge out of the mesh of stories. The identity of a person is therefore always

58 Cf. Nüssel, F., Narrative Identität?, 7f.

59 Ricœur, P., Time and Narrative III, 246.

open and un-closeable; it consists in a continuity of keeping one's word and the promises made to the other's face and received from the other.[60]

Narrative identity does not deal, as Strawson misunderstands the matter, with the power of a subject's self as a narrator, which relies on higher cognitive abilities. Verena Schlarb has also observed this, by pointing out that the eminent worth of telling stories consists in providing a space of freedom in the face of an apparently empirical loss of freedom – including in situations in which there is the loss of cognitive abilities, like in dementia.[61]

However, the question of how exactly primary-narrative identity and secondary-narrative identity have to be related cannot be completely closed in this philosophical part. Therefore, this subchapter remains a preview, and we will come back to this matter within the framework of anthropology and eschatology. The continuity of identity through keeping one's word and making promises, which is presupposed in *ipse*-identity, cannot be restricted to the social realm, but needs theological reflection.

60 Cf. NÜSSEL, F., Narrative Identität?, 7f.
61 Cf. SCHLARB, V., Narrative Freiheit, 224–246.

CHAPTER 20

Narration and Truth

The inquiry into the relationship between narration and truth implies a twofold task. On the one hand, we have to show that the concept of truth needs a narrative basis in order to be suitable. On the other hand, we have to show that truth – and therefore also falsity – can be predicated of stories and not in the sense of the distinction between historical and non-historical stories. This stage of our investigation is important, since narrative theologies in the last 40 years declared (e.g., Hauerwas) that 'we require […] not no story, but a true story'.[1] We, therefore, have to illuminate the concept of truth, even with the qualification that a strict definition of truth seems to be impossible, since any definition has to presuppose truth, with the consequence that a definition of truth would always presuppose an undefined, hidden concept of truth.

Any consideration of the concept of truth must acknowledge the insights Koch has developed in reference to Falk and McDowell (and implicitly Kant);[2] that is, the concept of truth consists of three equiprimordially related, irreducible aspects: a phenomenal one, a realistic one, and a pragmatic one. The phenomenal aspect refers to the state of affairs that truth is a phenomenon, something, that shows itself, that reveals itself, or that un-conceals itself, which is the aspect Heidegger called un-concealment (*Unverborgenheit*). The realist aspect means that true can be only what is the case. Here truth is distinguished from falsity. The so-called correspondence-theories of truth retained this aspect (in a problematic way) by seeing truth as a relation of congruence between two *relata*. The pragmatic aspect refers to the epistemic question of how truth can be known. Here, different theories like coherence-theories, pragmatic theories, and consensus-theories come into play.

The advantage of identifying these aspects is that the different truth-theories do not necessarily have to be understood as exclusive. The idea that the different theories of truth refer to different aspects of truth is of course not a new insight.[3] What Koch and Falk have done does not consist primarily in associating the different theories of truth with different non-concurring aspects, but in showing that these aspects are bound in an inner unity to the concept of truth. But here, too, this insight is not completely new. That the different aspects imply each other, has been seen by different philosophers,

1 HAUERWAS, S., Community of Character, 149.
2 Cf. KOCH, A.F., Versuch, 150–163.
3 Cf. SCHWÖBEL, C., Art. Wahrheit, 285f.

© WILHELM FINK VERLAG, 2020 | DOI:10.30965/9783846765852_021

(e.g., Heidegger[4] and William James). Usually, James' understanding of truth is seen as a variation of a pragmatic theory of truth, since true beliefs are 'invaluable instruments of action.'[5] But it is decisive to see in James not only the pragmatic aspects identified, since truth 'happens to an idea, it *becomes* true, is *made* true by events.'[6] Therefore, James also affirms the realist aspect, and he understands his considerations as a reformulation of the classical theory of correspondence.[7]

Since these aspects imply each other, one could be tempted to misunderstand their relation as one of equivalence, and therefore suppress the distinction. Perhaps this can explain the one-sidedness and falsely exclusive understandings of the traditional theories of truth.[8] Another reason for these false oppositions can be seen in the fact that the narrative embedding of truth is rarely explicated but frequently implicitly presupposed. Explicating this narrative embeddedness, then, is what distinguishes this work from Koch.

20.1 The Phenomenal Aspect of Truth

Truth appears, discloses itself, shows itself, or, truth is suffered. There is a passive aspect to truth, but not a passivity that excludes activity. Truth is a matter of the middle voice. In its appearance, truth is bound to our wayformational perspectives and to whatever appears on wayformational perspectives as carrying the truth claims that are impressed on us. Truth is based on the affordances (cf. ch. 5). They belong to the essential phenomenality of the courses of events; they appear as true and seem to be true. As un-concealment, truth is not bound to specific linguistic expressions, like statements or propositions. Propositional statements are a convenient means for speaking about the phenomenal aspect of truth, but it is not bound to this kind of expression. We can say that during our becoming and perceiving on wayformational perspectives it constantly *seems* that this or that is the case. This mountain seems to be larger than that one; this dog, baring its teeth, and running at me, seems to be bad, and this wall seems to be grey. If phenomena did not appear in wayformational perspectives, nothing would exist that could be true. The same is true for memories of past appearances on past sections of wayformational lines that are meaningful for the present. They, of course, have to appear as signs and

4 Cf. KOCH, A.F., Versuch, 159.
5 JAMES, W., Pragmatism, 97.
6 JAMES, W., Pragmatism, 97.
7 Cf. SEIBERT, C., William James, 333.
8 Cf. KOCH, A.F., Versuch, 162.

in the shape of secondary-narratives. And the same is even true for abstract concepts. It is not things that are this or that which appear as true, but things in their becoming or in primary stories. In the phenomenal aspect, no states appear as true, since states are always abstractions. Only stories or sequences of stories can appear as true.

The phenomenal aspect is veridical, insofar as in the most cases the appearance of truth is not consciously recognized, but it leads immediately to the orientation of the body's own movement: I do not think about the appearance of a low door, but I immediately seem to duck my head. In this example, to register the phenomenal, veridical truth happens in an enactive play between other's movement and my own movement, in an interplay between *pathos* and *response*, in perceiving and acting. In a minor amount of all cases, truth not only appears as this or that, but it appears that it appears that this or that is the case. Here the veridical truth becomes explicit. I will not understand these appearances of the appearing truth in all cases consciously as propositional statements or as secondary-narrative stories: the gap between platform and train reveals itself as dangerous, and the warning 'mind the gap' allows the appearance of danger to become thematic. Nevertheless, I do not in most cases think about this appearance of truth by thinking of propositional statements or as something important for my secondary narrativity. Only the fact that I have *successfully* used the subway indicates on the level of primary narrativity that the gap has appeared in a veridical way. A little part of that which appears thematically might be reformulated by signs, as propositions, or as integrated into secondary stories. Here it is the *logos* that let the speaker see what one has to speak about.[9] And of this last part, it will only be a little part wherein I am conscious that the appearance of truth is fallible. The fallibility of truth is expressed when I say 'It *seems* to be the case that x'. The appearance of truth therefore resembles an iceberg: its larger part is important for the primary story I undergo, but does not become known explicitly in secondary stories. And in still a smaller part of the case, I become aware of the distinction between apparent becoming and factual becoming. Perceptual trust (cf. ch. 5) is therefore also veridical trust as the trust in the truth of the course of events that present themselves to me. But by the help of this very small part, I can learn an important feature of the appearance of truth in general: the presupposition that the appearance of truth evokes trust and certainty, but never security: the presupposition that any appearance of truth can be deceptive:

9 Cf. HEIDEGGER, M., Being and Time, 28f.

> The 'being true' of *logos* as *alētheuein* means: to take beings that are being talked *about* in *legein* as *apophainesthai* out of their concealment; to let them be seen as something unconcealed (*alēthes*); to *discover* them. Similarly, 'being false,' *pseudesthai*, is tantamount to deceiving in the sense of covering up: putting something in front of something else (by way of letting it be seen) and thereby passing it off *as* something it is *not*.[10]

Thereby, the appearance of truth evokes two questions: whether the appearance is deceptive – i.e. the realist aspect of truth – and how I can know– i.e. the pragmatic aspect of truth. The phenomenal aspect of truth, correctly understood, implies the other two aspects as necessary questions. Therefore, it is not possible to give the phenomenal aspect of truth an absolute role in the framework of a narrative ontology – a mistake that Schapp makes[11] – because it itself includes the other aspects.

20.2 The Realistic Aspect of Truth, Representations, and (Re-)Sonances

Events and their course of becoming are essential and irreducibly phenomenal. That is the point of the phenomenal aspect of truth. However, events and becoming cannot be reduced to phenomena. If it could be reduced to phenomena, appearance and becoming would be identical. The possibility of error is constituted by the realistic aspect of truth. One could metaphorically call this the objectivity of becoming, but 'objectivity' is usually polluted by the idea that it is the remainder of what is not subjective, while the subjective is mistakenly identified with the phenomenal. However, in fact, the phenomenality of becoming belongs to its objectivity, without being restricted to it. The classical theories of correspondence try to explain the realistic aspect of truth by identifying a relation between two *relata*. Classically this relation is seen as *adaequatio rei et intellectus*, as a relation of adequacy between language and state of affairs, or simply as what is the case.[12] Which kinds of problems occur depends on the different descriptions of the relation as adequacy, representation, image or resonance, and on the understanding of the *relata* (mind, things, language, states of affairs, etc.). The semantics and the ontology on which it is based are both responsible for these different kinds of problems.

10 HEIDEGGER, M., Being and Time, 29.

11 SCHAPP, W., In Geschichten verstrickt (1953), 150, makes the mistake of making the phenomenal aspect of truth into an absolute, when he means that both of the other aspects would narratively coincide with the phenomenal. Nevertheless, Schapp is right in conceiving truth as a narrative relation.

12 Cf. WITTGENSTEIN, L., Tractatus Logico-Philosophicus (engl.), 4.024.

The difficulties associated with all kinds of correspondence theories, however, does not mean that talk about the realistic aspect, which itself remains essential, can be abandoned. Koch has therefore suggested that a coherent design for a theory of correspondence is not important at all, as long as one uses the simple method of disquotation without further interpretation[13] (which was used by Tarski[14] in his semantic theory of truth, for example) together with the principle of bivalence. Then it is ensured that the realist aspect of truth is not overlooked. Insofar as in a specific language the sentence 'snow is white' is true if and only if snow is white (disquotation), and insofar as the operation of negation can be applied to propositional statements (principle of bivalence), the realistic aspect is given. Formally this is correct, and we can use this method to express the realistic aspect of truth.

However, in the end, we cannot restrict ourselves to disquotations without interpretations. The interpretation of a disquotation is essential, if one wants to declare that the three aspects of truth are bound together. For example, if one conceives of truth exclusively as an attribute of propositions, then the correlated *relatum* cannot be the 'world' or 'things', but it has to be 'states of affairs.' If one conceives of one of the *relata* as '*intellectus*', perhaps '*res*' might be an adequately correlated *relatum*. But then numerous difficulties appear, and these difficulties rely on the ontology that one uses in order to interpret perception. We are able to unmask any naturalist, quasi-religious views by an *epoché*, but that does not mean we would be able to abandon any ontology. It only means that in the use of *epoché* we can substitute one particular ontology with another one. Therefore, the question of interpretation is an important one.

If one wants to claim that the phenomenal aspect and the realistic aspect of truth belong together, it is important to choose *relata* fitting to the perception of truth and value. Then both *relata* are basically narrative *relata*. In its realistic aspect, truth is then precisely a relation *between primary narrativity and secondary narrativity* – between the becoming of the world and our narrative conception of the world. By identifying both *relata* as stories, we gain the following advantages. First, both *relata* belong to the same class, which means that we get rid of specific problems. Second, any kind of linguistic use of signs (including propositions) is included, but it is not restricted to them. Third, in this way, the connection to the pragmatic aspect of truth is implied, as we will see later.

---

13 Cf. KOCH, A.F., Versuch, 157.
14 Cf. TARSKI, A., Concept of Truth.

Not only the identification of the *relata* is important, but also the identification of the relation between the *relata* must be determined. If one understands adequacy as congruence, one is forced to develop an image-theory of language (which is most probably a misleading endeavor). Whatever relation one uses, one has already made choices about our becoming in the midst of the becoming of the world. One strategy would be to determine a relation as broadly as possible in order to include many basic features. Perhaps this is the intention when the truth-relation is determined as a relation of representation. Then we could say that the phenomenal aspect expresses the presence of truth, whereas the realistic aspect is a representational one that binds what is not present with what is real. In this case, one uses the language of presence, presentation, and re-presentation.

However, there are serious objections against such an interpretation. The concept of representation is at best ambivalent, if not helplessly equivocal. In most cases it refers to external, non-constitutive relations, in which the *relata* are not essentially related and in which both belong to different spheres of being. Representationalism (i.e., the assumption that representations are basic for any kind of sign use) is laden with a lot of disadvantages that are not only disastrous for an understanding of truth, but also for its application in concrete sciences, like the neurosciences or evolutionary biology.[15] Representation is also the common root of both the maladies of naïve realism and constructivism, as Karen Barad observed:

> Indeed, the representationalist belief in the power of words to mirror preexisting phenomena is the metaphysical substrate that supports social constructivist, as well as traditional realist, beliefs, perpetuating the endless recycling of untenable options.[16] [...] The move toward performative alternatives to representationalism shifts the focus from questions of correspondence between descriptions and reality (e.g., do they mirror nature or culture?) to matters of practices, doings, and actions. Such an approach also brings to the forefront important questions of ontology, materiality, and agency, while social constructivist and traditional realist approaches get caught up in the geometrical optics of reflection where, much like the infinite play of images between two facing mirrors, the epistemological gets bounced back and forth, but nothing is seen. Moving away from the representationalist trap of geometrical optics, I shift the focus to physical optics, to questions of diffractions rather than reflection. [...] What often appears as separate entities [...] with sharp edges does not actually entail a relation of absolute exteriority at all. Like the diffraction patterns illuminating the indefinite nature of boundaries – displaying shadows in "light" regions and bright spots in

15 Cf. MÜHLING, M., Resonances, 36–38. 52–59. 154.

16 BARAD, K., Meeting the Universe Halfway, 133.

> 'dark' regions – the relationship of the cultural and the natural is a relation of 'exteriority within.'[17]

Representationalism suggests two sharply distinguished realms in which the *relatum* of the representing and the *relatum* of the represented are situated, and the relation is a secondary, non-constitutive one. Therefore, representationalism implies a strict kind of dualism.[18] However, if phenomenality belongs constitutively to the course of events of primary narrativity (i.e., if events are essentially phenomena grasped by perceiving truth and value), then perceiving truth and value with the means of secondary narrations is itself a part of the real course of the events of primary narrativity. In this case, any representational belief is impossible. We have to admit that not every use of representations is necessarily a representationalist one. If we restrict the use of representation to re-presenting in the sense of making something present again, there is no danger of representationalism. However, since the term is highly ambivalent and since the connotations of representationalism are so disastrous, it is better to avoid the term entirely.

We are confronted therefore with the question of how to name the relationship if not 'representation'. Barad uses the images of diffraction and interference gained through the well-known double-slit experiment. I am not sure if this might be a meaningful alternative or not. In the past, I have used acoustic metaphors instead of optical ones, by speaking of a 'resonance-theory of truth.'[19] In this case, truth would be a resonance between primary and secondary narrativity. They cannot be separated, just as we cannot distinguish between something that resonates and something that is resonating: A string without a resonating body is unable to oscillate at all. The resonating body has to be at least the two anchors of the string. The metaphor of resonance, therefore, can express internal or constitutive relationality, which belongs to truth. Truth can be understood in the model of a functional circuit: if one of the *relata* is missing, nothing remains. At the same time, the concept of resonance carries some difficulties due to its abundant use in recent years.

When I published 'Resonances' in 2014, a book that used 'resonances' as metaphor in the realm of the neurosciences, evolutionary biology, and theology, I could not know that in 2016 Hartmut Rosa would find great success by making resonance a key metaphor for a healthy social and personal life.[20] Here, the concept of resonance is

17 Barad, K., Meeting the Universe Halfway, 135.
18 Cf. Mühling, M., Resonances, 42–44.
19 Cf. Mühling, M., Voller Gnade und Wahrheit.
20 Cf. Rosa, H., Resonanz.

broadened in a problematic way, and this was criticized by Dieter Thomä.[21] One of his decisive arguments is that a resonance only appears, if the resonant frequency is responded to exactly. Therefore, the metaphor of resonance can also be used as a method to suppress legitimate alterity and deviance, not by explicitly excluding them, but by letting them vanish in a hidden way.[22] Therefore, the concept of resonance should not be used as the only key metaphor in a model design.

If we apply Thomä's objection to the resonance theory of truth, then we can say that the resonance-frequency would be the truth between primary and secondary narrativity. If it is met, there is truth; if it is not met, there is no truth. In this way, we could express bivalence. However, what this picture of resonance cannot show is how there can be an appearance of truth. If the resonance-frequency is not met, nothing will appear. And if it is met, all that can appear is the truth, but not the appearance of truth. In other words, if we use the metaphor of resonance to express the truth-relation, things would be reduced to their phenomenality and there would be nothing beyond their phenomenality. We have to prevent this. The problem does not occur in Barad's inference-metaphor, since this allows for light in shade and shade in light – or understood acoustically, silence in sound and sound in silence. Perhaps it would be possible to design an inference theory of truth, but we will not explore this line of thought. Another possibility would be to substitute representation not by resonance, but by *sonance*: we would have two oscillating stories, one of secondary narrativity that is embedded in the other of primary narrativity, which means that there can be harmonic interferences or sonances, or disharmonic interferences (or dissonances). Perhaps one can call this the sonance-theory of truth: harmonic sounds would mean truth or the appearance of truth, disharmonics would signify falsity or the appearance of falsity. Both primary narrativity and secondary narrativity would have their own sound, but there would be a joint frequency. That would express the idea of a constitutive relationality and at the same time that truth is not restricted to either an image or a representation, so that it is not possible to divide strictly positive from negative analogies: different instruments in the same orchestra sound different when playing the same melody. The same is true for stories: different secondary stories can be really different without losing their relatedness to primary narrativity. Therefore, this could also be called an 'accordance theory of truth', though this presupposes that one excludes the connotation of congruence and stresses the phenomenon of musical chords that are in tune.

21 Cf. THOMÄ, D., Soziologie mit der Stimmgabel.

22 Cf. CONNOLLY, W.E., Evangelical-Capitalist Resonance Machine.

In the end, we do not have to choose a terminology. The point is that the relation of truth is a constitutive relationship between primary and secondary narrativity, which is at the same time asymmetrical. This asymmetry guarantees the necessary distinction between primary and secondary narrativity. This distinction is necessary in order to speak of a realistic aspect of truth.

The realistic aspect implies the phenomenal as well as the pragmatic aspect. If truth did not appear, it would be possible that secondary stories could be true, but only purely by chance: Primary and secondary narrativity would not only be distinguished, but also separated in a radical manner, so that what really happens would be purely noumenal, which does not appear or cannot appear. The end would be the loss of any kind of realism and a radically skeptical approach, which is not viable. The pragmatic aspect is entailed, too, since we can now ask how to distinguish between the harmony or disharmony of the stories.

20.3 The Pragmatic Aspect of Truth

The pragmatic aspect of truth deals with the question of how we are able to know something as true or false. It is divided into at least two sub-aspects: a procedural and a criteriological. In regard to the latter, the ideas of coherence and inference play a large role. If one only puts stress on this criteriological sub-aspect, one ends up with a coherence theory of truth. Strictly speaking, coherence is a necessary, not a sufficient condition for truth, which means that coherence is more a criterion of falsity than of truth. To apply coherence to the question of truth presupposes that one is able to infer from true propositions and their concepts to other propositions. Therefore, semantical inferentialism also has its relative place. Furthermore, applying coherence presupposes that the whole of the word is a theoretically well-founded set. If this is not the case, then the antinomy of negation can appear anywhere. Then there is the problem that coherence becomes invalid even in its restricted role as a necessary condition of the concept of truth. Therefore, it is not coherence as such or conceptual coherence, but *dramatic coherence* (cf. ch. 16) that must be applied as a necessary criterion of truth. Conceptual coherence does not become superfluous, but can only be used in a regulative rule.

The questions of procedure are more interesting, which asks about the processes that are used to recognize something as true. Here, the narrativity of truth and the wayformational character of its appearance is immediately presupposed. We are, for example, able to apply the constant appearance of truth to itself, with respect to its phenomenal aspect. If I walk around two mountains, one of them might appear larger during a specific section of the way. If I believe in the identity of the two mountains, the constantly changing perspectives during my walk allows me to prove whether it is indeed the case that one of the mountains is larger – at least preliminarily. However, wayformational lines are always particular, and as ways they emerge out of walking, so they are not well-founded sets. Therefore, even an infinite hike would not allow for stepping outside of the whole field. Furthermore, narrative, wayformational perspectives are always social. This means that the pragmatic aspect must always be seen as a discursive one. In the discourse of communities, I can relate the appearance of truth in my wayformational perspective to the appearances of truth in the other wayformational perspectives by asking whether the veridical appearance of truth is trustworthy as dramatic coherence. This communicative process is itself a narrative and leads to the formation of traditions, out of which the historical emerges (i.e., what appears in respect to the process of tradition itself as true). The discourse means that the proving of truth always has the character of a process, in the sense that truth is always older than oneself. This means, on the one hand, that the appearance of truth for myself cannot be its final instance, but that it is connected with the authority of past traditions. On the other side, this means that the process of proving the truth is interminable. Since Peirce,[23] it has been assumed, as it is today (e.g., by Koch[24]), that truth could then be seen as an asymptotic limit value for an infinite future, since there could be a cumulative process of testing. However, wayformational lines can intertwine, overlap, and communicate with one another, but they cannot be cumulatively bound to sets. Therefore, there cannot be any asymptotic limit value for truth in an infinite future. But even if an accumulation is possible, the process remains open. Since it is dramatic coherence that governs this process, it would be possible that in the phenomenal aspect something un-inferably new emerges as true, which sets the whole history of proving truth at once in a new light – or in a new darkness.

This feature of a narrative basis of truth is seen correctly by Schapp: 'It is not possible to measure the story by the benchmarks of reality and truth from outside. The benchmarks gain their meaning only inside the story. The story can be corrected from its inside. Thereby it could appear as if these corrections were made from outside. Here we can refer to what we have said about the emergence of stories, [...] about the self-telling of stories. [...] We mean that one cannot say more than that stories emerge and that stories at the same time enlace us. [...] The possibility of a permanent change of

23 Cf. Peirce, C.S., Collected Papers, 5.565: 'Truth is that concordance of an abstract statement with the ideal limit towards which endless investigation would tend to bring scientific belief.'

24 Cf. Koch, A.F., Versuch, 162.

doubt and belief, the transition of hope into despair, of fear and salvation [...] belongs to the story and to being enlaced in stories. What yesterday was seen as true can be revealed today as false, and tomorrow once again as happy or sad truth. In the framework of the story, all this is possible. But one distorts the image if one views it with the eyes of an observer or with the eyes of one standing on the outside. [...] The one standing outside is not the ultimate canon, but he is only once again enlaced in his own story, which is manifold and it is not easy to disentangle its relation to the story of the other. [...] In this way, on the first story a sequel is built, perhaps in a we-story, and the same consideration has to be made about that new story, regarding reality and unreality, truth and falsity, without it ever being possible to escape this circle.'[25] Notwithstanding his observation about the interminability of the question of truth, Schapp's mistake is a tendency to abandon the concept of truth altogether.

An asymptotic proof of truth in an infinite future is therefore a fiction. The testing of truth – and therefore truth itself – is an *eschatological* process. Truth as such is a boundary concept between philosophy and faith. It leads toward faith and theological consideration, and it is only possible to say something really significant about truth from a theological perspective – the manner in which truth is essentially based on is *grace*.[26]

If, within the framework of procedure, one puts too much weight on the moment of discourse (e.g., by separating discourse from its narrative context), one gets one of the discursive theories of truth, like the consensus-theory of truth.[27]

In this framework, truth is what in an ideal situation, according to the rules of an ideal speech situation (i.e., everyone is allowed to participate, everyone is allowed to make any assertion or to question any assertion; it is coercion-free), is found to be the consensus.[28] In spite of the fact that no real consensus, but only a consensus that respects the rules of an ideal speech situation can represent truth,[29] a basic, quasi-religious and eschatological question arises: On the one hand the rules of an ideal speech situation can be disputed, and an ontology of ideal communication is

---

25 SCHAPP, W., In Geschichten verstrickt (1953), 150f (transl. MM).

26 Cf. MÜHLING, M., Resonanzen, 155f.

27 Cf. HABERMAS, J., Wahrheitstheorien, 218: 'We call "truth" the claim connected with constative speech-acts. A proposition is true if the claim of the speech-acts, which are used in sentences in order to make this proposition, is warranted" (Transl. MM), original: „Wahrheit nennen wir den Geltungsanspruch, den wir mit konstativen Sprechakten verbinden. Eine Aussage ist wahr, wenn der Geltungsanspruch der Sprechakte, mit denen wir, unter Verwendung von Sätzen, jene Aussage behaupten, berechtigt ist."

28 Cf. HABERMAS, J., Wahrheitstheorien, 255f.

29 Cf. HABERMAS, J., Wahrheitstheorien, 257: 'A reasonable consensus can only be distinguished from a misleading one by reference to an ideal situation of speech.' (Transl. MM), original: „Ein vernünftiger Konsensus kann von einem trügerischen in letzter Instanz allein durch Bezugnahme auf eine ideale Sprechsituation unterschieden werden."

presupposed. And here one has to ask whether such an ontology of ideal communication must already presuppose a concept of truth. On the other hand, it is obvious, that no historic situation whatsoever can be an ideal speech situation. Therefore, a hidden ideal-eschatological aspect is the basis of this conception.

The same objections that led to a rejection of universal coherence are valid against universal consensus. Additionally, discourse theories of truth carry the burden of – if they want to be more than sociology – having to abandon the phenomenological and realist aspects of truth: if truth is able to appear, and if things are reducible to their appearances (which is not a given), a test for truth would be superfluous. This is, of course, not the case. However, if the course of events cannot be reduced to its appearance, then there is no sequence of the discourse, and of a consensus that appears during the discourse, that would be able to represent the truth. If one wants to make the consensus theory of truth into an all-embracing theory of truth, then one must deny that there is a distinction between the phenomenal and the realist aspects. Furthermore, an implication of this is that radical theories of consensus are not able to bring real alterity and real plurality. In this respect, too, consensus-theories are not resonant with reality. In the end, consensus theories have to deny that there is a phenomenal and a realist aspect of truth. Truth would then only be what can be reasonably claimed, and this would be a constructivist concept of truth. In the end – *contra intentionem* – truth would become a matter of power and coercion. Here Nietzsche is clearer than Habermas. Absolutizing the element of discourse tends – even if one wants to lead the discourse in a coercion-free manner – to be a totalitarian endeavor that reduces tolerance. If one chose the other possibility by not abandoning the realist aspect of truth, a universal consensus could never have anything to do with truth. Also, after a universal consensus an event could occur that, by the phenomena, forces one to disagree by bearing witness: 'Here I stand. I can do no other'.[30]

I must admit that among all the problematic attempts to absolutize one of the aspects of truth, the reduction of truth to consensus seems to me the most implausible one. But perhaps this is only a result of the fact that I am simply consensually unmusical.

The pragmatic aspect of truth also implies both of the other aspects: without the realistic and the phenomenal aspect, it loses any ground. It might be especially helpful to inquire into the intrinsic connection between the pragmatic and the phenomenal aspect of truth. The basis of this connection is in

30 Cf. for more fundamental objections to the consensus theory of truth, see also RESCHER, N., Pluralism.

the end the narrative character of truth. Both the intrinsic connection and the narrative character can be observed in William James.

James regards true beliefs as 'invaluable instruments of action'.[31] He says, 'Truth happens to an idea, it *becomes* true, is *made* true by events.'[32] Here James acknowledges that the testing of truth without the phenomenal aspect is impossible. But James also knows about the realistic aspect and conceives of truth as a relation between two *relata*. In what way?

The first *relatum*, classically called *intellectus*, is not restricted by James to propositions, but any human referential activity, including ideas and beliefs that are able to be true, and are as such able to be experienced in the practical situation of participating in a world.[33] Since this practical situation has the features of the 'dramatic richness of the concrete world,'[34] James regards any formula for a definition of truth as problematic. The practical situation is dramatic insofar as it is a continual processing transition of presently non-determined possibilities into presently determined events by acts of selection. These acts of selection are contingent, not necessary, and they are as such in the need of orientation.[35] But orientation is only possible if there are beliefs and convictions, and, furthermore, if the action is guided by true convictions.[36]

The relation of truth is seen in the following way: true convictions are at the same time good convictions. In a classical way, James presupposes the identity of the good and the true. In contrast to the classical idea, however, he sees goodness as what is 'profitable to our lives'.[37] It is decisive that profitable usability is not understood in a mercantile way. This profitable usability is also by no means a sufficient, but only a necessary condition of truth. Therefore, profitable usability does not coincide with the reality-reference of truth. On the contrary, James means that usability and satisfiability presuppose a reference to reality, not the other way around. Therefore, in the end the truth relation consists in an *agreement* between convictions and reality.[38]

The second *relatum*, traditionally called reality, is according to James not made by the actor, but is previously given, yet it is nevertheless not independent of the actor. As reality that is in the need to be determined, it appears only in the particularly determined situations of acting and practicing. Therefore, it cannot be described without the actor. Nevertheless, the actor is not the basis of what is real, but the real appears in a situation of action as something that is in the need of becoming determined by the action.[39] The non-self-created personal interest of the actor is caused by the actor's personal narrative situation and the horizon of expectation that determines prelinguistically which aspects of the real can appear. James prefigures here an important aspect of Gibson's theory of affordances (cf. ch. 5). Truth, therefore, is always bound to perspectives and is prior to any predicative act that is narratively determined. James

31 JAMES, W., Pragmatism, 97.
32 JAMES, W., Pragmatism, 97.
33 Cf. SEIBERT, C., William James, 334.
34 JAMES, W., Will to Believe, 62.
35 Cf. SEIBERT, C., William James, 336.
36 Cf. SEIBERT, C., William James, 337.
37 JAMES, W., Pragmatism, 42.
38 Cf. SEIBERT, C., William James, 342.
39 Cf. SEIBERT, C., William James, 345–352.

knows the concept of an absolute truth as a limit-concept. In order to grasp such absolute truth, it would be necessary to know all possible practical situations and all of the possible interests of all of the possible actors – and this would mean knowing all possible narrative biographies of the actors.[40] Therefore, the idea of an absolute truth can only be a theoretical concept or a regulative idea in James' eyes. For us it is a chimera.

Due to an evolutionary-narrative understanding of reality, any testing of truth in a situation can only be a preliminary test. The storied dimension of the truth-relation consists, therefore, in the fact that it is, on the one hand, a manifestation of past true convictions, which inaugurates a horizon of expectation for the future, and that, on the other hand, only the future will show whether there is really an agreement with reality. Ideal truth as the agreement of conviction and reality is therefore not only dependent on the synchronic aspect, including all possible personal interests, but on a non-exceedable future, too.[41]

Let us illustrate this theory with the example of a hiker getting lost in the wilderness:

> If I am lost in the woods and starved, and find what looks like a cow-path, it is of the utmost importance that I should think of a human habitation at the end of it, for if I do so and follow it, I save myself. The true thought is useful here because the house which is its object is useful.[42]

The reality in need of being determined as one *relatum* of the situation of truth is here not independent of the actor, but is nevertheless previously given to her, since the preexisting biographic-narrative feature of being lost and hungry a personal interest is formed, which directs the attention automatically in such a way that things like trees, bushes, mountains or the blue sky do not arbitrarily appear, but something that looks like a cow-path. But that this can appear is a given for the actor. As the second *relatum*, the conviction consists in the opinion that what appears as a cow-path is a sign of civilization and an escape from hunger, and as a starting place for a further orientation in the world of civilization. Whether this appearance of truth is indeed true, depends on the one hand on the manifestation of truth itself, i.e. the path impresses itself to the hiker as a cow-path, but not as a path of wild animals. If the hiker follows it, a future test of truth is possible, when, in the course of following the way, troughs, fences, and the expected house appear, even if this only preliminary represents the definite future.

It is, therefore, characteristic of James' theory of truth that the determination of the personal *relatum* includes determinations of the situation that is in need of determination and *vice versa*. In this way, it resembles Gibson's theory of the affordances. There is, however, a significant difference. Whereas the affordances in Gibson are invitations of the environment to perceive and to act, James proceeds the other way around: he conceives of personal interest as the guide that lets the affordances appear. Both theories can be seen, perhaps, as completing each other. But even if we use James alone, truth is not an external relation, but an internal one, in which both *relata* are constitutive for each other. And therefore, James' theory is a non-representationalist one: although James calls the truth-relation an agreement, this is not representationalist.

40 Cf. SEIBERT, C., William James, 353–356.

41 Cf. SEIBERT, C., William James, 356–361.

42 JAMES, W., Pragmatism, 98.

20.4 The Truth of Narrations

So far, we have seen that truth must be considered from three perspectives, and that these three perspectives have, in themselves and in their relationship to one another, a narrative basis. Truth is an internal or constitutive relation between stories, i.e. between primary and secondary narrativity. Stories are the basis for any understanding of truth. At the beginning of this chapter, however, we also asked another question: what about the truth of stories? Are there criteria on which secondary stories can be judged true or false? Since all secondary stories are a part of primary narrativity, this question cannot be reduced to the narratological question about the difference between fictional and non-fictional stories. Fictional stories without any reality-claims are also a part of primary narrativity and co-determine primary narrativity and its course of events. For example, without Jules Verne's stories, astronautics most probably would not have appeared at the time and place in which it did in fact appear.[43] The question can also not to be reduced to a question about the difference between historical and non-historical stories. What we call the historical is essentially a process of tradition's self-reflection in a discursive practice of testing truth; therefore, the historic presupposes the truth of traditions.

If the distinction between true and false stories can neither be reduced to the distinction between fictional and non-fictional stories, nor to the distinction between historical and non-historical stories, a problem persists: According to the realistic aspect of truth, truth is a harmonic sonance between primary and secondary narrativity in dramatic coherence. Therefore, a secondary story is true if it resonates harmonically with the course of events. But on the one hand, we do not have any evaluative access apart from the appearance of truth, which always allows for the possibility of falsity. On the other hand, the idea of dramatic coherence allows for a revaluation of values in the unclosed course of events, possibly including the values of truth and falsehood. In regard to proving truth, the way, for example, Pannenberg[44] speaks of an eschatic, coherentist unity of truth is also impossible. But under these conditions, the result of this question seems to be a little bit disappointing. We started in ch. 5 with an analysis of perception and we have journeyed a long way since then. Along the way, we saw that the concept of truth presupposes the concept of

43 Konstantin Ziolkowski, Hermann Oberth, Wernher von Braun, and Robert Goddard were inspired in their work by the utopian novels of Jules Vernes, cf. ABRET H., Literatur und Technik, 121.

44 For Pannenberg's understanding of the entity of truth cf. LEPPEK, T.A., Wahrheit bei Pannenberg, 125–175.

stories, and that the concept of truth can be applied to stories. Therefore, there has to be a distinction between true and false stories, since the truth or falsity of propositions is only meaningful if they are embedded in a narrative nexus. Propositions and statements only have a truth-value in their narrative course of events, not apart from it. The fact that, in most cases, this narrative horizon remains implicit, supports this thesis more than it undermines it. Whereas we do not have many problems uttering and testing truth claims in everyday life, it is not possible to test our narrative horizons.

In other words, primary narrativity constitutes a horizon of primary and secondary stories, interwoven with one another and emerging out of the horizon. But they do not constitute a well-founded set of closed stories, but, if at all, a non-well-founded set. Truth then has to be understood as a relational attribute of the non-well-founded subset of secondary narrativity and the non-well-founded subset that consists 'exclusively' in primary narrativity. But what can 'exclusive' primary narrativity mean, if secondary narrativity belongs to primary narrativity, and if we cannot speak of well-founded sets? The best we can say is that it is a very fuzzy concept. 'Exclusive' primary narrativity is a broad metaphor. And there is another complication: With primary narrativity, harmonically resonating secondary stories (i.e. true stories) and dissonating stories (i.e. false stories) emerge out of the horizon of primary narrativity. The distinction between true and false would then be given and presupposed in the becoming of the horizon of primary narrativity itself. And the traditional truth of propositions also depends on this state of affairs: they can only be understood against the backdrop of their narrative context.

Does this not simply mean that so far, the question about the distinction between false and true stories remains unanswered, but also that the traditional concept of propositional truth becomes vague? Indeed, if philosophy, including the philosophy of religion, were all we had, this would be the case. Reflection on truth is an excellent example of how philosophical reflection can proceed into a wide field, how it can ask important questions, and how it can identify some conditions for answering these questions. Philosophical reflection itself, however, cannot answer these questions. Therefore, philosophical reflection turns to faith and to the phenomenality of revelation. Apart from technical details, this is the truth behind Tillich's so-called 'method of correlation'.[45] For our question of truth, this means: only by presupposing the phenomenality of revelation, and in the end presupposing pneumatology, can we answer the question of truth in a proper way.

---

45 Cf. Tillich, P., ST I, 73–80.

PART 3

Divine Self-Presentation

CHAPTER 21

Minimal Conditions for Speaking of God and the Divine Identifiability

Is it meaningful to speak of God in the mesh of narrative wayformational perspectives? That is what one expects from any kind of philosophy of religion or theology. But is it possible? We presuppose a specific order of questions one has to deal with if one wants to speak about something. This order is also important in the case of 'God'. This order, however, is not like the one used in classical dogmatics. *First*, we have to clarify what the term 'God' can mean, independently of the question, of how what is meant is identifiable, what attributes it has, and whether it exists or not. Only after this first question is solved, can we then ask, *second*, how God can be identified. The question of identifiability is therefore dependent on the question of what in a minimal sense 'God' can mean. It is, however, still independent of the question of which concrete and essential attributes 'God' can have, and whether 'God' exists. This order might be surprising, but it is purely logical: identifiability presupposes narrativity, and an entanglement of our primary narrativity with the narrativity of the one who shall be identified. What is not presupposed, however, is the existence of the one who is in need of identification in the common sense, e.g. as a phenomenon of primary narrativity. Snow White and Alice can also be narratively identified, without presupposing that there are spatio-temporal entities that match Snow White or Alice. And indeed, our survey into the minimal conditions for speech about God – after having clarified the first question – could reveal that God must not be thought of as a phenomenon that is embedded in primary narrativity like other phenomena. Only when something has been identified (i.e., when we have explicated an indexical reference in the entanglement of narrations) can we ask, *third*, which attributes the one identified may have. Only if we know the fairy-tale of Snow White is it meaningful to ask about her attributes (pretty, larger than many men, trusting, etc.). *Fourth*, the question of existence is then the last meaningful question, by no means the first one.

This chapter only deals with the first question concerning the minimal conditions for speaking of 'God'. The existence of God is by no means our theme, although we use arguments that have been traditionally used in order to deal with this other question. We will also not deal with the 'attributes' and the

 | DOI:10.30965/9783846765852_022

'essence' of 'God'. These questions belong to the material doctrine of God and therefore in the second volume.

21.1 The Necessity of the Theological Critique of Religion and the Question of Whether 'God' Signifies a Singular Term or Minimally a General Term

If one speaks of something, one needs to have an idea of what one is speaking about. Such is also the case regarding mundane phenomena as well as in regard to 'God'. About what is one talking about, if one uses the term 'God'? Obviously, 'God' is not a mundane phenomenon. Does this also mean that 'God' is not a phenomenon at all? Marion has tried to speak of 'God' as a 'saturated phenomenon' or as an 'absolute phenomenon',[1] but in principle this kind of speech is negative, as it means that 'God' is not a phenomenon, insofar as phenomena are bound to horizons – bound to what appears on wayformational perspectives.

Of course, it would be possible to use the word 'God' for a phenomenon, and indeed the history of myths reveals that 'God' and 'gods' were used for a plurality of different phenomena. An important insight of the philosophy of religion, rightly emphasized in the criticism of religion in every century, is, however, that this use is a mistake: 'God' should not signify any phenomenon, but a 'saturated', 'absolute' or 'unconditioned' phenomenon. But then, similar to the notion of God as a *causa sui*, as for example Dalferth has seen,[2] one only means that the category used – phenomenon or *causa* – cannot be used for God. At best, it is a specific kind of apophatic theology. These attributes serve in order to exclude God from the set of phenomena, and to give 'God' a transphenomenal or noumenal status. Therefore, it is claimed that the transphenomenal and noumenal is identical with a concrete phenomenon or a complex of phenomena, in a *completely arbitrary manner*. That is the structure of the better kind of religious criticism. Herms has recently expressed this in the following way:

> The structure of these ideas is well known from the myths of religions and ideologies. Equally well known is the basic critique of these ideas, which has been articulated and popularized by modernity's criticisms of religion. This critique says: The material determinations of the transphenomenal sphere are all derived from projections of the phenomenal sphere into a beyond, and there is no reason for these projections and no motivations apart from the wish to explain it in that

1 Cf. MARION, J.-L., État donné, and in addition DALFERTH, I.U., Radikale Theologie, 206.
2 Cf. DALFERTH, I.U., Radikale Theologie, 207.

> way – a wish that cannot be satisfied by any reasons. It is simply this wish that produces the whole idea. And one has to accept an apparent self-contradiction: The distinction between phenomenality and the basis that creates and preserves it, which is in need of being understood and conceived, is ignored – skipped or circumvented – by the fact that one ascribes without further ado features of the constituted to the constituting basis; nay, that it itself is thought of as based in what is constituted.[3]

This problem does not occur in the case of negative theology. But negative or apophatic theology, be it a traditional one, or be it in the shape of the critique of religion, is not a kind of natural theology that could claim to predicate anything about 'God'. It is the other way around: one only diagnoses here what one cannot say or must not say about God. The criterion that Herms mentions is important. It is not decisive that a particular, mythical kind of speech reflects an identification of the transphenomenal with the phenomenal, and thereby produces contradictions. We already saw that logical contradictions are allowed to some degree if we use dramatic instead of conceptual coherence. Therefore, revealing a logical contradiction is only a necessary condition for using apophatic religious criticism. The argument is only sufficient if one can show that this identification is built *arbitrarily* and is therefore unwarranted.

Karl Heim has explained the same state of affairs in regard to the question about 'God' as 'offspring' of 'transcendental ground', and he claims that this kind of apophatic religious criticism is a *biblical commandment*:

> Within the infinite succession of effects and causes opened up for us by our inquiry into the genesis of the world, we may halt at some particular member of the series and take that as the First Cause. [...] one member of the series of causes and effects is made absolute and is constituted by the *primum movens*. Such a solution to the question Why may be described by the biblical term, 'Idolatry,' [...] or 'Creature-worship.'[4]

At this point, we are far from explaining biblical authority in detail. Nevertheless, biblical reference belongs to the basic practices of the Christian faith. And since religious criticism is biblically commanded, this task of a philosophy of religion belongs to the obligatory tasks of theology. Therefore, reflecting on faith with the means of philosophy, as in this volume, is far more than prolegomena. From the practice of faith originates a critique that can be applied to this practice, too.

3 HERMS, E., Das Gehirn und seine Wirklichkeit, 99 (transl. MM).

4 HEIM, K., God Transcendent, 191.

Let us illustrate. The idea that God is an absolute person was criticized classically, on the one hand, by J.G. Fichte with the argument that a person or personality has to be particular and therefore finite, insofar as it is limited by other persons.[5] On the other hand, Feuerbach regarded the speech of an absolute person as a hypostasization or projection of the human nature to a single entity. Feuerbach regarded it as wrong to put God over love instead of love over God.[6] Critiques like these do not mean that we cannot use the concept of person meaningfully in regard to God, especially if one remembers the historical origin of the concept in theology. However, one has to respect the critiques in a double way: *First*, one has to show that it is not an arbitrary identification, and *second*, one has to show how in dramatic coherence the apparent contradiction is suspended or sublated. In the case of the concept of person, both are possible, as our analysis in the second volume will show. The outcome will be that we can use the concept of person in regard to God, but also that we are not able to call God a person.

Karl Barth is the most prominent for his theological critique of religion in the 20th century,[7] but of course he is not an exception. Tillich develops a similar critique, too, when he calls the 'demonic' that which substitutes participation in the ultimate (his concept of a symbol is presupposed here) for the ultimate itself.[8] If one takes a closer look, it is possible to find in any meaningful theological position analogies to these theologically necessary, apophatic critiques of religion.

Ingolf Dalferth is among those contemporary theologians who has applied this apophatic method in a radical way, from the beginning of his publications onward. He regards 'God' as a singular term.[9] 'God' is therefore not a general term and 'God' has none of the features of a general term. Whatever universal one might use in order to explain 'God', one ends up in the paradoxical trap of the apophatic. As a singular term, 'God' can only be understood within the framework of faith, or more, precisely in the practice of faith.[10] Among the many consequences of this position, one stands out: a general philosophy of religion, unbound to a particular practice of faith, becomes impossible. Interreligious dialogues or ecumenical dialogues also have to face a serious problem: how does one know that everyone means the same thing by 'God'?

5 Cf. FICHTE, J.G., Göttliche Weltregierung, esp. 20f

6 Cf. FEUERBACH, L., Wesen des Christentums, Bd. 1, 106f.

7 Cf. BARTH, K., CD, I/2, §17, 280–361.

8 Cf. TILLICH, P., Systematic Theology I, 34.

9 Cf. DALFERTH, I.U., Religiöse Rede von Gott, 571–583; DALFERTH, I.U., Existenz Gottes und christlicher Glaube, 96–99; DALFERTH, I.U., Der auferweckte Gekreuzigte, 224.

10 Cf. DALFERTH, I.U., Die Wirklichkeit des Möglichen. Hermeneutische Religionsphilosophie, 442–448. 466–470.

Of course, it is possible to use 'God' as a singular term, and in the contemporary practice of faith this might not be uncommon. For example, I use 'God' as a name and address in prayer. Whether this is a meaningful practice is a question we have to deal with later. But if it is possible, it presupposes that 'God', like every name, is embedded in a narration that illuminates its reference, as we have seen (ch. 14). And if 'God' refers to something, as narratively identifiable, then it is also presupposed that one can say, *what* it is that is identified. Narrative identity descriptions are not only based on indexicals, but on indexicals and metaphorically based, conceptual uses of signs. The indexical use of signs always refers to something that appears, i.e. to phenomena, whereas the conceptual use of signs refers to something general. It is true that God is not a phenomenon among other phenomena, but without phenomena 'God' is incomprehensible. One has to use concepts in the same manner – but only concepts embedded in stories – if the identification is to be intelligible. Even with the help of narrations, one cannot identify arbitrarily, but one always has to presuppose a universe of discourse. Such a universe of discourse is even presupposed in unmasking the paradoxes of the critique of religion and the paradoxes of the apophatic tradition. Otherwise these critiques would not be intelligible.

This conceptual core of the speech of 'God' cannot provide any definition of 'God', but only one or more minimal conditions for the talk of 'God'.[11] And in this sense, a 'God' (using the indefinite article explicitly) is absolutely not a singular term, but a minimal general term. In this sense, a 'God' is used in ordinary languages as well as in academic languages. The task of philosophy of religion is then to ask: *What is the content of this minimal general term and what is not its content?* Dalferth wants to avoid the speech of general minimal conditions for 'God', and instead he speaks of minimal rules of thinking God or of limit conceptions that have to be respected if one speaks of 'God'.[12] In this sense of rules of thinking, even Dalferth cannot avoid using minimal conditions in speaking of 'God' by using conceptual language. Whether one speaks of rules of thinking or minimal conditions, this is only a minor question of terminology that does not have to be resolved. The task of this whole chapter is then to analyze these minimal conditions in speaking of 'God.'

11 The use of the term 'minimal conditions' by the philosopy of religion for talk of God was already used by PANNENBERG, W., ST I (engl.), 394.

12 Cf. DALFERTH, I.U., Die Wirklichkeit des Möglichen. Hermeneutische Religionsphilosophie, 527.

21.2 'God' as Transcendence and Beyond?

A frequently used minimal condition for 'God' is as the transcendent. Frequently, 'transcendence' is used in an absolute manner, which is, in principle, an improper use of language, since transcendence is a relational concept. Something can only be transcendent in regard to something else, a limit or border of something. The concept of transcendence is here similar to the concept of the beyond. The beyond, too, is often used absolutely, but it is in its proper use a dyadic relation, signifying that something is beyond something else. Viewed from Europe, England is beyond the sea. The distinction between the concept of beyond and transcendence lies only in that, whereas beyond is a static expression of place, *transcendere* means 'to go across' and is therefore dynamic. From Europe, I could transcend the sea to England by a ferry, for example. Obviously, it is not this mundane use of 'beyond' and 'transcendence' that is used as minimal condition for God, but it is a metaphor: beyond the world as a whole or a transcendence of the world as all that there is. However, 'the world as a whole' is by no means a clear concept. Therefore, this explanation is far from being satisfactory. It might be meaningful to have a closer look at a position that uses the concept of transcendence intensively. For example, such a position can be found in the philosophy of religion as a foundation of theology by Karl Heim during the 20th century.

Heim criticizes the dogmatic tradition of the 19th and 20th century that mistakenly presupposed that 'God' or 'transcendence' are intelligible concepts:

> But they always take for granted that every one, even the sceptic, knows what is signified by the word 'God,' and how 'God' and 'world' are distinguished from each other. […] We take into account the possibility that some may challenge us here, may affirm that in this region beyond there is nothing at all; there is no God. But hitherto it has always been regarded as axiomatic that the prepositions 'above,' 'beyond,' 'over,' here employed have some definite easily intelligible meaning for all men. Today that is not the case. The idea of transcendence retained a clear and obvious significance in the history of human thought only so long as men looked on the universe as a self-inclosed system.[13]

However, from the time of Giordano Bruno onward, space is seen as infinite. Therefore, the concept of transcendence, including the presupposed concept of a limit, has become unintelligible.

> What kind of line is this that theology and the philosophy of religion would draw between the world and God, between immanence and transcendence? In every

13 HEIM, K., God Transcendent, 29f.

> act of worship, in every prayer, and every impulse of pious feeling, good men pass in spirit over this problematical boundary-line. [...] Thus we pass directly away from the 'immanent' theory to see things in the light of God's transcendence. This transition from one explanation to the other is what the secular mind cannot understand. It is dishonest double-dealing, 'double book-keeping.' [...] What exactly are we in search of when we inquire about the world beyond? What meaning do we attach to the prefix 'trans' when we speak of the transcendent and distinguish it from the immanent?[14]

But the reason for its unintelligibility is not only the tradition of Bruno's, which holds space to be infinite, but also the life-affirming nihilism of Nietzsche, which has become a common-place:

> Thus Nietzsche reaches the new 'world-conception,' which rejects as logically unframable the whole idea of transcendence and the connexion between Creator and creation. 'The world [...] will be, the world has been, but it has never begun to be, nor will ever cease to be. It maintains itself in both aspects [...] It lives on itself: if feeds on its own excrements.'[15]

In facing these circumstances, Heim does not abandon the concept of transcendence, but he tries to save it by giving it a meaning. He starts in explaining relationships of transcendence inside of the world, in order to arrive at a concept of transcendence beyond the world. Even the relationships of transcendence inside of the world can be categorized through two basic distinctions: they can refer to a boundary of content, or they can refer to a boundary of dimension. The former one, a material relationship of transcendence

> is a relation between two or more separate entities, both, or all of them, contents belonging to one and the same space.[16] [...] The case is different with the boundaries of dimension. Here it is two infinites which meet, two magnitudes which have neither beginning nor end. Consequently, it is impossible to indicate any point or any line at which the one limits the other. This being the case, is not a dimensional boundary-line something really quite inexpressible? [...] The boundary between two unbounded realms cannot be expressed otherwise than in paradox.[17]

Heim uses the idea of dimensional transcendence (or the idea of the dimensional limit) in order to explicate his philosophy of spaces, as we learned in ch. 11. Dimensional limits inside of the world can be found between time and space, between the spatial dimensions, between I and It, and between I and Thou. All these concepts refer to

14 HEIM, K., God Transcendent, 31–33.
15 HEIM, K., God Transcendent, 37. Here, Heim is referencing Nietzsche, F. Der Wille zur Macht, Stück 1066.
16 HEIM, K., God Transcendent, 51.
17 HEIM, K., God Transcendent, 51f.

different kinds of dimensional limits inside of the world, which he explains extensively. In contrast to this, he says:

> The kind of beyondness intended by belief in a Creator, in a transcendent Power [...] must be something altogether different from this intramundane transcendence. [...] How are we to distinguish the beyondness of the Creator from that intramundane transcendence? [...] Why must all intramundane relations of transcendence inevitably fail in the long-rung and become just ephemeral symbols and metaphors, when we use them to express the beyondness of God?[18]

Heim thinks that an answer to this question is both possible and necessary. It is prayer that necessitates an answer, since the one who prays dares to use the I-Thou relationship for something completely different, with the consequence that he assumes an omnipresent beyond, or a beyond omnipresence, that has to reveal itself. The result is the experience of a world-transcending beyond in prayer.[19] Every prayer has to be understood as 'a continuation of a dialogue inaugurated by the great unknown, who is beyond all that exists.'[20] Everyone, who does not take this experience of prayer seriously, 'has, of course, to regard prayer as a monologue, in which the lonely I speaks with itself, in other words, a kind of partial madness.'[21] But let's assume the contrary, that prayer is meaningful. How can we then understand the presupposed transcendence? First, Heim identifies what is common among all intra-mundane relationships of transcendence: They deal in all cases, including in cases of the dimensional transcendence of spaces, with polar spaces, in order to use expressions from Schelling and Schleiermacher. Therefore, the transcendence beyond the world that reveals itself is precisely transcendent beyond the world, because it transcends polarity:[22]

> This original being is not spatially beyond. If it is there, it is omnipresently there. [...] The manner in which the original being is beyond our being differs fundamentally from the manner in which spaces are beyond each other. Furthermore, the beyondness of the original being cannot be expressed by putting one of the intramundane relationships of transcendence into the superlative, by speaking of an infinite, qualitative difference or by speaking of an unbridgeable, abysmal opposition, or by speaking of an unmeasurable distance of heaven and earth, of time and eternity. All these spatial metaphors are misleading, since the original being is not distinct from us in a spatial way. It is closer to us than we could ever be close to ourselves. [...] The original being is non-polar. [...] If the original being is outside of polarity, the polar world, of which we are a part, cannot be besides or beyond it. Otherwise there is a new polar relationship between the original being and the world. God would be the counterpole of the world, and

18 HEIM, K., God Transcendent, 77f.

19 Cf. HEIM, K., Glaube und Denken, 172–178. These passages belong to the later, untranslated editions.

20 HEIM, K., Glaube und Denken, 175 (transl. MM).

21 HEIM, K., Glaube und Denken, 175 (transl. MM).

22 Cf. HEIM, K., Glaube und Denken, 179–184.

> the world would the counterpole of God. God and world would then constitute each other reciprocally.[23]

According to Heim, divine transcendence signifies precisely a beyond of polar being, a suprapolar space in which we, as humans, are set, and which signifies neither a spatial, nor a personal transcendence, but a polar transcendence that leads into suprapolarity. Only if one is determined to experience a stay in a super-ordered space, is this specific transcendence intelligible. The same is true in cases of intra-mundane transcendences and in the case of transcendences beyond the world. Both can only be *discovered*, and apparent contradictions *can, but do not have to* denote a transcendence. As we have seen in ch. 11, in most cases of intra-mundane transcendence, the tension vanishes in a dimensionally higher space. In such cases, an original discovery that is not at one's disposal is overcome by provability and comes to be at one's disposal. The case of the suprapolar transcendence is different: it does not remain at one's disposal and it needs a constant self-revelation. However, as we already saw in ch. 11, Heim's concept of the suprapolar space is contradictory. The structure of the argument does not exceed the arguments of apophatic theology. The same is true, then, with respect to hyper-polar transcendence: it is contradictory. It is negative theology not simply by claiming something beyond polarity; this would be nothing but vagueness. The claim is that polarity itself is denied in the hyper-polar space. A look at Heim's three corollaries makes this clear:

First, the movement of the I-Thou relationship comes to its rest in the realm of superpolar being.[24] Here he repeats the well-known structures of argumentation of the apophatic critics of religion, when he calls this kind of transcendence with Ferdinand Ebner a 'single Thou' or as the only one 'who does not need any Thou in order to be an I', specifically as a 'subject that never can become an object.'[25] *Second*, the movement of the I-It-relationship comes to a rest. In the realm of polarity, objectivity is

23 HEIM, K., Glaube und Denken, 203f (transl. MM). Interestingly, this solution can only be found in the newer German editions of *Glaube und Denken*. The early German editions, as well as the English translation, do not contain these passages. In these earlier editions, Heim does not use the term polarity. Instead, he says that the common structure of all intramundane relationships of transcendence, be it distinctions of content or distinctions of dimension, is their either/or-structure. But God stands above or beyond all possible either/ors. Cf. HEIM, K., God Transcendent, 205f. However, the idea of a suprapolar space can be found in HEIM, K., Christian Faith and Natural Science, 159–174. In fact, these passages in the later German edition of *Glaube und Denken* are improvements inaugurated by his later insights.

24 Cf. HEIM, K., Glaube und Denken, 205f.

25 HEIM, K., Glaube und Denken, 206 (transl. MM).

only perspectival because the I-It-relationship is dependent on the perspective of the I-Thou relationship,

> objective reality remains all-encompassing; beyond my consciousness. It remains an incomprehensible, unreachable X for my knowledge. If there is only polar being, we can never escape epistemological skepticism. [...] But if there is an I, in which the I-Thou relationship comes to a rest, the infinite series of all mundane aspects is comprehended in it. In God, the movement of human cognition comes to rest.[26]

Third, being in God means that

> restless movement, which always exists in the objective space, comes to a halt. [...] In the divine being, the whole structural law, which constituted the infinity of time and space, is abandoned. If God exists, the whole form of time and space, including its character of infinity, is not something ultimate, but something penultimate. There is, therefore, an establishment of the whole space-time out of eternity as well as a return of temporality into eternity.[27]

Heim's suprapolarity is at the same time non-polarity, which makes the contradiction complete, since it is not only claimed that God transcends any category (a traditional neoplatonic claim), but that God is beyond the category of transcendence. If one takes what Heim has written literally, the consequence would be that *the category of transcendence cannot be used for God.*

This conclusion can be reached not only from Heim's thinking, but it is supported by basic systematic arguments:

1. If polarity amounts to relationality, and if transcendence or beyondness is a kind of relationality, the negation of polarity is also the negation of relationality and a relation of transcendence.[28] Is Heim, then, a mystic? What we have quoted above in regard to 'rest' would support this suspicion.

2. Heim, then, delivers nothing but a variation on the traditional theme that God is an exception to any categorical scheme of being.

3. Let us escape from Heim's abstract declarations regarding space and instead look to what stands behind them: the basic idea is that all polar spaces are kinds of relations of order, and the most common relation of order is the

26 Heim, K., Glaube und Denken, 206f (transl. MM).

27 Heim, K., Glaube und Denken, 207 (transl. MM).

28 In chapter 11 we saw as well that Heesch, M., Theologie und Naturwissenschaften, 216–223, provided an interpretation of the concept of the suprapolar space that is not based on relationality *per se*, but only on the relationality of the subject-object-difference, which also allows at least a perspectival suprapolarity for us. Though this interpretation, which does not lead to the aporetic, seems to me less adequate due to the aforementioned reasons.

relation of space. If one wants to speak of transcendence within this framework, then transcendence would mean a 'place' beyond of any relation of order, i.e. what is classically called God's perspective, which is comprehensive. However, in ch. 19 we saw that this idea is impossible. We learned with Anton Koch that an implication of interindexicality is that it is impossible to assume an observer that is not interwoven bodily in a (spatio-temporal) relation of order. This order would not lead to the direct impossibility of a transcendence beyond a relation of order. Such a transcendence could be there, and, moreover, not only one, but there could be an infinite number of such transcendences. However, *first*, such a transcendence would be principally undiscoverable for us. *Second*, it would not be able to disclose itself to us. And *third*, such a transcendence has no way of knowing anything in the (spatial-temporal) series of the relation of order, or acting there. Such a transcendence would not be worth calling 'God'. Such a transcendence would be nothing that would be of any relevance to us. Such a transcendence would simply be blind.

4. We learned in ch. 11 that the concept of space, in any sense whatsoever, is not a basic concept, but a derivation and abstraction of narrative wayformational lines. It is not space-time itself that possesses a character of ordered relations, but it is the becoming of wayformational lines of primary narrativity that constitutes spatiotemporal relations. Consequently, if one wants to use the idea of transcendence in a radical way, one would have to apply it to narrativity. In this radical sense, transcendence would mean something that is beyond primary narrativity. In regard to such a transcendence, what we have said about interindexical transcendence would also be true. It would be completely unknowable; one could by no means discover it in the framework of primary narrativity, and it could not be affected in any kind by primary narrativity. Such a transcendence would not be worth calling 'God.'

5. All these difficulties disappear if one removes the concept of transcendence from the concept of beyond, which would be a non-radical, strictly relational understanding of transcendence. It would require abandoning the nominal use of transcendence and using only its verbal form.

6. To use the concept of transcendence in a relational manner is to say in what respect something is transcendent. But if one wants to say that divine transcendence means the transcendentality of transcendence – the condition for the possibility of a beyond with regard to anything – then the concept of transcendence expresses the same thing as the concept of alterity. In this relational-transcendental sense, transcendence means only that it is a feature of the becoming of narrative wayformational lines, which always appears in the mesh of other wayformational perspectives that are not identical with mine, but which are nevertheless constitutive for the becoming and formation

of my own wayformational perspective. And this is identical with the primary function of space: to enable alterity (ch. 11). In this relational-transcendental sense, the concept of transcendence is meaningful.

An example of such a concept of transcendence that also stresses the function of divine transcendence for human self-transcendence is Merold Westphal's. He liberates the concept of transcendence from the concept of space and distinguishes between cosmological, epistemological, and ethical, specifically religious transcendence.[29] All three of these levels of divine transcendence are correlated with human self-transcendence. Cosmological transcendence means 'the power that generates all finite things and gathers them into wholeness. By oneing the many, God provides identity in difference, unity in plurality.'[30] Epistemic transcendence not only means that God is the origin of all that is knowable, but that God is not at one's disposal, insofar as the cognition of God remains in hidden its revelation and a mystery. In a word, God transcends all our horizons of expectation, which leads instantly to the ethical or religious aspect of transcendence: 'God is the voice beyond my own who calls me to a life beyond my own through a promise and a command beyond any knowledge or will of my own.'[31] Westphal then tries to show that a theistic understanding of transcendence that is not subject to the verdicts of onto-theology is more appropriate for enabling human self-transcendence than pantheistic alternatives (Spinoza and Hegel). The kind of human self-transcendence that should be enabled is a movement that 'draws us away from our natural preoccupation with ourselves.'[32] Transcendence in all its forms, then, is an alterity that only refers to the wholly other: 'if it enters my experience on its own terms and not mine, if it permanently exceeds the forms and categories of my transcendental ego and permanently surprises my horizons of expectation.'[33]

In this relational sense, the concept of transcendence is not primarily a specific denotation of God, but something that expresses the relationship among wayformational lines. It expresses the essential feature of the narrative constitution of space. It is a kind of immanent transcendence. It stresses alterity, which is a given in any kind of relationality that is worth its name.

7. Yet more important is abandoning the nominal use of transcendence. Transcendence is derived from *transcendere*, 'to go across'. We can understand this in the sense of leaving any position behind and in the sense of being constantly on one's way to a new position, only to leave this one also behind. In this case, 'to transcend' refers to the unreality of standpoints. 'To transcend,' then, would be equivalent with becoming and moving on wayformational lines, that is, with the formation of stories, be it primary or secondary ones.

29 Cf. HENRIKSEN, J.-O., Life, Love and Hope, Pos. 3666.
30 WESTPHAL, M., Transcendence and Self-Transcendence, 9.
31 WESTPHAL, M., Transcendence and Self-Transcendence, 224.
32 WESTPHAL, M., Transcendence and Self-Transcendence, 2.
33 WESTPHAL, M., Transcendence and Self-Transcendence, 3.

This formulation of transcending is as such meaningful. But in this sense, it refers to something that is *not beyond* the mesh of becoming, and therefore, in that sense, it is questionable how it can refer to 'God', since any kind of becoming transcends: becoming *is* transcending.

We can summarize the results of this subchapter: The radical concept of transcendence, which is identical with radical beyondness, is not appropriate as a minimal condition of 'God.'[34] A non-radical, i.e. a relative concept of transcendence, that does not exclude the immanence of God, but is based on this immanence, would be possible. The latter could be developed in a nominal way as alterity and in a verbal way as transcending. However, in both cases such a non-radical concept of transcendence –not excluding immanence – would not deliver on what is promised. Although it would be right to say that God is transcendent and immanent, this would not only be true of God, but of all becoming – at least within the framework of a relational ontology of reciprocally constitutive relations.

21.3 God as Anarchic Event and as the Wholly Other

The concept of event has been used in manifold ways for 'God.' Here we must distinguish the concept of event within the framework of the doctrine of God, as it is used in Barth, Jüngel, and my own past writings, with that of the radical concept of event as it can be found exemplified in Žižek, Deleuze, or Caputo. Whereas the first type belongs to the doctrine of God in a way that presupposes both that the minimal conditions of 'God' are already determined, and that God has identified Godself, the latter is used, e.g. by Caputo, in order to determine something that we have called a minimal condition for speech about God – although in Caputo's opinion it is more a maximal determination of what can be said about God: beyond his philosophy of religion – which bears traces of the language of proclamation, as Henriksen has seen[35] – there is nothing to say. Theology therefore, is out of a job, in Caputo's view.

It is interesting that Caputo claims that he can 'name' radical alterity with the help of the concept of event without locating it in a conceptual, ontological system.

34 Cf. also recently HERMS, E., ST I, 177, who similarly refuses the concept of beyondness due to similar thoughts, but allows the concept of transcendence – not understood in the way of nominalized, verbal transcendence.

35 Cf. HENRIKSEN, J.-O., Life, Love and Hope, Pos. 3789.

Caputo presupposes a dialectic between event (in contrast to occasion) and name, as we saw in ch. 9.3. The name refers to the event, but, in contrast to the event, the name is incomprehensible, untranslatable, not literal, beyond any horizon, ethically ambivalent, and belongs neither to being nor to the perturbation of being. It is the truth behind the name, and irreducibly kairological. Caputo claims that classical theology was bipolar in the sense that it referred to the name as well as to the event. Insofar as it referred to the name, it was a theology of power, insofar as it referred to the event it was a theology of weakness.[36] Caputo presupposes the theological tradition and he regards his own, quasi meta-theological reflections as a kind of ironic language, by stressing (with Derrida) only the event and weakness. God as event is not real, but transcends the real in a hyper-real way to what is not yet real.[37] God is no *arche*, but an *anarche*, no essence, being or foundation of being, but the confusion or perturbation of being. God does not exist, but calls as *kerygma* and promises[38] – God promises the possibility of the impossible.[39] God inaugurates no ontological conceptualization, but an answer in prayer and deed,[40] or, at best, a quasi-phenomenological *epoché*.[41] What Caputo delivers is not a classical philosophy of religion, but he always presupposes the Christian tradition, its writings, and its theology. His meta-theology of the weakness of God is presented as an exegesis of St. Paul by means of Derrida. Thereby he conceives the kingdom of God as an event. We can hear its call in a narrative way, like in the parables of Jesus, but we cannot classify it in any ontological order. His meta-theology is more a confession than an argument:

> About God I confess to two heterodox hypotheses. First, the name of God is the name of an event rather than of an entity, of a call rather than of a cause, of a provocation or a promise rather than of a presence. Secondly, and this follows from the first, we will do better think of God in terms of weakness rather than of outright strength. So in sum, I shift from the register of strength to that of weakness, from a robust theology of divine power […] and omnipotence to a thin theology of the weakness of God, from the noise of being to the silence of an unconditional call.[42]

36 Cf. CAPUTO, J.D., Weakness of God, 7.
37 Cf. CAPUTO, J.D., Weakness of God, 11.
38 Cf. CAPUTO, J.D., Weakness of God, 9. 14. 16. 107.
39 Cf. CAPUTO, J.D., Weakness of God, 16. 18.
40 Cf. CAPUTO, J.D., Weakness of God, 5. 10.
41 Cf. CAPUTO, J.D., Weakness of God, 13.
42 CAPUTO, J.D., Weakness of God, 11f.

We have to acknowledge some advantages of this kind of thinking: Caputo is able to do something interesting with classical theology and piety. He also tries to exclude any remainder of strength, power, and omnipotence that might be mirrored in the speech of the all-determining reality as a minimal condition. In this way, he tries to take divine, radical alterity seriously. On the other side, there are disadvantages and Caputo has to pay a huge price, as Henriksen has observed.[43] Alterity is always a relational concept. And if one wants to stress alterity in a radical way as Caputo tries to do with the help of his concept of an event, then one is parasitically bound to the order of ontology – to the name. Furthermore, we have to add our own critique: by describing God as anarchical event, which disturbs any kind of order, which is not intelligible, but lovable and that calls to love,[44] Caputo is a victim of the Manichaean trap: He cannot explain why there is order, essence, being, becoming, and events in the sense of occasions. They represent the pole of the world that simply exists, and that is disturbed by the loving God of weakness, in the direction of a promise without any new kind of order. But God as disturbing, weak event is unthinkable without this presupposed order. Therefore, in Caputo there is a dualism of *arche* and *anarche*; of a occasion and being on the one, and of event and call on the other hand; of reason and love. This dualism is basic for Caputo – and more precisely, this dualism is – against Caputo's own intent – *ontologically* basic. Caputo is therefore a good example of the tragedy of all critics of ontology: They do not abandon ontology for the sake of something new, but they criticize certain ontologies on the basis of a different ontology – but which is not allowed to be called 'ontology.'

One can also see that alterity is bound ontologically to an ever-existing order when Caputo claims that space and time are primary over events and narratives,[45] and are therefore not based on narratives. It looks as though space and time, and the historical order founded upon them, would be the second pole of the dualistic God, to which the anarchical pole is opposed in weakness. And weakness is only weakness if it effects nothing. While the order of being and history is supposedly disturbed by God as the anarchical event, are being and history really affected? Or does the order of history not simply bury the weak event under its wheels, as Schweitzer said about Jesus' proclamation?[46]

---

43 Cf. HENRIKSEN, J.-O., Life, Love and Hope, Pos. 3815.

44 Cf. CAPUTO, J.D., Weakness of God, 36.

45 Cf. CAPUTO, J.D., Weakness of God, 6f.

46 Cf. SCHWEITZER, A., Quest of the Historical Jesus, 368f: 'The Baptist appears, and cries: "Repent, for the Kingdom of Heaven is at hand." Soon after that comes Jesus, and in the knowledge that He is the coming Son of Man lays hold of the wheel of the world to set it moving on that last revolution which is to bring all ordinary history to a close. It refuses

One could only give an answer to this question if one has some idea what truth is. But in the same way by that Caputo uses a dualistic concept of God, he also employs a dualistic concept of truth. In the realm of the order of being, truth means correspondence,[47] which is opposed to the higher truth of the anarchical God. There, truth has no correspondence relation, but a relation of action: he claims in an apparently biblical manner that one is in the truth, when one does the truth, i.e. the one who is moved by the call of the event of the kingdom of God – and who acts correspondingly.[48] The consequence is that human action becomes the only mode of actualizing God, because it is the only way by which the event transcends its hyper-reality to enter into reality. The consequences for non-believers are alarming: here is someone who acts in the name of a God, and claims – although it is called a God of weakness – the primacy for one's own human actions. This consequence might be the opposite of what Caputo intends. Nevertheless, viewed from any other wayformational perspective than Caputo's, it does not look like the victory of a God of weakness, but of a God of power. It looks like a commitment to one of Nietzsche's basic ideas. The danger of becoming totalitarian threatens. It is true that one's own actions might be understood as incomplete answers to the call of the event. But whoever has not heard this call, whoever has not heard the event, can only regard this as a strategy of self-immunizing or self-totalizing of the human believers. And that cannot be what is intended by the Gospel. Caputo's basic mistake consists in regarding truth primarily as action instead of passion.

With respect to methodology, the rupture between event and narration on the one hand and between name and concept on the other, is problematic. Names are not simply the origin of concepts, but constantly related to concepts. They are not anti-conceptual, since narrations are in need of concepts in order to work, as we saw in ch. 14.

The main thing that can be drawn from reading Caputo is that he illustrates the fact that radical alterity in the sense of absolute otherness is unthinkable. Alterity is always a relational concept, or, more precisely, a concept of difference. Therefore, it is important to explicate the particular relation at stake,

---

to turn, and He throws Himself upon it. Then it does turn; and crushes Him. Instead of bringing in the eschatological conditions, He has destroyed them. The wheel rolls onward, and the mangled body of the one immeasurably great Man, who was strong enough to think of Himself as the spiritual ruler of mankind and to bend history to His purpose, is hanging upon it still. That is His victory and His reign.' Schweitzer himself deleted this famous section in the later German editions.

47 Cf. CAPUTO, J.D., Weakness of God, 16.

48 Cf. CAPUTO, J.D., Weakness of God, 16: 'for in the kingdom, the meaning of truth is *facere veritatem*.'

since we can thereby see in what respect alterity and difference exists. The concept of difference, liberated from its post-modern, anarchic, or apocalyptic[49] connotations, is more precise than the concept of alterity, but at the same time it is less determined, since what can be meant concretely is dependent on particular wayformational perspectives.

Caputo's meta-theology illustrates the tragedy of thinking of God as alterity: whatever alterity means, it is determined through a known point of reference. The same true for the classical *via negative*, but also for Barth's dialectical period. The well-known metaphors of 'vertically, from above,'[50] the tangent that touches the circle without touching it,[51] the language of the wholly other, of being completely different, or of being utterly distinct,[52] etc. are not wrong. However, they remain limited in their ability to express alterity by including what is already known. In Barth, his handling of the problem of eternity is an example *par excellence*: he wants to liberate eternity from the opposition of time,[53] but his material explications of eternity remain captured by the opposition of time.[54]

However, Barth indicates another way of thinking of divine alterity not as relational, but (seemingly) as absolute, when he says, 'God is God.'[55] Only the proposition 'God is God' expresses divine alterity in a radical way, because it is not a determination of God, nor is it determined by minimal conditions. If it is seen as a minimal condition, one would have to say that the minimal condition is that there is no minimal condition anymore: One has to speak about something without being able to talk about it and not remain silent. Logically, this could be expressed in the following way: 'God' would be without any conceptual content, i.e. it would be a singular term, but a very special one. In contrast to all other kinds of names and singular terms, it would neither be bound to any identity description, nor to particular narrations. However, singular terms without reference to narration cease to be terms at all. If one wants to avoid this consequence, one has to acknowledge that the term 'God' requires the concepts of self-revelation, self-identification, or self-narration. And this is exactly what Barth stressed, at least after 1931.[56] The knowability

49 Cf. DERRIDA, J., Apokalypse.
50 BARTH, K., Romans, 30.
51 Cf. BARTH, K., Romans, 30.
52 Cf. BARTH, K., Romans, 28. 36. 107 etc.
53 Cf. BARTH, K., CD II/1, 611.
54 Cf. BARTH, K., CD II/1, 610–640, and for a review MÜHLING, M., Liebesgeschichte Gott, 255.
55 BARTH, K., Romans, 63.
56 Cf. BARTH, K., Fides quaerens intellectum.

of such a self-revelation presupposes once again minimal conditions for 'God' as concept, if one wants to avoid the trap of idolatry we mentioned in ch. 21.1. Retrospectively, after 1956, Barth deals with his dialectic period in an interesting way: What is known, the humanity of God, is grounded in the otherness of God:

> It is nevertheless true that it was pre-eminently the image and concept of a "wholly other" that fascinated us and which we, though not without examination, had dared to identify with the deity of Him who in the Bible is called Yahweh-Kyrios. We viewed this "wholly other" in isolation, abstracted and absolutized, and set it over against man, this miserable wretch – not to say boxed his ears with it – in such fashion that it continually showed greater similarity to the deity of the God of the philosophers than to the deity of the God of Abraham, Isaac, and Jacob. [...] Indeed [...] it is a matter of *God's* sovereign togetherness with man, a togetherness grounded in Him and determined, delimited, and ordered through Him alone. [...] Who God is and what He is in His deity He proves and reveals not in a vacuum as a divine being-for-Himself, but precisely and authentically in the fact that He exists, speaks and acts as the *partner* of man.[57]

This makes clear that Barth either abandoned the concept of an absolute, non-relative understanding of divine alterity or that he never really held that view.

Of course, the early Barth and his followers are not the only ones who tried to speak of a radical, absolute alterity as a minimal condition for speaking of the divine. In Jewish philosophy of religion, one might think of Levinas. His concept of alterity is significant, since it neither means the negation of being as non-being, nor the difference of an other-being in contrast with a particular, determined being. The idea is to speak of the radicalism of alterity as distinct of being, as beyond the alternative of to not-be and to be otherwise.[58] Is such an alterity thinkable? In no circumstance is it linguistically expressible. Herein, Levinas meets Derrida in his critique of logocentrism.[59] Therefore, it is no wonder that this kind of alterity manifests itself at most as shadow-like on the face of the other. What we can observe in examples like these are examples of the limits of any philosophy of religion: they cannot arrive at a minimal condition for 'God' that is in itself meaningful. All meaningful minimal concepts of 'God' – this is particularly clear in the case of the concept of alterity – exceed conceivability, and they are only meaningful if they meet a self-identification or self-representation of God. It is simply not true that religion can be sublated

57 BARTH, K., Humanity of God, 44f.

58 Cf. LÉVINAS, E., Otherwise than Being, 3, and to this also TIPPELSKIRCH, D.v., Liebe von fremd zu fremd, 42f.

59 Cf. DERRIDA, J., Grammatology, 3.

into philosophy. If, at all, philosophy has to be sublated into the trusting perception of what is revealed.

The result regarding the concept of alterity is similar to the result regarding transcendence (21.2): only in a strictly relational sense is the concept of alterity as well as the concept of difference meaningful.

21.4 God as Being Itself?

By trying to think God as other than being, Levinas presupposes a broad tradition that proceeds in a contrary way. To speak of God as being itself is classical, and one of its most radical originators can be found in Parmenides. From then on, it can be found in the whole history of Greek philosophy and in the theology influenced by it up to the 20th century.

Parmenides begins with the idea that non-being is unthinkable and unreal. Koch demonstrates convincingly[60] that the background for that kind of thinking is Parmenides' insight into the antinomy of negation (ch. 18.10). Parmenides deals with this antinomy in a radical way: he excludes not only the antinomy, but negation itself as limit. Then one gets the one, unchangeable, eternal being itself, without any plurality, alterity, becoming, changing, time, or temporal presence. There is only the simple, homogeneous being. Only in a metaphorical way can one think of it as a sphere. The presence, in which it exists, is a timeless presence, and therefore no presence at all, but simply the negation of time itself.[61] It is an open question whether Parmenides is a victim of his own trap: Is this Eleatic monism of being really the only thing that is thinkable and disclosed, whereas the phenomenal world is pure illusion – as Parmenides thought – or is Parmenides doing nothing but following the consequences of the operation of negation by denying all that is open to experience? In any event, Parmenides intends the former. Following Plato and Aristotle, the Eleatic understanding of being appears dissolved from its origin in the antinomy of negation,[62] and is quasi-independent. The consequences historically are that it unfolded from there with a disastrous influence on the history of theology and philosophy of religion. Here, the distinction between creator and creation softened the contrast somewhat, since the phenomenal could not simply be declared as unreal, but created being was seen in opposition to uncreated being itself. But even this relative salvation of the phenomena as created by

60 Cf. Koch, A.F., Versuch, 287f.
61 Cf. Koch, A.F., Versuch, 418, 433.
62 Cf. Koch, A.F., Versuch, 278.

God lead to the consequence that God as being-itself is beyond what can be expressed. An excellent example for this kind of thinking in the 20th century Paul Tillich's use of being-itself.

Beside his functional determination of God as ultimate concern, his main determination of God is the traditional *esse ipsum* or being-itself. According to his method of correlation, we have a kind of double access to it. On the one hand, we have the philosophical questions; on the other hand, we have the answers of revelation from the standpoint of the new being. The being-itself is therefore the intersection point of philosophy and theology. In Tillich's opinion, being-itself is far more than a minimal condition for the talk of God. Rather, he conceives it as the only proposition that is not a symbolic, but a literal statement about God:

> The statement that God is being-itself is a nonsymbolic statement. It does not point beyond itself. It means what is says directly and properly; if we speck of the actuality of God, we first assert that he is not God if he is not being-itself. Other assertions about God can be made theologically oinly on this basis. Of course, religious assertions do not require such a foundation for what they say about God; the foundation is implicit in every religious thought concerning God. Theologians must make explicit what is implicit in religious thought and expression; and, in order to do this, they must begin with the most abstract and completely unsymbolic statement which is possible, namely, that God is being-itself or the absolute. However, after this has been said, nothing else can be said about God as God which is not symbolic.[63]

Here, Tillich presupposes a genuine concept of the symbol, which is different than Peirce's concept that was used in ch. 12. In contrast to a conventional sign, a symbol participates in the being of that which it denotes, but is nevertheless distinct from it.[64] Therefore, the concept of being-itself is more than a purely minimal condition. His entire ensuing doctrine of God deals 'only' with symbolic statements. Of course, this 'only' is not the sign of a limitation, as, based on his theory of participation, symbols have an eminent dignity. Tillich asks whether this, as the only literal statement about God, could be a tautology.[65] But he denies that this is the case. Let us now consider *how* the philosophical and the theological epistemological approach culminates in being-itself, and *what* its content is.

Philosophically, the basic question is the question of the structure of being, which can be asked by the phenomenal being in the human manifestation of

63 Tillich, P., ST (engl.) I, 238f.
64 Cf. Tillich, P., ST (engl.) I, 239.
65 Cf. Tillich, P., ST (engl.) I, 164.

itself.[66] Since humans belong to being, they cannot ask this question in a disengaged way, but ask this question within their existence, including through the experience of anxiety and courage.[67] And this question is the same one Parmenides asked centuries ago: it is the question of being and non-being; it is the question about the threatening of being by its negation. And like Parmenides and Heidegger, Tillich also recognizes that the conceptual structure of reason itself presupposes the operation of negation.[68] Therefore he can call this the question of the 'depth of reason'.[69] In the face of the situation that the appearing being always emerges out of non-being and is threatened by non-being, it is in itself the question of being-itself.[70] The basic structure of phenomenal being is that in it being and non-being are quasi connected, with the effect that it is constituted as a polarity. Polarity means, according to Tillich, two things. First, it is dialectically constituted. The one pole includes the negation of the other and *vice versa*. Second, the relation between the poles is a reciprocally constitutive relation: the one pole implies the existence of the other and *vice versa*. These essential polarities are also reflected by the structure of Tillich's *Systematic Theology*. The essential polarities of being are the polarities of individuality and universality, of dynamics and form, and of freedom and destiny.[71] They mark all being as existence, which as a whole stand in a polarity to essence.[72]

Being-itself is the answer to these questions. It is outside these polarities, since otherwise it could not be the answer, as it itself would be threatened by non-being.[73] In order to express the polar character of being in its basic structure of negation, Plato and the Greek tradition used a different way than that of the Christian theological tradition. Tillich uses for this distinction the two Greek negations of being as *ouk on* and *me on*. *Ouk on* means the absolute negation, *me on* the relative negation which is related to being and its potentiality. Whereas in the Greek tradition, *me on* referred to the pure potentiality of matter, the theological tradition conceives of being as creation that is based on an *ouk on* according to the doctrine of *creatio ex nihilo*.[74] In order to express

66 Cf. TILLICH, P., ST (engl.) I, 168.
67 Cf. TILLICH, P., ST (engl.) I, 253.
68 Cf. TILLICH, P., ST (engl.) I, 187.
69 TILLICH, P., ST (engl.) I, 79.
70 Cf. TILLICH, P., ST (engl.) I, 163.
71 Cf. TILLICH, P., ST (engl.) I, 165.
72 Cf. TILLICH, P., ST (engl.) I, 165.
73 Cf. TILLICH, P., ST (engl.) I, 164.
74 Cf. TILLICH, P., ST (engl.) I, 187f.

the polar structure of being, *me*-ontic expressions are necessary. Christianity introduced these indirectly at another place.[75]

As an answer to the question of being, being-itself is also theologically comprehended. We can see this by noticing on the one hand that traditional theology has often used the concept of *esse ipsum* and, on the other hand, by the figure of the revelation of the new being that presupposes being-itself.[76]

Thus far, we have dealt with the epistemic question of how Tillich seeks to ground the concept of being-itself. Let us now deal with the material content of this concept.

The concept of being-itself is equivalent to the concept of the power of being (in everything and beyond everything),[77] the infinite ground of being,[78] the absolute,[79] and also the depth of reason.[80] As such, it is at once in all beings as it transcends all beings, i.e. it is beyond all polarities. The concept of being-itself is, therefore, constituted in the same structure as the concept of transcendence in Heim. Since the being-itself transcends every polarity, it also transcends the polarity between essence and existence.[81] All of this is mirrored by Tillich's whole doctrine of God. Therefore, it is understandable why the whole doctrine of God is a symbolic one: On the one hand, the polar beings participate in being-itself, otherwise they would not exist. On the other hand, being-itself is, in an Eleatic way, an exception to the polar structure of beings. The consequence is without any doubt that Tillich simply does not use being-itself as a negative, incomprehensible concept beyond all polarities, but that he, similar to the basic Eleatic, structure, *dissolves the polar structure in being itself for the sake of one pole* – in contradiction to what he claims. Here is the proof.

First, there is a basic argument concerning negation. Being-itself is the absolute opposition to *ouk on*. In contrast to the beings of creation there is no *me on*. Although Tillich acknowledged that theology did not try to conceive the meontic simply by ideas that concern creation, like *privatio boni*, but also by ideas concerning the doctrine of God that are not based on negative, but positive theology.[82] In the end, he sees the meontic negation restricted to creation.

75 Cf. Tillich, P., ST (engl.) I, 188f.
76 Cf. Tillich, P., ST (engl.) I, 55.
77 Cf. Tillich, P., ST (engl.) I, 235f.
78 Cf. Tillich, P., ST (engl.) I, 21.
79 Cf. Tillich, P., ST (engl.) I, 239.
80 Cf. Tillich, P., ST (engl.) I, 79.
81 Cf. Tillich, P., ST (engl.) I, 205.
82 Cf. Tillich, P., ST (engl.) I, 188f.

Second, the one-sidedness of Tillich's dissolution of polarity in favor of one pole is also reflected by his doctrine of the attributes of God. He presents the attributes in a specific order, and what he had designed in respect of being-itself governs all other attributes, the classical 'metaphysical' ones as well as the 'biblical' ones. Let's start with the 'metaphysical' attributes.

Omnipotence, on the one hand, cannot be understood as the ability to effect whatever one wants, since this would mean counting God with the polarity of created beings.[83] On the other hand, omnipotence must not be equated simply with the *determinatio* of all reality as a whole, which is how the Reformers conceived of it, since then the being of God would be restricted to spatio-temporal events, which would weaken divine transcendence.[84] Tillich defines omnipotence:

> It is more adequate to define divine omnipotence as the power of being which resists nonbeing in all its expressions and which is manifest in the creative process in all its forms. Faith in the almighty God is the answer to the quest for a courage which is sufficient to conquer the anxiety of finitude. Ultimate courage is based upon participation in the ultimate power of being. When the invocation "Almighty God" is seriously pronounced, a victory over the threat of nonbeing is experienced, and an ultimate, courageous affirmation of existence is expressed. Neither finitude nor anxiety disappears, but they are taken into infinity and courage. Only in this correlation should the symbol of omnipotence be interpreted.[85]

Omnipotence then means nothing but the fact that God as being itself is free of any negation, and this means hope for created, *me*-ontic beings

Eternity, omnipresence, and omniscience are nothing but omnipotence applied to the aspects of time, space, and the subject-object structure.[86]

Even the 'biblical' attributes are governed by the Eleatic dissolution of the negation in being itself.

Here Tillich subsumes most of the biblical, especially OT-predicates, under the idea of *God as living.* It signifies the principle of processuality that is reduced, by the classical argument of the *via causalitatis* in a transcendental way, to being-itself, with the effect that God is not really living, but only the ground of life:

83 Cf. TILLICH, P., ST (engl.) I, 273f.
84 Cf. TILLICH, P., ST (engl.) I, 273.
85 TILLICH, P., ST (engl.) I, 273.
86 TILLICH, P., ST (engl.) I, 274: 'With respect to time, omnipotence is eternity; with respect to space, it is omnipresence; and with respect to the subject-object structure of being, it is omniscience.'

> Most of the so-called anthropomorphisms of the biblical picture of God are expressions of his character as living. His actions, his passions, his remembrances and anticipations, his suffering and joy, his personal relations and his plans – all these make him a living God and distinguish him from the pure absolute, from being-itself. Life is the actuality of being, or, more exactly, it is the process in which potential being becomes actual being. But in God as God there is no distinction between potentiality and actuality. Therefore, we cannot speak of God as living in the proper or nonsymbolic sense of the word 'life.' We must speak of God as living in symbolic terms. Yet every true symbol participates in the reality which it symbolizes. God lives in so far as he is the ground of life. Anthropomorphic symbols are adequate for speaking of God religiously. Only in this way can he be the living God for man.[87]

Also, the question of *God as relation*, or, more accurately for Tillich, the question about divine relatedness, is reduced in the same manner. Although it might be thinkable that there are internal relations in God – and that is not a concern of the first volume of his *Systematic Theology* – it is clear for Tillich that God cannot be essentially related to something that is not God. Therefore, God is the ground of relatedness of created beings:

> "Relation" is a basic ontological category. It is valid of the correlation of the ontological elements as well as of the interrelations of everything finite. The distinctly theological question is: "Can God be related and, if so, in what sense?" God as being-itself is the ground of every relation; in his life all relations are present beyond the distinctions between potentiality and actuality. But they are not the relations of God with something else. They are the inner relations of the divine life. The internal relations are, of course, not conditioned by the actualization of finite freedom. But the question is whether there are external relations between God and the creature. [...] If God is said to be in relation, this statement is as symbolic as the statement that God is a living God. And every special relation participates in this symbolic character. Every relation in which God becomes an object to a subject, in knowledge or in action, must be affirmed and denied at the same time.[88]

It should be clear that such a conception cannot leave room for any kind of a relational ontology, in contrast to the contemporary approaches of the 'Trinitarian Renaissance,' like, e.g. Schwöbel's.

Also, the basic statement of theology that *God is love* is shaved away by the Eleatic razor of being-itself. Thereby, Tillich is not really able to treat this statement in a serious way. Even here, Tillich constructs a mystery:

---

87 Tillich, P., ST (engl.) I, 242.
88 Tillich, P., ST (engl.) I, 271.

> It is false to define love by its emotional side. This leads necessarily to sentimental misinterpretations of the meaning of love and calls into question its symbolic application to the divine life. But God is love. This, however, is understandable only because the actuality of being is life. The process of the divine life has the character of love. According to the ontological polarity of individualization and participation, every life-process unites a trend toward separation with a trend toward reunion. The unbroken unity of these two trends is the ontological nature of love. Its awareness as fulfilment of life is the emotional nature of love. Reunion presupposes separation. Love is absent where there is no individualization, and love can be fully realized only where there is full individualization, in man. But the individual also longs to return to the unity to which he belongs, in which he participates by his ontological nature. This longing for reunion is an element in every love, and its realization, however fragmentary, is experienced as bliss. If we say that God *is* love, we apply the experience of separation and reunion to the divine life. As in the case of life and spirit, one speaks symbolically of God as love. He *is* love; this means that the divine life has the character of love but beyond the distinction between potentiality and actuality. This means therefore that it is mystery for finite understanding.[89]

No one will be surprised by the fact that Tillich also places the deictic terms of address, like "Lord" or "Father" into the set of symbolic language, signifying only one side of the polarity that has to be balanced out by the other pole of non-personal contemplation. Both, prayer and contemplation, remain trapped in the meontic, polar being. Their use is justified be his theory of symbols, but this language is in the need of being corrected by being-itself:

> "Lord" and "Father" are the central symbols for the ego-thou relationship to God. But the ego-thou relation, although it is the central and most dynamic relation, is not the only one, for God is being-itself. In appellations like "Almighty God" the irresistible power of God's creativity is felt; in "Eternal God" the unchangeable ground of all life is indicated. In addition to such appellative symbols, there are symbols use in meditation in which the ego-thou relation is less explicit, although it always is implicit. Contemplating the mystery of the divine ground, considering the infinity of the divine life, intuiting the marvel of the divine creativity, adoring the inexhaustible meaning of the divine self-manifestation – all these experiences are related to god without involving an explicit ego-thou relation. Often a prayer which starts with addressing itself to God as Lord or Father moves over into a contemplation of the mystery of the divine ground. Conversely, a meditation about the divine mystery may end in a prayer to God as Lord or Father.[90]

It is not surprising, too, that Tillich – in the light of the Eleatic dissolution of the concept of God – has to reject the opposite approach of speaking of divine

89 Tillich, P., ST (engl.) I, 279f.

90 Tillich, P., ST (engl.) I, 289.

becoming, divine process, divine relationality and perhaps also divine contingency. All this would mean mingling the divine with the meontic beings:

> This situation has induced some thinkers – partly under the influence of Luther's dynamic conception of God and partly under the impact of the problem of evil – to emphasize the dynamics in God and to depreciate the stabilization of dynamics in pure actuality. They try to distinguish between two elements in God, and they assert that, in so far as God is a living God, these two elements must remain in tension. Whether the first element is called the *Ungrund* or the "nature in God" (Böhme), or the first potency (Schelling), or the will (Schopenhauer), or the "given" in God (Brightman), or *me-onic* freedom (Berdyaev), or the contingent (Hartshorne) – in all these cases it is an expression of what we have called "dynamics," and it is an attempt to prevent the dynamics in God from being transformed into pure actuality. Theological criticism of these attempts is easy if the concepts are taken in their proper sense, for then they make God finite, dependent on a fate or an accident which is not himself. [...] The divine creativity, God's participation in history, his outgoing character, are based on this dynamic element. It includes a "not yet" which is, however, always balanced by an "already" within the divine life. It is not an absolute "not yet," which would make it a divine-demonic power, nor is the "already" an absolute already. It also can be expressed as the negative element in the ground of being which is overcome as negative in the process of being-itself. As such it is the basis of the negative element in the creature, in which it is not overcome but is effective as a threat and a potential disruption. These assertions include a rejection of a nonsymbolic, ontological doctrine of God as becoming. [...] Being comprises becoming and rest, becoming as an implication of dynamics and rest as an implication of form. If we say that God is being-itself, this includes both rest and becoming, both the static and the dynamic elements. However, to speack of a "becoming" God disrupts the balance between dynamics and form and subjects God to a process which has the character of a fate of which is completely open to the future and has the character of an absolute accident. In both cases, the divinity of God is undercut. The basic error of these doctrines is their metaphysical-constructive character. They apply the ontological elements to God in a nonsymbolic manner and are driven to religiously offensive and theologically untenable consequences. If the element of form in the dynamic-form polarity is applied symbolically to the divine life, it expresses the actualization of its potentialities. The divine life inescapably unites possibility with fulfilment. Neither side threatens the other, not is there a threat of disruption. In terms of self-preservation one could say that God cannot cease to be God. His going-out from himself does not diminish or destroy his divinity. It is united with the eternal "resting in himself."[91]

Perhaps it is understandable that Tillich feels forced to regard the attribution of a dynamic becoming of God as idolatry, because he thinks that becoming is only possible in the realm of the created polar tension of beings. Therefore,

91 TILLICH, P., ST (engl.) I, 246f.

against his own declarations, he does not treat processes and becoming as basic ontological categories, neither in God nor in the world. Rather, he treats them as derived categories:

> Process philosophy is justified in its attempt to dissolve into processes everything which seems to be static. But it would become absurd if it tried to dissolve the structure of process into a process. This simply would mean that what we know as process has been superseded by something else, the nature of which is unknown at present. In the meantime, every philosophy of process has an explicit or implicit ontology, which is aprioristic in character.[92]

Tillich regards the phenomena of becoming as ontologically derived from the *apriori* categories of dynamism and form, which are polarized. In claiming this, he makes the mistake of deciding too quickly for a specific ontology of phenomena, which was not necessary. He does not see that the polarity of dynamism and form is itself a conceptual abstraction of phenomenal becoming, which as such is without ontological dignity. Nevertheless, one has to admit that the rejection of a becoming God *under these conditions* is understandable. However, these conditions must be questioned. Apart from this, two other state of affairs remain unclear.

First, it is not understandable why the Lutheran Tillich denies the staurological self-definition of God in the cross:

> The principle of participation drives us one step further. God himself is said to participate in the negativities of creaturely existence. This idea is supported by mystical as well as by christological thought. Nevertheless, the idea must be stated with reservations. Genuine partripassianism (the doctrine that God the Father has suffered in Christ) rightly was rejected by the early church. God as being-itself transcends nonbeing absolutely.[93]

It is unbelievable that here Tillich clearly argues with an intentional falsehood: The doctrine that God is able to suffer was accepted by the ancient church at the second council of Nicaea by proclaiming the theopaschitic formula.[94] Tillich seems to be (intentionally) confusing theopaschitism and patripassianism. Patripassianism is nothing but a pejorative name for modalism or Sabellianism, which was correctly rejected by the church. The reason for this rejection was, however, that patripassianism includes (in contrast to theopaschitism) the personal identity of Father and Son, and therefore the absurdity

---

92 TILLICH, P., ST (engl.) I, 167.

93 TILLICH, P., ST (engl.) I, 270.

94 Cf. BEYSCHLAG, K., Dogmengeschichte II/1, 149f.

that it was God the Father who became flesh, suffered and died at the cross. However, it was not divine ability to suffer that was rejected. The capability to suffer of God the Son and the ability of the Father of co-suffering (including the co-changeability of the Father, by implication) were explicitly *emphasized* in the theopaschitic formula. This lax and distorted handling of the tradition only befits a theologian that tries to make everything subject to the Eleatic razor.

Second, it is not really comprehensible why Tillich does not see that he is not arguing for a being-itself that is far from the polarities of beings, but that he dissolves the polarities in favor of one of the poles. He dissolves the *me*-ontic polarities of beings and their negation into the absolute being-itself without any negation; this is his Eleatic heritage. The only important difference from Parmenides is that he is not identifying being-itself with all that exists, but with the concept of God. This has, in comparison with Parmenides, the advantage that he can acknowledge *me*-ontic being in the created world, whereas Parmenides has to regard phenomena as illusions. But for Tillich, the *me*-ontic being is being fallen from essence into existence, and it awaits the new being – the actualization of essence under the conditions of existence –, and at last its essentialization. Therefore, to acknowledge *me*-ontic being is only seemingly an advantage, since in the last instance, i.e. eschatologically, there is no *me*-ontic being anymore.

Parmenides is brave: In facing the antinomy of negation, he denies the phenomena itself and claims that there is the pure, unchangeable being-itself without any negation. It is an irony that this negationlessness being-itself can only be expressed by using the figure of negation, when the phenomena of experience has to be denied. Tillich deals with the antinomy of negation in another way: he does not really acknowledge it, but he belongs to the many who try to interpret it away. This is shown on the one hand by all of the effort he invests in dealing with the negation, without taking the antinomy seriously. On the other hand, it can be seen in his attempts to escape polarity, but in the end simply retaining the pole of form, structure, and being, whereas he tries to get rid of the pole of becoming, change, process, and relations. Therefore, he is not overcoming the polarity, but trapped within it, with the effect that he succumbs to idolizing the creature, i.e. to the demonic. Interestingly, he cannot see this.

The language of being-itself cannot satisfy the role Tillich expects it to. It is simply wrong to call it the only literal statement about God. If used at all, it is nothing but one symbolic statement among others. It is a metaphorical statement. One might be tempted not to acknowledge this, because it is at the same time a very abstract statement. But abstraction is not the same as non-metaphorical. However, even the far humbler role of a minimal condition cannot be fulfilled in a satisfactory way by being-itself, since it is nothing but a one-sided solution to the polarity and not its transcendence. Even Tillich's speaking of being-itself is ensnared by the theologically necessary critique of religion. Speaking of being-itself as a minimal condition of God – and here it is similar to the language of the absolute – is not meaningful. One would do better to get rid of it.

A solution to this situation can perhaps be provided by a fruitful typographical error that appears in the German translation, and which survived several editions. Do you remember how Tillich explains omnipotence? He writes:

> Opposing such caricature of God's omnipotence, Luther, Calvin, and others interpreted omnipotence to mean the divine power through which God is creative in and through everything in every moment. The almighty God is the omniactive God.[95]

The German version includes no literal translation. It *tries* to translate the passage to mean 'the divine power through which God is creative in and through everything in every moment' with '*die göttliche Macht, durch die Gott in jedem Augenblick in allem und durch alles schöpferisch wirkt*'. Retranslated in English that would be 'the divine power by which God in every moment, in and through everything creatively acts'. Yes, that is in principle the same: the predicate is not the auxiliary verb 'to be' but the verb 'to act' (*wirken*). But that is not what is actually printed:

> Im Gegensatz zu einer solchen Karikatur von Allmacht haben Luther, Calvin und andere Allmacht so ausgelegt, als bedeute sie die göttliche Macht, durch die Gott in jedem Augenblick in allem und durch alles schöpferisch wird [sic!].[96]

So instead of '*wirkt*' it actually reads '*wird*', derived from '*werden*' (to become). This is an ironic typographical error – nothing more of course. But what if the cure for Tillich's disease would be to simply take that a little bit more literally? So, the literal retranslation reads: 'the divine power by which God in every moment, in and through everything creatively becomes.'

95 Tillich, P., ST (engl.) I, 273.
96 Tillich, P., ST I, 314.

21.5 God as Absolute Necessity and as Becoming a Semetipso

The theological tradition has ascribed necessity or absolute necessity to God in contrast to the contingent being of the world. This does not simply mean that God is a necessary condition for everything else that is not God, but that the divine being is necessary in itself. Consequently, divine necessity is not a relative necessity because it is related to another *relatum*, but an absolute necessity. This kind of necessity is generally thought to be found *par excellence* in Anselm.

In order to do so, one has to refer to *Proslogion 3*. Since the argument of *Proslogion 2* and *Proslogion 3* appear in the framework of an argument for the existence of God, there is a dispute whether there are one or two 'proofs' of God.[97] *Proslogion 2* deals with the *ens perfectissimum*, and *Proslogion 3* deals with the *ens necessarium* connected with the *ens perfectissimum*. This dispute is superficial in its own right, since, both are correct in different respects: Anselm himself does not deliver an independent argument in *Proslogion 3*, but he deepens the argument of *Proslogion 2*. It is, however, possible to use the *ens necessarium* as a basis for independent arguments.

The concept of *ens necessarium* in Proslogion 3 means a being, about which it is impossible to think of non-being (*non posse cogitari non esse*).[98] Strictly speaking, this is not an absolute necessity, since it is bound to thinking. Necessity is only used relative to reason and human argument. But a necessity of reason is not identical with absolute necessity. Another aspect of a necessary being can be found in a variation of the so called cosmological argument. With Kant, one assumes that necessity in the framework of the cosmological argument could only be a kind of relative necessity, since the basic structure of the argument is an inference from contingent beings.[99] Follow Kant's argument that cosmological arguments presuppose the ontological one,[100] and you can explain why

---

97 The thesis that there are two cases is held by MALCOLM, N., Anselm's Ontological Arguments.

98 Cf. ANSELM VON CANTERBURY, Proslogion, III (86).

99 Cf. Kant's reasoning in KANT, I., Critique of Pure Reason, B644–647.

100 Kant invokes *de facto* the same cosmological evidence for *e contingentia mundi* as in Leibniz's version. His reconstruction is far from sharp witted, but sure enough it suits his system: In KANT, I., Critique of Pure Reason, B632 he brings it to the shortest possible but also most unintelligible form. The actual evidence does not lead this way at all; it consists of a justification of the sentence above, which Kant inserts in a note afterwards, see ibid. B633. Because of the role that Kant concedes to causality, it is not surprising that he formulates it the way he does. It is, however, wrong. The better evidence for *ex contingentia mundi* does without the thought of causality as well as without the thought of the completeness of the sequence, but is based on the principle *ex nihilo nihil fit*: If there is just contingent ($\neg Np \wedge \neg N \neg p$) existence, then there must have been nothing sooner or later in a temporally endless regressive sequence. But nothing follows nothing. But there

the tradition dealt only infrequently with contingency-based variations of the cosmological type. Indeed, in regard to Aquinas' variation in the *summa theologiae* it might be true that it is not very interesting.[101] But that is not the only, and by no means the first, historical appearance of the cosmological argument in the modal shape. Under the influence of Aristotle, it can be found in the Arabic philosophy of religion after Al Farabi in the 10th century,[102] and in the Latin west without the influence of Al Farabi in Richard of St. Victor in the 12th century. The latter version is especially interesting. In contrast to Anselm, Richard's argument is not based on a necessity of reason, but on a specific conception of existence.[103] We learned in ch. 7 that Richard's particular concept of existence leads him on the way to the discovery of a new relational ontology. Existence means, in one word, that everything that is, is related to something other: Richard combines *relatum* and relation in a single concept: '*Ex*' of *existere* signifies the relation, '*sistere*' the *relatum*. Richard now defines divine necessity such that it is an existence related to itself, a being *a semetipso*. At the same time, it has to be conceived of as eternal, since a being *a semetipso* that is not eternal is seen as a contradiction.[104] For our purposes, the element of eternity can be ignored. A necessary being, then, would be a being related to itself. And this would be absolute necessity. In a similar way, Hegel tries to express the same in speaking of an absolute necessity.[105]

In ch. 18 we learned that Nicolai Hartmann regarded the concept of absolute necessity as a contradictory one, since, with Kant,[106] necessity is seen as a strictly relational concept. Whereas contingency and randomness is conceivable without necessity, the reverse case is impossible, since only in a relational nexus can necessity be discovered. Without a relational nexus, necessity becomes randomness. Therefore, necessity also vanishes from the relationship between the different spheres or realms of modalities.[107] The consequence for the concept of God as absolute necessity is thus: 'God as the absolutely necessary being is rather the absolutely random being.'[108] These are the details of his argument:

---

is something, so the basic assumption that there are only contingent beings is disproved. If there is something, there also has to be a necessary being.

101 Cf. THOMAS VON AQUIN, s.th., I, 2,3.

102 Cf. CLAYTON, J., Gottesbeweise, here 729–731.

103 Cf. MÜHLING, M., Gott ist Liebe, 157f.

104 Cf. RICHARD VON ST.VICTOR, De Trinitate, I,8 (78).

105 Cf. HEGEL, G.W.F., Wissenschaft der Logik I391: 'Das schlechthin Nothwendige *ist* nur, weil es *ist*; es hat sonst keine Bedingung noch Grund.'

106 Cf. KANT, I., Critique of Pure Reason, B621f.

107 Cf. HARTMANN, N., Möglichkeit und Wirklichkeit, 94f.

108 HARTMANN, N., Möglichkeit und Wirklichkeit, 94 (transl. MM).

> Applied to the "absolutely necessary being" this means nothing less than that it is in reality the "absolutely random being". If not, it had [...] to be a being necessarily out of itself. And exactly that is what one means by *causa sui*. Really, however, a being that is of itself necessary is a non-necessary being.[109] [...] The best example is the monstrous oxymoron the "absolutely necessary being". One intends thereby God as the first ground of all necessities internal to the world. [...] A ground for the necessity of something, must be necessary in itself; whatever is the first ground of all grounds and at the same time is the ground of all necessities, has to have absolute necessity; otherwise all other kinds of necessity would collapse and become random necessity. [... But here] reigns a simple misunderstanding concerning the nature of a ground. To be the ground of something does not mean that it is necessary, it only implies that there is a necessary consequence to follow.[110]

Is Richard's concept of a necessary being subject to this objection? Formally, Richard does not abandon relationality. Also, a necessary being must be an *ex*-sistence, but also one that is related to itself. On the other hand, Richard's expression '*a semetipso*' resembles the *causa sui* that Hartmann is criticizing. However, it is *not equivalent* with it. Richard is not talking about relations of causality, but of relations *per se*. Richard is not claiming that his being *a semetipso* is free from other (necessary!) relations: Richard's version of the cosmological argument does not intend an abstract, theistic God, but the person of the Father, who is necessarily related to the person of the Son and the person of the Spirit, as one can learn from Richard's argument for the Trinity. But Son and Spirit are beings *non a semetipso*. Therefore, they are not distinguished from created beings by the way they are related – self-relatedness versus other-relatedness – but by the concept of eternity. The Father is an *ex*-sistence *a semetipso et ab aeterna*, the Son and the Spirit are *ex*-sistences *non a semetipso et ab aeterna*. At the same time, the self-related Father is necessarily related to the other two, which can be seen from the concept of love: the Father's self-relatedness, therefore is not conceivable without his intra-divine other-relatedness.

The consequences are as follows:

If one isolates the concept of an existence *a semetipso* from its Trinitarian framework, one gets the concept of an existence exclusively related to itself, which would be the absolutely necessary being. In that case, Hartmann's argument is correct. Such a being is not necessary, but actually contingent and random. The absolute, if it is conceived as dissolved from all relationships apart from its self-relation, can only be a random being. In other words, the

109 HARTMANN, N., Möglichkeit und Wirklichkeit, 93 (transl. MM).
110 HARTMANN, N., Möglichkeit und Wirklichkeit, 92 (transl. MM).

application of modalities to such a being is questionable. Hartmann was not the first to recognize this, but Hegel did as well – and affirmed it. When Hegel, in contrast to Kant, regards the concept of a necessary being as meaningful, then it is, similarly to Richard, not in opposition to a random being.[111]

But what happens if one is not dissolving Richard's argument and speaking of an existence *a semetipso* from its proper Trinitarian frame? Then we get a sphere of relationality, the intra-Trinitarian one. Correctly understood, in Richard an existence *a semetipso* is not absolutely necessary but relative necessary. It is not necessary insofar it is *a semetipso*, but it is necessary for the existence of the other two eternal persons. Furthermore, due to the concept of love, the other persons are necessary for the person of the Father, and that means that they are necessary for the existence of the Father *a semetipso*. Now Hartmann's argument cannot be applied, since all necessities concerning God are attributed in an immanently Trinitarian way. Perhaps Hegel should also be understood in this way, when he affirms the concept of a necessary being, which is already a Trinitarian idea. However, this does not save the concept of necessity, because now we find that the being of the Father *a semetipso* has nothing to do at all with necessity. Necessity is defined in other ways, in intra-Trinitarian ones. This might be true, but this is no argument for saving the concept of absolute necessity for the whole God. If one wants to do so, one would have to have thought about the complete Trinitarian sphere as absolute necessary – and Hartmann's whole argument would begin anew. Also, such a necessity could only be conceived of as relationally necessary, in regard to the created world. But then it is not the absolute necessity we are looking for.

The whole language of necessity, is, however, highly problematic, since it presupposes, as the semantic of possible worlds has shown (ch. 18), conceiving of a relational sphere or a world as a well-founded set. However, as we saw with Evers, it is exactly this that is unthinkable. What then is the origin of the language of necessity and randomness? It is dependent on another horizon: the experience of perception on wayformational perspectives. An absolutely necessary being in a double sense – necessary, because it is dissolved from all that is not itself, and necessary, because it does not include in itself a relational nexus – would be something that is – similar to the concept of transcendence – dissolved from any wayformational line and from any narration. The consequence would be that it does not have any primary narrativity,

111 Cf. HEGEL, G.W.F., Wissenschaft der Logik I, 391. Cf. also in addition HENRICH, D., Hegel im Kontext, 164; JÜNGEL, E., Gott als Geheimnis der Welt, 34f; PANNENBERG, W., Die Bedeutung des Christentums in der Philosophie Hegels; EVERS, D., Gott und mögliche Welten, 286.

and that it cannot appear in primary narrativity. Perhaps this could exist. But everything that could be predicated about it, would be purely random. In itself it would have to be ontologically undetermined. It would rather resemble the *me*-ontic negation.

The result of this subchapter so far is that the concept of an absolutely necessary being cannot be a minimal condition for speaking of God. If one would nonetheless like to use modalities for speaking of minimal conditions of the divine, one would have to declare, like Hegel, that necessity and randomness collapse, or that, in Jüngel's language, God is 'more than necessary.'[112] In Jüngel's case, this is a terminological solution, since a being that is more than necessary cannot be distinguished from a random or contingent being.

At the same time, the concept of the absolutely necessary that coincides with the absolute random, is not meaningless. One has to apply it within the framework of speaking of a mesh of relations or wayformational lines, or a 'world', insofar events or becomings are claimed that are seen *a semetipso*. One must necessarily assume such an entity, but it cannot be assumed by what entity it is instantiated. It could also be an instance in the world, or it could be the world as a whole. It could be an instance that is partially transcendent, too. What is excluded, however, is, as we learned in ch. 21.2, that it is an absolutely transcendent entity. By speaking of becoming-itself, by experiencing something as somehow becoming, one has already asked the question of a becoming *a semetipso* – and at the same time one has given an answer, insofar as such an instance, whatever it may be, cannot not be thought or experienced.

A becoming *a semetipso* must be assumed and it is implied in experiencing becoming on wayformational perspectives. A becoming *a semetipso* is conceivable together with its becoming *ab alio*. These two kinds of becoming can be related in four types:

1. Becoming *a semetipso* that excludes becoming *ab alio*
2. Becoming *a semetipso* that includes reciprocally becoming *ab alio a se*
3. Becoming *a semetipso* that includes becoming *ab alio ab alio*. This is identical with a becoming *ab alio*, which includes a becoming *a semetipso ab alio*.
4. Becoming *ab alio* that excludes a becoming *a semetipso*.

Ad 4: The fourth type of a becoming *ab alio* that excludes any becoming *a semetipso* is observable in natural and technical processes. Naturalism is properly the claim that this kind of becoming is the only one. This is only possible if one regards the perception of becoming as wayfaring in the mesh as an illusion, while simultaneously claiming that actually there is only becoming as

112 Cf. JÜNGEL, E., God as the Mystery of the World, 24f, 28–30, 33f, 38, 365f, 378, 395f.

transport in the net. But also, in this case, one could ask the question whether the network of the world would exist *ab alio* or *a se*. If it exists *ab alio*, it could not be the complete network of transport. Then the question would not be answer at all, i.e. the network would be incomplete. Therefore, it can only exist *a se*. This would be the *aseity* of the world as a whole (and one can call it then necessary, contingent, or more than contingent, as one likes). This is the pantheistic option. Naturalism, therefore, can only be conceived coherently in a pantheistic way, i.e. under the claim that despite there being only particular becomings *ab alio*, the whole network of becoming is *a se*. However, whoever does not regard the experience of a becoming *a semetipso ab alio* as an illusion, has to reject naturalism. Becoming *ab alio* that excludes becoming *a semetipso* can only be observed in the 3rd person perspective. And we can never be sure whether even these processes that we conceive of as unequivocally mechanical do not have an 'inner-side', as we have seen in our analysis of the possibility of panpsychism in ch. 19.3.

Ad 3: A becoming *ab alio* that includes a becoming *a semetipso ab alio* is the basic experience of perceiving, as we saw in ch. 5. It describes phenomenality *per se* and cannot be denied. It can by necessity not be reduced to transport in the network, but it always remains wayfaring in the meshwork. If one regards a becoming *ab alio*, which includes a becoming *a semetipso ab alio* as the only kind of mundane becoming, one propagates the panpsychist option. Whether this is the case or whether mundane becoming is a mixture of type 3 and type 4 cannot be decided, not by empirical, phenomenal, nor logical means. Both possibilities are coherent. Since the whole of mundane becoming is not a network, but a mesh, the question of whether it is complete is nonsensical. Nevertheless, we can ask whether this mesh of mundane becoming becomes as an uncloseable whole *ab alio* or *a semetipso*. Both options may be coherent. If one holds to the view that the mesh of becoming *concerning the particular* is a becoming *ab alio*, which includes a becoming *a semetipso ab alio* (and that is mixed or not mixed with becomings *ab alio* that exclude a becoming *a semetipso*), then *the whole* of this mesh can become either *ab alio* or *a semetipso*. Due to the experience of perception, conceiving of oneself as always (passively) destined to becoming and further becoming, and identifying either oneself or a particular mundane instance as this destining instance is the only option that is excluded. Nevertheless, the two remaining possibilities (pantheism and panentheism) seem to be coherent.[113] If one chooses the pantheistic option, this would be a non-naturalist pantheism. If one chooses

113 Cf., put differently, HERMS, E., ST I, 175, who claims this possibility to be impossible and contradictory.

the panentheist option, two other possibilities remain: the instance signifying God can be a becoming according to type 1 or according to type 2. The first possibility is incoherent.

Ad 2: A becoming *a semetipso* that includes a becoming *ab alio* cannot be confused with the other kinds of becoming – i.e. being a divine instance – unless it includes the becoming *ab alio a se*. This reception of one's own becoming through one's self from another can be conceived of in a double manner. First, the determination of one's own becoming from another can be thought of as strictly asymmetrical by itself: that the other is a result of one's own becoming. The Christian, the Jewish, and partially also the Muslim tradition has called this creation. Second, the determination of one's own becoming from another by itself can be conceived of in a symmetrical way. In this case, the instance denoting God would include *a semetipso* alterity, which is not the alterity of creation. The Christian tradition has claimed that this is indeed the case: it is the immanent trinity. These last two possibilities do not exclude each other, but they amplify each other, as we will see in the second volume.

Ad 1: A becoming *a semetipso* that excludes any self-becoming *ab alio* is not completely incoherent. However, it cannot denote the divine instance. It would simply be what is absolutely hidden and absolutely ineffective. It could not have any relation to the mesh of mundane stories, including no conditional function. If it exists, it would be meaningless, because it would be a story completely parallel to the mesh of the world, without influencing this mesh and without being able to be imagined from inside the mesh. Furthermore, such becoming that excludes alterity would be a strange kind of becoming. It could only perpetuate itself, and as such it would exist without any content. It would amount to something that is a negation without any position. It would be an *Ungrund* and abyss, but not a ground. Perhaps it would amount to the Eleatic being-itself, which cannot be a minimal condition for speaking of God.

21.6 God as Relative Necessity and as Perfection

Something, that is not open to experience or thinkable, is, according to Proslogion 3, necessary, which is necessity as a necessity of reason embedded in a relational nexus. Therefore, it is a relative necessity. We saw that the concept of absolute necessity is not an appropriate one for a minimal condition of speaking about God. But what about relative necessity? Is it appropriate or not? In *Proslogion 3*, and for most of Anselm's followers, the concept of relative necessity is used together with the concept of perfection. It is at least historically, if not conceptually, reasonable to deal with relative necessity and perfection at once.

Anselm's concept of perfection, *id quo maius cogitari nequit*,[114] is used in *Proslogion 2* as an argument for the existence of God, insofar as it is said, first, that existence belongs essentially to the concept of perfection, and second, that existence is quantifiably greater in comparison to non-existence. Kant claimed, perhaps rightly, that existence is not an actual predicate.[115] This means that the concept of *id quo maius cogitari nequit* cannot meaningfully be used as an argument for the existence of God. But it does not mean that it cannot be used in an appropriate way as a minimal condition for speaking about God. The so-called ontological proofs of God do not function as a means for showing whether something exists, but they deal instead with the question of how to gain meaningful concepts that can serve as minimal conditions for saying 'God'. In this respect, the question of whether *id quo maius cogitari nequit* exists is not as important as the question whether it is a coherent concept.

Nevertheless, we have also to say some words about Kant's rejection of the ontological argument, insofar as it concerns existence. One frequently encounters the opinion that Kant got rid of the ontological argument once and for all. But this is not strictly correct, as he does not offer only a negative result. His claim is to have shown that if one thinks of the concept of *id quo maius cogitari nequit*, one is forced to think of the existence of *id quo maius cogitari nequit*, without it implying its real existence. And this means that one has to conceive of *id quo maius cogitari nequit* as existing. That is, in my opinion, no small thing, and something with which theologians can be satisfied.

Others have tried to say more by evading the argument that existence might not be a real predicate. For example, Hubertus G. Hubbeling introduced a distinction between existence *de re* and existence *de dicto*.[116] In this case, existence is not used as a predicate, but *de dicto* and *de re* are used as predicates. The 'proof' then works in a way that existence *de re* together with *de dicto* is greater than existence *de dicto*. Under the condition of comparability, this proof is valid. However, it does not show that *id quo maius cogitari nequit* actually exists, but 'only' that, if one has understood what *id quo maius cogitari nequit* means, one has to *conceive* it as existing *de dicto* and *de re*.

These implications seem closer to what Anselm intended, since for him *Proslogion 3* belongs to *Proslogion 2*. And in *Proslogion 3* it is shown that the

114 Cf. ANSELM VON CANTERBURY, Proslogion, 2 (84).

115 Cf. KANT, I., Critique of Pure Reason, B626–629.

116 Cf. HUBBELING, H.G., Einführung, 82–86.

perfection – *id quo maius cogitari nequit* – is only conceived if it is conceived of as implying a necessity of reason, as *non posse cogitari non esse.*

Charles Hartshorne is also right to claim that *Proslogion 3* can be used in order to design a stand-alone argument for the existence of God. Hartshorne's claim is an argument in which perfection and necessity are still bound together, but existence does not appear as a predicate. Therefore, one is able to circumvent Kant's objection. Hartshorne first defines *non posse cogitari non esse* as a necessary being that is at once perfection. If p reads 'perfection exists', then Np means 'It is necessary that perfection exists'. On this basis, Hartshorne designed his well-known argument in ten steps.[117] Nevertheless it is not difficult to shorten the proof to its core:

(1) $Np \lor N\neg p$
(2) $\neg N\neg p$
(3) Np

(1) means, that perfection cannot be conceived of as existing contingently, or, that one has to conceive of perfection as necessarily existing or as necessarily non-existent, because otherwise one has not conceived of what perfection means at all. If one now assumes in (2) that it is possible to conceive of perfection as existing, i.e. that it is not necessary to think that perfection does not exist, then the conclusion is (3): that it is necessary to conceive of perfection as existing. And since in systems of modal logic like T the conclusion $Np \to p$ is valid, one has to conceive of perfection as existing.

Findlay argued,[118] that it is possible to substitute the premise (2) by premise (2*), with the consequence that one now gets the conclusion (3*):

(1) $Np \lor N\neg p$
(2*) $\neg Np$
(3*) $N\neg p$

In (2*), it is claimed that it is not necessary to conceive of perfection as existing, i.e. that there is no contradiction in also conceiving of perfection as non-existing. But then we come to the conclusion that it is necessary to conceive of perfection as non-existing. Both diverse conclusions rely, according to Dalferth,[119] on the fact that in formal modal logics the possibility that there is something and the possibility that there is not something are not equivalent, in contrast to ordinary language. Nevertheless, the whole argument is not without worth. It shows that the question alone about the possibility of

117 Cf. Hartshorne, C., Logic of Perfection, 50f.
118 Cf. Findlay, J.N., Can God's Existence be Disproved?
119 Cf. Dalferth, I.U., Gott, 204f.

existence or the possibility of non-existence is not asked on a neutral ground, but bound to particular wayformational perspectives:

> The background in experience is decisive from which the concept of the possibility of God, which excludes the impossibility of God, is thought: from the background of the experience of the *presence of God*, which is why Christian faith lives, or the experience of the absence of God, which shapes our mundane experience.[120]

Dirk Evers noted[121] that this proof, which in any case presupposes S_5 as system of modal logic, can be abbreviated to the following shape:

PNp→Np

Materially this means: If it is possible that it is necessary to think of perfection as existing, then it is necessary to think of it as existing. In S_5, however, PNp→Np, is trivially true, since here all iterated modalities can be reduced to the last one. However, we have learned that we cannot use S_5. If modalities are nothing but extrapolations of experiences we have had during wayformational perspectives and primary narrations, without which it is possible to use well-founded possible worlds as an interpretation of the modalities, then this kind of reduction is impossible, since we cannot reduce modalities in this way, as we learned in ch. 18.

Evers notes another point, which is also important. The classical reformulations of the argument by means of modal logic carry the burden that they do not distinguish between modalities of reason, modalities of non-contradiction, and modalities of being. Therefore, they produce equivocations.[122] It is, however, possible to circumvent this problem by operating only with relative modalities of thinking and by evading the question of existence.

From the perspective of narrative wayformational lines, the reconstructions using modal logic exemplify an important state of affairs. If it is possible to imagine something like perfection, then it has to be thought or it must not to be thought. There is, then, no third possibility: indifference, or fashionable agnosticism, is, in this respect, a *contradictio in adiecto*.

If perfection is a minimal condition for describing what 'God' means, then either the necessity of thinking or imagining perfection or the impossibility of thinking or imagining perfection is given, too. However, this question so far remains an abstract one, as one has no further predicates to which to attribute

120 DALFERTH, I.U., Gott, 205 (transl. MM).
121 Cf. EVERS, D., Gott und mögliche Welten, 323f.
122 Cf. EVERS, D., Gott und mögliche Welten, 325–327.

perfection, besides this necessity or impossibility to think. Hartshorne and Plantinga deal with this important question in a very different manner.

Let us have a look to Plantinga's argument first. Although it is historically younger, and Plantinga also claims to have given a 'victorious' analysis,[123] Plantinga's argument is more traditional and weaker than Hartshorne's.

First, Plantinga materially conceives of perfection as the sum of the classical attributes: omniscience, omnipotence, and moral perfection.[124] Plantinga therefore reveals himself as a classical theist, and, more importantly, it is not perfection *per se* that is used as a minimal condition for 'God', but the predicates omniscience, omnipotence, and moral perfection.

Second, Plantinga distinguishes between greatness and excellence in speaking about perfection. Excellence means perfection in only one given possible world, whereas greatness means perfection in all possible worlds.[125] Analogously to Anselm's original argument, Plantinga understands greatness as greater in comparison to excellence. Therefore, he claims that the conjunction of omnipotence, omniscience, and moral perfection has to be thought of as existing in every possible world – or, in other words – that in every possible world, an omnipotent, omniscient, and morally perfect being has to be thought of as excellent. And this is what Plantinga sees as an advantage in comparison with the usual reconstructions of such arguments by means of modal logic.

At other points, Plantinga seems to be more humble: Since his variation also involves the double move from the possibility of existence to the necessity of existence on the one hand, and of the possibility of non-existence to the impossibility of existence on the other, he claims that both, the theistic and the atheistic, options are rational, although he decides for the theistic one.[126] This means that his use of the modal argument is embedded in his basic idea of warranted belief.[127]

However, all in all we have to reject Plantinga's concept of God for material reasons:

First, Plantinga does not conceive of God as a condition of the possibility of possible worlds, as Leibniz does, but he conceives of God as part of possible worlds. Therefore, his concept of God is a purely immanent one, perhaps the opposition to Heim's purely transcendent concept of God. Pure immanence, even if it is thought to be almighty, omniscient, and morally perfect, is subject

123 Cf. PLANTINGA, A., Nature of Necessity, 213–217.
124 Cf. EVERS, D., Gott und mögliche Welten, 319.
125 Cf. PLANTINGA, A., Nature of Necessity, 213f.
126 Cf. PLANTINGA, A., Nature of Necessity, 216f.
127 Cf. PLANTINGA, A., Nature of Necessity, 221.

to the arbitrary identification that we saw to be the basic target of the justified critique of religion (ch. 21.1).

Second, Plantinga not only presupposes the semantics of possible worlds (ch. 18), but also the complete accessibility of possible worlds to one another. But we saw that this cannot be assumed even for our actual world. The world is not a well-founded set of transport-like determinations of a network, but a mesh of narrative, wayformational lines. Plantinga's argument is therefore untenable, and its plausibility on the first glance has to pay the price of making transport omnipresent and of implying a radical decontingentization.

Third, the relative necessity of reason and perfection in the shape of greatness and excellence are second level attributes, dependent on omniscience, omnipotence, and moral perfection. Therefore, the applicability of Plantinga's concept of perfection is dependent on the applicability of these concepts. And there is a reason to object to precisely this, although we have so far not made use of it.

Far more fruitful is Hartshorne's material explanation of perfection, developed in dispute with Findlay's objection. We learned that the reconstruction of modal logic leads either to a necessity of thinking perfection or to an impossibility of thinking perfection, depending only on whether one regards perfection as possible or its negation as possible. Which side of the alternative should we chose? The answer depends on the material content of perfection. Hartshorne claims that the possibility of the non-existence of perfection – and therefore the impossibility of conceiving of perfection – is only given as long as one uses the classical concept of perfection. This classical concept means that perfection is thought of as *actus purus*, i.e. that in God all possibilities are actualized. This means that perfection has to be thought of as actualized (e.g., in contrast to mathematical infinity). Therefore, it excludes any kind of becoming: it is static.[128] Concerning such a concept it is easy to show that its non-existence is possible, if one treats it analogously to mathematical infinity: same way there is no greatest number, there is no greatest being.

But Hartshorne offers an alternative by using his di-polar theism, influenced by Whitehead. Here, existence and actuality are not the same. God as *actus purus* is rejected. Like any number, God can be surpassed – but by nothing that is alien to God, only by later sequential states of the divine story of actualization. According to Hartshorne, such a concept of perfection means that

128 Cf. HARTSHORNE, C., Logic of Perfection, 64.

a self-surpassing perfection is not subject to Findlay's objection. Concerning this new concept of God, one has to prefer the possibility of God's existence.[129]

Our task, however, is not to illustrate Hartshorne's doctrine of God. The only important thing is that Hartshorne suggests a minimal material determination of perfection that should be accepted; perfection as *actus purus* has to be rejected. Perfection surpasses itself, and that means that perfection is in itself a story, a kind of primary or transcendental narrativity. Only in the framework of a perfection conceived in this way can we assume the relative necessity of reason. But even then, it always remains a necessity of reason and it never becomes an ontological necessity. Dalferth fruitfully suggested that the value of the *ratio Anselmi* consists in providing a rule of thinking or a way of thinking, which is for believers a necessary condition of how the experienced God has to be thought.[130] We can express this rule in the following way:

It is a minimal condition of 'God' to think a storied actualizing perfection through the relative necessity of reason.

This statement does not mean, that such a storied actualizing perfection is actually perceived or experienced. It does not tell us *wherein* and *in respect of what* this story is perfecting itself. And it does not mean that this storied actualizing perfection is ontologically necessary, or that we are speaking of a pure necessity that is to be thought of by created perceivers. A self-perfecting story remains a random or a 'more than necessary' story. It is not necessary that such a self-perfecting story appears during the perception on wayformational lines. However, if perfection appears, it has to be conceived of as self-actualizing perfection, which for the perceiver has the relative necessity of reason.

21.7 God as the Reality determining All Else or as the All-determining Reality

In Plantinga's variation of the modal argument, the predicate of omnipotence appeared as a possible minimal condition of speaking of God. This is insofar unusual, as it normally belongs to the material doctrine of God. Nevertheless, a minimal condition that seems to be derived from the predicate of omnipotence appears in different ways in Bultmann and Pannenberg, when they use the formulas the 'reality determining all else' or the 'all-determining reality,'

129 Cf. HARTSHORNE, C., Logic of Perfection, 35: 'God cannot conceivably be surpassed or equalled by any other individual, but He can surpass himself, and thus His actual state is not the greatest possible state.'

130 Cf. DALFERTH, I.U., Gott, 94.

respectively. This concept is correlated, as Pannenberg remarks, to the totality of reality. But Pannenberg is wrong when he claims that Bultmann introduces this expression as undefined and without reference to the totality of the world.[131]

Although indeed the terms of the totality of the world or of reality do not appear in Bultmann, all that can be perceived appears in Bultmann under the distinction of subject and object. The totality of reality is therefore lost insofar as we perceive within the framework of the subject-object distinction. When Bultmann therefore says that 'the distinction between subject and object must be kept separate from the question of our own existence,'[132] then it is the term of 'our' or 'my' *existence* that plays the role of the totality of the world and that it is the necessary correlate for the reality determining all else. Since all talk 'of' or 'about' God already presupposes the subject-object separation as talk from a standpoint outside of the object one talks about, this kind of language is not appropriate for grasping what the reality determining all else means, since this would give us the totality of reality, in the sense of our existence, without the subject-object separation. Therefore, the theistic definition of omnipotence as the ability to do everything that one wants to do, as we found it in Plantinga, is a violation of the concept of the reality determining all else. Perhaps one can express it in this way: by better understanding what all-determining means, Bultmann gets rid of the theistic predication of omnipotence. In order to speak of God, one has to be able to speak of one's own existence. But that would imply a self-objectification, with the consequence that such a talk of my own existence would deny God's claim on my own existence, which is implied in the concept of the reality determining all else. Therefore, talk 'of' or 'about' God is not only misleading, but also sinful.[133] Bultmann's talk about the all-determining reality is, therefore, far more than a minimal condition in the realm of a possible philosophy of religion; it presupposes the whole of Christian faith. The only possibility for speaking 'of' God would presuppose speaking out of God, i.e. if it was the speech of Godself. But even this notion of a participation in divine self-revelation is not satisfying for Bultmann. The concept of the reality determining all else needs to be balanced with another concept as a minimal condition: the talk of God as the 'wholly other', which Bultmann conceives of as an implication of the reality determining all else. Even if it would be possible to speak out one's own existence without presupposing the separation of subject and object, then man would speak about

131 Cf. PANNENBERG, W., Theology and the Philosophy of Science, 301.

132 BULTMANN, R., What Does it Mean, 59.

133 Cf. BULTMANN, R., What Does it Mean, 54.

himself, but not of God as the 'wholly other'. The result is that man once more rejects the claim of God for human existence. But since the claim of God is a claim for my own existence, I would fail to talk out of my own existence. Bultmann is therefore also critical of Heidegger's existential analysis. It might be helpful in its approach, but it neither leads to possible speech of God nor does it reveal my own existence. The main point of divine alterity is not that it exists as a matter of spatial or personal transcendence, but in respect of sin, i.e. concerning a state of affairs, where it is necessary that I miss God and myself:

> The statement that the God who determines my existence is nevertheless the "Wholly Other" can only have the meaning that *as the* "Wholly Other" he confronts me who am a sinner. Furthermore, in so far as I am *world*, he confronts me *as the* "Wholly Other". To speak of God as the "Wholly Other" has meaning, then, only if I have understood that the actual situation of man is the situation of the sinner who wants to speak of God and cannot; who wants to speak of his own existence and cannot do that either. He must speak of it as an existence determined by God; but he can only speak of it as sinful, as an existence such that *he* cannot see God in it, an existence in which God confronts him as the "Wholly Other."[134]

In a dialectical manner, Bultmann sharpens the paradox. But the consequence is neither a kind of quietism nor simply a means of propagating a figure of divine self-revelation or self-disclosure, but its point is the *justification of the sinner*, i.e. the justification of my own missing and sinful talk of God and talk of my own existence by God, from God, and out of God.[135]

Bultmann's argument is remarkable insofar as he begins with two minimal conditions for the talk of God that are normally situated in the realm of philosophy of religion – the reality determining all else and the wholly other – which lead to a paradox that can only be dissolved by justification. Therefore, the effect can never be an understanding or world-view (*Weltbild*). What is remarkable is not the description of the paradox as such, which is a feature common to the whole of dialectical theology. What is remarkable here is that the way out consists not simply in an epistemological figure of revelation, but in the *soteriological* one of justification.

For our purposes, the way Bultmann delineates this justification – as an active answer in obedience to the claim of the *kerygma*, as it can be seen by the existential interpretation of the biblical writings after demythologizing – is not really interesting, and we can ignore these details here in the same way we can

134 BULTMANN, R., What Does it Mean, 57f.

135 Cf. BULTMANN, R., What Does it Mean, 63–65.

ignore the succession of this line of theology in the tradition of hermeneutical theology, e.g. in Gerhard Ebeling.[136]

In short: Bultmann applies the material doctrine of justification to the problem of the cognition of God. Thereby he stresses a central point of Protestant theology, if not Christian tradition proper. Even the seemingly self-evident minimal condition of God as the *reality determining all else* is in need of being corrected by God. The point then is, that 'God' can only be 'God': We cannot think about God in general, not even in the sense of a minimal condition. Bultmann here resembles the early Barth. If we take these implications seriously – which can easily be done without subscribing to the whole of Bultmann's theology – a consequence would be that 'God' or the 'gods' of the different religious traditions would necessarily have nothing in common.

At this point, Pannenberg's reception of God as reality determining all else comes into play, since he tries to defend this concept as a working minimal condition. Three points are important: *First*, the all-determining reality includes the concept of a 'determining reality', *second*, this concept enables the idea of the indirectness of divine revelation, and *third*, since it is the *all*-determining reality, it provides the correlate to the totality of reality.

First, to speak of God as the all-determining reality means that humans are always determined in such a way that they have the experience of power manifesting itself. All humans can do is respond to an experience of power, but not to act with priority out of oneself, which is not only the case in Christianity and other established religions. It is a basic feature of all religions, including polytheistic and animistic ones. Therefore, Pannenberg defends his concept of an all-determining reality against the naïve opinions of the weak discipline of religious studies, which accuse him of transferring a feature of monotheism to religion in general.[137] What is important here is that humans always experience themselves first as determined, not as determining. However much one is tempted to agree with Barth's view of religion as disbelief conceptually, it misses its target in the plurality of religions insofar as even the most primitive religious practices, like these who try to manipulate the power of future in a quasi-technical way, presuppose that humans are primarily determined, i.e. that humans find themselves in the realm of some power. It is possible that this experience of being primarily determined instead of determining is the only common feature of all religions. In this way, Pannenberg tries to take seriously the claims of the different religious traditions.

136 Cf. EBELING, G., Dogmatik I, 184–187.

137 Cf. PANNENBERG, W., ST I (engl.), 160, 163.

Second, the idea of the all-determining reality enables the indirectness of revelation to be an answer to the problem that God cannot be a phenomenon, including not an extraordinary phenomenon:

> On the assumption, then, that the word 'God' is to be understood as referring to an all-determining reality, substantiation of talk about God requires that everything which exists should be shown to be a trace of the divine reality. This requirement applies, however, not to objects in abstract isolation, but to their unbroken continuity: 'all', as used in the concept of an all-determining reality, refers not to each individual thing on its own but to each in its continuity with all others. Theology as the science of God would then mean the study of the totality of the real from the point of view of the reality which ultimately determines it both as a whole and in its parts.[138]

It is important not to underestimate the significance of this point. For example, within this framework, it is clear that contemporary projects like the so-called 'Cognitive Sciences of Religion' (CSR) or 'Neurotheologies' are completely misleading, since they miss that everything to do with experience is already accompanied by the term 'God'.[139] Furthermore, it is obvious that under these conditions there can be no separation between theology and other academic disciplines. Theology is from the beginning on not only inter- but also transdisciplinary in the best sense of this word, insofar as this means an orientation to the phenomena and not on tertiary issues as a function of society. Theology included all this, long before the word 'transdisciplinarity' or its discourse ever existed.[140] There is in principle no possible object of human experience that is unworthy of theological reflection. The question 'What has this to do with theology', which theologians sometimes hear, is always a sign that the questioner misunderstands the concept of God. The background of this second element comes from the material content of dogmatics, but not from soteriology, as for Bultmann, but from the doctrine of creation.

Third, it is not simply the experience of any power as power, but as an *all*-determining power that is decisive for the concept of God. This was an insight first discovered by Greek philosophical theology, and it necessarily requires the totality of reality as its correlate. However, Pannenberg conceives of the totality of reality differently than Bultmann. Whereas for Bultmann the

138 PANNENBERG, W., Theology and the Philosophy of Science, 303.

139 I give details on the relevant criticism in MÜHLING, M., Resonances, 92–96. For further criticism of the CSR cf. VISALA, A., Naturalism, Theism and the Cognitive Study of Religion, and for criticism of neurotheology RUNEHOV, A.L.C., Sacred or Neural?

140 A good introduction to, and attempted ordering of, transdisciplinary questions is given by VILSMAIER, U., Grenzarbeit.

language of the totality of reality would amount to overcoming the subject-object separation, that is, to be able to speak of one's own existence –seen as an impossible possibility – for Pannenberg the central question is how the particular and the general (or the whole) have to be related.

At this point we have to deal briefly with a misunderstanding that one might have: The fact that historically the idea of the *all-determining reality* is derived from the omnipotence-predicate does not mean that it is only another word for omnipotence. Therefore, all problems concerning omnipotence do not necessarily concern the all-determining reality. Furthermore, 'determination' has here nothing to do with the concept of determination as it appears in determinist naturalism. Whether divine action is a necessary and sufficient condition of all mundane events, or only a necessary, but not sufficient condition of mundane processes, whether God is responsible for everything that occurs in the world or not – all these are questions that have nothing to do with the understanding of the all-determining reality as a minimal condition for God-talk. The only point is that there is no phenomenal realm that is not related to God – without presupposing in what sense these relations have to be seen.

Only if the correlate of the totality of reality is a meaningful concept is the idea of the all-determining reality also a meaningful one. The problem, however, is that this idea of the totality of reality is nearly incomprehensible. In the Greek tradition, the idea of the totality of reality had to pay the price of the Eleatic razor, which erases all becoming and leads to a dehistoricization of the world. Since modernity, a dehistoricized world cannot meaningfully claimed, since the world is only viewed in its relation to man. Although a side-effect may consist in anthropological narrowness in some respects, one is principally justified in viewing the world historically. Therefore, one can read Pannenberg's modifications of the concept of the all-determining reality not necessarily as a critique of Bultmann's understanding, but as an extension. The becoming of the world in its relationship to man, however, carries the burden of history in the sense of the historical, that is, of the direction of history:

> But in what form does the *totality* of finite reality, and with it the correlative of the idea of God as the all-determining reality, exist in man's experience of the world and himself? The totality of reality is not available in our experience in a complete state. It is still incomplete; the future is still open, the world and mankind itself are still in the process of development. Because reality, and our own lives and our experience of the world, are temporal and historic, they are necessarily incomplete. In such a situation, what source is there for a concept of totality? [...] *The reality of God is always present only in subjective anticipations of the totality of reality, in models of the totality of meaning presupposed in all particular experience. These models, however, are historic, which means that they are subject to confirmation or refutation by subsequent experience.* Anticipation therefore always involves hypothesis. [...] Even in this view, however, the revelation of the

> divine reality must always be thought of as a self-revelation. The reason for this is that it would be a contradiction of the idea of God as the all-determining reality if he were to become accessible in any other way than by his own action. Nevertheless, this does not alter the fact that this anticipatory character of the experience of the totality of reality as a totality of meaning makes the historicality of the self-revelation of the divine reality intelligible.[141]

Pannenberg's main problem is the incompleteness of the totality of historical becoming. His solution lies in the anticipation of the totality of meaning, which is properly given at the end of history.

Therefore, Pannenberg has to conceive of the correlate of the totality of meaning, divine revelation, as history. Furthermore, within the framework of this kind of thinking his specific kind of a theology of religions, his ecumenical interest, his concept of truth (ch. 20), his apparent Hegelianism, etc., can be explained.

In order to evaluate this approach, we can say that Pannenberg stresses an important point concerning the idea of the totality of reality, whereas he nevertheless overlooks another important aspect.

He is right in stressing that the totality of becoming is not simply given, but only able to be experienced in a fragmentary manner. Therefore, he is also right to claim that we have access to the totality of reality only when attempting to anticipate meaning as the preliminary extrapolations of past historical becomings. It is very important that Pannenberg sees that the totality is unthinkable.

However, he misses how the totality of becoming is nevertheless a highly questionable idea, for the following reasons:

1. Pannenberg concentrates on becoming in the historical sense. He overlooks that the historic, i.e. what can be grasped by means of historical research, is a subset of the narrative, or more precisely, an entanglement of secondary narrativity within primary narrativity. Even the historical, or what can be grasped by means of history, concerns a perception of wayformational perspectives. Although Pannenberg claims that his presentation of salvation-history as universal history is more appropriate to its object – history – than secular historical approaches, he in fact presents nothing but a salvation-story as a universal story. And even secular approaches to history can only deal with history in the form of stories, in the same sense they are producing stories.

2. If it is correct that the totality of becoming is only conceivable as the totality of perceiving through narrative wayformational perspectives, this totality has to be understood as wayfaring in the mesh, not as transport in the net. But then the idea of a totality has to be rejected entirely, since it could never be a

141 PANNENBERG, W., Theology and the Philosophy of Science, 309–311.

well-founded set – even if there is an end to history. The mesh of the becoming of primary stories cannot be counted. Only in respect to secondary, applied categories of interpretation, in human acts, is the mesh represented as a net. For many technical applications, this might be sufficient. But this abstraction is meaningless if one wants to deal with the all-determining reality. This means that we have to understand the expression 'all' in 'all-determining reality' in such a way that everything is viewed *without any abstraction* – only under this condition can it be a minimal condition for 'God'. Therefore, concerning any kind of speaking of God, reduction and abstraction of the mesh of becoming to a net or to well-founded sets implies a self-contradiction. The correlate to the all-determining reality has to be understood as a mesh of wayformational lines, which can only be seen as a non-well-founded set. But then we have to reject the idea of totality.

3. Why should the idea of the end of history be plausible? Mundane becoming can be thought as being without any end. Only if one argues from the basis of the Christian story of salvation, might the end of history become plausible – or not. Only if one thinks in Hegelian terms does an end of history seem to be evident – or not. Be that as it may, to speak of an end of history always presupposes a specific, if nevertheless implicit, kind of eschatology. This approach might be indeed correct, but it is not self-evident. Suppose it is adequate, but even then, a problem occurs. It is possible that mundane becoming comes to an end. But such an end of becoming can mean at least two things Either it is a dissolution of becoming into being, in which movement resolves into rest, but then the concept of an all-determining reality would amount to the Eleatic being itself, which we rejected for other reasons. Or, it has to be thought of as a transition of one kind of becoming into another kind of becoming. Then we are confronted with the question of why the becoming before this transition should be seen as a totality. Why should 'totality' not refer to both processes including the transition of the first into the second? This would presuppose a connection between the two processes of becoming with regard to certain features. But only if one holds that there is a connection between the two kinds of processes, is one able to see the difference and so identify the 'old' and the 'new' becoming. Then the 'old' becoming would be a kind of relative totality, which might indeed be a meaningful presupposition for theology. Nevertheless, this would not be a self-evident idea from the realm of philosophy of religion, but a strictly theological idea.

4. The idea of a totality of mundane becoming is only meaningful if it is seen as a relative totality. An absolute totality would be as incomprehensible as an absolute necessity. Totality, therefore, is always a relational concept. However, it is not simply a dyadic relation, as Pannenberg seems to think, since he claims

that it is correlated with the all-determining reality. The relation is far more complex: *First*, the idea of a totality needs the relation between parts and wholes. Here we have seen that a well-founded set and the ability to count the parts has to be rejected. *Second*, any totality presupposes a principle of order that reconstructs the *per se* non-countable parts as countable ones, or in other words, which reduces the mesh to a net. The consequence is not that there are no totalities, but that totalities only appear in our reconstructions in secondary narrativity, not in primary narrativity. The other consequence is that a series can appear in relation to one category of order as a totality, whereas it lacks the features of totality in regards to another category.

Imagine a sum of cell junctions in an organism that interact in direct metabolism. If this is seen as the principle of order that builds the totality, then in most higher vertebrates this principle can be applied. The snail shell then belongs to the totality of the snail, but the beaver dam does not belong to the totality of the beaver. However, if one focuses on the functional relations between organism and environment, the above distinction vanishes, and the beaver dam belongs to the beaver in the same sense as the shell to the snail.[142] Functional totalities are not so easy to determine: the totality of a mouse would vanish if one presses the mouse through a sieve, since the mouse would die. But the cells of a sponge, pressed through a sieve, can reunite into a new functioning and living nexus. Does that mean that the sponge is not a totality in contrast to a mouse? This example illustrates that, in regards to biology, it depends on our abstract categories of interpretation, which are bound to our pragmatic interests, as to what can be seen as a totality.

A primary narration is only the totality of *one* narration in respect to particular rules of order. The becoming of primary narrativity is not the totality of a narration, but it is a non-well-founded mesh of narrations. For many practical, technical, and academic purposes it is highly important to make abstractions. However, it is a necessary condition for theology *not* to think along the lines of these abstractions. *Third*, among the relations that constitute a totality it is also the relation of one totality to other totalities, so that one totality is determined as a totality in an external way. We can illustrate this once more with the New Testament language of *old* and the *new*: To call the old 'the old', i.e. a totality, presupposes the experience of the 'new'. Here, everything which is called 'the old' does not have any internal principle of organization that makes it a totality like the totalities of organisms. As long as in this framework something becomes the 'old', the 'old' is no longer able to be experienced – as long as there is no entanglement between old and new becoming. *Fourth*, this

142 Cf. ODLING-SMEE, F.J./LALAND, K.N./FELDMAN, M.W., Niche Construction, 30. 62. 214–217. 334f.

external determination of a totality has to be applied to mundane becoming as such, and that means that only the concept of the all-determining reality as the wholly other in relation to what mundane processes can be determines the becoming of reality as a totality. And this argument would still be true, even if the processes of the world were a well-founded set, if there were no abstracting principle of order, and if there were no intramundane externalities.

In other words, it is not the case that concepts of God as the all-determining reality presuppose the concept of the totality of meaning, of becoming, or of reality. It is precisely the other way around: *Only in the light of the concept of God as the all-determining reality can the mesh of the becoming of the world appear as a whole of meaning, as one mesh or as relative totality*. The reverse, however, is only true in a restricted manner. If the all-determining reality were thought of in such a way that it could only be the all-determining reality, if it were related anyhow to another reality that would be a totality, then the all-determining reality could not be the all-determining reality. In this case, the all-determining reality would determine only everything that is not itself, whereas itself would be determined by a relative totality. Therefore: *Either*, the concept of the all-determining reality is inappropriate as a minimal condition of 'God' – this is the case if one understands the all determining reality in an ontological sense, since then it collides with the self-relatedness of God as a becoming *a semetipso* and *ab alio*. *Or*, one understands the concept of the all-determining reality not as an ontological but as a functional concept that describes a rule of thinking for creatures from narrative wayformational perspectives. But then the *term* of the *all-determining reality* is not a concept that can describe what 'God' means positively at all, but it is only a concept that determines the circumstances under which one does not have the thought 'God', that is, whenever one has thought anything that does not satisfy the criteria we have outlined for the concept of the all-determining reality. But this includes the possibility that the concept of the all-determining reality is an aporetic one.

21.8 God as the Condition of the Possibility of the World or as its Power of Origin

During our survey, we occasionally viewed transcendental concepts, i.e. minimal conditions for speaking of 'God', that analyze the condition of the possibility of *something*. This 'something' can be understood in different manners, as world, as being, as self-consciousness, etc. For example, when Tillich calls God the ground of being, he uses transcendental language. As such, the ground of being is not to be identified with being itself, as in Tillich. When we called God a becoming *a semetipso* that does not exclude divine becoming *ab alio*, this is also not only a relational, but also a transcendental notion. Transcendental understandings of the minimal conditions of 'God' are perhaps as old as human perceiving itself. Therefore, we must deal with transcendental understandings of 'God' explicitly.

For Protestant theology in modernity, the most important transcendental concept of 'God' can be found in Schleiermacher, when he calls God 'the *whence* co-posited in this self-consciousness, the whence of our receptive and self-initiated active existence.'[143]

Schleiermacher obscures the fact that he uses a transcendental argument instead of a proof of God by the way he argues: Formally he uses a disjunction and a *reductio ad absurdum*.[144] Furthermore, he shifts from relying on ontology to an ontology of consciousness. We will see that this is important for one point, but in principle it does not effect the transcendental argument.

Objects are, for Schleiermacher, always the contents of consciousness that have the features of being in interaction, of being receptive, and being active. Therefore, the subject itself always experiences itself in its temporal consciousness of senses, as partially receptive and partially active. Given this temporal consciousness of the senses, we can ask the transcendental question: 'What is the condition of the possibility of this temporal consciousness?' In the framework of his ontology of consciousness, it is clear that the answer can only consist in consciousness ('feeling') itself. But this cannot be a consciousness of interaction, because then the transcendental question would not be asked at all. But it also cannot be consciousness of pure activity, which would be seen as self-contradictory, since a feeling of absolute freedom could only exist 'if the given object were in every respect to come into being only by our activity; but this is always only relatively, and never absolutely, the case.'[145] Therefore, the possibility that remains is to assume a feeling of pure dependence as the condition of the possibility of the temporal consciousness of the senses. This consciousness of being non-relatively dependent can only be related to an unknown x, which is not situated in the realm of interaction and about which we can say nothing but that it is the 'Whence' of the feeling of absolute dependence. All statements in the framework of the classical doctrine of God, which appear as if they were statements about this 'Whence', are actually only one of

143 SCHLEIERMACHER, F., Christian Faith I, 24.
144 Cf. for analysis MÜHLING, M., Schleiermachers Gottesbeweis.
145 SCHLEIERMACHER, F., Christian Faith I, 23.

many modes for expressing this relation to the feeling of absolute dependence. They are not statements of the 'Whence'. That is, at least, Schleiermacher's claim.[146] Nevertheless, it is not true that such a Whence is, apart from its transcendental determination, completely undetermined, since within the transcendental argument there are always hidden the particular conditions of this ground. It can be seen in its correlation to the feeling of absolute dependence: it has to be absolutely active; i.e. not open to being influenced passively. Otherwise it would belong to the realm of the senses. Any kind of divine ability to suffer is therefore excluded, and divine changelessness must be claimed. If one does not want to inherit the Platonic heritage of this transcendental argument, one has to modify it.

Such a variation can be found, for example, in the recent work of Eilert Herms, who called the transcendental ground the 'power of origin.'[147] In comparison to Schleiermacher, two modifications are important: On the one hand, the empiric consciousness is seen as a relational consciousness, which includes a self-relation and a world-relation. The latter must be once more separated into a relation to personal beings and a relation to pre-personal beings. This three-fold relation is a dynamic one of becoming or 'proceeding'. 'Proceeding' here means that a 'basis' experiences becoming as determinations in acts of selection by a 'selector'.[148] Being pre-personal means that the selector is distinct from the basis, with the consequence that the becoming of the basis is purely selected for the basis, not by the basis. Being personal means that a basis, besides its experience of receiving selections of its becoming by other selectors, is also always able to select further determination of its own becoming. Being a personal becoming means not only having a self-relation, a relation to nature, and a relation to other persons, but also having the certainty of the constitution of this whole bunch of relations disclosed, i.e. a transcendental disclosure of the 'power of origin'. This power of origin is in no way undetermined, but, depending on one's 'state of disclosure', it has materially different content. The origin of the 'state of disclosure' has to be – in the case of mundane persons – only a self-disclosure or revelation of the power of origin, since a mundane personal basis experiences itself – although it is possible to determine its further becoming – primarily as determined for further self-determination. Therefore, the power of origin cannot be identified with the self, another mundane self or selves, or a pre-personal being.[149] Herms also

146 Cf. SCHLEIERMACHER, F., Christian Faith, §30f, 125–128.

147 Cf. HERMS, E., ST I, 27. 158. 177. 180–187. 210–214. 407 and elsewhere.

148 Cf. HERMS, E., ST I, 36. 136–147.

149 Cf. HERMS, E., ST I, 158. 175.

argues that, if one wants to avoid contradictions, it not only cannot be identified with particular other mundane states of affairs or sums of states of affairs, but also not with the world as a whole.[150] At this point, we do not want to judge whether this last argument is correct. If it is, pantheism is not a viable position. For Herms, it is clear that the power of origin cannot be exclusively immanent, but also not exclusively beyond. Therefore, he votes for a panentheistic option, and one of those is that of Christian theology.[151] Herein he is surely right. It is also clear that the author and the content of the disclosure-experience have to be identical, if it is a religious experience, i.e. an experience of the power of origin.[152] Moreover, the power of origin cannot be thought to be an apersonal or pre-personal one, since it has to be able to choose the determinations of its becoming on its own. Therefore, in the case of the power of origin, basis and selector have to be identical.[153] This identification is an important correction of Schleiermacher's view, and therefore a contribution to greater coherence. This personality of the power of origin *is not attribution in a derived sense, but in the literal sense*, because the power of origin is the only instance of basis and selector coinciding. Therefore, personality is *primarily* a divine attribute and only secondarily an attribute of creatures. In re-thinking this revelation, a Trinitarian description of the concept of person is needed,[154] which also implies that the self-presentation of the power of origin happens primarily for itself.[155]

Compared to Schleiermacher, Herms' transcendental concept of the power of origin has different advantages. It is embedded from the start in an ontology of becoming and does not suffer the Platonic or Eleatic disease of the changelessness of the transcendental ground. Further, Herms' concept of the transcendental original power leads to a revelation that is at the same time a self-determination of the power of origin.[156] Herms' concept is therefore open to a storied or a historical revelation and it provides more space for the plurality of religions and world-views. Not only can the disclosure of the Trinitarian God be understood as a revelation of the original power, the disclosure experiences of other world-views, including purely immanentist ones or atheist ones can also be understood in this way, though not necessarily as coherent.

Nevertheless, Herms' concept has a series of disadvantages, too.

---

150 Cf. HERMS, E., ST I, 175f.
151 Cf. HERMS, E., ST I, 177.
152 Cf. HERMS, E., Offenbarung, esp. 182.
153 Cf. HERMS, E., ST I, 152f. 178.
154 Cf. HERMS, E., ST I, 178. 414f; HERMS, E., Personbegriff, esp. 392. 394–399. 409–411.
155 Cf. HERMS, E., ST I, 413.
156 Cf. HERMS, E., ST I, 178. 410.

First, it remains unclear why Herms decided for the term 'power of origin.' Herms not only refers in this transcendental notion to an origin, but to an origin that is at once the aim and meaning of becoming. Therefore, the terms 'power of end' or 'power of meaning' would also be possible.[157] The 'power of origin' is thus not the basic minimal condition of 'God' as it includes other minimal conditions, like the all-determining reality.[158]

Second, and this is the most decisive, Herms' ontology of relational proceeding is not free of transport in the network, which is clear in the use of the terms 'basis' and 'selector', even in the case that basis and selector coincide. If becoming is only a selection, i.e. a choice and determination, then a realm of non-actualized possibilities – i.e. of all possible worlds[159] – seems to be a given. And such a realm would be a well-founded set or a network, which does not fit with the phenomenality of perceiving and it underestimates the radicalism of creation. But if in the mesh of mundane becoming transport is in the end impossible, and if all possibilities are non-well-founded sets emerging out of the perception of particular, wayformational lines, then new possibilities always emerge during the process from inferable alterity – inferable also for Laplace's demon.

If one really wants to use the concept of God as the transcendental ground of mundane becoming in the mesh, it cannot be designed as an exception to the ontological principles of becoming, as is the case in classical ontologies of substance, in Schleiermacher's ontology of consciousness, or in using Tillich's Eleatic razor. This was already demanded by Whitehead, and Tillich explicitly rejected this demand, as we learned (ch. 21.4). Herms satisfies this demand at least partially; therefore, his conception is more coherent. But Herms has to pay the price by also introducing – with the figure of selection in the frame of proceeding –features of the network and a transport-like understanding of becoming. The consequence is that he has no means for grasping radical contingency, alterity, and surprise.

21.9 God as that wherein Humans Find their Hearts Set and as that which is their Ultimate Concern

Immediately we find ourselves as becomings in becoming by other becomings and enmeshed with them. By finding ourselves, we experience ourselves first

157 Cf. Herms, E., ST I, 80f.

158 Cf. Herms, E., ST I, 411. 569.

159 Cf. Herms, E., ST I, 135. 176.

as pathic, and in *pathos* we are called to (re)action, but never the other way around. We are effected and addressed by others, before we can be anything else. Our 'heart' – understood as a term that stands in for our person, including the totality of all its aspects, but not as a term of romanticizing emotionality – is always relationally bound; it always hangs on something. It is possible to derive from this simple perception a functional concept of God. Aspects of this concept of God were already visible in discussing the other candidates for minimal conditions. Now we have to deal with it explicitly. The most prominent of them is Luther's famous explanation of the first commandment in his Large Catechism, followed perhaps by Paul Tillich's interpretation of the ultimate concern.

Although Luther's explanation of a God as that upon which a human sets her heart – or better: as that upon which a human's heart gets set passively – is well known, this classic passage is worth quoting:

> What does it mean to have a god? or, what is God? Answer: A "god" is the term for that to which we are to look for all good and in which we are to find refuge in all need. Therefore, to have a god is nothing else than to trust and believe in that one with your whole heart. As I have often said, it is the trust and faith of the heart alone that make both God and an idol. If your faith and trust are right, then your God is the true one. Conversely, where your trust is false and wrong, there you do not have the true God. For these two belong together, faith and God. Anything on which your heart relies and depends, I say, that is really your God.[160]

The concept of God is here a correlate of the concept of faith, whereby faith is, of course, understood primarily as *fiducia* (trust). In distinction from an everyday trust, the whole human is concerned. Therefore, it means a *sich verlassen*. This German expression normally means simply 'to rely on' or 'to trust', but the literal meaning is to 'leave oneself.' The point is that a human is constituted by a relational alterity. Another important point is that there is no alternative between faith and faithlessness, but only between faith and idolatry, and similarly between God and idol. Both, the concept of a complete abandoning oneself in trust and the concept of God as its correlate, are anthropologically constitutive. Therefore, we can expect that both, the concept of faith as well as the concept of God, are appropriate phenomenal descriptors, even in cases where there is nothing visibly 'religious' in the ordinary sense. Luther indeed confirms this in giving 'ordinary examples to the contrary'.[161] As gods or idols

---

160 LUTHER, M., LARGE CATECHISM, The Book of Concord: The Confessions of the Evangelical Lutheran Church (ed. Robert Kolb and Timothy J. Wengert; trans. Charles Arand, et al.; Minneapolis: Fortress, 2000), 386.

161 LUTHER, M., Large Catechism, 12.

he mentions 'Mammon',[162] 'great skill, prudence, power, favor, friendship, and honor',[163] and it would be easy to add healthiness and vitality.[164] Luther also mentions church practice in the realm of Papacy,[165] with a specific point: Here the true God becomes and idol, insofar as God is seen as nothing but a means for fulfilling one's own action and intentions: 'What is this but reducing God to an idol, yea, [a fig image or] an apple-god, and elevating and regarding ourselves as God?'[166] It is also interesting that the particular idol does not have to be really there in order to be in God's place: possessions, great skill, friendship, honor, healthiness, and vitality can also be powerful gods when people lack them. It is then that they preeminently control human pursuits.[167]

The distinction between God and idol, and therefore between faith and idolatry, is not made by humanity. When Luther says that right faith and trust implies a true God and *vice versa*, he is not making the concept of God dependent on psychological states. The true God is for Luther the Trinitarian one. To have the true God and true faith and trust is only possible if humans are able to surrender to the Trinitarian God; only then is the true God visible and perceivable.[168] But surrender to God is not an active human capacity. Therefore, the concept of God as that upon which one sets one's heart is a formal minimal condition, that is in need of material expansion by divine self-revelation, which can only befall humans. If one wants to express this properly, i.e. the fact that Luther teaches the priority of a *passio* before any *actio*, one has to express it in a passive way. Then, a God would be 'that, upon which one's heart gets set.' This is the same with idols: Here, too, the whole human being is passively determined, and it is hardly possible to resist their power.

Another important point is that the concept of God is neither an objective nor a subjective one for Luther. It is, like faith, prior to such distinctions.

In the 20th century, Paul Tillich adopted Luther's insights by paraphrasing Luther's concept as the 'ultimate concern'. Tillich claims that this minimal condition of 'God' is a philosophical paraphrase of the *Sh^ema Israel*.[169] Therefore, he stresses the totality of trust, which Luther only mentions *en passant*. The

162 LUTHER, M., Large Catechism, 12.
163 LUTHER, M., Large Catechism, 13.
164 Cf. MÜHLING, M., Wege des Heils und der Heilung.
165 Cf. LUTHER, M., Large Catechism, 13.
166 LUTHER, M., Large Catechism, 15.
167 Cf. LUTHER, M., Large Catechism, 13.
168 Cf. DINGEL, I./u.a. (Hg.), BSELK 1068 = BSLK 661.
169 Cf. TILLICH, P., ST (engl.) I, 11.

totality of trust is correlated to the concept of God that is 'existential'[170] in being prior to the subject-object-distinction:

> The religious concern is ultimate; it excludes all other concerns from ultimate significance; it makes them preliminary. The ultimate concern is unconditional, independent of any conditions of character, desire, or circumstance. The unconditional concern is total: no part of ourselves or of our world is excluded from it; there is no "place" to flee from it. [...] The word "concern" points to the "existential" character of religious experience. We cannot speak adequately of the "object of religion" without simultaneously removing its character as an object. [...] It is the correlate of an unconditional concern but not a "highest thing" called "the absolute" or "the unconditioned," about which we could argue in detached objectivity. It is the object of total surrender, demanding also the surrender of our subjectivity while we look at it. It is a matter of infinite passion and interest (Kierkegaard), making us its object whenever we try to make it our object.[171]

The formal minimal condition of God as the ultimate concern is the subject matter of theology,[172] and Tillich uses it as a criterion in order to exclude what cannot be seen as a God, and as a criterion for what theology does not deal with: nothing that is conditioned, that is preliminary, no aesthetic or ethical values, or things, can ultimately concern us. As in Luther, the ultimate concern has to be seen in the alternative of faith and idolatry, of God and idol.[173] Tillich divides the relation between a conditioned concern, i.e. whatever can appear in alterity on wayformational perspectives, and the ultimate concern in a threefold manner as indifference, identification, and mediation. Indifference

> is predominant in ordinary life with its oscillation between conditional, partial, finite situations and experiences and moments when the question of the ultimate meaning of existence takes hold of us. Such a division, however, contradicts the unconditional, total, and infinite character of the religious concern.[174]

Identification is of course idolatrous, since something preliminary and conditioned is elevated to something unconditioned.[175] Only mediation is the appropriate relation:

> The third relation between the ultimate concern and the preliminary concerns makes the latter bearers and vehicles of the former. That which is a finite concern

170 Cf. TILLICH, P., ST (engl.) I, 214.
171 TILLICH, P., ST (engl.) I, 11f.
172 Cf. TILLICH, P., ST (engl.), 11–13.
173 Cf. TILLICH, P., ST (engl.) I, 211.
174 TILLICH, P., ST (engl.) I, 13.
175 Cf. TILLICH, P., ST (engl.) I, 13.

> is not elevated to infinite significance, nor is it put beside the infinite, but in and through it the infinite becomes real. Nothing is excluded from this function. In and through every preliminary concern the ultimate concern becomes a possible object of theology. But theology deals with it only in so far, as it is a medium, a vehicle, pointing beyond itself.[176]

It is this understanding of mediation that enables revelation for Tillich, and it presupposes his understanding of symbols (ch. 21.4). The possibility of revelation in mediation is – like the possibility of idolatry – given in the concreteness of the perception of wayformational perspectives and what appears in those, since the 'more concrete a thing is, the more the possible concern about it. The completely concrete being, the individual person, is the object of the most radical concern – the concern of love. On the other hand, ultimate concern must transcend every preliminary finite and concrete concern.'[177] Tillich also applies this basic notion to the history of religions: He sees the one pole of concreteness of the concern predominantly actualized in polytheistic religions, whereas the pole transcending concreteness is expressed in monotheistic religions. And 'the need for a balance between the concrete and the absolute drives […] toward trinitarian structures.'[178]

Like Luther, Tillich regards such a minimal concept of God as anthropologically constitutive, and like Luther he does not restrict religion to what is ordinarily called 'religion'. Even wayformational perspectives usually called 'atheistic' are manners of trust that use a concept of God in the sense of the ultimate concern.[179]

Tillich not only tries to use this minimal condition of 'God' as ultimate trust in a formal and critical way, but he also attempts to give a material criterion for what can be of ultimate concern:

> Our ultimate concern is that which determines our being or not-being. Only those statements are theological which deal with their object in so far as it can become a matter of being or not-being for us.[180]

This criterion is not without problems and highly ambivalent, since now the content of what determines being or not-being is added as another minimal condition. When Tillich conceives being and non-being in the framework of ultimate concern as something that 'does not designate existence in time and

176 TILLICH, P., ST (engl.) I, 13.
177 TILLICH, P., ST (engl.) I, 211.
178 TILLICH, P., ST (engl.) I, 221.
179 Cf. TILLICH, P., ST (engl.) I, 220.
180 TILLICH, P., ST (engl.) I, 14.

space', but 'the whole of human reality, the structure, the meaning and the aim of existence', so that to be or not to be in *this* sense is a matter of ultimate, unconditional, total, and infinite concern,'[181] the component of unconditionedness is only one thing; the other is the material content of this 'structure' of being. And it is here that Tillich introduces via an intermediate step his second and third, previously discussed (ch. 21.4) minimal conditions of 'God' as the being-itself. This intermediate step is the argument that an ultimate concern is seen in a transcendental way, i.e. as the condition of the possibility of being and non-being, or as the power of origin: 'It must be the ground of our being, that which determines our being of not-being, the ultimate and unconditional power of being.'[182] In the next sentence, Tillich adds another determination to this transcendental one: 'But the power of being, its infinite ground of "being-itself," expresses itself in and through the structure of being.'[183] However, according to Tillich the analysis of the structure of being is not primarily a theological, but a philosophical task. If Tillich's 'method of correlation' was really coherent, then only a question should be asked without presupposing the answer. Tillich knows, of course, that a complete determination of the concept of God presupposes revelation,[184] and that therefore the ultimate concern has to be the 'New Being in Jesus as the Christ'.[185] However, this is in fact not the case, since the determination of being-itself now becomes the material content of the ultimate concern (including all other determinations Tillich sees bound to being itself, like omnipotence).[186] But these are things we recognized as dispensable (ch. 21.4).

Tillich therefore exceeds Luther's minimal condition by adding, via the intermediate step of the transcendental power of origin or power of being, at last being-itself. The consequence is that he identifies the ultimate concern with being-itself. We have to beware of subscribing to this identification! If one separates the ultimate concern, or that upon which one's heart gets set, from being-itself, it is an important minimal condition of the concept of God that has to be taken into account. An advantage is that both the concept of God and the concept of faith are liberated from illegitimate restrictions. A God who is not the ultimate concern, who is not worthy of this 'existential' trust, is not God at all, which means we have to exclude two things from being a God. First, wherever a God, even the apparently Trinitarian one, only appears

181 Tillich, P., ST (engl.) I, 14.
182 Tillich, P., ST (engl.) I, 21.
183 Tillich, P., ST (engl.) I, 21.
184 Cf. Tillich, P., ST (engl.) I, 106–146.
185 Tillich, P., ST (engl.) I, 50.
186 Cf. Tillich, P., ST (engl.) I, 273.

as traditional folklore or in apparently religious practices without one's heart being set upon him, is not God. Since godlessness is impossible, the only consequence is that humans in this case implicitly and perhaps without their knowledge have set their hearts on something else. Then they have become idolaters without knowing it. Second, wherever humans find their hearts set on something, be it explicitly or implicitly, it remains unclear whether this instance can be a God or an idol.

Tillich's criteria for distinguishing God and idol are partly helpful and partly misleading. What is helpful is that something that is purely concrete and something that is seen as purely absolute, cannot be that which is rightly called God. Furthermore, Tillich's distinction between the identification of the conditional and unconditional, as well as his notion of the mediation of the conditional and unconditional, is also helpful. What is not helpful, however, is Tillich's devaluation about being indifferent concerning the conditional and the unconditional. Here, Luther is more cautious, since he only uses a complete trust without specifying it in further ways. In contrast, Tillich's totality of concern excludes indifference or the oscillating concern of ordinary life. It seems as if he would – similarly to Schleiermacher – accept only that attitude in which the pure constancy of the consciousness of God dominates the temporal consciousness of the senses[187] can be a correlate to the concept of God. This conception would be far more radical than Schleiermacher, who regarded this dominance as a sign of salvation, but not as religiosity *per se*. More than Schleiermacher, Tillich here tacitly exhibits a radically pietistic heritage.

The matter becomes clearer when we remember that our perception is always one that is mediated by narrations, in narrations, and as narrations on wayformational perspectives. Tillich's demand for the totality of the concern therefore resembles the demand that all narrations of one's own life-story have to be actually experienced as logical coherent, the demand that they all have a single author, and the demand that they all have the same specific point. These demands, however, do not only appear unrealistic in the face of our life-world, but this demand is self-contradictory, too, since logical coherence is an abstraction from dramatic coherence. And only the latter can be applied to life-stories. In experiencing one's life-story, particular meta-narrations might impress themselves as unifying for a while and for specific realms, which implies that these meta-narrations acquire (preliminarily) qualities of a God. Whatever we regard as God, what concerns us ultimately, or upon which we find our heart set, might change during the becoming that is identical with ourselves. Totalities might be revealed only as preliminary

187 Cf. SCHLEIERMACHER, F., Christian Faith, §§ 66, 88, 89, 94.

constructions of totalities, and candidates for being a God might be revealed as idols. It is not so much the one who doubts who is in the need of justification, but it is more the one who is incoherently driven by this and that, the one who is impressed by different stories as the authority and canon of his own story of becoming.

Another point of Tillich's, however, should not be underestimated: it is the concrete that emerges in the stories of our becoming. As such the concrete has the power to impress itself as unconditional. But it is clear that everything that only emerges as something concrete in narrations is on the side of the idols, and that only leads to misplaced trust. It is something that cannot serve as a minimal condition of the true God. In the same way, the absolute, which is purely transcendent to any conceivable story, also cannot be that upon which humans can meaningfully set their hearts. We argued against absolute transcendence by way of interindexicality: something that is purely transcendent is not able to relate itself to a story. Now we find a correlative supporting argument: absolute transcendence – as well as Tillich's being-itself – is not something which we can trust unconditionally, or that could be our ultimate concern; it is excluded. Of course, what is not excluded is that one finds one's heart set upon the concept of transcendence, the absolute, or being-itself. A concept, however, has to be distinguished from its reference. A concept is always something that appears *in* narrations. Therefore, a concept, even if it seems to be a very abstract one, is always something concrete. As such, concepts of transcendence, the absolute, or being-itself carry the tragic burden of being able to invoke our ultimate concern, but not being able to do so without becoming idols. Whoever finds his heart set on the concept of being-itself, on the concept of transcendence, or on the concept of the absolute, suffers idolatry.

However, if neither something that emerges concretely in a story as perceivable, nor something that is beyond all stories, can serve as a minimal condition of 'God' or as our ultimate concern, then the answer to our basic question of what the minimal conditions for talk of 'God' must be situated on a new horizon: nothing that appears in a story, and nothing that is transcendent of a story, can be 'God', but only a story itself.

21.10 God as what Brackets Time and as the Episode-connecting Power

Existential concerns and ontological concerns meet in Robert Jenson's minimal definition of 'God'. His formulations have remained extraordinarily consistent during the years he has published. Jenson is therefore able to claim that this is a minimal condition that can also be used for other religions.[188]

His main thesis is that a God is what binds time together or what brackets time. A God, therefore, is a specific kind of eternity, understood as a nexus of time. An eternity of some kind is anthropologically necessary since it is the correlate of the basic experience of time, or, more precisely, since it is the correlate of the pursuit of coherence in human acting, which is threatened by the experience of the openness of time. In Jenson's earlier works, this aspect of the human quest for identity is only sporadically called 'religious', whereas in his mature *Systematic Theology* the concept of religion appears explicitly. At the beginning of the 1980s we read:

> The horizon of life and its concerns is time. [...] Every human act moves from what was to what is to be; it is carried and filled by tradition but intends new creation. Just so our acts hang between past and future, to be in fact temporal, to be the self-transcendence, the inherent and inevitable adventure, that is the theme of all religion and philosophy. But also, our acts threaten to fall between past and future, to become boring or fantastic or both, and all life threatens to become an unplotted sequence of merely causally joined events that happen to befall an actually impersonal entity, 'me.'[189]

His *Systematic Theology* supports this by further explaining what is seen as religious:

> Time is unmistakably the metaphysical horizon of specifically human life. All our self-understanding and action is ineluctably tensed; we can neither know nor act our world or ourselves without "will be", "was", and "is". Every human act moves from what was to what is to be: it is carried and filled by the intractable past yet intends free creation; it occurs at and as the juncture of memory and anticipation. Thus the substance of every specifically personal act is the particular way it rhymes past and future into lived present meaning. Just so human life is the ontological adventure that is the theme of all culture. Just so also our action and with them our lives threaten to fall or be torn between past and future, to become fantastic or empty, unplotted sequences of occurrences that merely happen to befall certain otherwise constituted entities. Human life is possible only if past and future are somehow bracketed by reality, that reconciles them in present meaning, so that sequences of events have plot and can be narrated.

188 Cf. JENSON, R.W., Triune God, 87: 'What do people use this word 'God' for, that we ask so urgently to whom or what it is truly applied?'; JENSON, R.W., ST I, 54: 'We must therefore undertake some analysis of the way in which the word 'God' has a common function across the religious spectrum.'

189 JENSON, R.W., Triune God, 87.

> Personal life posits an *embrace* around created time, to clasp its doings and sufferings in dramatic coherence.[190]

In the last sentence of the quotation, this minimal condition of God makes explicit reference to the notion of dramatic coherence, which Jenson derives from Hans Urs von Balthasar[191] much as we have, though not as extensively (ch. 16). The religious quest for coherence is necessarily related to the concept of God. Thereby, between 1984 and 1987, Jenson distinguishes a narrow and a broad concept of God. The broad concept of God refers to all things that claim to bracket time:

> Human life is possible – or, in recent jargon, meaningful – only if past and future are somehow bracketed, only if their disconnection is somehow transcended, only if our lives somehow cohere to make a story. Life in time is possible only if there is such a bracket, that is, if there is eternity. Thus in all we do we seek eternity. If our seeking becomes explicit, we practise 'religion.' If our religion perceives the bracket around time as in any way a particular something, as in any way the possible subjects of verbs [...] we tend to say 'God' instead of 'eternity.'[192]

Here we see that Jenson distinguishes implicit and explicit religion. Implicit religion is the pursuit of dramatic coherence in one's own perception in a story, which prevents time from falling apart. This pursuit is for Jenson a universal need. If it becomes explicit, the practice of religion appears. In the early Jenson, the minimal condition of 'God' is the correlate to that which brackets time, and, just as for Luther or Tillich, it is itself anthropologically constitutive. It appears in all religions, be they implicit or explicit, including in such cases as the branches of Buddhism that are called 'atheist', or in religions that reject this term and only call themselves 'philosophy', and so on. The specific manner of determining this eternity, i.e. introducing determinations more than this minimal condition, determines the religious attitude and how one perceives the world. Jenson gives examples:

> There are very many putative eternities. So, for example, many tribal cults honor an eternity that consists simply in the great age of the ancestors, of those with such long experience that nothing can surprise them, so that by their counsel established rhythms may avoid disruption by the onrushing future. Very differently, Platonic religion sought the sheer absence of time, a motionless geometric center of time's turning wheel. Different again is the eternity of 'existentialism',

190 JENSON, R.W., ST I, 54f.
191 Cf. JENSON, R.W., ST I, 55, note 86.
192 JENSON, R.W., Triune God, 87.

> the point-moment of decision that escapes time by location on time's line without extension on it.[193]

In the late Jenson, we find a small change, insofar as here the term 'God' is not signifying all kinds of eternity, but only specific kinds that embrace time, i.e. personal ones:

> The chief diagnostic question about a religion is, therefore, "What eternity does it posit?" As some religions answer that question, a second question presses: Can we *hear* and *speak* to the posited eternity? If we can, that religion has a God or gods.[194]

On the one hand, it seems that the late Jenson here is closer to the ordinary use of the word 'God.' On the other hand, it seems that he restricts the word 'God' to religions of revelation, although it is not clear what 'to hear' and 'to speak' means in this context. However, we have to remember that we are dealing with minimal conditions of 'God'. Therefore, this restriction of the late Jenson cannot be accepted. 'That which brackets time' suffices as a minimal condition. Therefore, this concept of God is also anthropologically constitutive.

The concept of God is a correlate of the human experience of time and of the human pursuit of dramatic coherence. All minimal conditions of 'God' are necessarily abstract and cannot appear in religious practices, but have to be occupied by concrete instances. And that means that the main target of a legitimate critique of religion (ch. 21.1) is unavoidable. After analyzing Feuerbach, Jenson declares:

> Discourse about God between the Gospel and the religions is possible because, although Feuerbach was right about the character of our religious projecting, he did not notice how we come into position to do it. [...] We are in position to project our identifications of good onto the screen of eternity and so to make worship idols only if we do identify some things as good. [...] Using the here premature concept of 'revelation', we may say that idolatry presupposes revelation of the God who is not an idol. Religious projection as described by Feuerbach and his epigones must be understood as *relapse* from a self-introduction of God that is the enabling truth of every grasp for eternity.[195]

Jenson here acknowledges the mechanism of projection that is at the core of Feuerbach's critique of religion, but at the same time he sees that it is parasitic on God's self-introduction. Indeed, in the light of faith this is the case. But

193 JENSON, R.W., ST I, 55.
194 JENSON, R.W., ST I, 55.
195 JENSON, R.W., ST I, 56f.

outside the light of faith one has to say that identifying a particular eternity in fact always means the identification of a trans-phenomenal eternity with some particular phenomenon. The distinction between religion and idolatry is thereby dependent on a necessary condition: the question of whether this identification is an arbitrary one or not (ch. 21.1). An arbitrary identification is one that is purely tacit and contingent, or one that is an intentional, active human construction, a product, or an interpretation. In all these cases, the specific concept of eternity is an idol and the corresponding religious practice is idolatry. However, in most practices that are explicitly called 'religious' this is exactly *not* the case. Most religious practices conceive of themselves as responses to an appearance of a deity, in the sense of the self-introduction of an eternity. In these cases, the condition for identifying idolatry is not given. However, this is only one condition. Therefore, the question of whether such a religious practice and the correlated concept of God may be true is still undecided.

It is important to see that it is the particular specification of the minimal understanding of God – the concretion of what brackets time – which determines human perceiving and acting in a comprehensive and distinctive way. Jenson discusses this at different times, too. We refer here to the later, shorter version:

> In a sentence with a religiously potent predicate and "god" as subject, such as, for example, "God redeems," the predicate remains materially undetermined until the referent of "god" is identified. For if we do not know which putative god is intended, "God redeems" says only that a somehow eternal someone somehow transcends whatever situation that someone regards as undesirable; when we learn that, we learn little enough. Only when "god" is identified as, for example, Baal, "God redeems" acquire religious meaning, in this case "God sends rain and so rescues the city."[196]

What Jenson here observes is not only true for his own minimal condition of 'God', but for every possible one. Every complete or partially affirming minimal condition we have dealt with in this chapter (or elsewhere) remains, without further specification, empty.

Interestingly, Jenson's critics also have not focused on his minimal condition of 'God' as that what brackets time. David Bentley Hart claims that Jenson's particular Trinitarian understanding of God would not satisfy Anselm's minimal condition of 'God' as *id quo maius cogitari nequit*,[197] but he does not relate

---

196 JENSON, R.W., ST I, 56.

197 Cf. HART, D.B., Beauty of the Infinite, Pos. 2559. 2583.

Jenson's Trinitarian story back to his minimal condition of God as that which brackets time. Francesca Murphy, who regards Jenson's decision to start and end with methodology as a mistake, as he winds up doing nothing but hypostasizing a grammatical methodology,[198] also does not refer to his minimal condition of 'God', although this minimal condition is free from linguistic determinations. At this point, we cannot inquire whether these critiques are justified or whether they miss the point, this can only be a task of the second volume and the doctrine of God. Be that as it may, to criticize Jenson's doctrine of God without referring to his minimal condition is, in any event, a shortcoming. It is neither the divine ability to choose, as Hart seems to think, nor grammar, as Murphy thinks, that are the root of Jenson's minimal condition, but his phenomenological understanding of time.

However, at this point I must offer my own critique of Jenson: Is it really time, the phenomenal observation of past, present, and future, and the attempt to prevent them from falling apart, that is decisive for Jenson's minimal condition for God? If this were true, then the story in which God is that which brackets time could lead to a narrative theology, but not to a narrative ontology. The concept of a story would be dependent on the concept of time and on the experience of time. However, our analysis of time showed that the experience of different aspects of time is not a basically given phenomenon, but an abstraction from a primarily narrative perception. Jenson is right to claim that in perceiving ourselves we are not able to bind the sequences of our life-story into a story, and consequentially we are longing for that which brackets the unbound episodes. However, it is this (not automatically coherent) narrative perception on the wayformational perspectives of our becoming that constitutes the paradoxes of time, not the other way around (ch. 10). Jenson's minimal condition for what brackets time is not so powerful because it elucidates the constitutive relation between time and eternity (that will be a task for the doctrine of God), but it is powerful because it is connected with the human need for a dramatic coherence to otherwise unbounded sequences. Strictly speaking, this minimal condition for 'God' is not what brackets time, but what brackets, embraces, or connects the episodes of our lives. Therefore, this minimal condition is a narrative one from the beginning onward. If we risk understanding Jenson better than he understood himself, we can say: a minimal condition for 'God' is that which connects episodes to a story.

'God', then, as the episode-connecting power can be specified in different ways. In the tradition of the Eleatic razor, one could claim that episodes cannot be connected by something that is itself becoming, i.e. that it is not possible

198 Cf. MURPHY, F., God is not a Story, 21.

to bracket episodes in a narrative manner. Meta-stories are thus simply impossible. Whatever can have the effect of connecting episodes would then only be a negation of becoming and an abstraction from the episodic. It would not really 'connect' episodes, but it would be the pure 'being' that remains. Logically, this way is possible, but it leads to a making all life-experience, all perception on wayformational perspectives, all mundane becoming, indifferent.

If one regards the episode-connecting power as beyond all episodes and as transcendent, then one is bound by the self-contradiction that is indicated by interindexicality: such a transcendent God might itself be or not be a story, but he would not be able to connect our episodes.

Viewed transcendentally, an episode-connecting power is only one if it is the condition of the possibility of episodes. As such it cannot be an episode among others. Episodes are unbounded or interact with one another, as Schleiermacher would say. Therefore, the concept of God cannot refer to an episode. But at the same time this also means that it cannot be exclusively transcendent of all episodes.

One might also ascribe relative necessity to the episode-connecting power, insofar as a connection of episodes is not possible without this episode-connecting power. However, it is not possible to attribute absolute necessity to it, since what connects episodes cannot be absolute (from *absolvere*) in this sense.

However, the episode-connecting power itself can be understood as becoming, as story or narration – but not as an episode. Whereas all other – mundane, primary, or secondary – narrations can become episodes of a larger narration, the power that constitutes and connects episodes, dramatic coherence, cannot be thought of outside of itself. Episodes get their dramatic coherence by the story that unites them. And this uniting story is in many cases nothing more than a narrative of secondary narrativity, i.e. a general structure. Such a narrative that always has a general structure might be psychologically, sociologically, or political effective, perhaps in that it might work as episode-connecting for humans in communities; it might lead to personal and social identities – but since a narrative is necessarily an abstraction of the particular, *every* narrative can be nothing but an idol. Therefore, every narrative necessarily leads to a false constitution of identity and to idolatry. *If God is storied, this means minimally that God can be a narration, but never a narrative*. Therefore, every narrative theology that does not claim at the same time to be also a narrative ontology, every theological use of narratological that is without a phenomenal basis, misses its subject-matter.

Such an episode-constituting-and-connecting power as a minimal condition of God can also be conceived as perfection. Therefore, it satisfies Anselm's minimal condition. But it would not be the perfection of the maximum in a series. It has to be thought of, much as Hartshorne does, as the perfection of a becoming that constantly surpasses itself. But even this concept of perfection is not without problems. It seems as if we would have to presuppose a countable, well-founded set of elements. However, since even the episodes, events, and sequences in which we perceive cannot be represented by well-founded sets, then this cannot be expected of the episode-constituting-and-connecting power. Therefore, it might be an open question as to how far the concept of perfection can be applied to the episode-connecting power. If it is possible to apply it, it has to be conceived of as the perfection of a constant self-surpassing in a realm of non-well-founded sets. In this case, Anselm's minimal condition is meaningful and compatible with a narrative concept of God. If not, *id quo maius cogitari nequit* would be nothing but an illusion. I have to admit that I think that the first possibility is the case.

The episode-determining-and-connecting power is *per se* the ultimate concern or that upon which we find our heart set. It is the dramatic coherence for which the perceiver longs during perception on her wayformational perspectives. And the perceiver needs to long for it. Therefore, the concept of the episode-determining-and-connecting power logically includes the concept of the ultimate concern.

We then have to ask how the concept of an episode-constituting-and-connecting power relates to the minimal condition of the all-determining reality. We learned that for Bultmann the all-determining reality means something that is beyond any subject-object separation and, at the same time, has to be true for the episode-connecting reality: it is neither subjective nor objective, because it has to be beyond this distinction. In the sense of the totality of the mundane mesh, it would be the episode-connecting reality, which would reveal the bunches of meshes as meshed into a whole mesh. In this double sense, talk of an all-determining reality is meaningful. However, we had to deal with so many difficulties in ch. 21.7 that it also seems fair enough if one wants to abandon this kind of talk about God.

Finally, what about the concept of alterity? The radical, absolute alterity, as it might be thought temporally by Levinas, still remains a difficult concept, although Levinas stresses the important point that this alterity has to be thought of as other than being, other than non-being, and other than other-being. But if we try to think the contrary, alterity seems to become identity. Therefore, we cannot use this concept of radical alterity, since it seems to be no concept at all. However, there is still Barth's relational alterity of difference, as he described it as the main point of his dialectical thinking of the 1920s, from the perspective of 1956. Here, Barth seems to identify a basic problem of any meaningful

minimal condition of 'God', including our talk of an episode-connecting reality. I am skeptical, however, whether the use of the concept of an event, in the sense of Caputo, Žižek, and others, is meaningful as a minimal condition for 'God'. I think that here nothing more is said than the concept of radical alterity claims to say, along with all its self-contradictions. However, a different concept of event has meaningful implications for a narrative concept of God, as our doctrine of God in the second volume will show.

21.11 God as the Narrative Integration of All Narrative Wayformational Perspectives in a Particular Wayformational Perspective

In the first 10 subchapters of this chapter we dealt with the discussion of 13 candidates of minimal conditions of a concept of God:

1. God as absolutely transcendent or as beyond.
2. God as relatively transcendent.
3. God as anarchic event and as the absolute other.
4. God as relative alterity.
5. God as being-itself.
6. God as absolute necessity.
7. God as contingent (more than necessary), not *ab alio* excluding becoming *a semetipso*.
8. God as relative necessity.
9. God as Godself surpassing perfection.
10. God as an all-determining reality.
11. God as transcendental ground of mundane becoming.
12. God as that upon which one finds one's heart set, or as the ultimate concern.
13. God as that which brackets time, or as episode-connecting reality.

We learned that conceptions of God as absolutely transcendent (1), as absolute alterity or as anarchical event (3), as being-itself (5), and as absolute necessity (6) have to be excluded. Therefore, 9 more or less meaningful minimal conditions for God remain:

1. God as relative transcendent.
2. God as relative alterity.
3. God as contingent (more than necessary), not *ab alio* excluding becoming *a semetipso*.
4. God as relative necessity.
5. God as self-surpassing perfection.
6. God as the all-determining reality.

7. God as the transcendental ground of mundane becoming.
8. God as that upon which one finds one's heart set, or as the ultimate concern.
13. God as that which brackets time, or as episode-connecting reality.

Even this list can be shortened once more. We saw that the concepts of relative transcendence and of relative alterity are parallels, and that the relative necessity of God can be identified with a transcendental understanding of God. The concept of an all-determining reality can only be used for a minimal understanding in the sense that all that is not God has to somehow have a relation to God. This, however, is satisfied by others, for example by the transcendental argument as well as by alterity. Therefore, we can reduce the options to 6 remaining candidates:

1. God as relative transcendence or alterity.
2. God as contingent (more than necessary), not *ab alio* excluding becoming *a semetipso*.
3. God as relative necessity or as transcendental ground of mundane becoming.
4. God as self-surpassing perfection.
5. God as that upon which one finds one's heart is setted, or as ultimate concern.
6. God as what brackets time, or as episode-connecting reality.

The first 4 minimal conditions can be seen as more or less independent rules for how to conceive of 'God', i.e. they do not imply one another. Therefore, we can use them in conjunction. The relation of the fifth and the sixth minimal conditions is one of concretion: indeed, a God has to be understood as anything upon which a heart is set or an ultimate concern. This concept becomes more concrete by the concept of God as the episode-connecting reality or as that which brackets time. Therefore, the concept of God as episode-connecting reality includes the concepts of ultimate concern, but not *vice versa*. This means, whenever one conceives of the concept of the episode-connecting reality, one has already conceived of the ultimate concern, but not *vice versa*. Therefore, we must ask how the conjunction of the first four concepts is to be related to the last two concepts.

Our thesis is that the first four concepts, be it on their own or in conjunction, are implications of the last two concepts; they are given by the last two.

The episode-connecting reality, upon which one finds one's heart set, cannot be itself an episode, as we learned above. Therefore, alterity and relative transcendence are givens. At the same time, transcendence and alterity must be seen in a strictly relative way, since absolute transcendence and alterity are excluded, for many reasons, especially for interindexicality. In ordinary language, we can say that God has to be at once transcendent and immanent, with the consequence that a kind of panentheism is most appropriate. If God is the episode-connecting reality that is our ultimate concern, then this means that the becoming of God – and we have to speak of a becoming instead of a being of God, since we are forced to reject God as being-itself – has to be a becoming *a semetipso*, since any kind of becoming exclusively *ab alio* has to face the problem that something that directs its becoming would be external to it. But that which would be external would need to be connected. But then the episode-connecting reality would be nothing other than another episode. This is, however, impossible. Therefore, God has to be a becoming *a semetipso*, but a becoming *a semetipso* that does not exclude, but includes its own becoming *ab alio*. Only a God whose own becoming can be affected by mundane becoming is trustworthy. In other words: whatever connects episodes, is altered by the particular episodes it connects and by the connection itself.

The episode connecting reality, on which a human finds his heart set, has to be the condition of the possibility to be an episode. Therefore, it is relatively necessary for the episodes. Of course, something can connect episodes without being the condition of the possibility of being an episode. And indeed, this is the case in the plurality of episode-connecting narratives that might impress us. However, these are not things that could be our ultimate concern; this is only possible if it is also at once episode-constituting. Something that connects episodes without being the transcendental ground of episodes would be an idol, while something that was the transcendental ground of episodes without connecting them would also be an idol.

At the same time, the episode-connecting reality has to be conceived of as perfection. Such a claim is not without problems, because we do not have that in relation to which something is supposed to be perfect. The perfection of love is something completely different to the perfection of strength, to give just one example. Nevertheless, we can use this unspecified perfection as a negative criterion. Whenever something can be thought that connects episodes, about which can be thought another thing that better connects episodes, we have in the first case thought not God, but an idol. We learned that this means that the episode-connecting reality has to surpass itself.

All that is only possible, if God in Godself is a narration, is a story. God is the story that connects primary episodes. God is the frame, in which episodes occur. And God is the plot that is the meaning of the episodes. Therefore, divine narrativity has to be the condition of the possibility of mundane narrativity, which also means that divine narrativity also has to be the condition of the possibility of the primary narrativity of becoming in the mesh. However, a God can only be a God, if God does not only connect the episodes of my own wayformational perspective, but if God is integral to all wayformational perspectives. Therefore, we could call the story that is God also the integration of all particular wayformational perspectives and of all primary narrations. However, precisely this concept has to face a serious problem: what is at stake is not only the connection of the episodes of my life in my own particular wayformational perspective, but the connection of all wayformational perspectives. The connection shows, in the radical sense, that the possibilities of narrative wayformational perspectives are not a preexisting space of possibilities out or which particular ones are selected, but that the possibilities only emerge *in actu* on the specific wayformational perspectives. Obviously, no one who becomes on a particular wayformational perspective can achieve this integration of all wayformational perspectives. No one who becomes on a wayformational perspective can tell, know, or grasp this integration. If we want to avoid abandoning the concept of God entirely, this means we have to conceive of God as a self-telling narration, which at once is able to communicate itself to the particular wayformational perspectives. However, due to interindexicality, this is only possible if, God is also the integral of all wayformational perspectives and, at the same time, a particular wayformational perspective. The transphenomenal becoming that God is – the integration and condition of the possibility of all mundane becoming und perceiving on wayformational perspectives – has to be identified with something phenomenal: it has to be itself a particular wayformational perspective. However, the claim that a particular wayformational perspective should be the integration of all wayformational perspectives seems to be a self-contradiction, at least a logical or conceptual contradiction. Therefore, the integration cannot be thought of as a conceptual one in a network. What we are talking about is a comprehensive dramatic coherence, which nevertheless occurs in a particular story that is not primarily my own story, that is distinct from my story, and that I nevertheless acknowledge as the dramatic coherence, as the canon, for myself. Even that seems to be a contradiction: if it is possible at all, God does not only have to be thought as a self-narrating story, but as a narration, which tells itself in such a way that the identification of the transphenomenal and the phenomenal – or of integration and integrated – is essential for this self-narration. In other words, it belongs to the minimal conditions of a deity that it can only be known by self-identification. Thinking in the realm of philosophy about what the minimal conditions of a concept of God might be, compels us towards revelation.

To sum up the results of this chapter: A minimal condition of God is that God has to be conceived of as *the narrative integration of all narrative wayformational perspectives in a particular wayformational perspective*. This concept is paradoxical. And this paradox is not an antinomy if what is integrative identifies itself with the particular. A narrative integration of all narrative wayformational perspectives is not logically constructible by secondary narrativity. It cannot rely on transport-like rules or laws, which might exist or not exist in primary narrativity. If one thinks that transport is the silver bullet, then only the general and universal, that is *per definitionem* opposed to the particular, can be integrative. In God, therefore, this difference and alterity has to appear somehow; it must be not external to God. A narration, however, is able to achieve this alterity-including integration, although we are not able to invent or construct such a story. Such a story can only be discovered. And it can only be discovered if it tells us of itself in the same way it tells itself for itself. Any secondary-narrative attempt from our side can only be a re-telling of this self-telling. And any kind of such re-telling is – under pre-eschatological conditions – not at our disposal. It can only be broken and fragmentary. If the integration of all narrative wayformational perspectives in a particular wayformational perspective is at stake, then God can be a narration as Godself, but never a narrative. If our re-telling of the divine self-identification has to use the means of secondary narrativity, and if it belongs to secondary narrativity to use narratives that always abstract, then any possible narrative answer to the self-identifying story that is God remains at best partial, independently of whether it is a narration of proclamation or a narration of academic theology. And all human attempts at re-telling by means of secondary narrativity are threatened constantly by the danger of idolatry. Idolatry automatically emerges whenever this secondary-narrative re-telling is *only* proclamation, i.e. my speech for other humans, or whenever it is *only* academic theology, i.e. conceptually reflexive re-thinking of the divine self-narrations. But even if both come together, when human proclamation and academic reflection meet perfectly, the problem remains. It necessarily has to be understood *that every re-telling of the self-identification of God as proclamation for other humans has to be at once an answer to the self-identification of God for Godself. Likewise, every kind of scientific re-telling of the narrative self-representation of God is only not automatically idolatry if it is at the same time a response and address to God.* Thereby, it is not the character of address as such that might prevent idolatry, but it is the address that is a request: that the episode-connecting reality may integrate even our deficient proclaiming and scientific babble, which are our attempts of re-telling the narrative self-presentation, into precisely this self-presentation. The only means of preventing idolatry in the end, is, in other words, to address and ask that God might justify our proclamations and scientific stammering.

CHAPTER 22

Revelation as Perceiving Truth and Value

22.1 Issues in the Concept of Revelation

In the last chapter, we saw that the minimal conditions for the concept of God implies that an abstract concept of God needs to be concretized. And any such concretion can only be done on the basis of a self-identification or self-presentation of God. At the same time, any divine self-identification cannot be conceived in terms of perceiving particular phenomena on wayformational perspectives, but only as a disclosure of the condition of the possibility of perceiving on wayformational perspectives in general. Therefore, divine self-presentations and the disclosure of the conditions of the possibility of perceiving coincide, which also implies that revelation cannot be conceived of as an operative or construed interpretation of independently given perceptual content. The discourse on revelation after Barth, as it was carried out by Gerhard Ebeling, Wolfhart Pannenberg, Eberhard Jüngel, Eilert Herms, and Christoph Schwöbel,[1] made clear that revelation cannot be seen as a contradiction to experience and cannot mean a particular experience or perception, but that it has to be understood as an 'experience with experience.'[2] Although one can show that this formulation is meaningful,[3] and that the mischaracterization of revelation as a particular extraordinary perception can be avoided, another misunderstanding, an operative-interpretative one, remains. 'Experience with experience' cannot mean that the sum of all particular experiences is reinterpreted in a new frame of interpretation in the sense of a network. Rather, the matter is something that grounds all kinds of perception. One can also say that revelation is a kind of perceiving, but not a perception of particular objects. The following issues are important:

1 Cf. e.g. EBELING, G., Klage über das Erfahrungsdefizit; EBELING, G., Dogmatik I, 246–256; PANNENBERG, W., Dogmatic Theses; PANNENBERG, W., ST I (engl.), 189–257; JÜNGEL, E., God as the Mystery of the World, 299–314; HERMS, E., Offenbarung; HERMS, E., Offenbarung und Erfahrung; SCHWÖBEL, C., Revelation and Experience; SCHWÖBEL, C., Offenbarung und Erfahrung.

2 Cf. EBELING, G., Klage über das Erfahrungsdefizit, 22f. 25f; JÜNGEL, E., God as the Mystery of the World, 32f; JÜNGEL, E., Unterwegs zur Sache, 8; JÜNGEL, E., Erfahrungen mit der Erfahrung, 9f.

3 Cf. MÜHLING, M., Resonances, 86–136.

 | DOI:10.30965/9783846765852_023

1. From the perspective of the divine self-presentation, revelation happens in the realm of primary narrativity that is prior to all perception. Here we have to make a distinction, because the expression 'the self-presentation of God' is ambiguous:

a) The self-presentation of God can mean that God is not presenting any other things, but Godself – for others. In this case, any presentation in the realm of primary narrativity would be something that happens prior to any form of its representation.

b) However, the self-presentation of God can also – and has to be – understood primarily as a presentation for Godself. A revelation is only such if it happens in truth, and that means, if God is in Godself as God discloses Godself for others. This presupposes that God is present for God, disclosed for God or revealed for God. This primary divine self-presentation is the transcendental narrativity, which is prior to any kind of primary narrativity.

2. As perceiving, and as the condition of the possibility of perceiving, divine self-presentation can only be grasped by secondary narrativity. Here two kinds are conceivable:

a) The secondary narrativity given in any kind of human perception involuntarily, in which human perceiving truth and value happens.

b) The reflexive secondary narrativity based on it that thinks about this involuntarily given narrativity in the life-world or through methodologies. This also includes thinking about revelation as primary narrativity and as transcendental narrativity.

Both aspects are related to each other in a specific manner. The order of 'first self-presentation, then perception' describes the ontological order, the reverse order, 'first perceiving, then self-representation' describes the epistemic order of knowledge. Forgetting these distinctions or not drawing enough attention to them, or, on the contrary, separating these aspects, has resulted in the many different conceptions of revelation to be found in the history of theology.

Let us illustrate this with some examples. The tradition distinguished between a *general* and a *special revelation*, or between *reason* and *revelation*. Sometimes, the general revelation could be simplified and reduced to a kind of a so-called natural theology. The whole field of problems associated with the distinction between a general revelation in nature or in reason versus special revelation, i.e. the old quarrel between theological rationalism and supra-rationalism, can be understood as separating too greatly the different aspects of perceiving the self-presentation of God. The theologians who acknowledged only a special revelation, separate the aspect of the *reflexive* secondary narrativity at the risk of losing *implicit* secondary narrativity. *Vice versa*, the proponents of a natural revelation – even in such cases where they were aware of their limitations and saw a supplement of special revelation as necessary – separated out the aspect of an implicit secondary narrativity, by understanding this aspect on the one hand as independent of reflexive secondary narrativity, and by negating its narrative structure (and thereby by negating the narrative basis of general reason) on the other. This problem is also repeated when one tries to avoid it analytically. An example is the typology of George Hunsinger, by which he distinguishes between five types of relating revelation and reason: (1) a reductionist understanding like in Lessing and Kant, that sees reason as sufficient, (2) a supplementing understanding, where reason is independent of revelation, but in which the experience of revelation completes reason, as in the Thomistic tradition, (3) a correlative understanding, in which revelation and reason appear as the two centers of an ellipse, as in Ritschl or Tillich, (4) a coherentist understanding, that is designed contrary to the first type as one, in which reason becomes an internal feature of revelation, with the consequence that one has to speak of reason within the boundaries of revelation, such as in Barth and T.F. Torrance, and (5) a fideist understanding, such as might be exemplified by D.Z. Philips.[4] The problem with that typology is that one has to accept the distinction of reason and revelation as a primarily given, essential problem – and simultaneously thereby one has to separate out the aspect of the implicit secondary narrativity against the explicit secondary narrativity.

Another example is associated with the debate inaugurated by Wolfhart Pannenberg against the hermeneutical tradition with its question as to whether revelation means primarily *revelation as word* or *revelation as history*. The proponents of the hermeneutical tradition like Bultmann, Fuchs, or Ebeling emphasized the perceptual aspect of divine self-representation. Therefore, they asked primarily about the relation between the two secondary-narrative aspects. Pannenberg, on the other hand, is more interested in the aspect of divine self-presentation as it is given first in primary narrativity and second in the transcendental narrativity for Godself. Pannenberg asks, like all kinds of theology that see a narrow relation between economic and immanent trinity, how both aspects are to be related. Similarly, Barth's Trinitarian understanding of revelation in CD I/2 is another example of stressing the aspect of divine self-presentation, though in contrast to Pannenberg, Barth puts greater emphasis on the aspect of transcendental narrativity.

That the aspect of divine self-presentation and the aspect of perceiving revelation belong together, is seen in the concepts of revelation by Eilert Herms and Christoph Schwöbel. Herms stresses, in his oft-repeated structural formula of revelation,[5] the aspect of self-presentation. Interestingly, the early Herms here emphasizes the aspect of primary narrativity more, whereas the later Herms stresses the aspect of transcendental narrativity.[6] With this move, Herms avoids problems of separation, which caused problems in the theologies of some of his epigones in the material doctrine of God.[7] With his structural formula of experience, Schwöbel emphasized the perceptual

4 Cf. HUNSINGER, G., Uncreated Light, and for discussion in detail MÜHLING, M , Resonances, 91f.

5 Cf. e.g. HERMS, E., Offenbarung, 176–178; HERMS, E., ST I, 126f.

6 The early remarks of Herms about revelation, like HERMS, E., Offenbarung, and HERMS, E., Offenbarung und Erfahrung, adhere to the highly formal description of the moment of disclosure in human experience, which is the primary-narrative level. The issue of the actual transcendental-narrative level of the condition of the possibility of these experiences of disclosure is not broached until later essays, e.g. in HERMS, E., Personbegriff.

7 This becomes apparent e.g. in the deficiencies, if not in the stated claims, in the understanding of God that still tends toward modalism in HÄRLE, W., Dogmatik. Specifically, this

aspect of revelation.[8] Schwöbel's material explanations show that the aspect of divine self-presentation is also not reduced.[9] What is more problematic is that the perceptual aspect is presented on the model of a conceptual predication,[10] which can lead to the misunderstanding of revelation in which it is seen as experience that relies on a non-interpretative, primarily given perception. However, since Schwöbel[11] explains his reflections on experience and revelation in the framework of an explanation of life-experience, this cannot be what is intended. Nevertheless, one can still ask critically whether the predicative model of experience presupposes an unjustified preference for the conceptual network.

Narrative approaches are also far from being free from these problems of unjustified separations or false connections. For example, Hauerwas seems to identify the implicit aspect of secondary narrativity of perception with the aspect of primary-narrative self-presentation, whereas he has no space for the transcendental narrative aspect and the reflexive aspect of secondary narrativity. Therefore, Hauerwas does not develop a conceptual theology, but devaluates it.[12] Other classics of the post-liberal tradition, like Hans Frei[13] or George Lindbeck,[14] which focus on the grammar of faith, emphasize the aspect of secondary narrativity. The explanations, however, of the aspect of transcendental narrativity or the primary-narrative aspect of self-presentation are insufficient. Interestingly, in doing so, they make exactly the same mistake as their 'modern' opponents, which accuse them of fideism and instead claim the universality of reason.[15] The only difference between them is how reflexive narrativity is understood and if secondary narrativity is understood as narrative at its root.

Robert Jenson does not seem to be so interested in the perceptual aspect of divine revelation, and puts greater emphasis on the aspect of self-presentation. His discovery that divine self-presentation has to be understood consequently as self-identification is an advantage that cannot be over-estimated,[16] and one that has influenced a lot of subsequent theology, including our own. However, Jenson makes the mistake of not distinguishing between transcendental narrativity and primary narrativity within the framework of the self-representational aspect. He identifies both aspects (by stressing the primary-narrative aspect more), with the consequence that Jenson identifies the

---

concerns a deficient understanding of the love that is God (236–247), the denial of the primary theological meaning of the concept of person (248–252), the associated denial of the theological concept of action (283f), as well as Härle's statements about the immanent Trinity as the economic Trinity, which prefers the modalist speech of ontological modes (397–408).

8 Cf. Schwöbel, C., Offenbarung und Erfahrung, 94.

9 Cf. Schwöbel, C., Offenbarung und Erfahrung, 103–111.

10 Cf. Schwöbel, C., Offenbarung und Erfahrung, 65. 87–91. 94. 98. 100. 102–105.

11 Cf. Schwöbel, C., Offenbarung und Erfahrung, 111–126.

12 Cf. e.g. Hauerwas, S., Community of Character, 59: 'the attempt to capture the ethical significance of scripture by a summary image or concept makes it difficult to be faithful to our growing awareness that the ethics in the scripture are bound in an intimate way with the life of Christ.' Cf. ibid., 95. 97f. 100, and elsewhere.

13 Cf. Frei, H., Ecolipse of Biblical Narrative; Frei, H., Theology and Narrative.

14 Cf. Lindbeck, G.A., Nature of Doctrine.

15 Cf. exemplarily Schärtl, T., Postliberale Theologie.

16 Cf. Jenson, R.W., Triune God, esp. 89–96; Jenson, R.W., ST I, Jenson, R.W., ST I, 42–89.

economic and immanent trinity[17] – in a far stricter manner than others like Barth, Rahner, Pannenberg, or Jüngel. The opposite mistake is made by John Zizioulas: for him the transcendental-narrative aspect is stressed, whereas the aspect of primary narrativity is nearly invisible.[18] Whereas in Jenson the immanent Trinity collapses into the economic one, in Zizioulas the economic one collapses into the immanent one.

Proponents of the 'neoliberal' theology, like Ulrich Barth or Christian Danz,[19] acknowledge the importance of the implicit secondary-narrative aspect of perceiving revelation. But by overstressing this aspect at the price of devaluing the self-presentational aspect, revelation seems to be dissolved into an omnipresence of the religious without any specifics.

Of course, the examples that could be given are nearly endless. An important problem for most positions is that the narrative basis of revelation is not seen, due to a one-sided and defective understanding of narration.

Even in Jüngel's theology such an example can be found. Although he stresses that the 'analogy of faith has a basic narrative aspect in its structure of perception' and that 'the humanity of God requires telling, as any love story',[20] he also doubts 'whether it is possible to carry out narrative theology in the form of a scientific dogmatic' and he regards 'narrative theology' as belonging rather 'to the practical expression of the church and have its *Sitz im Leben* in proclamation.'[21] This is surprising in the face of the fact that in the final parts of *God as the Mystery of the Word*, Jüngel discovers that only the concretion of a love-*story* is able to avoid false abstractions in regard of revelation:

> Obviously the being of the triune God is not to be deduced from the logic of the essence of love. Rather, the full understanding of the statement "God is love" will become understandable only on the basis of the history of the being of God, in which and as which he realizes his being as subject in a Trinitarian way. But even the understanding of the Trinitarian history as the history of love presupposes a pre-understanding of love. This pre-understanding may well be corrected or made more precise if the task is to identify God and love – just as any love story, what love is will be articulated in a new and special way in spite of the "general similarity" of the experience.[22]

First of all, we have to remark that the translator has made some unambiguous mistakes: in the original, Jüngel does not speak of a Trinitarian *history* or a *history* of love, which is meaningless, but of a *'trinitarischen Geschichte als Liebesgeschichte'*[23], i.e. a 'Trinitarian story as love story'. All instances of 'history' in this quotation must be

17 Cf. JENSON, R.W., ST I, 110. 114. 221–223.
18 Cf. e.g. ZIZIOULAS, J.D., Signifikanz des kappadozischen Beitrags.
19 Cf. e.g. BARTH, U., Religion in der Moderne; DANZ, C., Systematische Theologie.
20 JÜNGEL, E., God as the Mystery of the World, xi.
21 JÜNGEL, E., God as the Mystery of the World, xii.
22 JÜNGEL, E., God as the Mystery of the World, 316f.
23 JÜNGEL, E., Gott als Geheimnis der Welt, 433.

replaced by 'story' in order to get the original meaning. Therefore, in this quotation Jüngel shows that he is aware that the love-story God cannot be reduced to a narrative or a concept, which means that he also acknowledges this fact within the framework of the doctrine of God. Does it mean that he also acknowledges transcendental narrativity? If this is the case, how is it then possible to deny the reflexive secondary reconstruction of perceiving divine self-representation for the academic endeavor of dogmatics? Jüngel mentions here that Dietrich Ritschl's explanations of *'Story' als Rohmaterial der Theologie*[24] has encouraged his doubts.[25] And indeed, in Ritschl, one of the first proponents of an explicitly narrative theology in Germany, a similar problem occurs. Dietrich Ritschl is also not able to conceive of narrativity non-defectively, since he 'only' treats stories as 'raw-material', with the consequence that in a one-sided way the implicit secondary-narrative aspect is stressed, whereas the reflexive aspect is not acknowledged.[26]

If one wants to avoid these problems, the following has to be stressed:

1. All aspects of revelation are narrative phenomena. In order to show this, one has to use the comprehensive concept of a story, as we have done in ch. 5–20, and not any of the defective ones.

2. The self-presentational aspect of revelation is the ontological condition of the possibility of the perceptual aspect. *Vice versa*, the perceptual aspect is an epistemic condition of the possibility of the aspect of self-presentation.

3. Regarding the self-presentational aspect of revelation, the transcendental-narrative aspect is the material condition of the possibility of the aspect of primary narrativity. *Vice versa*, the aspect of primary narrativity is an epistemic condition of the transcendental-narrative aspect. In other words, against Rahner's hypothesis of the identity of economic and immanent trinity,[27] we have to stress that the immanent trinity is an ontological condition of the economic trinity, and that the economic trinity is an epistemic condition of the immanent trinity.[28] This thesis excludes both separation and identification.

4. Regarding the perceptual aspect, the reflexive aspect of secondary narrativity – in all its forms, including proclamation and theological reflection – is subsequent to the implicit secondary-narrative aspect and strictly bound to it. Nevertheless, the implicit aspect of secondary narrativity is not to be separated from its academic reflection, for two reasons: First, it is obvious that absolutizing the implicit aspect brings with it the danger, that, speaking with Schleiermacher,[29] the knot of history could be solved like the Gordian Knot, so that Christianity would be associated with barbarianism and

24 Cf. RITSCHL, D./JONES, H.O., "Story" als Rohmaterial der Theologie.
25 Cf. JÜNGEL, E., Gott als Geheimnis der Welt, XVII, note.
26 Cf. RITSCHL, D., Theologie ist explikativ und argumentativ.
27 Cf. RAHNER, K., Der dreifaltige Gott als transzendenter Urgrund, esp. 328.
28 Cf. MÜHLING, M., Immanent/Economic Trinity.
29 Cf. SCHLEIERMACHER, F., Sendschreiben an Lücke, esp. 347.

science with idolatry. Second, and more sophisticated, there is reason given in the content of revelation itself: God must be understood as the interaction of all wayformational lines under one particular line. This understanding of God is only possible if God is understood as a creator. And this is only possible if all the elements of human secondary narrativity including reason are also based on divine transcendental narrativity. Under these conditions, if one does not reflect on revelation in an academic or scientific way, one produces a self-contradiction. For perceiving truth and value from a Christian wayformational perspective, it is therefore true that it must necessarily include academic and scientific reflection. This is not to be done as an academic discipline on its own called 'theology', as Barth acknowledged[30] – this reflexive task could be done by other disciplines. But that would presuppose that these other disciplines would have to abandon their methodological atheism – and no one would regard this as an advantage.

In what follows, we will first explicate the implicit phenomenal or perceptual aspect of revelation (22.2), then the primary aspect of divine self-presentation (22.3). Implications for the transcendental-narrative aspect of divine self-presentation will then be mentioned in a nutshell (22.4), because its explication belongs to the realm of material dogmatics in the second volume. We will also talk about some implications for the reflexive, secondary-narrative aspect (22.5). The remaining chapters of this book will deal with its further explanations. This chapter will close with a summary by way of two (preliminary) structural formulas of revelation (22.6).

22.2 The Implicit Secondary-narrative Aspect of Revelation

In ch. 5, we saw that humans always perceive truth and value by means of narrations, including the means of secondary-narrative stories, which is of course the case at an age when stories can be understood or told. But even before such an age in an implicit sense this is the case, too, since all meaningful signs are embedded in a series of narrations. When children, from an age of 15 months on, are able to cooperate with adults in shared attention, or to support adults in their activities,[31] they are able to participate in secondary-narrative stories dramatically. They can take up roles and they are able to follow rules, without

30 Cf. BARTH, K., CD, I/1, 5f.

31 Cf. MELTZOFF, A.N./BROOKS, R., 'Like me' as Building Block for Understanding Other Minds; TOMASELLO, M., Origins of Human Communication, Pos. 1379–1388; LISZKOWSKI, U./CARPENTER, M./STRIANO, T./TOMASELLO, M., 12- and 18-Month-Olds Point to Provide Information for Others.

any explanation. The condition for this is the basic indexicality of the sign that was our theme in ch. 12. We learned, for example, that non-human primates were able to learn languages without any reflexive-symbolic understanding of signs.

The *first* consequence is that participation in a secondary-narrative wayformational story-line does not presuppose the reflexive abilities that are necessary to tell or retell stories. Participating in stories by acting and taking up roles does not presuppose reflection, but is based on perceiving truth and value in entangled, narrative wayformational perspectives that equiprimordially presuppose empathy and other kinds of receiving values in perceiving.

A *second* consequence is that these stories, in which persons inscribe themselves by acting, are not mental entities that subsist within the boundaries of a subject. They are bodily, in a double sense. In order to grasp them, it is not necessary to retell them, but to participate in them: a 15-month-old child that supports adults in their activities does not have to understand the secondary-narrative story and their aims, but does have to be able to grab, to go, and to perform the activities that are frustrating for adults by themselves. In order to be able to do so, it is necessary that there are other persons, who follow secondary-narrative rules themselves. Therefore the 2nd person-perspective is decisive, i.e. to be addressed by and in narrations, and to address others by and in narrations. Participation presupposes external personality.

A *third* consequence is that this structure of narratively mediated perceiving truth and value also subsists as a basis from an early age onward, when an autobiographical self is developed and reflexive capabilities appear, i.e. when a secondary-narrative retelling of one's own participation can be formed.

Perceiving, then, happens in being permanently entangled in three kinds of secondary-narrative stories:

1. the stories of our fragmentary, processual autobiographical consciousness,

2. the stories of the communities, that is, the social niches we inhabit as well as the stories of nature, i.e. the stories of the natural niches we inhabit, and

3. the stories of an integrative, meaning forming message. In the case of Christianity, these are the stories of the *Gospel*, i.e. the good news that has to appear as *viva vox evangelii*. What is at stake is the communication of actually told and communicated stories. They can appear in the form of re-telling the biblical stories, but they can also appear as stories of other witnesses of past and present. Formally, these stories are a subclass of the stories listed under (2), but distinguished from them by the fact that they are not only important during temporary sequences of wayformational lines, but that they often appear like a *cantus firmus* of one's own wayformational line. It is not necessary for them to be combined into a system of a network, or to be integrated into a

coherent meta-narration. Rather, it is important that in their light and in their feeling all other stories listed under (1) or (2) – i.e. self-stories, social stories, and natural stories – are perceived.

These stories of the meaning-constituting message, particularly the stories of the Gospel in case of Christianity, determine the manner of perceiving truth and value. According to the unity of perceiving truth and value, this does not mean that they color affectively and normatively the value of a previously 'objective', value-less perception, but that they enable the event of perceiving truth and value from the beginning onward.

These stories of the Gospel are the stories that shape the trust of human beings. And if it is not the stories of the Gospel, then it is the stories of other, identity-integrating Gospel substitutes. A necessary condition for their existence is their secondary-narrative, bodily communication, i.e. their actual appearance in all the means of the life-world. Or, in short, in what is classically called the *verbum externum*. Whether they really have the force to integrate wayformational lines is strictly not at the disposal of the mundane, neither at the disposal of biological processes, nor social processes, or one's own decision. If one could then describe them theoretically in a non-real, 3rd person perspective, one would find that whether they have this force is contingent. But from one's own wayformational perspective, this kind of contingency or chance is exposed, since the contents of the stories of the Gospel include hints that lead to a second necessary condition of their constitution: what can be, with Calvin, classically called the *testimonium internum*. The coherence of the content of the stories discloses their author in an indirect manner, but in all perceptions, including perceiving in everyday life.

The secondary-narrative stories of the Gospel do not have to be formed into a coherent meta-narration of a network or into a grand-narrative that could be understood completely by the believers (strictly speaking, this is impossible), but they have to be conjoined in a dramatic coherence if the meaningful perception and action of persons and communities is to be possible.

Perceiving all phenomena that appear in the life-world is a process that is shaped in the light of these Gospel stories that enable the perceiving of truth and value:

1. Trusting faith exists wherever the phenomena of our wayformational perspective, be it oneself or other phenomena, appear not simply as facts, but as creatures, i.e. where they appear as gifts and tasks for us. Therefore, attitudes like gratitude are included in perceiving truth and value. Perceiving here means the experience of experience itself as something that is previously given, and is not constituted by persons together with pre-personal beings. It is a special kind of the experience that there is something and not nothing. It

is the experience of creation. It can be described as the experience of *creatio ex nihilo*, i.e. the experience of the actuality and possibility of experiencing oneself as experiencing that is inaugurated by a divine entity, without the existence of mundane presuppositions. Creation primarily means not the creation of actuality, but the creation of the possible.[32]

2. Trusting faith lives wherever we do not simply perceive ourselves and others as perfect gifts and perfect tasks, but as distorted though restored gifts and tasks that are in need of further restoration or justification, which includes valuable attitudes like lament or requests for particular needs. The imaginative perception of a life better than the actual one is also included. Thereby, any shape of an imagined better life is also experienced as being made better passively by God. It is, in short, the experience of being saved *sola gratia* without any mundane presuppositions in the face of the permanently wrong orientation produced by one's own efforts. It is the experience of reconciliation. And it leads to a third point.

3. Trusting faith exists wherever we perceive ourselves and others in justified hope as destined to a non-ambivalent becoming, which includes attitudes such as enduring needs. It is the experience of a life of hope instead of fear, a hope for the perfection of the world. Also, this perfection is experienced *sola gratia*, i.e. it is hope for something that is completely beyond any prognosis or extrapolation of natural or social processes.

Oneself, other persons, and pre-personal entities are perceived as (1) created, (2) fallen and restored, and (3) destined to perfection. The implicit, secondary-narrative aspect of revelation is the entanglement of these secondary-narrative stories. If we view this aspect of a perceiving as enabling the entanglement of secondary-narrative stories isolated from the other aspects, it is not yet visible that it is actually an event of divine self-presentation.

However, since in this entanglement of stories it is the story of the Gospel that determines the ultimate or eschatological horizon of expectation (and therefore what makes an experience explicitly Christian), the story of the Gospel is in a specific sense prior in comparison with the other two kinds of stories. The entanglement of the stories has to resonate in a manner that excludes dramatic incoherence with the Gospel. If we then ask how these stories resonate, or if we ask about the origin of the narrative identity of the whole entanglement, the answer can only be – without excluding mundane actors or

32 Cf. DALFERTH, I.U., Die Wirklichkeit des Möglichen. Hermeneutische Religionsphilosophie, 139–141. Dalferth here describes the concept of a world as the horizon of possibilities of actualities.

co-authors, that the last author is 'what brackets time', or *id quo maius cogitari nequit*, a divine instance, in precisely the particular manner as it is identified by the story of the Gospel.

22.3 The Primary-narrative Aspect of Revelation

The stories of the Gospel's *viva vox* can be described as divine self-identification, as Robert Jenson and others following him have done.[33] Although our description is influenced by Jenson, as well, we stress some points differently:

1. Jesus Christ is the eschatological personal disclosure of the divine. He is the primary actor in the story through his implicit claims to be the kingdom of God, both, *in persona* and by his actions. This aspect of divine self-identification corresponds with the second aspect of phenomenal perceiving in the light of the Gospel, i.e. the aspect of perceiving any phenomena as fallen, restored, and in need of being restored.

2. The kingdom of God proclaimed and realized by Jesus, is the kingdom of the God of Israel, i.e. the God who is addressed as *abba* or Father by Jesus, and who is the creator of the world. This aspect of divine self-identification corresponds with the first aspect of phenomenal perception, i.e. the perception of all phenomena as gifts and tasks.

3. Jesus' identity claims lead him to his death on the cross, which seems to imply on a first glance the failure of his identity claims. However, the believers testify that Jesus was raised. Thereby they acknowledge his identity claim. If one asks any Christian, why she or he testifies to Jesus resurrection, she or he will answer that the reason for this conviction is that by divine action, Jesus is alive (Gal 1,15f). However, this kind of divine action is not a single one in the past, but an ongoing one: it is the same action that today results in the trusting faith of living humans. It is the same action that effects the entanglement of the life-stories of people with the stories told to them, which are resonantly entangled with the story of the Gospel. This story is unsurpassable, since it is directed toward an eschatological future. This aspect of divine self-identification corresponds with the third aspect of phenomenal perception in the light of the Gospel: the aspect of eschatological hope.

This threefold narrative structure of the Gospel is the identity-description of God, which can be abbreviated by personal names. Therefore, it is the story of the Father, the Son, and the Holy Spirit. However, this is only possible and

33 As e.g. in SCHWÖBEL, C., Trinitätslehre als Rahmentheorie des christlichen Glaubens.

meaningful, if it is not only a secondary-narrative description, but a *primary-narrative* one:

1. All primary-narrative events, i.e. all phenomenal perceivable becoming, all mundane processes, which can be later analyzed and interpreted by different scientific methods *etsi deus non daretur*, are by no means self-sufficient but they become due to the will of the one who is identified by the primary-narrative stories as Father.

2. All primary-narrative events, i.e. all phenomenal perceivable becoming of all mundane processes, independent of their secondary-narrative description, actually happens in distortion, but this becoming has also the possibility of being restored and redeemed, by the participation of the one who is identified by secondary-narrative means as the Son. At the same time, this participation of the Son in the processes of mundane becoming enables the reality-resonating perception in its distinction between perverted or fallen becoming and restored or justified becoming.

3. All primary-narrative events run towards a perfected becoming, liberated from ambiguities. In phenomenal perception, this aspect is only given by hope, which finds its reason in the secondary-narrative aspect of *promissio*. Therefore, it is *impossible* to derive from any scientific analysis and interpretation of becoming the fact that it is destined to achieve the aim of perfected becoming. This implies that there can be no 'objective' perceivable teleology of 'nature'. If there were one, it would rather be a falsification of Christian faith than a support to it.

In the story of Christian theology, theoretical reflection on this self-identifying story has led to the conceptual articulation of the classic doctrine of the Trinity. The identities of the Father, the Son, and the Spirit are conceived here as constitutively mutually related, i.e. as internal relations. This relation has been described in the tradition by different conceptualities. The eastern tradition speaks of two relations, the relations of *gennesis* and *ekporeusis*, whereas the western tradition from Richard of St. Victor onward uses the single *processio*, which allows it to express the personal proprieties together with the *filioque*.[34] It is possible to debate whether the one or the other conceptuality is more appropriate for expressing this state of affairs. It is also debateable whether we should use these traditional terms today or if we should use new terms, or whether we should add new terms to express this eschatological mesh

34 Cf. RICHARD VON ST.VICTOR, De Trinitate, 5. 13. 336; for interpretation cf. MÜHLING, M., Gott ist Liebe, 164.

of relations.[35] However, such debates are neither debates about the implicit secondary-narrative aspects of revelation nor about the disclosing primary-narrative aspect of revelation, but they regard theological reflection as part of the reflexive, secondary-narrative aspect. Nevertheless, these debates are highly valuable, since they indicate a relational structure that is given by the implicit secondary-narrative aspect of revelation, and which is a prior feature of the reality of the primary-narrative aspect itself.

Let us describe these structures first in their implicit secondary-narrative shape, independently of primary-narrative claims:

1. The story of the Father is not identical with story of Christ or the story of the Holy Spirit. The story of Christ is not identical with the story of the Father or with the story of the Spirit. The same is true for the story of the Spirit. Therefore, the relation among the three stories or identities is an *asymmetric* (but nevertheless reciprocal) relation.

2. The Father is related in a manner to the Son and the Spirit, in which he is not related to himself. Also, the Son is related in a manner to Father and Spirit, that is not identical with his self-relation. The same is true for the relationship of the Spirit to Father and Son. Therefore, the eschatological relation is an *irreflexive* relation.

3. a) Receiving faith means experiencing the action of the Holy Spirit. The Gospel communicated through Christianity tells us that the Spirit is related to Jesus Christ. Therefore, having experienced the action of the Spirit implies having experienced the activity of Jesus Christ, too. This is the reason that the main Christian traditions have rejected any attempts to express the action of the Spirit independently of Christ. b) Since the story of Christ implies the story of the God of Israel as creator of the world, experiencing the action of Christ means experiencing the action of the God of Israel as creator. Therefore, the church has rejected Marcionite positions that hold that the Christian faith can be understood without any positive relationship to the God of Israel. Both aspects, a) and b), imply that experiencing the action of the Spirit means experiencing the action of Christ, and, since the experience of the action of Christ also means experience of the action of the Father, experiencing the action of the Spirit also implies experiencing the activity of the Father. In other words: the relation between Father, Son and Spirit is a *transitive* relation.

---

35 As seen in e.g. Robert Jenson, who amended the the classic relations of origin to include relations of liberation, and Jürgen Moltmann, who distinguishes between a level of constitution and a level of execution within the innertrinitarian relations. Cf. JENSON, R.W., ST I , 156. 158. 161, and MOLTMANN, J., Trinity and the Kingdom of God, 182–185.

The logical structure of the divine identities of the divine meta-narration is therefore the structure of an *asymmetric*, *irreflexive*, and *transitive* relation.

I have to admit that this kind of talk about God does not seem very illustrative or vivid compared with other descriptions, such as 'love' or 'life'. We will, however, come to such vivid description in the second volume. The advantage of the formal descriptions that we have used here is that they can refer to the many different vivid descriptions of God as they appear in the language of faith, piety, and theology. This is possible, since they lack any concrete semantic content and concentrate on syntactic description. For reasons we will deal with later, we can add another formal feature: the eschatological relation of the three identities can also be described as an *open event*:[36] The story of the Gospel neither ends with the last sentences of Scripture nor with the present state of human development.

This relational structure of the entanglement of secondary-narrative stories also reflects the level of primary narrativity. This means: God is for humans as he discloses Godself for humanity.

If in the threefold narration of Christian experience, humans experience themselves not as self-created, not as self-reconciling, and not as self-perfectible, and if, in this experience, the threefold origin of this experience is identified as Father, Son, and Spirt, then we can conclude that the divine origin cannot be completely transcendent to experience and perception. The tradition expressed this insight with the help of the concept of *incarnation*: God is a bodily God in the crib, on the cross, between cross and crib, and, later, in the presence of Christ today. Therefore, this bodiliness of God also determines the other kinds of divine action, not only divine salvific action. Therefore, the Reformers have described the relation between the threefold narration of the experience of the identification of God as a threefold story of divine action. The decisive point here is that it is a threefold story of bodiliness, since it is a threefold story of action as *giving oneself*:

> For by this knowledge we obtain love and delight in all the commandments of God, because here we see that God gives Himself entire to us, with all that He has and is able to do, to aid and direct us in keeping the Ten Commandments – the Father, all creatures; the Son, His entire work; and the Holy Ghost, all His gifts.[37]

This quote can be found at the end of Luther's explanation of the Apostolic Creed as a summary of faith. Just as perception, experience, action, and

---

36 Cf. MÜHLING, M., Gott ist Liebe, 276. 308–315.

37 LUTHER, M., Large Catechism, 76. (BSLK 661, 35–42).

affectivity cannot be separated from one another, Luther speaks analogously of the knowledge or experience that provides us with love and delight, understood as affective states, which refer to the commandments, i.e. ethical human action. The basis for this combination of experience, action, and a specifically shaped affectivity is perception: Luther's says that we *see* that God gives, and seeing is a mode of perception. And what do we perceive? We perceive the perfect self-giving of God, the divine self-surrender in Godself's threefold identity as Father, Son, and Holy Spirit.

The consequence of this concept of divine action as self-giving is that divine identification has to be seen as self-identification. And since this self-identification is not simply a self-identification in the frame of the story of the Gospel alone, but a self-identification in the entanglement of the threefold stories of the Gospels with the stories of nature, the stories of communities, and the stories of the autobiographical self, this divine self-identification has to be conceived of as a self-presentation in, with, and under all kinds of perception and experience. Divine revelation therefore has to be understood as the self-presentation of self-giving. Therefore, God is experienced not as a particular phenomenon, but in, with, and under all experience. Revelation, therefore, is not a new source of information for a distinct human mind about anything that would be transcendent to any kind of everyday-experience, nor is revelation a kind of interpretation. Rather, divine self-presentation is perceived immediately by the believers. In this respect, is it not necessary to know theological theories about the Trinitarian God in order to perceive God as triune. In the same way as it is not necessary to have developed a theory of mind in order to be empathically related to others, it is not necessary to be acquainted with the doctrine of the Trinity. However, humans as creatures also have cognitive needs. Therefore, practicing conceptual theology is an important activity – but not a basic one. It relies on perceiving truth and value.

22.4 Implications for the Transcendental-narrative Aspect of Revelation

All description of divine self-presentation refers to a primary-narrative self-presentation by means of secondary-narrativity. In the same way as God discloses divine identity in the entanglement of the stories of the Gospel with the stories of self and world, God has to be Godself, at least for us. Godself, therefore, *is* – at least for us – a story. It is, however, a story that we can only retell by our secondary-narrative abilities and only in a highly fragmentary way. This story itself has to be able to really integrate all thinkable primary-narrative wayformational perspectives if it is really the story of God. And it is necessary that this cannot be done in the mode of relations of a network, but in a particular, self-developing wayformational perspective, which is the truth of the concept of divine incarnation. This claim cannot be resolved by logical means – only the actual experience of eschatological becoming will do so. For us today, we can only hope for this kind of dramatic coherence. Therefore, this feature of self-presentation is at once a bodily self-giving, a bodily offering, and a divine action by which God gives Godself to our power for our disposal – but at the same time, without reducing divine participation in the world, it is a withdrawal, a dispossession, and a hiddenness. However, this withdrawal need not be evaluated negatively, since only by this withdrawal can God be God in the sense of the all determining reality, which indicates that God is only perceivable prior to any kind of subject-object-separation. Without that divine withdrawal, divine self-giving would lead to an objectification of God. Is that all we can say? By no means! We learned in the last chapter that one minimal condition of God can be found in the transcendental understanding of God. And that means: if God discloses to us Godself, secondary-narratively and primary-narratively, as the becoming of the stories of Father, Son and Spirit, then this can only be understood as the self-presentation, self-identification, or self-revelation of God if the transcendental ground is not an abstract origin, an abstract 'whence' of this becoming. It is self-revelation only on the condition that the first address of self-revelation is neither man nor any other part of primary-narrative processes, but Godself. God does not primarily reveal Godself as a story of the becoming of Father, Son and Spirit for humans or other creatures, but for Godself. Like Barth and Rahner, all theologians of the 'Trinitarian renaissance' acknowledged this in different ways, when they were asked about the relation between the immanent and the economic trinity. That God has to be understood as the very first address of divine revelation has also been recently expressed by a theologian who is not normally associated with the movement of the Trinitarian renaissance, but interestingly more with the tradition of Schleiermacher. Eilert Herms writes:

> For whom does the essence of the power of origin become present? As the formula says, not only for the power of origin [...] but originally and, in the end, also for the power of origin itself. [...] Then one has to ask [...]: *for whom* this self-presentation of the essence of the power of origin happens. And the first answer is: for itself. This is also decided by the *essence* of the power of origin. This essence is determined by the power of origin itself and *ipso facto* for itself. The determination of the power of origin's mode of being actual through itself might be concretized in this or that way, but in whatever way it might happen, under every circumstance it is in its absolute *person*-presence a consummated determination *by itself* and at the same time *for itself*. The phrase 'the self-presentation of the

> power of origin' means under every condition and primarily: the presentation of the essence of the power of origin, as it is determined by itself, by itself for itself.[38]

Herms uses this divine self-presentation for Godself in order to derive his doctrine of the Trinity in a formal way by the following identifications: The Father is that which 'by itself determines itself,'[39] the Son is that which 'by itself is determined for itself,'[40] and the Sprit is that which 'is for itself present'[41] in its determination of its activity. This is nothing but a transcendentalist version of a figure that has already been seen in Barth's theology and his analysis of the sentence 'God reveals Himself as the Lord',[42] which leads to the triad of revealer, revelation, and being revealed.[43] The same structure, now informed by his minimal condition of God as what brackets time, can be found in Jenson when he identifies the Father with the divine whence, the Son with divine presence and the Spirit with the liberating divine whither.[44]

In all these three cases – Herms, Barth, and Jenson – we find *particula veri*, but mistakes as well.

The *particula veri* is that indeed in the framework of the transcendental aspect of divine self-presentation, self-revelation is primary a self-presentation for Godself. In the terminology of Herms: God is the one who determines Godself, who is God's self determination, and who is God's self presence of being or becoming determined. In the terminology of Barth, this means that God is not only revealer, but also revelation and being revealed. And in Jenson's terminology, this means that God indeed has to be understood as God's self whence, presence, and whither.

The mistake, however, is that in all three cases these structural aspects are identified with the divine persons. Pannenberg observed this mistake in Barth and correctly criticized him for violating his own plan to start with revelation, since he actually only analyzed revelation's grammatical structure.[45] But it is not this structure that has to be identified with the divine persons, but any identification of the person has to rely on the content of divine self-presentation.

As God reveals Godself, so, traditionally speaking, God has to 'be' – otherwise it would not be revelation at all. A self-presentation of God can only happen in an entanglement of implicit secondary-narrative and primary-narrative revelation, if it is identical with its conditions of possibility. This means that we have to speak primarily of a transcendental-narrative aspect of divine self-presentation and self-identification: *Etsi mundus non daretur*, even if there were no primary-narrative becoming at all, God has to be understood as narrative becoming. Godself, therefore, is a story, or more precisely,

38 HERMS, E., ST I, 410–413 (transl. MM).
39 HERMS, E., ST I, 414 (transl. MM).
40 HERMS, E., ST I, 414 (transl. MM).
41 HERMS, E., ST I, 414 (transl. MM).
42 BARTH, K., CD I/1, 378.
43 Cf. BARTH, K., CD I/1, §8, 295.
44 Cf. JENSON, R.W., ST I, 218f.
45 Cf. PANNENBERG, W., ST I (engl.), 303f.

becomes as story. And this story would be in all circumstances the story of these identities, by which God discloses Godself in a primary-narrative way by means of a secondary-narrative for us. It is under all circumstances, i.e. in a transcendental-narrative way, the story of Father, Son, and Holy Spirit in its asymmetric, irreflexive, and transitive process of becoming. God is in eternity a processual relation of order, i.e. a story. This order implies that God is his own frame of events, his own 'time', his own 'space' – even if there were nothing or no one besides God who could receive any divine self-disclosure. The primary-narrative becoming of the world, including all its secondary-narrative processes, has to be understood, consequently, as a part of the transcendental-narrative becoming of God. Echoing Jüngel,[46] we can say that divine being is in becoming. But it might be better, to abandon the language of a 'being' of God at all, in order to replace it with the becoming of God.

This becoming actually happens in the story of Father, Son, and Spirit. But without the concrete stories of the Gospel we would know absolutely nothing about the divine persons. It is only due to these contingent stories that we have insight into the performance of divine becoming as a Trinitarian love story. It does not rely on the structure of revelation as self-revelation, but on its content.

The concrete becoming of God as the condition of the possibility of mundane becoming cannot be known by analyzing the concepts of self-presentation, self-identification, or self-revelation, but only by the concrete stories in which God presents Godself for us. And these concrete stories are at the same time the story in which Godself becomes.

We can now ask which conditions have been met, and how the world has to be made, in order for this to be enabled. If the concrete story, in and as which God becomes, discloses itself as story for Godself and for us, a series of conditions have to be met, which we can address by a series of questions.

What does it mean to perceive (ch. 5), how do we have to speak about narrativity (ch. 6), in what way is narrativity related to relationality (ch. 7), and what has this to do with wayformational lines (ch. 7)? What is the relation between narrations and events (ch. 9), time (ch. 10), space (ch.11), signs (ch. 12), metaphors (ch. 13), concepts and names (ch. 14), and theories and models (ch. 15)? What is the function of conceptual and dramatic coherence in stories (ch. 16), causality (ch. 17), contingency, and chance (ch. 18)? What role does the distinction between subject and object play (ch. 19), and how do we have to think about truth (ch. 20)? And of course, at last: What do we mean minimally by 'God' (ch. 21)? We did not ask all of these questions independently of divine self-revelation, and, of course, they cannot find their answers independently

46 Cf. JÜNGEL, E., God's Being is in Becoming, 117.

of divine self-revelation. Indeed, it would be possible to give answers to these questions without referring to the self-revelation of God. However, in this case all answers were not necessary, but only possibilities, without any criteria to decide between competing answers. Our whole proposal of a narrative ontology in part II of this book (ch. 5–20) isolated on its own illustrates only that a narrative ontology of becoming is possible, and that human perceiving truth and value can be understood in the way we presented it, but by no means does one have to do anything in that way. From the perspective of this narrative ontology, the minimal concepts of God, which we detailed with in ch. 21, are possible concepts, but they cannot be inferred from this narrative ontology. Of course, the understanding of revelation presented in this chapter also cannot be derived from the narrative ontology of part II. It is simply only compatible with it through dramatic coherence.

However, we get another picture if we describe the whole thing from the concrete wayformational perspective of Christian faith, which is based on divine self-revelation, as we analyzed it in this chapter. Then we can ask: which conditions have to be met for such a self-revelation to be possible? And the answers are now the answers we gave in part II of this proposal of a narrative ontology. Part II can therefore be understood as a kind of theological philosophy. It really deals with philosophy, but the decisions made among different possibilities are only necessary if they are based on a theology of revelation. Indeed, it is a kind of theological circle, as Tillich has called it.[47] This circle is a sign of the coherence of the proposal. If there were no such circle, there would be manifold self-contradictions. Of course, one could ask: Why do you not present the whole thing in the reverse order?[48] Why do you not start like, for example, Barth and Jenson, with the divine self-presentation, so that all other things will follow? Why do you instead start with these quasi-philosophical reflections in part II? The answer is simply a pragmatic one. In this case, the philosophical issues from part II had to be presented as a kind of epilegomena, and we cannot present them directly after the analysis of divine self-presentation, but then consequently they would come after we have dealt with all dogmatic and ethical issues. However, in the presentation of these material issues, we have to use specific concepts, like truth, space, time, etc. And we cannot presuppose that these concepts are self-evident. Therefore, we have chosen this order of presentation.

47 Cf. TILLICH, P., ST (engl.) I, 8–11.

48 Also Schleiermacher thought already in SCHLEIERMACHER, F., Sendschreiben an Lücke, 338, in a similar way.

22.5 Implications for the Reflexive, Secondary-narrative Aspect of Revelation

So far, what we have said regards the implicit, secondary-narrative aspect of revelation, its primary-narrative aspect, and its transcendental-narrative aspect. What we have said, is of course a kind of theological reflection, and as such a part of the reflexive, secondary-narrative aspect of revelation. But it is not the most important part of the reflexive, secondary-narrative aspect, since theological reflection presupposes the real thing, that is, 'religion', whether organized or implicit in society's hidden communication of faith. It presupposes dealing with tradition and Scripture, it presupposes what we mean by theology as science or as an academic endeavor. In short, it presupposes everything that belongs to the other reflexive, secondary-narrative aspects of divine self-identification. Therefore, it would be appropriate to present all these themes as sub-topics of the reflexive, secondary-narrative aspect of revelation. To do so is attractive, since one could then show how Holy Scripture, tradition, the academic/scientific aspect of theology and its internal organization as well as its interdisciplinary relations, as well as the concrete practices of communicating faith, all cannot be simply understood as social realities, but can also be conceived of as aspects of divine self-identification. All these things are by no means isolated topics. Nevertheless, we refrain from this attractive mode of presentation in favor of a more traditional mode of presentation: we simply deal with these themes in their own chapters, which means that the explication of divine self-revelation is still incomplete in this chapter. Formally, the remaining chapters of this book belong to the present chapter, while materially, the whole work, including the following volumes, belong to it, too. At this stage of our inquiry, we will deal only with one central aspect.

Divine self-identification happens in resonance with divine transcendental-narrative becoming, in the performance of the primary-narrative revelation with the help of narrative means, and through human communication. In a basic way, the self-identification of God means that God addresses God's self indexically with the help of narrative means, i.e. by the entanglement of the stories of the believers with the stories of the Gospel, in such a way that it becomes clear that the stories of the believers are a part of the story of the Gospel. The narrative plurality, in which this self-identification happens, is materially irreducible – even a comprehensive work of dogmatics cannot grasp it – but structurally it is reducible to exactly the three stories of divine self-identification, which we dealt with in this chapter. These narrations of self-identification of God can be, like all narrative identity descriptions (see ch. 14), abbreviated with names. Traditionally, these are the names of Father, Son, and

Holy Spirit. 'Father', 'Son', and 'Spirit' are not predications in the usual sense. In this respect, i.e. in the framework of liturgy and of dogmatic reflection, their only meaning is to abbreviate these narrative-identity descriptions. The claim remains true in regard to addressing God in prayer and in dogmatic reflection. Therefore, they imply absolutely no (!) predicative implications like procreation, being male, being bodiless, and other things that are connoted with these expressions in ordinary language. In ordinary language, 'father', 'son', and 'spirit' are not names. In biblical language, we find a mixture of this ordinary predicative use and their use as names. Perhaps one can say that out of the predicative use of ordinary language and out of technical formulations such as, for example, we can find in the Psalms, their use as names emerged through time. The indexical use of Father as an abbreviation can be found originally in Jesus, who addresses the God of Israel as his *abba*, Father. *Abba* is an indexical that is used in addressing. It becomes a name only by the use of Jesus' use of it within the framework of the exclusive relationship between Jesus and *abba*. Although it is primarily an exclusive relationship, other created persons can be included subsequently. Perhaps it would have caused fewer misunderstandings if the tradition had only used *abba*, both in liturgical practices and in dogmatic writings. However, history took another course. Therefore, we are always forced to deal with the predicative misunderstanding of the name of the Father. Similar misunderstandings appear in the case of the name 'Son'. Perhaps it would sound more natural to replace it with 'Jesus Christ' or 'Jesus of Nazareth', which would make its use as a name clearer. Completely laden with misunderstandings is the name 'Holy Spirit', since here the indexical use as a name is polluted with manifold predicative connotations: Spirit is associated in ordinary language with bodilessness, and sometimes the name is derived theologically more or less from the Sprit's work of sanctification. Nevertheless, it is important at this point to exclude all these predicative connotations from the indexical use as a name.

A related problem regards the question of whether names can be substituted. In everyday life regarding human persons, this is possible. However, names can only be replaced by other names, (or by telling complete identity-narrations), which indicates that one cannot replace Trinitarian formulas like the opening of a liturgical service by predicative descriptions. It is not possible to meaningfully substitute 'in the name of the Father, the Son, and the Holy Spirit' by e.g. 'in the name of God who is the source of life, etc.', since this cannot satisfy the specific function of a name: identifying and addressing. One might ask if the Church could substitute 'Father, Son, and Spirit' by other names, like 'Sophie, Angela, and Carol.' This substitution is also excluded, and if it were possible, it would be nonsense, for two reasons. First, even in case of a universal consensus for such a replacement, it would presuppose the objectifying language of the 3rd person perspective. However, names have their primary use in addressing the 2nd person. Imagine a universal consensus of all other persons to change my name, ignoring my wish to stay with my old name; it would have no effect. On the other hand, if someone addressed me using a false name, and I responded, no consensus whatsoever is necessary. Transfer this to the use of 'Father, Son, and Holy Spirit': A name change would only be successful if Father, Son, and Holy Spirit responded to the new names. But how would we know? Another argument, from Jenson for example, is that the names Father, Son, and Holy Spirit are shadows of the transcendental-narrative, intra-divine communication. Of course, we do not know anything about the real intra-divine communication and its use of names. The names Father, Son, and Holy Spirit emerged during our contingent history of the human communication of faith. Therefore, it would be absurd to claim that Father, Son, and Holy Spirit would be exactly the names used by the divine persons to address each other around the 'throne.'[49] Nevertheless, this argument is correct in an ethical sense: to change names would be a sign of a lack of respect. Second, imagine that changing names were possible and that the arguments against it so far are invalid. It remains impractical. Even in daily life names cannot be simply substituted. They can only be substituted if an identifying story is told: 'Mrs. Smith is the one whose name was up to her marriage 2007 Miss Young.' Every attempt to substitute names leads back to narrative identity description. To substitute names cannot achieve what they are meant for, which is to abbreviate narrative identity descriptions.

Another question is whether the one name of God is 'Father, Son, and Holy Spirit' or whether the names of God are 'Father', 'Son', and 'Holy Spirit'. Answer: both are correct. In the same way that the three narrative identity descriptions are relationally entangled, the names are also entangled. This relational correlation is also visible in the case of the father-son pair in everyday-language, but this has to be claimed for all the three names: without Holy Spirit, no Father and Son; without Son, no Holy Spirit and no Father, without Father, no Holy Spirit and no Son.

The confusion of predicates and names, and the genesis of the name of God out of the use of predicative language inaugurated a whole series of other misunderstandings.

---

49 Cf. JENSON, R.W., What is the Point, esp. 34.

One example is the Pneumatomachian misunderstanding, which St. Basil argued against, as he changed the liturgical formula in such a way that it was able to express the *homotimeos* (the equality of honor) of the Spirit and to avoid dynamistic misconceptions of the Spirit.[50]

Another misunderstanding that arises in Christian- Muslim dialogue is comparing the doctrine of the Trinity with the so called '99 names' of *allah*. These 99 'names' are not names at all, but predications, i.e. attributes. If one wants to refer to the '99 names' in these inter-faith dialogues, the issue is neither divine self-revelation nor the doctrine of the Trinity, but the doctrine of material attributes. Unfortunately, it is common to ignore this.[51]

Even the dialogue between Christians and Jews is laden with the burden of misunderstandings regarding the name of God. In the Hebrew Bible, *YHWH* appears as the divine name. Its biblical predicative explanations like Ex 3,14 are linguistically incorrect; it is more a folk etymology.[52] Strictly speaking, *YHWH* is also a predicateless name. However, the history of this name has caused a state of affairs in which it is not possible to identify *YHWH* with the name of the Father. In ancient Hebrew practice, *YHWH* was not used orally, but replaced by the title *Adonai*. The LXX, instead of the tetragrammaton *YHWH* and the punctuation of *Adonai*, uses the Greek title *kyrios*. But the *kyrios*-title was used by the authors of the New Testament, as well as in later liturgical practice, exclusively in order to refer to the Son. And indeed, some Church Fathers, like Augustine, saw in all the mundane epiphanies of the Old Testament not epiphanies of the Father, but of the Son, since the Father was associated with pure transcendence. Nevertheless, all this cannot mean that we are allowed to identify *YHWH* with the Son.

There are several examples of misunderstandings like these. The German *Bible in a More Just Language* (*Bibel in gerechter Sprache*) allows misunderstandings implicitly to become programmatic, because the editors left the decision of how to translate the name *YHWH* and how to translate the *kyrios*-title in the hands of the different translators.

We can appreciate the intention of feminists to liberate the name 'Father, Son, and Holy Spirit' from predicative connotations of maleness, which are indeed nonsensical. However, in using predicative expressions, which have mostly the neutral gender, instead, one misunderstanding is replaced by another.

It is also unacceptable to substitute the formula 'in the name of the Father, the Son, and the Holy Spirit' with the, only on the very first glance identical, formula 'in the name of God the Father, the Son, and the Holy Spirit'. If spoken orally, one cannot hear whether this means 'in the name of God: the Father, the Son, and the Holy Spirit' or 'in the name of God the Father, and furthermore in the name of the Son and the Spirit.' The last case is simply wrong, because here the divine predicate 'God' is only attributed to the Father, not to the Son and Spirit. Therefore, the use of this formula promotes an Arian misunderstanding.

---

50 Cf. to this MÜHLING, M., The Work of the Holy Spirit.

51 This mistake is also made in the otherwise excellent essay by IPGRAVE, M., Trinity and Inter Faith Dialogue.

52 Cf. BECKING, B., Art. Jahwe, section 4.2.

To summarize this chapter:

God, i.e. the integration of all wayformational perspectives in a particular one, presents and identifies Godself in the narrative entanglement of the stories of the Gospel with the life-stories of humans by relational, threefold narrative identity-descriptions of the God of Israel with his people, with the life and destiny of Jesus Christ, and with the life and destiny of all believers at all times, as 'Father, Son, and Holy Spirit'.

22.6 Coda

My students like structural formulas, obviously, because they suggested that a complicated matter could be abbreviated to its essentials. I regard that as a misjudgment. Structural formulas are ambivalent. On the one hand, one could be tempted by them to oversimplify a state of affairs or to reduce it to transport in the net. On the other hand, they stress relational aspects. Be that as it may, elsewhere I have suggested such formulas of revelation and experience, and others have done something similar.[53] For the practical purposes of memorization, it might not be unhelpful to present two of them once more:[54]

Christian perception of self-disclosure according to the aspect of implicit, secondary narrativity:

Human person A perceives, on her/his bodily wayformational perspective in living a concrete sequence B, an event C as created, and who is in need of reconciliation and perfection through a passive change of her/his eschatological horizon of expectation D, which is a part of the communally constituted, dramatic meta-narration of her/his identity, into her/his new eschatological horizon of hope D in such a way that the dramatic story of the Gospel is entangled with her/his identity-narrations in an authoritative way.*

Revelation as divine, primary-narrative self-presentation:

Father, Son, and Holy Spirit disclose themselves in the bodily wayformational perspective in its sequence B for the created person A as God, which alters A's eschatological horizon of expectation D, to the eschatological horizon of hope D, which acknowledges the authority of the stories of the Gospel in which all things are perceived.*

53 Cf. e.g. Schwöbel, C., Revelation and Experience.

54 Cf. also similarly Mühling, M., Resonances, 136.

PART 4

Equipment

CHAPTER 23

Faith and Religion

23.1 Faith and Revelation as the Subject-matter of Theology

Christian faith is neither a system of doctrines, nor an understanding of reality, nor belief; although it is essentially trust (*fiducia*), it is not an individualist matter. Faith is not an operational interpretation, but determines the whole human person in a comprehensive way. Humans are persons in relation; their 'minds' are relationally extended: humans are narrative wayformational lines in becoming, always interwoven with other wayformational lines – not secondarily, but constitutively. Consequently, the notion of a single wayformational line existing without being interwoven with others is inconceivable. Faith can neither be attributed primarily to individuals, which later associate freely in societies like the church, nor can it be understood as a property of the church as a collective, in which human individuals subsequently become incorporated. Rather the concepts 'collective' and 'individual' are oversimplified abstractions from reality, where humans are always persons in communion. Just as the 'mind' does not reside within the boundaries of skin and skull,[1] faith is not a subjective event that could be attributed to a separate human. Human becomings are ecstatically constituted: the wayformational perspectives of others belong to my own faith as my wayformational perspective in and by which I perceive. In particular persons, faith comes into existence only by the communication of the communion. My wayformational perspective is 'older than itself', and it is *vice versa* a witness for others. Therefore, faith always remains in a 'state' of becoming.

Christian faith primarily understood as trust shapes and forms what we called in ch. 5. perceptional trust; it determines human affectivity, reason, and will. At the same time, the communitarian life of faith is not closed in on itself, but it is an expression of the reflexive, secondary-narrative revelation of God. The life of faith consists essentially in the secondary-narrative communication of faith, mediated by words, deeds, gestures, mimics, music, texts, etc. However, the sum of all mundane states of affairs are not sufficient to determine faith. This sum of all medial-communicative relations is only one part of faith, traditionally called the *verbum externum*. Its supplement is the divine

1 Cf. CLARK, A./CHALMERS, D.J., The Extended Mind.

 DOI:10.30965/9783846765852_024

self-giving in, with, and under human communication, traditionally called the *testimonium internum.*

However, the classical terminology of *verbum externum* and *testimonium internum* is as such capable of being misunderstood, as it suggests a dualism between an internal faith that could be attributed to a subject and an external communication of faith by different means. Protestant theology is not completely free from being responsible for this misunderstanding, because it has modelled both the relational aspects of human becoming – related to the world, and related to God – with the help of the pair 'external-internal'. This pair of concepts, that was used, for example, in Luther's famous *On the Freedom of a Christian*, is, however, only one model, and we have to refrain from absolutizing it – otherwise one produces myths. An example of such a production of myths can be seen today in theologies that try to follow Schleiermacher by simply using an ontology of consciousness. They must, therefore, restrict faith and piety to states of consciousness, which will be communicated externally and historically by the common spirit of the church. Such a reduction disrupts the constitutively relational interwovenness of faith. Actually, relational and narrative interwovenness is not something that simply constitutes faith as a distinct entity, but it is itself faith, or irreducibly a part of faith. To simply say grace, or participation in liturgical activities like the Lord's supper, etc. do not require inquiry into the participant's states of consciousness in order to determine if they are acts of faith: they are faith – as life-forms or wayformational perspectives, which cannot be separated into inner and outer. Faith is spiritual, but not mental. Rather, faith is bodily. Faith finds its concentration in trust, but trust is also not simply a subject's mental or affective state, but a bodily, personal phenomenon of communities. Christian faith is, in short, essentially a wayformational perspective, a way of perceiving truth and value, a way for shaping ways, or – speaking with Aristotle – a bodily *praxis*. This means that faith is initially not *poiesis*: Faith is indeed 'practical', but it is not practical because it is a function of something that is distinct, as the contemporary inversion of the concept of practice in ordinary language might wrongly suggest, but is practical precisely because it is an end in itself. Therefore, both, the constitutively interwoven wayformational perspectives of faith, and divine revelation are the subject matter of theology, because the self-revelation of God can only be found in the whole of the secondary-narrative mesh of the wayformational lines of faith. Theology is in this respect a particular, self-reflexive kind of medial communication of faith, and theology is an expression of faith itself: it is the methodology and criteria following self-explication (and self-*im*plication, and self-*com*plication, as we will learn in the last chapter of this volume) of the narrative communication of the life of faith, specifically the methodology and criteria following the self-explication (*im*-plication, and *com*-plication) of the proclamation of the self-disclosure of the Trinitarian God that is typical for the community of the church.

In face of these facts, the old quarrel as to whether a *theologia irregenitorum* is possible is superfluous. To distinguish between people that are born again and people that are not born again would presuppose a distinction between consciousness and bodiliness, and this separation is not meaningful. Everyone who does seriously engage in theology participates in faith and in the witness of faith. She or he might sometimes formulate statements and considerations hypothetically – nevertheless this is a witness to faith and to the Christian wayformational perspective, whether she or he intends to do so or not. From the moment in which the self-disclosure of God as ultimate concern is sought; from the moment in which the integration of all wayformational lines is reconstructed in the light of the particular wayformational perspective of Christ, Christian theology is born. Only when this is not the case, i.e. when there is the claim to speak about Christian faith from a quasi-objective standpoint, theology and its scientific character both cease to be.

23.2 Concepts of Religion

The Christian faith is a wayformational perspective or a manner of perceiving. Since it is essentially relational, it can be also described as a narrative community communicating the formation of identity. In all these descriptions, we use general terms. Therefore, we can ask whether these general terms actually refer to universal things in reality; we can ask, whether we can generalize some statements to every kind of narratively-shaped wayformational perspectives, manners of perceiving truth and value, or narrative communities communicating identity. In contemporary ordinary language, the concept of 'religion' (or of 'religious communities') is frequently used. However, the concept of religion is laden with problems.

1. The casual use of language seems to assume that whereas religions exist on the one hand, there could also be religion-less humans, which do not belong to any religion, or, in the words of the completely nonsensical phrase, who are 'religiously unmusical'.[2] In this way of speaking, 'religion' is understood as an organization with official membership-rules or social rules of participation, or as the possession of a specific predisposition, similar to a musical

2 This phrase, tracing back to Max Weber, emerged through HABERMAS, J.: Glauben und Wissen – Dankesrede.

predisposition, which some humans might possess whereas others lack them. This way of thinking about religion is something that is theologically irrelevant and inadequate, since a wayformational line or a narrative manner of perceiving truth and value is an anthropological constant, since it is inconceivable that there are humans not moving along wayformational lines, or not becoming on them. Also, being related to something that can be described by the minimal conditions of God, as we have used them in ch. 21, is not something that human becoming could lack. If one would use the concept of religion for this universalization, the problem is simply that religionlessness is as nonsensical as a person who describes themselves as 'biology-less'. The speech of being 'religiously unmusical' is as intelligible as the speech of being 'unmusical with regard to bodily movements.'

2. The history of the concept of religion, with its origins in the Roman philosophy of rights, its later developments in Christian Antiquity, and its transformation during Humanism or the Renaissance, is also not really helpful.[3]

3. The rise of the use of the concept of religion, first in the English Enlightenment, then in the Enlightenment in general, or the use of the term of a 'natural religion of reason', are also not really appropriate for determining what is at stake.[4]

4. If we have a closer look at the developments in the 19th century,[5] two tendencies that are on the way to the present use of 'religion' become visible, which cast doubt on its meaningfulness. On the one hand, an individualization and aestheticization took place from Romanticism onward that was intensified once again at the end of the 20th century.[6] On the other hand, the concept was coined by colonialist interests, which associated the concept of religion with the concept of the national state. It seems that the concept of religion could be a modern Western invention on behalf of protecting Western identity. If this is the case, it would not be appropriate to force it on non-Western cultures.[7]

5. Considering these last points, it is no surprise that there is an irreducible plurality of attempts to define 'religion' or 'religiosity',[8] and that the discipline of religious studies is unable to come up with a plausible definition of its subject-matter. Therefore, it has been suggested that the term 'religion' be

---

3 Cf. RATSCHOW, C.H., Art. Religion II–IV.

4 Cf. FEIL, E., Art. Religion IV.

5 For the conceptual history of the concept of religion and its difficulty cf. BERGUNDER, M., Was ist Religion?, esp. 20–47.

6 Cf. KRECH, V., Wo bleibt die Religion?, 20.

7 Cf. AHN, G., Art. Religion I; BERGUNDER, M., Was ist Religion?, 50–54.

8 Cf. e.g. POLLACK, D., Was ist Religion? and to this KRECH, V., Wo bleibt die Religion?, 14; BERGUNDER, M., Was ist Religion?, 6–13.

abandoned. It is either said that the discipline of religious studies is in no need of being related to a unified subject-matter,[9] or it is claimed its viability is implausible in the face of the impossibility of defining 'religion.'[10]

Although the difficulties of both the history as well as the contemporary use of 'religion' cannot be overestimated, one must address the phenomenon, for which the terms of 'religion' or 'religiosity' are sometimes used. Against all difficulties, ordinary language also seems to use the concept of religion in a phenomena-bound manner.[11] Recently, Eilert Herms has argued for the indispensability of the term of religion for phenomenological reasons, and he tried to define 'religion' in the following way:

> Religion signifies (1) phenomena of communal human life, which are (2) necessary for communal human life, and which (3) actualize universal content in a particular shape, and which (4) include certainties about the bodily, intra-mundane becoming of persons, specified as (5) certainty about the origin and end of the world, and which (6) concern semper-presently all of life's moments and sequences, and which (7) find their defining feature in the fact that the certainties about the meaning of the world and the aim of the world orients and motivates action, i.e. they determine an ethos, and which (8) become involuntarily manifest in the actions and behavior of people, and which (9) exist only in plurality.[12]

Herms' determination of 'religion' is echoed in his social theory, according to which the differentiation of society into sub-systems relies on specific tasks, which any conceivable society has to fulfil: (1) the acquisition and allocation of life-supporting goods (economy), (2) the acquisition and the communication of empirical knowledge about the world (science), (3) the communication of the rules for society's decision making (politics), and (4) certainties for ethical orientation (religion).[13]

Herms' concept is developed theologically, i.e. reflected from a particular wayformational perspective. How can such a concept of religion be related to concepts that claim implicitly or explicitly to not be derived from a specific wayformational perspective, like the concepts of religion that can be found in the disciplines of religious studies or the sociology of religion?

---

9 Cf. BERGUNDER, M., Was ist Religion?, 13f.

10 Cf. BERGUNDER, M., Was ist Religion?, 14–16, and HERMS, E., ST I, 78.

11 Cf. BERGUNDER, M., Was ist Religion?, 54f.

12 Cf. HERMS, E., ST I, 78–82.

13 Cf. e.g. HERMS, E., Kirche in der Zeit, esp. 237–253.

Volkard Krech's determination of religion using the theory of communication is exemplary of such attempts,[14] since he tries to critically integrate other concepts that were important in the 20th century for one reason or another:

a) Substantial concepts of religion, like Mensching's, conceive of religion as the 'experience-like encounter of humans with the reality of the holy, and the responding actions of humans determined by the holy.'[15] Such concepts are still oriented to Rudolf Otto, as the use of the holy illustrates, and they are not far from theological concepts of religion. Here, the 'holy' means a more or less transcendent point of reference, like our minimal descriptions of ch. 21, that shows itself empirically in the human world, preeminently in subjective experience.[16]

b) Functional concepts of religion try to define religion according to its anthropological and/or social function. According to Peter L. Berger, humans live in an ultimately uncontrollable world that challenges them to introduce orders by a *nomos* that is threatened by chaos, death, and the meaninglessness of mundane processes.[17] This *nomos* is always socially construed and as such it must fail constantly. Religion, then, is the human activity of projecting meaning onto the totality of being. Although this sphere is, like the other spheres of order, a human construct, it is distinguished from these other spheres by the ascription of an aura of ultimacy. Krech sees that Berger's conception has the advantage of being able to refer to phenomena of life that are not called 'religious' in ordinary language.[18]

c) According to Thomas Luckmann, religion refers to objectified and therefore symbolic systems of signs that symbolize the relation of everyday-experience to experiences transcending these ordinary experiences. This relation results in a process of the becoming of personal identity[19] by means of a threefold activity of transcending: first, the small transcending from something which is not actually experienced in ordinary life, but which is suggested by these experiences and that would be in principle experienceable; second, the middle transcending, which refer to the subjective world of the other person, that can only be experienced in a mediated way; and third, the great transcending that refers to extraordinary, ecstatic realities. In Luckmann, religion is a necessary correlate of becoming personal; it is an anthropological constant and always has a social shape.[20]

d) Such functional concepts of religion can be narrowed to the function of providing an orientation for actions. According to Talcott Parsons, every society has to satisfy four needs: It has to adapt to their environment, which is the task of the economic system; it has to provide aim-orientation for action, which is the task of the political system; it has to integrate functional positions and roles, which is the task of the

14 Cf. e.g. KRECH, V., Wo bleibt die Religion?
15 MENSCHING, G., Soziologie der Religionen, 18 (transl. MM).
16 Cf. KRECH, V., Wo bleibt die Religion?, 26f.
17 Cf. BERGER, P.L., Sacred Canopy, 19f–23.
18 Cf. KRECH, V., Wo bleibt die Religion?, 28.
19 Cf. LUCKMANN, T., Invisible Religion, 77.
20 Cf. KRECH, V., Wo bleibt die Religion?, 28–30.

juridical system; and it has to provide a system for the legitimation of values, which are dependent on an ordered relationship to an ultimate reality.[21]

e) Clifford Geerts conceives of religion in the frame of the relation between action and certainty of faith as '(1) a system of symbols which acts to, (2) establish powerful, pervasive, and long-lasting moods and motivations in men by (3) formulating conceptions of a general order of existence and (4) clothing these conceptions with such an aura of factuality that (5) the moods and motivations seem uniquely realistic.'[22] Here, it is important that these religious systems of symbols are not anchored in the individual, but in social communication.[23]

f) Krech also refers to Luhmann's concept of religion, which we already introduced in the framework of analyzing contingency in ch. 18. As a reminder: Every system is determined by the difference between a system and a system-relative environment. Systems can overlap and include each other. The last environment of any system is the world, which cannot be a system (since there is no environment for the world). What of the world appears in a system and what does not is a feature of double contingency. The task of the system of religion is to transfer this undeterminable contingency (or complexity) into determinable complexity, which is also an anthropological constant, justified by a sociology of systems.[24]

g) Krech's last point of reference is Oevermann's structural model of religions.[25] Humans always have to decide how to act on reasons that can only be based on past actions and therefore on routine. However, the future is open, therefore, it challenges one to act in a way that transcends past patterns. Nevertheless, these actions have to be justified. This paradox between the demand of justification and unjustifiability is transferred into a myth of justification, which always includes existential questions like 'who am I/are we?', 'Where do we/I come from?', 'where will we/I go?'. By posing such questions, this justifying myth is related to everyday life, and that is religion.[26]

In Krech's own model, religion is a specific kind of communication. What the models referred to all have in common is that the concept of communication is unavoidable, even if it is not emphasized in contrast to other concepts, like the concept of action. However, the concept of action is laden with a series of problems, like the problem of intentionality,[27] which is only meaningful for a small part of human life. For Krech, the 'primary function of religious communication is [...] to treat the contingency – which is constituted by the difference between the particular and the general, i.e. the insight that everything could be different, that every decision could be another one – in a specific manner [...] by translating the unfamiliar into the familiar.'[28] For Krech it is important for religion to treat the primary difference between immanence and transcendence as the difference between individual and society. And this work can

21 Cf. KRECH, V., Wo bleibt die Religion?, 30f.

22 GEERTZ, CLIFFORD, The Interpretations of Cultures. Selected Essays, New York: Basic Books 1973, 90.

23 Cf. KRECH, V., Wo bleibt die Religion?, 32.

24 Cf. LUHMANN, N., Funktion der Religion, and in addition KRECH, V., Wo bleibt die Religion?, 32–34.

25 Cf. OEVERMANN, U., Struktur von Religiosität.

26 Cf. KRECH, V., Wo bleibt die Religion?, 34f.

27 Cf. KRECH, V., Wo bleibt die Religion?, 15.

28 KRECH, V., Wo bleibt die Religion?, 38 (trans. MM).

only be done communicatively. However, not every kind of transcending is religious, therefore Krech has to concretize his definition: 'Religion deals with the problem of how it is possible to refer to non-describable transcendence by immanent means, how to transfer what is not at one's disposal into something that is at one's disposal, specifically how to translate the ineffable into something that can be communicated. This is, of course, a paradox, and it is not achievable once for all. [...] Therefore, religion must represent the transcendent by immanent signs, so that it can remain thereby within social communication. Out of this task, the necessarily tropic character of religious communication results.'[29]

If one compares Herms' theological definition of religion with the different definitions from the field of the sociology of religion, we can diagnose some similarities regarding the features of being an anthropological or social constant. Of course, this is not accidental, since Herms' definition was developed in discussion with different positions from the sociology of religion. However, at the same time one can also see that all attempts at defining religion in the field of sociology, of religion are far narrower, because they try to find the specific difference of 'religion' independently of concrete religions: as the transfer from the unfamiliar to the familiar, as the transfer of undeterminable contingency/complexity into determinable one, or as a specific kind of transcending. These definitions might be entailed by a *particula veri*, but they are not without problems, as we will see.

The reader who assumes the ordinary use of 'religion' might be unfamiliar with the necessity of religion that is claimed by Herms and the approaches of most sociologies of religion. Nevertheless, there are a lot of positions that deny that religion is an anthropological constant.[30] In this regard, Herms claims:

> Not only the first view [religion as anthropological constant], but also the second one [that denies that religion is universal] presupposes the following: One assumes that one can show that what is seen as constitutive for all elements of the set of life-phenomena that is called "religion", is not given permanently in all phases and states of human social life that is accessible to us, and therefore that it cannot belong to the universal conditions of living together, as it is manifest in all phases and states of social life. This claim, however, stands and falls with a) what the proponents identify as features of religion, and with b) what the proponents identify as the universal conditions of human social life.[31]

In other words, any kind of rejection of religion as an anthropological constant has to presuppose a notion of what it means universally to be human. Such

29 Krech, V., Wo bleibt die Religion?, 41 (transl. MM).

30 Cf. exemplarily the short overview in Herms, E., ST I, 79.

31 Herms, E., ST I, 79 (transl. MM).

notions, however, cannot be neutral, but are always religious or quasi-religious. Therefore, to reject religion as a universal phenomenon (if one does not use a notion of religion that is far too narrow) presupposes the validity of what is rejected. This is indeed true, if one uses a concept of religion that is as broad as Herms' is.

Here we come to a point where it is clear that the concept of religion presupposes discussions in material anthropology. Therefore, we once more have to restrict ourselves, since material anthropology is a subject for the later volumes. Nevertheless, we must note here that there are aspects of religious phenomenon that are neither addressed by Herms' theological reflection, nor by the reflections of the sociology of religion. However, reflections from the fields of social anthropology and philosophy stress these forgotten aspects. There are two folk-etymologies of the word religion, which are historically false, but nevertheless appropriate in addressing important specifics of the religious phenomenon.

The first etymology, which is historically incorrect but of hermeneutical value, is given, for example, by Michel Serres, who derives *religio* from *relegere*, 'to read again.'[32] Accordingly, religion would be a practice determined by reading and discovering the *traditio* again and again. Think about medieval reading in the monastery, where reading was a *bodily viva vox* in many respects. Without spaces between the words, following bodily with one's fingers was important, as well as reading aloud: the reader was heard as he read. Furthermore, the books that were read were not understood as representations of something, but as a mode of participation: One participates in the living text of the *traditio*, one is taken into it by reading, and *traditio* does not existing without reading; it is constituted by it. As spaces between words where invented in the 12th and 13th century, this practice changed.[33] Quiet reading becomes the rule, and thereby reading changed its character as a practice of bodily participation into a mental-representative activity. Whereas in the past books were open on the desk and were regarded as unclosed in their content, since the book proper was not the material object on the desk, but the practice of lecturing, so that it was in principle impossible to read the same book twice, now books became closed sources of information, which represent something out in the world and which can be represented in one's mind. Whereas before one read out of the text, or in the text, now one reads off the text. Then the decisive question was whether one could follow the text and if one can tell the story truthfully, now the important question becomes whether the story is a

32 Cf. SERRES, M., Natural Contract, 47.
33 Cf. INGOLD, T., Dreaming of Dragons, esp. 742.

true representation of something that is not a story. The logic of representation asks about the truth of a story. The logic of participation asks about following a story truthfully. This distinction in reading can also be applied to nature, which was called the book of nature – a metaphor that was important in the early scholasticism in Hugo of St. Victor, and which reappears also in Francis Bacon and Galileo.[34] According to the representationalist understanding, the book of nature is written in the language of mathematics; therefore, one has to ask whether a theory is true. A participatory understanding of the book of nature would be a different one: it is important to participate bodily in nature, to also hear non-human nature by reading it aloud in a participatory way – and this means to become or to emerge on one's own wayformational line in order to live the story truthfully. And this is what Serres means by the *relegere* of the religions. Compare this concept of religion with the ones from the discipline of sociology of religion referred to by Krech! The latter ones all use the logic of representation: what is transcendent shall be represented immanently, systems shall represent their environment or one another, etc. If Serres is right, the definitions of sociology of religion miss their phenomenon, because they try to not be bound to it by *relegere* in a participatory way, but by reading in the representationalist sense. Furthermore, it is interesting that the opposite of religion is, in Serres' view, not religionlessness or any kind of atheistic religion, but *neg-legere*, negligence. Wherever care is absent, i.e. bodily-participatory *re-legere*, there negligence reigns. Wherever a purely representative reading is promoted as the single appropriate one – be it in scriptural texts or in the book of nature – one has surrendered to negligence.

How can such a participatory concept of religion as *re-legere* be related to theological concepts like Herms' one? In contrast to the definitions from the field of the sociology of religion, Herms deals with the orientating function of religion without specifying it in a representationalist way. Therefore, Herms' understanding of religion is open to Serres' participatory understanding of religion.

However, one might object: does not the participatory concept of religion try to promote something that nobody actually experiences? Does not all our experience of our activities of perceiving truth and value presuppose the separation of subject and object, as well as the separation of culture and nature? Do we, therefore, have any chance of not reading in a representationalist way? Also, in the Christian faith, we do not first experience ourselves as part of the story of the Gospel, but the Gospel might be experienced as offending and attacking us as law, as something that denies us, or simply as something that is

34 Cf. CLINGERMAN, F., Reading the Book of Nature.

featureless for us in our attitude of *neg-legere*. Then our single reaction to the *patio* might be a shrug. Often, we do not experience ourselves as participating on the reality of becoming, but hovering over it. Therefore, there is a dilemma: if we conceive and perceive ourselves in the reality of becoming in the mesh of wayformational lines, we can ask how to tell the story, in which we become, in a truthful way. But we cannot ask anymore whether the story is true in the representationalist sense. In order to ask this question (not to solve it), we need the reflexive and discursive abstraction from our participatory perceiving truth and value. Then we are able to ask whether the story, by which we have perceived truth and value, is representationally true. However, then the other view is lost.

It is this problem that is addressed by the second folk-etymology of 'religion' that might be historically inaccurate, but which is hermeneutically fruitful, and that is a definition that can be found in Lactantius.[35] It is possible to derive *religio* from *re-ligare*, 'to bind again', or 'to weave again'. In this sense, religions are communicative practices that do not simply want to provide an orientation in action, but that want to mediate our reflexive and discursive abilities with our immediate perceiving of truth and value. Religions then, are not systems of representing reality or something that is beyond reality, but they are practices for finding new ways of reconciling participation in reality. In this case, we would again be interwoven with the reality of becoming by religion, whereas without religion we would face ourselves as detached, or at best as systems in the reality of an undeterminable world. Religion then, would be seen as wayformational perspectives or manners of perceiving in the proper sense, including the task of not simply providing abstract, orienting norms and motivations for action, but of forming and shaping our perceiving in a way that we will again be able to tell the story of our becoming truthfully. Tim Ingold uses such a concept of religion, influenced by Serres. But there is a problem: In contrast to the different notions from the field of sociology of religion and to Herms' theological concept of religion, Ingold's concept is from the outset a normative concept. Here, religion is a positive value, whereas its opposite, negligence, is a negative one. Therefore, the concept of religion is not identical with the concept of a wayformational perspective, but it is associated with a wayformational perspective that resonates or fits with reality. To absolutize the idea of transport in a network (ch. 8) would also be a wayformational perspective, but one that denies its own constitution and the constitution of mundane becoming.

35 Cf. INGOLD, T., Life of Lines, 155.

I think we have two possibilities for shedding light on the concept of religion, with the help of the concepts of wayformational perspectives or manners of perceiving truth and value:

1. 'Religion$_1$' means a secondary-narratively shaped manner of perceiving truth and value – or a wayformational perspective – independently of whether it resonates with the primary narrativity of reality in dramatic coherence, or not.
2. 'Religion$_2$' means a secondary-narratively shaped manner of perceiving truth and value – or a wayformational perspective – that leads to a harmonic resonance with the primary narrativity of reality.

However, here we reach a serious problem. It is almost impossible to use Religion$_2$ in a positive way. If religion refers on the one hand to a human practice of communication, that, on the other hand, will lead us back to a participatory mode by becoming interwoven again with reality, it is a self-contradictory and desperate practice. No one in the 20th century has seen this as clearly as Karl Barth in his theological critique of religion, as it can be exemplarily found in the famous §17 of his *Church Dogmatics*.[36] Here, revelation is understood as the sublation of human religion, which is primarily seen as unbelief,[37] insofar as 'religion' refers to human attempts to know God actively by means that are at one's own disposal. Barth's critique addresses Christian religion like other religions. If instead of 'God' we use here our minimal description of God as the integration of all wayformational lines in a particular one, then it is obvious, that the normative concept of religion we elaborated above, which claims to lead to a harmonically resonating, participatory mode of perceiving, is met by Barth's verdict. No human activity is able to do that. Perhaps one can also see this, at least partially, in Krech's determination of religion, because he acknowledges the paradoxical character of religion. If the endeavor is to form a human practice that leads back to a reality participating perception, then it is itself unbelief because humans do not trust their own abilities to do so, and as unbelief it is a sinful endeavor. Although sophisticated concepts of religion, for example in the framework of the mystic, or special kinds of atheism, can include a self-critical force, in this respect they remain religious. The problems we discovered in distinguishing between God and idols in ch. 21 are repeated here in regard of the concept of religion, which is then a correlate of the doctrine of the minimal conditions of God. It does not suffice to declare religion to be the human shape for receiving divine revelation (as Tillich did), but it is necessary to speak of a justification of religion by divine self-presentation. The

36 Cf. BARTH, K., CD I/2, §17, 280–361.
37 Cf. BARTH, K., CD I/2, §17, 299f.

implicit and explicit, human secondary-narrative communication can only become a means of the self-presentation of the triune God by being justified *sola gratia*. In this sense, Barth uses Hegel's term of the sublation (*Aufhebung*) for religion by revelation, although the English translation made the mistake of using 'abolition'.[38] Perhaps we can say that human, secondary-narrative communication is called into service by divine communication in dramatic coherence.

The notion of religion can be used in different manners, as we explored in this chapter. However, there is also no need to use it. For the wayformational perspective of Christian faith, the concept of faith is far more precise. And in order to develop a general approach, it is, at least within the framework of this book, more appropriate to speak of wayformational lines or modes of perceiving truth and value. The advantage is that there is no principal need to take on all of the problems of a concept that has been deformed by its use in contemporary ordinary language.

38 Cf. BARTH, K., KD I/2, 304. 324. 356 and BARTH, K., CD I/2, §17, 280. 297. 325f.

CHAPTER 24

Historicity and Holy Scripture

24.1 Secondary-narrative, Contemporary Communication, and the Historic

The secondary-narrative communication of faith is not restricted to specific means or media. The primary-medial way is always bodily communication, and the *viva vox evangelii* in all the variety of imaginable forms. However, the primary-medial communication of the body, and all secondary means that might be used, is dependent on the whole witness of the communication of faith as it was developed historically. The communication of faith always proceeds in a secondary-narrative way, but within the limits of the realm of secondary narrativity as a subclass it also has to deal with what is historic.

However, the difficulties in determining what historicity means are legion. Without claiming to treat the matter comprehensively, a few problems might be mentioned.

1. The historic cannot consist in objective protocols of past primary-narrative sequences of wayformational events, because past, primary-narrative events on wayformational lines are not objective 'facts', but something that is perceived in truth and value and therefore something that has already been shaped. Historical speech cannot be a reconstruction of what has actually happened, as, for example, 'in the 10th century Ranke thought…'[1] Rather, it relies on perceiving in truth and value what was perceived in truth and value in the past – with methodical means. Historical work is therefore always an operational interpretation, and therefore it is only distinguishable from non-operational kind of perceiving if it also constantly reflects on its hermeneutical principles. Whenever historical research claims to describe events objectively, it becomes a myth that unreflectively produces myths. This insight, as it is made exemplarily by Droysen in his critique of asking for the origins,[2] shows that historicist academic endeavors cease to be academic endeavors or sciences at all. What is thereby problematic is not the production of myths as such – myths are constantly produced by every secondary-narrative event[3] – but what is problematic is that the myth-producing subject – the historical

1 RANKE, L.v., Geschichten der romanischen und germanischen Völker, VI.
2 Cf. DROYSEN, J.G., Historik (1857/8), 160–163.
3 Cf. MÜHLING, M., Resonances, 33f.

© WILHELM FINK VERLAG, 2020 | DOI:10.30965/9783846765852_025

academic disciplines – are the ones that have the task of interpreting myths. Of course, interpreting historical myths can only happen on particular wayformational perspectives; therefore, the process cannot be neutral with respect to one's worldview. In this it resembles the *epoché*, which cannot mean abandoning ontological claims but means changing the ontology (ch. 5). However, in both cases, it is important also to reflect on the fact that one is bound to wayformational lines.

2. There are no single past events, but only events imbedded in a primary-narrative nexus. But the primary-narrative nexus can only be received by particular wayformational lines and it can only be described according to them. A consequence is that there can be no single secondary narration that can be called 'history', but that there are necessarily more than one.

3. The plurality of the secondary-narrative embeddedness of the historic can be illustrated by the simple question of the beginning, origin, aim, or end of what is historically reconstructed. Since there are no single events, only narrative sequences can be described. These need to have a beginning, an origin, an aim, or an end. Not only the decision of which sequence has to be described alters the explication, the decision of whether one decides for beginning or origin, aim or end alone, alters the whole view. Angehrn noted that beginning and origin are not the same: whoever sees a beginning, identifies a break with the past, sees what is new, and asks prospective questions. Whoever asks about origins, asks retrospectively about the basis of later processes and stresses continuity.[4] Analogously, to speak of an end stresses a closure and a discontinuity with what will follow, whereas speaking of an aim means identifying the result as a condition for what will follow. There are, in principle, no valueless expressions for structuring the field. It would be easy to specify the evaluative distinctions between other structuring expressions like middle, center, intermezzo, retarding element, preparation, post-history, etc.

4. The historic is a methodical, secondary-narrative mode of perceiving the past, and it is shaped by one's own historically constituted wayformational perspective. Therefore, the historical events to which it refers can be described in very many distinct ways; it cannot be fixed. *What is historic varies depending on sources and contemporary wayformational perspectives.* This thesis can be understood in two ways, a skeptical-realistic one, and a dynamic-realistic one.

The *skeptical-realistic* interpretation holds that there might have been past events, independent of present perception, but that it is inaccessible as such for historical research. It might be possible that contemporary, secondary-narrative

4 Cf. ANGEHRN, E., Frage nach dem Ursprung, 23–42, and HARTENSTEIN, F., Bleibende Bedeutung des AT, 171f.

research fits with what happened in the past, but it is purely contingent whether it fits; there is no proof of fitting at all (or in principle). This skeptical attitude towards historical research resembles metaphysical realism, as Koch described it.[5] It amounts to a metaphysical, skeptical historicism.

An example: The Israeli historian Yuval Harari seems to hold such a skeptical historicism. On the one hand, he acknowledges the priority of the narrative: 'I don't like the word 'abstractions' very much because most people don't think in abstractions. That is too difficult for them. They think in stories. And the best stories are not abstract; they are concrete.'[6] At the same time, Harari also claims that there is an important distinction between true and fictional stories. He claims that the fictional ones have more effect on what follows: 'In the book, I use the term "fiction", not abstraction, because what really unites humans are fictional stories.'[7] Although there are a distinction between true and false secondary-narrations (i.e. between secondary-narrations fitting to primary narration, or not fitting to them), this distinction is not seen as important for the actual course of primary-narrative processes, insofar as it is historically relevant: 'In big historical struggles, history does not go to the truth. It goes to the most effective story. And very often, the most effective story is not true. The idea that people sooner or later will discover that something is untrue usually doesn't happen, as in the case of all the big religions.'[8] Let us ignore that this quotation reveals Harari's defective understanding of religion. What is interesting is that it also reveals that Harari conceives the historic to be constituted by what is effective, not by what is true. In distinction to some post-modern thinkers influenced by Nietzsche, the motivation is not, however, that Harari rejects the concept of truth, but that he holds to this skeptical position despite his acknowledgment of the concept of truth. It is clear that such a position is laden with contradictions. However, in the face of the primacy of effectivity, these contradictions are irrelevant.

The *dynamic-realistic* interpretation allows for the possibility that contemporary historical reconstruction can also fit more or less with the past. In addition, it would also allow that the present (and future) pursuit of the past actually alters the past. Such a retroactive interpretation seems to be nonsensical at first glance. However, deeper thoughts reveal this seeming absurdity to be a naturalist prejudice that presupposes specific, implicit ontological commitments. The most important commitment is a causal interpretation of time, in which the concept of time is derived from the concept of causality: the past is what can be or was a cause of effects, whereas the future is what is or can be an effect of a cause. An advocate for such a causal understanding of time is

5 Cf. KOCH, A.F., Versuch, 55–57.
6 HARARI, Y.N., Dataism is Our New God, bes. 37.
7 HARARI, Y.N., Dataism is Our New God, 37.
8 HARARI, Y.N., Dataism is Our New God, 38.

Richard Swinburne.[9] However, we learned that neither causality nor time are basic states of affairs, but dependent on their narrative constitution (ch. 10 and 17). Whereas time is constituted by primary narrativity, causality is a far more complicated concept that presupposes a lot of ontological beliefs. Therefore, a causal interpretation of time is not really meaningful. But if time is constituted by primary narrativity, and if secondary narrativity is a subclass of what happens in primary narrativity, then we can neither exclude an interaction between secondary and primary narrativity, nor the retroactivity of the course of events. Past events are not facts, but a fuzzy cloud of what became. Therefore, we cannot exclude further becoming in that cloud by effects from the future. Of course, purely human secondary narrativity thereby has its limits. Perhaps a sometimes overused metaphor might be helpful in this respect: In the same way as quanta are spread over an extended, but definite space, so that they can become manifest at specific places with a certain probability according to the wave-function, whereas they cannot become manifest at other specific places, so present and future secondary-narrative activity can influence past events within strict limits. By this thesis, I do not intend to extend human or creaturely power to the past, which remains an excellent example of what is not at one's disposal. What I have in mind is more the prerogative of eschatology and the meaning of the last judgment – but these are topics for material dogmatics. While I want to acknowledge an interaction of what is future with what is past, it might be doubtful whether this interaction should really be called 'retroactivity'. The reason is that we opted for 'retroactivity' in terms of the constitution of time by primary narrativity, which creates the sequence of time. However, if in primary narrativity there actually is an interaction between what is future with the past, an observer in the midst of primary narrativity would hardly recognize it as being 'retroactive', but simply as a new insight about has happened, since the order of time is constituted by the narrative sequences of primary narrativity.

5. The historic is, as we claimed in ch. 20, a specific interaction or resonance in the realm of primary narrativity, that enables *a harmonic, i.e. true resonance between secondary narrativity and pure primary narrativity*. Two problems are bound up with this definition. The first is that pure primary narrativity that does not interact with secondary narrativity is hardly thinkable. The second is that this definition claims that the historic is a true secondary narration about the past. Our reflection on the concept of truth in ch. 20 showed that the concept of truth remains indefinable from the point of view of universal reason, and that it presupposes a material concept of grace. The consequence

9 Cf. SWINBURNE, R., Christian God, 81–90.

is that *truth is dependent on the primary-narrative aspect of revelation, not vice versa.* Applied to our problem, this means that *the historic is dependent on the primary-narrative aspect of revelation, not vice versa.* By that we have discovered the *particula veri* of the opinion that a secular understanding of the historical disciplines misses their subject-matter in contrast to an understanding of the historic in the framework of a history of salvation – which in fact means a narrative understanding of history.[10]

6. Our reflections on contingency in ch. 18 showed that in primary narrativity singular and new events occur, be they new in the sense of occurring the first time, or new in being actually singular. Pannenberg used this distinction in order to criticize a reductionist understanding of the historical sciences, which restrict themselves to only observations of analogies between events – if they do not try to explain everything by pure causality.[11] The features of novelty and singularity in history implies for us that the historic cannot be understood simply by means of a narratology, since narratology pre-eminently tries to identify narratives. But narratives are schemes, as we saw in ch. 6. The historic, if a harmonic interaction with primary-narrativity is its subject, cannot have the task of looking for narratives, but it is the task of looking for that which cannot be grasped by narrative and what is beyond all narratives. Exactly this is an identifying feature of historical language. It produces narrations, not narratives.

What does all this mean for our question about the relationship between faith and history? Of course, faith always implies a historical dimension, which is an important aspect within the boundaries of narrativity, but it becomes immediately self-contradictory if it is restricted in a historicist way.

For theology as the self-reflection of faith guided by methods, this means that it has to proceed primarily narratively, but that it has to go beyond a pure narratology to the development of a narrative ontology. Thereby, it has to integrate the historic. Theology is always also a historical discipline, but the historic is only one of its defining elements. Insofar as theology is a historical discipline, too, it is not methodologically distinguishable from other historical disciplines. However, historical theology realizes that neither itself nor other historical disciplines can simply use a general methodology of the historical sciences that rely on a concept of apparently universal reason or on a kind of pragmatic consensus. Theology is not forced to integrate the historic because

10 One has to maintain against PANNENBERG, W., ST I (engl.), 231f, that his insistence on the concept of history that is contrary to the concept of the *story* is based on a misunderstanding, which is that the concept of the *story* suspends the question of reality. This might be the case for James Barr, to which Pannenberg is referring here. But it was this kind of narrative thinking that we discovered in chapter 6 to be deficient.

11 Cf. PANNENBERG, W., Theology and the Philosophy of Science, 59–71.

this was the result of a development in the history of thought, but since faith as a bodily interwoven mesh of wayformational lines itself essentially incorporates a historical aspect.

Although it is not possible to do historical work without narratives, two universal narratives are excluded for the work of historical theology: the narrative of progress and the narrative of decay.[12] Apart from the fact that there is no general justification to opt for a universal decay or progress in history, the main problem is that to impose such narratives onto the actual mesh of stories is a de-contingentization of the historic. But the historic is an example of something that is contingent[13] *par excellence*. Interestingly, both narratives have appeared, up to now, in theology, although they are not only examples of de-contingentization, but of irreligiosity.

If it is true (1) that Christian faith is a narratively and temporally extended, bodily mesh of wayformational lines, and if it is true (2) that this faith is the secondary-narrative shape of the self-revelation of Godself, then to assume the idea of progress would imply the claim that the past is more remote from divine presence than the present and the future. Conversely, to assume a narrative of decay would imply that later times lack revelation in comparison to earlier ones. To assume both, however, is to claim that there is, at least a partial, historical period of godlessness in the world. The result is a historical Marcionism, i.e. the claim that while specific eras are saturated by revelation and happenings in God, others are far from the self-presentation of God. If this were true, a God could not be understood either as the integration of all wayformational perspectives in a particular wayformational perspective, or as the all determining reality, or an ultimate concern, or what brackets time. In whichever way one reconstructs the three meta-stores of Father, Son, and Holy Spirit, it cannot be done in a way in which the story of Jesus Christ is claimed to be more saturated by revelation than the pre-story (the story of the Father), or the post-story (the story of the Spirit). The history before Christ is not the pre-story of revelation, and present and future are not post-stories or post-histories of revelation. Although revelation is primarily a narrative and not a historical thing, it is always historical, *too*. And this historic aspect of revelation *cannot* be understood in such a way as if revelation occurs *in* history, but only, and here Pannenberg is right, in a way that conceives revelation *as* history. However, and this was overlooked by Pannenberg, revelation does not occur primarily or exclusively as history, but primarily and in a comprehensive way as a mesh of narrations of which one aspect is the historical one.

12 Cf. to this MÜHLING, M., Handbook of Christian Eschatology, 223–250.

13 Cf. PANNENBERG, W., Theology and the Philosophy of Science, 63f.

24.2 Narrativity and Textuality

A means in which secondary narrations can subsist are texts and literality. Texts are only one means among many others in which secondary-narrations happen and, in the framework of a theology of revelation, not an excellent one. Revelation is the actually occurring entanglement of the primary-narrative with the implicit secondary-narrative aspect of divine self-presentation, i.e. the actually occurring divine self-identification in the three identity-descriptions. The most important means, in regard to the secondary-narrative aspect, is the primary mediality of the body, and that means bodily communication. Nor is it to be expected that this will be altered in the immediate or distant future. Therefore, no text and no literal entity can be a primary means of revelation, and it would be completely wrong to call Christianity a 'scriptural religion'. Such nomenclature is, as self-description, strictly excluded. It might be meaningful for religions like Islam, in which the primary means of revelation is indeed a revelation of and in texts. And it might be possible that from such wayformational perspectives also Christianity looks like as it were a book religion, since Christians deal with texts. However, these texts have only a relative and mediated meaning for revelation. Texts, and therefore scriptures, are not the primary carriers of revelation. Indeed, linguisticality seems to play a pre-eminent role in Christianity, since from beginning on through the reception of Greek philosophy, the concept of *logos* was attributed with an eminent function for revelation by identifying it with the eternal Son. However, the concept of *logos* implies linguisticality, not textuality. As John 1 shows, it was understood bodily from the very beginning: the *logos* is the incarnate Son, and his story is at once the story of God. What John 1 wants to express by using the term *logos* is the identity of primary-narrative revelation with transcendental-narrative revelation.

With his doctrine of the threefold shape of the word of God in becoming, Barth correctly showed that it is primarily the person of Christ who *is* the Word of God, whereas the proclamation of the church in the *viva vox evangelii* and the witnesses of the Holy Scripture are only derived from it and can be called the Word of God in only a metaphorical way, insofar as they witness to the primary Word of God. However, Scripture does not become the Word of God by our reception, but by the divine revealing event.[14] 'Word of God' refers to an event, and the witness of the Bible is also not static. It can neither become the static Word of God, but can only metaphorically disclose itself as a witness of

14 For the doctrine of the trinitarian figure of God's Word in Barth cf. McCormack, B.L., Being of Holy Scripture.

the divine word in becoming.[15] However, we cannot simply follow Barth, since textuality and literality do not refer to Holy Scripture *per se*.

Insofar as the present communication of faith includes texts, and insofar as the historic dimension of the reflexive, secondary-communication of faith includes texts, texts are important. Both, the present and the past, are full of other media and sources, too, without the shape of textuality. True, the hermeneutics of human self-understanding between Bultmann and Ricœur might owe much the attempts to understand texts, but hermeneutics can neither be restricted to textual understanding, nor is this its primary aim. Theology is not a discipline of texts and not a discipline of literature, but it does include features from these disciplines. But even this fact, that theology includes a trace of textuality and literality among others, is not grounded in the concept of revelation, but it simply exists because of the pragmatic reason that texts can also be means of communication or historical sources. Therefore, we have to take care not to make textuality a paradigm, as, for example, happens when Boisen called human becomings 'living human documents.'[16]

Whereas we have to first relativize any absolute meaning of literality with the matter of theology, secondly, we have to acknowledge what is particularly precious in texts and in understanding texts. Perhaps more than any other means, texts exemplify the primary bodily communication with its two aspects of being available and withdrawing. As persons are at the disposal of other persons through their living bodies, but at the same time withdrawn, both aspects appear in the understanding of texts, since on the one hand, every text has authors and adaptors, and reflects their witness, on the other hand the authors and adaptors remain withdrawn in such a way that the *intentio auctoris* becomes irrelevant. Historically, the *intentio auctoris* has moved out of focus on behalf of the understanding of texts as a means of human self-understanding by an *intentio operis*.[17]

Ricœur stressed two functions of textuality and literality: First, texts and their methodical-hermeneutical interpretation save us from the arbitrariness of the recipient, and they safeguard the autonomy of the text. Second, texts let us imagine the new and alien, which would never come to our mind by the pure reflection of our self-consciousness.[18] Both points have their *particula veri*.

15 Cf. BARTH, K., CD I/1, §4, 110: 'The Bible, then, becomes God's Word in this event, and in the statement that the Bible is God's Word the little word "is" refers to its being in this becoming.'

16 Cf. ASQUITH, G.H.J., Boisen and 'Living Human Documents'.

17 Cf. MATTERN, J., Ricœur, 100f.

18 Cf. MATTERN, J., Ricœur, 106. 108.

However, I want to question Ricœur's first claim: A methodical access to texts, independent of the method which is used (hermeneutical, historic-critical, etc.) might save us of arbitrariness, but by no means from availableness. The contrary is true: Availableness is intensified, since the meaning that was once uncovered by a canonical method is now regarded as possibly being the *intentio operis*. With this move, however, the essential textual feature of withdrawal is illegitimately reduced. If one regards texts only as meaningful when methodologically interpreted, one deprives them of their possibility to be or to become means of revelation. Gadamer, therefore, was rightly seriously skeptical of all methods in the pursuit of truth.[19] It is not that which can be extracted by methods that is really precious in texts and textual communication, but in many cases that which is outside of any method, which cannot be observed through methodical interpretation, or which disturbs methods, that is precious. The eminent dignity of texts cannot be expressed by the fact that they can be interpreted methodically, but by the fact that by their means something alien addresses us, or that texts as instances of alterity disturb every method and push methods out into the realm of the preliminary and the deficient. If this were not the case, no text could become a means of revelation.

The second point Ricœur makes regarding textuality, including its methodical interpretation, cannot be overestimated: Precisely in that texts can be methodically interpreted, texts might disclose dimensions of meaning that would never enter the mind of the recipient without such methodical interpretation. Texts are eminent means of broadening horizons, in two ways: First, they enable a broadening of one's horizon in the course of receiving them, even if this happens without any method. Second, methodical interpretation enables an intensified broadening of one's horizon and the possibility that something new might disclose itself.

24.3 Holy Scripture as Canon

If one wants to reflect on the nexus of the mesh of secondary narrations in which Christian faith lives, it is necessary to deal with the whole of the tradition. Interestingly, it is not possible to refer to this narrative mesh of traditions without emphasis, i.e. without accepting particular threads of tradition as a norm, rule and guideline, i.e. as the canon, and so with a particular normative dignity. Nearly all attempts to either claim or reject the canonicity of certain writings illustrate this: to reject specific canonical claims means presupposing

19 Cf. MATTERN, J., Ricœur, 32–35.

other canonical claims, and to claim specific threads as canonical means to reject others. This is, however, not surprising, since we have known since chapter 5 that there is no perceiving without perceiving values, and that perceiving values leads to a narrative constitution of norms.

Nevertheless, to honor a particular thread of Christian secondary narrativity as canonical does not mean do devaluate the remaining traditions, as we will see after our reflection on what the canonicity of a particular threads means.

The church correctly claims that Holy Scripture, including both testaments, is canonical. Nevertheless, this causes a series of problems.

1. Historically, the canonicity of the first testament emerged through its liturgical and theological use in early Christianity, since it was these texts in the shape of the Greek LXX that was known as a collection of holy texts. Of course, the early church was originally a Jewish community that developed to be something different, which made using Scripture much more important. However, the problem is that neither the historical emergence nor the liturgical use can justify canonic normativity *per se*.

2. The canonicity of the texts later called the New Testament is also based on its use in the early church. It is thereby interesting that the constitution of the canon and its boundedness to the *regula fidei* was a reaction against Marcion's plan to introduce a canon with the help of specific material and predicative criteria. In the course of becoming canonical, specific criteria were named, like the apostolicity of the authors or the criterion of being a witness of Christ. Both criteria, however, are laden with further problems.

3. The criterion of apostolicity does not use a single concept of apostolicity. The canon includes both Luke's writings, in which apostolicity is bound to being acquainted with Christ in his *status exinanitionis*, and Paul's writings, in which apostolicity is bound to being a witness to the resurrection of Christ. Moreover, there are also writings like Mark, in which the 'second' generation of witnesses are included. Apostolicity is, therefore, in the regard to being a criterion for canonicity, not a clear concept, but a fuzzy set. This, as we will learn, is by no means a disadvantage.

4. The criterion of being a witness to Christ is also not without problems, although it has been consistently used: If one speaks in the Lutheran tradition of a canon within the canon, which is characterized by honoring specific elements of the canon, and by calling the criterion what *Christum treibet*, how then can the wider canon can be based on being a witness to Christ? The First Testament was conceived of during most eras of the church, especially in the very early church, as a witness to Christ. How is this possible, when this trait of being a witness to Christ is rejected by, for example, historical-critical means?

5. Applying both of the criteria from the ancient church can explain why specific texts from the 1st century did not become canonical, like the *Shepard of Hermas*, which does not claim apostolicity, or like late texts that wrongly claim to be apostolic, or like texts that distort the witness of Christ, like the *Gospel of Peter*. However, it cannot be explained why pseudepigraphic texts, like the deutero-pauline texts, were incorporated into and remain within the canon.

6. Historically, variations in the lists of canonical writings vanishes for the First Testament from the 2nd century onward, and for the New Testament from the 4th century onward. Nevertheless, the church refrained from defining a canonical list of texts. Only later, in the Florentine and Tridentine councils, did the Roman Catholic Church declare canonical lists.[20] In the Reformed tradition, there can be found the one or other symbolic writing like the *Confessio Gallica* or the *Confession Belgica*, that presents such a list as well.[21] However, in the Lutheran tradition, such a list was never declared. Does this mean that for the churches that never dogmatized such a list, the canon is not closed extensionally?

7. The fact that biblical writings are used in the communication of faith implies that these scriptures cannot be conceived of purely as human scriptures, because the reflexive, secondary-narrative communication of faith (including its use of the biblical scriptures) is not meaningful without divine cooperation, insofar as this reflexive, secondary communication of faith belongs to divine self-revelation. The tradition acknowledged this fact by naming the biblical texts in some sense as the 'Word of God', by conceiving them as constituted by divine theopneutic activity in the ancient church up to being constituted by inspiration in the framework of doctrine of verbal inspiration found in the old Protestant orthodoxy. Although all these arguments are very diverse, they coincide in claiming that human witness of divine self-revelation is not possible without divine collaboration. Therefore, these scriptures somehow must be evaluated as part of the divine self-presentation.

We could easily talk about more problems with the concept of canonicity. Instead of doing that, we will move to trying to justify the concept of canonicity in a material way. First, however, we will mention a specific example of denying canonicity. I have chosen an example from the early 21st century that attracted an astonishing amount of public interest.

---

20 Cf. DENZINGER, H./HÜNERMANN, P., DH, No. 706 and 784.

21 Cf. Conf. Gall. Art. 3 and Conf. Bel. Art. 4.

In 2013, Notger Slenczka rejected a part of Holy Scripture as canonical, with arguments going back to Schleiermacher, Harnack, and Bultmann.[22] I was for some time undecided whether this contemporary case should be mentioned in an overall presentation of theology. However, the interest of the media was immense, and specific material problems can be exemplified by the case. Therefore, it is meaningful to mention this case but not *en detail*.

1. Wherever parts of Holy Scripture are rejected as canonical, canonicity as such is not usually denied, but different understandings of canonicity are used.

2. This can be shown by the fact that in Schleiermacher's rejection of the canonicity of the OT – and similarly in Slenczka – the piety of the Christian self-consciousness is in fact seen as canonical,[23] and that for Harnack a specific material-predicative concept of the proclamation of Jesus as the unconditional love of the Father and the infinite value of the created soul[24] is actually used as the canonical principle.

3. It is interesting in these cases that it is only the canonicity of the Old Testament that is rejected, but not of parts of the New Testament. Marcion in the 2nd century was more coherent. He did not reject the canonicity of something, however, but he construed a canon as such. When it is claimed that the present consciousness of faith would 'have fear of the stranger'[25] in the face of the Old Testament, or that here the unchangeable love of the one God and the necessary correlate of the infinite value of the human soul cannot be found, then large parts of the New Testament would also be struck off by that accusation: think of Jesus's exorcisms, which are most probably historical; think of the relationship between male and female, or the understanding of the state in the Pastoral epistles; think of the rejection of the natural family in Jesus's proclamation, etc.

4. That it is only the rejection of the OT as canonical is not motivated by a central intention, but by secondary ones. In the case of Schleiermacher and Harnack, these consist in an image of history that is fueled by a conviction of the progress of the history of religions. But we saw already that progressive conceptions of history are highly questionable. In Slenczka, the deeper motivating reasons might consist in his intention to avoid a rivalry of the church as a canonical community of interpretation of the Hebrew Bible with contemporary Judaism,[26] and in conceiving of the non-Christian determinations of self-consciousness as sublated and overcome by the self-disclosure of Christ. Here, Slenczka refers to one of Bultmann's arguments,[27] according to which the OT might be of preeminent cultural value for our Western culture, which gives the OT the character of preparing for revelation, whereas this is not necessary for other areas of culture. Here, his argument resembles Raimundo Pannikkar's, who claimed nearly the same thing, but without the intent to reject the dignity of the OT, but with

---

22 Cf. SLENCZKA, N., Kirche und das AT. Cf. also Slenczka's own commentary in SLENCZKA, N., Was soll die These: „Das AT hat in der Kirche keine kanonische Geltung mehr"?, as well as his earlier underlying thoughts in SLENCZKA, N., Schrift.

23 Cf. SCHLEIERMACHER, F., Christian Faith, §11, 52–60; SLENCZKA, N., Kirche und das AT, 98–100.

24 Cf. HARNACK, A.v., Das Wesen des Christentums, 43. 52.

25 Cf. SLENCZKA, N., Kirche und das AT, 96. 100. 119.

26 Cf. SLENCZKA, N., Was soll die These: „Das AT hat in der Kirche keine kanonische Geltung mehr"?, 11.

27 Cf. SLENCZKA, N., Kirche und das AT, 106–110.

the intention of declaring a functional equivalence with other texts from other areas of culture.[28]

5. Without taking these secondary intentions into consideration, a shift in the principle of canonicity appears. In the case of Harnack, a shift to the material content of the proclamation of Jesus that can be reduced to two predicative statements. In the case of Schleiermacher and Slenczka, a shift to elements of an ontology of consciousness. Both kinds of shifts in the canonical principle of secondary narrativity are dangerous, but they nevertheless differ: Harnack transfers canonicity *contra intentionem* to a *doctrine* supposedly uncovered with historic-scientific means, and misses thereby the character of Christian faith from the very beginning. It is ironic that it is a doctrine that appears as the essence of Christianity. In the case of Schleiermacher and Slenczka, canonicity shifts to a historical manifestation of the content of the God-consciousness. Thereby any transcendental-narrative or primary-narrative of revelation is rejected, and only the implicit secondary-narrative aspect of revelation is placed in the center, which shall now function in order to regulate the reflexive secondary-narrative aspect canonically. This, however, is a reduction of revelation by means of an ontology of subjectivity.[29] This can be exemplified by the fact that the primary function of biblical and other texts for speaking to the dignity and normativity of what is alien to one's own wayformational perception is excluded. In this respect, it is remarkable how Slenczka uses the metaphor of having a fear of strangers in the face of the OT. First, I doubt if there really is a significant majority of those who are acquainted with the writings of the OT who really have a fear of strangers. Secondly, if the OT does really cause stranger anxieties in its readers, why is this used as an argument against its canonicity and not as one of its eminent characteristics? Yes, feeling anxiety around strangers and being bewildered might be the first *appropriate* response in some cases, for example, in cases in which physical violence is justified in the biblical writings. Such is true in the face of OT talk about a God who motivated the murder of little children (Hos 14:1) as well as in the face of NT statements about a God who punishes financial defraudment in the same way (Acts 5:1–10). Our response of such feelings of bewilderment and stranger anxiety are *not* arguments *against* canonicity, but *for* canonicity! Of course, this needs a concept of canonical authority that excludes blind obedience. But this should be normal for a religion that conceives of Holy Scripture as canonical and therefore not as direct self-revelation of God. Alienation can be an appropriate kind of perceiving the biblical texts in their truth and value, but it should not lead to a rejection of canonicity, because then a self-alienation from one's own perceiving truth and value becomes impossible. However, the reflexive secondary-narrative aspect of revelation deals with exactly that.

6. Slenczka also mentions and rejects possible alternatives to his concept of canonicity, like the so-called canonical approach of B.S. Childs, or a radical approach by way of reader-response criticism.[30] In cases like these, Slenczka might be right. However, these are not all the possible alternatives.

7. Slenczka rejects the thesis that the Old Testament is a witness for Christ (and therefore canonical) on the historicist grounds that this cannot be the case. The

---

28 Cf. PANIKKAR, R., Unknown Christ of Hinduism; PANIKKAR, R., Jordan, Tiber, Ganges.

29 Cf. similar HARTENSTEIN, F., Bleibende Bedeutung des AT, 33.

30 Cf. SLENCZKA, N., Kirche und das AT, 101–104; SLENCZKA, N., Was soll die These: 'Das AT hat in der Kirche keine kanonische Geltung mehr?,' 1.

argument that the OT is a witness for Christ has been used since the ancient church via the Reformation up to dialectical theology and to the followers of Gerhard von Rad, but it is no longer seen as tenable. Interestingly, Slenczka here refers in a very selective and distorting manner to Luther. Indeed, Luther identified the literal meaning of Scripture with the soteriological witness to Christ. And indeed, Luther saw this as given in the OT. However, whether there is such a witness is not something that is given by the letter of the texts, or by the text's historical conditions of origin, but whether they are, by the Spirit's action, transformed into the *pro me* of the Gospel through proclamation to the present situation. The character of the biblical texts' as a witness to Christ is not something that subsists in the texts as such, but is a result of a perceptual event that has to be understood as the self-revelation of God the Spirit in the midst of human activities.[31] This view is not only the opinion of hermeneutical theology, but is also the claim of Barth's doctrine of Scripture (see below), which did not understand the OT simply as a witness to Christ in a historical sense.

8. Whereas one is justified in diagnosing anti-Semitic tendencies in opponents of the canonicity of the OT in people like Emmanuel Hirsch, this would be absurd to do to those who argued against its canonicity and for it to be considered deuterocanonical at the beginning of the 21st century.

Examples of fruitful arguments for canonicity can be found in the tradition of hermeneutical theology.

Friedhelm Hartenstein recently noted correctly, with reference to Ricœur, that the canonicity of both testaments as parts of Holy Scripture consist in their being historically and hermeneutically given to be understood.[32] This givenness, as fact and task, is according to Hartenstein based in revelation itself, which is a boundary-phenomenon of the narrative witness of both testaments and is itself open.[33] Therefore, it is possible, within the framework of considering the canonicity of Holy Scripture, to speak of the Scripture Principle as long as *principium* is primarily associated with its meaning as *initium*, origin.[34] Revelation is understood here as crossing over of two narrations or worlds, the one of the text and the other of the reader,[35] with the result that 'the concrete (soteriological) events [...] are only given to us by means of narrations and confessions' and that faith, story, and history are in this manner insolubly interwoven.[36] Therefore, 'historical events and semiotic representations cannot (any longer) be distinguished.'[37] Confessions that serve as witnesses during the course of interpretation have the threefold character of witness, which was described in the tradition of Ricœur[38] as quasi-empirical, quasi-juridical, and (this is an expression

31 Cf. to this EBELING, G., Evangelische Evangelienauslegung, and HARTENSTEIN, F., Bleibende Bedeutung des AT, 21–23.
32 Cf. HARTENSTEIN, F., Bleibende Bedeutung des AT, 18.
33 Cf. HARTENSTEIN, F., Bleibende Bedeutung des AT, 33.
34 Cf. HARTENSTEIN, F., Bleibende Bedeutung des AT, 35f.
35 Cf. HARTENSTEIN, F., Bleibende Bedeutung des AT, 43.
36 HARTENSTEIN, F., Bleibende Bedeutung des AT, 44 (transl. MM).
37 HARTENSTEIN, F., Bleibende Bedeutung des AT, 43 (transl. MM).
38 Cf. RICŒUR, P., Hermeneutics of Testimony.

of Hartenstein's[39]) quasi-martyriological dimension. The quasi-empirical dimension means that only what is perceived bodily can be a subject of witness, but only in the shape of a report of a witness, and not independently from it. The quasi-juridical dimension is the internal process of finding the truth in a dispute. The quasi-martyriological dimension refers to the existential seriousness of the witness.

Revelation in this respect is itself a processual becoming that never produces a totality of meaning since it is able to re-bind the concretion and contingency of the events. Following Michael Moxter, Scripture is therefore the basis and limit of understanding.[40] The background of that is a functional understanding of the canon, in which, according to Herms, 'the sheer existence of contemporary Christianity [...] includes the actual and contemporary relevance of all the texts that count as canon.'[41] In using the canon, 'a polyphonic universe of meaning with large temporal depth and internal width, but without arbitrary plurality'[42] appears, that serves 'the collective and individual self-assurance with reference to the Bible.'[43]

This hermeneutical understanding of the canon, as it is exemplarily explicated by Hartenstein, can be conceived of within the framework of a broad understanding of revelation that does not separate the four aspects of revelation: the transcendental-narrative, the primary-narrative, the implicit secondary-narrative, and the reflexive secondary-narrative one. Its basis lies in the fact that Holy Scripture is actually used for the becoming of the identity of faith, which is its advantage. However, the question of why it is a Holy Scripture with both testaments that has these effects cannot be answered normatively. And that is a matter of principles: If one wants to find a norm for canonicity, this would mean basing canonicity on something that is non-biblical, that is, a conceptual principle, a doctrine, or whatever. But this would be a practical self-contradiction. Barth saw this with perfect clarity:

> It is the Canon because it imposed itself upon the Church as such, and continually does so. [...] If we thought we could say why this is so, we should again be acting as if we had in our hands a measure by which we could measure the Bible, and on this basis assign it its distinctive position. [...] No, the Bible is the Canon just because it is so. It is so by imposing itself as such.[44] [..] It is not in our own power to make this recollection, not even in the form of our grasping at the Bible. Only when and as the Bible grasps at us, when we are thus reminded, is this recollection achieved.[45]

39 Cf. HARTENSTEIN, F., Bleibende Bedeutung des AT, 46.

40 Cf. HARTENSTEIN, F., Bedeutung des AT für die evangelische Kirche, esp. 743, and MOXTER, M., Schrift als Grund und Grenze von Interpretationen.

41 HERMS, E., Was haben wir an der Bibel?, 102 (transl. MM).

42 HARTENSTEIN, F., Bedeutung des AT für die evangelische Kirche, 746 (transl. MM).

43 HARTENSTEIN, F., Bedeutung des AT für die evangelische Kirche, 746f (transl. MM).

44 BARTH, K., CD I/1, §4, 107.

45 BARTH, K., CD I/1, §4, 109.

Theological traditions as diverse as can be found in Ebeling, Herms, Hartenstein, and Barth acknowledge this point. Actually, it is not here simply the factuality of what had become to be the case historically, but that Holy Scripture imposes itself as an ever-new becoming of canonicity. Therefore, it is not to be underestimated. The theologians of the old Protestant orthodoxy spoke of the *efficacia* of Scripture, and this effectiveness consists preeminently in the Scripture's ability to impose itself in its canonicity on us. It is far more effective in doing so than the old Protestant theologians thought, who superficially invented the doctrine of verbal inspiration in order to support something that does not need to be supported. Does all this mean that canonicity can only be based on its facticity if one wants to avoid self-contradictory arguments? Or can we say a little bit more than that?

Ricœur is right in seeing in the concept of witness irreducibly (1) an aspect of perceiving, called the quasi-empirical aspect, (2) a discursive aspect, called the quasi-juridical aspect, and (3) an existential aspect that can be, with Hartenstein, called a quasi-martyriological one. Why, however, is the witness able to have these aspects? The answer to this question is essential. And the answer is that any kind of witness primarily has an indexical function, which is expressed in the entanglement of the narrations of the witnessing stories with the stories of what is witnessed. The same is true in the case of canonicity. *The essential point in the actuality of the canonicity of Holy Scripture in both testaments is that it is not an authority of the predicative contents of a doctrine or of conceptual truths, but that it is an authority of indexical-narrative content, and is so in a manifold sense.*

1. Since Holy Scripture is used for the communication of the believer's identity, they become entangled with the narrations of Scripture and are thereby inscribed into and addressed by it. In order to exclude self-contradictory arguments, this cannot be understood as a self-identification of the believers, but that believers conceive of themselves as passively addressed and identified by scripture.

2. Since Holy Scripture in both testaments collects so many witnesses, which cannot be predicatively unified by a doctrine, the indexicality of canonicity is emphasized, i.e. the texts of Holy Scripture witnesses to something by referring indexically to it that is distinct from the Scripture itself: the threefold shape of divine self-identification. This can be shown on the basis of the witness to Christ:

a) The texts of the New Testament witness to the divine self-identification in Christ and point on the one hand from themselves, and on the other hand, they do not establish a doctrinal principle or any predicative content as canonical. Whatever appears as a given task of preliminary predicative understanding is obligatory and important, but not canonical. Canonical is only this indexical entanglement with the story of the self-identification of Christ, which implies that neither our primary-narrative perceiving truth and value in the light of the Gospel, nor the reflexive interpretation on this basis is canonical.

b) The self-identification of God in Christ is, as we saw in chapter 22, asymmetrically bound to the story of God in Israel, who is addressed and identified by Jesus as his *abba*. In the entanglement of the life-stories of Christians today with the self-identification of God in Christ, the believers are then simultaneously related to the self-identification of God in Israel as Father. Transitivity matters here: since my identity is dependent on Christ's identity, and since Christ's identity is dependent on the identity of the God of Israel, so my identity is also bound to the identity of the God of Israel. The story of the God of Israel is not a doctrine that would be overcome in Christ, as the false logic of progressive historicism suggests, but it is a collection of narrative identity-descriptions that challenges us to understand the preliminary in predicative ways, too. To reflect on the story of the God of Israel, however, cannot be done without the reflecting the story of Christ, since by its inner biblical, indexical reference the identities of Christ and the identities of the God of Israel are entangled: whoever conceives his own identity as entangled with the identity of Christ is challenged to understand Christ in the context of the God of Israel. Conversely, the God of Israel can only be understood in the context of Christ (for believers). Therefore, in the framework of a narrative theory of identity, the Old Testament is indeed a witness to Christ from the very beginning. The fact that the Old Testament is not a historical witness to Christ is irrelevant, due to the fact that historicity is based on the narrativity. However, since the entanglement of the stories of the self-identification of God in Christ and of God in the Story of Israel is asymmetric, the logical conclusion is that while whoever is not perceiving his own identity as entangled with the story of Christ, the reverse cannot be said. This is, for example, the case in contemporary Judaism, which regards Christianity simply as another religion among many other religions. However, the reverse cannot be said from a Christian wayformational perspective. Contemporary Judaism conceives of themselves as a community of interpreting the Hebrew Bible, as Christianity conceives itself as a community of interpreting the First Testament. The problem of how the God of Israel is identical with God in Jesus Christ is a problem that is canonical, that is, indexically given by the narrative self-identification of the triune God for Christian theology as gift and as task – but not for Jewish theology.

c) The entanglement of the believers with the identity of Christ is not only irreducibly dependent on the self-identification of God in Israel, but also on the self-identification of God in the story of believers, i.e. in the story of the church. Why should the story of Christ be a story of divine self-identification at all? Christ's claim to be, in his actions and passion, the presence of the *basileia tou theou* can be contested. And whoever claims to be the *basileia tou theou* in person must face, according to John 5:18 and John 10:33, the charge of all critiques of religion: the idolizing of oneself. And indeed, the entanglement of one's own identity with the self-identification of God in Christ is not something that could be done by ourselves. If one did try to do so, one would experience the Cross as the failure of this claim. Therefore, the point of the synoptic confession of Peter, as well as the point of the identification of Christ on the Cross by the soldier, is that the story of the Spirit has begun: accepting the divine self-identification in Christ is not at the disposal of active human narrativity, it cannot be proven, and it can only be a result of the action of God the Spirit that constitutes certainty, if there are to be no contradictions. Therefore, the self-identification of God in the stories of the believers is an integral part of the entanglement of identities. Also, this third story is witnessed in the texts of the New Testament. The proper feature of this third story, however, is that it is not closed, but that it opens the entanglement to the whole of the tradition, including its presence and future. Does this mean a levelling of the relation between tradition and canon? Is the canon open? By no means. It is true that the indexical self-identification of God in the story of the believers is open, but its indexical function as witness is satisfactorily given in the biblical stories: whatever might reveal itself in the future tradition as self-identification of God, it is not another, new story, but is given to be understood in the story of the Holy Spirit.

The fact that the narrative meshes of the Holy Scripture are conceived as canonical, so that their canonicity consists in pointing themselves to the triune self-identification of God, provides protection against the self-absolutizing tendencies of the church, its practice of interpretation, and the texts themselves. The material ground of the canonicity of Holy Scripture in the threefold interwoven self-identification of God expresses itself for us in experiencing the facticity of canonicity that is epistemically unjustifiable. Its signs are the fact that the canon developed in a historically contingent manner, as well as in the contingent shape of the content of canonical texts. For example, when Luther on the one hand has problems with some doctrines of some biblical texts, like James, and on the other does not deny their canonical status, there is no contradiction, but an expression of the fact that canonicity is indexically given as gift and as task. Luther also declared that what *Christum treibet* is canonical; he also declared that an Apostle is whoever proclaims Christ, even if it be Judas, Ananias, Pilate, or Herod. He also declared that whoever contradicts what *Christum treibet* cannot be seen as apostolic, even if it be Peter or Paul.[46] In contrast to Harnack's material shift of canonicity, statements like these are in no way expressions of a supposed attempt on Luther's part to alter canonicity. It is more a sign that Luther acknowledges what is pre-given as gift and task to be understood by the biblical witness. Actually, Luther did not label his objections against particular texts of Scripture an opinion of the church, but simply as his own opinion.

It is now clear that the canon is may not be reduced in cases where we feel uncomfortable. But one could also ask whether it is possible to add texts to the canon – Barth had this possibility in mind when he spoke of the *relative* closedness of the canon.[47] What I have in mind are not other writings from the early church that are known to us, but sources and texts that might be discovered in the future and the texts that are called apocrypha or deuterocanonical writings, which are 'good and useful to read', i.e. the Greek texts of Hellenistic Judaism. These texts were for the early Christians a point of reference in the same sense as the texts of the Hebrew bible were points of reference. The fact that the Reformers decided to treat the Hebrew Bible as the 'original text' instead of the LXX is more driven by a historicist influence from humanism than by theological appropriateness. Nevertheless, the existence of apocryphal or deuterocanonical texts can be valued positively, because it indicates that canonicity does not mean a sharp set.

Karl Barth answered the question of why it is the texts we know today as biblical are canonical by reference to the self-imposing ability of the Bible or to the will of God. He did not thereby claim that the history of the canon is an absolute divine judgment.[48] He does not regard the canon as absolutely closed. Therefore, he regards discussions about canonicity as important.[49] This importance also remains under the condition that one knows the unjustifiability of canonicity. The reason why this is important consists in the fact that the community of faith is allowed to claim and to promise themselves and all those who receive their witness, that certainty about the entanglement of their identities with the threefold self-identification of God is something that should be expected from the canonical Scriptures.[50]

46 Cf. LUTHER, M., WA, DB 7, 385.
47 Cf. BARTH, K., CD I/2, §19, 476.
48 Cf. BARTH, K., CD I/2, §19, 479.
49 Cf. Cf. BARTH, K., CD I/2, §19, 478.
50 Cf. similarly Cf. BARTH, K., CD I/2, §19, 480.

CHAPTER 25

Enlightened Reason

Part of the reflexive, secondary-narrative aspect of divine self-presentation is also the human use of reason. But what is reason and how far it is dependent on divine self-presentation? A really concise analysis of this question would require digging anew into the themes we treated in part two. The themes of perceiving truth and value, of narrations, relations, wayformational lines, events, time, space, signs, metaphors, concepts, models, coherence, causality, contingency, subjectivity and truth would need to be explicated anew insofar as they can be conceived of as aspects of 'reason' and in the light of revelation. But even this would presuppose the whole explication of the material parts to follow. Reason would thus also be a topic for an epilegomena. For practical reasons, we have chosen another way by asking about the relationship between revelation and reason vis-à-vis possible types of relating them (ch. 22). Without repeating the discussions and the results of part two, the present chapter can be read as a reprise of it. What is new is that now the two approaches, from theology and from the philosophy of religion, have to meet. Therefore, we have to anticipate some material insights of later chapters, regarding bodiliness, anthropology, Christology, the doctrine of God, pneumatology, and eschatology.

What are the consequences for the theme of reason, if we treat reason by taking humans seriously as bodily human becomings, emerging on narrative wayformational lines?

25.1 The Living Body in its Meaning for Reason

Reason is primarily practical and epistemic reason, unmixed and unseparated, and only secondarily technical reason. Some of its features seem to follow a chiastic logic: On the one hand, reason is bound to bodily perceiving truth and value on particular wayformational perspectives, so that the epistemic aspect also presupposes the practical one. On the other hand, reason tries to integrate all wayformational perspectives in its endeavor for unity and coherence. Both aspects can only be mediated by dramatic coherence. Therefore, reason is – although it is bound to the body – not only concerned with validity relative to situations, but it claims to be directed to the general by the particular.

 | DOI:10.30965/9783846765852_026

Bodiliness, as we have seen, cannot be understood in the container-model, but at best in the model of whirlwinds.

1. Reason appears in different shapes: in the shape of technical reason, in the shape of practical reason, and in the shape of epistemic reason.[1] In the shape of technical reason, mathematical models of reality are foremost, offering a world-forming power that is at once something like a universal language for globalization. Nevertheless, technical reason is dependent on practical and epistemic reason. All forms of using reason, including mathematization, are bound to bodiliness, which can *per se* not be mathematized completely.

2. Reason is bound to the body, since reason presupposes the use of indexical words in order to be comprehensible. But indexes that are not bound to the body are not possible (ch. 12 and 19). They have to be anchored in the moving coordinate system of indexes which is bound to the bodily, wayformational perspectives. Here we have to remember the description of the body we gave in ch. 14.6: the body is a quasi-meteorological phenomenon, equipped with three perspectives: primary-narrative becoming, as means of inter-narrativity, and the secondary-narrative shaping of itself. We have to refer to these three perspectives if we want to analyze human reason.

3. Reason bound to the body is directed at what appears as gift and task to be understood in its own terms. In this way, reason is always directed to something that has to reveals itself, which shows how it is dependent on the unconcealment (*Unverborgenheit*) of things (according to Heidegger) or what appears as firstness (according to Peirce). At the same time, reason wants to grasp what appears. Grasping occurs in that everything that is and that is given in order to be understood (secondness) can be further determined by similarities and distinctions in relation to other appearances (thirdness). *Omnis determination negation est* is a description of the process, by which an entity becomes particular and is nevertheless integrated into a coherent whole. If a logical subject only possesses a single logical predicate (or *vice versa*), the statement would be uninformative. Therefore, every thought that is located in the wholeness of combinations can again be located in another wholeness of combinations, etc.[2] Neither reason itself, nor what appears for reason to be understood, allows for a limit, with the result that reason in its activity to determine the particular is always directed toward wholeness. This wholeness is the *particular veri* of the idea that truth is the whole, and also a reason for the fact that reason always has to use universalizations. This coherentist whole can, as we have seen, be understood in two ways: as transport

---

1 Cf. KOCH, A.F., Rationalität im Gespräch.

2 Cf. to this HINDRICHS, G., Das Absolute und das Subjekt, 167–169.

in the network of logical coherence, or as wayfaring in the meshwork of dramatic coherence. Logical coherence needs to understand the whole as a well-founded set, but dramatic coherence has no need to do so. If one is doing only conceptual work with a restricted vernacular, i.e. attributing predicates to logical subjects, regionally restricted, the abstraction of the network might lead to intelligible results. However, upon transcending to the whole, transport fails. Here we only have the option of wayfaring, which means we cannot think of the whole as a well-formed set. Ultimate wholeness is, paradoxically, always open.

This pursuit of unity includes all mundane entities and it motivates reason to ask about universal determination, i.e. the integration of all bodily wayformational lines. However, such an integration is only possible from particular wayformational perspectives. In other words, reason asks on its own about God in the sense of the minimal-conditions we have given in ch. 21. As the linguistic entities that humans are, this pursuit of universal coherence is always a narrative discussion that is in discourse with an other that enables the growth of one's own determination – and there is no limit to such narrative discussions. Therefore, reason is always chiastic, if not paradoxically constituted: on the one hand, bound bodily to particular wayformational perspectives of perceiving truth and value, on the other hand, bound to its pursuit of integration and universalization.

25.2 The Misery of Purified Reason

The modern project of pure reason could only be done in the sense of a purified reason, which reveals itself as a self-contradiction and as failing to fit with perception and reality. Purified reason regards its two only apparently opposite expressions: (a) realistic reason, and (b) constructivist reason. In both cases, the same mistake is committed, which is to regard the subject-object-distinction as a basic phenomenon.

1. 'Reason' is a term in need of clarification. It appears as a noun that seems to refer to a substantial, mental (i.e. non-bodily) entity, which governs the limits of the structures of the world, i.e. in the realms of nature and culture and in human life and action. In conceiving both aspects – the quasi-objective one and the quasi-subjective one – as positively related – which can be done in relations of correspondence, representation, correlation, etc. – an epistemic realism is postulated. It remains an open question as to why such a correlation is possible, and it remains open as to what exactly the material role reason is to play in that correlation.

2. A very simple attempt in the field of analytic philosophy it to identify the structure of reason with the correlation of statements and propositions. Statements on the human, mental side, seemed to be able to reduce the danger of arbitrary subjectivity by being related to a purified language (that is no longer necessarily bound to the users of language), which is what the propositions in a purified world consists of. However, semiotic considerations revealed that statements and language remain bound in semiosis to the users of signs. And phenomenological considerations reveal that propositions in the world are not perceivable phenomena. Propositions are therefore disclosed as abstract, theoretical entities, which – similar to memes, genes, the ether, the soul or strings – exist only as projections of a purified language in an 'objective' realm that is claimed to be beyond perception.

a) The Glass Bead Game – a game with statements and propositions that promised to make good on the belief in objectivity and universality of reason, which had been postulated for generations but never satisfied, in the hope that the logical structure of purified language could be at the same time the structure of the world and therefore the essence of reason. However, this attempt is falsified by the antinomy of reason, as we analyzed it in ch. 18. The goal of a purified reason has therefore failed once and for all, as is exemplified by Gödel's incompleteness theorems: at the point where language and world are purified to a maximum, the self-contradiction appears as a correlate between purified logic and the principle of the non-contradiction.

But imagine that this is not the case: what would be the point of such a purified reason? It is bound to the abstract structure of predicate logic, denies the reality of relations, the reality of the particular, the reality of temporal dynamics, and in the end, the reality of bodiliness. In short: it denies the reality of primary narrativity. However, it denies this reality in a very subtle manner: not by denying it explicitly, but simply because it has no means to speak about this reality. In reality, we never perceive external relations between atomistic individuals, but relational states of affairs, by which we extract, through highly interpretative and cognitive operations, separate *relata*, in order to relate them externally again.[3] In reality, we do not perceive tokens of humans, of the blue or the reasonable, but we perceive the offending Achilles, and draw back from this blue-greyish sky while in the Highlands. In reality, no timeless states of affairs are perceived, but dynamic processes, entangled with us, which cannot be modelled as logically coherent, since the principle of non-contradiction would need a timeless world in order to function properly. However, we can use *dramatic coherence*,[4] which

3 The emergence of *relata* out of interweavings is certainly not a random and not always a cognitive, interpretative act, but belongs to reality, including to the non-personal self; it resembles the 'intra-action' and the 'agential cut' in Karen Barad's theory, cf. BARAD, K., Meeting the Universe Halfway 139–140.

4 The concept of 'dramatic coherence' is not designed in opposition to the principle of non-contradiction, but it shows its basis in the world and how it appears. If you abstract the narrative-dynamic perception of the world, you release the world from the concept of time and bodyliness, which is how it is done in most logics, which are understood as timeless,

lives, ever and ever, from the unsatisfied promise of what is not yet and still remains open. In reality, we do not perceive materialistic matter, but we move bodily in a bodily world, without any primordial separation of is and ought, between reason, will, and affectivity. We do not perceive the world as points connected secondarily to lines, but dynamically in dynamic curves of unfinished, sketched lines.[5] In short: in reality, we perceive the world narratively, not classificatory. Therefore, all the distinctions of purified reason are unmasked as neither objective nor as universal. Since they are not able to describe perceptions, they can only describe *proposed* facts that are actually only constructs of abstract, purified reason. Therefore, the alleged realism of purified reason becomes what it intends to reject: constructivism.

b) However, this inversion of the problem, which claims that reason is culturally or subjectively relative, is also wrong in at least two respects. Primarily, the antinomy of negation appears here as an antinomy of the claim that the constructivist thesis includes as universal quantification: it is universally true that only particularly true, cultural-relative reasons exist. Here we find a contradiction between the logical form (a universal quantification) and its material content (plural particularity). Imagine that is not the case. Even under these counterfactual conditions, cultural relativism cannot explain the success of the use reason, including the perceptions of understanding and agreement. It cannot explain how humans are able to understand each other, why languages can be translated, why human becomings cooperate and behaving empathically most of the time. Although it is true that the indexical labelling of a phenomenon with, for example, 'gavagai', does not say anything about the ontology of the one who is using that word. However, it is also true that everyone who is acquainted with the Anglophone philosophy of the 20th century, be it a native speaker, a German, or an Italian, independently of whether she is philosopher, theologian or literary scholar, instantly knows what is meant if 'gavagai' is mentioned, regardless of whether one has read Quine, or Eco's novels.

The cultural-constructivist conception of reason is true, insofar as it acknowledges that a pure reason simply cannot exist, but that reason is always dependent reason – but it is false to assign this dependency of reason to the power of individual subjects or the cultural subject. The constructivist understanding, therefore, has to accept exactly what it wants to deny.

To postulate either a universal, pure, but in fact *purified* reason, or a subjective-particular reason, is to make the same mistake: to conceive of the subject-object separation as a primary one, whether it be epistemically the origin of all cognition, or ontologically as a fact. Neither the one nor the other is true. It is not a primary, immediate reality. The primary reality is narratively mediated perceiving truth and value, without any separation of subject and object, without any real distinction of primary and secondary qualities. To speak of a subject-object-distinction as well as to distinguish primary and secondary qualities is only possible due to sophisticated arguments combined with abstract acts of

then you get, without any compelling force, the classical concept of coherence. Cf. to this MÜHLING, M., Resonances, 123–128.

5 Cf. for the meaning of these two types of lines INGOLD, T., Lines, 152–170.

reflection related to these given perceptions. They are not basic in character, but interpretative. They are conceptual distinctions, not actual separations, products of abstracting from the perception of the narrative reality itself. The naked perception of facts, without perceiving values and without narrative mediation, is a *figmentum* and does not exist as such. It is always embedded in primary-narrative processes that *could be* described by secondary narrations and derivative of these by concepts as well. And if such a description is given, one has to pay the price of abstraction. Perception is always a narrative marked by perceiving truth and value. As such, it does not exclude conceptuality, but is always marked by narrative conceptualities.[6] Perceiving truth and value is the primary *pathos* and the primary activity not of a mental but of a bodily, and insofar relational and extended, 'subject' – the living body.[7]

25.3 Trusting Reason

The way out of the dilemma between purified and construed reason is only possible by a trusting or *sich verlassenden* ('relying', literally 'abandoning oneself') reason, which is an expression of a bodiliness that is constantly in movement.

Human reason is never without context, and it is never primarily creative or constructive. It only appears in the midst of and within the narratively perceived life-world, and it reflects on this life-world, since itself is a relatum or a sequence of this storied reality. Reality is not only perceived narratively; it consists in stories, since 'stories are lived before they are told.'[8] Reality is not conceived of on the model of stories, because human becomings are able to tell each other stories, or produce literature, but since reality itself is storied – because reality includes indexicality, change, novelty, alterity, relationality, exchange, discussion, and dramatic coherence – human becomings are able to have a storied, narratively embedded reason, by which they can produce second-order stories that can be applied once more to itself – e.g. by telling stories about a purified reason. Actually, every use of reason is not only dependent and bound if it is really critical reason, which reflects the conditions of its possibility, and so is actually *trusting* reason.

6 Cf. to this McDowell, J., Mind and World.

7 This phenomenological approach is also confirmed by the postanalytic philosphy, especially by the enactive theory of the human mind, cf. on this Clark, A./Chalmers, D.J., The Extended Mind, and Clark, A., Supersizing the Mind.

8 MacIntyre, A., After Virtue, 212: 'Stories are lived before they are told – except in the case of fiction.'

And then, of course, we have to face the problem of *in what* reason trusts *within the framework of which* narrations and narratives it does so. It is true: reality is storied, and reality becomes as a mesh of stories, but there is not the one secondary narration and of course not the one secondary-narrative that would be able to depict reality, since the antinomy of negation belongs to every narration. Reason is directed to the universal – but only from a particular, wayformational perspective of one's own story that is always in becoming.

Normally, perspectives are seen as 'standpoints' or 'positions'. However, in a world that is equiprimordially temporal and spatial, there cannot exist perspectives as standpoints, but only dynamically moving perspectives in constant change, as we learned in chapter 8. The body is always moved and moving, and any intentional movement is always an incomplete response to previously being moved. The concept of the wayformational perspective seeks to express this. It is important not to conceive of this wayformational perspective as an intrusion of the classical understanding of perspectives as positions, since such an understanding would cut off the dynamic character of the life-world. It would, in short, reduce wayfaring to transport. It would no longer be the moving perception that generates attention by perceiving alterities attentionally that is important, but the intention of a subject to impress invented aims upon the world.

Since reason is dependent on a narrative function in the becoming of the mesh of the stories of the world, and since reason itself is a partial sequence of this mesh, we can ask how reason that has to operate from particular wayformational perspectives in its activity of retelling reality is not fictive. On which line of narration should one move? Neither the story-line of the purified nor the story-line of constructive reason is able to correspond to reality. Only those wayformational perspectives can resonate reality harmonically that conceive of reason as embedded in the narrative reality, and which can develop the idea of a self-declaration of reality using reason in an entanglement of stories.

The incarnation of the eternal Son in Jesus Christ claims to be such a reason-informing story. Here, the story of the incarnation of the eternal Son in the bodily creature Jesus of Nazareth is not something that could be validated or falsified by any standards of purified reason. This story is also not a general narrative or general narrative structure that could be found in other stories, or conceptual systems. If it were such a narrative, it could never do what it claims to do: inform reason in a justified way. It is – as the story of the eternal Son – directed to universality, but from the particular wayformational perspective of the bodily human becoming Jesus. In this way, it claims that the abstract minimal condition of the concept of God, as the integration of all narrative wayformational lines in a particular one, is fulfilled in itself.

We therefore have to presuppose the narratological distinction between narration and narrative (ch. 6): Only narrations are particular, whereas narratives form the general structure and the space of possibilities of the repertoire of narrations. If the story of Christ was nothing but an instantiation of a general narrative (the appearance and proclamation of a hero, conflict with his environment, crisis [cross] and solution by a *deus ex machina* [resurrection], second solution on another level [spirit]), no real novelty is included in it, and it is not revelation of and by reality. Human expectations would then become the canon and guideline of the story of Christ. Then, the true God would be turned, as Luther knew, into an idol.[9] Christian theology, therefore, has to insist that the story of Jesus cannot be in its particularity a general narrative. Paradoxically, according to this claim, the story of Jesus is able to be understood as the actually comprehensive *logos* of reason, because only here can everything be included that has not appeared on our wayformational perspective, but which might appear in the future – not because it is a selection from the repertoire of a quasi-platonic realm of ideas, but because it is grounded in un-inferable and unpredictable novelty.

These are the concrete features enabling the incarnation to inform reason:

1. Incarnation is deep incarnation. This expression, coined by Gregersen,[10] means first that there is no flat incarnation, i.e. a kind of incarnation that excludes any dimension of reality. An incarnation that only consists in the self-consciousness of Jesus is a docetic incarnation, i.e. a flat incarnation, and that means no incarnation at all. Incarnation then means that the story of the eternal Son is, in a way, identical with the story of Jesus, that it is the eternal Son who is bodily, that it is the eternal Son who has a body constituted by relations of medial communication, and that it is the eternal Son who is relationally embedded in the storied mesh of the becoming of the human animal. In the incarnation, God does not only become man, but as Gregersen said, indirectly also becomes fox and dust.[11] In other words, the incarnation is only incarnation if something that a large part of the history of Christology has rejected is admitted: the *genus tapeinoticon*, i.e. the real communication of the passions of Christ to divinity or to the divine story. As we learned in ch. 19 to express it with the help of philosophy of religion: the point of the incarnation is that God's self becomes in the interindexicality of the world.

However, the idea of a deep incarnation is not designed in opposition to flat incarnation. Gregersen's intention is to critique Arne Naess'[12] idea of a

---

9 Cf. LUTHER, M., Large Catechism, 15 (BSLK 565): 'What is this but reducing God to an idol, yea, [a fig image or] an apple- god, and elevating and regarding ourselves as God?'

10 Cf. GREGERSEN, N.H., Deep Incarnation.

11 Cf. GREGERSEN, N.H., Deep Incarnation, 177. 182.

12 Cf. NAESS, A., Ecology, Community and Lifestyle.

deep ecology, in which a universal internal relationality is maintained, but in which also the particular, unique, and the other is not able to be understood – similarly to Hegel's system.[13] Therefore, incarnation is not at the same time the story of the deification of the world. It might be true that God became man in order that man became God. But this does not refer to the same narrative sequence. Incarnation is a particular story that determines the universal and open story of the becoming of the world – and which is influenced by it.

2. The incarnation is an informing story. It seems that the concept of information can be used in order to bring together insights from different disciplines, especially by transferring physical insights concerning the equivalence of matter and energy into the realms of natural philosophy and theology.

At the same time, the concept of information is also one of the most obscure concepts, so much so that reaching meaningful clarifications about it seems hopeless. Attempts to naturalize the concepts of information are very obscure.[14] Others – the authors mentioned below – do not intend to naturalize the concept, but nevertheless contribute *contra intentionem* something to the smokescreen surrounding the concept. One has to be careful here: the idea that the equivalence of matter and energy is not a basic state of affairs, but relies on information, belongs to the realm of natural philosophy, no matter what the proponents of this thesis may claim.

The idea that matter consists of information or quantum-information is not really new. J.A. Wheeler[15] and A. Zeilinger considered it.[16] Based on C.F. v. Weizsäcker's *Urtheorie*,[17] Th. Görnitz tried to popularize this idea with his protyposis-thesis,[18] in which a lot of quasi-religious content is visible. A lot of quasi-religious implications of another kind can be found in the theory of the feminist philosopher of science Karen Barad, in her reception of Niels Bohr. Instead of the term information, she speaks of an 'ongoing differentiating intelligibility' owing to 'intra-actions' of the yet undifferentiated.[19] In sum: There is no accepted theory in sight for how information could be the basis of matter. If all these theories have something in common besides the idea that the term information is primary, it consists in the idea that information is seen as a dynamic entity that differentiates itself in its becoming and thereby creates differences, events, and exchange.[20] Information that includes movement and thereby constitutes

13 Cf. GREGERSEN, N.H., Deep Incarnation, 178.

14 Cf. the instructive research of SCHÜTZ, G.M., Kann Information ein Naturgegenstand sein?, esp. 102.

15 Cf. WHEELER, J.A., Information, Physics, Quantum.

16 Cf. ZEILINGER, A., Einsteins Schleier, 117.

17 Cf. WEIZSÄCKER, C.F.v., Einheit der Natur.

18 Cf. e.g. GÖRNITZ, T./GÖRNITZ, B., Evolution des Geistigen, 134–164.

19 Cf. BARAD, K., Posthumanist Performativity, 824.

20 Cf. e.g. BARAD, K., Meeting the Universe Halfway, 181: 'Space, time, and matter are mutually constituted though the dynamics of iterative intra-actions. The spacetime manifold is iteratively (re)configured in terms of how material-discursive practices come to matter. The dynamics of enfolding involve the reconfiguring of the connectivity of the spacetimematter manifold itself (a changing topology). […] It should not be presumed that

or at least reconfigures time and indexicality can only be narratively, not predicatively, described, if indexicality is one of the main distinguishing features between both. Matter is not simply based on narrative information, but on a communication or an exchange of narrative information.[21] Other questions, such as the ones concerning whether and how information is to be related to signs and their semiotic dimensions,[22] are open, if not insoluble.

If the body is as an ecological body, intermeshed in its environment, with the consequence that 'our body is made of the same matter of which the universe is made,'[23] and if the body is always directed intentionally to intelligible orientation, and if all that is material can be understood as a communication or exchange of narrative information, then we can conclude: the body is made of a communicative narrative of interaction. In other words, the body itself is the subject of a dramatic-narrative becoming of information.[24] Here, the body shares an important feature with all that is material, as Luther knew.[25]

---

either the manifold itself or changes to the manifold are continuous. Discontinutity plays an important role.' Cf. also GÖRNITZ, T./GÖRNITZ, B., Evolution des Geistigen, 134.

21 BARAD, K., Posthumanist Performativity, 823: 'Material conditions matter, not because they 'support' particular discourses that are the actual generative factors in the formation of bodies but rather because *matter comes to matter* through the iterative intra-activity of the world in its becoming.' Ibid., 819: 'Discourse is not a synonym for language. Discourse does not refer to linguistic or signifying systems, grammars, speech acts, or conversations. To think of discourse as mere spoken or written words forming descriptive statements is to enact the mistake of representationalist thinking. Discourse is not what is said; it is that which constrains and enables what can be said. Discursive practices define what counts as meaningful statements. Statements are not the mere utterances of the originating consciousness of a unified subject; rather, statements and subjects emerge from a field of possibilities. This field of possibilities is not static or singular but rather is a dynamic and contingent multiplicity.'

22 Cf. SCHÜTZ, G.M., Kann Information ein Naturgegenstand sein? Related to the role of information to the question of matter-energy-equivalence is the newer use of the concept of information in evolutionary biology, where recently 'semantic information' has been spoken of (cf. ODLING-SMEE, F.J./LALAND, K.N./FELDMAN, M.W., Niche Construction, 177f). For analysis and criticism of this concept of information cf. as well MÜHLING, M., Resonances, 147f. 158.

23 SCHWÖBEL, C., Einleitung: Dimensionen der Leiblichkeit, 5 (transl. MM).

24 Similar also WILLIAMS, R., Edge of the Words, 102: 'Rather than looking to material processes, understood in a mechanical fashion, as the key to understanding what language is, it would be nearer to truth to say that we look at language to show us what matter is. [...] The material universe appears as an essentially symbolic complex. It is an exchange of 'messages' [...] because the unfolding story of material evolution leads to speech, to the expression and sharing of intelligent structure.'

25 Cf. LUTHER, M., WA, 42, 17, 17–19: „Sic Sol, Luna, Coelum, terra, Petrus, Paulus, Ego, tu etc. sumus vocabula Dei"; LUTHER, M., WA 42, 37, 6–8: 'Quaelibet igitur avis, piscis quilibet

Therefore, it is meaningful to claim that it is the story of Christ, as a story of bodily incarnation, that informs reason. In distinction to Barad's posthumanist, feminist ontology, the theology of creation can state that the communication of information, that causes matter to exist, is the *logos* of creation[26] that has become flesh in Jesus Christ. Since bodily reason orientates itself as trusting reason upon being informed by the story of Christ, according to a theology of creation it orients itself to the same story that informs every kind of mundane becoming.

3. The incarnation is an entanglement between the transcendental-narrative story of the eternal Son with the primary-narrative story of Jesus: The eternal Son has a story independent of the world, in its becoming related to Father and Spirit in eternity. This counterfactual and only theoretically existing independence of the story of the *logos* of the story of the world stresses the following points.

There are not stories because there is space and time, but since there is an eternal, transcendental-narrative story, this story has its own eternal time and its own space.

God does not incarnate Godself in a storied form because the world is spatial and temporal, but because Godself is transcendentally-narratively an eternal, relational process of storied becoming. God creates a primary-narrative world including a space and a time, which is an analogy of his own becoming, and which enables incarnation.

We do not have to talk about the incarnation of Christ because there is mundane materiality and bodiliness, but because the body is the primary means of communicative whence-and-whither becoming:[27] as the condition of the possibility of incarnation, the eternal Son becomes a body completely in Jesus Christ. In the context of the doctrine of God in the next volume, we

---

sund nihil nisi nomina divinae Grammaticae.' Cf. also WENDTE, M., Die Gabe und das Gestell, 404ff.

26 What is importnant here is a *theological* concept of information, which is then used as a bridge concept to natural philosophy. It is not intended to be in line with those authors who thereby seek to develop a theory of divine action, such as was done in Polkinghorne's theory of active information (on Polkinghorne's concept of information cf. LOSCH, A., Information ohne Energiebedarf). So it should be clear that every attempt to use the concept of information as an inmaterial idol that influences the material world, as has been recently proposed by representatives of creationism and and intelligent design, is strictly rejected.

27 For the backround to the concept of the person as an incommunicable whence-and-whither becoming cf. MÜHLING, M., Resonances, 184–186 (created persons) and 174f. (trinitarian persons).

will therefore have to ask: is, in inner-Trinitarian becoming *etsi mundus non daretur*,[28] there bodiliness in Godself?

Since Godself is transcendental-narrative reason, God creates a primary-narrative world in which analogously a secondary-narrative reason emerges that is able to comprehend itself and its creative ground – if it moves as trusting reason on the informing wayformational perspective of the incarnate Son.

The incarnation can only inform reason if it is not a story of the past, but if it consists in an entanglement and exchange or a communication between three meshes of stories: the mesh of stories of the incarnation of the eternal Son, the narrative mesh of my own identity in its becoming here and now, and the con-carnating story of the Spirit that draws the story of the becoming of my own identity into the identity story of the incarnated Son – and therefore into the story of God. In this way, human and creaturely reason is sublated in divine reason, since human becoming is sublated into divine becoming. This sublation, however, cannot be conceived as a kind of dissolution, but as a communication of real love, in which difference, particularity, alterity, and novelty irreducibly subsist by constituting the becoming of one's own identity. And this means that reason's necessarily concrete and indexical character is satisfied: I receive my my-ness only *mediated by* your your-ness *for* the their-ness of another *by* the Trinitarian God.

Since this primary entanglement of the identity-narration of the incarnation with my own identity-narration and the concarnation-narration of the Spirit happens under the condition of *formally* incarnational means, i.e. under the condition of the entanglement of the identities of my-ness, your-ness and their-ness, any explication of what reason can be is not an abstract one, but one that has to be made through the communication of different wayformational perspectives that might run parallel, cross over one another or stay apart. And that means: Any explication of reason has to acknowledge the pluralist conditions of its constitution. Wherever this pluralist communication of different wayformational perspectives of different disciplines, world-views, and religions is denied, the conditions of incarnationally informed reasons are denied. And that is a self-contradiction.

The communication between the different wayformational perspectives is not directed towards any historical consensus, since this would mean once more the unholy construction of purified reason, but its aim is simply its eschatological becoming that is not at its disposal. Wayformational perspectives

28 For this regulative principle of theological reflection, which is indeed not to be understood as speculative statement about God in principle, cf. MÜHLING, M., Resonances, 19–21.

cannot be altered into standpoints if they want to correspond with the reality of becoming. No universal consensus, no meta-narration of a grand, epic narrative is the aim of the conversation about reason. Nevertheless, wayformational perspectives are ways through the same reality – and therefore the success of technical reason is explainable. Technical reason is not universal consensus, but it is a minimal abstraction from wayformational lines done by ignoring their concretion and focusing only on their structural aspects. If the different partners communicate, this conversation about reason is always a dramatic story. This conversation can find its grand narrative, if at all, only eschatologically, and that means withdrawing from any intra-historical actualization. And even such an eschatologically realized grand narrative cannot be thought of in a way that contradicts its conditions in the incarnation. Eschatological life and eschatological reason – the sublation of the world in God by the story of *theosis* as the other correlate of the incarnation – can only be conceived of as a new becoming by informed reason, and that means as a discursively emerging narration. However, this has to be a story that excludes misunderstandings and sinful ambivalence.

25.4 The Antinomy of Reason and the Adventurous Contingency of God

The antinomy of reason resonates with the contingency of the becoming of God. If the description of the phenomenal perception of the phenomena of reason that we presented here is correct, insofar as it belongs to the universal in that it is withdrawn for the universal (which is to say that the antinomy of reason belongs to the experienceable and incarnationally grounded conditions of reason), then the antinomy of reason can in no way be external to incarnation. The antinomy of reason resonates with the state of affairs that the sum of all thinkable possibilities, in the sense of a well-founded-set, are not the real and intelligible world. Here we have to distinguish between true and logical contingency (ch. 18). Logical contingency means that, in the model of the network as a well-founded-set, everything is possible or is possibly not ($Pp \wedge P\neg p$). Under these conditions, everything that could be actualized in becoming would be a subset of this kind of logical contingency. Actuality would then only be the actualization of something that is already given as possible. True contingency, however, means that during the processes of becoming new possibilities (and impossibilities) emerge that did not previously belong to the set of logical contingencies. The 'set' of true contingency is therefore, always 'greater' than the set of logical contingency – however, it is not a well-founded set at all. The means of traditional modal logics cannot express true contingency, which is a mode of ontic becoming and appearing. Nevertheless, it is not epistemically illogical. On the level of reason, it resonates with the fact that there cannot be any closed system. And this is what the antinomy of reason or negation expresses.

The incarnation as process corresponds to this becoming in true contingency, with the consequence that true contingency, including true alterity and novelty, belong to the becoming of the world as well as to the transcendental-narrative becoming of God.

The incarnation means that divine becoming is incarnated in mundane becoming. The incarnation then is not a kind of crisis-management, but corresponds to the conditions of the identity of the becoming of God. In other words, if it is correct that creation belongs to the means that are necessary in order to actualize the incarnation, then both, the eternal becoming of the triune God and the eschatological becoming of the world in God, cannot be conceived without this condition. In the realm of divine, eternal becoming, truly new and truly contingent sequences and unpredictable possibilities are also included, which are also unpredictable for Father, Son, and Spirt as the centers of action in this divine becoming.[29] The emergence of novelty is grounded in divine becoming.

God seems to be – and this is an anticipation of what has to be said in the next volume – *adventurous*. Does this mean that God's self also becomes chaotically? No, that is not the case: the emergent and surprising becoming of new, un-inferable possibilities and actualities in the story of God satisfies the eternal, dramatic coherence of the conditions of incarnation in *cross and resurrection*: divine contingency neither re-introduces Tiamat as chaos-goddess, nor hypostasizes a *deus absconditus*, but it enables what is essentially divine in immanent alterity: love, a love story, or the adventure[30] of true love. Divine contingency is determined by the fact that it is a means for establishing what the triune God brings eschatologically up for discussion with his creatures by the life, crucifixion, and resurrection of Jesus Christ: that God is love, that spontaneously overcomes all resistances.

The emergence of true, contingent novelty in God and in the eschatological becoming of the world cannot be conceived of in the framework of a model of progress, as development from worse to better. We learned that such a view is

29 Cf. to this MÜHLING, M., Liebesgeschichte Gott, esp. 135–159.

30 For the thesis of God's becoming as an adventure cf. MÜHLING, M., Liebesgeschichte Gott, 156. 233. 256. 500–507. For the practical basics of this thought cf. among others, the instructive work of HAUERWAS, S., Community of Character, 147f., in SCHLARB, V., Narrative Freiheit, 88–90. 179f. 257–259. 263f.

in principal unreligious (ch. 24). Neither is it a chaotic change between good and bad. If this kind of becoming happens in harmonic resonance with the love that is presented in cross and resurrection, then the emerging differences can only be thought of as aesthetic differences, not as ethical differences.[31]

However, this cannot be a mechanistic, rational rule, but we have to remember the 'theological epoché',[32] i.e. the fact that any kind of theological reflection is bound to the cross, including its secondary-narrative ineffability. It is given only in the light of grace as hope for a spontaneous and surprising confirmation of the resonance of love and contingency in cross and resurrection by the Holy Spirit – *ubi et quando visum est deo.*

25.5 Reason in Need of Saving

Trusting reason, beyond skepticism and totalitarianism, is revealed as truly critical and enlightened reason. Deviations from it are therefore disclosed as results of a perversely informed reason that does not acknowledge its own constitutive conditions. Both, skepticism and totalitarianism are an expression of the fact that reason needs to be redeemed.

Truly enlightened reason that is critical regarding itself, can neither be the purified reason with its tendency to totalitarianism, nor the constructivist reason with its tendency to skepticism, but incarnationally informed reason. Both, the purified as well as the constructivist, forms of reason are revealed therefore not only as mirror variations on a shared theme, the rejection of the phenomenon of the antinomy of reason, but also, in the Christian wayformational perspective, as an expression of the actual human will to lead one's own becoming in contradiction to the divine becoming as it is incarnationally disclosed. Although purified and constructivist reason are expressions of the human consent to the false promise '*eritis sicut deus*', we have no occasion to demonize them. Why not? The basis on which both, purified and constructivist reason, deliver restricted results is only possible on the one ground of reason – and not the one which they wrongly identify as their ground, but the character of trust. Therefore, fallen reason also groans and longs for the revealing of the sons of God. Longing as an expression of the need for redemption, however, is always a sign of hope.

---

31 For detailed remarks cf. MÜHLING, M., Handbook of Christian Eschatology, 133–150. 325–336.

32 STOELLGER, P., Passivität aus Passion, 350.

CHAPTER 26

Theology, Philosophy, and Natural Science

26.1 Dialogue or Conversation?

Since the 1980s, simple classifications of the relationship between the natural sciences and theology have mostly been abandoned, and a variety of descriptions of diverse types of dialogue between science and theology have been proposed, most prominently the process-philosophy inspired typology of Ian Barbour (conflict, independence, dialogue, integration),[1] which has become a point of departure. Although these typologies have helped overcome problematic dichotomies, it was felt that they had shortcomings in describing the reality of the relationship between theology and science. Therefore, many improvements have been suggested, such as a cyclical alteration between the particular types[2] or a simultaneous appearance of the particular types in different respects.[3] Could it be, however, that the main problem with this and similar typologies is simply that they are too abstract, and that this abstraction relies on the fact that the notion of 'dialogue' underlies all types? A dialogue is a talk between two speakers, who talk *across a subject-matter* and who throw arguments and propositions at each other, pick up what they receive, alter it and return it like ping-pong players exchanging balls across the table. This simple metaphor also seems to be the basic model for conflict, which is simply a dialogue in which the players balk at everything they receive, for independence, where the players are at different tables, and for integration, where the play across the table is only possible between partners who change their positions and are able to be at two locations at the same time. The logic of dialogue has been described several times and fancy theories about dialogue are elaborated not only as a basis for the description of the relationship between science and theology, but more broadly to describe the work of human reason in general, such as Habermas' famous non-coercive discourse in the abstract, but ideal speech situation.[4]

But what if the model of a 'dialogue' is simply not adequate to describe what is going on between science and theology? What if a 'dialogue,' an exchange

1 Cf. Barbour, I.G., When Science Meets Religion.
2 Cf. Losch, A., Jenseits der Konflikte, 88f.
3 Cf. Mühling, M., Resonances, 24.
4 Cf. Habermas, J., Diskursethik – Notizen.

 | DOI:10.30965/9783846765852_027

of *logoi dia,* is not able to depict reality? If 'dialogue' expresses an exchange of speech-acts back and forth where the subject-matter functions only as the means for a medium 'across' which the exchange happens, then, like the table in ping-pong, it is not able to express what is going on in science and theology, and it is not able to deliver the basis for the claim that the sciences and theology somehow need each other. Surely, they need each other for conversation, but dialogue is not the essence of conversation.

26.2 Standpoints or Perspectives on the Move?

The first problem with 'dialogue' is that it requires the abstraction of a standpoint in order to work. A standpoint is a fixed point of perception, argumentation, and action from which the players act. And if it is necessary to leave this point for a while in order to get the arguments one wants to receive, then it is also necessary to come back to this point for the next course of exchange, like the ping-pong player who has a primary position to which she returns to after having lunged for the ball. But academic work – at least as long as one is doing research – cannot be depicted by certain moves back and forth from a standpoint, but is rather more like a constant movement into the unknown. Academic research means being on the way and the insights of research are shaped by constant movement along this way. It may be science or theology, but either way research is not done from a standpoint, but from a way into the unknown. The concrete perspective, from which all theories are made, all observations are done, and all arguments are exchanged, is not a point of view, it is a perspective on the move. And this constantly moving perspective is not a chain of connected points. Connected points (as visible in research articles) are only a very crude simplification of what is going on in everyday research.

26.3 Across or Along?

If it is true that the perspectives from which observing, theorizing, and arguing take place are on the move, there cannot be a table or a field that serves as something which one talks across. The subject matter is not a means for the interaction, but is rather the very ground one is moving through in research. In perception that is on the move, the terrain discloses itself only along the way one is walking. The observations, insights, discoveries, theories, and arguments that are expressions of research are formed by the way itself and the way is formed by walking *along, not across* it. The perspective is not only a perspective on the move, it is also a wayformational[5] perspective, i.e. a perspective that is formed by the way and that itself forms the way. In describing research as walking along a wayformational perspective, any radical kind of constructivism and any kind of naïve realism (like in neo-positivism) are unmasked as making the same mistake: they rely on the logic of depicting the environment from a standpoint and they both make the mistake of representationalism in very similar ways, either as projecting the pictures of the mind to the screen of reality, or by picturing the environment on the black wall of the closed *camera obscura* of the mind (naïve realism). On a wayformational perspective however, the way belongs to the environment and to the walker at the same time; they are interwoven, entangled, or resonant with one another. The way is part of both, meaning therefore that the researcher herself is not independent of the subject matter she is researching. The relationship between researcher and subject matter is not an external one, but rather internal. 'Subject and 'object' are, at most, simple abstractions from what is going on and they are in the danger of becoming myths[6] if the subject-object distinction is used as a basis for all knowledge.

26.4 Between or In-between?

Any conversation of two partners is not a dialogue *between* them, but rather a conversation *in-between* a way. Therefore, the different descriptions of both, inter- and trans-disciplinarity are not completely wrong, but they do have their vices. The main vice consists in the fact that they take the sure ground of specific disciplines as a standpoint and try somehow to transcend them, either by talking across the disciplines or by mixing up the two formerly independent disciplines into a new one. Regarding research as relying on a wayformational perspective, however, like life itself, means being guided by the phenomena. Every academic discipline becomes subsidiary to the appearance of the phenomena for practical reasons, and the history of academics, with the change and evolution of new disciplines, confirms that disciplines have no sacrosanct boundaries, be they physics, biology, philosophy, or theology. They have their relative right as long as they are meaningful for joint research on the walk in-between the subject-matter, but their boundaries are fuzzy and no methodology remains fixed forever, but is rather transient. Nevertheless, there

5 Cf. ch. 5 and 8.

6 On myths in science and religion cf. MÜHLING, M., Resonances, 33f and MACCORMAC, E.R., Metaphor and Myth.

are preliminary disciplines and approaches, and therefore one has to explain what the differences between them may be. This task is not so easy since, with regard to the subject matter of this chapter, there are no concrete disciplines, but the natural sciences, or 'science' as a whole on the one hand and theology as a whole on the other.

26.5 Perceiving in Faith and Theology

So far, we have used the concept of the wayformational perspective in order to describe academic work. But academics is not the example *par excellence* for perceiving on a wayformational perspective. The example *par excellence* is life itself and, more concretely, faith. Whatever one does, perception comes first. One is immersed into perception by the whole living body, including its inter-bodiliness. In perception, one perceives as one is perceived, driven completely by what is perceived. In a fission-fusion reaction,[7] the perceiver is with the perceived and the perceived forms the becoming of the perceiver. It was Merleau-Ponty who designated the unity of the perceiver and the perceived as '*flesh*,'[8] where the perceiver is enrolled[9] or immersed into the perceived, emerging distinctions notwithstanding. It is the world itself that perceives itself in the perceiver, but in some – not, of course, all – cases an asymmetry of perceived and perceiver is established in perception. In perception, there is no primary distinction between fact and value, but the perceiver responds to the affordances[10] of the situations, ways, or events of which she is a part. Perception is therefore always, in a specific way, immediate. It is immediate because there is no primary need to deliberately interpret what is perceived. The sun does not radiate, but shines, the stars do not beam but glow, driving a car is not simply an experience of acceleration, but excitement, and so on. In another sense, however, one must recognize that this immediate perception is at the same time mediated. It is mediated by the stories the entanglement of perceiver and perceived form – and by the attempt to retell of these stories in human narrative activity. 'Stories are lived before they can be told:'[11] but there is a resonance between the stories that are lived and the stories that are told. This understanding of perception has two consequences. First, no one is alone

7 Cf. INGOLD, T., Life of Lines, 99.
8 Cf. MERLEAU-PONTY, M., Visible and the Invisible, 248–251.
9 Cf. INGOLD, T., Life of Lines, 84–88.
10 Cf. GIBSON, J.J., Ecological Approach to Visual Perception, 119–134.
11 MACINTYRE, A., After Virtue, 212.

in perception, but perception is always a communal activity. Second, perception is always embedded in stories and stories are always laden with meaning, but it is not necessarily the case that all meaningful stories we inhabit cohere with one another. *Faith is nothing but the trust that despite all the incoherence and failure in perception that in the end it is worth living a life in this way. Christian faith is the trust, that the Christian narratives, the life of Jesus Christ as the Son of the Father who is present in the Holy Spirit, provide a wayformational perspective of life that is able to incorporate all dichotomies and that leads to a reality-resonating mode of perception.*

Therefore, the Christian faith is not a realm separate from culture. One cannot distinguish between activities that are 'religious' whereas others are not; it is not the case that performing a prayer is 'religious' or 'more religious' than meeting a fellow brother or sister during a walk on the street. There are no specifically 'religious' experiences like there are specifically gastronomic experiences. If the expression 'religious experience' is meaningful at all, it has to be an 'experience with experience'[12] and it is not possible to declare specific cultural activities as a subject-matter of 'religion,' which is the shared *crux* of the so-called 'cognitive sciences of religion' and 'neurotheology.'

Perceiving in Christ by the Spirit is as realistic as perception in general. But a decisive mark of any claim to be realistic is a capacity for fallibility. It is precisely the fact that a perception can be wrong that makes it realistic. Perception can resonate the affordances of situations, but they can also be dissonant to the affordances of the world we inhabit. In both cases, however, the perception is still immediately mediated; in both cases, perception appears as a disclosure of truth. *Theology, as an academic discipline, is nothing but the methodologically guided self-reflection on the conditions of perceiving, along the Christian wayformational perspective.* Therefore, on the deeper level of perception, there is no contradiction between the Barthian influenced descriptions of theology (or dogmatics) as 'the scientific self-examination of the Christian Church with respect to the content of its distinctive talk about God,'[13] and the Schleiermacherian discussion of the knowledge of the necessary capabilities for the life of the Christian community.[14] Theology, in short, has to start with the everyday experience of the Christian wayformational perspective,

---

12 Cf. EBELING, G., Klage über das Erfahrungsdefizit; JÜNGEL, E., Erfahrungen mit der Erfahrung; MÜHLING, M., Resonances, 86–96.

13 BARTH, K., CD, Vol. I,1; §1, 3.

14 Cf. SCHLEIERMACHER, F.D.E., Kurze Darstellung, §5. For the claim that the seemingly contradictory definitions are really only emphasizing different aspects of the same pheneomena cf. MÜHLING, M., Ethik, 37–40. A detailed analysis of the similarities between Schleiermacher and Barth can be found in STRATIS, J., God's Being toward Fellowship.

trusting that this perspective is only possible thanks to the constant self-disclosure of the triune God, and it has to claim that on this wayformational perspective or mode of perception, there is no distinction between facts and value. Theology is committed to concrete life and perception, meaning it can grasp the general only via the particular. Therefore, any theology that claims not to be a Christian theology, or a Jewish theology, or a Neo-platonic theology, or a biological theology, or any other kind of particular theology, would not be a theology at all.

26.6 Philosophy, Observation, and the Sciences

Immediate perception is mediated by stories we inhabit, but the stories we inhabit are also bodily stories. Our means of perception is our inter-bodiliness: skin, eyes, smell, our stomach, and our nervous system belong to these means as well. If perception is always inter-bodily perception, one may ask, must there not be any common kind of perception, common to all wayformational perspectives and common to all modes of perception? The answer can only be that there is no such common perception, but that some commonalities can be (re)constructed or made be visible by deliberate interpretation. One only has to have in mind that all such activity does not provide a representation of reality, but rather an abstraction from reality. In this case, the interpretative abstractions may be of immense value without producing myths. And these kinds of interpretations are twofold. On the one hand, one can reflect interpretatively on the conditions of perception or becoming on a wayformational perspective as such – that is the task of the endeavor called philosophy. On the other hand, one can investigate concrete perceptions by means of observations and their interpretation – and that is the task of the sciences. This task is, of course, not easy. One has to restrict oneself only to those features which are observable independent of the wayformational perspective; one has to, in other words, introduce the subject-object distinction, the ideal of objectivity, the idea of a separation between fact and value, and so on. Nothing is wrong in this endeavor – as long as no one is claiming to gain a picture of reality from it. It resembles somewhat what has been called the 'natural attitude.'[15]

On this basis, one could now dig into the history of theories of science in order to describe more precisely this scientific endeavor. But the task of this chapter is to describe the conversation between science and theology from the wayformational perspective of theology, perhaps a little more precisely than

15 Cf. HUSSERL, E., Husserliana 3/1, 63.

by using the metaphor of 'dialogue,' thus making an excursus into the theory of the science unnecessary.

At this point we can see that any conversation between science and theology has to be in reality a conversation between three partners, science, theology, and philosophy, independently of whether there is a professional philosopher involved or not.

When theologians, scientists, and philosophers walk along through the grounds and converse with each other, what kind of conversations can be distinguished? I want to suggest a very simple classification drawn from the model of possible conversations one could have while walking with others.

1. Following Conversations

In many situations during a walk, the terrain requires the walkers to follow one another. In this case, the first walker functions as a kind of guide, whose attention and whose story of formation allows for a specific kind of attention and perception. He will show the followers some of the experiences, will explain the background stories of what is perceived. He will encourage the followers to make their own observations and the others will follow in his steps. From time to time it might be necessary that the guides change; then the guide becomes a follower and *vice versa*.

What sounds natural during a walk seems to be out of fashion if one applies this model to the conversation between science, theology, and philosophy. No philosopher today wants to follow theology, at least in order to avoid the suspicion of the *old ancilla theologiae* model. Most philosophers, except perhaps some of the now old-fashioned naturalists, do not want to follow natural scientists by hypostasizing scientific research results. But many scientists would deny that it is meaningful to follow either theology or philosophy in their research. And the same seems to be true for the theologian: if he is following a particular philosophy, he would – at best – be accused of being 'creative' or denying the foundations of biblical faith. If he is following science, he would be accused of leaving his own terrain. Following each other in one's own discipline seems to be a bit more acceptable – at least as long as it does not last forever. Sometimes, however, it seems – after Kuhn – that not slaughtering one's academic forbears is regarded as a kind of intellectual suicide. Moreover, following in the footsteps of others is rather generally discredited in the intellectual sphere of liberal (post)modernity. Such relationships are pictured normally with the help of hierarchical models or models of suppression and liberation. But is slavery and exodus really the general pattern for academic work? Is not the model of going out for a walk where the terrain sometimes makes it necessary to follow one another a better model that comes closest to what is actually going on? Did not Faraday follow his Sandemanian religious commitments even in his experimental work and in his preference for field-theories instead of atomic ones (even if he also denied this at times)?[16] Did not Einstein follow, in his progression from the special principle of relativity to the general, intuitions that where impossible without his reading Hume and Schopenhauer?[17] Would not Karl Barth's theological commitment to revelation have been impossible without following his brother Heinrich in the latter's interpretation of epistemology?[18] We could mention endless examples of the same kind. What seems to be odd in the models of hierarchy, suppression, and liberation becomes quite natural in the model of hiking – and far more common than normally admitted. I have therefore started with the model of walkers following after one another, simply in order to liberate such following from its negative connotations. The blind spot, however, in interdisciplinary, phenomena-oriented research lies not in the fact that no one is following anyone else, because this happens independently of whether it is admitted or denied. The blind spot is that we have no methodology and no academic ethics for how to follow one another and how to follow one another through different disciplines. Following one another is not without its dangers, although these might have been overstressed in the past. But following one another also enables us to discover new ground, where one cannot go jointly without following someone else. There is a lot of work left to be done here.

2. Accompanying Conversations

Image a situation where the terrain is wide enough to walk side by side. Neither of the partners walking and conversing can have the same impression of their environment simultaneously, but due to their different stories of personal formation they will perceive things in a different manner that allows them to see more things than one would perceive alone or two would perceive when walking silently side-by-side. Accompanying conversations might be somehow similar to the old discourse model, but there is an important difference. Since the ground is constantly changing, the discussion cannot be guided mainly by the intentions of the partners or by attention to the other partner, but has to be guided by their way through the ever-changing ground itself. The discussion has to be had in response to what goes on, in response to what is perceived. It has to be an *attentional*[19] rather than an intentional conversation.

16 Cf. MÜHLING, M., Einstein und die Religion, 237–254.
17 Cf. MÜHLING, M., Einstein und die Religion, 84–105. 145–153.
18 Cf. GRUBE, D.-M., Unbegründbarkeit Gottes?, 102–147.
19 For the distinction between intentional/attentional cf. INGOLD, T., Life of Lines, 133.

Depicting academic conversations in this model seems to be far easier than in the first model. In a time where third-party funding is being provided more and more by non-academic institutions for inter- and transdisciplinary work, such conversations in the company of others appears be a new scholarly ideal. However, there is still a lot to do in order to find some meaningful guidelines for the academic ethics of such interdisciplinary discussions. For example, one has to avoid the danger of working in a purely intentional, results-oriented manner. In this case, accompanying each other would be nothing but a means for attaining third-party funding – to satisfy the expectations of the sponsors, to finish one's own publication or to reach one's own target agreements. It is instead decisive to remain attentional to phenomena as they appear and it is decisive to remain conscious of the fact that no one will close the door on the ever-enfolding ground of discovery.

3. Meandering Conversation

Imagine a long walk through difficult terrain. Imagine that it is not clear, which appearance will guide a fruitful way of travel. Imagine that it is necessary that the partners might partly follow each other, partly accompany each other, but that it is also possible to go different ways, to the right and to the left in order to meet up again in future, perhaps at the same time, perhaps later than the other one(s), so that it is necessary to be a follower for a short stretch in order to move forward at all. Imagine that this procedure will be necessary due to the shape of the terrain and will be necessary over and over again. And imagine the discussions that will happen during the periods of reunification. Will not all who have gone different ways give hints for the common way further on? Will they not from time to time insist that their perceptions while walking alone would provide the best guidance for going further? Will they not from time to time feel forced to contradict each other? And will not these contradictions also be fruitful for the way further on? Of course, this model of meandering conversation also has its risks. There is the risk of losing one another forever while walking separately and therefore of losing the joint endeavor. There is also the risk of insisting so much on one's own impressions that one cannot combine them with those of the others in a fruitful manner, and therefore there is once more the risk of losing the joint endeavor.

It might be easiest to apply this image to interdisciplinary academic discussions. And I hope that many might concur that the model of meandering conversations is the most comprehensive of the three I have tried to introduce. However, there is a decisive difference between going out voluntarily for a joint walk in a terrain that requires meandering pathways and academically meandering discussions. The latter is not voluntary. If it is correct that perceiver and perceived are shaping each other during perception, if it is true that walker and way are forming each other, and if it is true that the appearance of phenomena and disciplines and their tools are constantly shaping each other, then the danger of going apart forever without meeting once more means losing the phenomena and the subject matter. One might be tempted to explain situations like these with the remark that there is no world, or at least not one world. But losing the concept of one shared world means losing the concept of a world altogether. And losing the concept of the world – despite the fact that it might not be a sharp concept and it is not easy to define – means losing any resonance with it as well as the joy of discovery. Going apart independently forever without interfering is also not a possibility, neither for theology, nor for philosophy and the sciences. They might survive as doctrines or technologies or means of power, but the truth of philosophy is no less reducible to questions of power as science consists in technology and theology in teaching doctrines. They do not have to construct a common ground – their ongoing life as research is enabled by different appearances on the different wayformational perspectives of a common ground.

26.7 Conversations while Walking Together and Barbour's Abstraction

We started with a reference to Barbour's typology of conflict, independence, dialogue, and integration. We have seen that this typology is too abstract, and we have seen that this abstraction might rely on the mistake of depicting the relationship between science, theology, and philosophy as a dialogical ping-pong game. And we suggested that the model of a conversation during a walk, including the subsets of following conversations, accompanying conversations, and meandering conversations as a better model. If this last claim is true, one would expect that the third model could incorporate the virtues of the first one.

This is indeed the case. The model of meandering conversations is not only able to include conversations that occur side by side and conversations that occur forwards and backwards, but it is also able to include conflict, independence, dialogue, and integration. However, there could be no conversation that is purely conflict-laden. There could be also no independence that remains so forever. The model of a dialogue between partners of the same rank and right could also only be a short episode. And at last, if reality consists in ever changing alterations of processes and storied events, which surely can also be said by process-thinkers, any possible integration that might appear would necessarily be a transient one.

If one does not see academic endeavors in a quasi-platonic way that separates a possible 'essence' of a discipline from the researchers, their lives, and their activities, it is by no means unimportant how one conceives of inter- and transdisciplinary work. The models and pictures we use in an implicit way to structure our relationships shapes our modes of perceiving and our attitudes of behaving – in life as well as in academics. Barbour's typology is certainly able to give a certain frame for perception and it was decisive in overcoming false dichotomies, but at some points it also increases certain dangers; e.g. the danger of classifying oneself and one's conversation partners into one of the types, as well as the danger of conceiving of research in a purely intentional manner. Conceiving research on the model of conversations during a never-to-be-completed walk might be able to generate more fruitful attentional attitudes.

26.8 Why do Science, Theology, and Philosophy Need to Interact?

Theology is the self-explication of the concrete Christian wayformational perspective and it claims the inseparability of fact and value. The sciences rely on observations and their interpretations by theories abstracted from concrete perception. Nevertheless, they are immersed into the same changing ground and its appearances in perception. Without conversations shared by walking along together, they degenerate and lose their own identity.

Theology in this case would have the task of interpreting doctrines, which is harmless as long it remains a purely academic endeavor. But theology is related to different public realms – not only the academic one, but also to civil society and the church, and that means being in contact with people in everyday life, along with their perception and their activities. If academic theology were to degenerate into the art of interpreting doctrines, then the life of the church could all too easily be seen as a means for prescribing doctrines. But then theology would have lost its own signature of being: dependent on the grace of the triune God and his self-disclosure that leads humans into a Christian-storied way of perceiving in a reality resonating way. Someone who regards a doctrine as something to be prescribed also regards it as being at their disposal, and that is nothing but a contradiction of justification by grace alone. How can conversations with the sciences and philosophy be helpful in avoiding this danger? There are many good answers for this. I think the best one might be that we are bodily creatures and that the Son has also became flesh. Faith, therefore, has nothing to do with following doctrines and acting intentionally according to them, but firstly with perceiving oneself as intermeshed into the world in the way of the stories of the Son and the Spirit. Incarnation and concarnation (which describes the activity of the Holy Spirit better than the notion of fleshless inspiration) mean that the abstract way of the sciences in interpreting observations *etsi deus non daretur* has to be recognized by theology as the self-interpretation of bodily perceivers on a Christian wayformational perspective.

The sciences, on the other hand, are in danger of degenerating either into technologies or becoming quasi-religions. The degeneration into technology occurs when scientists claim that the methodologically useful distinction between fact and value becomes a strict separation. In this case, they no longer see that curiosity is not only a decisive attitude of research, but also of care. Curiosity and care are different sides of the same coin. And talking to theologians and philosophers (both!) could be a means for preventing the danger of separating curiosity and care.

Scientists have too often claimed that the results of their research are ethically neutral and that they can deliver the questions of applicability into other hands – the hands of theologians, philosophers, and politicians! Please do not allow me to give examples: the story would be far too depressing. In a pluralistic age, many scientists might not go the route of degeneration into technology, but rather of becoming founders of krypto- or quasi-religions. This danger emerges when science is not aware that in its interpretation of observables it relies on an abstraction from perceived reality. Sometimes the language of 'facts and nothing but the facts' suggests that the sciences describe the real world representationally. We could have observed this kind of degeneration in some branches of the neurosciences and of sociobiology, or in some of the dreams of the posthumanists. Both dangers can also emerge when scientists are in discussion with theologians and philosophers, but perhaps not so easily, because they can then partake in a joint discussion about the fact that not only what seem to be facts guide all of our actions and behavior, but also empirically non-testable presuppositions which emerge immediately in perception and which are bound to the wayformational perspectives of different faiths or religions. I am not sure whether the term 'religion' (in contrast to faith) really denotes something meaningful. However, there is one (though perhaps historically incorrect) etymology, coined by Lactantius, that makes good sense: If religion comes from *re-ligare*,[20] to re-tie or re-bind, then one can interpret religions as loosing us from our interpretations and naturalistic attitudes, and bind us back to the perception of reality.

Philosophy, finally, deals with the very basics of perception (epistemology in traditional terms), becoming (ontology in traditional terms), and the perception of values (ethics and aesthetics in traditional terms). As such, the danger

20 Cf. INGOLD, T., Dreaming of Dragons, Note 13, 750.

to philosophy is one that could emerge more easily when the conversational bonds to theology and the sciences are cut off: the danger of constructing systems and the danger of reducing their truth to their being accepted.

But this is also a degeneration because it ultimately means reducing all philosophical questions to those of power: the power to interpret, the power to accept, etc. In this case, philosophy degenerates into a provider of ideology for politics.

The dangers in our postmodern world are manifold, and it is not possible to mention even only a few without being far too simplistic. Nevertheless, I want to make some concluding remarks. The dangers of living unbound to reality, the dangers of perceiving in a non-reality resonating way and acting according to these kinds of perceptions and the attitudes they generate seems to be obvious to me. Living purely intentionally in an individualist way that subordinates everything and everyone to a means for one's own wealth seems to be one of the most plausible, but least reality-resonating temptations of our time. This attitude of reckoning with humans as 'autonomous' individuals rather than as particular persons in communion, of reckoning with humans as beings rather than becomings surely cannot be entirely thwarted by sharing conversations while the academic disciplines of theology, philosophy, and the natural sciences walk along together. But a separation and an absolute independence of these disciplines from one another surely furthers these temptations more than it liberates us from them.

CHAPTER 27

Theology as a Science

The 20th and 21st century experienced many debates about theology as an academic endeavor or as a science. There is no need to revisit these debates. After all that has been said so far, it should be clear that theology cannot work with any definition of science or academics that was developed out of theology. Furthermore, today one cannot expect that the non-theological sciences will find a consensus about what they conceive of as science or as academic endeavor. However, we also have to avoid any kind of explicit or implicit relativism of truth. Every discipline has to behave adequately in relation to its 'object,' be it theology or any other discipline. Nevertheless, theology is outstanding due to its particular 'object' not being at its disposal.

(Post-)systematic theology traditionally has the task of reflecting on the question of what science and academics can be for the whole of theology, including all its disciplines. In the following, we will talk about the criteria of post-systematic theology, and then about the intra-disciplinary nexus of theology.

Considering the criteria and methodology of post-systematic theology, a feature becomes visible that was apparent in nearly all of the previous chapters: the question of theology as a science, classically located in the 'prolegomena', cannot be treated independently of the material content of theology, if the criterion of fitness to its subject matter is applied. Also, this question could be more adequately discussed in the final section of an 'epilegomena.' However, this would require the reader to discern the criteria and methods implicit in the material parts herself. In order to avoid this, for practical reasons, it might be better to discuss the matter before dealing with material content. But even this discussion is not free of any imposition, since now the reader must envisage material content and decisions, or, at least, take theses that cannot be explicated here preliminarily for granted. In other words, there is a loop between material description and formal criteria. But this circle is in no way a *circulus vitiosus*, but a sign of an adequate, internal coherence – a kind of coherence that belongs in itself to the criteria of post-systematic theology, as we will see shortly.

First, we have to remember that the double-definition of what post-systematic reflection and discussion can do consists in viewing the same state of affairs from two different perspectives (ch. 3). Therefore, theology can be conceived of as science out of and in God, or as the science of Christian faith. Any theological criteria, therefore, cannot be foreign to the matter of theology:

 | DOI:10.30965/9783846765852_028

the criteria must somehow be implied by or in God, or by the Christian faith. This demand – that is only apparently twofold – is essential if theology is a particular, secondary-narrative kind of communication of the Christian faith. Theology as science is therefore a secondary-narrative activity that exists necessarily, if there is Christian faith or if there is divine self-presentation.

However, we have to distinguish between theology as science and the academic organization of theology. Whether there has to be academic theology, whether it has to be organized into sub-disciplines, how these have to be related, and how theology has to be related to other academic disciplines and to different realms of society – all these are secondary questions, questions that are more or less *adiaphora*. That these questions deal with *adiaphora* does not mean that they are unimportant, but it broadens the scope of its formal construction, since the questions are organized in relation to Church and society. Nevertheless, these organizing questions are not part of this final introductory chapter of our post-systematic theology.

The same can be repeated in regard to the methods of post-systematic theology. They are of secondary importance, compared with the criteria. We will not only find many methods, but in principle have an open canon of methods that have to be bound to the criteria. Not every method satisfies the demands of the post-systematic criteria.

27.1 The Criteria of Post-Systematic Theology

27.1.1 *Identity Criteria*

As speech that proceeds methodically out of and in God, theology presupposes the way of the divine narrative self-presentation of self-identification in the narrative of perceiving truth and value by believers. This self-identification has a narrative 'structure' of a threefold meta-narration, as we saw in ch. 22: God makes known Godself as the God of Israel, as God in the story of Jesus Christ, and as God in the story of the believers. We learned that this meta-story can never be reduced to a narrative or a structure, but that it must remain irreducibly a narration. Nevertheless, it can be abbreviated by the name Father, Son, and Holy Spirit. This threefold divine self-identification leads to three criteria for post-systematic reflection.

1. Post-systematic theological reflection has to be related to the reflection of the story of the God of Israel

The partial story of the God of Israel is only accessible by the means of the witnesses of the Hebrew Bible and the LXX. Therefore, methods dealing with the academic reflection of these scriptures belong to the methodology of post-systematic theology, at least in an indirect manner. In order to use this criterion, post-systematic theology does not have to invent new methods, but can refer to the plurality of methods that are used by Old Testament theology (hermeneutical methods, narratological method, biblical archeology, historical-critical exegesis, etc.). Thereby, post-systematic theology is neither in danger of degrading Old Testament theology to a handmaiden, nor of becoming dependent on its results. Rather, post-systematic theology has to critically weigh the themes, reflections, methods, and results of Old Testament theology. The need for post-systematic theology to make its own judgments is obvious: the discipline of Old Testament theology itself has not necessarily takes into account that its own value for theology consists in being a methodical, secondary-narrative reflection on the self-identification of God in the story of Israel. Old Testament theologians can understand themselves primarily as linguists, exegetes, or hermeneutical philosophers, etc., and they can shape their work and the selection of their subject matters according to their self-understanding and their chosen methods. Consequently, it is a task of post-systematic theology to assess to what extent Old-Testament theology can contribute to the reflection and discussion of the narrative self-identification of God in the story of Israel. Ideally, this post-systematic evaluation does not necessarily have to be done by the scholar of systematic theology. The post-systematic theologian will expect that the Old Testament scholar will conceive of this post-systematic reflection and discussion as a dimension of her own work, but not, of course, as its most important one.[1]

Vice versa, for the work of post-systematic itself, this means that the medial witnesses of the Old Testament in both languages have to be considered in relation to the self-presentation of God in the story of Israel. If this is not done, an essential criterion of post-systematic theology is violated and theology would cease to be (Christian) theology.

2. *Post-systematic theology is always related to a reflection on the story of God in Jesus Christ*

Without being positively related to the narrative self-identification of God in the story of Christ, there is no post-systematic reflection at all. In the same way, as the story of the God of Israel belongs irreducibly to the context of thinking about Jesus, also the narrative self-presentation of God in the story of Jesus Christ belongs irreducibly to the understanding of the story of the God

1 Cf. e.g. SCHWÖBEL, C., Erwartungen an eine Theologie des Alten Testaments and similarly HARTENSTEIN, F., Bleibende Bedeutung des AT, 15–54.

of Israel. Without reference to the story of Jesus Christ, post-systematic theology would cease to be theology. However, we do not have to confuse reference to the story of Jesus Christ with reference to the history of the so-called 'historical Jesus.' That would be far too narrow and it would artificially limit theological work. What we have said in the last section about the relationship of post-systematic theology and Old Testament theology is analogously true for the relationship between post-systematic theology and New Testament theology.

3. Post-systematic theological reflection is always related to the reflection of the story of God in the communion of believers

In the same way as the story of Christ is irreducibly entangled with the story of the God of Israel, the story of Christ is also irreducibly entangled with the story of the Holy Spirit, i.e. the narrative self-identification of the believers. Post-systematic theology, therefore, has to be related positively to the narrations of the community of faith. Here too, it is not necessary to do all the work on one's self, but it can rely on explicating the witnesses of the New Testament and the history of faith. In other words, post-systematic theology can refer here to historical theology. Here it is important, that in principle all eras of church history are important, not only particular ones. Otherwise, one produces a practical self-contradiction: if one focuses only on particular eras, e.g. the ancient church or the era of the reformers, one would take for granted that the activity of the Holy Spirit is missing entirely or subdued in other eras. Of course, a self-withdrawal of the Holy Spirit in particular historical times and places is possible in principal, but it is impossible for theology or any other human endeavor to judge whether this is the case or not – to do that would presuppose a God's eye view. Therefore, post-systematic theology is principally equally related to all eras and places in the history of faith. It is simply wrong that modernity is more important, or the era of the reformers, or that of the ancient church, or of the North-Atlantic, etc. We can see that the same is true for the contemporary history of faith. Therefore, post-systematic theology is not only related to the discipline of church history, but also to the disciplines of ecumenical theology and intercultural theology.

These first three criteria are criteria of the identity of Christian faith. If one (or more) of these criteria is violated, the identity of theology as a special part of the secondary-narrative self-reflection of Christian faith and of following divine self-presentation is lost. Nevertheless, these criteria are not criteria of truth. With the help of these criteria, we can only gain descriptive purchase on the identity of Christian theology, but we can say nothing about theology's truth claims. Therefore, it is necessary to add such criteria for truth.

27.1.2 *Truth Criteria*

The Christian faith is a communal wayformational perspective, or a mode of perceiving truth and value. From this feature we can derive sub-features and at last criteria for post-systematic judgment. These are the kind of criteria that are normally associated with the core work of systematic theology. And this is indeed justified, as we will see.

4. Dramatic Coherence

Christian perceiving of truth and value sets free a narrative-conceptual explication, im-plication, and com-plication of the truth of that narration in which it happens. Aligned with this is that it is a communal wayformational perspective, not an individual one – a contradiction in itself, since every particular/personal wayformational perspective is essentially intermeshed with those of others. One's own perceiving of truth and value is neither a prior nor a closed story, but every narration of only apparently individual stories of perceiving truth and value is drawn out of the mesh of the communal stories of the formation of persons.

Coherence is generally seen as a necessary condition of truth. Therefore, the eminent role of coherence must be stressed against false conceptions. In theology, there are no extraordinary fundamental statements that could be seen as 'properly basic' and could serve as axioms for logical inferences. None of the theological sentences, statements, secondary or partial narrations, stages, or episodes is more basic than any other. Therefore, it seems that theology would naturally tend towards a coherence theory of truth, if not to a coherentist holism.[2] However, this appearance is deceptive, and this misunderstanding might be responsible for many mistaken constructions. The criterion one has to use is not coherence in the sense of a logical exclusion of contradictions, but in the sense of the dramatic coherence of stories. If one uses logical coherence as the criterion, one violates dramatic coherence, and theology would cease to be theology. The reason is that logical coherence automatically leads to the construction of conceptual networks of transport. A 'theology' of logical coherence would simply be a well-founded set of true, timeless, non-contradictory propositions. But such a construction itself would be a contradiction to the conditions of perceiving truth and value. Since the Christian wayformational perspective is wayfaring in a mesh, we have to use the criterion of coherence so that the character of the mesh will remain intact. Therefore, we have to use

2 A coherentist holism in connection to the philosophical and theological debate has been developed by GRUBE, D.-M., Unbegründbarkeit Gottes?.

dramatic coherence, not logical coherence. We can discuss the criterion of dramatic coherence through the discussion of four sub-criteria.

a) Contradictions are allowed and their explication has to remain open
Since contradictions are allowed in dramatic coherence, if they can be sublated by following narrative sequences, systematic-theological activity has to allow contradictions. This path of theology is not only true in respect of paradoxes, which are primarily a stylistic device that one may like or dislike, but it is also true regarding real antinomies. If no antinomy appears, theological work is perverted into the construction of a system, into a doctrine of a network. Therefore, it would be wrong. It may sound paradoxical, but it is completely logical: an ironclad theological system would prove its wrongness by featuring a maximum of coherence in a network. However, one also has to refrain from the opposite mistake. One must not intentionally install antinomies or gaps in one's construction of a system. Nothing could be further from the truth. The kind of antinomies that are allowed by dramatic coherence cannot be constructed, they can only be *discovered*. They are secondary-narrative fractions constituted by the intermeshing of secondary and primary narrativity itself. There are two reasons that such fractures have to appear in secondary narrations: first, our analysis of the conditions of rationality have shown that the antinomy is inherent to reason. Therefore, it will appear, sooner or later. Second, we must consider what can be called the theological *epoché* of the cross:[3] everything that theology can say can only be said coming from the cross and by the cross. The cross, however, means, if one does not hastily put it into the background, a graspable *ineffability*. This alone – the cross as part of the story of divine self-presentation – is the reason why *apophatic theology* is relatively justified. The relative correctness of apophatic theology is neither justified by a kind of 'natural' theology, for example, as part of the classical 'three ways' for the knowledge of God, nor by epistemological considerations regarding the unknowability of God, but by the triune self-revelation of God, of which the cross is an essential part.

Whereas it is thus far theoretically clear what dramatic coherence is, it is difficult to apply it in practice. One is not allowed to suspend solutions to problems whenever it is convenient, or to remain with open problems. One is not allowed to produce temporary gaps with the hidden agenda of closing them later, since then it would not be a gap at all. We have seen that true, i.e. retrospective, surprise is an essential feature of dramatic coherence (ch. 16). Therefore, theological work has to itself be seen as structured in narrative

3 Cf. to this expression STOELLGER, P., Passivität aus Passion, 180–350.

sequences, which are interminable. Therefore, how should we deal with this sub-criterion that allows for contradictions and that demands the discourse to be open? There is only one possibility: one has to apply first and hypothetically logical coherence in rigorous way, *etsi antinomia non daretur*. If one then discovers fractions, gaps, and contradictions during this coherentist work, one has to inquire intensively whether they rely on methodological mistakes or not. If they do not rely on such mistakes, one can assume that they are true contradictions, gaps, or fractions. In order to discover contradictions with the intention of allowing their appearance, it is methodologically necessary to exclude them. In doing this kind of work, four possible scenarios appear:

First, (a) no contradiction appears at all. In this case, logical coherence would be satisfied, indicating that the reconstruction of the problem at stake ended in the construction of a conceptual network. The consequence is that the criterion of dramatic coherence is violated, and the whole reconstruction of the problem at stake is insufficient.

Second, one discovers contradictions that are most probably not constructed, which leaves open two further possibilities: *Either* (b) these contradictions are epiphanies of the antinomy of reason and/or of the *epoché* of the cross. Then post-systematic theological work has done well. *Or* (c) these contradictions simply indicate the wrongness of the proposed solution to the problem at stake.

The most important problem in practice is that it is not easy to distinguish between the cases (b) and (c), since the theological scholar can only work while moving on a primary-narrative sequence. Therefore, it is impossible to distinguish between (b) and (c) by somehow combining the allowance for contradictions with the principle of the excluded contradiction. Therefore, one can only weigh the options by considering also the other, following sub-criteria of dramatic coherence.

Third, one has to remember that there are no isolated theological problems, but that everything is related to everything else. Therefore, it is possible that (d) the inquiry into a partial problem reveals no contradiction at all, since a contradiction or fracture will only appear in the problem when it is seen in its broader context with the other problems of the *loci*.

It might appear as though the work of the post-systematic theologian is complicated. Well, perhaps. But the picture we have drawn here might really describe what is going on in academic work generally.

b) Renunciation of decontingentization

In ch. 18, we not only learned that the antinomy belongs to every possible use of reason, but also that a narrative reality without contingencies is unconceivable. More basically, the discussion of the threefold entangled self-presentation of God revealed a lot of (historical) contingencies. The inquiry into systematic-theological problems, therefore, cannot deal with the explication of necessary arguments of reason, as Anselm might have thought.[4] Rather, we have to consider irreducible contingency. Also, this sub-criterion is not easy to apply in practice. In principle, it only states that particular contingencies of the argument have to remain. If a systematic-theological description of a problem completely removed its contingency, it would be decontingentized and therefore necessarily wrong. Actually, as we will see in the second volume, it would not only be wrong, but sinful, since decontingentization is essentially an expression of sin.

Nevertheless, it is not easy to exclude decontingentization. What is not meant is that one would construct contingencies, since constructed contingencies are the opposite of real contingencies. Contingencies have to be discovered, too, which means that contingencies of secondary-narrative reflection have to resonate with contingencies in primary narrativity. In fact, the best way to proceed might be in a similar way to the case of contradictions: methodically one should try to exclude contingencies. If the result is a complete loss of contingencies, the procedure was wrong. If contingencies appear, two possibilities remain, and no one operating from one's own primary-narrative sequences, like every theologian, can ultimately decide between them. Either the contingencies are secondary-narrative ones that resonate with primary-narrative contingencies, or they are only secondary-narrative contingencies without resonating with primary-narrative ones that appear only because the paradigms, models, narratives, or metaphors used are defective. Here too, the only possibility is to judge with consideration of the other criteria.

c) *Internal relationality*

A third criterion of dramatic coherence concerns how the aspects of a problem are internally related. 'Objects' and persons are not primarily related in an external manner, but internally, with the effect that their essences consist in their relation to the other. This relation is only possible if the relations are essential for the *relata*. Internal or constitutive relations are on the one hand an implication of a narrative ontology (ch. 7), and on the other hand an implication of

4 Though the question is, if Anselm is actually concerned with necessity of reason in the narrow sense of necessity, cf. ANSELM VON CANTERBURY, Proslogion, chapter 1, 82–84: 'Non tento, Domine, penetrare altidudinam tuam, quia nullatenus comparo illi intellectum meum; sed desidero aliquatenus intelligere veritatem tuam, quam credit et amat cor meum. Neque enim quaero intelligere ut credam, sed credo ut intelligam. Nam et hoc credo. Quia nisi credidero, non intelligam.'

the doctrine of creation, as we will learn in the second volume. Since this is a state of affairs regarding the primary-narrative level, it has to resonate with the secondary-narrative level of theological reflection. However, we saw that it is meaningless to assume that *all* relations are internal ones (ch. 7), only the decisive part of the relational mesh. Therefore, one decisive part of the work of post-systematic theology has the aim of explicating such constitutive relations, equiprimordialities, etc., since the narrative reality is one of a meshwork, not of a network. The consequence is that any methodology that operates purely with the means of external relationality, like relations of causality (ch. 17) or relations of representation, is sharply restricted in their ability to resonate reality. Conclusion: if only external relations appear in a theory or in a theoretical approach, or if one does not specify whether relations are internal or external ones, the identity of the theological work is destroyed.

d) Witness in phenomenal alignment

(Post-)systematic theology is the explication, im-plication, and com-plication of the Christian wayformational perspective from the movements of this same wayformational perspective. This movement has to be reflected in the criteria, which cannot pretend to be quasi-objective. Every systematic-theological problem has to be explicated in an existential way by a phenomenal alignment with the perceiving truth and value of the theological scholar in his person. A theologian's own becoming is itself always a part of the narrative becoming, which is the subject matter of theology. However, what cannot be meant is that one's theology should resonate one's prejudices. Therefore, it is important for the (post-) systematic theologian to use particular philosophical means as they can be found in the realm of phenomenology, especially the phenomenology of perception.

At first glance, this criterion seems to exclude something like a *theologia irregenitorum*. However, this cannot be the case. To judge someone's faith, including one's own, is not a creaturely possibility, if our development on wayformational perspectives is owned not only the *verbum externum*, but also the *testimonium internum*. Personal doubts in faith, therefore, cannot be a hindrance to meaningful (post-)systematic theological work. To apply this sub-criterion of dramatic coherence correctly means that theology has to be done in a way that makes its engagement visible, which is to say it is not a disengaged operation. We can specify this kind of engagement in more detail. It is not arbitrary engagement for any possible reason, but an engagement for the concern of God as the integration of all possible wayformational perspectives in a particular one. This excludes both the quasi-objective as well as the quasi-subjective.

5. Discussions along the way

If theology deals with speaking out of and in God as the integration of all wayformational perspectives in a particular one, then there is (1) nothing that could appear on the Christian wayformational perspective that is theologically irrelevant. In other words, the Christian faith has always traditionally spoken of faith in creation. Nevertheless, the Christian wayformational perspective is (2) always intermeshed with other wayformational perspectives, at least in pluralist societies. These two features of the Christian faith lead to two more criteria regarding theology's communicability.

Theology is due to its own identity dependent on interdisciplinary discussions. The work on the phenomena by other disciplines, preeminently the natural sciences and philosophy, must be considered. The interdisciplinary, phenomena-oriented discussions are, in the theological view, not optional, but it is an obligation. It is an integral part of (post-)systematic work.

The Christian wayformational perspective is not only interwoven with the abstracted wayformational perspectives of the sciences, but also with concrete, non-Christian wayformational perspectives. Therefore, a theology of religions or a theology of pluralism also belongs to the genuine core of post-systematic work. Here one does not have to restrict oneself to discussions about phenomena traditionally called 'religious', but we have to look for a theology of wayformational perspectives that include kinds of faiths other than the traditional ones, including atheism, agnosticism, dataism,[5] or pantheism.

6. Unity of perceiving truth and value

Christian faith is not simply a mode of perceiving, but a mode of perceiving truth and value. It is an attentional behavior in respect to affordances that appear in narrative situations. This feature also has to be reflected by the secondary-narrative work of theologians. An excellent means to do so is to emphasize that in practice there is no basic distinction between fact and value. Dogmatics that is not at the same time ethics would not be theology at all, in the same way that ethics would not be itself if it was not at the same time dogmatics. If at all, we need a distinction of perspectives in order to explain the existence of these sub-disciplines of systematic theology. One might give different emphases, one may stress different points, but it has to be clear that both deal with the same subject matter. One can express this in the following way: any kind of solution to dogmatic problems also has to explicate the

5 For the quasi-religion of the dataism – meaning the perception that mundane and human being is reducible to data streams, so that being would always be *transport* in the network – is a scientistic replacement of religion, which has especially captured academics, cf. HARARI, Y.N., Dataism is Our New God.

implications for ethics (ethical implication), and every kind of ethical problem has a dogmatic dimension (dogmatic implication). So far, this distinction without separation might be helpful for contemporary academic work. Nevertheless, this way of expressing unity is also based on an abstract distinction. Rather, the problems we have in mind are not only the problems theological ethics deals with, but also the problems that practical theology, including its sub-disciplines, deals with.

The criteria of dramatic coherence, of discussions along the way, and of the unity of perceiving truth and value are the criteria for truth of post-systematic theological judgment. As such, they are necessary conditions of truth, in itself and in sum, but not sufficient criteria of truth. All three criteria might be satisfied, but the proposed solution can nevertheless be wrong. However, if the criteria are violated, then the proposal also has to be rejected. In other words, these latter three criteria are criteria of theological falsification (if one does not have the narrow empiricist understanding of falsification in mind). In regard of the most important of these latter three criteria, the criterion of dramatic coherence, including its sub-criteria, we saw that it may remain unclear whether it is satisfied and in what manner, or whether it is violated. However, if one has in mind that these criteria are not so much aimed at proving the truth of a theological proposal than the exclusion of false proposals, I hope they appear more acceptable.

In order to apply these criteria of truth, it is helpful to be trained in different disciplines: without detailed knowledge of logic, semiotics, and philosophy, dramatic coherence cannot be applied. Also, discussions along the way demand contact with other disciplines and with philosophy. To apply the criterion of the unity of perceiving truth and value presupposes skills and contact with all possible disciplines that somehow deal with the phenomena at stake. Post-systematic theology is therefore, an interdisciplinary endeavor from the very beginning.

Both sets of criteria, the criteria of identity as well as the criteria of truth, contain no specific methods. There are no methods which could be called genuinely (post-) systematic-theological ones. In principle, all the methods of all the disciplines are allowed – as long as they contribute something to the six criteria.

27.2 Post-Systematic Theology as Explication, Im-plication, and Com-plication

Beginning with ch. 3 onward, we called post-systematic theology the eminently practical activity of explication, im-plication, and com-plication. However, up to now we have not explained what this means. Now it is time to do so.

That the activity of systematic theology can be described as explication is not unusual.[6] Thereby, we do not have in mind some of the restrictive concepts of explication that might exist,[7] but a broad concept of explication. If the Christian faith is not a doctrine and not an understanding of reality, but a mode of perceiving truth and value, then theology as its secondary-narrative reflection also cannot consist of a collection of doctrinal propositions. Faith includes not only cognitive knowledge, but also knowledge that consists in attitudes, virtues, perceptions, skills, and the formation of feelings, which are in the widest (but also in the most concrete) sense bodily. This kind of knowledge was described by Michael Polanyi as tacit knowledge.[8] According to Polanyi, the task is to explicate this tacit knowledge, which would be a broad understanding of explication. Can theology be an explication in this sense? Yet we know what Polanyi wants to explicate, but we also have to ask what he conceives of as explication. According to Polanyi, explication consists of specification and articulation. Specification means the things that have to be explicated when ordering things into a system of concepts or a system of reference with specific coordinates. Articulation means binding them back into a structure. Of course, in many cases, this might indeed describe what systematic theology does normally. But can this be its only task, if systematic theology is bound to the Christian faith as a mode of perceiving truth and value or as a wayformational perspective? There is a serious objection against this understanding of explication that is, interestingly, not made by a theologian, but an anthropologist:

> To call this haptic dimension 'tacit' is a misnomer. If anything stops up knowledge and commits it so silence, it is the logic of explanation. [...] we specify when we plot dots on a graph, enter values in an equation, or type words on a page; we articulate when we join them up: dots with lines, values with plus or minus signs, words with spaces. The sentence of type – structured through and through, book-ended by a capital and a full stop – is the quintessence of literate articulation. Like the prisoner in his cell, also sentenced to a fixed term, its words are incarcerated, condemned to silence and immobility. Specification and articulation, the keys to logical explanation, lock the doors to feeling. What then escapes? Dies the unspecifiable part of knowledge – what Polanyi described as 'the residue left unsaid by defective articulation' – fall through the cracks into mute and illiterate incoherence? Or is the feeling for words as living things animated by the gestures of their production, enough to break open the gates of the prison? The dissolution of explication and the revocation of its sentences, far

6 Cf. e.g. SCHWÖBEL, C., Doing Systematic Theology (engl.); HERMS, E., ST I, 39, 65f.

7 Cf. e.g. CARNAP, R., Induktive Logik und Wahrscheinlichkeit, 12.

8 Cf. POLANYI, M., The Tacit Dimension. A good, readable introduction to the thinking of Polanyi is given LOSCH, A., Die Bedeutung Michael Polanyis.

> from putting a stop to study, reveal to us the poetry of words that carry on. [...] To communicate as a poet is to cherish words as the journeyman cherishes his equipment and materials. Every word is a jewel that sparkles like a pebble in the running water of a stream. We *feel* it in speaking. [...] Don't blame words for their incarceration; blame the court of explicators that has passed sentence on them.[9]

These words provide ample food for thought – and for feeling. Theology, if it wants to be resonate with its subject matter, cannot be the practical activity of explicating alone – even if we also think of an engaged explicating in the sense of *explicare* as *unfolding* and spreading. It also must be, if it resonates with its subject matter, the activity of *im-plicare* – of *folding* the theologians *in* the mesh of the light of the Gospel. But then it has also to be a *com-plicare* – a *folding together* of what it has explicated into the mesh of perceiving truth and value and its mediated immediateness. Well, does this sound complicated (in the normal sense of the word)? Indeed, and this impression is also not wrong, if complicating things serves what we have called in ch. 5 de-selfevidentialization. However, as explication, im-plication, and com-plication post-systematic theology is always 'plication' in the sense of *plicare*: a secondary-narrative wrapping, folding, and coiling of the narrative threads of the Gospel out of which it becomes.

27.3 Post-Systematic Theology and the Unity of the Theological Disciplines

We already referred to the contemporary academic sub-disciplines of theology in the previous section. The contemporary set of theological disciplines is historically contingent, and it is far from being sacrosanct. Pragmatic reasons were primarily responsible, and the set is still open. Further differentiations as well as a reduction of differentiations are possible in the future. However, this does not mean that the unity of theology is only the unity of a 'practical' discipline, which is united only pragmatically in serving an external end, be it beatitude or church-government, etc. The unity of theology as a whole relies on its reference to its subject-matter, which is the explication, implication, and complication of the Christian wayformational perspective, or the speaking that goings out of and is in God. The theme of theology as a whole is the same as the theme of (post-)systematic theology, which should not be misunderstood as a conquest by one sub-discipline. The contrary is true: it relativizes the work

9 INGOLD, T., Anthropology and/as Education, 51. The quotation is from POLANYI, M., Personal Knowledge, 91.

of (post-)systematic theology itself. That the existence of such a sub-discipline appears to be necessary is only true due to practical demands, since the other sub-disciplines can at least partially fulfil this task today. Theology is united in its subject matter, and therefore it is a unity in difference.

These remarks are not the end of post-systematic theology, rather they open the way up for more – for the genuine theological work, which is the explicating, im-plicating, and com-plicating of the ways of the triune God with us.

Literature

In the following, abbreviations are used according to

SCHWERTNER, SIEGFRIED M., Theologische Realenzyklopäde, Abkürzungsverzeichnis, Berlin et al. ²1994.

ABBOT, EDWIN A., Flatland. A Romance of Many Dimensions, London u.a. ²1884.

ABEL, GÜNTER, Interpretationswelten. Gegenwartsphilosophie jenseits von Essentialismus und Relativismus, Frankfurt/M 1993.

ABRET, HELGA, Literatur und Technik, in ESSELBORN, HANS (Hg.), Utopie, Antiutopie und Science Fiction, Würzburg 2003, 118–132.

ACZEL, PETER, Non-Well-Founded Sets, Stanford 1988.

AHN, GREGOR, Art. Religion I, Theologische Realenzyklopädie, 28, 1997, 513–522.

ANGEHRN, EMIL, Die Frage nach dem Ursprung. Philosophie zwischen Ursprungsdenken und Ursprungskritik, München 2007.

ANSELM VON CANTERBURY, Proslogion (lat.-dt.), Stuttgart – Bad Cannstatt ³1995.

ARISTOTELES, De Arte Poetica Liber, Oxford 1966.

–, Peri Poietikes,

–, phys.,

ARISTOTLE, The Nicomachean Ethics, London 1954.

–, The Poetics of Aristotle (engl.), University Park 2000.

Art. Nahwirkungstheorie, Lexikon der Physik, 1998–2000, http://www.spektrum.de/lexikon/physik/nahwirkungstheorie/10108.

ASQUITH, GLENN H. JR., Anton T. Boisen and the Study of 'Living Human Documents', Journal of Presbyterian History 60 (1982), 244–265.

AUGUSTINUS, AURELIUS, Conf.,

–, Confessiones Buch 11, lat.-dt., Frankfurt/M. 1993.

–, De ordine, Paderborn 1966.

–, De trinitate, in CChr.SL 50.

–, De vera religione, Stuttgart 1986.

BALTHASAR, HANS URS VON, Theo-Drama I: Prolegomena, San Francisco 1988.

–, Theo-Drama II: The Dramatis Personae. Man in God, San Francisco 1990.

–, Theo-Drama III: The Dramatis Personae. Persons in Christ, San Francisco 1992.

–, Theo-Drama V: The Last Act, San Francisco 1998.

–, Theodrama IV: The Action, San Francisco 1994.

BARAD, KAREN, Agential Realism. How Material-discursive Practices Matter, Signs. Journal of Woman in Culture and Society 28 (2003), 803–831.

–, Meeting the Universe Halfway, Durham – London 2007.

–, Posthumanist Performativity. Toward an Understanding of how Matter comes to Matter, Signs. Journal of Woman in Culture and Society 28 (2003), 801–831.

Barbour, Ian G., Myths, Models and Paradigms, New York u.a. 1974.
–, When Science Meets Religion, New York u.a. ¹2000.
Barth, Karl, Church Dogmatics, Edinburgh 1957ff.
–, The Epistle to the Romans (1922), Oxford u.a. 1933.
–, Fides quaerens intellectum (1931), Zürich ²1986.
–, The Humanity of God, in Barth, Karl (Hg.), The Humanity of God, Louisville 1960, 37–68.
–, Kirchliche Dogmatik, Zürich 1932–1967.
Barth, Ulrich, Religion in der Moderne, Tübingen 2003.
Barwise, Jon, The Situation in Logic, Stanford 1989.
Barwise, Jon/Perry, John, Situations and Attitudes, Stanford ²1999.
Becker, Jürgen, Jesus von Nazareth, Berlin u.a. 1996.
–, Paulus. Der Apostel der Völker, Tübingen ³1998.
Becking, Bob, Art. Jahwe, WiBiLex, 2006, https://www.bibelwissenschaft.de/stichwort/22127/.
Bell, John Stewart, On the Einstein-Podolsky-Rosen Paradox, Physics 1 (1964), 195–200.
Berger, Peter L., The Heretical Imperative, New York u.a. 1979.
–, The Sacred Canopy. Elements of a Sociological Theory of Religion (1967), New York 2911.
Bergson, Henri, Matter and Memory, London 1913.
Bergunder, Michael, Was ist Religion? Kulturwissenschaftliche Überlegungen zum Gegenstand der Religionswissenschaft, Zeitschrift für Religionswissenschaft 19 (2011), 3–55.
Bermes, Christian, Maurice Merleau-Ponty zur Einführung, Hamburg ²2012.
Bermúdez, José Luis, Transcendental Arguments and Psychology. The example of O'Shaughnessy on Intentional Action, Metaphilosophy 26 (1995), 379–401.
Beuttler, Ulrich, Gott und Raum – Theologie der Weltgegenwart Gottes, Göttingen u.a. 2010.
Beyschlag, Karlmann, Grundriß der Dogmengeschichte, Bd. 1, Darmstadt ²1987.
–, Grundriß der Dogmengeschichte. Gott und Mensch: Das christologische Dogma, Darmstadt 1991.
Black, Max, The Identity of Indiscernibles, Mind 61 (1952), 153–164.
–, Metaphor, Proceedings of the Aristotelian Soicety 55 (1954), 273–294.
–, Models and Metaphors, Ithaca 1962.
–, More about Metaphor, Dialectica 31 (1977), 431–457.
Blumenberg, Hans, Lebenswelt und Technisierung unter Aspekten der Phänomenologie (1963), in Blumenberg, Hans (Hg.), Wirklichkeiten in denen wir leben, Stuttgart 1986, 7–54.

–, Paradigmen zu einer Metaphorologie, Frankfurt/M. 1997.
–, Theorie der Lebenswelt, Berlin 2010.
–, Wirklichkeiten in denen wir leben. Aufsätze und eine Rede, Stuttgart 1981.
BOESCH, CHRISTOPHE, Symbolic Communication in Wild Chimpanzes?, Human Evolution 6 (1991), 81–90.
BOHM, DAVID, A Suggested Interpretation of the Quantum Theory in Terms of "Hidden Varibles" Physical Review 85 (1952), 166–193.
–, Wholeness and the Implicate Order, London – New York 1980.
BÖHNER, PHILOTHEUS/GILSON, ETIENNE, Christliche Philosophie von Ihren Anfängen bis Nikolaus von Cues, Paderborn ²1954.
BOHR, NIELS, Can Quantum-mechanical Description of Physical Reality be Considered Complete?, Phys. Rev. 48 (1935), 696–702.
BOOST, MAXIMILIAN, Naturphhilosophische Emergenz. Vermittler im Dialog zwischen Naturwissenschaft und Religion, Würzburg 2012.
BOVON, FRANCOIS, Das Evangelium nach Lukas. 2. Teilband (Lk 9.5–14.35), Neukirchen-Vluyn u.a. 1996.
BOYD, RICHARD, Metaphor and Theory Change. What is 'Metaphor' a Metaphor for?, in ORTONY, ANDREW (Hg.), Metaphor and Thought, Cambridge 1979, 356–408.
BRADLEY, FRANCIS HERBERT, Appearance and Reality, London ²1893.
BROCK, BRIAN, Singing the Ethos of God. On the Place of Christian Ethics in Scripture, Grand Rapids – Cambridge 2007.
BROUWER, LUITZEN E.J., Begründung der Mengenlehre unabhängig vom logischen Satz vom ausgeschlossenen Dritten, in BROUWER, LUITZEN E.J. (Hg.), Collected Works, Amsterdam – Oxford 1975, 150–190.
BRÜMMER, VINCENT, The Model of Love, Cambridge 1993.
–, Speaking of a Personal God, Cambridge 1992.
BRUNER, JERRY, Acts of Meaning, Cambridge, MA 1990.
–, Life as Narrative, Soial Research 54 (1987), 11–32.
BULTMANN, RUDOLF, What Does it Mean to Speak of God? (1925), in BULTMANN, RUDOLF/FUNK, R.W. (Hg.), Faith and Understanding I, London 53–65.
BUNGE, MARIO, The Mind-Body Problem. A Psychological Approach, Oxford u.a. 1980.
–, Philosophy of Physics, Dordrecht 1973.
CAPUTO, JOHN D., The Weakness of God. A Theology of the Event, Bloomington – Indianapolis 2006.
CARCATERRA, GAETANO, Le nome constitutive, Mailand 1979.
CARNAP, RUDOLF, Induktive Logik und Wahrscheinlichkeit, Wien 1959.
CARTWRIGHT, NANCY, How the Laws of Physics Lie, Oxford 1983.

CARTWRIGHT, NANCY/SHOMAR, TOWFIC/SUÁREZ, MAURICIO, The Tool Box of Science, in HERFEL, W./U.A. (Hg.), Theories and Models in Scientific Processes, 1995, 137–149.

CASSIRER, ERNST, Nachgelassene Manuskripte und Texte, Bd. 1–18, Hamburg 1995–2009.

–, Philosophie der Symbolischen Formen. Neuausgabe, Hamburg 2001–2002.

CHALMERS, DAVID J., The Conscious Mind. In Search of a Fundamental Theory, New York 1996.

CHARBONNIER, GEORGES, Le monologue du peintre, Paris 1959.

CHISHOLM, RODERICK M., Events without Times, Nous 24 (1990), 413–427.

CICERO, MARCUS TULLIUS, De natura deorum, Stuttgart 1995.

CLARK, ANDY, Supersizing the Mind. Embodiment, Action and Cognitive Extension, Oxford – New York 2011.

CLARK, ANDY/CHALMERS, DAVID J., The Extended Mind, Analysis 58 (1998), 10–23.

CLARKE, SAMUEL/LEIBNIZ, GOTTFRIED WILHELM, Der Briefwechsel mit Gottfried Wilhelm Leibniz von 1715/1716, Hamburg 1990.

CLAYTON, JOHN, Gottesbeweise, TRE Bd. 13 708–784.

CLAYTON, PHILIP, Mind and Emergence. From Quantum to Consciousness, Oxford u.a. 2006.

CLINGERMAN, FORREST, Reading the Book of Nature. A Hermeneutical account of Nature for Philosophical Theology, Worldviews. Global Religions, Culture Ecology 13 (2009), 72–91.

COBB, JOHN/GRIFFIN, DAVID RAY, Process Theology. An Introductory Exposition, Louisville ²1976.

CONNOLLY, WILLIAM E., The Evangelical-Capitalist Resonance Machine, Political Theory 33 (2005), 869–886.

CONTE, AMADEO G., Art. Regel IV, Historisches Wörterbuch der Philosophie, 8, 1992, 446–450.

–, Idealtypen für eine Theorie der konstitutiven Regeln, in ECKHOFF, TORSTEIN/FRIEDMANN, LAWRENCE M./UUSITALO, JYRKI (Hg.), Vernunft und Erfahrung im Rechtsdenken der Gegenwart, Berlin 1986, 243–250.

–, Konstitutive Regeln und Deontik, in MORSCHER, EDGAR/STRANZINGER, RUDOLF (Hg.), Ethik. Grundlagen, Probleme, Anwendungen, Wien 1981, 82–86.

–, Variationen über Wittgensteins Regelbegriff, in HALLER, RUDOLF (Hg.), Sprache und Erkenntnis als soziale Tatsache, Wien 1981, 69–78.

CROUCH, COLIN, Post-Democracy, Cambridge u.a. 2004.

CRUIKSHANK, JULIE, Do Glaciers Listen? Local Knowledge, Colonial Encounters and Social Imagination, Vancouver – Seattle 2005.

DALFERTH, INGOLF U., Der auferweckte Gekreuzigte, Tübingen 1994.

–, Die Wirklichkeit des Möglichen. Hermeneutische Religionsphilosophie, Tübingen 2003.
–, Existenz Gottes und christlicher Glaube, München 1984.
–, Gott. Philosophisch-theologische Denkversuche, Tübingen 1992.
–, Inkarnation: Der Mythos vom inkarnierten Gott, in DALFERTH, INGOLF U. (Hg.), Der auferweckte Gekreuzigte, Tübingen 1994, 1–37.
–, Radikale Theologie, Leipzig 2010.
–, Religiöse Rede von Gott, München 1981.
–, Sprachlogik des Glaubens, München 1974.
DANZ, CHRISTIAN, Systematische Theologie, Tübingen 2016.
DAVENPORT, JOHN J., Narrative Identity, Autonomy and Mortality. From Frankfurt and MacIntyre to Kierkegaard, New York 2012.
DAVIDSON, DONALD, Essays on Action and Event, Oxford ²2001.
–, The Individuation of Events, in RESCHER, NICHOLAS (Hg.), Essay in Honor of Carl G. Hempel, Dordrecht 1969, 216–234.
–, Truth and Interpretation, Oxford 1984.
–, What Metaphors Mean, Critical Inquiry 5 (1978), 31–47.
DE MONTICELLI, ROBERTA, The Feeling of Values. For a phenomenological theory of affectivity, in BAGNARA, SEBASTIANO/CRAMPTON SMITH, GILLIAN (Hg.), Theories and Practice in Interaction Design., Mahwah (NJ) 2006.
–, Perceiving Values. A Phenomenological Approach, in MÜHLING, MARKUS/GILLAND, DAVID/FÖRSTER, YVONNE (Hg.), Perceiving Truth and Value, Göttingen – Bristol (CT) 2010, 37–53.
–, Sensibility and Values. Toward a Phenomenological Theory of the Emotional Life, in RINOFNER-KREIDL, SONJA/WILTSCHE, HARALD A. (Hg.), Analytic and Continental Philosophy. Methods and Perspectives. Proceedings of the 37th International Wittgenstein Symposion, Berlin – New York 2016, 381–400.
DEACON, TERENCE, The Symbolic Species. The Co-evolution of Language and the Human Brain, New York – London 1997.
DEANE-DRUMMOND, CELIA, Christ and Evolution. A Drama of Wisdom?, Zygon 47 (2012), 524–541.
–, Christ and Evolution. Wonder and Wisdom, Minneapolis 2009.
DELEUZE, GILLES, The Logic of Sense, London 1990.
DELEUZE, GILLES/GUATTARI, FELIX, What is Philosophy?, New York 1994.
DELEUZE, GILLES/GUATTARI, FÉLIX, A Thousand Plateaus. Capitalism and Schizophrenia, Minneapolis – London 1987.
DENNETT, DANIEL C., Why Everyone is a Novelist, Times Literary Supplement 16–22 Sept. (1988),

Denzinger, Heinrich/Hünermann, Peter, Enchiridion Symbolorum, Definitionum et Declarationum de Rebus Fidei et Morum – Kompendium der Glaubensbekenntnisse und kirchlichen Lehrentscheidungen, Freiburg u.a. ^{39}2001.

Derrida, Jaques, Apokalypse. Von einem neuerdings erhobenen apokalypltischen Ton in der Philosophie Köln – Wien 1985.

–, Margins of Philosophy, Brighton 1982.

–, Of Grammatology, Baltimore 1976.

Dingel, Irene/u.a. (Hg.), Die Bekenntnisschriften der Evangelisch-Lutherischen Kirche. Vollständige Neuedition, Göttingen – Bristol (CT) 2014.

Dornes, Martin, Der kompetente Säugling. Die präverbiale Entwicklung des Menschen, Frankfurt am Main 1993.

Drechsel, Wolfgang, Lebensgeschichte und Lebens-Geschichten. Zugänge zur Seelsorge aus biographischer Perspektive, Gütersloh 2002.

Droysen, Johann Gustav, Historik (1857/8), Stuttgart – Bad Cannstatt 1977.

Dunbar, Robin I.M., The Social Brain Hypothesis, Evolutionary Anthropology 6 (1998), 178–190.

Ebbersmeyer, S., Art. Spekulation, HWPh 9, 1995, 1355–1372.

Ebeling, Gerhard, Die Klage über das Erfahrungsdefizit in der Theologie als Frage nach ihrer Sache, in Ebeling, Gerhard (Hg.), Wort und Glaube, Bd. 2: Beiträge zur Fundamentaltheologie, Tübingen 1975, 3–28.

–, Dogmatik des christlichen Glaubens I, Tübingen 1979.

–, Evangelische Evangelienauslegung. Eine Untersuchung zu Luthers Hermeneutik (1942), Darmstadt 1962.

Ebert, Theodor, Praxis und Poiesis. Zu einer handlungstheoretischen Unterscheidung des Aristoteles, Zeitschrift für philosophische Forschung 30 (1976), 12–30.

Eco, Umberto, The Open Work, Cambridge (Mass.) 1989.

Eichler, Klaus-Dieter, Wilhelm Schapps narrative Ontologie, in Joisten, Karen (Hg.), Das Denken Wilhelm Schapps, München – Freiburg 2010, 102–125.

Einstein, Albert, The Collected Papers of Albert Einstein. Bd. 2. The Swiss Years: Writings, 1900–1909, Princeton – Jerusalem 1989.

–, Über die spezielle und die allgemeine Relativitätstheorie, Berling, Heidelberg u.a. ^{23}2001.

Einstein, Albert/Podolsky, Boris/Rosen, Nathan, Can Quantum-Mechanical Description of Physical Reality Be Considered Complete?, Physical Review 47 (1935), 777–780.

Evers, Dirk, Art. Law/Natural Law, ^{4}Religion Past and Present, 2011, <http://dx.doi.org.ubproxy.ub.uni-heidelberg.de/10.1163/1877-5888_rpp_COM_08581>.

–, Gott und mögliche Welten. Studien zur Logik theologischer Aussagen über das Mögliche, Tübingen 2006.

–, Raum – Materie – Zeit. Schöpfungstheologie im Dialog mit naturwissenschaftlicher Kosmologie, Tübingen 2000.

FEIL, E., Art. Religion IV, Historisches Wörterbuch der Philosophie, 1992, 644–653.

FELDMAN, RICHARD/FELDMAN, FRED, Art. Roderick Chisholm, The Stanford Encyclopedia of Philosophy, Winter 2016.

FEUERBACH, LUDWIG, Das Wesen des Christentums, Bd. 1–2, Berlin 1956.

FICHTE, JOHANN GOTTLIEB, Über den Grund unseres Glaubens an eine göttliche Weltregierung, in RÖHR, WERNER (Hg.), Appellation an das Publikum. Dokumente zum Atheismusstreit um Fichte, Forberg, Niethammer, Jena 1898/99, Leipzig 1991, 11–22.

FINDLAY, JOHN N., Can God's Existence be Disproved?, Mind 57 (1948), 176–183.

FINE, ARTHUR, The Shaky Game. Einstein, Realism and the Quantum Theory, Chicago – London ²1996.

FISCHER, JOHANNES, Theologische Ethik. Grundwissen und Orientierung, Stuttgart u.a. 2002.

FLASCH, KURT/AUGUSTINUS, AURELIUS, Was ist Zeit? Augustinus von Hippo, das XI. Buch der Confessiones. Historisch-philosophische Studie. Text Übersetzung, Kommentar, Frankfurt/M. 1993.

FOERSTER, HEINZ VON, Cybernetics of Cybernetics, in KRIPPENDORF, K. (Hg.), Communication and Control, New York 1979, 5–8.

FORD, LEWIS S., Transforming Process Theism, Albany, NY 2000.

FÖRSTER-BEUTHAN, YVONNE, Zeiterfahrung und Ontologie. Perspektiven moderner Zeitphilosophie, München u.a. 2012.

FREGE, GOTTLOB, Über Sinn und Bedeutung, Zeitschrift für Philosophie und philosophische Kritik NF 100 (1892), 25–50.

FREI, HANS, The Eclipse of Biblical Narrative. A Study in Eighteenth and Nineteenth Century Hermeneutics, New Haven – London 1974.

–, Theology and Narrative. Selected Essays, New York u.a. 1993.

FUCHS, THOMAS, Das Gehirn – ein Beziehungsorgan. Eine phänomenologisch-ökologische Konzeption, Stuttgart ⁴2013.

–, Neurobiology and Psychotherapy. An Emerging Dialogue, Current Opinions in Psychiatry 17 (2004), 479–485.

–, Selbst und Schizophrenie, DZPhil 60 (2012), 887–901.

–, Values as Relational Phenomena. A Sketch of an Enactive Theory of Values, in MÜHLING, MARKUS/GILLAND, DAVID/FÖRSTER, YVONNE (Hg.), Perceiving Truth and Value, Göttingen – Bristol (CT) 2020, 19–36.

FUENTES, AGUSTÍN, A New Synthesis. Resituating Approaches to the Evolution of Human Behaviour, Anthropology Today 25 (2009), 12–17.

–, Race, Monogamy, and Other Lies They Told You. Busting Myths about Human Nature, Berkeley – Los Angeles – London 2012.

FUENTES, AGUSTIN/KISSEL, MARC/PETERSON, JEFFREY, Semiose in der Evolution von Primaten und Menschen, in HEMMINGER, HANSJÖRG/BEUTTLER, ULRICH/MÜHLING, MARKUS/ROTHGANGEL, MARTIN (Hg.), Geschaffen nach ihrer Art. Was unterscheidet Tiere und Menschen?, Frankfurt/M. 2017, 33–51.

GALLAGHER, SHAUN/ZAHAVI, DAN, The Phenomenological Mind, London – New York ²2013.

GAZZANIGA, MICHAEL S., Who's in Charge? Free Will and the Science of the Brain, New York 2011.

GERTZ, JAN CHRISTIAN, Die Stellung des kleinen geschichtlichen Credos in der Redaktionsgeschichte von Deuteronomium und Pentateuch, in KRATZ, R.G./SPIECKERMANN, H. (Hg.), Liebe und Gebot. Studien zum Deuteronomium. FS L. PERLITT, Göttingen 2000, 30–45.

GIBSON, JAMES JEROME, The Ecological Approach to Visual Perception, New York – London 2015.

GÖDEL, KURT, Über formal unentscheidbare Sätze der Principia Mathematica und verwandter Systeme, Monatsheft für Mathematik und Physik 38 (1931), 173–198.

–, Zum Entscheidungsproblem des logischen Funktionenkalküls, Monatsheft für Mathematik und Physik 40 (1933), 433–443.

GOFFMAN, ERVING, The Presentation of Self in Everyday Life, New York 1959.

GOODSON, IVOR F./SCHERTO, R. GILL, The Narrative Turn in Social Research, Counterpoints 386 (2011), 17–33.

GOPNIK, ALISON/MELTZOFF, ANDREW N./KUHL, PATRICIA K., The Scientist in the Crib. What Early Learning Tells us About the Mind, New York u.a. 2001.

GÖRNITZ, THOMAS/GÖRNITZ, BRIGITTE, Die Evolution des Geistigen, Göttingen ²2009.

GRÄßER, ERICH, Das wandernde Gottesvolk. Zum Basismotiv des Hebräerbriefs, ZNW 77 (1986), 160–179.

GREGERSEN, NIELS HENRIK, Deep Incarnation. Why Evolutionary Continuity Matters in Christology, Toronto Journal of Theology 26 (2010), 173–188.

GRESHAKE, GISBERT, Der dreieine Gott, Freiburg u.a. 1997.

GRIFFIN, DAVID RAY, Process Theology. On Postmodernism, Morality, Pluralism, Eschatology, and Demonic Evil, Anoka 2017.

GRÖBLACHER, SIMON/PATEREK, TOMASZ/KALTENBAEK, RAINER/BRUKNER, CASLAV/ZUKOWSKI, MAREK/ASPELMEYER, MARKUS/ZEILINGER, ANTON, An Experimental Test of Non-local Realism, Nature 446–449 (2007), 871–875–252.

GROßHANS, PETER, Theologischer Realismus, Tübingen 1996.

GRUBE, DIRK-MARTIN, Unbegründbarkeit Gottes?, Marburg 1998.

GUASTINI, RICCARDO, Six Concepts of 'Constitutive Rule', in ECKHOFF, TORSTEIN/FRIEDMANN, LAWRENCE M./UUSITALO, JYRKI (Hg.), Vernunft und Erfahrung im Rechtsdenken der Gegenwart, Berlin 1986, 261–269.

GUGUTZER, ROBERT, Soziologie des Körpers, Bielefeld 2004.
GUNTON, COLIN E., The Actuality of Atonement. A Study of Metaphor, Rationality and the Christian Tradition, Edinburgh 1988.
–, The One, the Three and the Many, Cambridge 1993.
–, The Promise of Trinitarian Theology, Edinburgh 1991.
HABERMAS, JÜRGEN, Diskursethik – Notizen zu einem Begründungsprogramm, in HABERMAS, JÜRGEN (Hg.), Moralbewußtsein und kommunikatives Handeln, Frankfurt/M. 1983, 53–135.
–, Glauben und Wissen – Dankesrede anläßlich der Verleihung des Friedenspreises des deutschen Buchhandelns, http://www.friedenspreis-des-deutschen-buchhandels.de/sixcms/media.php/1290/2001_habermas.pdf (2001), 9–15.
–, Wahrheitstheorien, in FAHRENBACH, HELMUT (Hg.), Wirklichkeit und Reflexion, Pfullingen 1973, 211–265.
HANSON, NORWOOD RUSSELL, Patterns of Discovery, Cambridge 1958.
HARARI, YUVAL NOAH, Dataism is Our New God, New Perspectives Quaterly 34 (2017), 36–43.
HÄRLE, WILFRIED, Dogmatik, Berlin u.a. 1995.
–, Dogmatik, Berlin u.a. ²2000.
– (Hg.), Im Kontinuum. Annäherungen an eine relationale Erkenntnistheorie und Ontologie, Marburg 1999.
HARMAN, GRAHAM, The Road to Objects, Contiment 3 (2011), 171–179.
HARNACK, ADOLF VON, Das Wesen des Christentums, 1999.
HART, DAVID BENTLEY, The Beauty of the Infinity. The Aesthetics of Christian Truth, Grand Rapids 2003.
HARTENSTEIN, FRIEDHELM, Die bleibende Bedeutung des Alten Testaments, Göttingen 2017.
–, Zur Bedeutung des Alten Testaments für die evangelische Kirche. Eine Auseinandersetuzung mit den Thesen von Notger Slenczka, ThLZ 140 (2015), 738–751.
HARTMANN, NICOLAI, Möglichkeit und Wirklichkeit, Meisenheim am Glan ²1949.
HARTSHORNE, CHARLES, The Logic of Perfection and Other Essays in Neoclassical Metaphysics, LaSalle ³1973.
HAUERWAS, STANLEY, A Community of Character. Toward a Constructive Christian Social Ethic, Notre Dame 1981.
–, The Peaceable Kingdom. A Primer in Christian Ethics, Notre Dame 1983.
HAWKING, STEPHEN W, A Brief History of Time. From the Big Bang to Black Holes, London u.a. 1995.
HEESCH, MATTHIAS, Theologie und Naturwissenschaften. Historische und Systematische Erwägungen, Würzburg 2017.

HEGEL, GEORG WILHELM FRIEDRICH, The Difference Between Fichte's and Schelling's System of Philosophy (1801)., Albany 1977.
–, The Encyclopaedia Logic (with the Zusätze). Part I of the Encyclopaedia of Philosophical Sciences, Indianapolis – Cambridge 1991.
–, Vorlesungen über die Philosophie der Religion I – III, hg. v. W. Jaeschke, Hamburg 1993–1995.
–, Wissenschaft der Logik I, in HEGEL, GEORG WILHELM FRIEDRICH (Hg.), Gesammelte Werke, Bd. II, 1978.
HEIDEGGER, MARTIN, Being and Time, Albany 1996.
–, Das Ding, in HEIDEGGER, MARTIN (Hg.), Vorträge und Aufsätze, Stuttgart 1954, 157–169.
–, The Question Concerning Technology, in HEIDEGGER, MARTIN (Hg.), The Question Concerning Technilogy and Other Essays, New York – London 1877, 3–35.
–, Vom Ereignis. Beiträge zur Philosohie. Gesamtausgabe III/65, Frankfurt/M. 1989.
HEIM, KARL, Christian Faith and Natural Science, New York 1953.
–, Glaube und Denken (6. Aufl. n. d. 5. Aufl. 1957), Wuppertal ^{6}1975.
–, God Transcendent. Foundation for a Christian Metaphysic, New York 1936.
HENRICH, DIETER, Hegel im Kontext, Frankfurt/M. ^{2}1975.
HENRIKSEN, JAN-OLAV, Life, Love and Hope. God and Human Experience, Grand Rapids 2014.
HERMS, EILERT, „Das Gehirn und seine Wirklichkeit". Hirnphysiologie als Theologie bei Gerhard Roth, in HERMS, EILERT (Hg.), Zusammenleben im Widerstreit der Weltanschauungen, Tübingen 2007, 90–101.
–, Kirche in der Zeit, in HERMS, EILERT (Hg.), Kirche für die Welt, Tübingen 1995, 231–317.
–, Kosmologische Aspekte des Gesetzesbegriffs, in HERMS, EILERT (Hg.), Offenbarung und Glaube, Tübingen 1992, 408–430.
–, "Meine Zeit in Gottes Händen", in STOCK, KONRAD (Hg.), Zeit und Schöpfung, Gütersloh 1997, 67–90.
–, Offenbarung, in HERMS, EILERT (Hg.), Offenbarung und Glaube, Tübingen 1992, 168–220.
–, Offenbarung und Erfahrung, in HERMS, EILERT (Hg.), Offenbarung und Glaube, Tübingen 1992, 246–272.
–, Offenbarung und Glaube, Tübingen 1990.
–, Systematische Theologie. Das Wesen des Christentums: In Wahrheit und aus Gnade leben. Bd. 1 §§ 1–59, Tübingen 2017.
–, Systematische Theologie. Das Wesen des Christentums: In Wahrheit und aus Gnade leben. Bd. 2, §§ 60–84, Tübingen 2017.
–, Systematische Theologie. Das Wesen des Christentums: In Wahrheit und aus Gnade leben. Bd. 3, §§ 85–100, Tübingen 2017.

–, Was haben wir an der Bibel?, Neukirchen-Vluyn 1998.

–, Zur Systematik des Personbegriffs in reformatorischer Tradition, NZSTh 49 (2008), 377–413.

HESSE, MARY B., The Cognitive Claims of Metaphor, The Journal of Speculative Philosophy New Series 2 (1988), 1–16.

–, Models and Analogies in Science, London u.a. 1963.

–, Theory and Observation. Is There an Independent Observation Language?, in COLODNY, ROBERT (Hg.), The Nature and Function of Scientific Theories IV, Pittsburgh 1970, 256–275.

HEYTING, AREND, Die formalen Regeln der intuitionistischen Logik, Sitzungsberichte der Preußischen Akademie der Wissenschaften, physikalisch-mathematische Klasse (1930), 42–65. 57–71. 158–169.

HICK, JOHN, Jesus and the World Religions, in HICK, JOHN (Hg.), The Myth of God Incarnate, London 1977, 167–185.

HILLER, DORIS, Gottes Geschichte. Hermeneutische und theologische Reflexionen zum Geschehen der Gottesgeschichte orientiert an der Erzählkonzeption Paul Ricœurs, Neukirchen-Vluyn 2009.

HINDRICHS, GUNNAR, Das Absolute und das Subjekt. Untersuchungen zum Verhältnis von Metaphysik und Nachmetaphysik, Frankfurt/M. 2008.

HOBBES, THOMAS, Leviathan or the Matter, Forme, and Power of a Common-Wealth Ecclesiastical and Civill, London 1651.

HOFHEINZ, MARCO/MATHWIG, FRANK/ZEINDLER, MATTHIAS (Hg.), Ethik und Erzählung. Theologische und philosophische Beiträge zur narrativen Ethik, Zürich 2009.

HOFIUS, OTTO, Katapausis. Die Vorstellung vom endzeitlichen Ruheort im Hebräerbrief, Tübingen 1970.

HOFSTADTER, DOUGLAS, Gödel, Escher, Bach. An Eternal Golden Braid, New York 1979.

–, Nomic, Scientific American 246 (1982), 16–28.

HOYE, WILLIAM J., The Emergence of Eternal Life, Cambridge 2013.

HUBBELING, HUBERTUS GEZINUS, Einführung in die Religionsphilosophie, Göttingen 1981.

HUGHES, GEORGE EDWARD/CRESSWELL, MAXWELL J., A New Introduction to Modal Logic, London u.a. 1996.

HUIZING, KLAAS, Ästhetische Theologie, Gütersloh 2015.

HUME, DAVID, A Treatise of Human Nature, Vol. 1, London u.a. 1911.

HUNSINGER, GEORGE, Uncreated Light. From Irenaeus and Torrance to Aquinas and Barth, in O'COLLINGS, GERALD/MEYERS, MARY ANN (Hg.), Light from Light, Grand Rapids u.a. 2012, 208–235.

HUSSERL, EDMUND, Erste Philosophie (1923/24). Zweiter Teil: Theorie der phänomenologischen Reduktion, Hua VIII, Den Haag 1959.
–, Ideen zu einer reinen Phänomenologie und phänomenologischen Philosophie 1. Husserliana 3/1, Den Haag 1952.
HUTTER, AXEL, Der kritische Sinn des Gottesbegriffs, in BUCHHEIM, THOMAS/HERMANNI, FRIEDRICH/HUTTER, AXEL/SCHWÖBEL, CHRISTOPH (Hg.), Gottesbeweise als Herausforderung für die moderne Vernunft, Tübingen 2012, 149–177.
–, Narrative Ontologie, Tübingen 2017.
HUTTO, DANIEL D., Folk Psychological Narratives. The Socio-cultural Basis of Understanding Reasons, Cambridge (MA) 2008.
IJJAS, ANNA, Der Alte mit dem Würfel. Ein Beitrag zur Metaphysik der Quantenmechanik, Göttingen 2011.
INGOLD, TIM, Anthropology and/as Education, London 2018.
–, Being Alive. Essays on Movement, Knowledge and Description, New York u.a. 2011.
–, Dreaming of Dragons. On the Imagination of Real Life, Journal of the Royal Anthropological Institute 19 (2013), 734–752.
–, The Impediments of Objectivity and the Pursuit of Truth, in MÜHLING, MARKUS/GILLAND, DAVID/FÖRSTER, YVONNE (Hg.), Perceiving Truth and Values, Göttingen – Bristol (CT) 2020, 133–139.
–, The Life of Lines, London – New York 2015.
–, Lines. A Brief History, London – New York 2007.
–, A Storied World, in INGOLD, TIM (Hg.), Being Alive, Oxon – New York 2011, 141–176.
IPGRAVE, MICHAEL, Trinity and Inter Faith Dialogue. Plenitude and Plurality, Frankfurt/M. u.a. 2003.
JABLONKA, EVA/LAMB, MARION, Evolution in Four Dimensions. Genetic, Epigenetic, Behavioral and Symbolic Variation in the History of Life, Cambridge (Mass.) 2005.
JACKSON, B. DARRELL, The Theory of Signs in St. Augustine's *De doctrina christiana*, Revue d'Etudes Augustiniennes et Patristiques 15 (1969), 9–49.
JAMES, WILLIAM, Pragmatism (1890), Cambridge 1975.
–, The Will to Believe (1897), Cambridge 1979.
JENSON, ROBERT W., "Gott" als "Antwort", in SALAQUARDA, J. (Hg.), Philosophische Theologie im Schatten des Nihilismus, Berlin 1971, 146–159.
–, On Thinking the Human. Resolutions of Difficult Notions, Grand Rapids 2003.
–, Systematic Theology I: The Triune God, New York u.a. 1997.
–, The Triune God, in JENSON, ROBERT W./BRAATEN, CARL E. (Hg.), Christian Dogmatics, Bd. 1, Philadelphia 1984, 79–191.
–, What is the Point of Trinitarian Theology?, in SCHWÖBEL, CHRISTOPH (Hg.), Trinitarian Theology Today, Edinburgh 1995, 31–43.
JOEST, WILFRIED, Ontologie der Person bei Luther, Göttingen [2]1987.

JOHANNES SCOTUS ERIUGENA, De divisione naturae, PL 122, 1853.

JOOSS, ELISABETH, Raum. Eine theologische Interpretation, Gütersloh 2005.

JÜNGEL, EBERHARD, Erfahrungen mit der Erfahrung. Unterwegs bemerkt, Stuttgart 2008.

–, God as the Mystery of the World, Grand Rapids 1983.

–, God's Being is in Becoming, London u.a. 2001.

–, Gott als Geheimnis der Welt, Tübingen [6]1992.

–, Unterwegs zur Sache. Theologische Bemerkungen, München 1972.

JÜNGEL, EBERHARD/RICŒUR, PAUL, Thesen zur theologischen Metaphorologie, in NOPPEN, JEAN-PIERRE VAN (Hg.), Erinnern um Neues zu sagen, Frankfurt/M. 1988, 52–67.

KANT, IMMANUEL, Critique of Pure Reason. The Cambridge Edition of the Works of Immanuel Kant, New York [15]2009.

KÄSEMANN, ERNST, Das wandernde Gottesvolk. Eine Untersuchung zum Hebräerbrief, Göttingen 1939.

–, Der Ruf der Freiheit, Tübingen [3]1968.

–, Kirchliche Konflikte, Bd.1, Göttingen 1982.

KEGLER, JÜRGEN, Biblische Begriffe und Vorstellungen von „Seele", in BEUTTLER, ULRICH/MÜHLING, MARKUS/ROTHGANGEL, MARTIN (Hg.), Seelenphänomene, Frankfurt/M. u.a. 2016, 95–109.

KELLER, CATHERINE, On the Mystery. Discerning Divinity in Process, Minneapolis 2008.

KELLER, JAMES A., Problems of Evil and the Power of God, Aldershot u.a. 2007.

KERSTIENS, L., Art. Kontemplation, HWPh 4, 1976, 1024–1026.

KIERKEGAARD, SÖREN, Abschließende unwissenschaftliche Nachschrift (1846), Gesammelte Werke 16/1, Jena 1957.

KIM, JAEGWON, Causation, Nomic Subsumption, and the Concept of Event, The Journal of Philosophy 70 (1973), 217–236.

–, Events as Property Exemplifications. Proceedings of the Winnipeg Conference on Human Action, Held at Winnipeg, Manitoba, Canada, 9–11 May 1975, in BRAND, MYLES/WALTON, DOUGLAS (Hg.), Action Theory, Dordrecht 1976, 310–326.

–, Physicalism, or Something near Enough, Princeton 2005.

KLEE, PAUL, Beiträge zur bildnerischen Formenlehre, Bern (http://www.klee-gestaltungslehre.zpk.org) 1921/22.

KOCH, ANTON FRIEDRICH, Rationalität im Gespräch. Grundlegendes aus philosophischer Perspektive, in MÜHLING, MARKUS/U.A. (Hg.), Rationalität im Gespräch – Rationality in Conversation, Leipzig 2016, 11–22.

–, Versuch über Wahrheit und Zeit, Paderborn 2006.

–, Wahrheit, Zeit und Freiheit. Einführung in eine philosophische Theorie, Paderborn 2006.

KOFFKA, KURT, Principles of Gestalt Psychology, New York 1935.

KÖNIG, G., Art. Theorie I, HWPh 10, 1998, 1128–1146.

KÖPPE, TILMANN/KINDT, TOM, Erzähltheorie. Eine Einführung, Stuttgart 2014.

KOSCHORKE, ALBRECHT, Wahrheit und Erfindung. Grundzüge einer Allgemeinen Erzähltheorie, Frankfurt/M. 2012.

KOSELLECK, REINHART, Fiktion und geschichtliche Wirklichkeit, Zeitschrift für Ideengeschichte I.3 (2007), 39–54.

KRAUTZ, JOCHEN, Bildung als Anpassung? Das Kompetenz-Konzept im Kontext einer ökonomisierten Bildung, Fromm Forum 13 (2009), 87–100.

KRECH, VOLKHARD, Wo bleibt die Religion? Zur Ambivalenz des Religiösen in der modernen Gesellschaft, Bielefeld 2011.

KREITZSCHECK, DAGMAR, Zeitgewinn. Theorie und Praxis der erzählenden Predigt, Leipzig 2004.

KRIPKE, SAUL A., Naming and Necessity, Cambridge (Mass.) 1980.

KUHN, THOMAS S., The Structure of Scientific Revolutions, Chicago [4]2012.

KÜHNE, HARTMUT, Art. Wallfahrt V., Theologische Realenzyklopädie 35, 2003, 423–429.

KÜNG, HANS, On Being a Christian, Garden City 1984.

LAI, PAN-CHIU, Confucian Understanding of Humanity and Rationality in Conversation, in MÜHLING, MARKUS (Hg.), Rationalität im Gespräch – Rationality in Conversation, Leipzig 2016, 333–346.

–, Die letztgültige Realität im chinesischen Buddhismus und die christliche Gotteslehre, in MÜHLING, MARKUS (Hg.), Gott und Götter in den Weltreligionen, Göttingen 2014, 219–249.

–, Trinitarische Perichorese und Hua-yen Buddhismus, in MÜHLING, MARKUS/WENDTE, MARTIN (Hg.), Entzogenheit in Gott, Utrecht 2005, 45–62.

LAKOFF, GEORGE/JOHNSON, MARK, Metaphors We Live by. With a New Afterword, Chicago – London [2]2003.

–, Philosophy in the Flesh. The Embodied Mind and its Challenge to Western Thought, New York 1999.

LEBOWITZ, JOEL L., Time's Arrow and Boltzmann's Entropy, Scholarpedia, 3(4):3448, 2008, 1–11.

LEFEBVRE, HENRI, The Production of Space, Oxford (UK)–Cambridge (USA) 1991.

LEIBNIZ, GOTTFRIED WILHELM, Die kleineren philosophisch wichtigen Schriften, hg. v. J.H. von Kirchmann, Leipzig 1879.

–, Die philosophischen Schriften von Gottfried Wilhelm Leibniz I – VII, Berlin 1875–1890.

–, Philosophische Schriften. 4 Bände in 6 Teilbänden, Frankfurt/M 1996.

–, Philosophischer Briefwechsel Bd. 1. Der Briefwechsel mit Antoine Arnauld, frz.-dt. hg. v. R. Finster, Hamburg 1997.

LEPPEK, THORSTEN A., Wahrheit bei Wolfhart Pannenberg. Eine philosophisch-theologische Untersuchung, Göttingen – Bristol (CT) 2017.

LÉVINAS, EMMANUEL, Otherwise than Being, or, Beyond Essence, Drrdrecht 1991.

LEWIS, CLARENCE I., Implication and the Algebra of Logic, Mind 21 (1912), 522–531.

LEWIS, DAVID, Anselm and Actuality, Nous 4 (1970), 175–188.

–, Counterpart Theory and Quantified Modal Logic, in LEWIS, DAVID (Hg.), Philosophical Papers I, Oxford 1983, 26–46.

–, On the Plurality of Worlds, Oxford 1986.

LINDBECK, GEORGE A., The Nature of Doctrine. Religion and Theology in a Post-liberal Age, Philadelphia 1984.

LIPPITT, JOHN, Getting the Story Straight. Kierkegaard, MacIntyre and some Problems with Narrative Unity, Inquiry 50 (2007), 34–69.

LIST, ELISABETH, Einleitung, in LIST, ELISABETH/FIALA, ERWIN (Hg.), Leib, Maschine, Bild. Körperdiskurse der Moderne und Postmoderne, Wien 1997, 9–16.

LISZKOWSKI, ULF/CARPENTER, MALINDA/STRIANO, TRICIA/TOMASELLO, MICHAEL, 12- and 18-Month-Olds Point to Provide Information for Others, Journal of Cognitive Development 7 (2006), 173–187.

LOCKE, JOHN, An Essay Concerning Human Understanding, Oxford 1979.

–, An Essay Concerning Human Understanding. Part 1. Of Identity and Diversity, II, 27, in (Hg.), The Works of John Locke in Nine Volumes, London ^{12}1824.

LOHFINK, NORBERT, Zum „kleinen geschichtlichen Credo“ Dtn 26,5–9, ThPh 46 (1971), 19–39.

LOSCH, ANDREAS, Die Bedeutung Michael Polanyis für das Gespräch von Theologie und Naturwissenschaft, Glaube und Denken 21 (2008), 151–181.

–, Information ohne Energiebedarf. Das Konzept der “aktiven Information” bei John Polkinghorne, Evangelium und Wissenschaft 36 (2015), 119–124.

–, Jenseits der Konflikte. Eine konstruktiv-kritische Auseinandersetzung von Theologie und Naturwissenschaft, Göttingen 2011.

LOTMAN, JURIJ M., Universe of the Mind. A Semiotic Theory of Culture, Bloomington – Indianapolis 1990.

LUCKMANN, THOMAS, The Invisible Religion, London 1967.

LUHMANN, NIKLAS, Funktion der Religion, Frankfurt/M. 1982.

LUI, LEONG TING/YANG, Z. RON/ROBINSON, ANDREW/SOUTHGATE, CHRISTOPHER, Interpretation and the Origin of Life, Biological Theory 5 (2010), 112–116.

LUTHER, HENNING, Religion und Alltag. Bausteine zu einer Praktischen Theologie des Subjekts, Stuttgart 1992.

LUTHER, MARTIN, D. Martin Luthers Werke (WA), Weimar u.a. 1883–2009.

–, The Large Catechism, University Park 2000.

LYOTARD, JEAN-FRANCOIS, The Postmodern Condition. A Report on Knowledge, Manchester 1984.

MACCORMAC, EARL R., Metaphor and Fuzzy Sets, Fuzzy Sets and Systems 7 (1982), 243–256.
–, Metaphor and Myth in Science and Religion, Durham (NC) 1976.
MACINTYRE, ALASDAIR, After Virtue. A Study in Moral Theory, London ³2007.
–, Dependent Rational Animals. Why Human Beings Need the Virtues, Chicago – La Salle 1999.
MALCOLM, NORMAN, Anselm's Ontological Arguments, The Philosophical Review 69 (1960), 41–62.
–, Thought and Knowledge, Ithaca 1977.
MARION, JEAN-LUC, The Erotic Phenomenon, Chacago u.a. 2007.
–, État donné. Essai d'une phénoménologie de la donation, Paris ²1997.
MARKSCHIES, CHRISTOPH, Gibt es eine einheitliche „kappadozische Trinitätstheologie"?, in PREUL, REINER/U.A. (Hg.), Trinität (MJTh X), Marburg 1998, 51–94.
MARTY, ROBERT, Sur la réduction triadique, Semiosis 17/18 (1980), 5–9.
MARX, KARL, Capital Volume I, in Marx, Karl/Engels, Frederick, Collected Works, vol. 35.
MASSCHELEIN, JAN, E-ducating the gaze. The Idea of a Poor Pedagogy, Ethics and Education 5 (2010), 43–53.
MASSEY, DOREEN, For Space, London 2005.
MATTERN, JENS, Ricœur zur Einführung, Hamburg 1996.
MATTHEWS, GARETH B., Aristotelian Essentialism, Philosophy and Phenomenological Research 50 (1990), 251–262.
MATURANA, HUMBERTO, Neurophysiology of Cognition, in GARVIN, R. (Hg.), Cognition. A Multiple View, New York 1970, 2–23.
MATURANA, HUMBERTO/VARELA, FRANCISCO J., Autopoiesis and Cognition, Dordrecht–Boston–London 1980.
MAURER, ERNSTPETER, Narrative Strukturen im theologischen Denken Karl Barths, ZDTh 23 (2007), 9–21.
MCCORMACK, BRUCE L., The Being of Holy Scripture is in Becoming, in BACOTE, V. (Hg.), Evangelicals and Scripture. Tradition, Authority, and Hermeneutics, Downer Grove, IL 2004, 55–75.
MCDOWELL, JOHN, Mind and World. With a New Introduction, Cambridge (MA) ⁵2000.
MCFAGUE, SALLIE, Metaphorical Theology. Models of God in Religious Language, London 1983.
MCTAGGART, JOHN M.E., The Unreality of Time, Mind 17 (1908), 457–474.
MELANCHTHON, PHILIPP, CR.
MELTZOFF, ANDREW N., Understanding the Intentions of Others. Re-enactment of Intended Acts by 18-month-old Children, Developmental Psychology 31 (1995), 835–850.

MELTZOFF, ANDREW N./BROOKS, RECHELE, 'Like me' as Building Block for Understanding Other Minds. Bodily Acts, Attention, and Intention, in MALLE, B.F./ MOSES, L.J./BALDWIN, D.A. (Hg.), Intentions and Intentionality. Foundations of Social Cognition, Cambridge (Mass.) 2001, 171–191.

MENNE, ALBERT, Was ist Analogie?, in MENNE, ALBERT (Hg.), Folgerichtig Denken, Darmstadt 1988, 45–53.

MENSCHING, GUSTAV, Soziologie der Religionen, Bonn 1969.

MERLEAU-PONTY, MAURICE, Phenomenology of Perception, London–New York 2002.

–, The Visible and the Invisible, Evanston 1968.

MEYER ZU HÖRSTE-BÜHRER, RAPHAELA, Gott und Menschen in Beziehungen. Impulse Karl Barths für relationale Ansätze zum Verständnis christlichen Glaubens, Neukirchen-Vluyn 2916.

MINKOWSKI, HERMANN, Raum und Zeit, in H.A., LORENTZ/EINSTEIN, A./ MINKOWSKI, H./WEYL, H. (Hg.), Das Relativitätsprinzip, Darmstadt [6]1958, 54–66.

MOLTMANN, JÜRGEN, The Trinity and the Kingdom of God, Minneapolis 1993.

MORRIS, CHARLES W., Foundations of the Theory of Signs, Chicago [3]1944.

MÖRTH, EVELINE, Der Leib als Subjekt der Wahrnehmung. Zur Philosophie der Leiblichkeit bei Merleau-Ponty, in LIST, ELISABETH/FIALA, ERWIN (Hg.), Leib, Maschine, Bild. Körperdiskurse der Moderne und Postmoderne, Wien 1997, 75–87.

MOXTER, MICHAEL, Kultur als Lebenswelt. Studien zum Problem einer Kulturtheologie, Tübingen 2000.

–, Schrift als Grund und Grenze von Interpretationen, ZThK 105 (2008), 146–169.

MÜHLING, ANKE, Blickt auf Abraham, euren Vater. Abraham als Identifikationsfigur des Judentums in der Zeit des Exils und des Zweiten Tempels, Göttingen 2011.

MÜHLING, MARKUS, Art. Paradigm III+IV: Fundamental Theology + Ethics, 4Religion Past and Present, 2011, <http://dx.doi.org.ubproxy.ub.uni-heidelberg.de/10.1163/1877-5888_rpp_COM_024265>.

–, Einstein und die Religion. Das Wechselverhältnis zwischen religiös-weltanschaulichen Gehalten und naturwissenschaftlicher Theoriebildung Albert Einsteins in seiner Entwicklung, Göttingen 2011.

–, Gefühle, Werte und das ausgedehnte Selbst, Kerygma und Dogma 63 (2017), 115–131.

–, Gegenständlichkeit Gottes und Quantentheorie, Evangelium und Wissenschaft 32 (2000), 45–64.

–, Gott ist Liebe. Studien zum Verständnis der Liebe als Modell des trinitarischen Redens von Gott, Marburg [2]2005.

–, Grundinformation Eschatologie. Systematische Theologie aus der Perspektive der Hoffnung, Göttingen 2007.

–, Immanent/Economic Trinity, Religion Past and Present, 2011, http://referenceworks.brillonline.com/entries/religion-past-and-present/immanent-economic-trinity-SIM_10307.

–, Liebesgeschichte Gott. Systematische Theologie im Konzept, Göttingen 2013.

–, Logic, Religion Past and Present, 2011, http://referenceworks.brillonline.com/entries/religion-past- and-present/logic-COM_13166.

–, Metaphor III+IV: Philosophy of Religion + Fundamental Theology, Religion Past and Present, 2011, http://referenceworks.brillonline.com/entries/religion-past-and-present/metaphor-COM_14023.

–, Resonances: Neurobiology, Evolution and Theology. Evolutionary Niche Construction, the Ecological Brain and Relational-Narrative Theology, Göttingen – Bristol (CT) 2014.

–, Resonanzen: Neurobiologie, Evolution und Theologie. Evolutionäre Nischenkonstruktion, das ökologische Gehirn und narrativ-relationale Theologie, Göttingen – Bristol (CT) 2016.

–, Schleiermachers Gottesbeweis? Die De/Re-Konstruktion subjektiver Selbstgewißheit und die Erkenntnis Gottes, in Dalferth, Ingolf U./Stoellger, Philipp (Hg.), Krisen der Subjektivität, Tübingen 2005, 125–141.

–, Systematische Theologie: Ethik. Eine christliche Theorie vorzuziehenden Handelns, Göttingen 2012.

–, The T&T Clark Handbook of Christian Eschatology, New York – London 2015.

–, Versöhnendes Handeln – Handeln in Versöhnung. Gottes Opfer an die Menschen, Göttingen 2005.

–, „Voller Gnade und Wahrheit". Eine theologische Resonanztheorie der Wahrheit, in Rothgangel, Martin/Beuttler, Ulrich (Hg.), Glaube und Denken. Jahrbuch der Karl-Heim-Gesellschaft 27, Frankfurt u.a. 2014, 81–102.

–, Wege des Heils und der Heilung. Öffnende Überlegungen zum Christus medicus, in Wendte, Martin (Hg.), Jesus der Heiler und die Gesundheitsgesellschaft, Leipzig 2018, 19–34.

–, The Work of the Holy Spirit. The Differentiation of Human and Divine Salvific Acts in the Pneumatomachian Controversy, in Knight, Douglas (Hg.) (Hg.), The Theology of John Zizioulas: Personhood and the Church, Aldershot – Burlington 2007, 87–96.

Murphy, Francesca, God is not a Story. Realism Revisited, Oxford 2007.

Murray, Lynne/Trevarthen, Colwyn, Emotional Regulations of Interactions between Two-month-olds and their Mothers, in Field, T.M./Fox, N.A. (Hg.), Social Perception in Infants, Norwood 1995, 177–197.

Mutschler, Hans Dieter, Von der Form zur Formel. Metaphysik und Naturwissenschaft, Zug 2011.

NAESS, ARNE, Ecology, Community and Lifestyle. Outline of an Ecosophy, Cambridge 1989.

NAGEL, THOMAS, Mind and Cosmos. Why the Materialist Neo-Darwinian Conception of Nature is Almost Certainly False, 2012.

NAZIANZ, GREGOR VON, Orationes theologicae (FC 22), Freiburg u.a. 1996.

NELSON, KATHERINE, Narrative and the Emergence of a Consciousness of Self, in FIREMAN, G.D./MCVAY, T.E.J./FLANAGAN, O. (Hg.), Narrative and Consciousness, Oxford 2003, 17–36.

NEUMANN, JOHN VON, Eine Axiomatisierung der Mengenlehre, Journal für die reine und angewandte Mathematik 154 (1925), 219–240.

NIETZSCHE, FRIEDRICH, Der Antichrist, in (Hg.), Werke VI/3.

–, Über Wahrheit und Lüge im außermoralischen Sinne (1873), in (Hg.), Kritische Studienausgabe, ²1988.

NOVIKOVA, NATALIA, Self Government of the Indigenous Minority Peoples of West Siberia, in KASTEN, ERICH (Hg.), People and the Land. Pathways to Reform in Post-Soviet Russia, Berlin 2002, 83–97.

NÜSSEL, FRIEDERIKE, Narrative Identität? Dogmatische Überlegungen zu einer philosophischen Debatte, unveröffentlichter Vortrag LMU München (2014), 28.6.2014.

NYSSA, GREGOR VON, In Canticum canticorum homiliae – Homilien zum Hohenlied, Freiburg 1994.

O'REGAN, JOHN KEVIN/NOE, ALVA, A Sensorimotor account of Vision and Visual Consciousness, Behavioral and Brain Scienses 24 (2001), 939–1011.

ODLING-SMEE, F. JOHN/LALAND, KEVIN N./FELDMAN, MARCUS W., Niche Construction. The Neglected Process in Evolution, Princeton – Oxford 2003.

OEVERMANN, ULRICH, Ein Modell der Struktur von Religiosität. Zugleich ein Strukturmodell von Lebenspraxis und sozialer zeit, in WOHRAB-SAHR, MONIKA (Hg.), Biographie und Religion, Frankfurt/M. – New York 1995, 27–102.

ORR, H. ALLEN, Awaiting a New Darwin. Rev. of Nagel, Thomas: Mind and Cosmos. Why the Materialist Neo-Darwinian Conception of Nature is Almost Certainly False, The New York Review of Books February (2013).

OYAMA, SUSAN, Evolution's Eye. A Systems View of the Biology-Culture Divide, Durham (NC) 2000.

PANIKKAR, RAIMUNDO, The Jordan, the Tiber, and the Ganges. Three Kairological Moments of Christic Self-Conscoiousness, in HICK, JOHN/KNITTER, PAUL F. (Hg.), The Myth of Christian Uniquenss. Towards a Pluralistic Theology of Religions, Maryknoll 1987, 89–116.

–, The Unknown Christ of Hinduism, London ²1981.

PANNENBERG, WOLFHART, Der Gott der Geschichte, in PANNENBERG, WOLFHART (Hg.), Grundfragen Systematischer Theologie, Bd. 2, Göttingen 1980, 112–128.

–, Die Bedeutung des Christentums in der Philosophie Hegels, in PANNENBERG, WOLFHART (Hg.), Gottesgedanke und menschliche Freiheit, Göttingen 1972, 78–113.

–, Dogmatic Theses on the Doctrine of Revelation, in PANNENBERG, WOLFHART (Hg.), Revelation as History, Toronto 1968, 123–158.

–, Systematic Theology, Vol. I, London u.a. 2004.

–, Systematic Theology, Vol. II, London u.a. 2004.

–, Systematic Theology, Vol. III, London u.a. 2004.

–, Theology and the Philosophy of Science, Philadelphia 1976.

–, Wahrheit, Gewißheit und Glaube, in PANNENBERG, WOLFHART (Hg.), Grundfragen Systematischer Theologie, Bd. 2, Göttingen 1980, 226–264.

–, Was ist Wahrheit?, in PANNENBERG, WOLFHART (Hg.), Grundfragen Systematischer Theologie (Bd.1), Göttingen 1967, 202–222.

PARK, WOOSUK, Common Nature and Haecceitas, Franziskanische Studien 71 (1989), 188–192.

PEIRCE, CHARLES S., Collected Papers, Cambridge (MA) 1960.

–, Evolutionary Love (CP 6), in HARTSHORNE, CHARLES/WEISS, PAUL (Hg.), The Collected Papers of Charles Peirce, Vol. 6, 1960, 287–317.

–, Letters to Lady Welby MS [R] L463, unpublished manuscript 1906.

–, The New Elements of Mathematics, Vol. 1–5, The Hague – Atlantic Highlands 1976.

–, On a New List of Categories, Proceedings of the American Academy of Arts and Sciences 7 (1868), 287–298 (CP1.545–559).

PEPPER, STEPHEN C., World Hypotheses, Berkeley u.a. 1942.

PETERSEN, UWE, Dialetheism and Paradoxes of the Berry Family, Logique & Analyse 139–140 (1992), 273–289.

–, Die logischen Grundlagen der Dialektik. Ein Beitrag zur exakten Begründung der spekulativen Philosophie, München 1980.

PINNOCK, CLARK/RICE, RICHARD/SANDERS, JOHN/HASKER, WILLIAM/BASINGER, DAVID, The Openness of God. A Biblical Challenge to the Traditional Understanding of God, Westmond 1994.

PLANTINGA, ALVIN, The Nature of Necessity, Oxford 1974.

–, Reason and Belief in God, in PLANTINGA, ALVIN/WOLTERSTORFF, NICHOLAS (Hg.), Faith and Rationality, Notre Dame (IN) 1983, 16–93.

PLATON, Politeia, Stuttgart 1958.

POLANYI, MICHAEL, Personal Knowledge. Towards a Post-Critical Philosophy, London 1962.

–, The Tacit Dimension, Gloucester (Mass.) 1983.

POLLACK, DETLEF, Was ist Religion? Probleme einer Definition, Zeitschrift für Religionswissenschaft 3 (1995), 163–190.

PÖPPEL, ERNST, Grenzen des Bewußtseins, Frankfurt/M. – Leipzig [2]1997.

PORZIG, PETER C., Die Lade Jahwes im Alten Testament und in den Texten vom Toten Meer, Berlin – New York 2009.

PRIEST, GRAHAM, Beyond the Limits of Thought, Oxford 2002.

–, In Contradiction. A Study of the Inconsistent, Dordrecht 1987.

PUTNAM, HILARY, The Meaning of 'Meaning', in PUTNAM, HILARY (Hg.), Mind, Language and Reality. Philosophical Papers Vol. 2, Cambridge 1996, 215–271.

QUASH, BEN, Theology and the Drama of History, Cambridge 2005.

QUINE, WILLARD VAN ORMAN, Intensions Revisited, Midwest Studies in Philosophy 2 (1977), 5–11.

–, On Universals, J. Symbolic Logic 12 (1947), 74–84.

–, Ontological Relativity, in QUINE, WILLARD VAN ORMAN (Hg.), Ontological Relativity and other Essays, New York 1969, 26–68.

–, A Postscript on Metaphor, Critical Inquiry 5 (1978), 161–162.

–, Three Grades of Modal Involvement, in QUINE, WILLARD VAN ORMAN (Hg.), The Ways of Paradox, New York 1966, 156–174.

–, Word and Object, Cambridge (Mass.) u.a. 1960.

QUINE, WILLARD VAN ORMAN, From a Logical Point of View. 9 Logico-philosophical Essays, Cambridge, Mass. [u.a.] 2. ed., rev., 12. print 1999.

RAD, GERHARD VON, Old Testament Theology, vol. 1, Edingburgh 1962.

RAHNER, KARL, Der dreifaltige Gott als transzendenter Urgrund der Heilsgeschichte, in FEINER, JOHANNES U.A. (Hg.), Mysterium Salutis, Bd. 2, Einsiedeln 1967, 317–401.

RANKE, LEOPOLD VON, Geschichten der romanischen und germanischen Völker von 1494 bis 1535, Leipzig – Berlin 1824.

RATSCHOW, CARL HEINZ, Art. Religion II (Antike und Alte Kirche) + III (Mittelalter) + IV (Humanismus und Reformation), Historisches Wörterbuch der Philosophie, 8, 1992, 633–644.

RESCHER, NICOLAS, Cognitive Systematization. A Systems-theoretic Approach to a coherentist theory of knowledge, Oxford 1979.

–, Pluralism. Against the Demand for Consensus, Oxford – New York u.a. 1993.

RICHARD VON ST. VICTOR, De Trinitate, Paris 1958.

RICŒUR, PAUL, Die lebendige Metapher. Mit einem Vorwort zur deutschen Ausgabe, München 1986.

–, The Hermeneutics of Testimony, in RICŒUR, PAUL (Hg.), Essays on Biblical Interpretation, Philadelphia 1980, 119–153.

–, The Rule of Metaphor, Toronto u.a. 1981.

–, Time and Narrative I, Chicago – London ²1990.

–, Time and Narrative II, Chicago – London 1985.

–, Time and Narrative III, Chicago – London ²1990.

RITSCHL, DIETRICH, Theologie ist explikativ und argumentativ, nicht narrativ – auch bei Karl Barth, ZDTh 23 (2007), 22–33.

Ritschl, Dietrich/Jones, Hugh O., "Story" als Rohmaterial der Theologie, München 1976.

Robinson, Andrew, Traces of the Trinity. Signs, Sacraments and Sharing God's Life, Cambridge 2014.

Robinson, Andrew/Southgate, Christopher, A General Definition of Interpretation and its Application to the Origin of Life Research, Biology and Philosophy 25 (2010), 163–181.

Rohls, Jan, Protestantische Theologie der Neuzeit, 2 Bde., Tübingen 1997.

Rolf, Eckhard, Metapherntheorien. Typologie, Darstellung, Bibliographie, 2005.

Römer, Thomas, Israels Väter. Untersuchungen zur Väterthematik im Deuteronomium und in der deuteronomistischen Tradition, Fribourg – Göttingen 1990.

Rosa, Hartmut, Beschleunigung und Entfremdung, Berlin 2013.

–, Resonanz. Eine Soziologie der Weltbeziehung, Berlin 2016.

Rosch, Eleanor, Human Categorization, in Warren, Neil (Hg.), Advances in Cross-Cultural Psychology I, New York 1977, 1–71.

Rosenberg, Jay F., On a Certain Antinomy. Properties, Concepts and Items in Space, in Tomberlin, James E. (Hg.), Philosophical Perspectives 10, Metaphysics, Atascadero 1996, 357–383.

Rost, Leonhard, Das kleine geschichtliche Credo, in Rost, Leonhard (Hg.), Das kleine geschichtliche Credo und andere Studien zum AT, Heidelberg 1965, 11–25.

Rubin, David C., Go for the Skill, in Neisser, Ulric/Winograd, Eugene (Hg.), Remembering Reconsidered. Ecological and Traditional Approaches to the Study of Memory, Cambridge 1988, 374–382.

Rubin, David C./Wetzler, S.E./Nebes, R.D., Autobiographical Memory across the Adult Lifespan, in Rubin, David C. (Hg.), Autobiographical Memory, New York 1986, 202–221.

Runehov, Anne L.C, Sacred or Neural? The Potentiality of Neuroscience to Explain Religious Experience, Göttingen 2007.

Russell, Bertrand, My Philosophical Development, New York 1959.

Russell, Bertrand/Whitehead, Alfred North, Principia Mathematica, Cambridge ^{2192}7.

Russell, Robert J., Entropy and Evil, Zygon 19 (1984), 449–468.

Sacks, Oliver, The Man who Mistook his Wife for a Hat, London 1985.

Saussure, Ferdinand de, Course in General Linguistics (1916), New York 2011.

Schapp, Wilhelm, In Geschichten verstrickt. Zum Sein von Mensch und Ding (1953), Frankfurt/M. ^{4}2004.

–, Philosophie der Geschichten (1959), Frankfurt/M. ^{2}1981.

Schärtl, Thomas, Postliberale Theologie und die Standortbestimmung von Fundamentaltheologie, ZKTh 132 (2010), 47–64.

Schechtman, Marya, The Constitution of Selves, Ithaca, NY 1996.

Scheler, Max, Der Formalismus in der Ethik und die materiale Wertethik. Neuer Versuch der Grundlegung eines ethischen Personalismus, Halle 1916.

–, Formalism in Ethics and Non-Formal Ethics of Values, Evanston 1973.

–, The Nature of Sympathy, London 1954.

–, Wesen und Formen der Sympathie, Bonn ^{6}1973.

Schlapkohl, Corinna, Persona est naturae rationabilis individua substantia. Boethius und die Debatte über den Personbegriff, Marburg 1999.

Schlarb, Verena, Narrative Freiheit. Freiheit und Erzählen im Zusammenhang der Altenseelsorge, Leipzig 2015.

Schleiermacher, Friedrich, Brief Outline of the Study of Theology, Edinburgh 1850.

–, The Christian Faith, London u.a. ^{3}2016.

–, Christian Faith I, Louisville 2016.

–, Über die Glaubenslehre. Zwei Sendschreiben an Lücke (1829), in Schleiermacher, Friedrich (Hg.), Kritische Gesamtausgabe (KGA) I/10, Berlin – New York 1990, 307–394.

Schleiermacher, Friedrich Daniel Ernst, Dialektik (1811), Hamburg 1986.

–, Kurze Darstellung des theologischen Studiums zum Behuf einleitender Vorlesungen (1811/1830), Berlin u.a. 2002.

Schmidt, Jochen, Die Geschichte des Genie-Gedankens in der deutschen Literatur, Philosophie und Politik 1750–1945, Darmstadt 1985.

Schopenhauer, Arthur, Die Welt als Wille und Vorstellung, in Hansen, Frank-Peter (Hg.), Philosophie von Platon bis Nietzsche. Digitale Bibliothek 2, Brasov/Romania 1998, 63077–65445.

Schultz, Werner, Der Gedanke der Peregrinatio bei Augustin und das Motiv der Wanderschaft bei Goethe, NZSTh 8 (1966), 79–110.

Schütz, Gunther M., Kann Information ein Naturgegenstand sein?, Evangelium und Wissenschaft 36 (2015), 66–105.

Schweitzer, Albert, The Quest of the Historical Jesus. A Critical Stiudy of its Progress From Reimarus to Wrede, London 1910.

Schwelger, Helmut, Modelle als Theorien? Wo sind die Originale?, in Sandkühler, Hans Jörg (Hg.), Theorien, Modelle und Tatsachen, Frankfurt/M. 1994, 61–77.

Schwöbel, Christoph, Art. Law and Gospel, ^{4}Religion Past and Present, 2011, <http://dx.doi.org.ubproxy.ub.uni-heidelberg.de/10.1163/1877-5888_rpp_SIM_08576>.

–, Art. Systematic Theology, ^{4}Religion Past and Present, 2011, <http://dx.doi.org.ubproxy.ub.uni-heidelberg.de/10.1163/1877-5888_rpp_COM_025037>.

–, Art. Wahrheit, Taschenlexikon Religion und Theologie, Bd. 5, 1983, 283–289.

–, Doing Systematic Theology (engl.), in Schwöbel, Christoph (Hg.), God: Action and Revelation, Kampen 1992, 9–22.

–, Einleitung: Dimensionen der Leiblichkeit, in JANOWSKI, BERND/SCHWÖBEL, CHRISTOPH (Hg.), Dimensionen der Leiblichkeit, Neukirchen – Vluyn 2015, 1–9.

–, Erwartungen an eine Theologie des Alten Testaments aus der Sicht der Systematischen Theologie, in JANOWSKI, BERND (Hg.), Theologie und Exegese des Alten Testaments/der Hebräischen Bibel. Zwischenbilanz und Zukunftsperspektiven, Stuttgart 2005, 159–185.

–, Gott in Beziehung. Studien zur Dogmatik, Tübingen 2002.

–, Offenbarung und Erfahrung – Glaube und Lebenserfahrung. Systematisch-theologische Überlegungen zu ihrer Verhältnisbestimmung, in SCHWÖBEL, CHRISTOPH (Hg.), Gott in Beziehung, Tübingen 2002, 53–129.

–, Revelation and Experience, in SCHWÖBEL, CHRISTOPH (Hg.), God: Action and Revelation, Kampen 1992, 83–120.

–, Trinitätslehre als Rahmentheorie des christlichen Glaubens, in SCHWÖBEL, CHRISTOPH (Hg.), Gott in Beziehung, Tübingen 2002, 25–51.

SEAGER, WILLIAM/ALLEN-HERMANSON, SEAN, Art. Panpsychism, The Stanford Encyclopedia of Philosophy, 2015, https://plato.stanford.edu/archives/fall2015/entries/panpsychism/.

SEARLE, JOHN R., Animal Minds, in FRENCH, P.A./UEHLING, T.E./WETTSTEIN, H.K. (Hg.), Midwest Studies in Philosophy XIX: Philosophical Naturalism, Notre Dame (IN) 1994,

–, How to derive "Ought" from "Is", The Philosophical Review 73 (1964), 43–58.

–, The Rediscovery of the Mind, Cambridge (Mass.) 1992.

SEIBERT, CHRISTOPH, Religion im Denken von William James. Eine Interpretation seiner Philosophie, Tübingen 2009.

SELLARS, WILFRID, Empiricism and the Philosophy of Mind, in FEIGL, HERBERT/SCIRVEN, MICHAEL (Hg.), Minnesota Studies in the Philosophy of Science I, Minneapolis 1956, 253–329.

SELLIN, GERHARD, Lukas der Gleichniserzähler, ZNW 65 (1974–1975), 166–189.19–60.

SERRES, MICHEL, Gnomon. The Beginnings of Geometry in Greece, in SERRES, MICHEL (Hg.), A History of Scientific Thought. Elements of a History of Science, Oxford 1995, 73–123.

–, The Natural Contract, Ann Arbor 1995.

SLENCZKA, NOTGER, Die Kirche und das Alte Testament, in GRÄB-SCHMIDT, ELISABETH/PREUL, REINER (Hg.), Das Alte Testament in der Theologie, Leipzig 2013, 83–119.

–, Die Schrift als ‚einige Norm und Richtschnur', in KANDLER, K.-H. (Hg.), Die Autorität der Heiligen Schrift für Lehre und Verkündigung der Kirche, Neuendettelsau 2000, 53–78.

–, Was soll die These: „Das AT hat in der Kirche keine kanonische Geltung mehr"?, https://www.theologie.hu-berlin.de/de/professuren/professuren/st/was-soll-die-these.pdf (2015), 1–16.

SOSKICE, JANET MARTIN, Metaphor and Religious Language, Oxford 1992.
SPARN, WALTER, Art. Law and Legislation IV, [4]Religion Past and Present, 2011, <http://dx.doi.org.ubproxy.ub.uni-heidelberg.de/10.1163/1877-5888_rpp_COM_08565>.
SPINOZA, BARUCH, Ethica, in SPINOZA, BARUCH (Hg.), Opera – Werke, Bd. 2, Darmstadt 1967, 84–557.
STÖCKLER, MANFRED, Theoretische Modelle, in SANDKÜHLER, HANS HÖRG (Hg.), Theorien, Modelle und Tatsachen, Frankfurt/M. 1994, 45–60.
STOECKER, RALF, Was sind Ereignisse? Eine Studie zur analytischen Ontologie, Berlin – New York 1992.
STOELLGER, PHILIPP, Die Metapher als Modell symbolischer Prägnanz. Zur Bearbeitung eines Problems von Ernst Cassirers Prägnanzthese, in KORSCH, DIETRICH/RUDOLPH, ENNO (Hg.), Die Prägnanz der Religion in der Kultur, Tübingen 2000, 100–138.
–, The Interpreting of Perception and the Perception of Interpreting. On the Relation between Interpretive Patterns and Perception, or on the Interpretativity of Perception, in MÜHLING, MARKUS/FÖRSTER, YVONNE/GILLAND DAVID (Hg.), Perceiving Truth and Values, Göttingen – Bristol (CT) 2018, 69–103.
–, Metapher und Lebenswelt. Hans Blumenbergs Metaphorologie als Lebensweltthermeneutik und ihr religionsphänomenologischer Horizont, Tübingen 2000.
–, Passivität aus Passion. Zur Problemgeschichte einer 'categoria non grata', Tübingen 2010.
–, Über die Grenzen der Metaphorologie. Zur Kritik der Metaphorologie Hans Blumenbergs und deren Perspektiven in der Fortschreibung, in HAVERKAMP, ANSELM/MENDE, DIRK (Hg.), Metaphorologie. Zur Praxis von Theorie, Frankfurt/M. 2009, 203–234.
–, Vom vierfachen Sinn der Metapher. Eine Orientierung über ihre Formen und Funktionen, in BÜHLER, PIERRE/FABINY, TIBOR (Hg.), Interpretation of Texts. Sacred and Secular, Zürich – Budapest 1999, 87–116.
STRATIS, JUSTIN, God's Being toward Fellowship. The Meaning of 'God is Love' in Dialogue with the Theologies of Friedrich Schleiermacher and Karl Barth, Aberdeen (Diss. Masch.) 2012.
STRAWSON, GALEN, Against Narrativity, Ratio 17 (2003), 428–452.
STRAWSON, PETER F., Individuals. An Essay in Descriptive Metaphysics, London–New York 1959.
STRUB, CH., Art. System, HWPh, 10, 1998, 824–856.
SUBER, PETER, The Paradox of Self-Amendment, Frankfurt/M. – New York 1990.
SWINBURNE, RICHARD, The Christian God, Oxford 1994.
–, Thisness, Australian Journal of Philosophy 73 (1995), 389–400.
SWINTON, JOHN, Dementia. Living in the Memories of God, Grand Rapids 2012.
TARSKI, ALFRED, The Concept of Truth in Formalized Languages, in TARSKI, ALFRED (Hg.), Logic, Semantics, Mathematics, Oxford 1936, 152–278.

TAYLOR, CHARLES, Sources of the Self. The Making of the Modern Identity, Cambridge (Mass.) 1989.

THEIẞEN, GERD, Die Jesusbewegung. Sozialgeschichte einer Revolution der Werte, Gütersloh 2004.

–, Soziologie der Jesusbewegung, München 1977.

THIEMANN, THOMAS, Lectures on Loop Quantum Gravity, Lect.Notes Phy. 631 (2003), 41–135.

THIMANN, THOMAS, Auf der Suche nach dem Heiligen Gral. Schleifen-Quantengravitation, Physik in unserer Zeit 39 (2008), 116–124.

THOMÄ, DIETER, Soziologie mit der Stimmgabel, Die Zeit 2016 (30.6.2016),

THOMAS VON AQUIN, s.th., THOMPSON, EVAN T., Mind in Life. Biology, Phenomenology, and the Sciences of Mind, Cambridge (Mass.) 2007.

TILLICH, PAUL, Systematic Theology I, Chicago 1967.

–, Systematic Theology. Three Volumes in One, Chicago 1967.

–, Systematische Theologie I, Stuttgart ^{6}1980.

TIPPELSKIRCH, DOROTHEE VON, „Liebe von fremd zu fremd ...“ Menschlichkeit des Menschen und Göttlichkeit Gottes bei Emmanuel Lévinas und Karl Barth, Freiburg-München 2002.

TOMASELLO, MICHAEL, Die kulturelle Entwicklung des menschlichen Denkens. Zur Evolution der Kognition, Darmstadt 2002.

–, Origins of Human Communication, Cambridge (MA) 2008.

TORRANCE, ALAN, Persons in Communion, Edinburgh 1996.

TRENDELENBURG, FRIEDRICH ADOLF, Historische Beiträge zur Philosophie I, Berlin 1946.

TRONICK, ED Z., Things Still to be Done on the Still-Face Effect, Infancy 4 (2003), 475–482.

TURNER, BRYAN, The Body in Western Society. Social Theory and its Perspectives, in COAKLEY, SARAH (Hg.), Religion and the Body, New York – Cambridge 1997, 15–41.

UEXKÜLL, JAKOB VON, Theoretische Biologie (1928), Frankfurt am Main 1973.

VAN KAMPEN, NICO G., Entropie, Plus Lucis 97 (1997), 7–8.

VILSMAIER, ULLI, Grenzarbeit in integrativer und grenzüberschreitender Forschung, in HEINTEL, MARTIN/MUSIL, ROBERT/WEIXLBAUMER, NORBERT (Hg.), Grenzen, Wiesbaden 2018, 113–134.

VISALA, AKU, Naturalism, Theism and the Cognitive Study of Religion, Farnham – Burlington 2011.

VON RAD, GERHARD, Theologie des Alten Testaments, Bd. 1: Die Theologie der geschichtlichen Überlieferungen Israels, München ^{9}1987.

WALDENFELS, BERNHARD, Bodily Experience between Selfhood and Otherness, Phenomenology and the Cognitive Sciences 3 (2004), 235–248.

–, Das leibliche Selbst. Vorlesungen zur Phänomenologie des Leibes, Frankfurt/M. 2000.

WALTER, GREGORY, Rev. Mühling, Liebesgeschichte Gott, Lutheran Quarterly 29 (2015), 351–352.

WEINRICH, HARALD, Allgemeine Semantik der Metapher, in WEINRICH, HARALD (Hg.), Sprache in Texten, Stuttgart 1976, 317–327.

WEIZSÄCKER, CARL FRIEDRICH VON, Die Einheit der Natur, München 1972.

WELKER, MICHAEL, Universalität Gottes und Relativität der Welt, Neukirchen-Vluyn ²1988.

WENDTE, MARTIN, Die Gabe und das Gestell. Luthers Metaphysik des Abendmahls im technischen Zeitalter, Tübingen 2013.

–, Raumzeitimplosion und Schöpfungsfülle. Soziologisches, Philosophisches und Theologisches zur gesellschaftlichen Gestaltung von Raum und Zeit in der Spätmoderne, in GRÄB-SCHMIDT, ELISABETH (Hg.), Was heißt Natur? Philosophischer Ort und Begründungsfunktion des Naturbegriffs, Leipzig 2015, 55–81.

WESTPHAL, MEROLD, Transcendence and Self-Transcendence. On God and the Soul, Bloomington 2004.

WHEELER, JOHN ARCHIBALD, Information, Physics, Quantum. The Search for Links, in ZUREK, WOJCIECH H. (Hg.), Complexity, Entropy, and the Physics of Information, Redwood City 1990, 309–336.

WHITE, LESLIE, The Symbol. Origin and Basis of Human Behavior, Philosophy of Science 7 (1940), 451–463.

WHITEHEAD, ALFRED NORTH, Process and Reality. Gifford Lectures Delivered in the University of Edinburgh during the Session 1927–28, New York 1978.

WIECKOWSKI, BARTOSZ, Gott in möglichen Welten. Eine Analyse des modalen ontologischen Arguments für die Existenz Gottes von Alvin Plantinga, Münster u.a. 1999.

WILELAND, G., Art. Gesetz, ewiges, HWPh, 3, 1974, 514–516.

WILLIAMS, BERNARD, Life as Narrative, European Journal of Philosophy 17 (2009), 305–314.

WILLIAMS, ROWAN, The Edge of the Words, London – New York – New Delhi – Sydney 2014.

WITTGENSTEIN, LUDWIG, Philosophical Investigations, Oxford ²1958.

–, Tractatus Logico-Philosophicus (engl.), London – New York 1922.

WÖLFEL, EBERHARD, Endet die Zeit? Bemerkungen zum Zeitproblem im Aspekt naturwissenschaftlicher Erschließung, in STOCK, KONRAD (Hg.), Zeit und Schöpfung, Gütersloh 1997, 11–40.

WOLTER, MICHAEL, Das Lukasevangelium, Tübingen 2008.

WRIGHT, GEORG HENRIK VON, Art. Logik, deontische, HWPh, 5, 1980, 384–389.

WÜTHRICH, MATTHIAS, Raum Gottes. Ein systematisch-theologischer Versuch, Raum zu denken, Göttingen – Bristol (CT) 2015.

YOUNG, EUGENE B./GENOSKO, GARY/WATSON, JANELL, The Deleuze and Guattari Dictionary, London – New York – New Delhi – Sydney 2013.

YOUNG, N.Y., The Commandment to Love your Neighbor as Yourself and the Parable of the Good Samaritan, AUSS 21 (1983), 265–272.

ZADEH, LOFTI A., Fuzzy Sets, Information and Control 8 (1965), 338–353.

ZEILINGER, ANTON, Einsteins Schleier. Die neue Welt der Quantenphysik, München ^{3}2005.

ZEILINGER, ANTON/WEIHS, GREGOR/JENNEWEIN, THOMAS/ASPELMEYER, MARKUS, Happy Centenary, Photon, Nature 433 (2005), 230–238.

ZERMELO, ERNST, Über Grenzzahnlen und Mengenbereiche, Fundamenta Mathematicae 16 (1930), 29–47.

ZGOLL, CHRISTIAN, Phänomenologie der Metamorphose. Verwandlungen und Verwandtes in der augusteischen Dichtung, Tübingen 2004.

ŽIŽEK, SLAVOJ, Event. Philosophy in Transit, London u.a. 2014.

ZIZIOULAS, JOHN, The Doctrine of the Holy Trinity: The Significance of the Cappadocian Contribution, in SCHWÖBEL, CHRISTOPH (Hg.), Trinitarian Theology Today, Edinburgh 1995, 44–60.

ZIZIOULAS, JOHN D., Being as Communion, Crestwood 1985.

–, Die Signifikanz des kappadozischen Beitrags zur Lehre von der Heiligen Trinität, in MÜHLING, MARKUS (Hg.), Gezwungene Freiheit?, Göttingen 2009, 69–81.

Index

Index of Authors

Index of Things